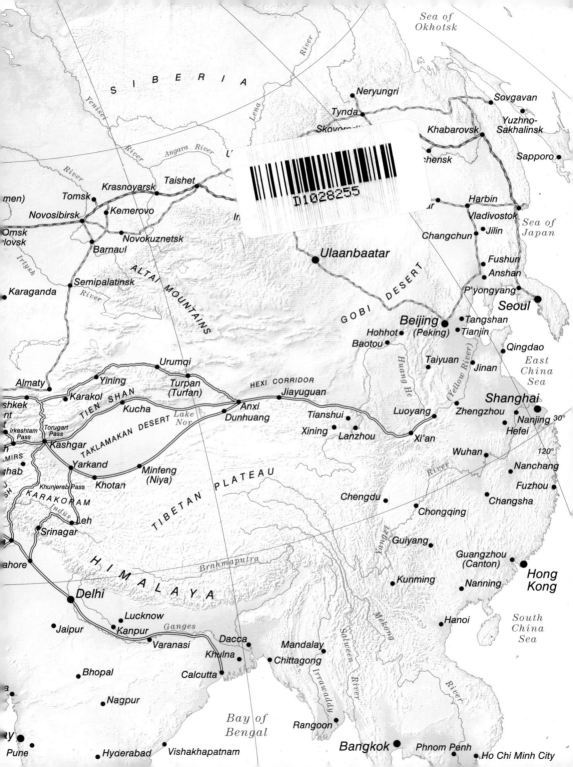

Sea of
Okhotsk

SIBERIA

Neryungri

Sovgavan

Tynda

Yuzhno-
Sakhalinsk

Skovoro...

Khabarovsk

...chensk

Sapporo

Taishet

Krasnoyarsk

D1028255

Tomsk

Harbin

...men)

Novosibirsk

Kemerovo

Vladivostok

Sea of
Japan

Omsk
...lovsk

Novokuznetsk

Changchun

Jilin

Barnaul

Fushun

Ulaanbaatar

Anshan

Karaganda

Semipalatinsk

ALTAI MOUNTAINS

GOBI DESERT

P'yongyang

Seoul

Beijing
(Peking)

Tangshan

Hohhot

Tianjin

Baotou

Qingdao

Urumqi

Taiyuan

Jinan

East
China
Sea

Almaty

Yining

Turpan
(Turfan)

HEXI CORRIDOR

Jiayuguan

Huang He

Yellow River

Shanghai

...shkek...
...nt

Karakol

TIEN SHAN

Kucha

Anxi

Tianshui

Luoyang

Zhengzhou

Nanjing 30°

Irkeshtam
Pass

Torugart
Pass

Lake
Nor

Dunhuang

Xining

Lanzhou

Xi'an

Hefei

...h

Kashgar

TAKLAMAKAN DESERT

Wuhan

120°

MIRS

Yarkand

Minfeng
(Niya)

River

Nanchang

...hab

Khotan

TIBETAN PLATEAU

Chengdu

Fuzhou

Khunjerab Pass

Changsha

KARAKORAM

Indus

Leh

Chongqing

Srinagar

Yangtze

Guiyang

Guangzhou
(Canton)

...ahore

HIMALAYA

Brahmaputra

Kunming

Nanning

Hong
Kong

Delhi

Lucknow

Mekong

Hanoi

South
China
Sea

Jaipur

Kanpur

Ganges

Varanasi

Dacca

Mandalay

Salween River

Khulna

Chittagong

Bhopal

Calcutta

Irrawaddy

Nagpur

Bay of
Bengal

Rangoon

Bangkok

Phnom Penh

...y

Pune

Hyderabad

Vishakhapatnam

Ho Chi Minh City

Recent Reviews of other Odyssey Guides...

(Above) *A string of camels stride across the dunes in Xinjiang's Taklamakan Desert; today tourists take turns riding for short distances through the harsh but bewitching landscape, but in days of yore merchants spent gruelling months traversing this enormous sea of sand.*

(Previous page) *The magnificent Hall of Prayer for a Good Harvest in Beijing's Temple of Heaven complex.*

(Following page) *The great Cascade Fountain in Peterhof, Peter the Great's Summer Palace on the outskirts of St Petersburg.*

ASIA OVERLAND

TALES OF
TRAVEL ON THE
TRANS-SIBERIAN &
SILK ROAD

BIJAN OMRANI

WITH

ADDITIONAL MATERIAL BY

JEREMY TREDINNICK

Backed by the mighty peaks of the Karakoram, Baltit Fort in Pakistan's Hunza Valley occupied an important strategic point for merchants and armies crossing between Central Asia and the subcontinent.

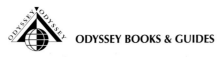
ODYSSEY BOOKS & GUIDES

Odyssey Books & Guides is a division of Airphoto International Ltd.

1401 Chung Ying Building, 20–20A Connaught Road West, Sheung Wan, Hong Kong

Tel: (852) 2856 3896; Fax: (852) 3012 1825

E-mail: magnus@odysseypublications.com; www.odysseypublications.com

Distribution in the USA by W.W. Norton & Company, Inc, 500 Fifth Avenue, New York, NY 10110, USA. Tel: 800-233-4830; Fax: 800-458-6515; www.wwnorton.com

Distribution in the UK and Europe by Cordee Ltd, 11 Jacknell Road, Dodwells Bridge Industrial Estate, Hinckley, Leicestershire LE10 3BS, UK. Tel: 01455-611185; info@cordee.co.uk; www.cordee.co.uk

Distribution in Australia by Tower Books Pty Ltd, a member of the Scribo Group. Unit 18 Rodborough Road, Frenchs Forest, NSW 2086, Australia. www.towerbooks.com.au

Asia Overland: Tales of Travel on the Trans–Siberian & Silk Road

ISBN: 978-962-217-811-3

Library of Congress Catalog Card Number has been requested.

Copyright © 2010 Airphoto International Ltd.

Grateful acknowledgement is made to the following authors, photographers and publishers; all photography/illustrations remain the property of their respective copyright owners as indicated:

Pavel Ageychenko/©BaikalNature 127 (top), 161, 165 (bottom), 166, 167, 492 (bottom left); Courtesy of the **Asian Art Museum, National Museums in Berlin** 277 (top right), 278 (bottom left); **George Grantham Bain Collection**, Library of Congress, Prints & Photographs Division 381; **David Lewis Baker** 482; **Magnus Bartlett** 1, 225, 226 (top), 228, 229 (bottom right), 230, 231, 232, 233, 275 (bottom), 276, 287 (top), 328, 353, 354, 496 (bottom right); **Christoph Baumer** 284, 396–397, 400; **Joan Bellver** 430–431, 432 (top); Courtesy of the **Bodleian Library, University of Oxford** 446 (bottom x2, Shelfmark 2063 a: 1 and 5); Courtesy of the **British Library** 271, 272, 289; **Anthony Cassidy** 385, 388 (bottom), 389, 390–391, 392, 393 (top left and bottom), 394 (bottom), 395 (top); Courtesy of **Dennis George Crow** 209, 241; **Yolande Crowe** 281 (bottom), 451 (top); **Jacques Descloitres, MODIS Land Rapid Response Team, NASA/GSFC** 164, 322–323, 422 (bottom); Archive of the **German Alpine Club, Munich** 313; **Earth Observations Laboratory, NASA-Johnson Space Center** 423 (top left); **Earth Sciences and Image Analysis Laboratory, NASA Johnson Space Center** 280, 452 (bottom); **Abdullah Frères Collection**, Library of Congress, Prints & Photographs Division 383, 438; **Amar Grover** 273; **Marc Guitard** 128; **Atif Gulzar** 470; **GW Travel Ltd** 64 (bottom), 124 (top), 162–163, 226 (bottom), 234 (top), 503 (bottom); **Paul Harris** 321, 324 (top); **Markus Hauser** 330–331, 332 (bottom); **The *Illustrated London News*** 207, 208, 211, 214, 219, 220, 222; **William Henry Jackson**, Library of Congress, Prints & Photographs Division 473 (bottom); **George Kennan Collection**, Library of Congress, Prints & Photographs Division 106, 108, 111, 126 (bottom), 134, 142, 184, 185 (left), 187, 189, 192; **S.C. Keung** 2–3; **Bob King/Sundowners Overland** 171 (bottom), 172, 174, 175; Courtesy of **Klimovka** 117 (bottom); Courtesy of **Anton Lange/Russian Railways** 118 (bottom), 121 (top), 165 (top), 484; **Patricia Lanza** 52, 62, 63 (top); **Library of Congress, Prints & Photographs Division**: 28, 32 (bottom), 35, 36, 37, 40, 48, 66, 69, 70, 71, 100, 169 (bottom), 196, 318, 339, 340, 342, 343, 345, 346, 347, 348, 349, 401, 474 (bottom); **William Lindesay** 243, 251, 255, 256, 275 (top); **Keith Macgregor** 50 (top), 56; **Calum MacLeod** 335, 360 (bottom), 361 (bottom), 363 (top), 364, 366 (bottom); **Bradley Mayhew** 362; **Y.S. Mehmet** (licensed under the GFDL) 424–425 (top); **Paul Mooney** 234 (bottom);

Moscow History Museum 60–61; Leo Murray 492 (middle); NASA/Visible Earth (http://visibleearth.nasa.gov) 398 (bottom); National Library of Russia, Siberian Postcards Collection, Prints Division 141, 143, 144, 145, 167; Tom Nebbia 277 (bottom), 285 (top left), 456 (top), 496 (top left); Kazuyoshi Nomachi 274; Masha Nordbye 57; Gürkan Öztürk 20–21; Sergei Mikhailovich Prokudin-Gorskii, Prokudin-Gorskii Collection, Library of Congress, Prints & Photographs Division 11, 79, 113, 114–115, 120 (top), 125, 137, 341, 350, 359 (top), 365 (bottom), 367 (bottom), 368, 416; Carl Robinson 492 (bottom right); Robino Robokow 432 (bottom); Courtesy of the Roerich Museum 306; Mikhail Romanyuk 327 (top left), 332 (top), 333; Russian State Library, Department of Printed Art 157, 159, 177, 178; Jonas Satkauskas 363 (bottom); Jeff Schmaltz/NASA 293; Courtesy of Sphinx Fine Art 245, 334, 336, 359 (bottom), 367 (top), 395 (bottom), 424 (bottom), 425 (bottom), 426, 429 (bottom); Jane Sweeney/Sundowners Overland 4, 12, 14–15, 16–17, 24–25, 49, 51 (top), 54, 58, 59 (bottom), 63 (bottom right), 64 (top), 117 (top), 170 (top), 171 (top), 176, 229 (bottom left), 287 (bottom), 288, 355, 356–357, 358, 360 (top), 419, 420–421, 485, 488–489 (top), 496 (top right); Wendy Tanner 447 (bottom), 448, 450 (top) 451 (bottom); Jeremy Tredinnick 122–123, 139, 224, 235, 236, 237, 238, 239, 240, 254, 257, 278 (top and bottom right), 281 (top), 282–283, 285 (top right and bottom), 286, 305, 316, 317, 324 (bottom), 325, 326, 327 (top right), 452 (top), 453, 456 (bottom), 458, 459 (top), 460

A Mughal miniature painting shows Emperor Akbar hunting with cheetahs.

(top), 462, 463, 464, 467, 468 (top), 473 (top), 496 (bottom left), 499, 502, 506, 507 (top, middle and bottom left); Trillium Studios/Cary Wollinsky 61 (inset); Bruce Wallace 398 (top left); Courtesy of Wattis Fine Art 217, 227 (top); Wong How Man/CERS 327 (bottom); Bill Woodburn 446 (top), 449, 450 (bottom); Adam Woolfitt 417, 418 (top), 427; Yao Pey Yong 6–7, 454–455; and Zhong Ling 277 (top left).

The following images are used under licence by Creative Commons Attribution-Share Alike (CCAS, http://creativecommons.org). Under CCA 1.0 Licence: Marc Heiden 168. Under CCA 2.0 Licence: Dennis Mark Mulhall 270; David Wilmot 203; M@Mad 386 (top left); Flydime 371. Under CCA 2.5 Licence: Murdjo 422 (top); PlaneMad 461 (top). Under CCA 3.0 Licence: 124 (bottom); 386 (bottom left); Alaexis 418 (bottom); S. Barnes 428 (bottom); Aleksey Beloborodov 116 (bottom); Captmondo 268 (left); CyArk 366 (top); Vera Donk 121 (bottom); John Hill 398 (top right); Iahsan 388; Guillaume Jacquet 268 (right); Yuri Karamazov 169 (top); Alex Kofman 120 (bottom); Evgenia Kononova 361 (top); Matthew Laird 461 (bottom); Edal Anton Lefterov 429 (top); PetarM 489 (bottom left); Yves Picq 447 (top); Hans A. Rosbach 459 (bottom); Tiarescott 173; Bjørn Christian Tørrissen 503 (top); Untifler 118 (top); Leonti Andreevich Usov 136; Anton Ottl/Gert Wrigge 468 (bottom); Yaan 492 (top).

Managing Editor: Jeremy Tredinnick

Designer: Alex Ng Kin Man

Production and printing by

Twin Age Ltd, Hong Kong

E-mail: twinage@netvigator.com

Manufactured in Hong Kong

ACKNOWLEDGEMENTS & THANKS

This book ultimately was the genesis of many long conversations between Magnus Bartlett, Simon Maddison and Tony Glynn. To them, and to the other staff of Sundowners Overland, I owe a great debt of gratitude for conceiving this project, and giving it their sustained support.

Much of the historical research was done at the libraries of the School of Oriental and African Studies, the School of Slavonic and East European Studies, the Royal Society for Asian Affairs and The Royal Asiatic Society, all in London, and the Indian Institute Library in Oxford. My thanks to the many members of staff and librarians – unfortunately too numerous to name individually – for sharing their knowledge, and the many small acts of helpfulness and kindness which lightened the long hours of study.

The staff of Odyssey Books & Guides have done everything in their power to support the wayward author in every aspect of his work. My thanks not only to Magnus, but also Margarita, Helen, Cecilia, Au Yeung, Suk Woon, Tony and Alex, and especially to my editor, Jeremy Tredinnick, whose hard work, professionalism, and unerring eye for a good photograph have brought the book together.

To my friends in London and Oxford, who happily distracted me after a long day's writing (or as often as not when I should have actually been writing) – especially Fran and Paul, Theo and Sarah, Dockar, Oakes, Breen, the PGCE Cohort, Gail in Oxford, Michael and Judy in Sussex: *Non possum reticere qua me vos omnes in re iuveritis aut quantis iuveritis officiis.* And finally to my parents, and most of all to Sam, I must apologise for the huge distraction of these constant literary productions, and say what their support and love has done to sustain me through them.

Bijan Omrani
Eton College, January 2010

The publisher and editor would also like to acknowledge, with thanks, the valuable contributions of the following individuals and organisations:

Tony Glynn of Sundowners Overland, and through him photographers Jane Sweeney and Bob King; Timothy Littler of GW Travel Ltd; and Sergey Sloutskov of Russian Railways for the images by Anton Lange, part of a joint project by Mr Lange and Russian Railways entitled "Russia through a Train Window".

For kindly giving permission for us to use their excellent images, Wendy Tanner, Yao Pey Yong, S.C. Keung, Gürkan Öztürk, Marc Guitard, Robino Robokow, David Lewis Baker, Vladimir Klimov

Tobolsk, on the Siberian steppe, in the early 1900s. As imperial Russia spread across Eurasia, towns and cities grew along the banks of rivers that punctuated the endless open land. This image (among others in this book) was made by the great Russian photographer Sergei Mikhailovich Prokudin-Gorskii, who pioneered an early type of colour photography using a camera that took a series of three monochrome pictures in sequence, each through a different coloured filter, which were then reconstructed as a colour image. While the results sometimes showed multiple "ghost" images, Prokudin-Gorskii's work is an astonishing and wonderful documentation of the Russian Empire's expansion into Central Asia and the Far East.

(of the Klimovka Recreation Centre in East Kazakhstan), and Pavel Ageychenko and Natalya Zolotareva of Baikal Nature in Irkutsk (www.baikalnature.com).

We would also like to extend our gratitude to Roy Bolton at Sphinx Fine Art in London (www.sphinxfineart.com), who generously gave us access to a wonderful collection of 19th and 20th century artworks; to the Asian Art Museum, National Museums in Berlin; the British Library; the Roerich Museum; the Deutsches Alpines Museum; the Department of Printed Art of the Russian State Library; and the Prints Division of the National Library of Russia.

A special thanks is due indirectly to the family of Sergei Mikhailovich Prokudin-Gorskii – his visionary approach to the documentation of Central Asia and the newly built Trans-Siberian Railway at the turn of the 20th century illuminates this book in a unique manner.

EDITOR'S NOTE

The production of this book presented us with some interesting challenges due to its vast geographical and historical scope. Consider Eurasia's great land routes: offspring of the ambition of Russian tsars, Chinese emperors and Mughal khans, they have served human history well, acting as conduits for trade, religion and cultural conventions, and as avenues down which conquering armies and commercial pioneers swarmed in the forging of empires. But what was it really like to travel the iron rails of the Trans-Siberian Railway in its early years, the dusty, parched tracks of the Silk Road in its heyday, or the rugged, dangerous mountain passes into and out of the Indian subcontinent?

In answering this question, author Bijan Omrani has woven a tapestry of fascinating tales and reports by a panoply of travellers down the centuries, taking the reader on an exciting journey that crosses continents and spans epochs. In illustrating his text we were inevitably limited – in the main – to the 19th century development of photography, but the sheer volume of material available, once research had begun, took us on our own journey of discovery, complete with no little consternation at first, but eventually a great sense of fulfilment. With hindsight it was a wholly appropriate process.

A note on place and name spellings: The constant ebb and flow of empires, kingdoms and their cultures into and out of Siberia, China, Central Asia and the Near East has resulted in an often bewildering list of possible spellings for towns, regions and peoples. Some spellings differ only slightly (ie Yekaterinburg/Ekaterinburg, or Bukhara/Bokhara), while others are entirely distinct (ie Khanbaliq/Peking/Beijing, or Yarkand/Shache); romanization and other forms of transliteration from different sources create literary conflict wherever one looks. We have tried to remain consistent in using what we believe to be the most common English usage of a place or person, with historical names in brackets where these are entirely different to the modern day. However, if you do venture into these lands, either physically on an adventurous holiday or from the comfort of home through the avenue of literature, be prepared for the confusing range of nomenclature that will present itself.

A note on dates: Varied religions are represented in the diverse countries through which this book's tales take us, from Orthodox Russia to Taoist and Buddhist China and Islamic Central Asia. With deference to this, when referring to dates the conventional Christian terms "BC" (Before Christ) and "AD" (Anno Domini) have been replaced by the more neutral "BCE" (before Common Era) and "CE" (Common Era), whereby "Common" simply refers to the Gregorian Calendar, the most widely recognised and used timeline reference in the world today.

Jeremy Tredinnick

(Left) *Colourfully dressed Uzbek women share a joke in Bukhara, once one of the great trading cities of the ancient "Silk Road", now part of the modern state of Uzbekistan.*

A close-up view of the Monument to Kozma Minin and Prince Dmitri Pozharsky in Moscow's Red Square, with the remarkable coloured domes of St Basil's Cathedral in the background.

The 48-metre (157-foot) Kalon Minaret in Bukhara was an impressive and welcome sight for caravans toiling across the desert steppe. An awed Genghis Khan was said to have bowed at its base and ordered it not to be destroyed, but in later years it was known as the "Tower of Death" for the practice of tying criminals in a sack and throwing them from its heights.

Contents

The island of Akdamar in Turkey's Lake Van, located in the far east of the country, is home to the 10th century Armenian Church of the Holy Cross. Travellers heading for Constantinople from Persia passed between the lake and the high mountain range dominated by Mt Ararat (not shown here).

INTRODUCTION

O f all the fatuities uttered in the English poetic corpus, perhaps nothing more foolish has been written than "East is East and West is West and ne'er the twain shall meet".

Anyone conscious of the history of travel will be aware of the absurdity of the statement. There was never any time that the West or East were cloistered away from each other. From the earliest times of humanity across the great routes of Asia, there have been exchanges of people, of goods and ideas. Lapis lazuli from the most distant corners of Afghanistan adorned the funerary masks of the Egyptian Pharaohs 2,000 years before Christ; the war chariots of ancient Assyria in modern-day Iraq were owed to the nomads of the great steppe of today's Kazakhstan; and it was to the same region that the early empires of China turned their gaze when they sought the fabled "blood-sweating" horses, a breed which would be worthy to defend their frontiers.

As legion and varied as these goods and ideas were the travellers themselves who – at great personal risk and with no small courage – brought them across the vast intervening distances. They might be hardy migrants in search of a better life or refugees from war and invasion; empire-builders and conquerors; merchants in pursuit of gain; ambassadors or adventurers; holy men seeking scriptures or even converts; unwilling prisoners, disciplined soldiers or ingenious spies. There were botanists and antiquaries, hearty builders of railways and highways, lunatics on quixotic quests, and others who came driven purely by a lust for knowing.

So great was their number, and so many were their works, that many, on account of space, I have been compelled to omit. No tome of reasonable size could hope on so grand a subject to be comprehensive, and it has been grievous to leave aside much that was worthy of inclusion. For all this, I hope that this book will not only act as a satisfactory introduction to the ways of travel in Asia and Siberia before the luxuries of the aeroplane and the contemporary age, but also serve to remind the reader of how intertwined, by means of travel, the West and the East have always been, and the abiding importance of each to the other.

Bijan Omrani

A 19th century albumen print by William Carrick shows two local women outside a bark shelter in Siberia, a good example of local ingenuity in using the most readily available material in the taiga forest regions.

A passenger boat cruises along the Neva River in front of the Hermitage façade in St Petersburg.

THE STEEL ROAD

ST PETERSBURG AND
THE WAY THERE

n a warm summer's day in 1891, an English traveller, Harry de Windt, crossed the German frontier with Russia, at the beginning of a journey that was to take him over 6,000 miles (almost 10,000 kilometres) to the farthest regions of Siberia. De Windt was a seasoned explorer, a Fellow of the Royal Geographical Society, and no stranger to Russia. A few years earlier, he had travelled overland in the opposite direction from Peking to Calais across the Russian Empire, and he knew as well as any the discomforts that his forthcoming journey would entail. As the post train from Paris carried him eastwards on its four-day journey across Europe towards St Petersburg, he could barely help thinking on the discomforts that he would shortly be facing. He foresaw endless hours and days in a sledge, or *tarantass*, jolting madly over pot-holed roads at the mercy of a vodka-soaked coachman; the prospect of waiting hungry hours in a vermin-ridden post-station while replacement horses were sought; the danger of collisions on the way; of robbery by escaped convicts hiding out in the forests; of crashing through the ice and drowning as they crossed an imperfectly frozen river. As he pondered over these things from the luxury of his first-class *wagon lit*, the anticipation seemed to make him appreciate all the more the comforts which at that moment he still enjoyed, and become all the more angry when anything failed to come up to standard.

"Will the Germans never understand the art of travelling in comfort?" he asked in his journal, as he was hustled out of his sleeping compartment at 8 o'clock in the morning, and forced to cover a great part of the German leg of the journey towards Russia in a small stuffy carriage, tackily furnished in red velvet and antimacassars, reeking of orange peel and stale cigar smoke. Things got little better when they stopped at Hanover for lunch: "A cup of tepid, gritty coffee, some tough, half-raw beef floating in grease, are the only provisions procurable the whole livelong day."

The sights of the German countryside, however, served to mollify him as he drew closer to the Russian border. It being a Sunday, the fields were deserted, and the train was filled with holidaymakers being dropped off at rural stations along the way. The German railway stations, he noted, were like chalets, enfolded in lime trees, rosebushes and honeysuckle. The narrow platforms were turned into the sites of impromptu parties: "Plain and perspiring German females, still plainer and somewhat inebriated German men, with a sprinkling of soldiers in stiffly starched white uniforms, looking as if they had walked out of a toy-box, shared out trays of beer, fruit and punch, singing folk songs, laughing and enjoying the fresh pine-scented country air."

These last bucolic memories of Germany were strong in de Windt's mind as the train pulled across the Russo-German frontier. The train departed the final German outpost, Eydtkunen, and then moved slowly over the physical marks of the border: a strip of neutral territory, wild, uncultivated and overgrown, and then an iron bridge above a small stream. By the crossing was a solitary figure, a Cossack standing to attention in a black and white sentry box, alone and enveloped in a drab-coloured greatcoat, high boots, a white linen cap, leaning slightly on his rifle. Beyond him, everything seemed to be strangely and suddenly reversed.

It was hardly favourable to the country he had entered. The snug homesteads, trim hedgerows and well-cultivated fields of Germany gave place to tumbledown log huts and carelessly sown crops, intersected by vast tracts of wild wasteland and pine forest. However, by the same token, the amenities for travellers enjoyed a wonderful transformation. At Eydtkunen, all had been dirt, discomfort and confusion. Stopping at the first station in the Russian Empire, Wirballen, for Customs and an inspection of passports, de Windt was almost overwhelmed to discover a cool and spacious dining room decked out in immaculate linen, glass and bright silver. "No greasy scalding soup or petrified sandwiches nor warm lemonade," he joyfully recorded as he helped himself to iced wine and Russian tea.

The quality of officialdom was equally improved. The Customs officers, he declared, were the least troublesome in Europe. They might occasionally prove obstructive to a German traveller, but a Frenchman seldom, and an Englishman never. His 300 cigars and near unlimited supply of tobacco were waived through without interest, and although his Kodak camera was taken into another room for close examination, he was given permission to proceed. His passport, and those of his fellow travellers, were handed back – save one, belonging to a rather shabby-looking fellow from Switzerland – and they returned to the St Petersburg train.

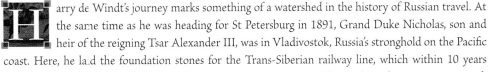

arry de Windt's journey marks something of a watershed in the history of Russian travel. At the same time as he was heading for St Petersburg in 1891, Grand Duke Nicholas, son and heir of the reigning Tsar Alexander III, was in Vladivostok, Russia's stronghold on the Pacific coast. Here, he laid the foundation stones for the Trans-Siberian railway line, which within 10 years was to consign to oblivion the old-fashioned sledge journeys across Siberia along the ancient post road. Yet, although de Windt was one of the last to travel in that fashion, he was only one of an innumerable succession of travellers who were to be drawn over the centuries into the deep heart of Asiatic Russia.

Before him there had been convicts and colonists, fur-trappers and gold prospectors. There had been political exiles, princes and princesses condemned to hard labour in the mines of Chita or Nerchinsk, or else to languish away from their families and the cosmopolitan society of the capital in the peasant villages of the Siberian steppe. There were ambassadors and tea traders, headed for Peking across the wilds of the Mongolian desert, seeking favour or good fortune at the hand of the Emperor of China. There were missionaries and ethnographers, horrified or fascinated in equal measure by the shamanism and sacrifices of the aboriginal tribes, seeking either to eradicate or else to save from oblivion the extraordinary beliefs and customs that they found. And after the time of de Windt, when the new Trans-Siberian Railway slashed the journey time across Asia from months to days, and for a fare of £12 (US$20) one could view

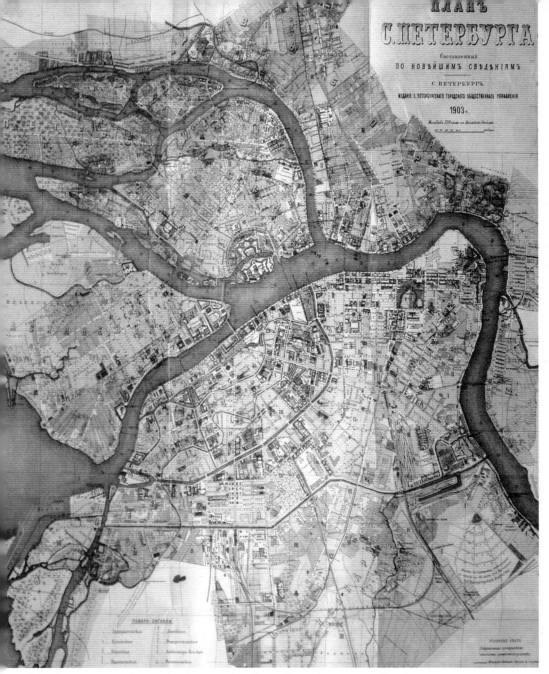

(Above) A Russian map of St Petersburg from 1903 shows the significance of water in its low-lying location.

(Top left) A colour photomechanical print of St Isaac's Cathedral and the Nicholas I monument in St Petersburg in the late 19th century.

(Bottom left) A similar colour rendition of Moscow's Kremlin, circa 1890–1900.

the immensities of the undiscovered continent from the comfort of a dining carriage, dressed in a lounge suit and eating soup, a different class of traveller began to emerge.

Although the train journey was not without its rigours, it began to attract a more genteel, professional tourist, thirsty for different adventures. Foreign families and single women began to make the trip. Even the famous Baedeker compiled notes for the voyage. Besides these, there were also businessmen, who saw in Russia's Far East an exact analogy to the American West. The old image of snow-bound Siberia, an icy tract of convicts, torture and desolation, was, in their mind, beginning to pass away. Instead, they conjured up a pristine empty land of boundless opportunity, fertile and rich with resources, waiting for the energy of entrepreneurs and the magic of technology to turn its potential into wealth.

For many of these travellers, whether convict or ambassador, explorer or businessman, whether bound for Siberia or Vladivostok, Mongolia or Peking, it was from St Petersburg that they would ultimately make their way. More than any other place, it was the elegant streets and the grand façades of St Petersburg that would serve as the backdrop for the start of a multitude of journeys far into the Asian hinterland.

According to the old legend, it was in 1703 that Peter the Great, Tsar of Russia, rode into the marshy swamps at the mouth of the Neva River, and amidst the scattered hamlets and isolated fisherman's cottages, cut out a cross of turf with his sword and declared "here shall be a city". Yet, for hundreds of years before this, the very site of St Petersburg was heavy with associations. In the mid-ninth century, a Viking chieftain, Rurik, sailed in from the Baltic and established a base in the area where St Petersburg was later to be founded. From here, an area known as Ingria, he was able to make forays inland, and by 862, establish the first Russian dynasty – an association of Viking kings with Slavic subjects, that was to endure for over six centuries until the time of Ivan the Terrible.

The Russian Chroniclers hold Rurik's establishment of this Ingrian base as being the first act of Russian history. They point to the first emergence of the Russian nation as being a result of the very character of the land of St Petersburg. It was the fact that the nature of Ingria acted as a point of departure for travellers, where interaction between East and West could occur, that allowed Rurik to build the Russian dynasty, and bring the Russian nation into being. Pushkin was to characterise St Petersburg as Russia's window onto Europe, but a thousand years before he wrote this, the same was true of the land itself, though in the absence of the city. There were few other locations in Russia that could be said to have such profound importance for Russian history, or indeed, for the history of travel, and where the two in so fertile a fashion have been so closely interlinked.

Despite this, many of the travellers who went through St Petersburg seem to give the city only light treatment in their writings, or none at all. It is perhaps the prospect they faced beyond St Petersburg – of a journey of several months and several thousand miles – that distracted them from taking note of the city, or else the wearying hunt for travelling equipment, trustworthy servants, letters of introduction and government passports. Yet, those who did choose to concentrate on it often evince a certain sense of disappointment. It begins with their portrayal of the approach to the city. George Dobson, a *Times* correspondent who made the same journey by rail into St Petersburg several years before de Windt, noted the same immediate reversal of conditions between Germany and Russia; a sudden movement from discipline and neatness, tidy farms and homesteads, deer-stocked parks and well-kept woods, to clusters of "wretched wooden huts… without the least traces of comfort". Villages composed of these huts, each exactly like the other, continued in monotonous repetition, all the way from the German border to St Petersburg, giving a "poverty-stricken look [to] the dreary, flat landscape".

The slow, meandering journey did not displease de Windt. He enjoyed the frequent stops at the small stations along the line, picturesque one-storey buildings painted red with green sheet-iron roofs, often surrounded with gardens and over-bowered with vines. Frequently no one got on, and no one got off. Beyond them, the peasants were toiling in the fields, their scarlet kaftans adding dabs of colour to the background, breaking up the dull brown monotony of the landscape of which Dobson had earlier complained. De Windt noted the peasants' industry. Both men and women would work frequently until after 8pm. It was this aspect of the approach to St Petersburg, the contrast between town and country life which, more than anything, unsettled Adolf Erman, a German anthropologist of the 1840s. In travelling to St Petersburg, he said, "we see only tedious plains, inhabited by a labouring population, apparently without repose or enjoyment; but the capital itself looks like the abode of a people living only for enjoyment."

any 19th century travellers were surprised at the abruptness with which they arrived in the city. In the time of Dobson and de Windt, there "were no suburbs to serve as an introduction". Approaching St Petersburg, the train would first pass through the Ingrian Marshes, great swamps reaching to the horizon broken up by the occasional sedge-bound lake, heavy with waterfowl and wildlife. Nearer the city, it would then plunge through a succession of forests, pine, white birch and black poplar. Getting closer, these gave way to orchards and gardens, villages and villas, the residences of Grand Dukes and high nobility. Erman, travelling before the abolition of serfdom, noted how these villas would have a board in front with the name of the owner, and the number of serfs attached to his estate. Trout streams transected the landscape; Swiss-style chalets abounded. The peasants' cottages and posthouses were neatly painted yellow and red, and servants from the local estates dressed in coloured livery of white, silver and green, might be seen at the stations waiting to attend on their masters arriving from abroad. And then, suddenly, one left behind these rural scenes, and found oneself in the midst of the city. There was no "running of the train between miles of houses on a level with the first-floor windows", as Dobson and others were used to from travel elsewhere in Europe. St Petersburg's station stood on the edge of the city, and without any warning, one was immediately presented with a *coup d'oeil* of the capital.

It was similar for the traveller arriving by sea. For the liners that steamed towards St Petersburg by way of the Gulf of Finland, there was little to indicate, even within a few miles, the impending presence of the Russian capital. The approach to the city, complained Dobson, was certainly not inviting. A French diplomat and traveller, the Marquis de Custine, who travelled there in 1839, was more outspoken: "There is nothing so mournful as the approach to St Petersburg. As you proceed into the Gulf, the Ingrian marshes, ever more flat, are eventually reduced to a little wavering line between earth and sky: that line is Russia, a soggy moorland, low-lying and scattered as far as the eye can see with birch trees that appear scanty and meagre. This landscape, uniform, void, featureless, colourless, without limits, is so lit as to be barely visible."

(Above) *St Petersburg in the early 1800s, showing the Strelka and lighthouse with the Peter and Paul Fortress in the distance. The city was a busy port even then, with thousands of ships arriving from all over the world during the summer months.*

(Right) *A hand-coloured print based on a daguerreotype by Noel Paymal Lerebours shows Moscow's St Basil's Cathedral in 1842.*

nother traveller, the American explorer George Kennan, made the journey from England (Hull) to St Petersburg by sea in July 1870. His sense of the arrival, though similar to de Custine's, is portrayed with rather finer a brush. He travelled second class on a brigantine-rigged steamer, the *Thomas Wilson*, one of only three passengers. The ship was otherwise laden with thousands of tons of iron rails, and the deck with engines and boilers for export. The route, he observed, swarmed with ships. North of Copenhagen – where, under protest, he was hauled up onto the cold, rainy deck at 5am by his travelling companion to see Hamlet's Castle, Elsinore – he counted the sails of 97 vessels. Going east, two days later the *Wilson* entered the Finnish Gulf. The channel narrowed to a distance of 30 miles (50 kilometres) in width, and the *Wilson* bore towards the middle of it to avoid the danger of rocks, steaming towards St Petersburg at a speed of nine knots. The way was misty and clogged with rain, and little was visible from the deck, aside from the warning beacons at night, and the distant view of the low-lying shores by day. In the middle of the hazy channel, although he could smell the damp odour of the earth and sense the proximity of land, there was little to be seen on the two green shores on either side except the occasional church, house or light tower. Before long, a pilot boat came forward to guide the ship, and it shortly reached the outpost of Kronstadt, the narrow fortified island which guards the entrance to the Neva River – a forbidding place, festooned with parapets, granite ramparts, guns and sea forts. As larger ships could proceed no further, here Kennan disembarked, and was ushered into the cabin of a little steamer, a long vessel with no skylight, but portholes just above the water's edge. He was joined by a Russian solider drinking beer, and a crowd of Russian Mujiks looking dishevelled and miserable in long sheepskin coats, with ragged beards and long, dirty hair. It was from this viewpoint, and amongst such a crowd that, with the vessel fighting against the current of a Neva River swollen by rain, Kennan caught his first and unexpected sight of St Petersburg: the golden dome of St Isaac's Cathedral, standing high over the city skyline.

Dobson similarly remembered the moment. After leaving Kronstadt, "there was no sign of St Petersburg being in front of us until we caught sight of a brilliant glitter in the hazy distance, which… was a reflection from the gilded dome of the St Isaac Cathedral, the Russian St Paul's, and the highest building in the city. As the boat brought us closer to this luminous landmark, the city seemed literally to rise out of the water." The quality of the scene had not changed for over 150 years. In the mid-18th century Count Francesco Algarotti, following the same route, was overwhelmed on his arrival by the sudden appearance, apparition-like, of the city: "On either shore sumptuous edifices ground together; turrets with gilded spires rising every here and there like pyramids; ships, which, by their masts and floating streamers, mark the separation of the streets, and distinguish the several quarters; such was the brilliant sight which struck our eyes: we were told, here is the Admiralty, there is the Arsenal, here the Citadel, yonder is the Academy, on that side the Tsarina's winter palace."

Count Algarotti said of the way that St Petersburg appeared without warning that it was like a "scene changing in an instant, as at an opera." His comment, likening the city to the backdrop of a stage or theatrical set, more than anything neatly encapsulates the reason why such a number of travellers have been unnerved by their visit. They felt that St Petersburg, despite its grandeur, the size and extent of its palaces, its wealth and its power, was an insubstantial, superficial and almost impermanent place. As the

Marquis de Custine wrote, "no one can believe that this marvellous capital city will endure". A change of circumstances, of politics, a mischance of war, and "this marvellous creation of Peter I [will] vanish like a soap bubble in a puff of wind".

I f there was a city to which Prospero's image in Shakespeare's *The Tempest* of "the cloud-capped towers… the gorgeous palaces… this insubstantial pageant" dissolving and leaving "not a rack behind" might apply, that place, in the minds of many travellers, was St Petersburg. This sense is perhaps symptomatic of the circumstances under which the city came to be built. The location, although closely entwined with the earliest of Russian history, was marshy, low-lying, and dangerously prone to flooding. Dobson said of the view from the top of St Isaac's that the entire city seemed to be floating on an immense volume of water. The city emerged not from a process of organic growth or of economic necessity, as was usual with European cities, but was constructed and peopled almost within an instant, on the strength of imperial diktat. From the moment of the city's foundation, labourers and prisoners were corralled not only from Russia but also from Finland, Sweden and Russia's Asiatic and Siberian provinces to work on the building. They laboured in squalid conditions, proper tools were in short supply, and the workers were compelled to heap up ramparts and embankments by carrying mud over the swampy ground with their bare hands, or else the tails of their shirts. Tens of thousands are thought to have perished in the city's earliest days.

The higher classes of Russian society were not immune to sharing the travails of the poor. In 1712, Peter made a decree compelling 1,000 families of the nobility, 1,000 merchant families, and 2,000 artisans "of every kind – painters, tailors, joiners, blacksmiths, etc" to settle on the banks of the Neva, and to build fine houses according to their means. On account of its scarcity in the region, each person coming to the city was ordered to bring with them a piece of stone, and in order to secure greater supplies of the material and the people who could work it, the building of stone houses was forbidden anywhere else in Russia, aside from the new capital.

The sense of a literal superficiality, perhaps best summed up in Orlando Figes' phrase that St Petersburg was a "city of imported stone built on water", found its practical effect in the simple stability of the buildings. Of the early buildings, despite their number, few survive, on account of the rapidity of construction and the poor nature of the ground. It is on this account that Algarotti held the city to be nowhere as impressive as it was on its first appearance. The palaces of the nobility whom Peter compelled to live in Petersburg, he writes, "are upon the banks of the Neva, and it is easy to see that they were built out of obedience rather than choice. Their walls are cracked, quite out of perpendicular, and ready to fall. It has been wittily enough said, that ruins make themselves in other places, but that they were built at Petersburg."

This literal superficiality of the buildings found an echo in the casual nature of their style. The architecture of the city did not draw from Russian antecedents; the examples of Moscow, the earlier capital, were ignored. Peter's whole mission in the foundation of the city was to escape the backward-looking medieval obscurantism of the old capital, and to modernise Russia by opening the new capital to the influences of the West. Thus, he similarly imported Western designs, as well as architects, artisans

A panoramic view of St Petersburg, dedicated by permission to his Imperial Majesty Alexander I, drawn on the spot by J.A. Atkinson from the observatory of the Academy of Sciences, circa 1805–07.

and craftsmen, and, with his autocratic power, imposed them on the new Russian capital, and its Russian society. Hence, many travellers perceived a dual rootlessness in the capital's architecture. The first was that there was such a mixture of different European styles, that the city's architecture in itself expressed no style at all, relating to no place. "There reigns in this capital," said Algarotti, "a kind of bastard architecture, which partakes of the Italian, the French, and the Dutch." The Russian writer Aleksandr Herzen summed it up later in the 19th century by remarking that St Petersburg looked unlike any other western European city, because it looked like all of them at once. On top of what one might call this cosmopolitan architectural rootlessness, many travellers evinced a sense of unease that a foreign idiom was imposed wholesale on a Russian city, that the buildings were not just imported stone on water, but imported ideas on a foreign and unsuitable soil.

The Marquis de Custine summed up this idea, this feeling of anomie held by many, in a letter sent from St Petersburg: "Here, we find no concordance between what nature has given and art has created, and this lack of harmony constantly shocks me. As I walk through the town, I experience the same unease as when speaking to a person of affected manners". He went on to elaborate the point: "My first impressions were of some gilded spires, slender as lightning conductors; porticos, the base of which almost disappears beneath the water; squares, colonnaded, vanishing into the vastness of their surroundings; statues, imitations of the antique, their features, style and manner of dress clashing with the nature of the land, the colour of the sky and the climate, as well as with the faces, costumes and customs of the inhabitants, until they seem like heroes held captive among their enemies; buildings in exile, temples fallen from the summit of some Greek mountain into the Lappish marshlands and which, as a result, seem dwarfed by a setting into which they have been transported, not knowing why."

The everyday annoyances of the traveller were as much in the mind of Harry de Windt as the abstract peculiarities of St Petersburg. Checking into his room at the Hotel de France, he was at first disturbed by the inhabitants of the room opposite to his. They were a general and his daughter, as peculiar and detached a pair of characters as one might have encountered in one of Gogol's short stories on the city. The general was in his 60s, and was never seen except in his uniform. His daughter was 16, beautiful and grey eyed, but had the fault of incessantly strumming the piano, all day, every day, taking only short breaks for "rest, refreshment and exercise". De Windt would have found this bearable, except for the fact that she knew only one tune, an air called "Some Day", which she rehearsed some 200-300 times daily. "Practise makes perfect," thought de Windt to himself, but she still failed to get it quite right. This did not disturb the general, however, who sat placidly by the window, drinking endless cups of tea and nodding his head to the music. Wondering whether he had been driven mad by his daughter, or else also only knew one tune, de Windt stole down to lunch, and found the dining room colonised by Thomas Cook's travellers.

"I really cannot do the Winter Palace this afternoon," gasped one of the women, white and trembling with fatigue. "May I not go for a drive instead?" De Windt looked with sympathy at the tour guide as argument flared at the table of 40 tourists, and wondered how he was going to calm the mob. Quitting the hotel, he found the streets quiet and the heat intense. Many of the residents had quit for the summer, leaving for the cooler spots of Helsinki or Viborg. Those people whom de Windt did see puzzled him. Despite the temperature being over 90 degrees Fahrenheit (32°C) in the shade, they carried thick greatcoats over their

shoulders. He later found that the temperature in the summer had a propensity to drop all of a sudden as much as 40 degrees, and anyone unprotected was open to catching a fever. The streets themselves, he discovered, were swept daily but not watered, so that from morning to evening the air was thick with clouds of dust. These combined with the smells which rose from the canals, so that for de Windt St Petersburg possessed an odour which brought to mind the back streets of a Chinese town.

St Petersburg's Bolschaya Morskaya, with the War Office Arch behind, in 1901.

Nevsky Prospect, St Petersburg's main thoroughfare, in the early 20th century, a time of horse-drawn carriages and trolley buses.

His walk around the streets bolstered him in his conviction that St Petersburg was not a "taking city". Although he admired the broadness and regularity of the principal thoroughfares – as Pushkin put it, St Petersburg's "stern symmetric form" – on closer inspection he declared that the private buildings were "ugly and stunted", and that the ironwork lattices and porticoes which decorated a number of the houses, being painted in garish light blues or greens, increased the "tawdry gimcrack appearance of the streets". Even Nevsky Prospect, the great avenue of St Petersburg, did not escape his condemnation. Everything had a cheerless, squalid appearance, even on the brightest day. The very plaques which bore the legend "Nevsky Prospect" had long since lost their blue enamel, and the name had been crudely repainted in white letters over the rusty background. Despite the length of the street, three miles, there were only a dozen shops – mainly French jewellers – which came up to de Windt's exacting standards. Their windows, he decided, were marvels of riches and taste, and their prices would put their countrymen in Paris's Rue de la Paix to shame. As for the others, their shoddy appearance was not improved by a plethora of crudely painted, gaudy signboards, advertising the wares for sale.

A 1930 silver gelatin print shows an unusual angle of one of the entrances to the State Hermitage Museum, founded by Catherine the Great and occupying a number of historic buildings including the Winter Palace, former residence of Russia's emperors.

The one thing that did impress de Windt as he walked along Nevsky Prospect was the succession of different places of worship, each of a different denomination. As he passed by the Orthodox Cathedral of Our Lady of Kazan, the Dutch Church, then Lutheran and Catholic churches, and even a synagogue, he marvelled not only at the tolerance that the city displayed, but also at the variety of people congregated within it. The earlier traveller Adolf Erman, who made the same walk down Nevsky Prospect over 60 years before de Windt, being an anthropologist and ethnographer, was also taken with this diversity. Perhaps on account of his profession, he was also more precise in his description, and possessed a greater sympathy than de Windt for the people and places that he encountered.

For him, a walk along Nevsky Prospect was an experience far more exciting, exotic and sensuous. Surveying the canals that intersected the Prospect, he found that the lower stories of the houses had been turned into warehouses and shops. Their proprietors were as international a crowd as he had ever seen. Not only were they held by some of Russia's near European neighbours, the Germans, English and French, but amongst these were traders from much farther afield – Armenians, Persians, "Bokharans" from Central Asia, and Chinese. These merchants had, he maintained contrary to de Windt, "carried to perfection the arts of attractive display". His eye was caught by the bright colours of their goods, imported cloth, and the gleam of damasked sword blades. The air around was perfumed with the scent of attar of roses.

Carrying on down Nevsky Prospect away from the Admiralty and the fashionable heart of the city, the more singular and characteristic, according to Erman, St Petersburg became. Crowds thronged around Our Lady of Kazan, but on the streets, horse-drawn vehicles were more numerous than pedestrians. Their wheels were near silent, being held together with wooden, not iron stakes, and the predominant noise in the air was the clatter of hoofs and the calls of drivers. Guards clutching halberds stood in sentry boxes, calling out "*Prava*" (keep to the right) in an attempt to stave off collisions and to keep the traffic flowing.

A little beyond, he found the Gostinnoi Dvor (Gostiny Dvor), or Great Bazaar, a giant colonnaded building of irregular shape, whose longest side was over 1,200 feet (365 metres) long. Today, the site is occupied by a department store, expressing at least a continuity of purpose, but in Erman's time it was something much rarer: a great market in plan and in spirit such as one might find in one of the Silk Road cities of Central Asia. Indeed, it could be counted as one of the westernmost outposts of that culture. There was even a reservoir in the centre of it for camels to drink.

As with its cousins in Central Asia, the Gostiny Dvor of St Petersburg was divided up into a succession of rows or streets, each dedicated to a specific class of merchandise. Erman found the "Iron Row" for blades, the "Peltry Row" for furs from Siberia, even a "Book Row". The goldsmiths and silversmiths had rows to themselves, as did the sellers of ikons (icons). Anything could be found in the alleys of the bazaar, from a toy watch to a ship's anchor. Each row was divided into narrow compartments, which were then allotted to particular merchants. Sitting outside these little shops, they would lay some of their goods around them, but would keep the finer merchandise hidden within for the trusted customer, or else in magazines above on the first floor. They manned their stalls from dawn until dusk, when the shutters would be drawn, and tripwires rigged with bells tied to the doors to act as an alarm against intruders.

Here, remarked Erman, returning to the theme of diversity, "Russian traffic is seen in all its nationality". He saw traders who had brought their wares from the different khanates of Central Asia. He saw seasonal migrant workers, peasants who flocked into St Petersburg to act as drivers of vehicles or boatmen on the Neva. These workers lived simply; they dressed in the most primitive homemade sheepskin clothes, ate bread, drank mead and *kvass*, and slept near the Bazaar in carts or else on the canals in their boats. At the other end of the social scale, he found another sort of Russian, the members of the old mercantile class, more Eastern and Asiatic in bearing than many of the Westernised inhabitants of St Petersburg. They clung fast to their archaic customs and ways of dress. While government officials and ordinary townspeople affected Western costume, neckties and frock coats, the merchants in the bazaar preserved their antiquated outfits of long beards, kaftans and girdles. Despite their wealth, and in contrast to others in the city, they maintained a strict simplicity of conduct, abstaining from any pleasure or indulgence. Their women, as was the Russian custom dating back to the Middle Ages, were generally kept sequestered indoors. One of the few times that they might be seen was at the matchmaking bride-shows in May, where, bedecked with old-fashioned headdresses dripping with ornaments, their marriageable daughters were allowed to promenade with potential mates along the alleys of the summer garden on the Neva.

The Tartar Bazaar in St Petersburg, where merchandise of every description could be found.

Despite the unease that many travellers felt about St Petersburg, few of them were insensible to its beauty. Although for Erman, the impress of perfection possessed by many of the streets near the centre of town was partly dependent on the absence of anything in those places "to remind us of the vulgar wants of life... no sign of trade, handicraft or... labour... but that the inhabitants here seem to live only for the tranquil enjoyment of their opulence", he was still capable of falling into raptures at their splendour. When contemplating the majesty of the thoroughfares, the frequent clatter of coaches drawn by "high-mettled horses" was not enough to withdraw his attention from the "fine forms and massive grandeur around", nor encroach on the more transcendent "solemn stillness" of the place.

As the evenings fell in summer, still light in the northern sky – de Windt was able to read the small print in his newspaper until 10pm – many of the people would go to promenade on the banks of the Neva, or even take their ships to sail upon the river. For Erman, this was one of the chief pleasures of St Petersburg, and one of the best ways to appreciate its beauty. The river was always alive at this time of day with gondolas and boats perpetually gliding backwards and forwards. From them, as the river narrowed upstream, the buildings of the city on either side seemed more colossal. "The golden cupolas of the church towers, the glittering windows of the palaces," all appeared to him "doubly gay and brilliant when reflected from the clear waters of the Neva."

For an earlier traveller, Andrew Swinton, who visited St Petersburg in the 1790s, 40 years before Erman, the sight of the river at dusk was enhanced by the custom of the nobility to have music as they sailed. Their boats, observed Swinton, were elegantly canopied in silk, and the rowers would be chosen from those among their servants who had the best voices. At first, they would sing as they rowed, keeping time to their songs by the beat of their stroke. Yet, having gone upstream for a while against the current, they would ship oars, gather in a circle at one end of the boat, and at that moment, freed from the constraints of rowing, exert their vocal powers to the utmost. At this moment, they would make "such exquisite harmony", that they drew people out onto the galleries and balconies of the houses overlooking the water. Others outside would stand on the edge of the banks, and follow the boat as it drifted downstream to listen to its songs. The nobility brought instruments, and would play in ensembles to provide an interlude to the singing, or sometimes accompany it. When the music was done, the people on the banks, said Swinton, would go their way, repeating and echoing the songs to every corner of the city.

Another option for the citizen of St Petersburg was to resort to the parks and pleasure gardens around the city. Here they might eat, drink, stroll or watch performances at the open-air theatres. One evening, de Windt, who was suffering an interminable wait in St Petersburg for his travelling documents and permissions from the Russian government to visit the Siberian prisons (such was the object of his journey), decided to follow the fashionable crowds in these recreations. Crossing the Troitski Bridge, he paused for the view, and in spite of his earlier dislike for the city, he was almost moved to poetry at what he saw. The sun was setting, and transfused the western quarter of the sky with the colour of rose, against which the spires and domes of the city stood out, clear and distinct. One or two stars shone above in the darkening sky, which merged into grey haze and light saffron on the horizon, as the Neva flowed on below him, gleaming like a sheet of burnished steel in the twilight.

As the bells of the Fortress of St Peter and St Paul boomed across the water, the crash of orchestral music suddenly rose from the Livadia Gardens on the right bank of the River, but softened by the distance. Hurrying across to the crowded gardens, he was able to watch the most part of a "grand spectacular performance", somewhat incongruously, on Stanley and his explorations of Africa. In the St Petersburg version, Stanley was accompanied on his travels by two women, one white and one black, not to mention a comic servant; and his travels were somehow concluded by the procession of the Star-Spangled Banner across the stage to the accompaniment of the orchestra, its percussion section enhanced by enormous squibs of gunpowder, playing "Yankee Doodle Dandy". The enthusiasm of the audience, related de Windt, knew no bounds. Yet, for all the incongruity of the performance, de Windt was not at all put out, but rather returned to his hotel elated by the beauty and the quiet of the night.

The times after such performances, as the crowds returned home from the pleasure gardens and resorts around the city, were equally uplifting for Erman. As their clamour was suddenly lulled into silence of the rural edges of the city towards the sea, the stillness of the night was enhanced. The outlines of distant objects in the whiteness of the summer night were still visible, and nightingales sang in every grove. Fishermen, with little fires burning in their canoes, pursued salmon between the islands at the mouth of the river. Dense cloud would come down at midnight, but melt away early at the falling of the morning dew.

MOSCOW AND THE WAY THERE

he road by way of St Petersburg and Ingria into Russia was by no means the only route towards Moscow. For the earliest travellers from Europe, particularly before the foundation of St Petersburg, there were several other ways that they might take. One route was from the Gulf of Finland down the River Neva to Lake Ladoga, and then south via the Volkhov River to the great trading city of Novgorod, Tver and then Moscow. Others travelling overland might come from Central Europe eastwards by way of Smolensk.

The first English travellers reached Moscow in 1553. As was typical, they were not at all intending to go there, and happened upon it only by accident whilst seeking a northeastern sea passage, by way of the North Pole, to China. Their small fleet of three ships, which set off from Deptford in London, having rounded the northernmost tip of Scandinavia were scattered by a storm. One of them, the *Edward Bonaventure*, under its Captain Richard Chancellor, was able to regain its bearings. However, instead of proceeding eastwards along the northern coast of Siberia, it was forced by the cold and lack of provisions to turn south. Chancellor eventually was able to navigate into the White Sea on the northern coast of Russia, and put into the bay opposite Kholmogory (Colmogro), where the natives, astonished at these visitors, told them that their country was Russia, and that "Ivan Vasiliwich", or Ivan the Terrible "governed farre and wide in those places".

An albumen print panorama of Moscow in the 1890s shows the imposing nature of the central Kremlin.

Chancellor, though unable to proceed any farther in the search for the Northeast Passage and the fabulous wealth that it would ensure him, instead decided to turn his attention to the country on which he had unwittingly stumbled, and had beforehand known absolutely nothing. His actions, on his return to London a year later, would lead to the foundation of the Muscovy Company (1555) and the emergence of trade between the two countries. Stranded as he was, he requested an audience with the Tsar (Grand Duke), so that he might open relations between England and Russia, and propose the establishment of commerce and traffic. He was conducted south towards Moscow by sledge from Kholmogory by way of Yaroslavl on a journey that was "very long and most troublesome", astonished at the "hardnesse of the ground" and the "force of the colde, which in those places is very extreme and horrible".

Despite the freezing conditions, Chancellor was able to make a description of his journey, and the country between the northern coast and Moscow. The way he went was to become the initial route for commerce between England and Russia. Bearing always in mind the possibility of trade, he noted as he went anything that might have a potential for business, particularly in the field of goods. In the northern regions, by the White Sea and Dvina River, he observed that they were "very great fishers for Salmons and small Coddes". There was also a great industry in extracting salt from seawater. Kholmogory served Moscow, Novgorod and all the cities in the region not only with salt, but with salt fish also. Besides this, the country in the north was rich with valuable furs. He found for sale "Sables, marterns, greese Bevers, Foxes white, blacke, and redde, Minkes, Ermines, Miniver, and Harts". Other commodities he noted were tallow (for the manufacture of candles), wax, flax, and perhaps most importantly hemp, used in the making of rope. There was at this time a shortage of hemp in England, and the new supply from Russia was to prove vital. The British fleet that defeated the Spanish Armada in 1588 was rigged with rope made from imported Russian hemp.

After he passed the city of Yaroslavl, 155 miles (250 kilometres) north of Moscow, the traffic began to grow greater. The country between the two cities was "well replenished with small Villages, which are so well filled with people, that it is a wonder to see them". The fields were rich with corn, and the roads were busy with sledges carrying it south to Moscow, or else up to supply the northern regions, which were too cold for proper agriculture. "You shall meete in a morning seven or eight hundred sleds comming or going thither, that carrie corne," he noted, and coming from the north towards the capital were sledges laden with "fishes, furres and beastes skinnes". However, of the appearance of the towns and villages he passed, he said that they were built "out of order, and with no hansomeness: their streetes and wayes are not paved with stone as ours are: the walles of their houses are of wood: the roofes for the most part are covered with shingle boords."

Sigismund von Herberstein, an ambassador who visited Moscow in 1526 on behalf of Maximilian I, the Holy Roman Emperor, did not find the surrounding country nearly as bucolic as Chancellor. Travelling in the depth of one of the harshest winters that there had been for many years, he was drawn to comment on the area's extremes of climate. Fruit trees along the way had perished for the cold. Whenever he spat, the saliva had frozen solid before it reached the ground. And, as his party went on its way, they found endless bodies along the road of those who had expired in the cold. Couriers were found frozen in their carriages. Cattle-herders, bringing their livestock to Moscow, died huddled together with their animals. Worse, a number of poor itinerants, who wandered the area leading troops of dancing bears, were numbered amongst the dead. Their bears, crazed with hunger, flew into the neighbouring villages and rushed into the houses, driving out the "rustic multitude", which, terrified, fled and perished miserably out of doors as well. This winter tragedy followed a summer that had been one of the hottest known. Everything that had been sown in the cornfields had been burnt up and withered in the sun. Forest fires catching in the adjacent districts to Moscow gave rise to clouds of smoke that so filled the country, that "the eyes of those who walked out were severely injured by it".

he city that von Herberstein and Chancellor found was a city of wood. Neither had it been a city long established. Moscow had scarcely existed before the beginning of the 12th century, except perhaps as a village. It rose to prominence in the 13th century as its lords volunteered to act on behalf of the Mongol hordes, who then ruled Russia, in collecting taxes from the other cities and princedoms into which Russia was then divided. The decision of Metropolitan Peter in 1327 to make Moscow the permanent seat of the leaders of the Russian Orthodox added to its prestige, and it was at this time that work began to give the Kremlin, which was then a fortress of oak, an outer rampart of white limestone.

"Mosco it selfe is great," wrote Chancellor. "I take the whole towne to bee greater then London with the suburbs: but it is very rude, and standeth without all order." Von Herberstein agreed, and went on to make an important observation on the layout of the city. Although it was "tolerably large", at a distance it appeared larger than it really was, "for the gardens and spacious courtyards in every house" along with the "houses of smiths and artificers" standing detached in their own grounds, "make a great addition to the size of the city". These houses, he continued, "extend in a long row at the end of the city, interspersed with

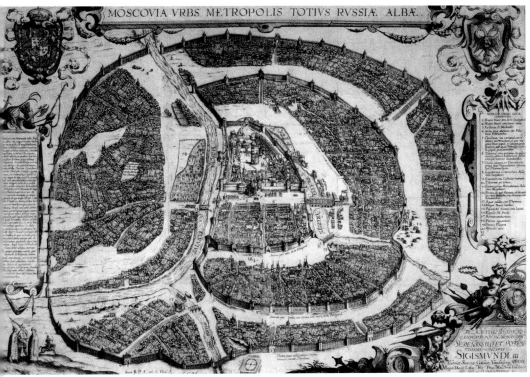

A Polish map of Moscow dating to 1610, when they had invaded and taken control of the city – though they were soon to be driven out by a Cossack army.

fields and meadows". In this fashion, Moscow in history was never a very densely packed city. In its design, inasmuch as there was any design, it was almost like a garden city, having something of the suburban. It eschewed the compact or the claustrophobic, but rather had a tendency to spread out.

Edward Clarke, an English academic and traveller who journeyed to Moscow 250 years after Chancellor, found that even into the 1800s, it still preserved this characteristic of being a city full of room, even a miscellany of a place. Of arriving in the city at the beginning of the 19th century, he wrote: "Numerous spires, glittering with gold, amidst burnished domes and painted palaces, appear in the midst of an open plain, for several versts..." [a *verst* was equal to approximately one kilometre]. Having passed the city's gate, "you look about, and wonder what is become of the city, or where you are; and are ready to ask, once more, How far is it to Moscow? They will tell you, 'This is Moscow!' and you behold nothing but a wide and scattered suburb, huts, gardens, pig-sties, brick walls, churches, dunghills, palaces, timber-yards, warehouses, and a refuse, as it were, of materials sufficient to stock an empire with miserable towns and miserable villages. One might imagine all the States of Europe and Asia had sent a building, by way of representative to Moscow: and under this impression the eye is presented with deputies from all countries, holding congress: timber-huts from regions beyond the Arctic; plastered palaces from Sweden and Denmark, not white-washed since their arrival; painted walls from the Tirol; mosques from Constantinople; Tartar temples from Bucharia [Bokharia]; pagodas, pavilions, and verandahs from China;

cabarets from Spain; dungeons, prisons and public offices from France; architectural ruins from Rome; terraces and trellises from Naples; and warehouses from Wapping."

Another English academic and traveller of the same period, William Coxe, agreed and put it more succinctly: "In a word, some parts of this vast city have the appearance of a sequestered desert, other quarters, of a populous town; some of a contemptible village, others of a great capital."

Although four-fifths of the city was burnt down shortly after Clarke's visit in its capture by Napoleon, when rebuilt it still preserved this open and rustic feel. Even towards the end of the 19th century and the time of the great novelists, the streets were so muddy that it was not uncommon to see horses sunk into the mire up to their middles, according to George Carrington in *Behind the Scenes in Russia*. Another traveller, G.T. Lowth, exclaimed that cows would be kept in the garden courtyards of the houses, let out at sunrise to wander and graze in the streets, and then at evening, like cats, would find their own way home.

Clarke's description highlights another important characteristic of Moscow. Not only with its feel of being an agricultural centre, but also with the chaos of styles and influences, it betrayed how closely it was linked not only to the wider countryside, but also to the Asiatic realms of the Russian Empire. It was this feeling of being grounded, of being more deeply a part of Russia, which has historically marked out Moscow from St Petersburg.

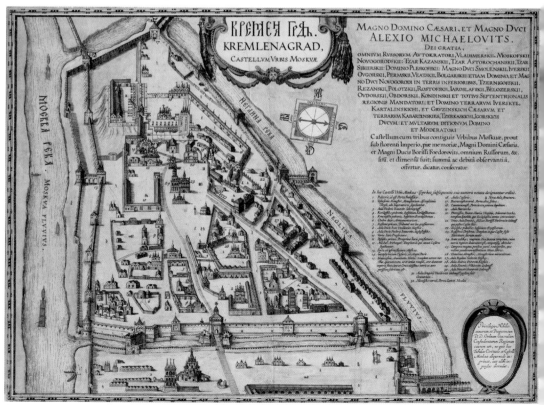

hen Chancellor arrived in Moscow, he waited in the city for 12 days and then was summoned to see the Tsar. The Kremlin by this time had begun to assume the appearance with which we are now familiar, being given its red brick walls and towers during the course of the 1400s, replacing the earlier white limestone of the 14th century. It was now the residence not only of the Tsar's family, but also contained the residence of the Patriarch of the Orthodox Church, and many members of the Russian nobility. Full of great houses of stone and wood together, von Herberstein commented that "from its size it might itself almost be taken for a city". Chancellor saw the nine cathedrals within its walls, "fayre churches" he said, "but I will not stande in description of their buildings nor of the strength thereof because we have better in all points in England". He was similarly underwhelmed by the Tsar's palace: "The Emperours or Dukes house [the Tsar was originally known as the 'Grand Duke of Muscovy'] neither in building nor in the outward shew, nor yet within the house is so sumptuous as I have seene. It is very lowe built in eight square, much like the olde building of England, with small windowes, and so in other points."

He was more impressed by the dignity of the noblemen and the court ceremonial. Entering the palace, he was welcomed by an interpreter and one of the officials responsible for foreign ambassadors. First, he was led into an outer chamber, where 100 gentlemen "all in cloth of golde very sumptuous" sat in attendance. Then, he was conducted into the Tsar's council chamber, where the Tsar himself sat, surrounded by his noblemen. "A faire company," said Chancellor. They sat around the chamber on raised seats, and in the midst of them was the Tsar. His figure, thought Chancellor, was kingly. He sat above the others on a throne of gilt, and wore "a long garment of beaten golde, with an emperial crowne upon his head, and a staffe of Cristall and golde in his right hand".

After Chancellor had given letters to the Tsar from his master, King Edward VI, the Tsar enquired, as was customary, after the King's health, and then invited Chancellor to dinner. Later in the day, he was shown to another palace called the golden palace, "but I saw no cause why it should be so called, for I have seene many fayrer then it in all points"; he was brought into the hall, "which was small and not as great as is the Kings Majesties of England". Beyond this was a dining chamber, where the Tsar sat alone at his table on a high dais. He still wore his crown, but had changed his gold vestment for one of silver. Around the room, there were long trestle tables covered in white cloth at which 200 nobles sat, but they were far off from the Tsar himself: "There sate none neare him by a great way." In the middle of the chamber was a table on which was kept all the plate for use at dinner. It was laden with cups of gold, and four "marvellous great pottes" of gold and silver, "a good yarde and a halfe hie". A marshall, bearing a white wand of office, kept order, and two butlers with white napkins over their shoulders acted as cupbearers to the Tsar, bringing him his drinking vessels, not only of pure gold but also set with pearls and precious stones.

The food, when it came, was brought in no order, but "commeth in dish by dish". It was served on gold platters, and whether it was bread, roast swan or wine, everything was brought first to the table of the Tsar, who would then send helpings of it to each of the noblemen in turn, in the manner of a

A 1664 map of Kremlenagrad, the "Kremlin Castle", during the reign of Alexei I, father of Peter the Great.

Children play on the frozen Moscow River embankment by the Kremlin in winter, circa 1919.

present. The intention was to emphasise the personal dependence of all upon the Tsar. The servants who took it from the Tsar to the guests, when they brought the food addressed each one of them by name, and said "Ivan Vasilevich Emperour of Russia and great Duke of Moscovia doth reward thee with bread", at which the guest had to stand out of respect to the Tsar.

As trade and diplomatic connections with Russia increased over the course of the 16th and 17th centuries, more and more accounts came to be published about life in the Russian capital. One of the most prominent and most graphic was that left behind by Adam Olearius, an envoy from the Duke of Holstein in Germany, who visited Moscow on four occasions between 1633 and 1643. Olearius's memoirs were hugely successful in his own lifetime and for years afterwards, perhaps for two reasons. Not only did he have a vivid eye for the transactions of everyday life, but his descriptions of Russia seemed to chime in with a growing unease about Russia in Western Europe. They fed a general anxiety that the Russians, thanks to their long detachment from the European mainstream, were profoundly different, and should be treated as a people apart. His work can perhaps be seen as one of the early texts of European "Russophobia", which was to become so prevalent later in the 19th century.

Olearius's accounts dwell rather less on the courtly than did those of Chancellor. He formed a gloomy view of the Russian character: "...a very quarrelsome people who assail each other like dogs, with fierce, harsh words. Again and again on the streets one sees such quarrels; the old women shout with such fury that he who is unaccustomed to it expects them at any moment to seize each other's hair. They very rarely come to blows, however; but when they do, they strike with their fists, beating one another with all their might on the sides and genitals..."

Their pugnacity, wrote Olearius, was also reflected in their language: "When their indignation flares and they use swearwords, they do not resort to imprecations involving the sacraments – as unfortunately is often the case with us – consigning to the devil, etc. Instead they use many vile and loathsome words, which, if the historical records did not demand it, I should not impart to chaste ears. They have nothing on their tongue more often than 'son of a whore', 'son of a bitch', 'cur', 'I fuck your mother', to which they add 'into the grave', and similar scandalous speech. Not only adults and old people behave thus, but also little children who do not yet know the name of God, or father, or mother, already have on their lips 'fuck you', and say it as well to their parents as their parents to them."

Baroque onion dome roofs adorn Catherine's Palace, built by Peter the Great for his wife and future empress, Catherine I, in the town of Tsarskoye Selo 24 kilometres south of St Petersburg.

(Top) *Russian folk singers perform for tourists in the grounds of Catherine's Palace at Tsarskoye Selo.*
(Bottom) *A lithograph from the 1840s by L.J. Arnout shows the majestic Cathedral of Our Lady of Kazan on St Petersburg's Nevsky Prospect during winter.*

(Top) *The Cascade Fountain, in Peter the Great's Summer Palace, boasts 17 waterfalls, 142 water jets and 39 gilded statues.*
(Bottom) *A view of the Mikhailovskii Palace in the 1850s during a St Petersburg summer, when residents would promenade and make good use of its parks and gardens (lithograph by E. Chevalier and Smidt from an original by I.I. Charlemagne).*

(Above) *A statue of Alexander Pushkin stands proudly in St Petersburg's Arts Square.*

(Right) *An 1851 painting by V.S. Sadovnikov shows Nikolaevskii Station on St Petersburg's Znamenskaia Square – in the distance a train can just be seen steaming towards the station.*

(Above) *The Front Staircase in the Winter Palace, St Petersburg, 1842 (a lithograph by F. Kellerhoven, from an original painting by V.S. Sadovnikov). It is now called the Jordan Staircase and is part of the State Hermitage Museum.*
(Left) *St Petersburg's famous Church of the Savior on Spilled Blood, erected in 1881 on the site of the assassination of Tsar Alexander II, killed by a bomb on the very day he was to sign the constitutional reforms demanded by the revolutionaries.*

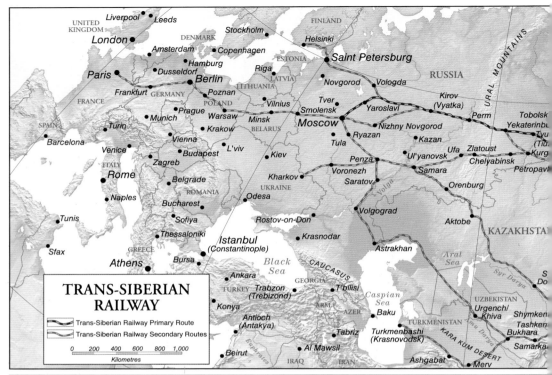

TRANS-SIBERIAN RAILWAY

〰 Trans-Siberian Railway Primary Route
〰 Trans-Siberian Railway Secondary Routes

0   200   400   600   800   1,000
Kilometres

(Above) The front façade of the Pavlovsk Palace (built 1782–86) is graced with a statue of Paul I, a copy of the statue at Gatchina, Paul's other summer residence.

(Right) The "Hut on Chicken Legs," a small dacha designed by artist Viktor Vasnetsov, named after the home of the witch Baba Yaga from a popular Russian fairy tale, and part of an artist colony created in 1870 on the Abramtsevo Estate north of Moscow.

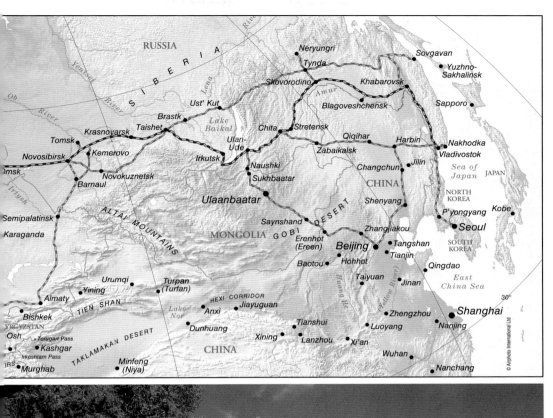

(Top) The Morning of the Execution of the Streltsy, an 1881 painting by Vasily Ivanovich Surikov depicting the aftermath of the failed 1698 revolt by the Streltsy Palace Guard, put down swiftly and violently by Peter the Great.
(Bottom) Russian folk dancers perform Cossack dancing.
(Opposite top) One of countless beautiful Russian Orthodox churches in the Golden Ring area.
(Opposite bottom) The Emperor Cannon in Moscow, the world's largest existing cannon (each cannon ball weighs a ton).

(Right) *In 1908, Henrik Wigstrom made a nephrite egg whose interior was a model of Tsarskoye Selo's Alexander Palace in St Petersburg. The surface of the egg is encrusted with elegant gold garlands, decorated by miniature portraits in frames made out of small diamonds.*
(Below) *An early 19th-century view of the Moscow Kremlin from the Stone Bridge; this scene is exhibited in Moscow's State Historical Museum.*

(Above) *The Old Arbat is one of the most popular shopping areas in Moscow. Everything from antique stores and portrait painters to McDonald's can be found along this pedestrian thoroughfare.*

(Left) *Matryoshka dolls are one of the most popular Russian souvenirs.*

(Far left) *A 15th century icon of Metropolitan Peter, who moved his see to Moscow in 1325, paving the way for its rise in influence and power. He is now the patron saint of the city.*

(Opposite page) *The interior of the GUM Department Store on Red Square. Built in 1893, it is Russia's largest store and has a large glass roof and ornate bridges that lead to over 200 shops on three levels. Compare it to the old photo on page 70.*

The Sukharev Tower, Moscow. Built in the 1690s in the Baroque style, it was first used as the barracks of the Streltsy regiment, then as the Moscow Admiralty, and eventually as the centre of a market. Unfortunately it was destroyed by the Soviets in 1934.

Not long before his time, records Olearius, there was an attempt to put an end to the use of foul language on the Moscow streets. Secret agents were appointed whose job was to mingle with the crowds and listen out for obscenities, and, with the help of the militia (*streltsi*/musketeers) and executioners, pluck out offenders and have them whipped on the spot. However, "this habitual and deeply rooted swearing demanded more surveillance than could be provided… and caused the observers, judges and executioners such an intolerable burden of work that they tired of spying out and punishing that which they themselves could not refrain from, and gave it up as a bad job."

Unless Chancellor was less than frank in his account of his banquet with the Tsar, Olearius had nowhere near as pleasant an experience in dining with his hosts: "After a meal, they do not refrain, in the presence and hearing of all, from releasing what nature produces, fore and aft. Since they eat a great deal of garlic and onion, it is rather trying to be in their company. Perhaps against their will these good people fart and belch noisily – as indeed they did during the secret audiences with us."

(Opposite top) *Fortified towns were essential in the Russian countryside to ward off attack from countless foes.*
(Opposite bottom) *The dining car of the Golden Eagle, a luxury private train that travels the Trans-Siberian Railway line.*

Drunkenness, which was by no means confined to Russia, was seen as being their pre-eminent vice. All classes, says Olearius, succumbed to the lure of drink: men and women, high and low, young and old, even priests and clergy who were supposed to abstain. Walking in the streets of Moscow, to find people lying dead drunk in the streets was perfectly run of the mill. Coachmen, coming across their unconscious friends in the street, would scoop them up, throw them in their wagon and cart them off home. Around the Kremlin and amongst the market stalls of Red Square, there were hundreds of idlers, with nothing to do but drink. Taverns and drinking houses were everywhere. Amongst the company were

Moscow's bustling Khitai-Gorod Market, circa 1898. This area, which formed Moscow's second ring, was originally where foreign merchants lived – Khitai-Gorod means "China Town".

musicians, who improvised songs on lewd subjects to the delight of the crowds. The most outrageous that Olearius heard involved sodomy with horses. Puppeteers would improvise little theatres and booths out of blankets, and devise performances on similar themes. No one, "anywhere, anytime, or under any circumstance lets pass an opportunity to have a draught or a drinking bout". Vodka, as now, was still the drink of choice, and all manner of people would come and spend every last bit of their money and time in such places. "The common people would bring all their earnings into the tavern and sit there until, having emptied their purses, they gave away their clothing, and even their nightshirts, to the keeper, and then went home as naked as they had come into the world."

Olearius records, as an example, one incident that he had seen on the way to Moscow. "I saw such besotted and naked brethren coming out of the nearby tavern, some bareheaded, some barefooted, and others only in their nightshirts. One of them had drunk away his cloak and emerged from the tavern in his nightshirt; when he met a friend who was on his way to the same tavern, he went in again. Several hours later he came out without his nightshirt, wearing only a pair of under-drawers. I had him called to ask what had become of his nightshirt, who had stolen it? He answered, with the customary 'Fuck your mother', that it was the tavern keeper, and the drawers might as well go where the cloak and nightshirt had gone. With that, he returned to the tavern, and later came out entirely naked. Taking a handful of dog-fennel that grew near the tavern, he held it over his private parts, and went home singing gaily."

For all the discourse on the customs of Moscow, many of the travellers were in awe of the harshness of life, and the hardiness of the people. "The poore is very innumerable," said Chancellor, "and live most miserably: for I have seen them eate the pickle of Hearring and other stinking fish: nor the fish cannot be so stinking nor rotten, but they will eate it and praise it to be more wholesome then other fish or fresh meate." It was a similar case for the soldiers that Muscovy put into the field: "they be such men for hard living as are not under the sun." When campaigning in the field, even though the ground might be utterly frozen solid, they had no thought of using a tent. Their only protection was a piece of felt, which they would set against the wind. When the snow came, they would lie upon it, and make a fire to warm themselves. As for food, the soldiers for months could live upon just "water & otemeale mingled together cold, and drinke water thereto: his horse shall eat green wood, & such like baggage, & shall stand open in the cold field without covert, & yet will he labour & serve him right well." If Chancellor had thought that there were better things than the Kremlin in the architecture of England, he was not so sure about the fighting men: "I pray you amongst all our boasting warriors how many we should find to endure the field with them but one moneth."

The harshness of life was reflected in the punishments that the Muscovites were compelled to endure. Although Russia was one of the first places to abolish the death penalty (if only briefly) in 1753, during the 17th and 18th centuries there were a variety of public punishments, part of the many spectacles of Moscow life, which visitors such as Olearius regarded as horrible and barbaric. Torture was used to extract evidence from suspects. A prisoner might have his arms tied behind his back and have them drawn up high; an executioner would then tie a heavy beam to his feet and jump on it to stretch his limbs, or even light a fire underneath him to scorch his feet. In other cases, a patch of their hair might be shaved, and they would be tied in a seat and cold water dripped onto their head, a drop at a time. Debtors might be kept in prison, and beaten daily on the shins with a supple stick of a finger's width. Users of snuff – an illegal substance in the 1600s, it being declared an offence against religion – would have their nostrils slit with a razor. The worst and most notorious punishment, however, Olearius reckoned to be the knout. This was a long whip to the end of which were attached three thongs made of "hard, tanned elk hide, each the length of a finger, which cut like knives".

n one of his visits to Moscow in 1634, Olearius watched the punishment of eight men and one woman by this method; they had been convicted for illegally selling tobacco and vodka: "Before the chancellery called the Novaia Chetvert, they had to bare their bodies down to the waist. Then each in turn was obliged to place his stomach to the back of one of the executioner's servants, while holding him around the neck. The legs of the offender were bound together, and a special person held them down with a rope, so that the one being punished could move neither up nor down. The executioner retired a good three paces behind the offender and flailed as hard as he could… making the blood gush forth freely after each stroke… A servant of the court stood by and read from a paper the number of strokes each was to receive. When the prescribed number had been fulfilled, he cried Pol'no!, that is, 'Enough!' Each was given 20–26 strokes, and the woman 16, after which she fell unconscious. Their backs retained not so much a finger's thickness of skin intact. They looked like animals whose skins had been flayed."

Despite, or perhaps on account of the harshness of life in Moscow, the whole of life seemed instinct with a sense of the spiritual. The observation of the grand religious festivals was one of the most conspicuous sights of Muscovite life. One of the most striking to another early English traveller, Robert Best, who visited Moscow in 1558 shortly after Chancellor, was the blessing of the waters of the Moscow River on the 12th day of Christmas. A square hole about 10 feet wide (three metres) was sawn in the deeply frozen river to the water below, and a grand procession of over 100 priests bearing lighted tapers, lanterns and ikons, would troop onto the ice, followed by the Patriarch and the Tsar with his courtiers. The Tsar would go to the water's edge, and after the clergy had chanted prayers, burnt incense and blessed the water, the Patriarch would take up a handful and cast it on him, as well as his followers. After this, when the royal party had retired, a huge crowd of the Moscow citizens would descend upon the hole with pots and vessels to scoop up some of the water, now holy. Men and women stripped to dive naked into the freezing torrent. Babies, unclothed, were immersed, and riders led their horses there to drink, by which means, comments Best, "they make their horses as holy as themselves."

he sense of spirituality pervaded the private as much as the public sphere. Every cottage or hovel, no matter how so humble, would be provided with an ikon in the corner. A visitor would not so much as greet the host, before finding in which corner the holy picture was displayed and crossing oneself before it. All of the inhabitants appeared to possess a feeling for the numinous, but many European travellers, particularly after the Enlightenment, were accustomed to dismiss this as so much superstition. A German visitor, George von Reinbeck, who travelled to Moscow at the turn of the 19th century, claimed that superstition pervaded all ranks of Russian society: "They believe in their *domowoys* (house-demons), prognostic, prophecies, fortune-telling by means of coffee, cards, or the melting of tin on the eve of saint's day." Many of these practices were much in favour with the nobility and ladies of high society, and anyone who could become an adept in these rituals to predict the course of love and liaisons was apt to be richly rewarded. But everything, according to von Reinbeck, was seen as portentous, even dropping salt, spilling wine or water. "He who is the involuntary cause of any bad prognostic, often makes the person whom it regards, pass suddenly from the most cheerful, to the worst of humours."

It was not every traveller, however, who eschewed the stirrings of the numinous. De Windt, for example, on gaining a view of the skyline at dusk from the tower of Ivan Veliki in the Kremlin, was moved with the sense of Moscow as a unique and spiritual place. At his feet was a mass of the white buildings of Moscow, all confused together, with their red roofs and green gardens. Amongst them were

A general view of Moscow circa 1890–1900. This photomechanical print was made for the Detroit Publishing Company, whose extensive collection is now housed by the US Library of Congress.

the 600 churches of the city topped with their star-spangled domes and gold crosses flashing in the sun. The Moscow River, crossed by innumerable stone bridges, moved sluggishly through the crowded streets and out into the green plains beyond the city, before diminishing to a silver thread, and losing itself in the blue haze on the horizon. From his vantage point, the stillness of the evening was only disturbed by the buzz of insects and the cooing of pigeons. The scene was transfused with stillness and colour, the crimson light against the soft grey masonry of the streets, the setting sun catching against the windowpanes. And then, as he was drawn almost into the midst of abstraction, suddenly and simultaneously a thousand bells pealed for evening prayer. Some were loud and crashing, some deep and sonorous, and others light and delicate, a ring of pure silver. It was, he declared, a "grand indefinable melody over the darkening sky". It marked out Moscow as an "ideal holy city".

"There is but one Moscow," he mused. It was not only that he found it the most beautiful city in Europe, or that he was beguiled by the heavy sense of history in the Kremlin, its dim, dark churches with "priceless tapestries rotting with age and incense", and its massive gold ikons blistered with jewels. It was also that the amenities of the place lived up to his expectations as a modern late-19th century traveller. His hotel, the Slavianski Bazaar near the Kremlin, was the best in Moscow, he claimed, if not in Europe. The prices might have been equal to Claridges or the Hotel Bristol, but the cuisine was unsurpassed, and the rooms palatial. The cuisine seemed to matter to him more than the rooms, however, and he dilated at length on his experiences in the restaurant. In the centre of it, he recorded, there was a grand fountain, "wherein lazily disporting themselves among cool green leaves are starlet from the Volga fresh every morning". The hungry diner was given a net to pick one of his own choosing, and in 10 minutes it would arrive *à la tartare*, plain, boiled or fried. An expensive luxury, he conceded, but fresh from the water, nothing could touch its delicacy or flavour. The only difficulty, he complained, was that a good cigar to follow dinner was to be found nowhere in Russia. If you should ask for one at any first-class restaurant, it would be brought to you in a tiny wooden box, the glass lid of which would disclose "a pale musty flavourless weed, exorbitantly dear, and of which cabbage forms the most harmless component".

side from the cigars, he found the shopping in Moscow a superior experience. Strolling down the fashionable streets and Westernised boulevards (Beloi Gorod, Alexander Garden), he came across new arcades built after the fashion of those in Piccadilly, lofty galleries with glass roofs and marble pavements. The shops were universally fine, bristling with luxury goods, jewellery, furs and expensive perfumes. There was no incongruity, he noted, as on the Nevsky Prospect in St Petersburg, where a jeweller's shop, refulgent with gold and precious gems would often be seen next to "a dirty little fly-blown window, disclosing a few boxes of cheap cigarettes, packets of tea, and perhaps half-a-dozen

vodka bottles, blown into rough shapes representing the Czar, Bismarck, or the Eiffel Tower". On a summer's afternoon, the parks and boulevards would be crowded with the Muscovite bourgeoisie promenading or window shopping. There would be officers and civil servants clad in greatcoats, despite the heat, and children with their nurses and governesses in ruby headscarves and dresses of blue satin.

Yet, de Windt seems to have stuck to the modernised streets. The sheer internationality and antiquity of Moscow's traditional commerce seems to have escaped him. Even up to his time, the great bazaars of the city near the Red Square and in the district of Kitai Gorod were still trading. They far surpassed in

variety and business, said Adlof Erman, anything to be seen in St Petersburg. The current coin of every country, he adds, was to be found in these places. The same went for the merchants: Greeks, Turks, Tartars, Cossacks, Chinese, Muscovites, English, French, Italians, Poles and Germans were all enumerated by Edward Clarke, parading the bazaars in the costumes of their respective countries. As in St Petersburg, the Muscovite merchants stuck to their old-fashioned customs, as well as their antique dress of kaftans and large beards. It was difficult, according to a 19th century traveller, J.G. Kohl, to find a more jovial and pleasant sort than these merchants in the bazaars. Notwithstanding their lust of gain, they had a cheerfulness of temperament that was quite absent elsewhere. They carried on their business in the bazaars in the midst of "praying, tea-drinking... and draughts", and in the narrow passages between their shops would "play at ball... making use of a great leathern ball filled with air, which is struck by the foot".

The goods that could be found in the city were legion. John George Korb, an ambassador to Moscow at the end of the 17th century, was able to find markets for silks, cloth, gold, furs, shoes, linen, ikons, garments, fruit, fish and poultry. Wine, imported by way of Archangel, was also available, as were wheat, cattle, beer and brandy. The exports that passed by way of Moscow included the skins brought in by way of the north and Siberia; the honey which was not used in the manufacture of mead; beeswax, over 20,000 pounds a year; tallow for candles; oil, made from the boiling down of the carcases of seals; caviar, harvested from the Volga delta; salt; tar; flax; hemp; and iron. Flowers were to be obtained from the flower market beneath the walls of the Kremlin. A range of painted huts surrounded by flowerbeds were spread out at one side, and anything from beds of violets to roses and cherry trees could be bought, or, as was more frequent, rented by the night to decorate a dinner party. It was here, according to J.G. Kohl, that commerce and pleasure came most closely together, and there were few pleasures equal to wandering about the huts, discussing the flower trade with their keepers, and listening to the evening song of the birds as they sang in the branches of the trees.

(Above) A wealthy merchant's house, replete with varying cultural elements, in Moscow at the turn of the 20th century. (Left) The interior of Moscow's Grand Bazaar in 1903; today it houses Russia's most famous shopping mall – the State Department Store, or GUM – but you need a big bank account to shop there.

THE STEEL ROAD: BUILDING THE TRANS-SIBERIAN RAILWAY

or the Muscovites of the fin-de-siècle period leading into the 20th century, an equally popular evening recreation to promenading in the parks or walking in the flower markets, was to gather at Yaroslavsky Station, and watch the departure of the trains for Siberia. The Scottish journalist and travel writer, Sir John Foster Fraser, who left Moscow on such a journey in 1901, was a vivid observer of this ritual. They would arrive in their hundreds, the nobility and wealthy in their furs and their pearls, and equally the peasants in their matted hair and baggy red shirts. Some would be coming to see off a friend or relative, others might turn up in the hope of catching an acquaintance in the throng, and others still would be there merely for the spectacle. They watched the departing hordes as one might watch an astronaut bound for Mars. Amongst the crowds there were myriad individual tableaux that betrayed a multitude of stories and reasons for departure.

A host of peasants set for emigration to the fertile lands of the east, their worldly belongings enfolded in bundles, took leave of their wives – "dumpy, unattractive women" commented Fraser – in short skirts with bright handkerchiefs tied around their heads. Their eyes were red, their lips quivering, but they were silent, unable to find words for their thoughts. They did not, Fraser conjectured, understand the language of farewell. A number of mechanics, their eyes glazed with drink, came reeling along the platform, laden with bags of kit, lurching about with incoherent grins, bumping into the crowds as they embarked. From the window of one of the carriages, a group of neatly dressed officers in white tunics with gold epaulettes leant out, and laughing, bid farewell to their friends.

A bell was rung, the signal that the train was soon to depart, and the farewells grew all the more passionate. Fraser caught sight of a nervous young man, an ordinary soldier, fair-haired, slim and beardless. Standing to attention, his arms stiffly straight by his side, he was embraced and clasped passionately by his mother, wizened and hunched, her face wrinkled and tanned, wetting his tunic with her tears, kissing him, and invoking blessings for his safety. The bell rang a second time, indicating the imminent departure of the train. Hands were grasped through the windows. Other peasants, brawny and black-bearded, took off their caps and threw their arms around each other, kissing on the lips – in Russia, a brotherly custom – before scurrying aboard the train. A third time, the doors were slammed shut, a whistle was blown, and the cars began to rattle and creak as the locomotive shuffled forward. Everyone on the platform made the sign of the cross. The passengers, standing at the windows, returned the gesture. Staying where they were, they waited to catch the last sight of the domes and towers of the city receding slowly into the twilight, as the train started its long journey bound for Siberia.

Fraser displayed a faint note of condescension for the awestruck crowds who came to watch the hordes departing for Siberia. "The Russians are an enthusiastic and credulous people, and in all the world they think there is nothing so magnificent as this Siberian Express." In this, he spoke unjustly. For all of its imperfections, the Trans-Siberian railway was an achievement of which the Russians could justifiably be proud. Not only was it an extraordinary feat of construction, spanning some 6,000 miles (9,656 kilometres) of territory, often barely known or accessible, mountainous, marshy, icebound, and bereft of resources, natural materials or manpower for hundreds of miles around. It was also a triumph of the vision of farsighted men, battling against the forces of bureaucratic inertia, vested interests and penury that so often dogged the government of Russia. The fact that the debate over whether the railway should be built at all lasted three times as long as its construction demonstrated that the greatest challenge was more a battle of ideas than a problem of engineering.

The railways were slow in coming to Russia. Whereas in England there were regular public services by steam locomotives in the northeast from 1812 on, even 20 years later there was no such thing anywhere in the Russian Empire. Transport, whether across Siberia or else within the Russian heartland, was still dependent on riverboats, sledges, carriages and animal traction – the traditional methods that had remained unchanged for hundreds of years. A number of proposals even for horse-drawn railways were obstructed either under pressure from the owners of river shipping companies, who feared the collapse of their business, or else from traditionalists, who thought that the railways were not suited to Russia.

The first tentative steps came in 1834, when a Viennese professor, Franz Anton von Gerstner, was invited to inspect the mining industry in the Urals. Aside from mining, another accomplishment of the professor had been the construction of the first public railway on the European continent (the Danube-Moldavia line), and he took the opportunity of his visit to point out to the Tsar the slowness of communications within Russia. He suggested that the Tsar should grant him a 20-year concession to build railways within the empire, and that before long, he would be able to produce a line from St Petersburg to Moscow, Nizhny Novgorod and Kazan, that could move 5,000 infantrymen and 500 cavalry, along with horses and artillery, between the cities at a speed of 200 versts (130 miles or just over 200 kilometres) a day.

The Emperor and Autocrat of All the Russias, Nicholas I, was tempted by the power that this apparatus would place in his hands, but the proposal was bogged down in a host of committees. Some doubted von Gerstner's ability to raise the necessary capital, some were indignant that money which could be spent on the welfare of people by investing in agriculture might be diverted to what many thought a white elephant; others complained that the sledge men or carters would suffer, and that the forests of Russia would be consumed as fuel. In the end, the proposal for a line of over 1,000 miles of track was whittled down to one of about 15, linking St Petersburg not to the strategic cities of Central Russia, but to the Tsar's summer residence of Tsarskoye Selo, and then on to the nearby village of Pavlosk. The line was to be treated as an experiment to see whether steam locomotion would work in the Russian winter, and also if such a venture could be made commercially viable.

Although it had likely been the secret hope of many that the railway would fail, it instead proved to be an immediate success. Opened in 1837 using three English (and one Belgian) locomotives, and the occasional extra horse-drawn service in the first few months, the line carried nearly three-quarters of a million people in its first year. Pavlosk, now only a little more than a half-hour journey away, became an immediately fashionable resort for day-trippers from the capital, and the railway company capitalised on their business by building buffets and a ballroom near the terminus. In the 1860s, they even engaged Johann Strauss for a summer season of free concerts. The episode led to the despairing remark of Kankrin, the Russian Minister of Finance, that whereas in other countries railways were built to industrial centres, in Russia the first railway led to a tavern.

In spite of this success, it was still several years before the full railway between Moscow and St Petersburg was even begun. Members of official committees, in the face of the evidence of a railway's utility, still grumbled of the threat of "this modern sickness", and it was not until various of their number retired or died that the construction of the line could begin in 1843.

For the materials and the technology, Russia found itself dependent on external help. Despite being a major producer of iron, it was only able to produce a small fraction of the rails required for the venture. England made up the deficit, supplying a million tons of rails, as opposed to Russia with just 10,000 tons. Although the locomotives were manufactured in Russia, the technical expertise was imported from America. A Russian factory was established at St Petersburg for the manufacture of engines and carriages, but it was under the management of two American locomotive builders, Winan of Baltimore, and Eastwick and Harrison of Philadelphia. From the United States they brought machinery and craftsmen, and were required to train a new generation of Russian artisans and engine drivers.

The construction of the line itself was in the hands of the Russians. Such were the demands of the railway, and so few were the engineers in Russia, that the work consumed nearly the entire graduate output of the Imperial School of Engineering in the first year of construction. Some of the engineers who worked on the line became famous in other fields. One of them, Zhuravskii, who was responsible for many of the original bridges (now replaced), was later to design the spire of the Peter and Paul Fortress in St Petersburg.

As for brute manpower, there was no such scarcity. Over 50,000 serfs were hired from their owners by contractors to participate in the earthwork. Their treatment, as might be expected, was harsh: their wages were minimal, and they worked from sunrise to sunset, as well as Sundays and holidays. Only heavy rain could be guaranteed to secure them any time off. As a great deal of their work involved draining the marshes and swamps which the line was to traverse, they would spend much of their time immersed in mud and stagnant water rife with mosquitoes. Epidemics were commonplace, particularly typhoid, and complaints from malnourishment such as scurvy and diarrhoea were also prevalent. Thousands are believed to have died in the course of the work. Dissent was rewarded by flogging, and it is likely that the peace was kept thanks only to the free-flowing supply of vodka. Although little of the suffering endured by the labourers was known to the public at the time, several years later a poet, Nekrasov, was moved to publish a verse on the matter:

The way is straight, the embankment narrow,

Telegraph poles, rails, bridges.

And everywhere on both sides are Russian bones –

Vanechka, do you know how many?

For all the suffering that the workers endured, their abundance at least meant that the St Petersburg–Moscow line was the best and most sturdily constructed in the whole of the Russian railway network. It was eventually opened in November 1851, and with its express trains travelling at an average of 21mph (34kph), cut down the journey time between the two cities to just under 18 hours. On Peter the Great's old corduroy road (logs laid transversely over marshy ground to make it passable for carriages, though bumpy), the journey might ordinarily have taken two to three uncomfortable days.

Over the next two decades, the railways began to take a greater hold in Russia. Further lines were constructed linking the great cities of the Russian Empire – Kiev, Riga, Smolensk, Vilnius, Voronezh, Yaroslavl, Rostov-on-Don, and Odessa on the Black Sea Coast – into a unified and growing network. A further line out of Vilnius to Warsaw and on to Vienna also made overland travel from Europe a more practical matter.

Yet, for the boom in construction that was taking place in European Russia, there was little appetite on the part of the government to extend the railway east. The first known proposal for a Trans-Siberian Railway came in the 1850s from Count Nicholas Muravyev, the Governor-General of East Siberia. Muravyev was a leader of huge energy in every sphere. In military terms, he was able to wrest from the decadent Chinese empire enormous swathes of Manchuria along the borders of the Amur River even up as far as the frontiers of Korea. In terms of exploration and commerce, he sent expeditions to survey the full reaches of the Amur River, Okhotsk and Sakhalin, establishing towns, factories, fortresses, trading outposts, cutting roads through virgin forest and swamps, exploiting deposits of minerals and coal, and bringing Russian settlers to cultivate the territory. Eager to protect Eastern Siberia and the Amur River from any encroachment by the British Empire or Japanese, and also to exploit the area's vast natural resources, he sought a concession from the government to build a railway linking the region into the national network. This would tie more firmly the scarce accessible Russian possessions in Siberia and on the Pacific Ocean to the Russian heartland, and allow for them to be more easily defended. Yet, for all his achievements and foresight, his proposal was turned down. The idea of building a railway so far away was, commented an official, "too novel for the central administration to support".

After Muravyev there came a flurry of further proposals, most of them foreign, and most of them outlandish. An English engineer, of whom nothing except his name, Dull, is known, proposed a railway to run from Nizhny Novgorod to Perm and the Urals, and thence, "by the best route" to the Amur and the Pacific. The trains would initially be drawn by capturing some of the four million wild horses he believed to be roaming free in Siberia, until the government was able to build enough steam locomotives fit for the job. The Minister of Communications, Chevkin, was not enthusiastic. Sighing that, like many

Englishmen, Dull knew nothing of Siberia, he turned down his plans on the grounds of adverse "climatic conditions". Not long afterwards, a former governor of Tomsk attempted to revive the idea, suggesting a horse-tramway from the west Siberian city of Tyumen to Irkutsk, which, for its entire 1,900-mile (3,000-kilometre) length, would be enclosed in a colossal wooden tunnel. Chevkin turned this down too.

He also turned down proposals for a steam railway by a company of three Englishmen, Morrison, Sleigh and Horn. The first was a banker of dubious repute, the second an actual bankrupt, but it was the fact that the third was a lawyer which gave Chevkin his grounds. No one in Russia, at a time of assassinations and political ferment, caused more unease or fell under more suspicion than anyone employed in the legal profession. They were reckoned as one of the primary sources of subversive and revolutionary ideas.

A more formidable challenge to Chevkin's intransigence came from an American, Perry McDonough Collins. Collins' original business was as a banker and gold-dust trader in San Francisco in the 1849 gold rush. However, he became infatuated with the idea of Siberia as another and grander version of the American West, an undeveloped and undiscovered land of opportunity. Studying obsessively whatever literature he could find about it, he eventually contrived in 1856 to get himself appointed as the "US Commercial Agent on the Amoor River". Immediately he launched into an exploration of Siberia, collecting data on the trade passing through the area, and looking for commercial opportunities. The first of these, he considered, was a railway, and soon he was at work on one of the most detailed early plans for a Siberian railway that was to come to the attention of the Russian Government. Chevkin, confronted with a comprehensive proposal, including costings, a scheme for raising 20 million dollars in share capital, estimates for labour requirements and a plan to hire workers from China should their number be deficient in Siberia, was forced to find more convincing reasons for his refusal. The terrain to be crossed, he held, was not well enough defined. The construction methods to be used were unclear, and there was by no means enough food in Siberia to cater to the welfare of the workforce of tens of thousands that Collins proposed to import.

The ultimate reluctance on the part of the Russian bureaucrats of attempting to build a railway into Siberia can be traced back to a few simple factors. They were unwilling to upset the present order, and to harm the business of the boatmen and sledge drivers who were still responsible for Siberian transport. They feared the potential for spiralling costs and demands on Russian manpower. Many believed that especially in a time of economic crisis, wars and famine – all of which occurred in Russia in the 1870s – it would be senseless and almost immoral to spend what might amount to many tens of millions of dollars and many tens of thousands of men on a railway whose purpose to them remained unclear. They lacked the foresight to understand that the railway would allow them to exploit the enormous potential for wealth that Siberia offered, and also bring greater unity to a country which, although spanning several time zones, was held together from end to end only by a tenuous muddy track that, for a body of marching soldiers, could take over two years to traverse.

One thing perhaps beyond this, and less definable, was an ingrained fear of the railway itself, and a raw inertia that was comfortable and settled in the old ways, despising the new as unsettling and deviant. Orlando Figes reminds us that originally many Russians saw the railways as an agent of the malign. Tolstoy, in his novels, rarely fails to associate them with evil. In *Anna Karenina*, it is on a train that Anna first meets the anti-hero Vronsky, her forbidden and immoral love, an encounter which ultimately leads her to destruction. Later, it is again at the hand of the railway, under the wheels of a train, that she eventually meets her death.

Amongst many of the ordinary people, as much as among officialdom, it is perhaps possible to trace the reluctance to embrace the advance of the railway into Siberia as a result of this primal suspicion. There was also, however, a sheer unwillingness to change an old and settled custom, no matter how toilsome or inconvenient, for anything new and more advanced, no matter that it might be much better or more comfortable. Although the horse-drawn ride was slow, unpredictable, dirty, prone to delay and dangerous, one official of a Siberian city would not have it any other way. "We like better to travel by Tarantass... One leaves when one likes, stops when one likes, and at post stations of one's choice. With trains, you must board them at a fixed hour and ride in a carriage full of strange and unpleasant people; you are transported like a trunk, and you haven't the right to stop the train when you please."

But this inertia of preference was not able to detain the necessity of progress for much longer. As the 1880s drew on, Russia became increasingly concerned about a resurgent China. In 1885, Count Alexis Ignatiev, the Governor-General of Irkutsk, sent an anxious submission to the government in St Petersburg. There were reports (quite overblown, as it happened) that China was experimenting with railways northeast of Peking in Manchuria. Their military strength, after decades of torpor, was on the rise, and their agents and soldiers were beginning to infiltrate Russian territory east of Lake Baikal. Without a railway connecting Irkutsk to Europe, and the Russian territories east of Lake Baikal to Irkutsk, Russia's possessions in the east, only meagrely defended, were desperately vulnerable, and Vladivostok, her best port on the Pacific Ocean, might be completely cut off.

The Tsar, Alexander III, on reading the submission, could barely restrain his anger. In the margin of Ignatiev's despatch, he wrote: "How many times have I read such reports from the Governors-General of Siberia. I must own with grief and shame that up to the present the Govt has done scarcely anything to meet the needs of this rich but forsaken country. It is time, it is high time!"

The Tsar's personal commitment and active interest in the matter corralled his officials and ministers into action, and teams were sent out into Siberia to survey possible routes between Tomsk and Sretensk, near the source of the Amur River. Nonetheless, the parsimonious Minister of Finance, Vyshnegradski, continued to temporise. There was no money in the treasury to construct such a long-distance line, he pleaded. He would have to raise international loans, or print tens of millions of roubles and lay the currency open to being debauched by foreign speculators. It would be better, he argued, if they proceeded tentatively. A small stretch could be built in western Siberia going easterly out of Tomsk, which could be reached by river, towards Irkutsk. When the financial climate should favour it, it could slowly be extended east.

However, a new wave of officials appointed by the Tsar who were unshakeably committed to the project, no matter the financial dangers, finally began to sweep away all objections. The Trans-Siberian line, they decreed, should be built in its entirety, not piecemeal. The route, all the way from Chelyabinsk at the western end of Siberia to Vladivostok in the east, should be divided into six sections, and construction work should be undertaken on all of the sections as simultaneously as possible.

As to the problems of finance, a new and brilliant minister, Sergius Witte, was appointed in the place of Vyshnegradski. Witte had spent much of his early career managing the Russian railways in Georgia, but he showed a genius for arranging the Russian budget. Determined to allow nothing to prevent the construction of the railway, he did everything in his power to make it financially possible. The rouble was stabilised by establishing a gold standard. Foreign reserves were drawn into Russia. Funds were magically produced from the Treasury and Central Bank through wondrous feats of creative accountancy. Tariffs on imports and exports were rationalised, and cash was harvested from the people by the imposition of a state monopoly on the sale of vodka: a move which in its first year brought in nearly US$12 million, nearly a 10th of the original estimated cost for the line.

On 24 February 1891, the decision to embark on the construction of the line was finally and officially approved. To underline the importance with which he treated the undertaking, Alexander III issued a weighty Imperial proclamation ordering his son and heir, the Tsarevich Nicholas, who was on a tour of India, Southeast Asia and Japan, to lay the inaugural stone of the railway on his return to Vladivostok. On 23 March, the following letter was despatched to Nicholas:

YOUR IMPERIAL HIGHNESS!

Having given the order to begin the construction of a continuous railroad line across the whole of Siberia, destined to unite the Siberian lands, so rich in natural endowments, with the railway network of the interior, I entrust You to proclaim My will on this matter upon Your return to the Russian land after Your inspection of the foreign countries of the East. Furthermore, I charge You with the duty of laying the foundation stone, in Vladivostok, of the Ussuri section of the Great Siberian Railway, which is to be built at State expense and under direction of the Government.

Your significant role in the commencement of this truly national task which I have undertaken will give fresh evidence of My sincere desire to facilitate communications between Siberia and the other parts of the Empire and thus will demonstrate to this region, which is so dear to My heart, My very keen interest in its peaceful prosperity.

Beseeching the Lord's blessing upon the long journey through Russia which lies ahead of You,

I remain Your sincerely affectionate ALEXANDER.

By the end of May 1891, when the 23-year-old heir to the Russian throne laid the foundation stone for the Vladivostok railway terminus, and heaped up the first wheelbarrow of mud for the embankment of the line, the Russian railways had already started to make some progress towards Siberia. By the mid-1880s, a single-track line had already been constructed from Samara to Zlatoust, a town on the western side of the Urals, at the eastern extremity of European Russia. This was connected to the general Russian railway network and could be reached from Moscow. A freestanding line had also been constructed between the more northerly cities of Perm and Yekaterinburg (Ekaterinburg). It led at that time to a strange variety of modes of transport for travellers heading into Siberia. Aside from taking the direct route to Zlatoust, many would also travel from Moscow to Nizhny Novgorod by train; from there to Perm by steamer; again onto the train at Perm, and then embark on a tarantass at Yekaterinburg.

The six sections into which the railway was to be broken were the West-Siberian section from Chelyabinsk (which would link to Zlatoust on the opposite side of the Urals, and also to Yekaterinburg) to the Ob River; the Mid-Siberian, from the Ob to Irkutsk; the Circumbaikal, which marked the short but difficult loop running south of Lake Baikal, which would require a precipitous ledge and many tunnels to be blasted through the winding mountains surrounding it; the Transbaikal from the eastern side of Lake Baikal up to Sretensk on the Amur River; the Amur section, running parallel to the Amur up to the trading town of Khabarovsk; and finally the Ussuri section, the north-south line which linked Khabarovsk to Vladivostok.

Although the original idea was to construct the six sections simultaneously, the plan did not work so easily in practice. By the end of 1900, the West- and Mid-Siberian, as well as the Transbaikal and Ussuri Lines had been completed and opened to traffic. However, the Circumbaikal loop and the Amur section had not been attempted at all. For several years, the journey was still composed of a mixture of mediums: travellers would disembark at Irkutsk, to be taken by boat across Lake Baikal. Similarly, at Sretensk they would leave the train to join a paddle steamer which would make a slow journey down the shallows of the Amur River, arriving several days later at Khabarovsk, from whence they could reach Vladivostok by train in just over a day.

A Trans-Siberian Railway train on one of countless bridges that had to be constructed across the vast steppe lands stretching into the Far East. This bridge is wooden, its pilings protected from floodwaters by large triangular wedges.

For a time, the Russian government was distracted from completing the Amur section by the notion of finding a shortcut. It thought to build a line that would link Vladivostok directly with Chita on the Transbaikal section, bypassing the Amur but crossing directly over the Chinese territory of Manchuria. By these means, it hoped to save not only 250 miles (400 kilometres) of track, but also to avoid the engineering difficulties of the difficult and little known land north of the Amur. In 1897 Russian officials obtained a concession from the Chinese Government to build such a line and, with Chinese assistance, it made good progress. However, in the Boxer Rebellion of 1900, almost two-thirds of the line was destroyed by Chinese troops, who bombarded it with field guns. Although the Trans-Manchurian line was completed in 1904, Russian fears for its security led to them reviving work on the Amur line. It was thus only in 1914, with the final opening of this section, that it became possible to travel by train, uninterrupted, from Moscow, to the furthest extremity of the Empire in Vladivostok.

I n terms of engineering standards, the Trans-Siberian was to be a "Pioneer Line". That is, it would be built according to standards far inferior to those normal in Europe, or even in Russia. Witte might have worked his magic to produce as much as possible in the way of funds for the project, but it was beyond even his means to conjure up enough capital to pay for the levels of safety which had by now become common in other places. To get the project done, economy was paramount. The railway would be single track. The rails would be of the most lightweight variety, the sleepers would be fewer, and the ballast below the track thinner. Bridges, in general, would be timber instead of metal or stone. Passing places would be kept to a minimum. They would attempt as much as possible to avoid making tunnels or cutting through hills, unless it was absolutely unavoidable. They were willing to subject the line to sharp bends and steep gradients, no matter how hair-raising this might be for the passengers or challenging for the drivers. Such was the initial nature of the line that passenger trains were limited to speeds of 13mph (21kph), and freight trains to a mere nine.

Each section of the railway, depending on its terrain, population and natural resources, possessed its own individual engineering problems. The West-Siberian section, which was started in July 1892, was perhaps the easiest of the six, but even then the difficulties which presented themselves were immense. Although it passed through the most populous part of Siberia, artisans and labourers were scarce. Workers had to be imported not only from European Russia, but also from Turkey, Persia and, particularly for the experienced bridge-builders, from Italy. Heavy frosts limited the construction season to just four months of the year.

The winter months were spent in bridge construction, clearing roads and accumulating supplies, which were most easily brought in on horse-drawn sledges. Despite the eight months of the year that were devoted to this latter activity, the work was still crippled by shortages. The bulkier items such as wagons, carts and horses were in short supply, but even the simplest tools such as shovels and spades were hard to come by. Many workers had to make do with spades made entirely of wood, instead of iron. Horse-drawn machines for excavating were generally unavailable, and the workers had to make do with picks and wheel-less wheelbarrows, hauled along planks. Improvisation was a sine qua non. Smithies, brickworks and limekilns had to be set up on site. Instead of mechanical pile drivers to drive in the stakes for bridges,

"Prisoners destined for Siberia pass the Kremlin," a sketch made by Bayard Taylor in 1862 that only hints at the misery and hardship to come for the unlucky convicts.

labourers would hammer them in with a boulder hauled aloft by a rope slung over an improvised tripod of logs.

The raw materials were as much of a problem as equipment. Much of western Siberia was treeless, and the wood that was available there, small birches and willows, was only good for fence-making and firewood. Heavier timber, suitable for sleepers, had to be brought in from Ufa, over 300 miles (483 kilometres) away, and sawn up on site. Stone for ballast was hardly to be had. For this, the engineers had to resort to the Ural Mountains, or else to the upper reaches of the Irtysh River, 600 miles south of the line. Sand became the normal material for ballasting the track, and even for this they had to make journeys of over 50 miles from the site of construction.

The labourers' working conditions, as can be imagined, were hardly comfortable. In the summer months they were able to camp outside; in winter, they retreated to log cabins, or railway trucks which had been shunted down the line. Although their diet was meat, usually boiled in communal cauldrons, and they had rudimentary access to surgeons in the rural areas between the cities, some of the terrain in which they had to work must have detracted from even these small comforts. On the near 400-mile (644-kilometre) stretch of steppe between Omsk and the Ob River, the conditions were as bad as those between Moscow and St Petersburg. The rolling green plains, broken up by numerous shallow lakes and ponds, might have seemed benign at a distance. However, in reality they were boggy and marsh-like; dense thickets of reeds concealed an endless succession of swamps and peat bogs, where solid ground was rarely to be found. In some places, acres of stinging nettles, 2.5 metres tall, straddled the line of the route. Gnats and mosquitoes were abundant in the summer heat. For weeks, the labourers would toil in the stagnant, insect-ridden water to build canals for drainage, and then haul tons of rubble over the stinking earth to make a solid foundation for the track.

It was the bridge-builders who encountered the most severe danger. As mentioned, many of these were Italian, particularly those responsible for the masonry. Their most frequent complaint was not the cold of Siberia, but that they missed the wine of their country, and found Russian vodka a poor substitute. However, it was the freezing Siberian winter, a time in which most of the bridge-building took place, which caused them the greater peril. Perched on the middle of a span, perhaps 350 feet (107 metres) in length, they would dress the stonework, or bolt and rivet the beams and girders with no harness, hoarding or safety net to protect them from falling. Often, their hands benumbed and useless from the freezing temperatures and wind, they would lose their grip on the beams – a hundred-foot drop into the ice-choked waters below, without hope of rescue, was the inevitable result. Such hazards were accepted, at least by the management, as a part of the job. Russian statistics, privately compiled at the time, reckoned on four deaths per million roubles spent on bridge-building as a perfectly acceptable average.

Foreign engineers who came to observe the building of the track were amazed at the speed with which it was constructed. Observers noted that, on a good day, the line would advance by two and a half miles (four kilometres). However, it was only thanks to the cavalier attitude towards safety and poor construction standards that such a pace could be set. As construction trains began to roll along the track, they were beset by the rails shifting out of place. The use of lightweight rails (weighing 49 pounds a yard, much lighter than the European standard), and the scanty provision of sleepers and bolts led to frequent derailments. On some occasions, the locomotives would crash through the exiguous ballast and sink into the marshy ground below. In this early period, drivers feared to take the trains much above walking pace on the regular track. And although the many bridges had not only been weight-tested by engineers but individually blessed by priests of the Orthodox Church for good measure, their crossing occasioned much worry. The engines would slow to a crawl, and the drivers would throw coins into bowls positioned at the feet of ikons displayed at each end of the bridge, relying more on divine assistance than the quality of engineering to reach the opposite bank safely.

A startling illustration of the extraordinary ideas about what constituted safe and acceptable practice during the period of construction is provided by the means used to cross the great rivers before the building of the bridges. The lines up to rivers such as the Irtysh and Ob were often completed many months in advance of the bridges over the rivers themselves. In winter, so that goods could be taken across the river in the absence of bridges, the workers did not, as might seem sensible, unload the trains and ferry the goods across. Rather, they laid rails directly onto the ice of the frozen rivers. Once they had frozen these in place by pouring buckets of cold water over them, the locomotives and wagons would descend onto them from the banks, and steam slowly from one side of the river to the other.

 contemporary eyewitness, Robert Jefferson, who had not long before risen to fame by being the first person to cycle from London to Moscow and back within 50 days, and who by this time was travelling down the unfinished line as a steerage passenger, described such a crossing of a stretch of the Chulym River, twice the width of the Thames at London Bridge: "The engine snorted, puffed, snorted again, puffed three or four times and got up way slowly, drew to the shelving bank and laboriously descended on to the ice. There was a distinct crunch as it did so, and another crunch when the first car rolled on; but gradually the whole train descended, and, at a pace not exceeding five miles an hour, moved across the frozen surface. As it passed us we felt the ice quiver, and heard innumerable cracks, like the reports of pistols in the distance; but the train got across the centre safely, spurted when near the bank, climbed up, and was on *terra firma* again."

The same sort of problems, but far more intense, were suffered on the other sections of the line farther east. Labour was exceedingly scarce; for example, in the Mid-Siberian section between the Ob River and Irkutsk, the population density was less than one person per square mile. Of those, many were "Old Believers", early settlers who had fled from European Russia after reforms to the Orthodox Church in the 17th century. They clung to an older version of the faith, and refused to have anything to do with the railway, believing it to be a work of the devil. It was difficult to draft in soldiers to do the work, as they regarded it as beneath their dignity. It was similar for the Cossacks, who were responsible for guarding the borders in the east. Many of the aboriginal Siberian tribes who lived in the region had neither the training nor the temperament for such employment. On the Ussuri section in the Far East, the Chinese farmers, who were more abundant, refused to leave their fields and the highly profitable cultivation of ginseng. Chinese coolies, imported every season from spring until December, proved a slightly more reliable source of labour. But despite their industry, they were not without their problems. Many, it appears, had to be taught how to use shovels and wheelbarrows, the summer temperatures were ruinous to their health, and they refused to work in the rain. Most disruptive of all, they lived in abject fear of the tiger, and would abandon their tools and run at the slightest suspicion that one might be near.

In the end, much of the labour in these regions was provided by exiled Siberian convicts. Any criminal who volunteered for work on the line would be granted not only a year's remission of their sentence for every eight months' work, but also a salary of 25 kopeks a day. The response to this offer was enthusiastic, and many offenders given this opportunity proved themselves to be honest workers. Nonetheless, the success of the scheme was not universal. On the Ussuri Line, many of the convicts were brought from the island of Sakhalin, where the most brutal and violent of the convicts were kept, including murderers and rapists. At first, they were obedient and worked well. However, as time went on they began to steal away, committing robberies and thefts throughout the countryside and villages. Fear descended on the people of Vladivostok, as it became impossible to venture out of their houses without the danger of

Exiled convicts at the Nerchenskii Penal Colony, a photograph taken by A. Kuznetsov in 1891. Life in the penal colonies of Siberia was desperate, described as inhuman by many Europeans and Americans, such as George Kennan, who visited them.

being accosted. The crisis was reached when a French naval officer was killed in the city in broad daylight, after which the Sakhalin convicts were withdrawn. The citizens of Vladivostok breathed a sigh of relief, but the speed of construction of that section suffered accordingly. Although the stretch was only 475 miles (764 kilometres) long, the problems of labour meant it took over five years to bring to completion.

The problems of climate farther east were just as vexatious as those of labour. Aside from the West-Siberian section, the working season was little more than three months of the year. In winter, temperatures would plunge as low as -60°F (-51°C). On the Ussuri section, when the temperatures did climb high enough in the summer to allow work to commence, progress would be blighted by week-long showers.

The makeshift roads would turn into swamps of mud, clogging up the progress of men, carts and baggage animals alike. From the mire rose heavy clouds of humidity, which led to epidemics of fever among the labourers and even anthrax among the animals. The level of the Ussuri River, thanks to these rains, was liable to rise over 35 feet (10 metres), and in the first year, when this phenomenon was unknown, swept away a long section of newly laid track. There were similar disasters in the Transbaikal section up to Sretensk. In 1897, the rivers in the area suffered from serious flooding; 230 miles (370 kilometres) of new track were damaged, a landslide near Sretensk submerged a great section of the workings, and 15 bridges were swept away by the water.

Similarly, the terrain in the eastern regions gave rise to enormous difficulties. In the Mid-Siberian section between the River Ob and Irkutsk, the course of the railway crossed the taiga, or dense Siberian forest. The planners had determined that the route should not be on top of the old Post Road, so an entirely new way had to be cut through the primeval growth of trees. For hundreds of miles a road 250 feet (76 metres) wide – to avoid the danger of sparks from the locomotives setting fire to the forest – was carved out across the continent. Canals were dug to drain the sodden ground, but the shallow-rooted trees alongside the route, as the land was dried out, became destabilised and crashed to the ground. Towards Irkutsk, the land became exceedingly mountainous. On account of the economy required by Witte, tunnels and cuttings were avoided at all costs. The requirement for bridges to smooth out the line was huge. In one 44-mile (71-kilometre) stretch, 82 bridges had to be built.

The problems with supplies were more acute than in the west. Despite the abundance of wood, most of it was of the softwood variety – pines, larch, spruce and birch. None of it could be used for sleepers or bridge construction. Hardwood for these purposes had to be imported many hundreds of miles, along with the stone and iron rails. Such were the distances involved, it was decided that the easiest route in for the latter might be by river, and it fell to a British sea captain, Joseph Wiggins, to import them to the region by sailing them via the Arctic Circle to the mouth of the Yenisei River, and then south to the site of construction.

On the Transbaikal section, the climate and terrain conspired together to deliver one of the most difficult problems for the railway, that of permafrost. Little more than a few metres below the surface was a thick stratum of earth, perennially frozen and quite impenetrable. Iron tools made no impression on it, and to shift it nothing could be done except blast away at it with dynamite, or else thaw it along the line with an endless succession of great bonfires. The track laid across this surface was at the mercy of the seasons. In winter, the topsoil above the permafrost layer would also freeze solid and expand, forcing the line to arch and buckle upwards, undulating for miles like waves. In summer, by contrast, the surface layer would melt and turn sodden. The line would then sink into the newly generated marsh, and subside beneath puddles or disappear into the mire. Cuttings and embankments would dissolve away like snow. Colossal efforts were made to drain and stabilise the soil, and to anchor it with wooden piles, but in the regions where nothing could prevail against nature, entirely new courses over more stable ground had to be sought out for the route of the track.

A NEW WORLD OPENS UP

nce the main sections of the railway had been completed, the travails and cost of their construction were quickly forgotten in the newfound convenience and comfort of the journey. European public opinion, which for so many years had been brought up to regard Siberia as a place of grinding misery, and the voyage there as terrible an undertaking as a descent into the Underworld, was astonished when the new mode of transport was unveiled. To mark the opening of the railway in 1900, the Paris Universal Exposition featured an exhibition by the Franco-Belgian Sleeping Car Company, which was contracted to supply the rolling stock for one of the two weekly express services from Moscow. Their stand created a sensation.

Four of the luxury coaches which were ready for export to Russia had been brought bodily into the exposition: two *wagons-restaurants* and two *wagons-salons*. Visitors marvelled at the opulence with which they were furnished. The styles would vary from carriage to carriage, from French Empire to Louis

For those with the wherewithal, travel on the Trans-Siberian Railway could be a comfortable, even sophisticated, affair. Here an old photograph shows the library in the first-class dining salon.

The overtly pious need not worry about lack of religious ministering onboard the Trans-Siberian: a purpose-built church carriage complete with priest allowed access to God whilst in transit.

XVI, even to Chinese. There were sleeping compartments, lounges provided with pianos, and smoking rooms. The panelling was of mahogany and gilded oak. The walls were adorned with large mirrors or frescoes, hand-painted, of nymphs and bucolic swains. The furniture was gilt or white-lacquered lime. The windows were shielded by curtains and heavy drapes, richly and beautifully embroidered. Visitors could sit in the restaurant car and enjoy the five Franc menu, as the passengers would on their travels, whilst a long canvas panorama, depicting the sights of the journey into Siberia, was turned like a piano roll outside the windows.

Correspondents wrote gushingly about the new trains, which, they said, would be "a veritable Waldorf-Astoria on wheels" – the American and Canadian trains would have to "hide their diminished heads". Beyond the carriages displayed at the Exposition, even more was promised. The journalists described the library-cars, bath-cars and gymnasium-cars still to come. There would be barbershops where the travellers would receive a free morning shave; fireproof safes for the deposit of jewellery and documents; bathtubs in sycamore so elegantly designed that not a drop of water would spill out on the many curves in the track; exercise bicycles where, before breakfast, one could make a "century run". Such would be the magnificence of the service, they wrote, that its luxuries would be too numerous to catalogue.

The reality, as the first European travellers embarked on the Trans-Siberian services, was naturally different, but not too different. As the provision of rolling stock at this early date was split between the Sleeping Car Company and the Russian State, variations in quality were frequently encountered. Besides this, the finest of the Sleeping Car Company's carriages were held back, so that such innovations as the free haircuts were never ultimately, as promised, introduced. Nonetheless, this did not prevent many of the original passengers from being suitably impressed.

One among their number was Annette Meakin, who is the first Englishwoman known to have travelled on the Trans-Siberian. She made the journey on a whim in May 1900 after seeing the display at the Paris Exposition. With her was her elderly mother, whom she took as a travelling companion. On the first leg of the journey to Omsk, they shared a luxury *coupé* with two other ladies. For Meakin, the Siberian Express was, unlike other trains, "a kind of Liberty Hall". One was free to sleep all day without interruption if one desired, or else to eat, drink, smoke or play cards, entirely as one's impulse dictated. The modern amenities, combined with the ambling pace of the journey – no more than 16 miles an hour – made the trip a thoroughly restful experience. "Time passes very pleasantly on such a train, and it is quite possible to enjoy the scenery, for there is none of that fearful hurry that makes railway travelling so risky for body and nerves in Europe and America," she enthused.

Meakin revelled in the array of electric buttons and switches in her cabin, which gave her a satisfying sense of control: "An electric bell on one side of your door summons a servingman to make your bed or sweep your floor, as the case may be, while a bell on the other side summons a waiter from the buffet." The novelty of such new technology was still fresh and impressive, and she lingered over the personal electric reading lamp "by which you may read all night if you choose".

The British MP Sir Henry Norman, who travelled on the Express the year after Meakin as part of a fact-finding mission, had an even sharper eye for the new technology employed on the train. For him, the journey was a delightful medley of Heath Robinson contraptions. In the sleeping compartments, aside from the electric buttons to summon the waiters, two mechanical levers controlled the temperature. One admitted fresh air through wire gauze to keep out the dust and sparks; the other filled the heating apparatus with hot water. In the salons and dining cars during the summer, ingenious filter-ventilators would be filled with slabs of ice to blow pleasingly chilled air over the passengers to prevent them from being stifled.

A particular touch that Norman especially appreciated, but which again gives one pause over the safety arrangements of the early Trans-Siberian, was that his first-class carriage was entirely unencumbered by brakes. These were relegated only to the other carriages on the train. The first-class passenger was thus "undisturbed by the grinding and jolting which even the best-regulated brake produces, and can read and sleep peacefully through stoppages and down grades and hostile signals". Such an apparently dangerous arrangement was, he wrote "surely the height of railway consideration". However, the steam turbine that drove the dynamo for the train's electricity could not be similarly silenced. Driven by one of the boilers, its shrill and persistent note became noticeably audible whenever the train came to a halt after dark.

For all his admiration of the Trans-Siberian's modern technology, Norman was unable similarly to praise the service. A particular bugbear was the dining carriage, which would "not bear a moment's comparison with the Orient Express or the Riviera Express". He found himself, like many, waiting interminably for meals. Other passengers were similarly frustrated: he noted the vignette of a man who, having sat in expectation of his main course and a bottle of beer for over 50 minutes, could only get served by jumping up and screaming for the complaints book which the trains were compelled to carry. Yet, he found it in himself to be more indulgent over this problem, as he came to recognise its ultimate cause. As hour merged into hour, and the uneventful days of the journey telescoped into an indeterminable mass, the sense of time began to evaporate. And among the Russians, at least in the view of many travellers, this was a sense that was little developed in the first place. "Whether they arrive at their destination tomorrow or next week is a matter of indifference," says John Foster Fraser. In this strange and disconnected atmosphere, food would start to occupy the forefront of attention. The travellers would take every opportunity to eat, and any notion of fixed mealtimes, of breakfast, lunch and dinner, would fall entirely by the wayside. Passengers besieged the dining car at every hour of the day and night – one had to intrigue and struggle for a table. As for the staff, there was "no time to sweep up and set tables; no time when the servants can feel free to rest, sleep, or eat; no time when the wearied kitchen fire can 'go down' as it does at home."

Whatever time of day Norman ventured into the dining car, he would find it peopled. If he called for an early morning cup of tea, he would find the "inevitable nameless official in his dark-blue uniform piped with green or blue magenta cloth, with crossed pick-axes or hammers or bill-hooks on his collar and cap… thoughtfully spitting out the bones of a fried carp upon his plate while he selected a fresh mouthful with his knife." When he crept in at midnight for a sandwich, a party of rugged-looking men were sat round an empty *cafetière* drinking champagne out of tumblers, in front of them a saucer with a tottering pile of ash from many dozens of cigarettes.

The recreation of eating on the Trans-Siberian became a matter of comment for many travellers. Fraser confirmed the observations of Norman: "How the Russian eats! He has no fixed mealtime, but takes food when he is hungry, which is often. He has about six square meals a day. He has at least a dozen lunches, a little bit of salt fish or some caviar, a piece of bread and cheese, an onion and some red cabbage, a sardine and a slice of tomato, all washed down with many nips of fiery vodka."

For another early recreational traveller, the American Lindon Bates Jr, the repast in the dining carriage was even more extensive. The first item was, of course, the shot of cold vodka. "While we still gasp and blink over this, [the waiter] has gotten the cold *zakuska* of black rye-bread and butter, *sardinka*, salty beluga, and cold ham… Then comes in… a big pot of cabbage-soup which we are to season with a swimming spoonful of thick sour cream. The chunky pieces of half-boiled meat floating in it are left high and dry by the consumption of the liquid. The meat becomes the third course, which we garnish with mustard and taste." There was the option of sturgeon and starlet, "parboiled so that it tastes like blotting paper", or else the "filet that is called 'biftek', and the oil-sodden 'Hamburger', that is dubbed 'filet.'" Passing these, they moved on to roast partridge with sugared cranberries, red wine from the Imperial Crimean estates, and then two dessert courses of a "hard German-like" apple tart followed by cheese. The conclusion of the "mighty meal" was marked with tea and cigarettes, taken as they stretched out in armchairs to digest.

The dining car was by no means the sole supplier of food. At the many stations along the way, the train would stop for long intervals as the passengers took the opportunity to disembark and stock up at the station buffets. These, says Fraser, were sometimes small, sometimes large, but always good and clean. Though a station might be in the midst of a wilderness, with not another building to be seen for miles around, they were always stocked with a multitude of produce. The food would be arrayed on two or three long tables decked out with clean tablecloths and potted plants for decoration. Presiding over all would be a host of waiters, dressed the same as those in the best London hotels. There would be white or rye bread covered with napkins; rows of wine bottles with the price on the label; hot dishes, "half fowls, beef steaks, meat pies, basins of soup". Outside, the local peasants would gather with produce of their own to sell, which passengers would take on to the train to eat picnic-fashion: "cooked fowls, hot or cold, as you liked, for a shilling, very hot dumplings, with hashed meat and seasoning inside, for twopence-halfpenny, huge loaves of new made bread… pats of excellent butter, pails of milk, apples and grapes, and fifty other things." Others found boiled eggs for 10 kopeks a dozen, chunks of fried meat and fried fish, fish tarts, jam turnovers, pickled cucumbers, and, most characteristically of all, bottles of home-brewed *kvass*: "a kind of innocent pop beer", one traveller remarked. Also on the station platform would be a great cauldron-like samovar. Passengers would normally carry their own tea, sugar and brewing equipment, and all classes of people would cluster round and clamour for hot water.

Surveying the scramble for food that took place at every station, Fraser was moved to comment on how the pace of the trains was a function of the Russian appetite: "Foreigners grumble about the slowness of the Russian trains. They are not particularly slow. The time is spent at the railway stations while the passengers eat. And while the Russians have appetites in proportion to the size of their country those waits are not likely to be shortened."

 s the train rolled out of Moscow, the passengers who were booked in for the long journey to the Urals, or as far as Irkutsk, began to make themselves at home. Wandering through the corridors towards the parlour in search of company, Lindon Bates Jr drank in the atmosphere around him: "Along the broad aisles you walk, past the staterooms, filled with baggage, littered with bedding, kettles, novels, and fur overcoats. Everything is in direst confusion, and the owners are sandwiched precariously between their belongings. On the little tables which are raised between the seats, they are playing endless games of cards, sipping tea and nonchalantly smoking cigarettes the while." Along he went, past the niches where iron stoves burned wood to heat the train, through the covered bridges between the carriages, sharp zones of cold air with accumulations of snow that had seeped in through the gaps. At length, he reached the parlour. Throwing off his fur hat, he crossed himself before the ikon in the corner, and settled himself in one of the broad sofas near the bookcase. He was now at liberty to indulge himself in the other activity that was good for passing time on the Trans-Siberian: the observation of characters and life.

The initial sight of the company in the first-class parlour was exotic and raffish enough at first sight: the variety was a tonic to the imagination; the air was a babble of conversation and languages. A uniformed Russian officer sits down with a French couple and finds some excuse to order a bottle of champagne. Snippets of the latest Parisian argot rise up above the din: *"Ces sont des betteraves là-bas!"* This is outdone by a group of German technicians clutching schooners of beer, one of whom hammers the table with his fist: *"Arbeit in Sibirien nimmer geendet ist* – they always want more advice about their gas-plants." An English medical missionary bound for north China discusses his work with an American engineer on his way to the mines of Nerchinsk.

A burly man in a frock coat and gaudy jewellery introduces himself to Bates, and tells him his life story – a convict who had marched for seven years in Siberia, before being released to make his fortune there in gold. He is joined by a travelling official, a judge with his family heading east to take up a new posting; he complains bitterly of the danger of the Japanese. After a while, another man reels to the piano and strikes up a tune, singing at first to himself: "You can hear the girls declare, He must be a millionaire..." His playing is far from perfect, and from time to time he skips a note, but is not embarrassed in the least. He forges ahead in his song, and before long, all around, clutching their cigarettes, bottles of beer or cups of tea, begin to join in. The chorus rises to a crescendo of accents, German and French, English and Russian, united in an untroubled accord: "The man that broke the bank at Monte Carlo!"

A newspaper correspondent, George Lynch, who used the Trans-Siberian to travel back to Europe from China, noted how even shortly after its construction, the service had begun to attract an extraordinary range of rootless and inexplicable eccentrics. He noted a number of them who were travelling with him on his journey.

There was, first of all, a representative of "that type of wandering English spinster on whose face an east wind seems always to be blowing". Her hair was iron grey, with a fringe of an even sterner shade. She wore a sailor hat and a golf cape no matter the weather, and sniffed suspiciously at the foreign food proffered to her. She kept a rigorous check on her spending, and would always compare prices for food or anything else, before reluctantly extracting her money from a bag suspended by a string from her neck.

There was a man, perhaps from Burma, whom Lynch dubbed "The Professor". Tall and gaunt, his height was exaggerated by a gigantic colonial pith helmet, which he was never seen without. He would either wear a lounge suit of drab silk whose trousers stopped an inch above a pair of bright yellow shoes, or else a golf suit, consisting of a bright-red jacket with matching knee-length socks and plus-fours. His habit of wearing an immense pair of blue goggles in addition to his ordinary glasses gave him the appearance, says Lynch, of a "goblin-like ferocity". In his luggage he carried golf clubs, fishing rods and a gun. He was obsessed with exercise. Whenever the train came to a station he would eschew the buffet, but attired in his strange costume and pith helmet he would jog unsteadily up and down the platform to the astonishment of the ordinary Russians, until the bell rang for the train's departure.

There was a peculiar and obsessive American academic, to Lynch "The Fishman", who was making a collection of Siberian fish for a US university. Whenever possible, he would rush to the fish markets near the stations and gather from the mystified dealers an enormous bundle of strange and inedible specimens. Bringing these back to his room, the Russian passengers watched in mounting bewilderment as he immersed them in formalin (a mixture of formaldehyde, water and, usually, methanol) and packed them away in empty kerosene tins. He did little to explain himself to the spectating Russians, and Lynch attempted to reassure them, saying that the man was from a tribe of Americans who lived on raw fish. It did little to allay their suspicion, and one of the servants crossed himself with much trepidation.

Further down the carriage, there was an Anglican vicar, a mild-mannered young man, shy, with straw-coloured hair. Deeply impressionable, he was thoroughly moved by a long peroration by "The Professor" on the wholesomeness of the Russian diet, and particularly the health benefits of Russian sausages. Taking the opportunity of a stop at one of the stations, he went out and bought "one of the most formidable high-powered sausages" that Lynch had ever seen. Lynch put this out of his mind until the evening, when the time came for him to turn in. The evening was hot and close, and he kept the window open for fresh air. However, a strange odour began to pervade his room. He thought it might be smouldering oil leaking from the engine, but closing his window, he failed to exclude it. Fearing that the formalin of the Fishman's collections had begun to seep out, he rushed to check, but found it secure. In the corridor, the smell was more insistent. The "Professor" paced restlessly up and down in a Japanese kimono, slippers and pith helmet. Lynch followed the odour and found it strongest by the vicar's door. Lynch knocked, and a weak, hollow voice told him to come in. Within, he found the man of God sitting on his bunk in a Jaeger flannel shirt and trousers, his clerical collar twisted to one side, and his hair a dishevelled mess. Before him lay the sausage, which he regarded, said Lynch, rather like a picture he had seen of Oliver Cromwell contemplating the body of Charles I.

The vicar confessed responsibility for the smell. He could not bear to throw the sausage away, such had been the capital sunk in its purchase. He had tried to carry it by putting it in a bag and hanging it out of the window of his carriage, but crowds of barking dogs would congregate at every station and attempt to chase the train. Lynch decided to take the initiative and hunt for a safe place to stash the offensive purchase. Burying it under the mattress had no effect on its power, and an attempt to seal it in a switch box plunged the carriage into darkness. Eventually, Lynch consented to isolate the sausage for the duration of the journey in his typewriter tin, which solution was able to conceal the stench, but led later to complaints from his editors that his typescripts were inexplicably offensive to the nose.

Of all the strange characters to be found in the first-class parlour, the officials, merchants, prospectors, speculators, decadents, eccentrics, "c'est magnifique," said one observer, "mais ce n'est pas le Russe." The real spirit of the early Trans-Siberian, contended many, was to be found at the other end of the train in the third-class carriages. Here would be found the huddled masses of the poor European Russian peasantry heading for a new life in Siberia. It was a mirror image of the process that was playing itself out at the same time, with emigrants from Europe seeking a new beginning in the new lands of the United States.

A number of Western travellers eschewed the comforts of the parlour to be able to travel with the peasants. Among these were Sir John Foster Fraser, and also two American journalists, R.L. Wright and Bassett Digby. A third-class carriage, they found, was a Spartan affair. The décor was none of the mahogany or oak to be found in the trains de luxe, but merely a grimy wash of drab-looking paint. Instead of compartments, there were larger rooms, lined with backrests which could be unfolded into sleeping benches at night. The travellers would bring their own quilts, camelhair blankets, and bundles of rags to serve as a pillow. With these, they would make their beds. The cabins would be congested with bundles of goods, the few items that the migrants could salvage from their old lives, rolls of tattered clothing and blankets, rugs or else kettles, and the occasional wooden spoon.

Despite the apparent grimness of the surroundings, the Western travellers found their journeys both congenial and interesting. There was none of the conventional stiffness of demeanour, said Wright and Digby, that one would usually meet with in the West. Easy comradeship and fraternisation was the norm. No one was ashamed to ask of any other traveller, whom they had just met, the most personal and forward of questions: "Where do you come from?" "Where are you going, and what is your business?" "How much money have you? Have you your money by you, or in the trunk? What have you in that box?"

During the day, picnicking and the telling of anecdotes was the main occupation. As with anyone else, the peasants would rush off the train at every stop to obtain food from the buffet, and hot water for their tea. Their staple food, according to Fraser, was melon and black bread. The floor would be a mess of breadcrumbs and melon rind, further sodden when a clumsy wayfarer would knock over one of the kettles to a mass of hearty fraternal expletives. The other main occupation was to smoke. The cigarettes carried by the peasants, said Fraser, were tiny, unsatisfying things, half cardboard tube. They "provide three modest puffs, and then are to be thrown away. You could smoke a hundred a day and deserve no lecture on being a slave to tobacco."

The characters and types of people to be seen amongst the peasants were as remarkable and arresting as those travelling at the other end of the train in first class. Equally, there was variety in terms of background, occupation and ethnicity. There were "decent-looking artisans;" there were hearty young bloods, "harum-scarum… fellows… diving into every buffet and shouting for *pevo* (beer), and making mock attempts to pitch one another out of the window". There were a greater mass of more staid rural *mujiks*, "shaggy men with big sheepskin hats that gave them a ferocious air". They wore rough-spun cloaks and often, instead of boots, nothing more than sacking tied closely around their feet. Their wives were "fat and plain", but always brightly dressed, with shawls and headscarves, short skirts, often in bright orange, and knee-length felt boots. There were Tartar women, clothed similarly to their Russian cousins, but enveloped in a thick white veil from head to foot. There were, side by side with them, more modernised Russian women, who wore "hideous military jackets, fur toques tilted over the brow, and… execrably hung skirts".

The individual characters to be spied in third class were as legion as those described by George Lynch. Wright and Digby were among their premier observers. Amongst the masses playing cards or drinking tea, a young engineer student took out a tattered paperback book of quadratic equations, and busied himself amongst the din. In the meantime, two soldiers with musical inclinations did their best to distract him, one strumming on a balalaika, the other on an improvised three-string fiddle. A sailor moved about, collecting up all the cigarettes from his fellow passengers that he could muster. Next to him was a man inexplicably dressed in a fashion not dissimilar to the Pied Piper of Hamlin: "… a conical green felt hat, a long, pinkish sheep-skin coat, a neck cloth flaming with scarlet and pink and salmon and orange, great pink felt boots to the thigh, boots embroidered with trailing red flowers"; by him, another student, tall and mop-headed, clutching a book of poetry, teaching a child of 10 to learn and recite a litany of marked passages out loud.

At night, when darkness fell, the conductors would pass through and fix up candles, two for each room, that would flicker onward late into the night. Extra candles might be purchased by those wishing to carry on their games of cards, but in general the carriages would descend into near darkness and silence. It was at this time that Fraser found them at their most forbidding. Although he believed the emigrants to be, in general, happy, he could not but help be depressed at their condition:

"The place was all gaunt shadow. The men lay back loungingly, like weary labourers caught with sleep in the midst of toil. On the seat beside the man, huddled up, with her face hid in her arms, was the wife. Lying on the floor, with a bundle of rags as a pillow, were the children. I had to step over a grey-whiskered old man, who was curled up in the gangway – a feeble, tottering creature to emigrate. Close to the door was an old woman, her face hanging forward and hidden, and her long, bare, skinny arms drooping over her knees. It was all very pathetic in that dim, uncertain candle flare. There was no sound but the snore of deep-sleeping men and the slow rumble of the moving train.

"I stood looking upon the woeful picture and thinking. Then a child cried, and its mother turned testily and slapped it."

Before the construction of the Trans-Siberian railway, the main route from Europe to Siberia was the Old Post Road, or *Trakt*. This came into being over the 16th and 17th centuries, as the European Russians explored, conquered and colonised Siberia, all the way to the Pacific Ocean. The road was little more than a muddy track, in places compacted into a "corduroy road", smoothed down by a panel of logs dragged over it by a horse or pack animal. Every *verst* (two-thirds of a mile, or just over one kilometre) a post, painted black and white, marked out the distance. In its essentials and the way it operated, it was remarkably similar to the other great routes of history, although distant from many of them in time and space. In its operation, it bears close comparison, for example, to the 6th century BCE Royal Road of Ancient Persia, which stretches from Persepolis in southern Iran to Sardis near the western Turkish coast, or many of the roads built and maintained by the Roman Empire. As with these, the maintenance of the Trakt was an imperial concern. The crown would mandate for post houses to be stationed at regular intervals along the way. Each had to be supplied with a certain number of horses, which must be kept ready for the use of travellers at subsidised

A wheeled tarantass *labours through soft ground in a pine forest (albumen print by Maksim Dmitriev).*

prices. A number were held back for the exclusive use of royal messengers, who had an absolute priority of claim. The post houses also doubled as inns, and were required to provide subsidised food and shelter for travellers, whenever they should choose to rest.

The first concern of a traveller about to embark on the Trakt was to obtain a "*podorojna*", or passport/permit. There were three types. The first, or courier's passport, was only available to messengers on urgent government business or people of importance, and, as has been said, would guarantee them the first use of available horses in the post houses along the way. Those travelling in such a fashion were likely to ride fast, travelling for days without intermission, barely leaving their carriage. Such a passport would allow one to travel with relative speed – for example, one traveller notes that he heard of a courier making the journey from Irkutsk to St Petersburg, a journey of nearly 3,700 miles (5,955 kilometres), in only 11 days. But it could scarcely have been a comfortable ride.

The second variety was a "crown" passport. It was distinguished from the other passports by bearing two seals, and thus could be recognised by the illiterate postmasters and horsemen on the way. It was given to army officers, officials travelling on government service, and could also be obtained by well-connected private travellers. Not only did it allow one a preferential claim, only behind the couriers, to the horses at the government post houses; it also allowed one to avoid many of the charges and tolls, for example on bridges and ferries, or for greasing the wheels of one's carriage. The third sort of permit was that allowed to ordinary travellers. Unlike the second, which was given out free, the ordinary passport had to be purchased. A charge was levied for every verst that the applicant intended to travel.

Having collected the passport, the next concern of the traveller was for his vehicle. The passport entitled travellers to the hire of a carriage, a number of which were also held at every post station. However, these government vehicles were hardly inviting. Dr The Rev. Henry Lansdell, an English missionary who travelled on the Siberian Post Road in 1879 to inspect the prisons and distribute Bibles, described the manner of these conveyances as "a roofless, seatless, springless, semi-cylindrical tumbril, mounted on poles which connect two wooden axletrees". Not only were they bumpy and ramshackle, but one was also compelled to change them at every post station like the horses. On a journey from St Petersburg to Vladivostok, this could mean packing and unpacking a vehicle over 400 times. Most travellers preferred to buy a tarantass. This was not dissimilar to the government vehicles, but was of rather a better standard. Its shape, mentioned de Windt, was more boat-like. Its size might be around six feet (two metres) in width, and between five and eight feet in length. The bodywork and axles were iron, rather than wood. Instead of being open, shelter would be provided for the traveller with a hood and curtain that could keep out the weather and keep in the warmth.

The tarantass was a low carriage used throughout Russia; during winter wheels were replaced by runners to turn it into a sled, and journeys were usually swifter across frozen or snow-covered ground.

For those travelling over the snow in winter, a tarantass rather than a carriage would be the order of the day. Of these, there were many varieties, some entirely open, some entirely covered back and front in a thick canvas hood lined with felt, and some just hooded at the back. However, all of them were equipped with stout ash poles on either side to act as outriggers. These prevented the vehicle from overturning when it was travelling at speed, and also, as collisions were frequent, to mitigate the damage when running into another vehicle.

The packing of the sledge was an extremely fine science. As there was no separate perch for the traveller to sit, one's luggage became not only one's seat, but frequently one's bed. The wise traveller avoided wooden trunks, solid cases and sharp corners. Lansdell and de Windt both opted for soft, cornerless leather bags. These they would lay down at the bottom of the carriage on a layer of hay, and then cover them with mattresses and rugs. On top of this, finding contortions that would allow them to lie down in the confined space, they made themselves comfortable as best they could.

n important part of the packing was the choice of clothing to keep out the extreme temperatures. Aside from three travelling rugs, de Windt chose a thick fur pelisse, made of reindeer lined with lynx, and also a *bashlik*, a type of head and neck covering, woven from camel hair, often used by Russian soldiers. Lionel Gowing, an English traveller who made the journey from Vladivostok to St Petersburg in 1887, took even greater precautions. He wore a *kuklinka*, a type of buttonless hooded smock double-lined with deerskin, and over this a long *shuba*, or rough sheepskin coat with the wool turned inwards. In addition to a bashlik, he took a fur-lined cap and fur-lined gloves, with one compartment for the four fingers together. On his feet were goat-hair stockings, dogskin socks "of Chinese manufacture", and thick felt boots going up above the knees.

For all these precautions against the cold and the rigours of travel, in the 19th century sartorial considerations were never allowed to be forgotten. In Harry de Windt's bag, next to his reindeer pelisse, nestled his frock coat and dress suit – "*costume de rigueur*," he comments, "for morning calls in Siberia".

Once the tarantass had been packed and the horses secured, a *yemschik*, or driver, would be secured for the stage. He would choose a set of three horses, lash them to the *douga*, the distinctive arched Russian horse harness, and hang from this a large and discordant bell. Its jangling, which made a characteristic background music for the journey, served not only to provide warning to others, but also to keep the driver awake. As soon as the set of three horses, or *troika*, had been tied to the vehicle, it only took the driver to jump into his seat for them to surge forward, such was their instinct for the road. Often, they had to be held back while the driver mounted, and when freed, would start with a bound.

No matter how carefully the traveller packed, the softness of his leather cases or the depth of rugs and pillows with which he lined the tarantass, the journey was only occasionally marked by comfort. "The roughness of the roads and the lack of springs combine to cause a shaking up, the very remembrance of which is painful," wrote Lansdell. Charles Wenyon, an English doctor who travelled on the Post Road from Vladivostok in 1893, agreed. "None of my joints were actually dislocated, though several of them felt as if they were, and for a week or more every bone in my body ached."

The fashion in which the yemschiks drove was scarcely an aid to a serene journey. It was rare to find one not drunk. In expectation of a 10- or 20-kopek tip to buy vodka to preserve them in this state, they would urge the horses on as quickly as they could, often winding them or knocking them up in the pursuit of speed. The bodies of horses that had dropped from exhaustion were a not infrequent sight on the wayside. Although the yemschik would carry a whip to spur on the horses, it was only infrequently that he resorted to its use. It was usually by pure force of personality that he would drive them on to speed. When the horses rode fast and went obediently, the yemschik would pour out his terms of endearment on them. A mare was *sudaruina*, "good woman", a tired horse who had gone well was *starik*, "old man". A *troika* at a good gallop were *golubki*, "little doves". When, by contrast, the horses began to flag, the yemschik altered his language to use terms that were "not so complimentary or endearing," says Wenyon. So fearful or crude were the curses that the yemschik would pour upon his steeds' heads, that not only did the travellers not care to record them, but at the sound of them the horses would usually rush off in terror.

The condition of the roads only aggravated the behaviour of the yemschiks. In the summer, if a road should be muddy and the tarantass sink up to its axles in the mire, the yemschik would pull off the track and take a cross-country detour, speeding willy-nilly over roots, stones and tussocks. Holes in the road were commonplace, sometimes more than a foot deep. Sometimes these were mended by having a few logs rolled over them, but it scarcely improved the smoothness of the journey. Encountering any of these obstacles, the tarantass would judder uncontrollably. The worst moments, claim the travellers with one accord, was the descent of the hills. The yemschik would whip up the troika into an unbearable pace, and they would shoot down the gradient of the hill in order to build up a momentum to preserve their speed for the moment they reached the flat. However, the moment they hit the bottom, they would often strike a stone, a hole, or even the side of a wooden bridge over a stream. The luggage and anything moveable would crash about from side to side, the passengers would be shot vertically out of their seats, and it was sometimes the case that they could give themselves concussion by hitting their heads on the stiff canvas hood.

Safety on the journey was not at a premium. Accidents on the way were a common occurrence, and many of the travellers record at least two or three in the space of their journey. Gowing's troika, for example, was driven directly into a tree, which got fearfully wedged between two of the horses. On another occasion, his yemschik misjudged an attempt to overtake another vehicle, and the travellers in front were surprised to have their privacy disturbed by one of the horse's heads being thrust up to its neck through the canvas hood. Despite rules against overtaking couriers or other priority travellers, the yemschiks would often show a keen competitive edge, and attempt to engage them in races, with predictable consequences. Fenders would be shattered, and wheels broken in pieces. The results would be similar when they attempted to pull ahead of the slow trade caravans on the route carrying tea or other goods, crashing into other vehicles, or coming near to upsetting their own.

Yet collisions were not the only source of danger. If the wheels were not greased and the yemschik drove too fast, the friction against the axles would cause them to burst into flames – a problem that was often reported. Otherwise, if the yemschik had tired himself out with his exertions, he was liable to fall asleep on the box. This was a problem that Lansdell encountered on his travels. He woke late at night to

Lunch in the fields – a typically bucolic peasant scene in central Russia in 1934 (gelatin silver print by Georgii Petrusov).

find his tarantass barely ambling, and the sound of loud snoring proceeding from up front. Not only the yemschik, but two of the horses were slumbering. Opening the curtain and giving the yemschik a shove, he was soon able to whip him back up to the customary speed.

The post houses, more often than not, would do little to enhance the comfort of the journey. They were in general, reports Lansdell, of highly varying quality. The best would have all the appearance and comfort of "a roomy, well-established English farm-house or country inn". The worst – and these were generally more common – were little better than hovels. Nonetheless, they all shared certain characteristics. Usually, they were divided into two rooms: one would be the accommodation for the postmaster and his family; the other would be set aside for the use of travellers. At the very least, one could expect it to be furnished with a table and chair, a candlestick, a bed in the better houses, or else an unpadded bench, the customary ikon in the corner with a devotional lamp before it, and also a number of framed official notices. One of these was an extensive menu of food and drink along with the officially mandated prices, "not that you are to suppose for a moment," says Lansdell with some bitterness, "that any amount of money would purchase the luxuries named thereon... the government makes every post-master take out a victualler's licence, and named thereupon are the prices which he would charge for the delicacies IF HE HAD THEM!" Such occasions, it seems, were infrequent. One could just about count upon getting a helping of black bread, and also a supply of boiling water for tea, which like on the Trans-Siberian, one would bring one's self, along with the kettle (teapot).

On account of this uncertainty of supply, it was customary for the traveller to carry a considerable stock of provisions. This was easier in winter than in summer. When the temperatures outside descended to -60°F (-51°C), icicles formed on the nostrils of the horses, the moustachioed learned to tell the temperature to within five degrees by the stiffness and condition of their facial hair, and the outside air was more effective than any refrigerator might ever be. Travellers would merely place a piece of meat, chicken or game in a sack, hang it to the side of the vehicle, and within a few hours it would be frozen solid. At any of the stops, they could hack off as much as they needed with a hatchet, and warm it through on the stove of the post house. Frozen meat pies, recommended Lansdell, were particularly convenient. Thrown in water, he said, they were eatable in a few minutes, and it was similarly the case for frozen cream. Loaves of white bread could be picked up at major cities and likewise frozen; tinned meat, butter, anchovy paste and marmalade would serve along with this as a base for the diet. "If anything better fell in the way, it was so much to the good; if white bread and butter failed, then we hoped for improved circumstances."

It was not pleasant to dawdle too long in the post houses. Often, travellers would sleep in the vehicles whilst still on the road, or take rest in them outside the post houses when they were compelled to stop. However, if one did not have the luck of possessing a "crown" passport, one might suffer the agony of waiting hours or days for new horses, as others with priority jumped the queue. The annoyances of the accommodation, according to travellers, were manifold. It was not just that it might be cramped, with a selection of unwashed and drunken yemschiks huddled asleep on the floor. The stuffy atmosphere and the absolute absence of cleanliness – the stove was kept perpetually burning, and the windows were never opened for fresh air – encouraged in many places the presence of insects and vermin.

 number of travellers complained of the persistence of fleas and lice. Lansdell himself, when he came to a post house at Rasdolnoi near Vladivostok, found it completely infested with cockroaches. "By day they hid themselves, but at night they came out on to the table, the couch, and everywhere, great grandfathers and grandmothers with their offspring to the third and fourth generation." To wage general warfare against them, he said, would be hopeless, so he therefore set himself the task of at least keeping the table free. He recalled a trick he had seen at the Huntley and Palmer's biscuit factory in Reading, which in his time suffered a similar plague. To keep them from climbing the tables, their legs were placed in pans of water, which the insects were averse from attempting to swim. This plan, says Lansdell, he adopted with modifications. Taking a box of insect powder, he surrounded each leg of the table with a generous rampart of it. "...great was my delight to see the enemy advance, evidently thinking to scale the ramparts and mount as usual, but, instead, suddenly stop, hold a council of war, wave feelers, and then beat a retreat!"

With the development of the various railway lines, the routes that travellers took from Moscow through eastern Russia to Siberia varied throughout time. Up to the mid-19th century, the most usual way was to proceed towards Nizhny Novgorod where, taking ship first on the Volga then the Kama River, one would sail to Perm, before crossing the Ural Mountains to Yekaterinburg. Later, with the development of the Trans-Siberian railway, the bulk of the traffic moved south. Yekaterinburg was bypassed, and the Urals were crossed lower down at the town of Chelyabinsk.

A traveller who made the former journey on more than one occasion was the American George Kennan. Originally a committed Russophile, he made his first travels in Eastern Siberia in the 1860s as an engineer on a failed venture to run an undersea telegraph cable from the US to Russia by way of the Bering Straits. Having learnt the language, he was drawn to travel further in Russia, the Caucasus and Siberia in the 1870s and 1880s where, so horrified at the living conditions of Siberian prisoners, he resolved to campaign for their better treatment and the abolition of the exile system. Despite his disgust at this aspect of Russian life and the political objective of his travels, he still retained his fascination and enchantment with the people and the land itself. Such enchantment is especially visible in the descriptions he made of his journey to Nizhny Novgorod and onwards to the Urals, far more perceptive and extensive in their detail than many others who took the same route.

In the late 19th century, merchants stand in front of the Government Palace in Nizhny Novgorod, site of the Great Russian Fair.

Nizhny Novgorod (called Gorky for much of the 20th century) sits on the Volga, at its junction with the Oka River. Its position ensured that its lifeblood would be trade. By land, it looked west towards Moscow, and east towards Siberia and the steppe of Central Asia. By river, its place on the Volga tied it directly to the Caspian. It led to the traffic of the Caucasus and Persia, as well as the Turkish Empire and the Mediterranean. In the early 19th century, the city became the receptacle for an enormous trade fair, held every autumn, which united the commerce of these regions. Outside this season, however, the city was a deserted and eerie place. Kennan describes arriving there one January (1868) to find it near abandoned, "an extraordinary picture of loneliness and desolation". Churches, mosques, theatres, banks, markets, hotels, exchanges and the city's 6,000 shops sat empty and barred. Untrodden snow lay two foot deep on the pavements, and there was not a sign of a single human being. However, with the onset of autumn, all was changed. Over half a million merchants and tradesmen came from every direction, bringing hundreds of millions of roubles worth of goods, and the city burst into a riot of colourful but ephemeral life.

When Kennan arrived at the city during the fair in 1870, he was overwhelmed by this extraordinary contrast. Along the banks of the Volga, below the massive walls of the upper citadel and the church domes of silver and gold, green and blue, over eight miles of the riverfront was occupied by shipping. An endless tangle of masts ran across the vista, flags waved in the dusty breeze, and steamers blew their whistles. Huge black barges ferried goods either way along the river, and other vessels were being loaded or unloaded by hosts of swarthy Tatars on the multitude of wharves and landing stages. Small four-wheeled, one-horse wagons, or *telegas*, were carting away bags, boxes and crates from the piles of merchandise on the riverside towards the bazaars on the city's streets. Looking on were an innumerable crowd of traders and peddlers, sailors and labourers, pilgrims and tramps. As if to cap the theatricality of the scene, a military band were drawn up on the boulevard in front of the governor's house, playing airs from the operas of Offenbach.

Descending into the commercial area below the city's Kremlin, Kennan found a variety and confusion that far exceeded anything that might have been seen on a bazaar of the old Silk Road. Modernity and antiquity, luxury goods and everyday wares jostled together in confusion. Fashionable stores with gilded signs and plate-glass windows stood next to the rough, unpainted stalls of petty hawkers. Antique churches nestled in the corners and by-ways, giving an air of sanctity to otherwise disreputable neighbourhoods. Banks, elegant hotels, and the offices of steamship companies were distributed amongst the ship's chandlers, the sellers of old clothes, and the humble teahouses. It was a spot where anything and everything in the world could be bought, from "a paper of pins, a wooden comb, or a string of dried mushrooms, to a ship's anchor, a church bell, or a steam-engine". The more obvious goods, such as tea brought overland from China, or furs from Siberia were on sale. Yet traders also offered him prices on articles from battered samovars and sleigh bells to swords and revolvers, elk horns, tins of biscuits from London, accordions, iron crucifixes and a bathtub.

he variety of peoples in the bazaar was equally legion. Tatars in skullcaps and *khalats*, or loose silken gowns, were seen side by side with Russian peasants clad in greasy sheepskin coats and wickerwork shoes, their legs bound in dirty bandages of coarse linen cloth. There were Persians and Turks, Circassians, Parsis from India, and even Chinese. Monks with long hair and longer beards moved amongst the crowds, begging alms for churches or hospitals. They held out boards lined with black velvet to receive any coins, which they would scoop up and deposit in jangling tin boxes hung from their neck, secured with massive iron padlocks. There would be dealers in kvass, mead and sherbet, peddlers of brass jewellery, salted cucumbers, and sellers of printed handkerchiefs, displaying the nascent railway network of Russia. Even the children were not to be denied their part in the city's commerce. Kennan noted a ragged boy, not more than eight or nine years old, carrying nothing but a few meagre strings of dried mushrooms. Nevertheless, he pushed and shoved his way through the crowd with all the assurance of one with many years' experience, crying "Mushrooms! Fine mushrooms! Sustain commerce, gentlemen! Buy my mushrooms and sustain commerce!"

From Nizhny Novgorod, Kennan took a place on a steamer that carried him along the Volga to Kazan, where, joining the Kama River, he was eventually taken onwards towards Perm and the Urals. It was a route that was shared by Harry de Windt a few years afterwards, and although they both had eyes for the beauty of the journey, it is, as is typical, de Windt who tells us more about the minutiae of life onboard ship for the 1,000-mile (1,600-kilometre) passage.

Around 450 steamships would ply the Volga between Nizhny Novgorod and Perm during the season of the fair. De Windt booked a first-class ticket aboard one of them, the *Alexis*. Although his ticket was first class, the conditions of his journey were hardly as pleasant as he had hoped. Boarding the ship, he found the first-class saloon. The décor was of threadbare red velvet. Although the sun was bright and hot, the windows were kept tightly shut, and the atmosphere was stifling. The heat of the day, amplified by the thin metal roof, accentuated the fug of the room, a mixture of cooking, sweat and cigarette smoke. It was only fit, thought de Windt, for a salamander, but the Russian travellers seemed to prefer it like this. All around, they lounged on hard wooden benches smoking and chatting. Others sat at the deal tables covered in dirty white cloths, eating heartily, spilling breadcrumbs and scraps onto the oilcloth floor. Resolving to make the best of it, de Windt decided to join in the eating. He was cheered to find the food excellent, well-cooked starlet (a type of fish) and stewed plums, and his mood was slowly mellowed by glasses of fine Crimean wine.

As the steamship pulled out, de Windt was able to find space on deck and admire the passing scenery of the landscape. By day, the river continued to be crowded, with other passenger boats, tugs, and strings of barges roped together, bringing heaps of timber down to market. The riverbanks presented an extraordinary beauty. The left bank was low and flat, but the right was more varied, with the land rising sharply into cliffs over 400 feet (122 metres) in height, breaking up the view of the river into stretches. Kennan marvelled at the white-walled churches with silver domes on the promontories, surrounded by little villages of wooden houses. In the secluded coves, half-hidden amongst the great thickets of green foliage, were nestled small monasteries, their gilded domes rising above the tops of the trees. Deep valleys allowed the sight of rich farmland beyond. Between the breaks in the woods of hazel and pine could be seen dells of flowers or rich fields of clover. As, from time to time, the steamer came close to the bank, one could make out the features of laughing peasant girls who ran down to the water's edge to wave their handkerchiefs at the steamer, or else even talk to the red-shirted mujiks who were lying on the grassy slopes.

Cossacks returning from the hunt, 1875 (albumen print by Ivan Boldyrev). Note the fellow in the background, who is pouring the vodka even before dismounting!

The greatest pleasure of the journey, agreed Kennan and de Windt, was to be had by staying on deck for the fall of night. The warm air was moved and cooled by the breezes on the river. The scent of the flowery meadows, the damp forest glens and the dewy grass rose from the banks. The sidelights of passing steamers streaked across the heavy darkness. In the background was the comforting patter of the paddlewheels against the water. Except for this, there was silence, aside from the faint barking of sheepdogs, the faint call of a timber rafter, or else an occasional fisherman singing the most traditional of the river boatmen's songs, *V'nis po matushke po Volge*, "Down the Mother Volga". Although de Windt was pestered until 3am by a drunken Russian official who had found an English phrasebook and was trying to practise his knowledge of the

A family in the Nizhny Novgorod region, 1870s (albumen print by Ivan Raoult), showing a fascinating view of traditional life and culture in the rural Volga region of Russia.

language by repeatedly toasting Queen Victoria, he was moved by the serenity of the scene. Sometimes the passengers on deck would join in when they heard the snatches of the fishermen's music, and the deepening darkness was accompanied by a litany of melancholy song.

hether one travelled by the new route of the Trans-Siberian railway, or the old route of the Volga, one could not escape the sense of the impending east, and the lingering departure from Europe. Embarking on John Foster Fraser's train at Samara were crowds of Mongolians who might have come west for work, and "fine set Cossacks, carrying themselves proudly", wearing white sheepskin hats, belts of cartridges slung over plum-coloured coats, and long riding boots of red morocco leather. On the northern route of the Volga, Kennan steamed past the old (Muslim) Tatar capital of Kazan, which had been conquered by Moscow and incorporated into its empire in the middle of the 16th century. The Volga at that time had washed the walls of its citadel, but by the 19th century its bed had receded six miles from the city, and its towers, domes and minarets could now only be seen at a distance from the river. Nevertheless, the landing stage that had been built on the bank of the river gave something of the flavour of the city. The settlement, said Kennan, was like a "materialised architectural aurora borealis", its houses painted in the most extraordinary range of clashing and diverse colours. Chocolate-brown houses would be finished with yellow shutters and green roofs; an orange house with an olive roof; a sky-blue house with a red roof; a lavender house with a shining tin roof; and amongst them one house "which displayed the whole chromatic scale within the compass of three stories and an attic". In the streets, wrote de Windt, between the droshkies that vied to take travellers into town, were green-turbaned hajjis, water and melon sellers clanging metal cymbals to gain attention, and women in balloon-like dresses with headscarves of delicate muslin.

Joining the River Kama, still closer to the Urals, the landscape became less cultivated, stranger, more wild. By the banks were poplars, aspens and silver birch, and inland there were meadows blue with forget-me-nots, but which in the distance were swallowed up by the grey-green steppe. The villages became less frequent, more tumbledown. The churches were not of stone, but only of whitewashed wood with high, green roofs and gilt crosses. The houses came down to the water's edge, and cattle, pigs and dogs roamed freely in their neglected gardens. The number of inhabitants also seemed to be fewer. Those that one glimpsed from the deck seemed to have assumed the motif of garish colours; both men and women boasted clothing ranging in colour from blue and crimson, to purple, lemon, scarlet and pink. Although the occurrence of inhabitants was less frequent, one would still see the mujiks lounging on the bank; and, at every stop along the way, peasant girls would rush to sell the travellers armfuls of lilies of the valley, which went some way to perfuming the heavy fug of the first-class saloon of the steamer.

he crossing of the Urals, the great boundary line between Europe and Asia, is often an event that many western European travellers let pass with little remark. The mountains themselves are low, irregular, broken by frequent passes, and often are characterised only as hills. Certainly throughout history, they formed little barrier towards movement, and during the periods of eastern invasion, such as the time of Mongol rule in the 13th and 14th centuries, they provided little defence against the attacks of Tatar cavalry. John Foster Fraser remarked that every Russian to whom he mentioned the Urals broke out in raptures of adjectives: "beautiful, lovely, picturesque, magnificent, grand". Certainly in comparison with the unremittingly flat landscape of the Russian and Asian steppe, they might seem so. But, goes on Fraser with his usual bluntness, "naturally when you have spent years on a desert you regard a hillock with some trees as charming... The scenery of the Urals is beautiful because you have travelled days on a featureless plain."

Despite his curmudgeonly remarks, Fraser did not deny that the range was at the least picturesque; he travelled in autumn, and enjoyed the golden tints of the trees along the grey rocks, backed by a rich crimson sunset. However, he, among others, held that the Urals were little different to parts of Derbyshire, and for grandeur and scale, one would need to look to the other mountain ranges of Europe, America or India.

Perhaps one of the other reasons for disappointment in crossing the border between Europe and Asia was that there seemed to be so little apparent difference between the two. This is often a symptom of crossing a boundary, particularly one artificial and man-made, but in this case it is frequently, especially among the travellers of the 19th and early 20th centuries, a feeling that is particularly pronounced. When the likes of Kennan, Lansdell, Fraser and de Windt were travelling, western Siberia was already in the throes of modernisation and Westernisation. Many of the characteristics that served to make it distinct were already in decline. When Fraser reached Chelyabinsk, the first Asiatic stop on the Trans-Siberian, it was the forwarding station for the tens of thousands of poor Russian emigrants who were going to settle in Siberia. On the day of his arrival, the rain fell in torrents, and hundreds of the settlers poured out of the train clutching their bundles, wrapping themselves in musty sheepskins to act as waterproofs. Scuffles for provisions broke out at the station buffet. Said Fraser, "I have joined in a scramble for food at an English railway station, but that was the decorum of a court reception compared with the fight at Chelyabinsk." They marched through the streets knee-deep in mud to the strip of ramshackle sheds where they were to take up residence for several weeks, until they received their forwarding papers and grants to proceed further along their way. The whole scene did not inspire Fraser: "Conceive a field in which a cattle show has been held for a week, and it has been raining all the week. That will give you some idea of Chelyabinsk."

When Kennan and de Windt took the train over the Urals from Perm to Yekaterinburg – the first line to cross the range, predating the more southerly Trans-Siberian line by over 20 years – the experience was altogether more pleasant, but it was hardly redolent of the Asiatic. The line, unlike the Trans-Siberian, was better financed, and built without the same pressures of time or the shortages of labour. It was thus was one of the best-constructed railway routes that any of them had seen in Russia. Kennan commented on the solidity of the well-ballasted track, the rolling stock as good as anywhere in the Russian Empire, the verst-posts on the side of the line beautifully set in mosaics of coloured stones.

De Windt, characteristically, remarked on the buffet at Nizhny Tagil, the first stop on the Asiatic side. This, he said, was as fine as the top restaurants of Paris or London. Outside there were well-maintained flowerbeds and neatly trimmed hedges. Within, the décor was of marble and inlaid oak with stucco cornices and crystal candelabra. A long refectory table in the middle of the room was laid with starched white linen napkins and tablecloths, costly china and fresh-cut flowers. Pyramids of wine bottles, an aquarium of fish, a giant clock and a bronze heating stove occupied various sides of the room. Waiters attired spotlessly in white tie and tails moved noiselessly around, bringing from the white-capped chefs wines that were "iced and delicious", and "viands well cooked". The rest of the company consisted of beribboned colonels and ladies in long suede gloves with straw hats. Kennan, who also thought it "one of the neatest... and most attractive public dining-rooms that I entered in any part of the world", expressed the strangeness of his feelings, the sense that he had hardly left home. As he helped himself to a four-course dinner, he reflected that he found it utterly impossible to believe that he was in the "unheard-of mining settlement of Nizhni Tagil, on the Asiatic side of the mountains of the Ural".

The feeling persisted on reaching Yekaterinburg, the first major Asiatic settlement. At the station, liveried footmen bustled to collect their masters, "prosperous-looking gentlemen" in private droshkies, and drive them home along the wide and elegant boulevards, already by 1880 illumined at night with the white globes of electric street lamps. It would be many years before the city gained its melancholy associations with the murder of the last Tsar in the Bolshevik uprising in 1917. In the mid- to late-19th century, Yekaterinburg was thought of as an industrial boomtown, its prosperity based on the extensive mineral wealth of the surrounding territories. Not only did it produce a wealth of manufacturing staples such as iron, coal, copper and salt, but also a multitude of precious stones and metals, gold, silver and platinum, as well as emeralds and topaz, amethysts and aquamarine.

Visitors to the city, such as the English artist Thomas Atkinson, who was travelling in Siberia with his wife in the 1850s, marvelled at the great workshop, the *Granilnoi Fabric*, where the gems were cut and polished using machines, lathes and saws, with the latest water-driven technology. Great blocks of jasper and porphyry were sawn into slabs for use as tabletops, or else carved into columns, pedestals or semi-transparent vases for furnishing the homes of the rich. The wealth generated by this industry went to pay for hospitals and schools, theatres and performances of opera, as well as financing a lifestyle of dissipation for many of the wealthier inhabitants of the city. There were those, reported Atkinson, whose routine of playing cards in Yekaterinburg was as regular as a merchant turning up to the office. 10am was the hour of business, and the games would continue, with breaks only for meals, well into the evening. Thus, with all its amenities and amusements, life on the Asiatic side of the Urals could be said to offer as much as the great cities of St Petersburg or Moscow in Russia proper.

By the mid-19th century, when many of these travellers made their journeys, the influx of Russian migration had already changed life in Siberia forever. In 1850, the population of Siberia was reckoned to be 2,176,000, including men, women and children. Of these, two million were Russians; the native Siberian tribes, the original inhabitants of the region, only made up the small remainder. It is necessary to turn to the travellers who visited Siberia before this period of colonisation in order to find a sense of entering a different and foreign world, and of coming amongst a different and foreign people.

River ferries were numerous and essential for travellers in Siberia, as George Kennan discovered in the 1880s.

One example of such a traveller is Evert Ysbrants Ides. Ides was a Dutch merchant from Holstein who was sent as Peter the Great's ambassador to Peking in 1692. Taking the same route along the River Kama as Kennan and de Windt, he recalls in detail his crossing of the Urals from Europe into Asia. For him, this transition was endowed with a great sense of moment. To mark his final evening on the western side of the Urals, he came ashore from the river and climbed a "high and beautiful green hill" to eat his last dinner in Europe on the grass, and drink a glass of wine "as a farewell to dear Europe". Having made the crossing, he was soon confronted not with iron works, great boulevards or camps of Russian immigrants, but rather with a sight that would become a rarity in later years: a traditional settlement of a native Siberian tribe.

Beyond the Urals, he sailed slowly along the banks of the Chusovaya River. The lands around it, he wrote, "deserve really to be reckoned amongst the most charming in the world". Everywhere he went ashore, he found "the most beautiful plants and flowers, which emitted a most agreeable scent, and all sorts of great and small wild beasts running about in great quantities". However, the river led to a settlement of Vogul Tartars. The fact that they were "stupid heathens" made him eager to find out more about their religion, customs and ways of life, to which end he paused on his journey to lodge for a night among them.

The people, he found, were naturally strong, and had "large heads". Their dwellings were wooden huts not unlike those of the Russian peasants, lined with broad benches for both sitting and sleeping. Instead of heating their dwellings with the usual Russian stove, they would keep an open fire in the middle of the floor, which they would use for both warmth and cooking. They had an ingenious – although somewhat dangerous – method of preserving the heat in the room. After the wood had burnt down to glowing embers, they would cover the smoke hole in the roof with a block of ice, thus keeping in the heat, but allowing the sunlight to shine in. They did not husband livestock such as pigs or chickens, as was usual with Russian peasants, but rather took most of their food by hunting, their main quarry being elk. Ides admired a number of traps they showed him for game. The simpler of these consisted of pits dug in the floor of the woods covered with reeds and grass. The more elaborate included bows and arrows rigged up with tripwires, designed to shoot at any animal that should take up a bait in the snare. The captured animals would be taken back to the settlements, cut up and hung out to dry around the houses, where, even if they should "stink abominably", they were still treated as a delicacy.

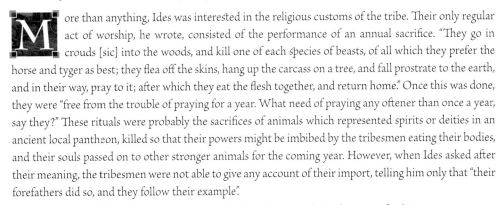

ore than anything, Ides was interested in the religious customs of the tribe. Their only regular act of worship, he wrote, consisted of the performance of an annual sacrifice. "They go in crouds [sic] into the woods, and kill one of each species of beasts, of all which they prefer the horse and tyger as best; they flea off the skins, hang up the carcass on a tree, and fall prostrate to the earth, and in their way, pray to it; after which they eat the flesh together, and return home." Once this was done, they were "free from the trouble of praying for a year. What need of praying any oftener than once a year, say they?" These rituals were probably the sacrifices of animals which represented spirits or deities in an ancient local pantheon, killed so that their powers might be imbibed by the tribesmen eating their bodies, and their souls passed on to other stronger animals for the coming year. However, when Ides asked after their meaning, the tribesmen were not able to give any account of their import, telling him only that "their forefathers did so, and they follow their example".

The lives of the tribesmen seemed to be free from much in the way of religious ceremony or strictures. Marriages were conducted without priests. Men could take as many wives as they pleased, and no rites were observed aside from a feast. Burials were similar in nature; there was no gravestone, but the corpse was bewailed by the relatives, and buried with fine clothes, ornaments and money, so that the deceased would have provisions for the afterlife. They had a particular care of dogs; should one die, particularly in the course of hunting, they would erect in its honour a small hut or kennel on four props of earth, and lay its body there "as long as the hutt lasts".

When Ides questioned the tribe further, asking "whether they did not believe that there was a God and Lord in Heaven above, that had created, and did at present preserve and govern all things, and also gave rain and fair weather," they replied, "We may very well believe that, for we see, that the Sun and Moon, those two bright lights which we worship, and the stars also, are in heaven, and that there is one which rules them." However, they would not in the least accept the idea of the Devil. How could they know anything at all about him, they asked "since he never appeared, or revealed himself to them". Pressing them again, he admonished them "that it was time to acknowledge Christ the saviour of the whole world, and turn to him; which would secure their not only temporal, but eternal welfare". The tribesmen were not enthusiastic, pointing to the strange behaviour of the inhabitants of the west, who would concern themselves more over the spiritual life than the matter of their daily bread. "...As for what concerns temporals, we daily see vast numbers of poor wretched Russians, that can hardly get a piece of dry bread, and yet nevertheless some of them believe in Christ: and as for the eternal things they would accommodate themselves". Better it was, declared the tribe, to "live and die in the opinion of their forefathers, whether right or wrong".

George Kennan, on his visit to Siberia in June 1885, left Yekaterinburg by tarantass, and travelled by the Great Post Road towards Tiumen (Tyumen). Its course was still to the north of the later Trans-Siberian railway, and in its absence it still carried a great deal of the commerce of Siberia. Great horse-drawn freight caravans of 50 or 100 wagons, piled high with goods and covered in coarse matting, were frequent on the road. In the course of his first day's journey, he counted 1,445 wagons, indicating the sheer volume of trade. Despite the congestion on the Road, the journey was still bucolic. The Road itself at this point was more like the driveway of an English country house. When the way did not lead through forest, the road was lined on each side with a double or triple row of birches, 70 or 80 feet (21 or 24 metres) high, their branches touching in the middle to form a natural arcade, providing shade to the traveller under a magnificent canopy of white and green foliage. These were planted, according to tradition, on the order of Catharine II, and that part of the way became known as "Catharine's Alley". Beyond them, there were great fields and banks of flowers, whole meadows yellow with trollius or blue with forget-me-nots. The trees were filled with the song of sparrows and warblers. The roadside was rich with wild roses, buttercups, primroses, marsh marigolds, yellow pea, iris and honeysuckles. At intervals

A Siberian post sled using the troika, or "three of a kind", horse-drawn system that is still popular today (see page 117). George Kennan utilised this one during his trip across Siberia in 1885 – one of the figures may or may not be Kennan himself.

towards the evening, he would find groups of the caravan drivers who had stopped for refreshment by the way. Their horses had been hobbled and turned loose to graze around the fields, and the men themselves relaxed on the flowery roadside, stretching out around campfires in their scarlet kaftans and shirts, drinking tea, conversing, and making a "peculiarly Russian picture".

However, the pastoral air of Kennan's journey was upset on the second day after leaving Yekaterinburg. Passing through a forest between the villages of Markova and Tugulimskaya, the tarantass driver suddenly pulled up the horses and shouted "*Vot granitsa!*" – "Here is the boundary!" By the side of the road was a square pillar of brick covered in white plaster, around 12 feet high, on the western side bearing the coat of arms of the Russian province of Perm, and on the other the arms of the Siberian province of Tobolsk. This point was regarded as the start of Siberia proper. Although the Urals were regarded as the frontier between Europe and Asia, the boundary between Russia and Siberia was administratively considered to fall at the border of these two provinces. The sight of the pillar put Kennan immediately in mind of the hordes of convicts who had marched the road into exile – over half a million between 1800 and the time of Kennan's visit in 1885 – and who were allowed to pause at this spot, rest, and bid a final farewell to the motherland of European Russia.

The "grief-consecrated" pillar was notorious for its association with the march into exile. Kennan immediately conjured up for himself scenes of the convicts, their arms in chains and their legs in fetters, some weeping, others comforting them; some kissing the earth of the Russian side, and collecting handfuls of it to take away into exile, others pressing their lips to the European side of the pillar and scratching graffiti into its plaster. At the time of his visit, many of these inscriptions had been effaced, but a number could still be made out. Kennan discerned names and initials, and in one place the phrase *prashchai Marya!* (goodbye Mary!). Although Kennan was to learn much about the life of the convicts over the course of his journey, visiting prisons and mines, forwarding stations and secure hospitals, little could sum up so effectively the human misery associated with the exile system as emotively as the simple sight of this monument on the frontier of Siberia.

he system of sending convicts into exile in Russia dates back to at least 1648, not long after the first colonisation by the Russian Empire of Siberia. In the beginning it was a system sparingly used; the first offenders to suffer the penalty were those who had already been subjected to one of the torture-like punishments described earlier by Olearius, such as the knout or whip, or else branding or amputation. Its original intention was to put out of sight those criminals who had been permanently disabled by these punishments, and who were reckoned by contemporary society to be physically useless and morally corrupt. It was also a means of escape chosen by religious dissenters, such as the "Old Believers", who refused to accept reforms to the Orthodox Church during the period.

However, towards the end of the 17th century, the system of punishments in Russia was reformed. The Russian government, realising that they needed a large and able-bodied population to exploit the newfound resources of Siberia, abolished bodily mutilation, many forms of corporal punishment and even many occasions of the death penalty, and substituted exile as a sentence for a huge variety of crimes. In this way, they hoped to encourage settlement in their new territories.

Thus, soon after the reforms one could expect to be sent to Siberia even for the most petty misdemeanour. The list included fortune-telling, prizefighting, snuff taking, driving horses with reins (the use of reins was considered in the 17th century to be a European and un-Russian innovation), begging whilst falsely claiming to be in distress, and accidental arson. After the accession of Catherine II in 1762, and the discovery of the huge mineral reserves around Yekaterinburg that led to an even greater demand for labour, the number of ways to be condemned to Siberia increased. Government decrees turned prisoners in Russian jails into exiles. Army officers were sent away at the slightest breach of discipline. It was similar for Jews who failed to pay their taxes correctly. Landowners could banish their serfs to Siberia if they felt they had any valid cause, while if any village was troubled by a vagabond, or else one of its inhabitants refused to work, or behaved as a drunkard or wastrel, the village elders and council could elect to send him into exile.

he future that awaited exiles in Siberia depended on the reason they had been sent. The worst offenders, for example those convicted of murder or violent crimes, were generally sentenced to a number of years hard labour within an institution, such as a jail or mine. Lesser offenders were sent as penal colonists, ordered to reside in a certain place for a number of years but not imprisoned, and left to earn their own livelihood however they pleased. These two grades of offender were forbidden from returning to European Russia on the expiration of their sentences, and forfeited their civil rights upon conviction. Upon entering Siberia, their heirs could inherit their property as if they were legally dead, and their spouses were free to remarry, unless they should choose to follow them into exile. By contrast, those who had been exiled by the village councils were merely banished without any stipulation as to where in Siberia they should live.

From the earliest days, the convicts were expected to march from European Russia all the way to the place of their sentence in Siberia. In many cases, following the Post Road, this journey could take over two years, depending on the final destination. Originally, in the 17th and 18th centuries, little thought was given to the welfare of the prisoners on the journey. No provision was made for their accommodation on the way, and they were often compelled to sleep in the open and beg for food as they travelled. Death from starvation on the road is not thought to have been uncommon. The relative chaos of the administration of the system also led to great injustice. Identification of prisoners was difficult, and their documentation scanty. Hard-labour prisoners were able to swap identities with ordinary exiles for small bribes of money, vodka or warm clothing, thus escaping jail or the mines. Many prisoners were also able to abscond and live in the forest as outlaws. They were able to communicate with other prisoners by means of gossip scratched on trees along the Post Road. If they were recaptured, they gave their names as "Ivan Don't-remember" or "Feodor Know-nothing"; those recaptured without passports or any means of identification were only treated as vagrants, and by these means the hard labour convicts were also able to escape their sentences.

However, from the beginning of the 19th century, some reforms were slowly introduced. Resting houses, or *étapes*, were built at stages along the Post Road to allow the prisoners shelter. A bureau of Exile Administration was established, its headquarters in Tobolsk and later in Tiumen, charged with monitoring and registering the prisoners at every stage along the route, and inspecting the conditions in which they

Convicts in Siberia – George Kennan's documentation of the late 19th century penal colonies uncovered horrendous living conditions, though this summer shot shows them in better shape than was the norm, by most accounts.

were kept. Later, with the onset of steam power for riverboats and the construction of sections of the railway network, portions of the journey into Siberia began to be made by these forms of transport.

Nonetheless, well into the 1890s, the sight of gangs of Siberian prisoners being marched into exile was still common on the Post Road, and was remarked upon by many of the Western travellers. They would proceed in great columns of up to 500 convicts. Usually, they were lightly guarded, with escorts of no more than two-dozen soldiers bearing rifles with fixed bayonets. On the march, the prisoners wore shirts and trousers in grey linen, grey linen wrappings round the feet in place of socks, a long overcoat and a peakless cap. Women were given a grey linen skirt in place of trousers. The back of the overcoat was sewn with yellow or black cloth diamonds, determining their category. The prisoners who had been sentenced to hard labour or the penal colonies also had half of their heads shaved as a mark of the depravation of their civil liberties, and wore five-pound iron leg fetters around their ankles, using leather guards to protect them from chafing. Following the main body of prisoners were the families who had chosen to follow their condemned members into exile, baggage wagons, three or four telegas for those who were too sick or infirm to march, and a tarantass for the military officer in charge of the column.

The convicts were each given a small sum of money, usually ten kopeks a day, and were responsible for the purchase of their own food along the way. Nevertheless, they would still attempt to supplement whatever they could buy by means of begging, whenever they passed through villages or settlements. Whenever they reached such places, they would sing a traditional begging song, while a few of their number went around the houses collecting food or alms from the locals. George Kennan, who saw this ritual and heard the song while waiting at a post station in a Siberian village, deserves quotation at length:

> I shall never forget the emotions roused in me by this song when I heard it for the first time. We were sitting, one cold, raw, autumnal day, in a dirty post-station on the Great Siberian road, waiting for horses. Suddenly my attention was attracted by a peculiar, low-pitched, quavering sound which came to us from a distance, and which, although made apparently by human voices, did not resemble anything that I had ever before heard. It

was not singing, nor chanting, nor wailing for the dead, but a strange blending of all three. It suggested vaguely the confused and commingled sobs, moans, and entreaties of human beings who were being subjected to torture, but whose sufferings were not acute enough to seek expression in shrieks or high pitched cries. As the sound came nearer we went out into the street in front of the station-house and saw approaching a chained party of about a hundred bare-headed convicts, who, surrounded by a cordon of soldiers, were marching slowly through the settlement, singing the "exile's begging song". No attempt was made by the singers to pitch their voices in harmony, or to pronounce the words in unison; there were no pauses or rests at the ends of the lines; and I could not make out any distinctly marked rhythm. The singers seemed to be constantly breaking in upon one another with slightly modulated variations of the same slow, melancholy air, and the effect produced was that of a rude fugue, or of a funeral chant, so arranged as to be sung like a round or catch by a hundred male voices, each independent of the others in time and melody, but all following a certain scheme of vocalization, and taking up by turns the same, dreary, wailing theme. The words were as follows:

Have pity on us O our fathers!
Don't forget the unwilling travellers
Don't forget the long-imprisoned.
Feed us, O our fathers – help us!
Feed and help the poor and needy!
Have compassion, O our fathers!
Have compassion, O our mothers!
For the sake of Christ, have mercy
On the prisoners – the shut-up ones!
Behind the walls of stone and gratings,
Behind oaken doors and padlocks,
Behind bars and locks of iron,
We are held in close confinement.
We have parted from our fathers,
From our mothers;
We from all our kin have parted,
We are prisoners;
Pity us, O our fathers!

If you can imagine these words, half sung, half chanted, slowly, in broken time and on a low key, by a hundred voices, to an accompaniment made by the jingling and clashing of chains, you will have a faint idea of the miloserdnaya, or exiles' begging song. Rude, artless, and inharmonious as the appeal for pity was, I had never in my life heard anything so mournful and depressing. It seemed to be the half-articulate expression of all the grief, the misery, and the despair that had been felt by generations of human beings in the étapes, the forwarding prisons, and the mines.

(Opposite) A guard on the rail line, taken in the early 20th century by Sergei Mikhailovich Prokudin-Gorskii as part of his documentation of the Trans-Siberian Railway, which was sponsored by Tsar Nicholas II.

A metal truss bridge on stone piers provided the best protection against annual floodwaters. Prokudin-Gorskii photographed this particularly impressive example on the Kama River near Perm in the Urals.

(Right) *A modern Trans-Sib carriage waits in a station.*

(Below) *Kanavinsky Bridge crosses the Oka River in Nizhny Novgorod, an important city founded at the confluence of the Oka and Volga rivers, named Gorky between 1932 and 1990, and now the fourth largest city in Russia.*

(Opposite top) *Rural Russians sit in front of a wooden house with typically pretty decorative carvings framing the windows.*

(Opposite bottom) *A troika sled or sleigh pulls through deep snow in the taiga region of the Altai Mountains. This system of three horses was developed centuries ago and is still popular today, as the three animals provide great speed and combine for a harmonious and smooth ride.*

(Top) *The Kazan Kremlin, a World Heritage site since 2000. It was built by Ivan the Terrible in the 16th century on the ruins of the castle belonging to the former Kazan khanate. Kazan is capital of the Russian Republic of Tatarstan and is situated on the Volga River.*

(Bottom) *A misty panorama taken from a Trans-Sib train – a common sight on the long journey into and out of the east.*

(Right) *A Kalmyk couple in the Orenburg region, an 1872 albumen print of a watercolour by Mikhail Bukhar.*

(Top) *A modern Trans-Siberian train courses through the steppe.* (Bottom) *Engines on display at Novosibirsk's Train Museum.*
(Opposite top) *Prokudin-Gorskii's early 20th century image of Mary Magdalene Church in Perm.*
(Opposite bottom) *A riverside view of Yekaterinburg, located on the eastern side of the Ural Mountains. Pictured is the Church on the Blood, built on the site of the Ipatiev House where the Romanovs – Nicholas II and his family – were executed following the Bolshevik Revolution.*

A typical village in the Altai region, surrounded by thick taiga forest made up of numerous species of mainly coniferous trees. With so much wood available, it is not surprising that this is still the main construction material for the region's inhabitants.

(Above) The sumptuous interior of the private Golden Eagle train, which represents the most luxurious and upmarket way of crossing Eurasia by land.

(Right) The Epiphany Cathedral and Lenin Statue in Tomsk, one of Siberia's oldest urban centres, having been founded in 1604. Unfortunately, it declined in importance when it was bypassed by the Trans-Siberian Railway in favour of a village to the south, which eventually grew to become the city of Novosibirsk.

(Opposite) Another type of railroad bridge construction documented by Prokudin-Gorskii in the early 1900s, this one using massive rectangular wooden pilings.

(Above) *The railway station at Krasnoyarsk on the mighty Yenisei River. This city was founded in 1628 as an imperial border fort, but today has grown wealthy through its place on the Trans-Siberian rail line and a booming aluminium industry.*

(Right) *George Kennan's image of a Tatar family evocatively illustrated the need for inhabitants of the Siberian steppe to be warmly clothed!*

(Opposite top) *A traditional wooden house in modern-day Irkutsk – though these are becoming less common as the city modernises.*

(Opposite bottom) *Crossing the Angara in Winter, an 1886 painting by Nikolay Dobrovolsky.*

A view of the town of Kurgan, east of the Ural Mountains and south of Tiumen and Yekaterinburg, at the end of the 19th century. Note the featureless steppe landscape as far as the eye can see, and the only building of any height, the church – a common theme of Siberia's towns in the early years of their growth.

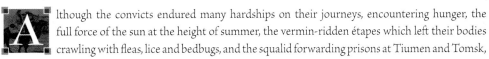

lthough the convicts endured many hardships on their journeys, encountering hunger, the full force of the sun at the height of summer, the vermin-ridden étapes which left their bodies crawling with fleas, lice and bedbugs, and the squalid forwarding prisons at Tiumen and Tomsk, constantly overcrowded and foetid with the smells of disease and excrement, for ordinary travellers the conditions were not much more comfortable.

Arriving in Tiumen, Harry de Windt was looking forward to a decent bed for the night, having slept in his tarantass or in the post houses. He thought it would not be overoptimistic to expect a decent hotel, the town being an important trading post; it had grown wealthy on the export of carpets, leather goods, boots and gloves, and also boasted a dockyard for the construction of steamers to ply the Rivers Ob and Irtysh. He was to be deeply disappointed. "Were I a cruel, vindictive despot, with the power of wreaking vengeance on my deadliest enemy, I would not confine myself to inflicting torture by such old fashioned means as molten lead, the rack or thumbscrew. My victim should undergo mental misery as well, in the shape of a month's residence at the Hotel Sherbakoff, Tiumen, Siberia. If he survived that, I should give it up as a bad job, and forgive him."

De Windt arrived before dawn, and rang the loud and discordant doorbell. He continued to do so at 30-second intervals, standing in the freezing cold, until it was broad daylight, when the door was answered. The host, he found, a stout, bald-headed man, had at one time been a sailor who had picked up a few words of English on a visit to Hull. His invariable reply to any statement by de Windt was "very good, why not?" no matter the topic of conversation.

When de Windt was shown to his room, he had an opportunity to fully appreciate what was supposed to be the best hotel in Tiumen. Great pieces of plaster had fallen from the once whitewashed

(Left) Built in the early 18th century, the Church of the Epiphany has been renovated and is one of modern Irkutsk's main attractions, with its stone Bell Tower (pictured here) showing elements of old Russian wooden architecture.

ceiling, exposing the rafters and showing gaps into the room above. The wallpaper was filthy, peeling and mildewed. The floor had no carpet, but rather was of rotten and insecure wooden boards. The only furniture was a small truckle bedstead covered with a ragged mattress, standing in one corner of the room. Any thought of reclining on it was soon banished on closer inspection. It was infested with an army of white bugs which could inflict an irritating and poisonous bite. The floor was not much more promising. Large grey rats disported themselves both day and night, impervious to any attempt to scare them away, and apparently resentful of the intrusion of de Windt into their domain.

De Windt thought that he might at the very least be able to wash after the journey. He asked the landlord, who replied "very good, why not?" and then went on in Russian "Nice pond in the yard", pointing outdoors to a "shallow puddle of brown and stagnant water, coated with slime and duckweed".

With such accommodation in the towns, it was often a relief for travellers to be back on the road. Beyond Tiumen and Tobolsk, up to and beyond the western Siberian capital of Tomsk, if one did not make the journey by steamer along the River Ob, the more laborious overland route would take one across the Barabinska Steppe. The land was once part of a great inland sea that united the Caspian, Aral and Arctic Seas. From this origin, it derived its present character of a vast, flat and unchanging plain. For hundreds of miles, the flatness of the landscape was only relieved by the occasional copse of willow, alder bushes and small birches. The terrain itself was only varied by sand banks and salt marshes, beds of clay and swampy lakes.

Orlando Figes discusses the contrary Russian cultural responses to this near overwhelming feature of the country's landscape. For some writers like Gogol, it was a symbol of liberty, expansiveness, a freedom to roam. In his short story *Taras Bulba*, about the Zaphorozhian Cossacks, the unbounded steppe evolved into an image of the Cossacks' unrestrained and freedom-loving character. Some, pointing to its infinite horizon, would even see it as a spur to contemplation, transcendence, communion with higher things. This instinct in the Russian character, as the scholar Edgar Knobloch has pointed out, can be traced back to the earliest dwellers of the steppe: their god was the sky, and the tribal leader drew his authority as the sole representative of the sky on Earth.

For other writers, the steppe was oppressive, monotonous and stifling. Its unremitting evenness and lack of feature exercised an almost hypnotic quality. For the gentry, they were isolated and cut off from the stimulation of civic life. For the ordinary peasants in everyday communion with the earth and landscape, the flatness seemed to drain from its inhabitants every last trace of vigour and the will to action. Although Chekhov was drawn by the vast majesty of the steppe, he still conceived of its enormity being almost prison-like; when in other frames of mind, he lambasted it for its sheer tedium. Writing about his journey across Siberia to Sakhalin, he says: "If, while travelling, the countryside possesses any significance at all for you, then going from Russia to Siberia you could have a very boring time from the Urals right up to the Yenisey. The chilly plain, the twisted birch trees, the pools, the occasional islands, snow in May and the barren, bleak banks of the tributaries of the Ob – these are all that the memory succeeds in retaining from the first 2,000 versts."

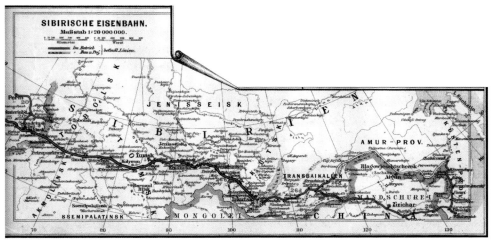

An old German map from 1897 shows the eastern section of the Trans-Siberian Railway from Perm and the Urals all the way to Vladivostok on the Pacific coast.

There were more strident views. Figes quotes Gorky, who could not at all, like Chekhov on occasion, see its positive aspects. The steppe, he writes, had "the poisonous peculiarity of emptying a man, of sucking dry his desires. The peasant has only to go out past the bounds of the village and look at the emptiness around him to feel in a short time that this emptiness is creeping into his very soul. Nowhere around can one see the results of creative labour. The estates of the landowners? But they are few and inhabited by enemies. The towns? But they are far away and not much more cultured. Round about lie endless plains and in the centre of them, insignificant, tiny man abandoned on this dull earth for penal labour. And man is filled with the feeling of indifference killing his ability to think, to remember his past, to work out his ideas from experience."

Many travellers across the steppe would probably have agreed with this assessment of Gorky. John Foster Fraser, crossing it by train, exclaimed, "Wasn't a journey though this great lone land dreary? Of course it was. The eye began to ache with the monotony of the horizon line, and peasants ceased to be picturesque because every group at every station was exactly like the other groups."

One aspect of the journey that he and the other travellers on the Trans-Siberian found strangely haunting at this point was the operation of the signalling system. At every verst along the line was a small wooden hut. Each was inhabited by a good-conduct convict, and sometimes by his family. When the train approached by day, he would come and stand by the track with a green flag to indicate that all was clear; at night, he would do the same with a green lamp, shining it down the track to the next signalman to warn him of the coming of the train. No matter how distant and cut off from civilisation, these little huts extended for hundreds and thousands of miles all the way down the line, across the steppe, and across all Russia and Siberia. Nothing spoke more powerfully of the sheer immensity of the country, and the isolation of life in its midst.

Nevertheless, travel across the steppe was certainly not without its interests, particularly for those who went before the advent of the train, and who were thus able to observe more closely such life as there was along the road.

One thing that forcefully struck many travellers in the region was the absence of human habitation in the landscape. Although parts of the steppe could boast of great and untouched beauty, with rich green grass or endless oceans of wild roses, harebells or tiger lilies, the lack of any trace of human activity unsettled many. There were no detached farmhouses, barns or outhouses outside the villages. Even these were infrequent, sometimes being more than two or three hours' journey by horse apart. Although the landscape was well cultivated, fences and hedges were not used to separate fields. Livestock were not allowed to roam free, but were rather enclosed in pastureland that surrounded the villages.

The villages themselves were rarely prepossessing. The first sight of them to greet the traveller was usually the village gatekeeper. They dwelt on the edge of the settlement, outside the wattled fences that encircled the villages, often in makeshift half-underground huts constructed of branches of trees and mud. One of the first that Kennan saw was "a dirty, forlorn-looking old man with inflamed eyes and a long white beard, who reminded me of Rip Van Winkle after his twenty years' sleep". In general, they rarely deviated from this pattern, of being "wild, neglected picturesque embodiments of poverty and wretchedness clothed in rags".

Once this official had been passed, the road would run through the village common where the livestock were put out to graze, and where, on occasion, a windmill would stand, its sails revolving from the top of a log-gabled house. Beyond this was the main street of the village. This thoroughfare was lined on either side with one-storey log houses, wearing always an air of rickety dilapidation. Their walls were crooked. Their roofs were either of nailed boards, of birch bark, of straw, or even of the heavy black earth of the steppe covered with the sprouting of grasses, weeds and buttercups. Yards containing sheds and granaries stood behind and between them, but these did not function as gardens, and no vegetation, no grass and no plants were cultivated in them.

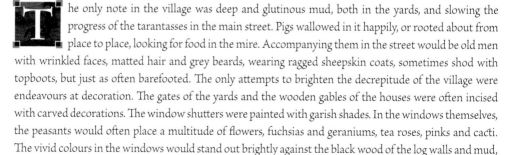

he only note in the village was deep and glutinous mud, both in the yards, and slowing the progress of the tarantasses in the main street. Pigs wallowed in it happily, or rooted about from place to place, looking for food in the mire. Accompanying them in the street would be old men with wrinkled faces, matted hair and grey beards, wearing ragged sheepskin coats, sometimes shod with topboots, but just as often barefooted. The only attempts to brighten the decrepitude of the village were endeavours at decoration. The gates of the yards and the wooden gables of the houses were often incised with carved decorations. The window shutters were painted with garish shades. In the windows themselves, the peasants would often place a multitude of flowers, fuchsias and geraniums, tea roses, pinks and cacti. The vivid colours in the windows would stand out brightly against the black wood of the log walls and mud, but these small gestures did little to save the villages in the estimation of most travellers. As Kennan wrote, "It is with a feeling of intense pleasure and relief that one leaves such a village and rides out upon the wide, clean breezy steppe where the air is filled with the fragrance of clover and the singing of birds."

The further east the travellers penetrated, the more they discerned that there was an essential contrast between European Russia and Asiatic Siberia. As has been said, it did not lie in ethnic differences; even by the late 19th century, the native tribes had been all but effaced by the influx of settling Westerners. Between the Russian heartland and Siberia, there was one Tsar and one Church, albeit with dissenters. From the Baltic Sea to the Arctic permafrost, there was a community of custom and language. In the furthest Russian settlement in the most distant corner of the steppe, one would still bow before the ikon in the corner of the room, or fear to upset the resident house spirit, or *domovoy*, just as one would in Moscow or St Petersburg thousands of miles to the west.

The passenger station at Omsk, on the Irtysh River, which became a major Siberian centre and an important stop on the Trans-Siberian Railway, with both the main line and a secondary branching route from Samara passing through it.

The travellers perceived that the essential difference was in spirit. Compared to European Russia, Siberia was a place of freedom and endeavour. Although it was a land of prisoners and penal colonies, it was also a magnet for the energetic; a place of refuge for contrarians and free thinkers. It drew dissenters, both religious and political, hoping to build new societies. As for convicts, they might for a time be enjoined to forced labour or confinement, but once their sentence was spent, they were at liberty, and encouraged, to make new lives for themselves and seek wealth. It was a land where there had been no serfdom. The old social structures and power of the nobility held less sway. There was a greater premium on deciding one's destiny for oneself, and attempting to bring it about. Entrepreneurship was in the air. As the potential of Siberia's resources began to filter into the Russian imagination, vigorous new colonists motivated by these ideals came with government support, either to farm, or else to try their hand at mining or in industry. Fortunes were won and lost, and peasants rose from obscurity to positions of wealth and even power.

The point was made eloquently by N.V. Basargin, an exile who was sent to Siberia after being involved in the Decembrist plot against the life of the Tsar in 1825. "The common people seemed to me much more free, more clever, even more educated than our Russian peasants and especially more so than the peasants of the landlords. Here they have better understood human dignity, and have valued men's rights more highly. Later I happened to hear from those who visited the US and lived there that Siberians have much in common with Americans in their manners, customs, and even in their way of life." The similarity was not one that was dwelt upon by rebels against the system. Such was the sense of potential and free enterprise that one 19th century Governor-General of East Siberia even suggested the land would evolve into a "United States of Siberia", to become a partner of the USA.

This impression of potential and dynamism impressed itself most forcefully on travellers when they reached towns such as Tomsk and Irkutsk. Tomsk is counted as being at the eastern end of the steppe. It acted as a major stop on the old Post Road, but the Trans-Siberian Railway left it behind, passing 50 miles (80 kilometres) to the south (through Novosibirsk), only approaching it by means of a branch line. The story in general circulation to explain this peculiarity, than which no better reason has been found, holds that the engineers of the line demanded of the city a bribe to ensure the line ran close to it. The magnates of the city refused, and all of a sudden, insurmountable technical difficulties were produced, compelling the line to turn its course far to the south. Even the branch line ended three miles away from the town centre. Yet, the breakneck droshky ride downhill through the mud to the city put travellers in mind to appreciate the energy of this place which, as Fraser remarked, had "a flavour of the Californian gold-digging days."

A panorama of Tomsk in 1885, taken during George Kennan's Siberian sojourn.

The first sight of Tomsk was not particularly promising. "Another unpaved, miry, over-grown village," said Fraser, "but with electric light everywhere." Yet, the recently exploited gold fields left their mark on the city far beyond this innovation. Not only did it boast Siberia's first university, a handsome building with 1,000 students at the faculties for law and medicine, a technical college for scientific study into Siberia, and large public library; for travellers, it offered accommodation which left anything else in western Siberia entirely in the shade.

Fraser stayed at the largest hotel in town, the Europe. When he arrived, it had only been opened a fortnight, and not only did it reek of fresh paint, but the paint on the floor of his room came off on his feet "like the tar on a freshly asphalted sidewalk." The colours were garish, an incessant mixture of blue, red and gold. The great pride of the hotel, installed in the dining room, was an enormous barrel organ, such as were found on the roundabouts at English funfairs, but bigger. "There were the harsh brass and rattling drums, clanging cymbals, and in front was a toy figure of a man with right arm jerking up and down, beating time wrong." All Tomsk, it seemed, was talking about the new organ, and they clustered into the hotel with great revelry to listen while it played the night away, only ceasing at four in the morning.

"Tomsk is a rollicking wealthy city," wrote Fraser, "and its evenings are given to dissipation... To squander money in drunken carousal, and to load his womenkind with pearls and sables, is the ambition of the average Tomsk man." The attitude of many of the gold workers and merchants, said de Windt, was "winter for pleasure, summer for work". In the warmer months, they would live a healthy and frugal life in the gold fields, sleeping under canvas or the stars, rising with the sun, eating healthily and working hard. As autumn came to a close, they returned to the town, laden with money, and ready to revel with equal vigour.

Amusement was to be had in theatricals and masquerades, horseracing, tobogganing and sleighing expeditions. Picnics would be held on the riverboats on the Tom and Ob, millionaires and peasants together, drinking

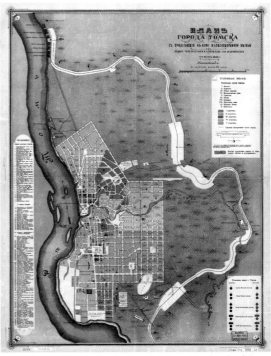

An 1898 map of Tomsk, showing its orderly layout by the side of the Tom River.

kvas, claret and champagne, as musicians played their serenades. Parties and dances were endless in number, and formed an opportunity for the conspicuous display of new-gotten money, and uneasy attempts at social self-promotion. Harry de Windt was invited to a ball by the wife of one of the self-made magnates, and watched in fascination as their grand townhouse was filled by men in the most tatterdemalion, motley attempts at evening dress that he had ever seen. Black tailcoats were worn with blue neckties, canvas trousers, jackboots and grey flannel shirts. Others in tweeds and hobnail boots soiled from the fields danced on the polished parquet floor with women in muslin skirts of loud colours, wrinkled cotton gloves, and hair done in fashions 20 years behind St Petersburg.

Wright and Digby, travelling a few years after Fraser, and staying at a rival hotel, the Russia, found people better dressed, but equally raucous. Arriving just after midnight on a Sunday, they went through the triple swing doors of the hotel to find a uniformed brass band playing, accompanied by bursts of laughter and the popping of champagne corks. "Around us floated ravishing creatures in high spirits and ultra-abbreviated crimson silk skirts," wrote Digby. "Sloe-eyed maidens, attired as for the ballet, flitted by to join peroxide blondes in tight pale blue knickerbockers; and bewigged fairies in fleshings dived hither and thither in the throng. Every now and again came a crash of broken glass or a prodigious stamping of feet from the long restaurant, the stage at the end of which was given up to vaudeville."

Going out into the street, Fraser saw a procession of the characters who had accumulated and were spending the wealth. A dirty old man writhing in the mud of the street was pointed out to him. "The richest man in Tomsk, a rouble millionaire four times over," he was told. Two ladies, fashionably dressed, sped past in a horse-drawn carriage. "One is the daughter of a convict, and the other is engaged to be married to a convict's son." Another man rode by in their wake: "That man is a prince; he belongs to an older family than the reigning house of Romanoff." The head of a gang of swindlers, he had conned an Englishman out of 30,000 roubles, and was sent into exile. "He's a solicitor here," explained Fraser's companion.

As with anywhere that conspicuous wealth had suddenly emerged, conspicuous poverty was also apparent. This was no more so than at the great market on the banks of the Tom River, visited by Wright and Digby. They wandered through the ranks of permanent wooden booths spread out along the riverfront. Between the stalls where frozen butter and fish were sold, broken into the required measure by the blow of a hatchet, dozens of men and women presided over pathetic bales of merchandise. These might consist merely of "a few old lamp burners, a battered picture frame or two, a single boot that has seen better days, and a scrap of frayed oilcloth". Even less fortunate than these were the beggars. Some stood at the corners, deformed and covered in vermin, ready to give a blessing in return for a few kopecks. Others went around the eating stalls of the market, begging and receiving lumps of good fresh bread, and stowing them away in the folds of their garments. Blue-cheeked children, young girls without coats, their very skirts in rags and covered in snow, barely able to open the door of the shop, followed the adults to the counter, making the sign of the cross and eagerly hugging the slices of bread to them as they shuffled away into the cold.

Wandering musicians at least gave some needed jollity to the scene. At one cookhouse, stationed

in a barn, sheepskin-clad peasants, eating fish and drinking vodka, clustered round to listen to a band consisting of a singer with bandaged stumps in place of hands, a boy and a girl playing two harps, a young man with a hurdy-gurdy strapped round his neck, and three Jews playing an accordion. Everyone appeared very dirty, said Basset and Digby, but very happy.

In the end, Tomsk left a sour taste in the mouth of many travellers. Fraser, the son of an Edinburgh clergyman, allowed his Presbyterian scruples to take the lead in his judgement: "...in Tomsk, pleasure is the one pursuit. Not to be immoral is to be suspected of revolutionary ideas. Laxity of conduct is the best sign of good fellowship... On the whole, I was not favourably impressed with the capital of Siberia. It is a caravanserai for orgies."

A modern-day statue along the river in Tomsk satirises Anton Chekhov, who visited the city in 1890 and was less than complimentary about it.

Another visitor, Chekhov, who visited in 1890, was even more slighting. "I shall not describe Tomsk. In Russia all cities are alike. Tomsk is a boring town, not sober, no beautiful women at all, Asiatic lawlessness. The city is remarkable by reason of the fact that Provincial Governors die in it."

B eyond Tomsk, the landscape began to change. The flatness of the plains began to be broken by the upturn of hills, and woods grew more dense as the travellers approached the taiga, or deep Siberian forest. Scarcely any settlement of note, save villages, broke the way of the journey. The Post Road became dire, as under the profounder canopy of trees it failed to dry after the rains and became almost a waterway of mud, the wheels of tarantasses crunching over hidden stones, logs and concealed ruts. Chekhov, whose spirits had not been raised by the initial part of the journey over the steppe, or what he perceived as the tedium of Tomsk, was almost broken by this section of the voyage. They got held up by a convoy of tea wagons, their drivers knee deep in the mud. A sledge carrying his travelling companions – two army officers and a military doctor – overturned, throwing not only the travellers but their trunks, bundles, sabres, and even a case containing a violin into the deep mud. Juddering over the uneven ground, a vital bolt in his own tarantass broke, leaving the front to drag along against the mud. Huddling around a paraffin lamp in the next post house, the other travellers told horror stories of how the road was even worse farther on. A member of the Imperial Russian Geographical Society smashed up his coach twice between stations, and was

A road bridge crosses one of Siberia's innumerable rivers, here with thick forest crowding both banks.

forced to spend the night in the forest. A lady had cracked her head open from the jolting of her carriage. An exciseman who had been stuck in the mud for 16 hours had to bribe the local peasants 25 roubles just to drag him out and convey him somewhere warm.

Chekhov was only cheered when he came to Krasnoyarsk, and beneath it the great Yenisey (Yenisei) River. His paean to it is near ecstatic: "Let it be said to the jealous admirers of the Volga that I have never seen a more magnificent river than the Yenisey. A beautifully dressed, modest, melancholy beauty the Volga may be, but, at the other extreme, the Yenisey is a mighty, raging Hercules, who does not know what to do with his power and youth. On the Volga a man starts out with spirit, but finishes up with a groan which is called a song; his radiant golden hopes are replaced by an infirmity which it is the done thing to term 'Russian pessimism,' whereas on the Yenisey life commences with a groan and finishes with the kind of high spirits we cannot even dream about."

F or Chekhov, Krasnoyarsk was the "best and most beautiful of all Siberian towns". Annette Meakin, who spent several days there, was in agreement. She was similarly taken with its situation by the river, sitting in a hollow surrounded by hills of red sandstone, from which it took its name (*krasni* meaning red, and *iar* cliff). It lacked the raucousness of Tomsk, possessing instead a quiet and dignified prosperity. Meakin visited the opera, a museum of shamanist costumes, and a shop kept by Chinese traders selling imported tea in beautifully decorated boxes, silks, embroideries and china. As she strolled round the gardens beside the river, such was the unexpected serenity of the place, she fancied that she might be in a town on the River Rhine rather than travelling in the depths of Siberia.

Beyond Krasnoyarsk, the taiga proper began. It was only from this point that Chekhov was able to take any pleasure in the scenery. Beyond the Yenisey, he wrote, the land became "distinctive, majestic and beautiful". The stimulation of the changing views and undulating landscape was a refreshing treat after the heaviness of the steppe. Travelling in May through the unending forest of pine and larch, spruce and birch, birds poured out of the trees, insects hummed, the glades were covered with sheets of blue, pink and yellow flowers, and the pine needles in the warmth of the sun gave off their distinctive odour. Unlike the steppe, Chekhov was able to revel in the sheer scale of the taiga, without feeling it oppressive, stultifying or tedious. "The power and enchantment of the taiga lie not in titanic trees or the silence of the graveyard, but in the fact that only birds of passage know where it ends," he enthused. "Over the first 24 hours you pay no attention to it; on the second and third you are full of wonderment, and by the fourth and fifth you are experiencing the sensation that you will never manage to emerge from this green monster."

Its size and its capacity for mystery and surprises appealed strongly to Chekhov's imagination: "... how many secrets the taiga conceals within itself! Over there a road or pathway skulks off and disappears into the gloaming of the forests. Where does it lead? To a secret distillery, or to a village about whose existence neither the District Police Chief nor the magistrate has yet heard, or, perhaps, to gold workings discovered by a trade association of vagabonds? And what devil-may-care seductive freedom wafts from this enigmatic pathway!"

Other travellers, whilst appreciating the ominous power of the taiga, reacted not with Chekhov's light-hearted elation, but with fear. Charles Wenyon, who travelled through the taiga by sledge in the depths of winter, had a sense, like Chekhov, that the forest brooded with some great secret. But for Wenyon, on this account, the fir trees made "morose companions". He could not help recalling the beliefs of one of the native Siberian tribes, the Orotchis, who held that a certain menacing spirit haunted the depths of the forest. Passing through, especially at night, he almost felt the need to follow the Orotchis' custom, and attempt to propitiate the spirit's favour. The snow of winter had put an end to the noises and wildlife that had so charmed Chekhov. "The very air seemed to palpitate with supernatural life; and, with no chirp of bird or hum of insect to disturb the silence, one could almost hear the music of the spheres; the tread of spirits on the vault of heaven; the heart-throb of the universe; and it was a positive relief when a crash among the shadows recalled one's thoughts to material concerns, as some bear plunged through the saplings, or some decayed giant of the forest fell."

Seemingly impenetrable taiga forest offers a mesmerising palette of shades and tones for window gazers on the long journey across eastern Siberia.

Chekhov, transported by the scenery, was blithe about the danger of being attacked by the many bears in the forest. Wenyon, however, was more circumspect. He feared to camp out at night, and was hesitant even about allowing the sledge to come to a halt. The only suitable defence against bears, if one was not armed, was to set one's encampment within a ring of fire or hot charcoal. Yet Wenyon knew that even this precaution was of little avail against them: "...a hungry bear is cunning enough to know that, having first got dripping wet in a brook, he has only to roll over on the burning brands and extinguish them".

Wenyon's greatest fear, however, was of wolves. He had been filled with horror stories of their depredations. He heard that they caused havoc among the livestock of smallholders, but their great preference "with a sort of cannibal propensity" was the flesh of a dog, and they would often be able to pluck them away from their masters whilst towing a sleigh, or sheltered in a tarantass. Nor would they hesitate in winter, driven crazy by hunger, to attack humans. He trembled to think of a story he had been told of a Siberian priest in the forest, shortly before his own journey, who had been killed and eaten by a pack of wolves. His horse brought a cart without a driver into a village, and when a search was made, the bones of a man were found, licked clean.

Wenyon was careful to remember the means whereby the wolves could be kept under control. A mounted Cossack on a good horse would not hesitate to ride into the midst of a pack, and by thrashing them with an executioner's knout, drive the pack howling with fear into the woods. However, ordinary travellers, should their tarantass be pursued by a pack, must take a cord, tie to it an old rag or piece of clothing, and allow it to trail behind the vehicle. The wolves would shy at the mysterious object, in the same fashion as a timid horse, and not dare to overtake it.

However, for all his fears, Wenyon had a somewhat shamefaced confession to make: "At night the cold compelled me to keep well under my rugs and blankets, but sometimes I ventured to look out; and if those black things which I saw beside the road were not what they looked like – wolves, but only what the driver said they were – burnt stumps of trees, I cannot say that I ever saw a wolf in Siberia."

I n Irkutsk, "In the spring, a young man's fancy fondly turns to thoughts of blood." Thus wrote Wright and Digby after their fortnight in the capital of East Siberia in 1910. As a city of commerce and wealth, consumption and crime, inequality and excess, Irkutsk was like Tomsk, but writ large. Not only to Wright and Digby, but also to others such as Fraser, it was a place where dwelt the old-fashioned spirit of the American gold rush. "What San Francisco was in '49 when it flourished as

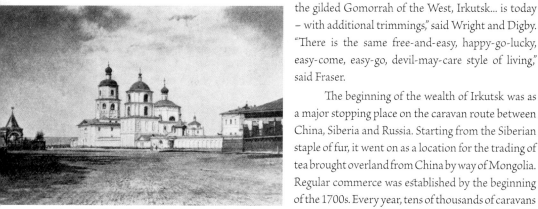

the gilded Gomorrah of the West, Irkutsk... is today – with additional trimmings," said Wright and Digby. "There is the same free-and-easy, happy-go-lucky, easy-come, easy-go, devil-may-care style of living," said Fraser.

The beginning of the wealth of Irkutsk was as a major stopping place on the caravan route between China, Siberia and Russia. Starting from the Siberian staple of fur, it went on as a location for the trading of tea brought overland from China by way of Mongolia. Regular commerce was established by the beginning of the 1700s. Every year, tens of thousands of caravans of brick tea – compressed blocks of the leaves held together with gum and occasionally bullocks' blood

Irkutsk's Epiphany Cathedral at the turn of the 20th century – today the city crowds in on all sides.

– would be imported by way of Irkutsk. Even after the advent of shipping, Irkutsk retained its place as a tea-trading outpost; many Russians refused to drink tea that had not been brought overland, saying that tea imported by sea lost its flavour.

After this, with the development of the nearby gold fields, it was decreed that all the gold mined in eastern Siberia had to be brought to Irkutsk to be processed at the government laboratories. Towards the end of the 19th century, the weight of gold annually exported to European Russia by this route was on average around 40,000lbs (18,000kg). Just as much was fenced from the miners by Chinese traders and smuggled duty-free out of the country. Their most notorious method was to fill the coffins, and sometimes even the embalmed corpses of their countrymen with gold dust, before sending them back to their family plots in China for burial.

Two paupers pose for a photographer in the 1870s – hopefully they were paid or fed for their time (albumen print by Iosif Kordysh).

Irkutsk was a haven for past as well as present criminals. Many of the convicts of eastern Siberia, having served their sentences, resorted there to see where life might take them. Many of the high-class political prisoners were able to prosper as lawyers, doctors and clerks. As for the more serious offenders, the hard-labour and penal convicts, some were able to find work in menial occupations; others tried their hand at mining and business, making fortunes in the process; and others retained their interest in crime, turning to swindling and extortion, theft,

A view of the market in Irkutsk, at the time a rough and tumble place reminiscent of America's Wild West.

robbery and murder. A great part of the city's population was made up of such convicts, or else their families and descendants.

The mix of such people and such wealth made Irkutsk a hair-raising place. From its earliest days it possessed a reputation. In 1787, it was visited by an American traveller, John Ledyard, the first man known to have attempted to walk from Europe to the northwest coast of America via Siberia and Kamchatka. Calling on the governor, a perpetually inebriated Frenchman who had been there for over 30 years, he asked if the local area had any specimens of note in natural history. The governor replied that indeed it did: "thieves, liars, rascals, whores, rogues, and villains of every description".

By the late 19th century, the city boasted the same temptations to dissipation as were to be found in Tomsk. "The fun in Irkutsk starts at midnight," said Wright and Digby. The theatres and motion picture houses – of which there were many in Irkutsk by this time – shut their doors, and the fur-clad crowds clustered in their masses to the restaurants. Throwing off their overcoats and their felt snow boots, they would crowd into the dining rooms, full of officers in full-dress uniform, women in the latest Parisian fashions, mining engineers, fur traders, and self-made peasant or convict millionaires who clung to their unkempt beards and voluminous red kaftans. A stage was set before the diners, and "a score of young maidens in a minimum of skirt and a maximum of smile" would go through "fatuous double-shuffles and fancy dances" before leaping down to mingle with the rich below, ordering for them "the costliest fruits and the rarest wines that the management can provide", entertaining them until dawn with "gay music" and crude but spirited vaudeville.

Yet outdoors, danger lurked round every corner. "Residence in Irkutsk is not altogether a rest cure for the nerves," warned Wright and Digby. The population at the turn of the century was just over 100,000, but the annual murder rate ran into the hundreds. Life was held cheap; quarrels escalated into killings, and thieves did not scruple to murder for the sake of even a few roubles. All were at risk, from the wealthiest magnate to the lowest pauper. The favourite method was a variation on the garrotte. The thief would steal up on his victim, and throw over his head a loop of cord attached to a stick. After a sharp and sudden tug, the victim would fall down dead, his neck broken as if he had been hung.

George Kennan's view of Irkutsk's main road in 1885 – a very different prospect to the city you will find today.

The patchy lighting in the streets of Irkutsk at night did little to help the situation, leaving pools of darkness for the thieves to practise their work. The discovery of corpses in the streets at morning was seldom an occasion for comment. The police force was of little effect, rarely competent and frequently corrupt. Their usual method of deterring the thieves at night was to hide in the dark by-ways with football rattles, making as much noise as possible to let the criminals know that the streets were being watched. Householders, however, had a more direct approach to deterrence. At nightfall, they would open their windows and loose off a volley of gunshots into the street so that anyone with nefarious intentions could see that there were guns on the premises which would willingly be used. Otherwise, ferocious mastiffs patrolled the streets, and one guidebook of the time warned travellers never to dawdle in the streets after dark, lest they provoke attack.

For many travellers, the distant sight of Irkutsk belied the city's reputation. For Dr The Rev. Francis E. Clark, a devout American clergyman travelling with his wife and young son in January 1900 as a missionary representative of the Young People's Society of Christian Endeavour, Irkutsk appeared from the railway as a city of churches. 20 years earlier, approaching it from the Post Road, George Kennan recalls it with a bucolic tinge. Seeing it against a backdrop of autumn, the way there was fringed with the intense red leaves of the poplar, and birches with their foliage of brilliant canary yellow. The fields were thick with ripe corn, and hundreds of men and women in horsehair mosquito nets toiled with sickles to reap the grain and bind it together in sheaves. Closer to the outskirts of Irkutsk was the great white-walled monastery of Voznesensk, around which thronged a picturesque if none too salubrious horde of ragged long-haired pilgrims muddied by their journey, unarmed soldiers, peasants, peddlers, tramps and nondescript vagabonds, wandering the road towards the heart of the city.

However, Francis Clark spoke for many travellers in saying that "distance lends considerable enchantment to Irkutsk, and nearer approach does not bear out the remoter promise...". From its foundation in 1652 until the late 19th century, despite its burgeoning wealth, the city was nothing more than a sprawling collection of low wooden shacks; a cluster of hovels and warehouses, relieved by only the occasional stone house, church or broad square.

The later appearance of Irkutsk was dictated by the great fire of July 1879, in which three-quarters of the old city was destroyed. Henry Lansdell, who had just arrived there by tarantass, had the fortune to be an eyewitness to the catastrophe. Lansdell had an eye for the human tableaux and tragedies in the midst of the disaster an old woman tottering under a pile of furs on her head; a half-blind nun hugging an ikon; a delicate young lady in tears clutching a kitten; a group of boys dragging a samovar through the streets. Although he remembered with near amusement the sight of drunk beggars helping themselves to looted furniture, paintings and chandeliers from warehouses, or working men, drunk on stolen rye brandy, jumping into burning shops to taste for the first time chunks of tinned West Indian pineapple or imported peaches and apricots, it was the fall of the buildings to the flames which seemed to strike him most.

As the fire engines, made in Britain by Merryweather and Sons, stood useless, the Irkutsk Fire Brigade not knowing how to use them, and as the clergy formed processions in the streets to pray for deliverance, Lansdell watched the fire progress, mesmerised. Church bells rang in the towers to call for help, but before long the flames began to play up the wooden steeples. The bells would fall quiet, and the fire, first bursting

An Irkutsk panorama – part of the Siberian Postcards collection held by the National Library of Russia.

through the highest windows, would work its way back downwards from the top, dancing playfully first out of the middle and then the lowest windows in the towers. The flames could jump across wide streets, such was their intensity, setting alight first the shutters of the wooden houses. Otherwise they would feed on the piles of firewood stacked outside each dwelling, gathering strength as they advanced.

Having seen the scale of destruction – 3,600 buildings destroyed and over 20,000 people left homeless – Lansdell doubted at first that the city would be rebuilt. The day afterwards genteel families camped in the mud, sheltering under tables or chests of drawers. Ikons lay strewn about in the wreckage, along with personal belongings, and, noted Landsell, desks and scientific instruments from the laboratory of the High School. Yet, the mood of the survivors was far from despondent. The atmosphere was rather that of a party. People stood alongside the carts of goods they had saved, dispensing tea from samovars, enjoying themselves, laughing, and savouring the absurdity of the situation. Not the least amongst them was the deputy governor of the city, who had lost everything in the blaze, and stood directing the relief efforts wearing a threadbare borrowed shirt.

A museum in Irkutsk in the early 1900s. Religious and official buildings were grand affairs that stood out among the otherwise wooden architecture of Siberia's towns.

The indomitability of their spirit was evinced by the speed at which the city was rebuilt. Much of the city's sense of its early past was lost with the disappearance of its universal medium of wooden architecture, such as was preserved at Tomsk. However, it did not lose its sense of being a pioneer town, a place of raucous new wealth. The opportunity for general and sensible improvement, however, was spurned. Shops as opulent as those on Regent Street were opened to absorb the surpluses of the wealthy. Money was lavished by the entrepreneurial millionaires on new houses of grand ostentation. A number of these, said John Foster Fraser, in outward appearance rivalled those in Park Lane. Harry de Windt, shown round one of them by its proprietor, caught sight of a large gold nugget being used as an ashtray. This lost him $1,500 in annual income, boasted the proud magnate. Many of these tycoons, who not many years previously had been prisoners or peasants, compiled heaps of luxuries that they feared to approach. In the house of another self-made millionaire, de Windt was shown a magnificent bed with an ebony frame, rich hangings and backed with a Gobelin tapestry. "This is my bed," de Windt was told, "but I sleep under it, you know. It is too good to use."

Aside from this self-denying form of conspicuous consumption, the millionaires bestowed funds on new churches, schools, museums, learned societies, philanthropic missions, even a theatre with two permanent dramatic companies to perform in it. Yet, these same benefactors thought it absurd to spend a kopek on the cleanliness or the maintenance of the streets. Instead of stone pavements, there were walkways of wooden duckboards, many of which were rotten or missing, running over or besides open sewers flowing in the streets. They were little more than mantraps for the unwary passenger, wrote Clark. The roads remained of mud, and in the summer suffocating clouds of dust were whipped up by the horses, animals and even bicycles that traversed the fashionable boulevards. Clustering around and between the grand houses, little shanties of cheap brick lean-to shacks grew up in the spaces left by the fire. It was for this reason that despite its wealth, Fraser could think of Irkutsk as nothing different to a "mushroom city" in Western America, and Clark was not sorry to leave behind the city's few tourist attractions, obscured as they were by the stifling dust of the streets.

THE SACRED BAIKAL

ot far beyond the city of Irkutsk, following the torrent of the Angara River upstream to the southeast, you come to its source – the great lake of Siberia, Baikal. Few travellers who encountered it came away with anything less than a sense of respect and dread, even extending to a profound and spiritual awe. Native Siberian tribesmen venerated it as holy. For the local Buriat tribesmen, each crag and outcrop had a particular religious significance. The common people would swear oaths by the Lake. For Siberian shamans, and even the lamas who travelled there from Mongolia to the south, the near submerged granite cliff dividing the Angara from Baikal, named Shamanka, was the dwelling place of the invincible White God. They would travel from miles around to make sacrifices, even human sacrifices, at this spot. Such veneration, though of less extreme a form, was inherited later by the Russian colonists. One of the most famous Siberian folk songs, describing the emotions of an escaped convict from the East first setting sight on its waters, begins by praising it as "The sacred Baikal, the glorious Sea". Indeed, it was held to be bad luck ever to describe Baikal as a "lake". If one failed to refer to it as a Sea, the insulted waters would stir up terrible winds and storms to overwhelm the impious offender. More benignly, the waters of its nearby springs were held to possess miraculous powers of healing, and travellers even into the 20th century heard tales of the dead raised by their agency, or at the very least severed limbs being regrown thanks to their curative powers.

For those more scientifically minded, to whom such notions were little more than superstitious nonsense, a bare recitation of Baikal's statistics would nonetheless serve to stir up similar feelings of respect. It is the largest freshwater lake in Europe or Asia, with a surface area of 11,780 square miles (30,510 square kilometres), which makes it slightly smaller than Lake Superior in the US or Africa's

A steamer leaves the Irkutsk river dock, heading upstream to the Angara River's outflow from Lake Baikal.

Lake Victoria. It is just over 395 miles (636 kilometres) long, and varies from 15.5 to 50 miles (25–80 kilometres) in width, the average being about 35 miles (56 kilometres). It is fed by 336 rivers, but is only drained by one, the Angara.

Baikal's surface is 1,496 feet (456 metres) above sea level, yet it is the deepest lake in the world, its maximum confirmed depth being 5,314 feet (1,620 metres), well over a mile. Two-thirds of the lake is over 1,600 feet (488 metres) in depth, and a quarter over 3,280 feet (1,000 metres) deep – on average, the depth is 2,395 feet (730 metres), far exceeding that of any of the Great Lakes in America. (For the sake of comparison, the maximum depth of Lake Superior is only 1,333 feet or 406 metres). Hence, Baikal is also the largest reservoir of surface fresh water on Earth. Its volume is 5,700 cubic miles (23,600km^3), around 18 percent of the world's total, or as much as all five of the American Great Lakes put together. The exceptional depth of the water, which means that its sediments, even when disturbed, do not come near to the surface, and its low content of salts and minerals, lend the water an unrivalled transparency and blueness. In the deeper parts of the lake, one might see objects in the water at a depth of up to 130 feet (40 metres).

Baikal claims to be the oldest large lake in the world – it is thought to have existed in its present form for at least 23 million years. It was never part of any sea, and as a result of its detachment has developed a unique ecosystem of its own, with distinct varieties of flora and fauna, many of which find no parallel anywhere else in the world. It boasts 500 distinct forms of plant and 1,200 animals, of which two-thirds are found nowhere else. These range from unique forms of worms and shrimp-like creatures, to insects, and the salmon-like *omul* fish, a popular food throughout much of Siberia. The omul is unique among fish, as it cries out when hauled from the water.

The most peculiar of its species is the *golomianka*, a strange fish that lives in the cold waters at a depth of over 700 feet (213 metres). It is composed mainly of an oily transparent fat, much of which is concentrated in its translucent head, which occupies a third of its body, usually up to eight inches (20 centimetres) long. It gives birth to live young in early autumn, around 2,000 at a time, at which point many of the parents die and float to the surface in great masses. Washed to the shore, their bodies evaporate in the hot sun within hours, leaving nothing behind but the skeleton of the head and backbone. The local tribesmen, on seeing them appear, would rush to harvest the oil for use in their lamps, or else for incorporation in traditional remedies. Baikal is remarkable for one species that is common elsewhere: the Arctic Seal. A population of around 20,000 seals live on the lake, the only fresh water population of seals in the world, more than 2,000 miles (3,220 kilometres) south of their native habitat. It is conjectured that they could only have reached Baikal by a slow process of migration, making their way down from the Arctic for thousands of miles up the Yenisey, and then along the Angara into the Lake.

Despite its relatively slender width at the normal crossing place, 20 miles (32 kilometres) between the landing stages of Listvyanka (Listvinichnaya) on the western side and Boyarskaya on the east, Baikal was always a formidable and dangerous obstacle for the traveller. In the age of the Post Road, the Lake would be crossed during summer by barge or by steamship, and in winter by sledge. Each mode of transport presented its own peculiar perils. The size and climatic peculiarities of Baikal meant that navigation of the lake, especially under sail, was fraught with hazard: impenetrable fogs rose up and lingered for days; immense winds would appear out of a blue sky, and whip the lake up into a frenzy. One of these, the *Sarma*, would burst unpredictably through the gorge of the river of the same name feeding the Baikal, assaulting it with hurricane force winds of over 100 miles per hour. The Sarma has been known to tear up animals and houses and throw them into the water, or, by whipping up fine sprays of water which turned to ice in the wind, engulf fishing vessels, overwhelm them in the freezing haze, and sink them. Another wind, the *Gornyi*, although not as intense as the Sarma, can persist over the whole lake for days. In the days before steam it was said that this wind could keep a vessel on the lake and prevent it from reaching either shore for weeks. It is not for nothing that a Russian saying was repeated by nearly every traveller who made the lake crossing in this way: "It is only on the Baikal that a man learns to pray from his heart."

The temperature of Baikal is always slow to change. Hence, it freezes very late on in the year, usually only in December, and traditionally from this time onwards travellers would resort to a crossing by sledge. This would be pulled by horses with specially sharpened shoes to grip to the ice, with one of the animals attached to the back of the sledge to provide an instant reverse gear should cracks appear ahead of the vehicle. Every year, a contract was given to a private operator, who was required to mark out a road with the trunks of pine trees, keep it clear of obstructions, and lay boards on top of it should cracks appear in the ice. Until around the mid-1870s a rest station was also maintained at the halfway point of the journey, where travellers could stop at a small wooden hut for tea and refreshment. However, this institution was abandoned after the ice broke one winter, and swallowed the station and its proprietor whole.

In this lay the great danger of a winter crossing. The ice ranged in depth from three to six feet (1–2 metres). However, variations of air pressure and currents in the water beneath could lead to giant rents in the ice opening up unpredictably and so quickly that there were no means of escape. With a sound like thunder, fissures could tear across the lake, opening up to a distance of 20 miles, and a width of over six feet. However, this terrible danger did little to deter the travellers. In the summer, there might only be one steamboat crossing a week. In the winter, the amount of traffic increased substantially, the uninterrupted sledge journey being far more suited to the transport of merchandise such as tea than the crossing by boat.

The problems of crossing Baikal were heightened substantially with the advent of the railway. The construction of the railway around the southern loop of the Lake to link Irkutsk to the Transbaikal section of the line was at first postponed. The mountainous and unfriendly nature of the terrain would make the work of building extremely slow, requiring a ledge to be blasted into the precipitous rock for a distance of around 200 miles (320 kilometres). Such was the projected cost, over $60,000 per mile compared to the average of around $30,000 per mile for the rest of the railway, a different solution was found for the first few years of the railway's operation. This was the commissioning, from the British shipping firm of Armstrong, of two great ice-breaking ferries, the *Baikal* and the *Angara*. These were manufactured in England, the first in 1895 and the second in 1898, taken to pieces, and transported across Siberia to the banks of the Lake, where they were painstakingly reassembled under British supervision.

Of the two vessels, the *Baikal* was the grander. "A huge four-funnelled vessel," wrote John Foster Fraser, who glimpsed it on his crossing of the lake, "by no means pretty, and rather like a barn that had

An icebreaker on Lake Baikal, which in winter could freeze to a depth of six feet (two metres).

slipped afloat." At 4,000 tons, 290 feet long and with a beam of 57 feet, it drew 20 feet of water and was designed to hold up to 28 railway carriages, which would be rolled on at the terminus of Listvyanka, and restored to the rails at Mysovsk on the other side, 40 miles (64 kilometres) distant. Special jetties were built in each of these villages, designed to grip the vessels fast, so that the trains could roll onto the three parallel sets of rails in the hold. Upstairs, the passengers were accommodated in grand luxury, with lounges, buffets, cabins for 150 first- and second-class passengers, a chapel, and deck space for 650 third-class passengers. The *Baikal's* sister ship, the *Angara*, was similar but smaller, at only 200 feet in length and 35 feet across the beam. Unlike the *Baikal*, she was designed to carry only passengers, not trains, and act as a backup should the *Baikal* encounter difficulties.

The ships worked tolerably well in the summer. Fraser, who travelled on the *Angara* in September 1900, found the crossing comfortable, "like a holiday cruise". An old hobbling waiter, seeing that Fraser was foreign and therefore likely to have the wealth to give him a good tip, secured him a superior cabin and ministered to him assiduously, bringing him plates of cutlets and peas, and ample supplies of bottled beer. On deck, the higher-class passengers strode about taking photographs of each other and the scenery, unfolding maps and scoping the view with their binoculars. Only the third-class passengers huddled below with their bundles, some of them fearful, never having before seen such a vast expanse of water. Such worries for their safety were unfounded. Although a wind blew from the northwest over the mountains, filling the rigging of the ship with "Valkyrie cries", and boiling up from the waters a smoking mist, the red and green harbour lights of Mysovsk were soon in sight, and all safely disembarked on the eastern shore.

It was a very different matter in winter. For her work as an icebreaker, the hull of the _Baikal_ was armour plated with an inch-thick casing of steel, re-enforced with a two-foot layer of heavy wood beneath. At the rear, she had two grand engines, and a third at the bow attached to a screw, with which to make inroads in the ice. Moreover, her bow was built with a sweeping curve, so that should the screw make no inroads, she could be backed up to charge against the ice, climb on top of it, and so smash down through it to create a way. A crossing in this fashion could take over a week to accomplish, and often could never be finished. On account of a miscalculation over the depth of the winter ice, the _Baikal_ was only designed to break through a covering of three feet (one metre), whereas often she encountered six feet of ice. The _Angara_ was quite unable to make her own way, and became dependent on the _Baikal_ to clear a path for her. Even when she did so, often her engines failed, and passengers had to disembark onto the ice and be driven to land in the old-fashioned way by hundreds of sledges commandeered to her side.

By February 1904, when Russia had to move troops quickly in considerable numbers to combat Japanese attacks in the Far East, the situation became intolerable. To prevent Baikal from becoming a bottleneck, the expedient used to transport trains across the frozen rivers farther west before the building of bridges was tried. Workers, labouring in temperatures of up to minus 60 degrees Celsius, laid tracks across the ice, in the hope that the trains would safely be able to cross the 40-mile expanse under their own steam. The first of these, having traversed 28 miles, hit a weak spot caused by a previously unknown warm underwater spring, and plunged through the ice to the bottom of the lake. A four-foot crack burst open for over 12 miles, and huge lengths of the line were destroyed or warped beyond repair.

B y a great effort of determination, at length the extraordinary scheme was made to work: the line was re-laid with 30-foot (nine-metre) sleepers to distribute the weight on the ice; the troops were disembarked and led across by sledge; the locomotives were drawn by an army of 600 men and 1,000 horses; lookout stations on the ice, connected by telegraph line, watched for new fissures, and sheltered troops as they made their way across. However, these difficulties finally decided the authorities in St Petersburg, and abandoning their reliance on the ice-breaking vessels, they pressed ahead with construction of the expensive and difficult line along the south side of the lake. A few years later, as the new line became operational, the customary difficulties associated with the Lake evaporated, and travellers, who before were accustomed to devote pages to the crossing of the water, now scarcely gave the traverse of its edge a few paragraphs, serene encomiums of its grandeur.

The journey towards and beyond Lake Baikal often left as much of an impression, in some cases more favourable, than the sight of the lake itself. Lionel Gowing, who crossed in winter 1887, admired the great caves of ice, adorned with great stalactites, which formed around the Lake's edge with the onset of the cold. He also wondered at the strange atmospheric phenomena that the expanse of ice engendered. For example, as the sun sank in the evening sky, two immense concentric circles of light, two grand mock suns, burst onto the horizon, which hung suspended, alternately growing in brilliancy and then falling dim.

Charles Wenyon, who travelled in the spring five years later, had equal eyes for its beauty. He admired the crystal-clear waters, blue as sapphire at a short distance from its margin, and the small crags of ice floating by left over from the winter freeze, which broke up the sunbeams as a prism, skirting themselves with colours as a rainbow. Perhaps more prosaically, he also cast a longing eye over the many fish rising in the evenings after grey flies on the surface of the water: "...very provoking, when with so much leisure there was no angling apparatus within reach".

However, both travellers were as haunted by the lake as transported by its beauty. Gowing spoke of the ghostly moaning of the waves of the lake, howling as they passed by underneath the ice. Wenyon complained of its loneliness, and the sense of overwhelming solitude on its banks. He bore in mind also how the area was liable to constant seismic activity: "...rumblings and quaking and even rendings of the earth... the constant apprehension of these portents makes the stillness weird and painful". It was no wonder, he went on, that the early Russian settlers, "looking out upon the surface of the lake from the gloom of the forest which overspreads its bordering mountains, were so impressed with the mystic silence of that vast solitude that they named it 'the Holy Sea.'"

Lansdell, by contrast, journeying towards the lake from Irkutsk, was not at all upset by such brooding presentiments. Following the Angara along its sweeping wooded valley, he stopped frequently to admire the majesty of the views: enormous sandstone cliffs rising out of the water, topped with dark pines, or great forests along steep ravines reaching down to the edge of the bank. More often, he paused entranced by the sheer power of the river. Falling through a depth of 400 feet (122 metres) over the 40 miles (64 kilometres) between the Lake and Irkutsk, and a mile across at its mouth, the water rushed through the rapids with a fierce impetuosity, throwing up enormous jets of spray. So fast was the flow of water that even in the depths of winter, with the temperature at minus 24 degrees Fahrenheit and six feet of ice on the Lake, the water at the mouth of the river never froze. Clouds of steam breathed from the surface of the water, and ducks swam about untroubled in its currents. Having crossed the Lake, he immediately found a redoubled beauty. There were red and yellow lilies on the roadside, an abundance of wild strawberries, raspberries and whortleberries (bilberries), giant cedars 120 feet (36 metres) in height, cherry trees, and the balsam poplar, so wide in girth that a single trunk hollowed out would serve the native tribesmen for an ample canoe.

TO THE GREAT OCEAN

eyond Lake Baikal, the landscape of Siberia sees a dramatic change. The territory, which towards Irkutsk begins to rise, concertinas into a near unremitting extent of great mountains and steep valleys, softened only by a few exiguous stretches of steppe around the Rivers Onon and Argun. Although rich with minerals, the land is thickly wooded, swampy, difficult for cultivation, and transport becomes even more of a difficulty than in the west. The old Post Road became muddier, heavier going, and much of the transportation was entrusted to flat-bottomed barges and river steamers, which made their way along the treacherous shallows of the rivers that flowed towards the Pacific.

The population, similarly, saw a change. The number of inhabitants became scarcer, more widely scattered. The number of farms and settlements dwindled, as did the number of great towns and their size. The composition of the people also altered. The number of Russian settlers was far lower; not only were the native tribesmen, the Buriats and Tungus, more in evidence, but so also were workers and families from China and the Korean Peninsula.

The character of Siberia east of Baikal was always accounted as something different to that of the western regions. Undoubtedly it could boast to an even greater extent of the wild antics of Irkutsk and Tomsk, with fortunes being made and lost in an instant among the gold mines and gambling tables in the rough towns along the Shilka River. However, more than this, it had the sense of a marchland, a frontier area of Russia whose links to the motherland were scarce established and always in danger. Russian colonists had reached the area in the mid-17th century, but been unable to secure much of it, especially the areas around the Amur River, for the empire of the Tsar. The Chinese Qing (Manchu) Dynasty, then more of a power in the land, forced the Russian colonists back for over two centuries, before ceding the area north of the Amur to Russia in 1858, and east of the Ussuri in 1860, unable to hold it on account of their then weakness. By the time that Western travellers began to reach these far eastern regions, by far the greatest expressions of Russian colonisation were military garrisons living in perpetual anticipation of conflict with China, Japan or even Britain, some of the most notorious convict prisons and forced labour mines, and unbounded Cossacks on the very fringes of civilisation. Everything else partook of an uncultivated rawness, of which even the most difficult regions west of Baikal could not imagine to boast.

Different travellers owned to different views about the temperament of the inhabitants of Eastern Siberia. For John Foster Fraser, the free democratic spirit which characterised Western Siberia, untainted by serfdom and unafraid to speak its mind, stopped at Lake Baikal. Beyond here, he reminds us, nearly all of the Russians had come directly from European Russia, and had never come under the influence of "Siberian freedom". Many were there under temporary military or official postings, and had travelled not overland, but by sea from Odessa via Vladivostok. "They were Russians proper, and all the severe, rigid, official discipline was in evidence. Everything was in accordance with regulation."

R.L. Wright, by contrast, took a very different view: "West of Baikal the steppe land and *taiga* are dreary; east is a country whose scenery is more diversified, whose people are imbued with modern ideas, and, in a measure, have a freer hand to live and do as they please. Amurland and the maritime regions showed marked traces of American influence and of that inimitable Far East cosmopolitanism. The people have a cheery slap-dash about them. In the cities, they seem to live, not barely exist; and they hurry now and then. Little wonder that Siberia east of Baikal is called 'Russian America.'"

What they could all agree on was the region's essential rawness. The Englishwoman Anette Meakin, who was travelling as a tourist with her aged mother in 1900, had perhaps the most direct experience of this the moment she reached the eastern shore of Lake Baikal. It will be remembered that Meakin had found the Trans-Siberian out of Moscow an opulent sort of "liberty hall"; now, disembarking from the steamer, she found that the only luxury carriages on the Transbaikal railway line had just been commandeered by an official delegation. For the other passengers, "a train composed of fourth-class carriages stood waiting..." The compartments were bare and austere, furnished only with wooden shelves for bunk beds in three tiers. "We got into a compartment and tried to keep it to ourselves," but the train showing no sign of starting, "more and more people kept coming in." As the compartment filled to bursting point with people not of her class, the trepidation of the Meakins grew greater and greater. Finally, when the bunk above her became "an object of desire to two men of so dirty and unkempt appearance..." who allowed their "wretched... feet" to hang out and dangle above her head, it became too much for her. "I put up my hands to ward them off and cried 'Conductor' in the most threatening tones I could muster..."

Returning with Miss Meakin, he grimly surveyed their quarters. "'This is not a fit place for ladies,' said our new friend, looking round at our grimy companions – 'and *English* ladies too!'" After several hours waiting in a huddle, with the offensive feet still swinging above their heads, the Meakins were eventually ushered through the darkness and pouring rain into a luggage van which held a detachment of six soldiers with their captain. One end had been partitioned off with curtains that the kindly conductor had taken from his own house. The Meakins thus had a makeshift coupé, ten feet by eight (3 x 2.5 metres), deal boards to sleep on, and for warmth a wood stove, whose chimney penetrated the roof of the carriage. They travelled for three days in these conditions, drinking tea and milk, and sharing brown bread with the soldiers, "with sour lumps of uncooked dough here and there". They doubled up their rugs to keep out the hardness of the boards on which they slept, but they ached after only 10 minutes in one position. "My mother had the side nearest the curtain; a soldier slept on a similar board to ours on the other side of it, and she occasionally felt his elbow. We had a tiny window in the corner, so high up that to look out we had to stand on the seat. *Still, we had it all to ourselves.*"

The Meakins' journey to Stretensk (Streitinsk) would have been harrowing enough to try anyone. The two carriages next along were prison vans, their windows strongly barred and the sliding doors bolted with a lock. Whenever the train stopped, four of the soldiers jumped out into the unceasing rain and stood guard on either side, with rifles and fixed bayonets. "Whenever I looked up at the prison bars I saw a cluster of children's faces peering out – hardly ever a man's face... One of the soldiers picked some flowers and handed them in to the children. They stretched out their hands eagerly, and looked so pleased to get them."

This fragment of Meakins' journey demonstrates in epitome what many others experienced over the whole course of their travels in Eastern Siberia, whether it was squalor and difficulty in travel, the military and frontier character of the territory, or else its reputation for the most degrading settlements of prisoners and convicts. It was to investigate the latter that brought George Kennan this far out in Siberia, and his travels in the region degenerate into a harrowing refrain of misery and institutional inhumanity. He trekked from place to place, searching out the most notorious penal institutions, and surveying them at close hand, unfolded a terrible inventory of suffering. He found the worst prison at the convict mine of Ust Kara, somewhat north of the Post Road. This was one of a set of seven prisons, working a mine which was the private property of the Tsar, and which produced for him 4,000 lbs of gold every year.

Back on the Post Road in Nerchinsk, in whose prison he found convicts being kept naked as a punishment for overindulgence in liquor, Kennan was overwhelmed at the extreme disparities in wealth that the town of 4,000 people presented. The town's hotel was scarcely better than the habitation of the prisoners. The stale air was full of the scent of burning charcoal, rotting wallpaper hung limply in torn shreds from the walls, and the floor of warped, uncovered planks was interrupted by rat holes, and the occasional cockroach. His bedroom contained no bed. When he asked for the wherewithal to wash himself, the only servant, a "half-grown boy" in top boots and a red flannel shirt brought him a yellow brass bedpan in which to clean his hands, which had recently been "put to a more ignoble purpose" and had not since been washed.

By contrast to this squalor, he had the opportunity to see one of the local landmarks, the house of the mercantile Butin family, which had grown rich on distilling vodka, iron manufacture, and the construction of river steamers. On seeing it, he had to rub his eyes to make sure he was awake. A dazzling and extensive palace, it was an extraordinary complex in an array of architectural styles from the gothic to the classical. Indoors, he went from room to room, stunned by its sheer opulence. There were hardwood marquetry floors, silken curtains, tapestries, stained-glass windows, chandeliers, oriental rugs, white-and-gold furniture upholstered with satin, Flemish old master paintings, marble statues, and a glass conservatory filled with palms, lemon trees, and rare orchids from the tropics. There was a ballroom with a grand staircase, galleries, and a library fully stocked with books. "Such luxury would excite no remark in a wealthy and prosperous city; but in the snowy wilderness of the Trans-Baikal, 3,000 miles from the boundary-line of Europe, it comes to the unprepared traveller with the shock of a complete surprise."

ohn Foster Fraser was rather more lucky than the Meakins with the train journey from Baikal to the then terminus of the section at Stretensk. He was able to secure a normal train carriage, and every evening spent hours looking out mesmerised over "the rich hues of the fading year", not hearing the clatter of the wheels on the tracks, but rather enjoying the rich masses of brilliant wild flowers on the banks, "flaunting red, and pale puce, and strong yellow, and gentle blue" and the days "dying in exquisite sunset, and the rippled reflections in the rivers". His ecstasies died away, however, when he reached Stretensk. Here, the Transbaikal section of the line ended, and travellers had to take a steamer down the Shilka and Amur rivers, past the town of Blagvostchensk to Khabarovsk, where the train line restarted for the last section of the journey towards the Pacific port of Vladivostok. Day after day he visited the shipping office, but none of the officials had any idea when a steamer might turn up, or indeed even seemed to know anything about it at all. But "*nitchevo*," they would repeat to him – "what did it matter?" He therefore resigned himself to an extended wait in a town that was, to him, a "melancholy hole".

"Let me try to describe Streitinsk," he begins. "All along the banks of the Shilka stretch a higgledy-piggledy lot of shanties all unpainted, all with little dirty windows, and all with a yard that is more than ankle deep in cattle filth. There is usually a rude fence, but broken. The cows, poor thin brutes, and the pigs, ridge-backed, flabby, and bristled, wander anywhere." By day, the place seemed generally deserted. On the roadways, covered in a six-inch layer of dust which became a foot-deep mess of slush in the rain, herds of Siberian ponies cantered by, driven by Tatars in huge sheepskin hats and dressed in all-enveloping sheepskin coats. From time to time, a Cossack officer might be seen in a white linen jacket and a yellow band around his cap, and even less frequently a "lady hurrying along" in the improbable finery of Europe.

The shops, however, came as a surprise to Fraser. Dingy and apparently quiet on the outside, within they were full of imported commodities, Attendants, clattering on abacuses to reckon their takings, saw to the shelves, and buyers from the far interior of the country, distinguishable by their full native dress, surveyed the many goods on offer. George Kennan noted that US goods had penetrated this far, including tinned peaches and tinned tomatoes. The Chinese added to the trade of the place by a cottage industry of cigarette manufacture, but whose products, declared the American traveller R.L. Wright, were vile and unsmokable. Fraser lamented that the only signs of British commerce in this corner of the world were tomato ketchup and brown sauce, which seemed to be ubiquitous, and used to season any of the traditional Russian dishes. "These shops in so wretched a place amaze you till you remember that Streitinsk, like all other towns in Russia with railways and water communication, is the centre of trade for many hundreds of miles around."

Every day as he waited for news of a steamer to take him down the River Shilka, Fraser paced his way through the town. "I confess its sordidness weighed heavily. One was indeed right out of the world. There were no newspapers. No news ever came there." R.L. Wright felt similarly. "We have not yet said much about the amusements of Stretensk. Well, there are none." Occasionally, a troupe of wandering actors might appear on their way to Irkutsk, and a little while before his arrival an amateur company had put on Bizet's *Carmen*, performing it on a hotel stage 15 feet square, a single pianist undertaking the whole of the orchestral duties. By the waterfront, a Chinese man with a Punch and Judy-style booth would regularly perform, for a fee of three kopeks, a repertoire of four lectures in Chinese to the uncomprehending Russian onlookers. On the little stage of the booth, with the aid of a printed backdrop of a lamasery, a picture of the steamer *Odessa*, a pile of sardine tins, and "a row of Parisian photographs in questionable taste", he would discourse on subjects ranging from the export of tea to the principles of Tibetan Buddhism. Otherwise, the only other entertainment seemed to be drunkenness. Wright was in Stretensk over the period of Easter. On Easter day, men saluted each other with the words "Christ is risen", kissed, and then went home to drink vodka. Seven days later, the revels were still in full swing. The vision of two priests, "maudlin with drink, rolling down the main street in their blue cassocks shouting at the top of their lungs 'Christ is risen!'" was the sight that greeted him on the first Sunday in Easter.

The passenger steamer Amur, owned by the Ministry of Ways of Communication.

Every night at around 10pm the wearying lassitude of the town, says Fraser, would at least lift for a spell. By then, his hotel, the best in Stretensk, would undergo a wonderful transformation. "In the daytime it was just a barn with some gewgaws on the walls and imitation plants on the table to make a dining room. So dilatory was everybody that if I could get a modest lunch of two courses in two hours I was fortunate." However, by night, it burst into a sudden and unexpected rollicking uproar. The hordes of officials in the multitude of uniforms, soldiers from the barracks, the river police, the post office, telegraph officials and endless others, with caps, gilt buttons and multicoloured braids, piled in, drank deeply of vodka and beer, and were "uproariously merry before the food was ready". A "wheezy" pianola would crown the evening with music, and the card-playing and eating continued daily until four in the morning. "And this in a shed of a hotel, where your clothes hook was a nail, and the gaps in the woodwork so open that you could easily see your neighbour going to bed."

Fraser was eventually able to escape from the tedium of Stretensk on the arrival of one of the steamboats which plied between there and Khabarovsk, connecting the Transbaikal section of the railway to the Ussuri Line which led to Vladivostok. Such a journey by steamboat was the standard means of passage until 1914, when the Amur section of the Trans-Siberian connected these two lines, making a continuous journey by train on Russian territory possible all the way to the Pacific. Like Fraser, there were many others anxious to be on their way. Every first- and second-class place on the *Admiral Tschchachoff* (also called the *Chicachoff*) was taken, and the third-class deck passengers were only allowed to embark after the loading of the mails. Fraser watched the entire process from on board. First, the post sacks were taken on, giant leather bags of whole cowhides fastened shut with locks and heavy steel chains, each being carried by half a dozen Chinese coolies staggering under their colossal weight. Then a siren was sounded, and the jostling crowd of steerage passengers charged for the narrow gangplank, all trying to force their way down it at once. There were Russians, Tatars, Chinese, all laden down with their life possessions, bundles of bedding, clothing, food for the journey, hunks of bread, kettles and, noted Fraser, "often a big flapping-tailed dried fish which would slap the face of the next person". Scuffles would break out as the purser insisted on checking every ticket. People would have to untie their bundles to hunt for their documents, stashed deep away for safekeeping. On more than one occasion, Chinese passengers who declared that their friends had gone ahead with the tickets and then tried to rush on board were hauled back down the gangplank by the pigtail.

his far into Siberia, the concept of first-class travel had become somewhat diluted. The first-class dining saloon consisted of a table covered with a ragged oilcloth and perennially unwashed serviettes. The midday meal was usually a great platter of "a hash of meat and onions, undercooked peas and macaroni, and oil-smeared potatoes". Each passenger dived in, hauling out what they wanted with their own knives and forks. The level of table manners left Fraser somewhat out of sorts: bread was brought to the table in a big pile, the diners would grab four or five rolls, examine each carefully, and sling back into the middle those they did not fancy. When tea was brought, everybody produced toothpicks, and proceeded to scratch at and suck their teeth for prolonged periods of time. "I've an idea some fastidious Britishers would think this rather disgusting," said Fraser.

The American traveller Francis Clark found the worst manners in this situation belonged not to any of the local travellers, but to two Frenchmen. However, the real breach of etiquette was not the way they held their knife and fork, but the refusal to pitch in and endure cheerfully the discomforts of travel. Making themselves generally disagreeable, "the climax was reached when one of these irascible Gauls found that sugar had been put in his cabbage. His gastronomic canons were all outraged, and, throwing the cabbage, dish and all, out of the window into the river, he flung a full bottle of beer at the waiter, narrowly missing a lady's head, and only then felt that his outraged culinary taste had been fully avenged."

Nonetheless, the first-class passengers were still relatively well off. The second- and third-class passengers had no dining saloon, only a stove for common use and a cauldron of water perpetually boiling under one of the hatches. As was the case with the railway, there seemed to be no regular hours for eating, except that none seemed to occur between midnight and four in the morning. The second-class passengers could at least retreat to their cabins to eat, but the third-class messed on deck with their kettles and fragments of dried fish strewn around.

For all their dubious table manners, Fraser found his travelling companions generally an agreeable crowd. The most important, a general and his wife, stayed in their cabin, eating alone and bringing down silent derision from the other travellers who revelled in the Siberian travelling spirit of piling in together. Below the general, the next senior was the colonel of a Tatar regiment travelling to Manchuria: "a drab-faced man with black, cropped whiskers and spectacles of black glass (for his eyes were weak)... He ate with his fingers and salivated after the manner of a Mexican cow-puncher." Beside him was a military wife on her way to join her officer husband at Vladivostok. Travelling alone, she smoked incessantly, and even at mealtimes, rather than using an ashtray threw the cardboard cigarette ends about indiscriminately. As for civilian travellers, there was a jovial fur merchant who knew one word of English, "porter", although there was none on the ship, and his kindly old wife, whom Fraser found agreeable, even though at the dinner table she would pass lumps of butter to him with her fingers.

Fraser shared his cabin with an inspector of schools. By day, he spent most of his time lying on his back smoking and drinking Crimean wine. By night, he snored "with the snort of a tugboat". This, however, was not the cause of Fraser's greatest discomfort. Having managed to get to sleep on his first night, he awoke to the sensation of unidentified things dropping from the ceiling on his neck, crawling about on his cheek and then making their way down his arm. He struck a light, and found the cabin, and himself,

A landscape drawing of the Amur River, from A Journey to the Amur, Completed by the Siberian Division of the Russian Emperor's Geographic Society: An Album of Drawings, *held by the Russian State Library's Department of Printed Art.*

awash with cockroaches. When the inspector of schools, on being awoken, laughed at Fraser's complaint with a hearty "*nitchevo*", Fraser snatched up his belongings muttering "*nitchevo* be hanged", and then strode upstairs to pace the deck.

The *Admiral Tschchachoff* and its sister vessels which plied these reaches of the Shilka and Amur rivers were flat-bottomed steam-driven paddle boats. In the words of Francis Clark, they were stately side-wheelers, "such as might have done duty on the Mississippi before the railroads robbed her of her commercial glory". Although grand, they only drew four feet of water. Such vessels had to be used, as the rivers, for much of their lengths, were shallow, seldom dredged, and treacherous with perpetually shifting sandbanks lurking just below the surface of the water. Every mile's progress along the river was painfully won. For the entire duration of the journey, both day and night, a sailor would stand on the bow of the ship, and every minute take a sounding with a 10-foot (three-metre) coloured rod. If the depth of the water were more than this, he would say nothing, but anything below this, he would shout up a warning to the helmsman, "*shest*" (six foot), or "*pyat polovina*" (five and a half foot). Below five foot the boat was lowered to half speed, and anything beneath this the boat could not proceed, but had to reverse and look for a deeper channel.

Despite the caution shown by the sailors, it was a frequent occurrence that the sound of the keel of the boat grating on the bottom of the river could be heard, and the boat could be marooned on a sandbank for hours or even days. The passengers would often be disembarked whilst the sailors went into the river to try and displace the steamer by digging it out, or using main force. On some of these occasions, the passengers were even called upon to wait on the convict barges that the steamers frequently towed, and could fraternise freely with the prisoners. Francis Clark, peering at his "fellow-passengers behind the bars", who were probably in the highest category of offender, murderers and the like, felt moved to confess "that they were not bad-looking fellows... and the impartial visitor, had he been asked to pick out the convicts by their looks, would, very likely, have chosen the hardened criminals from among the free men on top of the barge, instead from among those whom the law had put into the cage below."

Whether or not the steamers sailed freely or ran aground, the travellers in general were never too weary to neglect enjoying the scenery of the river. The Amur, along with the Shilka, which in reality is only the upper stretch of the Amur, is one of the greatest, but perhaps least well-known rivers of the world. It is longer than anything in Europe, is exceeded only by the Nile, Amazon, Yangzi, Mississippi-Missouri, Yenisey, Yellow, Ob-Irtysh and Congo rivers, and drains an area of land something in excess of half a million square miles (1.3 million square kilometres). However, despite its size it never seemed to overawe travellers with grandeur and majesty. An approachable beauty was the sole note of the river. The banks were little cultivated, and the settlements infrequent. Travellers such as Clark and Lansdell talk of a profusion of flora. They describe lilies of the valley, violets, blue and white forget-me-not, and a mass of wild orchids. There were woods thick with larch and birch, and the sound of the cuckoo could be heard from on board.

One of the great sights was the high cliffs, over 200 feet (61 metres) high, with veins of coal which had some time in the distant past caught fire, and burned deep within the rock, glowing with an unquenchable flame. Every so often, the ship would near a village, and the captain would give a blast on the ship's whistle. The peasants would rush out with armfuls of bread, bottles of milk, butter, eggs, or even live geese to sell on board. The sailors would jump out to fetch logs from the woodpiles left at intervals along the banks, and the passengers would take the opportunity to bathe in the river, or else walk in the meadows, gathering up armfuls of wildflowers to lighten their journey.

he other traffic on the river was slight. Rafts conveying wood were frequent, and so were smaller barges, laden with emigrant families continuing to make their journey eastwards into the territories newly acquired by Russia. Tugboats drew them, and they were crowded not only with men, women and children, but also horses, cattle and dogs, sometimes so tightly packed that they could barely sit or lie down. However, the sight that many travellers seemed to find most evocative was the dugout canoe. Towards sunset, people were to be seen paddling these along the edge of the stream to light the lamps which marked out the shipping channel; red lanterns on the Chinese side of the river, and white on the Russian. If there were no fog, the steamers would navigate through the night by their aid. The men charged with this responsibility reminded many travellers of the solitary signalmen posted at every verst along the Trans-Siberian. "What lonely lives these men must lead," commented Fraser.

It was often the case that travellers would disembark and change boats at Blagoveshchensk. Again, like Stretensk, this was the commercial and military centre for an area hundreds of miles in extent, but unlike Stretensk it had nothing of its lassitude. At the turn of the 20th century, the city had a population, huge for Siberia, of 40,000 people – it called itself "The New York of Siberia". Even if it wasn't that, as Fraser asserted, the Americans, he said would still call it "quite a town". The American Francis Clark assented. Admiring the wide streets and "fine blocks", it was as good as any of the smaller cities that the United States could boast. The streets swarmed with activity. Construction materials, timber and brick, were heaped up ready for use. Masons, carpenters and stonecutters plied their trades. Consumerism was in full bud: two department stores, "palatial in proportions and equipment", one German-owned and one Russian with Chinese staff behind the tills, offered everything from shirts and linen collars (at New York prices, noted Clark) to "pipes and pickles, flowers and flat-irons, oil and oysters, waistcoats and watches, indigo and icons".

For the traveller, it had every convenience. The hotels were clean, well furnished and reasonable. The inhabitants were helpful. There were libraries, local newspapers, a museum, banks, a hospital, and a clubhouse where a dramatic society and amateur orchestra performed regularly. There were also beautiful gardens that were maintained on a bund that stood between the main street and the river. Perhaps the motive

Locals in a shallow boat, from A Journey to the Amur *(see page 157) – note the more Oriental appearance in this region.*

force behind the city's energy was the fact that it was the seat of a group of religious dissenters called the *Molokans*, or Milk-drinkers, on account of the fact that they only drank milk on fasting days. They abstained from smoking, drinking, as well as the use of ikons or clergy in worship. They rose early, had a reputation for industry, and were the founders of many of the city's successful businesses and merchant ventures.

However, for all of its freshness and dynamism, Blagoveshchensk had a far darker side. Like other great Siberian cities, it was a mining metropolis. The miners were not only Russians, but also Koreans and Chinese. The workers, laden with wages, would return to the town, ready for pleasure and dissipation. Fraser commented on the Chinese coolies, who having a few spare kopeks, delighted to call a droshky, and so be able to have a Russian under their command. The Koreans, he observed, took to Russian dress, with loose open shirts, thick belts, and "big slouching Californian hats, and judging from the way they swaggered along, were full of the Korean equivalent for picturesque though unprintable Californian oaths". At night, said R.L. Wright, fortunes were made and lost over the gaming tables. As much responsible as the miners were the colony of young German merchants, or the military officers posted this far out as Russia found them too hot to handle. The city rivalled Irkutsk in murder statistics: "It is a poor week that does not see five or six cold-blooded murders," wrote Wright. Suicide was also popular, he also observed, particularly at Easter, with 15 people on average taking their own life over the week after Easter Sunday.

Most egregious was the sight of a massacre of Chinese residents in July 1900, made in response to an unfounded rumour that all of the Western residents of Peking had been slaughtered in the Boxer Rebellion. The Chinese community were rounded up and ordered to return to China, but given no means of crossing the Amur River, which marked the border, and at Blagoveshchensk was over a mile wide. Protesting they could not cross, they were forced into the river by the military garrison at bayonet point. It is thought that over 4,500 drowned. The offending governor who ordered the outrage was demoted, but otherwise no other action was taken by the government. More Chinese workers returned to take the place of the dead and life continued as before, but the act, according to Fraser, hung heavy on the conscience of the Russian inhabitants. Some refused to talk about it; others were stirred with indignation. As a traveller, inspecting the spot where the incident took place, the knowledge of the fact gave him pause. It would have reminded him that he was travelling through an area that was recently won by Russia, and potentially still under dispute. For all the veneer of development, the chaos of frontier politics could still bring normal life in those regions sharply to a halt, and travel in these regions was still a deeply precarious undertaking.

Korean workers were employed on the construction of the Trans-Siberian Railway in the Ussuri region.

The early travellers left the Amur River and rejoined the railway line at Khabarovsk, the head of the Ussuri line, which led to Vladivostok. Khabarovsk itself, after the agonies of Stretensk and the excitements of Blagoveshchensk, was not for the travellers on the Trans-Siberian a particularly remarkable town. Grandly situated on the ravines carved out by the Amur at its junction with the Ussuri River, it was a place of brick-built offices, Russian barracks and Chinese shopkeepers. The streets were full of Koreans, wearing "singular" black hats that reminded Fraser of those sported by "countrymen in out-of-the-way corners of Wales". Women, noted Fraser, were scarce to be seen. A census at the turn of the century discovered that there was a ratio of 11 men to every woman. A museum boasted a selection of Manchurian artefacts, the spoils of war against the Chinese Empire. The only Russians in the town appeared to be soldiers and uniformed bureaucrats. The railway line itself seemed to be administered more by the army than the civilian authorities, and its stations, according to Annette Meakin, partook of a military appearance. As befitted the frontier, the line was ready to be commandeered by the army, and used solely for the transport of troops in the event of further conflict.

This far on the way towards the Pacific, a certain travel-hardened attitude appeared to steal over many. Meakin, after the ordeal of her journey on the Transbaikal line, was at ease among her fellow passengers, and warmly greeted the familiar faces she recognised from earlier in the journey. The barriers and guards of English reserve were tottering. "When people have been travelling for weeks and weeks they meet more or less as old friends even if they have never exchanged a word," she observed. The great press at the train station and the throng of nationalities was not at all trying, but rather a great curiosity to her. Aside from the Koreans dressed in white and Chinese ladies hobbling on bound feet, she observed Serbian gypsies mingling amongst the crowd, offering to tell fortunes. There were Japanese travellers, and even a Circassian family from Tiflis, their women in long velvet caps topped with lace handkerchiefs, and the son of the family, a priest, sporting a long grey coat lined with bright purple silk.

(Right) *Stunning scenery and crystal-clear water can be seen along the west coast of Lake Baikal. The largest freshwater lake in Europe and Asia, Baikal is 395 miles (636 kilometres) long and contains just under a fifth of the world's freshwater, as much as all the Great Lakes of America combined. So significant is the lake that it creates its own microclimate, allowing cities like Irkutsk to enjoy less harsh weather than elsewhere in eastern Siberia… relatively speaking, of course.*

The Golden Eagle *luxury train skirts Lake Baikal, with snow-covered mountains rising from the eastern shore in the distance.*

(Top) *A boat moored to the shore is silhouetted by the sun on a balmy summer's day on Lake Baikal.*

(Bottom) *Winter on Baikal is a different experience altogether; here, thick ice has been churned up into ice hummocks, hinting at the enormous crushing power that through the centuries has left so many vessels at the bottom of the lake.*

(Left) *A NASA satellite image of Lake Baikal; 336 rivers feed it, but only one flows out from the lake, the Angara River which can be seen emerging from its southwestern end and heading north. The lake, in combination with the mountains to the north and south, were an engineering nightmare for the builders of the Trans-Siberian Railway.*

(Above) *A rock headland on Orkhon, Baikal's largest island.*

(Right) *Old Believers in the Baikal region, where their families fled many generations ago from persecution by 17th century reformists of the Russian Orthdox Church.*

(Opposite top left and right) *A Buriat shepherd and Buriat girl wearing traditional clothing – the round-faced Buriats are of Mongol origin.*

(Opposite bottom) *A Buriat family ger, or yurt, the nomad's easily erected and transported home. Buriats are the northernmost ethnic Mongol group, traditionally living in the Ulan-Ude area and along the Angara River.*

(Above) Vladivostok Railway Station, the end of the line – or the beginning – for a Trans-Siberian railway trip.
(Top right) Vladivostok harbour, the major Pacific port for Russia's Navy, its Eastern fishing fleet and commercial shipping.
(Bottom right) "The landing of the Japanese army – Welcomed by every nation at Vladivostok", a colour lithograph of a Japanese propaganda poster, circa 1906, taken from The Illustration of the Siberian War No. 1.

皇軍浦鹽斯德上陸各國官民熱狂的歡迎

救露討獨遠征軍畫報（其一）

THE ILLUSTRATION OF THE SIBERIAN WAR. №1. The Landing of The Japanese Army Welcomed By Every Nation, At Vladivostok.

(Top) *The Temple of Boddhisattva Avalokiteshvara at Gandan Monastery in Ulaanbaatar, containing a 26.5-metre gilded statue.* (Bottom) *A "brochure" for the Kiakhta Tea-Trade Company in 1900, whose head office was in St Petersburg – the back of the card shows price lists, stores and agencies. (Opposite top) The smiling face of Mongolian hospitality. (Opposite bottom) A Tsam dance mask at a national festival in Ulaanbaatar.*

An archer at a competition during the
Naadam festival – archery is one of the
"three manly sports" of Mongolian culture.

A truck looks tiny against the vast Mongolian landscape, which moves from desert to steppe to mountain in a roughly south to north configuration.

(Above) *The easily named Turtle Rock, a short way outside Ulaanbaatar – look at the livestock grazing below it and you will get some perspective on its size. (Below) Horse racing is a popular sport in Mongolia, but during the Naadam festival only children are used as jockeys, and the cross-country courses can be up to 20 miles (30 kilometres) long.*

(Above) *A typical tourist ger camp in the Mongolian steppe – though built on stone and concrete platforms with wooden floorboards for extra insulation and comfort, the gers are otherwise exactly the same in construction as a nomad family's.*
(Below) *Inside a ger, its ingenious design is plain to see – a central stove warms it up nicely for guests.*

A ticket lady looks smart in her uniform on the
Trans-Mongolian Railway, which connects Ulan-Ude
in Russia with China and ultimately Beijing – a
"short cut" for many transcontinental travellers.

The train journey from Khabarovsk to Vladivostok was, compared to the scale of the whole Trans-Siberian, comparatively slight. The distance was about 480 miles (772 kilometres), and took a mere day-and-a-half to complete. The carriages, according to Meakin, were nothing more than post-wagons with a dining car tacked on, but against this, now inured to the hardships of travel, she made no complaint. The poor quality of the track also seemed to cause her little distress. The "pioneer" nature of the original line, with the stress being on getting the rails laid as cheaply as possible with scant regard to safety, meant that the journey was, in the words of Fraser, "jolt and

Excavation of a railcut at Chaldonka, verst 120, in 1913, from The Amur Railroad Album, *held by the Russian State Library.*

jerk and bump all day and all night long". However, great sections of the track were being improved all the time, and Fraser watched as soldiers laboured on the line, putting down new ballast and sturdier rails. Meakin, troubled only by the mosquitoes endemic in the riverine territory, sat the afternoon through with her mother, delighting herself at the sight of flowers along the track, purple and white iris, lilies both yellow, red and white, and even disembarked at the wayside stations to pick a few handfuls.

But ensconced in their train carriages, only able to see the wayside flowers or the toiling soldiers against the backdrop of the swampy grassland and thinner woodlands rising up into "huge, round-shouldered hills", the detail of the land passed them by in the ease of the journey. The close observation of the region belongs to the small handful of earlier travellers, making their way without the benefit of the train. One of the most prominent of these was the missionary Henry Lansdell. Making his way about the most inaccessible parts of the Siberian hinterland, laden with a stock of bibles, tracts and New Testaments in Russian and all the native languages that he had been able to procure, he stands as one of the most readable, if occasionally vain and bizarre, amateur ethnographers to encounter the native tribes in the region before the full onset of modernity.

Travelling the length of the Amur and Ussuri rivers, he was able to record glimpses of life on both the Chinese and Russian sides of the border. In Chinese Manchuria, he was able to visit the tiny local settlements – poverty-stricken hamlets of a few thatched houses with hollowed-out tree trunks for chimneys, set in the midst of scanty fields of millet, raging with mosquitoes. Outside, men – and only men were seen – laboured to scratch a living from the land. They ground corn between millstones by hand, pulled hemp into threads, fed slender cattle from troughs outside their doors, and carted about their meagre produce in wagons with clumsy juddering wheels. Little shrines, the size and shape of a sentry box, stood in their yards to lend a benediction, and were adorned with tattered pictures of the gods, pans, vases, joss sticks and fishhooks.

On the Russian side, he was also able to survey the dwellings of the Cossack colonists, who were responsible for protecting the frontier and keeping the Manchurians at bay. Their cottages, built of logs, he found were "cleanly and orderly", if somewhat sparse. The floors were strewn with hay, the walls were whitewashed, and on them were proudly hung the only tableware the dwellers might possess. In one cottage where he was received, the sum total of it was seven forks, four spoons, a ladle, four plates, one mug, one cup and two glasses. A hand-grinder was used to mill the corn, the occupation of the women of the household. For the Cossack soldier himself, there were fishhooks and an antique flint-lock hunting rifle. Hanging by the door there were two bundles of valuable squirrel fur, the token of his expeditions to the wild.

Lansdell was able to spend time with and observe many of the native Siberian tribes that still then dwelt throughout the region. Their numbers were dwindling, and their populations could perhaps even then be counted in the thousands. Nonetheless, in his time they still lived according to old customs, and eked out a living in ways unaffected by modern technology or agriculture.

One such people he was able to visit were the Nivkhi, also known as the Gilyaks, who inhabited the lands around the Amur River and the island of Sakhalin. It was an act of heroism, he wrote, to spend any time in the house of a Gilyak. They were a people who were almost entirely devoted to fish. Their dwellings, square huts plastered with mud, were hung with drying fish, dried fish, fish entrails, fish nets and fish baskets. The summer clothes of the people were made of waterproof fish skins, which had been scraped, made supple and sewn together. The same was used for windows, travel bags and boat sails. Some of the tribesmen even boasted tobacco pouches made out of sturgeon skin. The houses, needless to say, were trying on the nose. If one got over this, one might be alarmed that

Two dwellings in the Amur region, from A Journey to the Amur, Completed by the Siberian Division of the Russian Emperor's Geographic Society: An Album of Drawings, *held by the Russian State Library's Department of Printed Art.*

some families kept a tethered bear or sled-dogs in the centre of the single room, or be worried that one would bump into the dog sledges, oars and birch-bark canoes which also hung from the rafters.

he Gilyaks were generally short, less than five feet (1.5 metres) tall, tawny skinned, with thin dark hair. Their families were small, and it was rare for a woman to have any more than six children. Babies would be placed in cradles that were hung amongst the fish and hunting gear from the roof beams. Lansdell marvelled at the resourcefulness of the people. Aside from fish skins, their winter clothes were animal furs and dog pelts, and their sewing threads or larger ropes were made of fibres extracted from stinging nettles, as strong as anything made in a factory. Their living was almost entirely from hunting and from the wild things of the land. Large-eared owls, hawks and jays were kept for rat-catching and a supply of feathers for arrows. Agriculture and cultivation were near unknown; millet seeds might be collected on special occasions, but their food was either fish or animal flesh. This included their sled dogs when they reached the end of their lives. Tea, in Lansdell's time, was only just being discovered, as was sugar, while scraps of bread, brought in by outsiders, were considered a rare and precious delicacy. Brandy, however, had become well known. By day, they would fish on the rivers using nets, or else spear salmon from canoes. Women would row larger boats in expeditions on the rivers, while the men steered, puffing on Chinese long-stemmed amber pipes.

Their habits, said Lansdell, were "filthy beyond description". They never washed. He relates a story that a telegraph engineer once gave a Gilyak tribesman a bar of soap. The tribesman took it, put it in his mouth, chewed it to a lather, and pronounced it "very good". They practised polygamy, married early, and were betrothed at infancy. A girl would fetch £10–50 in silk stuffs, or a team of up to 10 dogs, a sledge, and a crate of brandy thrown in. A good nose would ensure a better price. Marriages were raucous affairs, with the consumption of much Chinese spirits, and intoxicated violence akin to madness.

The Gilyaks were also, according to Lansdell, the "most thorough heathen I saw in Siberia". A few had been baptised, but most of them adhered to their ancestral shamanistic and animistic beliefs. They feared to be photographed, thinking that the camera would steal away their souls. They did not dare to mention their ancestors, for fear of disturbing or conjuring their spirits. They carried wooden idols and charms to ward off disease or promote healing. On the principles of sympathetic magic, a lame person would carry a wooden leg, a wooden arm for a broken arm. The souls of the dead were thought to pass into the body of one's favourite dog. The dog, after the soul had been teased out by magic, was sacrificed.

Despite their entire dependence of killing animals for survival, they held them in deep reverence. Cats had a half-religious character. Tigers were seen as portents of evil. A man or animal killed by a tiger was immediately buried on the spot without ceremony. No one would attempt to hunt a tiger or a wolf. Bears, however, were bringers of joy. If a cow was found slaughtered by a bear, it would be eaten with rapture. It was accounted as a great honour for a man to be mauled or killed by a bear. Every year, each settlement would go out to capture a bear alive. They would attempt to seize one by jumping on its back out of a tree and grasping it by the ears. Led back to the village, it would be kept in a cage, called by the name *Mafa Sakhle*, or "black chief" and fattened on fish. On a great occasion, it would be brought out with its paws in chains,

A shaman holding an animal-skin drum, an integral part of the many rituals that were part of tribal culture in Siberia.

sacrificed, and its flesh shared by the village in a sacramental feast. Its head and paws were treated with veneration, and were afterwards hung up in the trees to ward off pestilence. The branches of trees were often also, in winter, the receptacles for the bodies of the dead.

Moving about the Amur and the Ussuri, Lansdell was able to meet with shamans, and observe the practice of their rituals. The shamans were figures whose function was difficult to define. Their roles included that of a seer, a religious leader and a healer. They had knowledge of medicines and natural cures for disease. Later research showed that they had an intimate knowledge of the *material medica* of the Siberian territories, and could produce a number of preparations with curative and antibiotic properties. They might be called on to rid lands of pestilence, or uncover the location of possessions lost or stolen. They have been known in Siberia since the earliest times, and even when later religions such as Buddhism or even Islam made an appearance, the shamans were able to accommodate themselves to the change, and the institution to continue up to the beginning of the modern age.

Evert Ysbrants Ides, the Russian ambassador sent to Peking at the end of the 17th century, like Lansdell was able to witness the shamanistic rites amongst the Tungus people in Eastern Siberia. Being introduced to an old shaman with 12 wives, he was first shown the extraordinary outfit he assumed for his work. His coat was "made of joined iron work, consisting of all manner of representations of Birds fishes ravens owls, &c, besides several Beasts and Birds Claws and Bills, saws, hammers, knives, Sabirs, and the images of several beasts &c, so that all the parts of this Diabolical robe being fixed together by joints, might at pleasure be taken to pieces. He had also Iron stockings for his feet and legs, suitable to his robe, and two great bears claws over his hands. His head was likewise adorned, with suchlike images, and fixed to his forehead were two Iron bucks horns." The coat of iron was so heavy that Ides could scarcely lift it with one hand. Yet, wearing this garb, the shaman would perform his exhausting rites.

When something had been stolen amongst the Tungus, the shaman would be besought, and asked to uncover who was responsible. After being paid by the petitioner, he would assume his outfit and heavy mantle, and begin the fearsome ceremonies. "When he designs to conjure he takes a drum made after their fashion in his left hand, and a flat staff covered with the skins of mountain mice in his right hand; thus equipped he jumps cross legged, which motion shakes all these iron plates, and makes a great clangor; besides which, he at the same time beats his drum, and with eyes distorted upwards, a strong bearish voice makes a dismal noise." The shaman would continue to jump, leap and roar around his hut, until a blackbird came to perch on its roof. At this point, he fell into a faint, and lay unconscious for around a quarter of an hour, at which point he would revive, and then be able to tell his customer who was responsible for the theft, or give him answers to other questions as well. "And they tell us," goes on Ides, "that all that he saith proves true." His huge wealth in cattle, brought to him by eager customers, was testament to his reputation and his art.

Lansdell observed similar rituals for the cure of illness. When a man was laid up with an illness, the shaman was called. Wearing his jingling coat of iron, he arranged charms around the man's hut, and decorated it with strips of wood and shavings of birch. A table was laid, on which were arranged wooden idols, fish, squirrels' skin, millet and brandy. Beneath it would be tied a dog. The food and brandy would be offered to the idols, and shared among the audience who crowded into the room to watch the rite. Then the shaman would shake his tambourine, cry out, dance, and sometimes fall to the floor in a daze. The ritual in some cases could last for up to three days. The object in the proceeding was for the shaman to take upon himself and then expel the essence of the illness. Some, it seems, were revered for having such an apparent ability. They were wealthy in life and possessed magnificent tombs in death, bearing witness to the cures they had been able to effect.

"M ost of us," wrote John Foster Fraser, "take to towns as we do to persons – at the first blush or not at all. I felt attracted to Vladivostok before I had been there ten minutes." Many travellers, it seems, felt similarly. Their feelings about the town might have been enhanced by the strong sense of serenity encountered by a wayfarer on reaching the goal of his travels. Similarly, the first sight of the sea after an interminable journey on land touched many with a powerful emotion. Fraser was a prey to both of these. Weaving between hills on the Ussuri line, he was sitting in the carriage when he heard a shout, and then suddenly saw out of the window far off "like the gleam of a sword blade... the glitter of the Pacific Ocean". He watched astonished as the train crawled up an incline to follow the edge of the sea, on which a scattering of Chinese junks floated, and watched above it an astonishing sunset: "a mass of gold and blood, like a great cauldron into which other worlds were thrown, banking up the heavens behind a mass of clouds".

A panorama of Vladivostok in the 1890s, before the new railway linked it to western Russia and allowed it to boom.

The passenger station in Vladivostok, inaugurated on 19 May 1891 in the presence of Nicholas II.

T he meadows beyond the city, rich in fodder and scattered with lilies and wildflowers, came to an end. The railway ran past the back gardens of rows of houses, just as they did in English or European towns. This was then unusual for Siberia, where stations were often built far from the settlements they served. Other travellers described the private gardens of Vladivostok as rich with trees, oak, lime, maple, walnut, apple, pear and cherry. In the summer, they lent the city a backdrop of rich verdure. The line carried on slowly past level crossings with iron barriers holding back a swarm of traffic. Finally, it reached Vladivostok station. As Fraser jumped from the train, he caught sight of a huge board above the end of the track. It read, in pained letters: "Vladivostok to St Petersburg, 9,877 versts".

It was not just the fact that Vladivostok stood at the end of the journey that gave it its attractive qualities. The town, according to travellers, possessed an intrinsic merit. In the words of Francis Clark, "Vladivostok, on nearer approach, unlike many towns, carries out its more distant promise". Aside from the beauty of its location, the place seemed a hive of excitement and activity. Visitors seemed to draw from its energy. Its harbour, a grand 50-acre (20-hectare) bay protected by a grand sweep of hills, was a profusion of bustle. Russian warships, painted white, were anchored in a row at the ready; boats of foreign navies were given liberty to anchor there, no more than two at a time; one could hear shots of courtesy being fired, and see the pomp of naval hospitality. Japanese liners disembarked their passengers. Chinese junks threw out bales of wood to float to the shore. Other vessels unloaded their goods. Little launches steamed between the ships, and in winter an icebreaker would circle, keeping the harbour open. On the quayside, Chinese gangs sang as they staggered under the weight of bales of merchandise, while bunches of sailors reeled about drunkenly. Passengers were met by droshky drivers, wearing cloaks of blue velvet and astrakhan hats, who "swung up their horses with a crack", and clattered "harum-scarum" up and down the steep streets, not for a moment pausing to moderate their speed.

The city was as cosmopolitan as any to be found in Siberia. There were Russians, Chinese and Koreans; also Japanese, Germans, French, Italians, English and Americans. People moved briskly, each with a sense of purpose. The signs of new trade and new money were manifold; the roads and pavements were being paved and asphalted, and buildings were rising everywhere, hotels, department stores and offices. In pride of place were an orthodox church and a triumphal arch, which marked the 1891 visit of the Tsarevitch to lay the foundation of the Trans-Siberian line. Although the town was half-finished, everywhere lay optimism, as Clark said, for the "great future" of the place, the "natural port of Siberia, with a limitless country of vast resources behind her".

At the conclusion of the journey, it is perhaps interesting to consider John Foster Fraser's verdict on Vladivostok, and also the whole of his travels throughout Russia at the turn of the 20th century.

> No man can come through Siberia to such a place as Vladivostok and give a thought to what Russia has done in the generation without being amazed. We may criticise Russian manners and growl at Russian diplomacy, and wonder how people can live under an autocratic government! But Russia has laid hold on the East.
>
> I went for a walk one evening in the public gardens. There was a statue fronting the Pacific to General Nevelskof, who laboured long and successfully for Russian dominion. On the plinth are inscribed his own words: "When a Russian flag is once hoisted it must never be lowered!"

(Above and left) *Two views of Vladivostok in the 1950s, part of the Siberian Postcards collection held by the National Library of Russia. They give the impression of a rather genteel seaside town, but today this is Russia's largest port on the Pacific Ocean, a bustling, polluted city that is home to the Russian Pacific Fleet.*

SIBERIA TO PEKING:
TRAVELLING THE TEA ROAD

Vladivostok and the Pacific Ocean were by no means the only destinations for travellers who had made their way eastwards from European Russia. At Verkhni Udinsk (now called Ulan-Ude), the route of the Trans-Siberian bifurcated, and one of the branches turned south towards Mongolia and Peking. Although this line was only completed in 1955, the route it followed, linking Siberian Russia to the Chinese capital, was longer established and originally more important than the tenuous Post Road which led towards the fledgling Russian possessions in the Far East. Since at least the mid-17th century, the route acted as the main conduit for Sino-Russian trade. Tea came northwards in great caravans from China, and bundles of Siberian fur were sent south. Ambassadors between Moscow and the Forbidden City also followed the path, as did monks who came professing Tibetan Buddhism from the south, and later explorers from the west. Until the great expansion of shipping in the late 19th century, the route maintained its position as one of the main highways linking the European World to China.

For travellers who chose to turn south at Verkhni Udinsk, the first sign of the influence of the highway was the impact it had brought on the religion of the area. The native Siberians who dwelt in the area south and east of Lake Baikal were Buriats. Short, and of a Mongol appearance, they dwelt in tents and simple huts, and herded sheep amongst the hilly pastureland towards the Mongolian border. Their staple food was lamb and mutton broth, and they drank tea flavoured with salt. The men wore their hair in long plaits, and the women adorned themselves with headdresses of silver, coral and mother-of-pearl. Originally, their religious beliefs reflected those of the broader mass of Siberia,

Portrait of a Buriat man and his wife in 1885, taken on George Kennan's trip to the Baikal region.

shamanism and primal animism. Yet by the 18th century, Tibetan monks had spread their doctrine to the north, and Lamaistic Buddhism had overwritten the animism of the Buriats. Characteristic signs of the religion were obvious everywhere to travellers. By the roadside there were little shrines in the form of heaps of stones, decorated with rags; in the huts, the people kept altars, and most importantly of all, the area boasted one of the great regional institutions of Lamaistic Buddhism: the Monastery of Goose Lake, the seat of the Khamba Lama, near the wayside town of Selenginsk.

(Above) *The Tibetan Buddhist* datsan (*monastery*) *at Lake Gusinoe near the Mongolian border.*
(Left) *Captain Christopher Fomich Makofskii, Irkutsk chief of police at the time of George Kennan's visit in 1885 (photo by T.A. Milevskaio of Irkutsk, from the George Kennan collection).*

At one point during his research into the conditions of Siberian convicts in 1880, George Kennan was in the vicinity of Selenginsk. He had wearied from the depressing round of chain gangs and prison hospitals, and was suffering from all of the maladies that could beset a traveller in Siberia: sleeplessness and fatigue, hunger and the attentions of countless bedbugs. He therefore decided to make a detour to visit the monastery, and follow the southward road.

Had Kennan not been malnourished and covered in sores, he would have been in a better position to appreciate the beauty of the route at that spot. The way followed the valley of the Selenginsk River. The air, he recalled, was filled with "an autumnal fragrance like that of ripe pippins". The meadows were covered with flowers, forget-me-nots and yellow alpine poppies. The land was divided by neat fences and scattered with haystacks, and the log huts of Buriat farmers gave the scene a note of homely warmth. When he reached Selenginsk, had rested and attempted somewhat to recover, he looked to find a Buriat interpreter who had sufficient connections to the monastery to negotiate their entrance. Before long, none other than the Buriat chief of police, a man called Khainuief Manku, had offered to be their guide. The man, "hard-featured, bullet-headed", was clad in a plain grey Buriat gown and a black felt Mongol hat "shaped like a pie-dish, and worn with a sort of devil-may-care tilt to one side". However, transported with excitement at the prospect of escorting two visitors to the monastery, he rushed off to dress for the occasion. An hour later, he returned in a gig, "transfigured and glorified beyond recognition". Already drunk when Kennan had met him, he had fortified himself with "six or eight more drinks" and had put on a "long, loose, ultramarine-blue silk gown with circular watered figures in it, girt about the waist with a scarlet sash and a light blue silken scarf... A dishpan-shaped hat of bright red felt was secured to his large round head by means of a colored string tied under his chin, and from this red hat dangled two long narrow streamers of sky-blue ribbon." Kennan had never seen such a chief of police before: "...he looked like an intoxicated Tatar prize-fighter masquerading in the gala dress of some color-loving peasant girl".

As they approached the site of the monastery, the landscape took on a more barren, less hospitable appearance. Trees were only to be seen on the mountaintops, and the floor of the valley was covered in parched and yellowing grass. The monastery itself sat on the edge of the tranquil lake, a cluster of over a hundred mean log huts around a grand, three-roofed temple, covered in white stucco and ornaments in red and black. The police chief, who had pestered Kennan throughout the journey for his "insanity drops", as he referred to the contents of his hip flask, grew grave and reverent at the sight. On arrival, he began to treat Kennan with cringing deference in front of the monks, doffing his cap and claiming that Kennan was something of the order of a "Lord High Commissioner" from the "Great American Republic". Although Kennan was wearing a dirty tattered jacket and covered in insect bites, the story won him admittance from the clergy, and he was invited to view the rites of the temple.

ithin the building the profusion of colour and activity, sound and smell, made an intense contrast to the barren setting beyond the walls. The riot of decoration was near overwhelming for Kennan. He was ushered in just before the beginning of a service. Within, there was a large and dimly lit hall, supported by columns. However, these and the walls were almost entirely hidden by portraits of saints, pictures of holy places, and festoons of scarlet drapery. In front of these were hung coloured banners, lanterns and silk streamers. Subsidiary chapels contained a multiplicity of Buddhist statues, idols, and even a sacred white elephant carved in wood, before which were laid offerings of millet and rice, oil, incense and holy water. At one end there stood three large thrones for the Khamba Lama and the other senior Lamas (priors of the monastery), covered in old-gold silk and piled with cushions and yellow felt. Before them were two parallel ranks of lamas, dressed in robes of orange silk, red silk scarves, and yellow hats, trimmed with red. Students and other acolytes in black gowns clustered at one end of the hall. All around there were musical instruments; beside the doors were two enormous drums, the size of barrels. Two lamas each supported great iron trumpets, at least eight feet long and the bells 10 inches (25cm) in diameter. On tables were placed cymbals, horns and conches.

At the beginning of the service, for a moment, all was stillness. Then, one of the senior lamas picked up a small rattle. In response to the signal, "there burst forth a most tremendous musical uproar, made by the clashing of cymbals, the deep-toned boom of the immense drums, the jangling of bells, the moaning of conch-shells, the tooting of horns, the liquid tinkle of triangles, and the hoarse bellowing of the great iron trumpets. It was not melody, it was not music; it was simply a tremendous instrumental uproar." For a minute it continued in such a way, and then suddenly it ceased. Immediately it was followed by a chant from the orange-robed lamas, "peculiar, wild, rapid... in a deep, low monotone". Their voices were exactly

Onanski Datsan (Monastery) in the Trans-Baikal region, visited by George Kennan in 1885.

in time, and at the end of every stanza of their chant the cymbals were sounded and the drums beaten. After several verses of this chanting, there was another "orchestral charivari which would have levelled the walls of Jericho without any supernatural intervention", followed by further chanting, and thus they alternated in turn. The service lasted in this way for about 15 minutes. "It was interesting," says Kennan, "but it was quite long enough."

Afterwards, they were entertained to a sacred dance outdoors before the temple. The drums and trumpets were brought out, and yellow cushions were set out for the lamas. Again, at the signal of a rattle, a dozen dancers rushed out. As the instruments struck up a heavy, crashing beat, the performers began to swirl and leap about in a slow, rhythmic dance. The costumes they wore were beyond anything that Kennan had ever seen. The colours were orange and crimson, scarlet and blue, in silks, satins and velvet, heightened with gold brocade. They were further ornamented with cords, fringes and tassels, brooches, beads, and jewels with gold and silver. The dancers, it seemed to Kennan, were divided into two groups, and the performance was a sort of mystery play, representing a cosmic struggle between good and evil spirits. The evil powers were masked. Some wore great helmets with the faces of Mongolian demons, and flags on short sticks radiated from their edges. Some bore human skulls on their shoulders, stag antlers or bullhorns. The opposing group wore great hats heavy with gold latticework, and flourished naked daggers.

Kennan concluded his visit by having dinner with the Khamba Lama himself. Over glasses of fruit cordial and madeira, and a bottle of vodka for the Buriat police chief, the Grand Lama began to question Kennan closely on a delicate matter of cosmology.

"You have been in many countries," he said to Kennan, "and have talked with the wise men of the West; what is your opinion with regard to the shape of the earth."

"I think," replied Kennan, "that it is shaped like a great ball."

The Khamba Lama looked thoughtful. "I have heard so before. The Russian officers whom I have met have told me that the world is round. Such a belief is contrary to the teachings of our old Tibetan books, but I have observed that the Russian wise men predict eclipses accurately; and if they can tell beforehand when the sun and the moon are to be darkened, they probably know something about the shape of the earth. Why do you think the earth is round?"

"I have many reasons for thinking so," replied Kennan, "but perhaps the best and strongest reason is that I have been around it."

The Lama looked shocked.

"How have you been around it? What do you mean by 'around it'? How do you know that you have been around it?"

"I turned my back upon my home," replied Kennan, "and travelled many months in the course taken by the sun. I crossed wide continents and great oceans. Every night the sun set before my face and every morning it rose behind my back. The earth always seemed flat, but I could not find anywhere an end nor an edge; and at last, when I had travelled more than thirty thousand versts, I found myself again in my own country and returned to my home from a direction exactly opposite to that which I had taken in leaving it. If the world was flat, do you think I could have done this?"

After a long conversation on the subject, the Lama gave a great sigh.

"It is not in accordance with the teachings of our books, but the Russians must be right."

ontinuing south from Selenginsk, the road reaches the border between Siberia and Mongolia. The way passes through desolate sandy regions, with stunted grass and occasional low hills covered with birches, larches or fir trees. Before long, the settlements that marked the border, Troitskosavsk, Kiakhta (Kyachta) and Maimachin came into view. The first two were Russian, and the latter Chinese; Mongolia remained a Chinese protectorate until the end of the First World War. Kiakhta and Maimachin sat on either side of the border, and were separated by a no-man's land of neutral territory, about 200 metres in width. The towns sat in a shallow valley on a tributary of the Selenga River, and in the distance above them could be seen the hazy blue mountains south towards Mongolia.

Kiakhta and Troitskosavsk did not appear at first sight to be particularly important or remarkable settlements. Their populations were perhaps no more than 5,000 each, and they each presented the usual appearance of a moderately well-to-do East Siberian town. There were streets with two-storey log huts, and a couple of Orthodox churches with white walls and gilded onion domes. However, entering either of them, it became immediately apparent that they were by no means ordinary. Strings of camels were led through the streets; Mongols and Chinese bustled about, unloading carts and organising the affairs of trade caravans; Mongolian and Chinese shops competed for custom in the town markets. All these were outward signs of the true significance of the settlements – through Kiakhta passed nearly the entire sum of Sino-Russian trade. Every year, tens of millions of roubles' worth of goods went in transit through the town. Aside from the great caravans of the more common brick tea, fine yellow teas were presented to the resident merchants, unpacked and sewn up in raw hides, before being transported via Irkutsk across Siberia to the great fair at Nizhny Novgorod. Silks, crapes and fine porcelain also made up

A tea store and bazaar in Kiakhta, on the Russian side of the border with Mongolia, at the turn of the 20th century.

part of the trade. Aside from animal furs, passing also in the opposite direction were deer horns and ginseng, all of importance to the Chinese medicine industry, and quantities of bullion in the form of Russian, English and American coins.

To pass over the border from Kiakhta to Maimachin (now known as Altanbulag) was to undergo a sudden and sharp cultural shock. Maimachin was maintained by the Chinese government as its trading and customs outpost on the border of its Mongolian protectorate, and was as thoroughly a Chinese town in its form and constitution as Kiakhta was Russian. Kennan recalled the abruptness of the change: "One

George Kennan arrived in the Mongolian border town of Maimachin to find Chinese influence much stronger than Russian.

moment you are in a Russian provincial village with its characteristic shops, log houses, golden-domed churches, droshkies, soldiers, and familiar peasant faces; the next moment you pass behind the high screen that conceals the entrance to the Mongolian town and find yourself apparently in the middle of the Chinese Empire." For many travellers, Maimachin was their very first encounter with China and Chinese culture. It would be the place they first saw Chinese streets, first ate Chinese food, and for the first time even saw goldfish. Consequently the town never failed to leave a deep impression.

The town stood within a square wooden palisade, about 400 metres long on each side. The four or five main streets were narrow, "just wide enough for a London omnibus," said Henry Lansdell. The houses, their walls made of straw and clay, presented grey and generally windowless walls to the outside world. The roofs, however, bore ornaments and wooden carvings, and curved upwards, as was characteristic, at the corners. The streets were generally kept clean, but nevertheless were thronged with traffic. Two-wheeled ox-carts loaded with boxes of tea were guided on their way by Mongol merchants, and lamas in orange robes rode in on horseback, wild-looking and sunburnt having arrived from the depths of the desert. In the streets there were hawkers selling all manner of everyday Chinese cottage-made household goods and trinkets. There were beads and hats, brushes and combs, cutlery and razors. Lansdell did not like the thought of shaving with the latter, which looked, he thought, like miniature hatchets. Others went around selling the paraphernalia of Buddhism, sacred vessels and perfumed rosaries. Men sat around on benches at crossroads, boiling kettles for tea on common fires, and exchanging gossip. Women, however, were never seen. It is not that they were kept indoors, but rather that the Chinese government would not allow them to reside in the town at all. Thus they hoped to concentrate the minds of their merchants on trade.

Lansdell, who visited in the 1880s, was invited into the house of a merchant. Like many other houses in the settlements of the Silk Road, it was based around a courtyard, the windows looking inwards, rather than out onto the street. The house was as much a place of business as of residence, and performed both functions not only for the merchant, but also for the two-dozen clerks who worked for him there. In one section of the house there ranged a long and elevated divan, where the clerks would sleep altogether, rising early, and rolling up their bedding and cushions into neat bundles for storage by day. The window frames were covered with paper. Small birds were kept, sitting on little perches. The walls within were hung with scrolls of Confucian sayings, and also paintings of Cai Shen, the Chinese God of Prosperity. "A very stout personage he looked," mused Lansdell, "strictly in keeping with Chinese notions, for they delight to load their deities with collops of fat, prosperity and abundance of flesh in their eyes having great affinity."

The clerks were nearly all dressed alike in suits of blue Nankin cloth and black skullcaps. Conical straw hats with horsehair tassels hung from the walls for use in summer. One of their number, however, was in a half-mourning outfit, which had to be worn for three years after the death of a relative (full mourning, requiring an entirely white suit not made of silk, lasted for 100 days). The half-mourning suit was black edged with white, and a small white ball was fastened to the top of the skullcap. The chief clerk was treated with especial deference. He grew a straggling moustache, and was permitted to grow his fingernails long, a sign of gentility and abstinence from manual work. All of them smoked slender pipes, which were so slim that they only allowed of five puffs. On seeing Lansdell and learning that he was English, they were overcome with curiosity. They swarmed about him seeking to know his affairs, turned over all of his possessions down to his pencils, and attempted to imitate his language and even his laughter.

Having made their acquaintance, Lansdell enquired after buying some souvenirs of his trip. Immediately, the clerks pulled open an endless stream of concealed drawers and cupboards, brimming with hidden merchandise. The house was like a larger version

Tea was transported by different means on its long journey to the West from China, depending on the terrain to be crossed – camel caravans were used for the dry desert regions, and horse carts for the rolling hill steppe.

of a Chinese box, full of secret compartments, keeping the goods hidden from the prying eyes of the taxman. The house brimmed with teas and cotton, silks, satins and furs. There were balls to play with in the palm of one's hand, crafted with jade that would flash with sparks of static electricity. There were gilt buttons which had reached the city from Birmingham. There was musk and little bags of perfume, crackers, fireworks and rockets. There were wooden lacquered bowls that could hold boiling water, or fine porcelain cups and saucers.

Travellers other than Lansdell were not so impressed by these items. The German ethnographer Adolf Erman, travelling 50 years before Lansdell, found himself being offered teacups painted with nude couples in "licentious" attitudes. Such porcelain, it appeared, was the preserve of the wealthy, and the prices of the items increased in proportion to their obscenity. Scroll paintings of similar subjects hung from the walls of many houses, and seemed to be of unbridled popularity. He could not but admire the fineness and delicacy of Chinese craftsmanship of some of the less indecent items he was offered. He saw nephrite spherical bowls, oval vases of chalcedony and agate. However, he was dismissive of their opulence. They were, he held, a "proof of luxury and profuse expenditure" indicating "enervation and an effeminacy of manners". Lansdell, it seems, was loath to agree, and was exceedingly contented with his eventual purchase: a pair of earmuffs, lined with Siberian fur.

Preparations for the journey across Mongolia to Peking usually began in Kiakhta. As with travel across Siberia, the modes of travel were various. Mongols in general would travel by camel, taking with them a tent for shelter. Usually, they would travel as light as possible. The Reverend James Gilmour, an English missionary who went to live amongst the Mongols in the 1880s to learn their language and immerse himself in their culture, left a check-list of the few items they were accustomed to take. "A spare sheep-skin coat for bedding; a few calf-skin bags (looking like the original calves themselves), with provisions; a small blue cloth tent, black with smoke and a good deal patched; a pot, a grate, two water buckets, and a few odd pieces of felt." Thus lightly encumbered, with strong camels and favourable weather, over 40 miles (64 kilometres) could be accomplished in a single day's march.

Travel on horseback was preferable to many Mongol travellers. The swaying motion of the camel exposed them to a feeling of seasickness, and the horse, aside from being much faster, was also more pleasant to ride. Nonetheless, horse travel was fraught with greater difficulty. The horse could not carry nearly so much as a camel, while the care that it required was greater. Unlike the camel, which could go for

great distances without water, eating nothing but the remnants of a few scratchy thorn bushes, a daily regard had to be given to feeding the horse. There were no inns at which to buy fodder on the way. Pasture in the neighbourhood of the tented Mongol settlements was always poor, trodden down by so much livestock. The horse had to be turned out at night to seek what it could. However, if it found any food in the heat of the day, it had to be held back from satisfying itself (horses which ate in the hot sun grew sores on their backs, according to Mongol horsemen). Usually, travellers on horseback would seek out and follow a camel caravan. Although they were constrained to move more slowly, they would travel away from settlements where there was plenty of good grass to be found, as well as the security of a convoy.

The poorest of the Mongol travellers would simply walk. The greatest number of these foot travellers were those on religious pilgrimage, or students heading towards monasteries and seats of Buddhist learning. Their expenses were slight, and they could beg most of what they needed from tents and temples on their

Portrait of a Mongolian man in traditional deel and fur cap.

way. However, they did not neglect to bring food and equipment for survival, even though it was of the simplest description, weighing no more than a few pounds. Gilmour saw many of these travellers in his time. Their gear in general was nothing more than a simple tent, a pot, a water bucket, a ladle, a piece of felt and a skin bag. With these accoutrements, they would travel for hundreds of miles, walking for up to four or five months. Their daily fare was millet seed boiled up in water, and if they were lucky they would be able to procure some cheese to throw into the mixture for added flavour. It was not unknown for a number of these travellers, despite their hardiness and determination, to suffer a breakdown through exhaustion and find themselves unable to go on. Such travellers would take themselves painfully to the nearest monastery or shrine, where it was regarded as a meritorious act for benefactors to pay their way, by horse or camel, back to their native place.

Well-to-do Chinese travellers, particularly merchants, would contract a Mongol Lama as their guide, and elect to travel in a Chinese cart. This was also the vehicle of choice for Russian and Western travellers as well. This was a large square wooden box that rode on two great wheels on an axle just below its back. It could be attached to the Russian post-horses that took the mail for most of the way between Kiakhta and Peking, or else more usually to camels. A Chinese cart had the advantage of not requiring much in the way of maintenance. Travellers only had to take a few items for the cart's upkeep: a jar of oil with a brush to apply to the wheels; an iron lantern with some candles for light at night; some paper to act as glass for the windows (this, of course, was frequently torn) and some wooden chocks to stop the wheels when the cart was untied from its camel. However, although it supplied some comfort, it was not of the most certain sort. In general, it was large enough for a traveller to recline, but not horizontally. Nonetheless, this was not the greatest problem. The great Russian explorer Colonel Nikolai Przhevalsky (also spelt Prjevalsky or Przewalski), who travelled all over Central Asia, China and Mongolia in the late 19th century, complained that "the shaking in this kind of car baffles description. The smallest stone or lump of earth over which one of the wheels may chance to roll produces a violent jolting of the whole vehicle and consequently of its unfortunate occupant. It may easily be imagined how his sufferings may be aggravated when travelling with post horses at a trot."

"No matter how smooth or level the road," complained another traveller, Julius Price, "the cart jolts about as vigorously as when it is passing over rocks, and the smallest pebble under the wheels will send a spasm through the whole vehicle like an electric shock. I felt if it went over smoothest asphalt road, it would be affected by geological substrata, and jolt accordingly."

William Athenry Whyte, an Englishman who chose to travel back overland to England from Hong Kong, discovered this property of the Chinese cart to his cost. On first obtaining his vehicle, he packed his belongings beautifully, hanging up his toiletries and necessaries from hooks that hung from the ceiling, and laid out his other possessions about him ready for the journey. Climbing in and reclining, the cart had scarcely covered any ground when he called for a halt. Such was the unforeseen juddering that the stony road had engendered, that everything about him, his rugs, pillows, brushes, books and candles, were all thrown together in a heap on top of him in the middle of the cart. His head was nearly broken by a large bag, and the vital bottle of sherry he kept by him lay on the floor, "broken into small atoms". The shakiness of the cart, after a couple more efforts at proceeding, caused Whyte to defect to the ranks of the foot traveller.

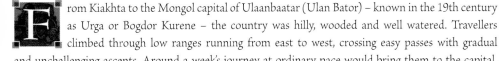

rom Kiakhta to the Mongol capital of Ulaanbaatar (Ulan Bator) – known in the 19th century as Urga or Bogdor Kurene – the country was hilly, wooded and well watered. Travellers climbed through low ranges running from east to west, crossing easy passes with gradual and unchallenging ascents. Around a week's journey at ordinary pace would bring them to the capital. It was a place that was revered by the Mongolian Buddhists. They regarded it as second only to Lhasa in Tibet for sanctity. It was the seat of the Kutukhtu of Urga, a reincarnated lama who was regarded by Tibetan (Lamaist) Buddhists as the third most senior in the faith behind the Dalai Lama and the Panchen Lama. The city boasted a temple with a massive 40-foot-high (12-metre) figure of a Buddha in painted bronze gilt. Its fluctuating population, which estimates in the late 19th century placed between 15,000 and 30,000, was principally composed of lamas. It also possessed one of the great schools for training the clergy, where they studied in the three faculties of Divinity, Medicine and Astrology. Grand processions of lamas to mark high days in the religious calendar were some of the most brilliant sights of the city, and the roads would be thronged with chanting monks in orange robes, people dressed in silk and opulent jewels, waving aloft banners, beating drums and holding up multicoloured umbrellas.

The city, however, was less pleasing to many of its foreign visitors. Urga, wrote Julius Price, the Special Artist of the *Illustrated London News*, who was travelling in the 1890s attached to a commercial expedition, made no pretentions to architectural beauty. Aside from a small Chinese administrative quarter, also confusingly called Maimachin, the city was made up of long and dreary rows of wooden palisades. Behind them were not wood or stone houses. Rather, such was the nomadic instinct of the Mongol people that they chose to live in yurts in these enclosures, rather than build anything more permanent. The streets, said Przhevalsky, were disgustingly dirty: "All the filth is thrown out into the streets, and the habits of the people are loathsome." Starving beggars thronged the thoroughfares and marketplace, and penniless old women, without homes or relations, would take up their abode in whatever nook or cranny they could find, waiting for charity or death. It was a sight that was to be seen no matter the season. In summer, they fainted in the heat, and in winter would be covered by snowdrifts. The ferocious dogs that stalked around the city devouring the waste and any scraps they could find, would seek out the dying. Gathering round, they would wait patiently for the poor soul to expire, at which they would devour the corpse, leaving a vacant space for other beggars in their turn.

To be devoured by dogs was not only the fate of the expired beggar. It was something that befell the living as well as the dead. The dogs, which looked to Price like larger and fiercer versions of the border collie, would hunt down old women in the streets and eat them up, or pull frail lamas from horseback to maul them. People feared to go out of their houses alone, especially at night, and were foolish to travel without a stout stick. The nighttimes were a cacophony of howling. However, the dogs were tolerated and maintained, as they performed a vital office of religion. Their duty to man was in the cemetery. Here, the dead bodies of all, as Przhevalsky wrote, "instead of being interred, are flung to the dogs and birds of prey. An awful impression is produced on the mind by such a place as this, littered with heaps of bones, through which packs of dogs prowl, like ghosts, to seek their daily repast of human flesh... No sooner is a fresh corpse thrown in than the dogs tear it to pieces, and in a couple of hours nothing remains of the dead man... The dogs are so accustomed to feed in this way that when a corpse is being carried through the streets of the town to the cemetery the relations of the deceased are invariably followed by dogs, sometimes belonging to his own encampment." Such a practice of burial was a normal part of Tibetan Buddhism, and one of the public manifestations of the doctrine. It was thought a good sign if the body was quickly devoured, indicating that the departed had lived a pious life.

Other signs of piety were certainly not lacking. Prayer flags and rags fluttered throughout the city streets and from poles surrounding the yurts in their encampments. Under wooden canopies like little barns on the roads and street corners were large prayer wheels, which one would spin about at will by hand. Price was somewhat flummoxed at the sight of what appeared to be diving boards fixed at ankle height in various public places throughout the city. These were in fact prayer boards, on which people would lie prostrate to pray or contemplate. Even when he discovered their true function, he could not get the first association out of his head. The whole action of a person using them, he confessed, seemed to him more like someone "preparing to make a run along the board and take a 'header' rather than a prelude to a devotional exercise". People, however, did not always depend on the use of the prayer boards for their orisons. People would throw themselves down unexpectedly in the street for the sake of prayer as the fit took them, and many was the time that Price had to swerve on his horse so as to avoid trampling a devout worshipper.

he character of the land changes beyond Ulaanbaatar. Crossing the Tola (Tuul) River, the little hills ebb away into nothing, and the streams that water the country disappear. For over 100 miles (161 kilometres) southwest, the caravan road transects a band of steppe. The soil is of clay and sand, and frequent nomad settlements exploit the rich grass which the territory supports. Beyond this point, there is a further change: the clay begins to disappear, and the steppe gives way almost imperceptibly to the sterile plains of the Gobi Desert. The landscape is intersected by the traces of dry watercourses, full for only a few hours after the infrequent heavy rains. The earth turns to a coarse reddish gravel sometimes covered by a shifting drift of yellow sand, and shines with the occasional small pebble of agate. Coarse grass, no more than a foot high and tough as wire, clings to the occasional fertile patch where moisture has persisted since the rains, as does budarhana (a small, hardy shrub), one of the desert staples of the camel, the wild onion, and scrub wormwood. The population is similarly thin, and for the 250 miles (400 kilometres) from the end of the steppe to the borders of China, few Mongol encampments were met by the traveller.

The journey along the desert caravan route in general presented little variety. Although the actual course taken by travellers towards China was never unchanging, as the caravans had to adapt the road every year to wherever there might be fresh vegetation or recharged wells, the voyage rarely presented much in the way of incident. Julius Price gave a summary of the daily route. Camp would be struck at sunrise. Although the dawn was barely visible as a red streak on the flat horizon, the leaders would wake the rest of the party, and in a few minutes everything would become a great bustle of activity. Preparations were immediately made, everything was packed, and the animals harnessed in little more than an instant. No time was set aside for breakfast, "and, although I would often have given anything for a cup of hot coffee or Bouillon Fleet before starting," said Price, "I did not like to disarrange the evidently invariable custom of making an early start..."

There passed many "dreary, weary hours" before the first stop was made. This usually took place at noon, and was, "after eight hours jolting a veritable oasis in the discomfort of the day". The tents were shortly pitched, the camels turned loose to rest and scratch about for fodder, and for the company there was a chance to take breakfast. For Price, this consisted of a "bite of biscuit, perhaps some preserved icy-cold tinned meat, washed down by a limited quantity of stale water sucked through a pocket filter". Such water was found at wells, for which the leaders aimed at the end of each stage of the journey, or else could be dug up at the bottom of the dry watercourses. In some cases, "in appearance and consistency it had the cut between chocolate and coffee and milk", clogging up the filter and compelling Price not so much to drink it as eat it. "It was a breakfast so complete in its discomfort as to require the very keenest appetite to do justice to it," said Price, yet such an appetite he possessed, for "the air of the desert acted on one like the strongest tonic".

The halt lasted for around 2.5 hours. After this, the procedure was repeated. The tents were struck, the camels recalled, and the road rejoined. The distance between daily halts varied from 15 to 30 miles

Harriet Chalmers Adams, an intrepid early 20th century traveller, poses with a camel in the Gobi Desert.

(25–50 kilometres) depending on the conditions, but the camels would keep a constant speed of around three miles per hour. The monotony of the journey meant that the smallest incident was magnified to the greatest proportions. A meeting with another traveller or the sight of a post convoy was an occasion for great rejoicing. The camels would be pulled up, the vodka produced, the travellers would embrace, drink toasts and exchange whatever news they had of the way.

The heavy stretches of unbroken time and tedium encouraged many to brood on the smallest irritations. Price began to grow enraged at his camel. "Till I went to Mongolia I had always thought that the camel was the most patient and docile of animals. I soon, however, saw that for absolute bad temper and stubbornness he has not his equal anywhere; and, as added to these gentle traits of character, nature has also provided him with a unique and disgusting means of defence, in the form of a power to spit, or rather eject, almost on the slightest provocation, a mass of undigested food, at anyone who may be unlucky enough to incur his displeasure..." Such heavy and hypnotic brooding on the constant sight of the camel also afflicted Alexander Michie, who travelled the same route in the 1860s, complaining bitterly at "...the unpleasant nearness to the odour which exudes from the pores of a camel's hide, to which it requires long apprenticeship to get accustomed. [It is] Most uninteresting besides to sit for an hour or two contemplating the ungainly form of the ugliest of all created things, and to watch his soft spongy foot spreading itself out on the sand, while you reckon that each of these four feet must move 700,000 times before your journey is accomplished."

Przhevalsky suffered a similar fixation with the desert crows. With nothing else to distract his attention in the desert, they won his personal and bitter enmity. Soon after starting, he noticed that they would pursue the baggage camels that followed his cart, and having perched on them, fly away with something in their beaks. On inspection, he found that they had torn open the provision bags, and were stealing their rusks (hard, dry biscuits ideal for lengthy travel). After hiding one load in a secret place on the side of the road, they would fly back and return for more. "The rapacity of the crow in Mongolia surpasses belief," complained Przhevalsky. "These birds, so shy with us, are there so impudent as to steal provisions almost out of the tents of the Mongols. Nay, they will actually perch on the backs of the grazing camels, and tear their humps with their beaks. The foolish, timid animal only cries at the top of its voice, and spits at its tormentor, who returns again and again to the back of the camel until it has inflicted a large wound by means of its powerful beak..." Shooting the birds, which distressed the Mongol guides, was of little avail. Others immediately came to fill their place, and Przhevalsky's expedition, like all other caravans, was followed across the desert by a flock of voracious crows and predatory kites.

The expanse of the desert would always play its customary tricks on the minds of the travellers. Mirages were a common affliction. For Whyte, they were a frequent occurrence. The most powerful he saw was a large blue lake in the midst of the desert, surrounded by mountains covered by trees. On its banks were small hills, surmounted by ruined castles. Another time, he saw a sea before him, its surface as still as glass, but pierced by an archipelago of little islands. As he advanced towards them, the sights receded, and would vanish altogether towards dusk. Strangely, Whyte welcomed these apparitions as a pleasant relief from the desperate monotony of the desert landscape. Objects far away seemed magnified. A man on a camel might seem like a hill, and a dog like a gigantic animal. The judgement of distances similarly grew deceptive, and impossible to calculate. One might enter a little plain that appeared at first sight just ten miles long, bounded by a slight incline in the ground. However, after a full day's journey the same landmark seemed just as far, or even farther away, than when one started. The wind and sand, acting together, also made themselves enemies to the traveller. The northeast wind was accounted the most terrible, and was of a freezing power, especially in winter. Lamas, experienced in travel through the desert, could predict the onset of certain winds by the curious appearance of three suns in the sky. The gales that followed these portents could rise to an incredible force. In the face of them, the camels were unable to stand, and whirlwinds of stones were sucked up. The desert sand penetrated the whole equipage of the traveller, and choked up eyes, mouths and food alike.

At the end of a day's march, the traveller might be lucky enough to find a Mongol encampment. A number were maintained to act as makeshift post stations for the Russian mail service between Kiakhta and the Chinese frontier, but they were as likely to be clustered round a religious shrine, or else simply the property of wandering pastoralists looking for fodder. Gilmour describes the pleasure of the sight after many long and indistinguishable days of travel. The yurts in the daytime seemed to shine from afar. Nearby, there might be a flock of sheep grazing on an incline, or ox-carts, the oxen unbound, browsing on a patch of tough grass. The luxury of finding a yurt, along with its attendant supply of fresh food and milk, and the joy of stretching out on a comfortable and spacious bed, along with different company and a modicum of mental stimulation, was a pleasure that few travellers were willing to pass by.

A hospitable welcome was all but guaranteed, if the visitor should observe a few simple rules of etiquette. "The Mongols," says Gilmour, "are the first to forgive people ignorant of their ways, yet it is better to know some of the more important customs to be observed." The first of these is that a yurt must always be approached from the front. If one approaches from a way off one should ride around it at a distance, so as to make the nearer approach directly opposite the door. The rule holds equally strong for travellers on foot, who also should not go near the tents without carrying two strong sticks or a whip.

On drawing close, the traveller should shout *"nohoi"* (dog). At, or even before this point, the savage dogs who guard the encampment, like those in the city, will rush out to challenge the traveller. Close behind them come the women and children of the yurt, whose duty it is to restrain them. They do so by scolding the tamer ones, and sitting on top of the more ferocious. Until the dogs have thus been put under control, the traveller on horseback does not dismount, and the traveller on foot does his best to hold them back by thrashing them with the whip, or using the sticks: "One long one in the left hand to keep the dogs at bay, a shorter and stronger one in the right hand to drop on Towser's nose if he venture too near," wrote John Hedley, another English traveller who followed in the footsteps of Gilmour. When they have been quieted, the traveller seizes his moment, and rushes into the yurt. However, he should be careful to deposit his sticks or his whip at the door. To take them into the tent is regarded as a grave insult. Bearing them, the traveller conducts himself as if he had come inside the tent to beat the inhabitants in the same way as the dogs.

n entering and taking his allotted seat – one should sit cross-legged, or with the feet pointing towards the door – the first ritual is an interchange of snuff. Mongol travellers would all carry small bottles, and allow the other to take a sniff from them as a sign of friendship. Even if the foreign visitor did not possess one, the Mongol would still make the offer. "The bottle should be received in the palm of the right hand, carried deferentially towards the nose, the stopper should be raised a little, then a sniff, the stopper may be readjusted, and the bottle handed slowly and deferentially back to its owner." All the while, the host and guest would make the normal complimentary enquiries after each other's state. They would not usually ask first after each other's health, but rather after the health of the animals. "How are your cattle?" might be the first query, followed by more detailed questions such as "in whose care did you leave your cattle before leaving on such a long journey," or "what was the weight of the *kurdiuk* (fat tail) on each of your sheep?" Such questions could pose problems for Western travellers whose wealth did not consist of such items, and the Mongol hosts would often react incredulously when travellers of such apparent prosperity did not even lay claim to ownership of a single camel back at home. Whilst these misunderstandings were being negotiated, the women of the yurt would lay out tea and dishes of food, and pipes of tobacco might even be produced as an enhanced sign of goodwill.

For many travellers, the yurts were cosy and welcoming, particularly in winter. Their size varied, often being between 12 and 15 feet (4–5 metres) in diameter and 10 feet high, allowing for a balance of roominess and intimacy. At the back of the tent were placed the Buddhist idols, and near them the household goods, bows and arrows, and flintlock guns for hunting. The walls were double-lined with felt, as were the floors, and in some cases, where the proprietors were well off, there would be silk or cotton also on the walls, and carpets to soften the floor. However, there were many aspects of yurt life that could be especially trying for the visitor. The most immediate of these was the method of heating. In the middle of the tent was placed the hearth, ventilated by a metre-wide hole in the middle of the roof. Here, a perpetual fire was kept burning, fed by the only fuel of which there was a steady supply in the wilderness: *argols*, or dried animal dung. It had the merit of lighting easily and giving off much heat, but its smoke was blinding. Its particular odour asides, it was probably responsible for the high level of eye complaints that were found among the yurt dwellers, and the travellers, not at all used to its fumes, found it difficult to bear for any length of time.

If the traveller could grow accustomed to the smoke, it was not long before he became troubled by a more general problem: the endemic lack of hygiene in the Mongol way of life. It is a characteristic that was observed by travellers throughout the history of exploration, and was remarkably unchanging through the generations. In 1253, William of Rubruck, a Franciscan missionary-explorer under orders from Louis IX to convert the "Tartars", travelled to the Mongol capital of Karakorum, around 150 miles (241 kilometres) southwest of Ulaanbaatar, and observed of the Mongols in their yurts that they never washed their clothes. In fact, washing was under some sort of religious taboo. They believed that it not only made the gods angry, but also that washing one's clothes and hanging them out to dry would bring about terrible storms and cataclysmic flooding. Anyone who did wash was beaten, and their clothes were taken from them as a further punishment.

Over 600 years later, the habits had not changed. "The first thing that strikes the traveller in the life of the Mongol," wrote Przhevalsky, "is his excessive dirtiness: he never washes his body, and very seldom his face and hands. Owing to constant dirt, his clothing swarms with parasites, which he amuses himself by killing in the most unceremonious way. It is a common sight to see a Mongol, even an official or lama of high rank, in the midst of a large circle of his acquaintances, open his sheepskin or kaftan to catch an offending insect and execute him on the spot between his front teeth."

Another 13th century European ambassador to the Mongol count, John da Plano Carpini (Giovanni da Pian del Carpine), complained that the Mongols were "unmannerly and uncleanly in taking meat, and drink". Przhevalsky, in the late 19th century, concurred. Of the tea, the first thing to be offered to a guest in a yurt aside from snuff, he wrote that its "mode of preparation is disgusting; the vessel in which the tea is boiled is never cleansed, and is occasionally scrubbed with *argols*", the dried animal dung. The brick tea itself, which was often rock hard, had to be softened, and in order to do this it was placed for several minutes in the dung fire itself, which imparted "a flavour and aroma to the whole beverage", as Przhevalsky nicely put it. They would always eat with their fingers, he went on, "which are always disgustingly dirty; raising a large piece of meat and seizing it in their teeth, they cut off with a knife close to the mouth, the portion remaining in their hand. The bones are licked clean, and sometimes cracked for the sake of the marrow; the shoulder-blade of mutton is always broken and thrown aside, it being considered unlucky to leave it unbroken." The gluttony of the people was also conspicuous. A single person might consume an entire sheep in the space of 24 hours. Yet, such was their hardiness that they could go without food for long periods of time without problem. Even if they should fast for a day or two, commented Carpini, they would still "sing and be as merry as if their bellies were full".

Between the visits of the 13th century ambassadors and the 19th century explorers, the whole palette of the Mongols did not seem to have changed in the slightest. Rubruck was entertained with sodden millet, roasted mutton and broth, and it was the same for Przhevalsky. The millet would be placed in a cup of tea, and, as a relish, butter or raw fat from a sheep's tail would be added. "The reader may now imagine what a revolting compound of nastiness is produced, and yet they consume any quantity of it! Ten to fifteen large cupfuls is the daily allowance for a girl, but full-grown men take twice as much." The diet of meat and millet was enhanced by milk from the herds, cheese, curds, whey and *kumiss*, or fermented mare's milk, in which "they are all inclined to indulge too freely, although drunkenness is not so rife among them as it is in some more civilised countries". Of the kumiss itself, Rubruck had mixed feelings. "It leaves behind a taste of almond milk, and intoxicates weak brains. It also causes urine to be voided in great measure."

In general, there was an equal ambivalence about the lifestyle and character of the nomadic Mongols. Their knowledge of the land was astonishing, and their ability to find directions in a barren landscape devoid of any landmark, judge distances and forecast weather seemed to every traveller amazing. They thrived on the hardness of nomadic life. They could travel for days throughout the winter on horseback, accompanying the tea caravans, with the temperature at least -20 degrees Fahrenheit, and a bitter wind blowing in their faces. Some made the journey from China to Kiakhta four times during the winter, travelling over 3,000 miles. Their health not only endured but flourished in these conditions, despite the limited diet and the uncleanliness, and many would still be seen out riding and herding well into an advanced age.

Yet, visitors were troubled by their apparent sloth. "Their whole lives are passed in holiday making," wrote Przhevalsky, "which harmonises with their pastoral pursuits. Their cattle are their only care, and even they do not cause them much trouble. The camels and horses graze on the steppe without any watch, only requiring to be watered once a day in summer at the neighbouring well." As a result, observed Hedley, "he revels in such luxury as suits his environment. He smokes, he drinks whisky, and likes a lot of it; he gambles; he talks; he idles round all day and every day, and only wakes up when the hunting falls due, and then he spends three days each month chasing terrified hares across the plains, or trying to bring them down with his matchlock." The hard work was taken up by the women, who were responsible for the everyday tasks of milking the animals, churning the butter and preparing the meals. It was rare that they would take to anything beyond the normal realm of their habits. So accustomed were the men to riding, even using a horse to go from yurt to yurt within an encampment, they would be tired out after attempting to walk a few hundred yards.

Nonetheless, the liberality, openness and hospitality of the nomad Mongols seemed to win over many travellers. William Athenry Whyte, a traveller outspoken in many matters, is one of the most eloquent in their defence. When entering their yurts, he found a hearty welcome, was seated in the best place, and everything that they had would be shared unstintingly. "It is quite refreshing," he wrote, "after the falseness and absurdities of what is called polite society to find oneself thrown amongst a barbarian people. I believe in true manners and real innocence and kindness the latter are immeasurably superior to the former. I know that I benefited much by my intercourse with the Mongols. They opened my mind to the fact that after all our system is very imperfect. I would not for a moment say in all cases that civilisation is not better than what is falsely called barbarism, but I most unhesitatingly do aver that these people are better as they are, and would shame, even by their rude breeding, many polite people who consider themselves highly bred."

The spiritual dividing line between China and Mongolia could be said to lie along the Great Wall of China. Its original was built in the third century BCE by the Emperor Qin Shi Huangdi, famous for unifying and reforming China. He intended that the Wall should stand as a bulwark to protect his kingdom from the attacks of the Xiongnu, the nomadic warrior horsemen who then were the power in Mongolia. Although the wall was rarely able to fulfil its defensive function, and northern China was prey to the steppe nomads from the Xiongnu in the third century BCE to the Mongols and Genghis Khan in the 13th century CE, the wall still provided a function of identity. North of it, life was pastoral and nomadic. Fixed settlements were rare, and held in contempt. It was similarly the case for agriculture. Cultivated fields were never to be seen. The wealth of man consisted in his animals, and from animals came his food. It was a land of milk and meat.

outh of the Wall, it was a different matter. Here was a land of settlement, of agriculture, of industry and tillage. Animals were not a staple, but people rather depended on their plots and farmsteads, and what they could bring out of the ground. With settlement and the division of land there came the need for powerful governments and great cities. The carefree life of desert and steppe gave way in the settled lands to the daily round of toil and regulation.

As the travellers from Siberia to Peking neared the Great Wall, they became more and more aware of this grand contrast in ways of life. As they picked their way southwards through the desert, vegetation began to appear. Before long, rolling grasslands and prairies took the place of the stony gravel and sands of the desert. About 60 miles (96 kilometres) before reaching the Great Wall, villages inhabited by Chinese farmers began to appear. It was the first sight of bricks and mortar that many travellers had had for weeks. Around the settlements plantations and fields were laid out, in which industrious Chinese peasants would labour all day. The distinction between these border regions and the empty desert was already striking. The traffic on the road grew busier. The fields and the land seethed with inhabitants. "...I saw everywhere such crowds of people and children that I could not help wondering where they all managed to live in the place..." comments Price.

Before long, the geographical boundary which distinguished Mongolia and China came into view. The road began to pick its way down from the edge of the Mongolian Plateau, around 4,000 feet (1,200 metres) in height, and slowly descend through ranges of hills and valleys, circling and winding beneath sheer granite cliffs. On every available space, even on precarious ledges high up on the rock faces, the Chinese farmers had built huts, laid out terraces for growing vegetables, and made the land fit for cultivation. Travellers like Price watched astonished as they saw the "blue-coated inhabitants" of these places, moving between tiny houses, "dotted here and there like dolls".

The travellers finally encountered the Great Wall at the frontier town of Kalgan (modern-day Zhangjiakou). In reality, the Great Wall stood in two ranks. That at Kalgan was built first in the third century BCE. The second rank stood further back, and was crossed a little later by travellers at the Nankaou Pass. At the sight of it, many were moved by the sense of antiquity and its achievement. Although thinking it a white elephant, Przhevalsky was moved to apostrophise: "What could have been the object of this gigantic work? How many millions of human hands must have laboured at it!" Others, however, felt an inexplicable sense of disappointment. "I scarce know why," said William Athenry Whyte, "I do not think, except to say that one has been close to it, that it repays even a climb up the hills to see it." It is perhaps that the travellers might have expected something grander. At first sight, wrote Price, the Great Wall at Kalgan "looks... more like an Irish stone fence than anything else. I could hardly realize, on first being shown it from the valley, that this almost shapeless mass of rubble, looking not unlike some huge fossilized serpent, winding away over the tops even of the highest mountains, had been raised as a serious defence of the empire in bygone days... I found I could sit astride it at the top, so it is not very wide."

t was the sight of the Great Wall from a distance that often proved overwhelming for travellers. Although Whyte, when close by, was dismissive, from far off he was moved to almost a state of religious rapture. "Never had I seen such a sight," he said, "the ranges of hills, the snow clad mountains like confused waves tossing in the distance. I could trace the Great Wall extending its span over the mountain tops, and see various towers solitary in ruins." Over the hills were shades of deep purple, the colours changing and ever bewildering in their variety. Deeply he felt its grandeur of the landscape "so rugged and variegated... remembering that all these wonders were made for man."

Travellers were often keen to move on from Kalgan. Although the place was full of interest, the town, with its low-built houses and booths presenting the impression of being "in some immense fair," was indescribably dirty. The streets were near impassable, not only through being "fearfully badly paved," but also such was the throng of people that it was almost impossible to move. As quickly as possible, they would make preparations to move on. Western travellers would cash letters of credit with the Russian tea merchants who lived in a settlement just outside Kalgan, beyond the wall. They would also exchange their Mongolian currency – brick tea – for silver Chinese coinage. (In Mongolia, brick tea was the only generally accepted means of exchange, and despite Russian attempts to make banknotes to represent it, the genuine article had to be carried by travellers. Each brick was 16 x 8 x 1½ inches in size, and was reckoned to be worth around 60 kopeks, or 1s 6d sterling. It would only be made into a drink once it was too chipped to continue in circulation.)

The Chinese cart would also be abandoned, and travellers to Peking would substitute it for a mule litter, rather like a sedan chair but lashed between two mules. "This is not only a novel conveyance to the average European, but owing to its subtle peculiarities affords also a continuous vein of excitement, which is a great change after the monotony of the bumping and shaking of a camel-cart," wrote Price. The excitement he refers to includes the mules, without being led by any driver, being allowed to pick their own way over the "frailest of bridges" or yawning precipices. Only a boy would walk ahead, guiding the animals with an occasional command. The journey, aside from these hair-raising moments, was usually much more pleasant than a Chinese cart, but not always: "If the mules behave themselves and don't walk in step, the motion is simply delightful; but this state of beatitude is unfortunately the exception, and the bad qualities of the mule seem to develop themselves to an exasperating degree as soon as the animals find themselves attached to one of these litters."

Passing along the road, the population grew denser and denser. "Village followed village so closely at times as to give the road the appearance of passing through an immense street, whilst everywhere was the same teeming population of

A modern view of the Great Wall in Inner Mongolia – many sections of the Wall have been reconstructed after centuries of disuse.

blue-coated Celestials." The walls and battlements of great towns loomed up against the sky. Often, by the 19th century, they were little more than dilapidated ruins inside, but earlier travellers give a better picture of how they used to be in their heyday. The Russian Cossack Ivan Petlin, travelling as an ambassador from Moscow to China in 1618, gives a description of what was to be found in the towns on the road to Peking. "The trade is so great in all kinds of goods, that of a morning you can hardly force a way beyond the crowd... The shops are of stone painted in all colours, and the shutters painted in the same colours; and all kinds of goods are there, save only cloth; nor are there any precious stones; but velvets and damasks, *doroghi* (striped silk stuffs) and taffetas, and silk on gold and with copper in plenty. And there were all kinds of flowers and different kinds of sugar, cloves and cinnamon, and anise, and apples, and melons, and water-melons, and pumpkins, and cucumbers, and garlic, and radishes, and onions, and turnips, and cabbages, and parsnips, and horse-radish, and poppy, and Muscat, almond kernels, rhubarb, and other fruit and vegetables as we know not. And there was a shop-row in the town with all sorts of wares, and eating houses with food, and drink-shops, and in there all kinds of drinks, and many drunkards and prostitutes in the drink shops, and stone prisons stand in plenty."

Soon, the road came to the Nankaou Pass, where the second line of the Great Wall stood. This branch of it was erected during the Ming Dynasty in the 17th century, and consequently was better built, and in much better condition than the earlier branch at Kalgan. It is this photogenic stretch of the Wall with which the world is familiar today, and certainly it was then a monument that could bring travellers to a halt in a stupor of amazement. "Some time before reaching it," wrote Price, "I could distinguish the mighty structure standing out in bold relief against the sky, where in places it actually crossed the very tops of the highest mountains. I had fully prepared myself for something wonderful, but this marvellous work more than realised my expectation, and fairly held me spellbound for a few minutes... What struck me about it was its wonderful state of preservation, the symmetrically hewn stones of which it is composed showing but few signs of the ravages of time. I persuaded Nicolaieff to halt the caravan long enough for me to make a rough sketch; but it is too overpowering and colossal for an ordinary pencil to be able to do justice to."

Little more than a day's journey beyond this, there was a monument of equal grandeur, and the final object of all the long journey. The city of Peking came in sight.

THE SILK ROAD

PEKING

The histories of Peking and Moscow bear strange and similar echoes. Although now both great capitals boasting centuries of rich history, they are in fact relative newcomers to the recent world stage. Neither can lay claim to any great significance in the ancient past of their respective countries. Moscow, before the 13th century, was probably no more than a village. Peking, although at various times a metropolis of some importance, was equally often under the rule of the northern barbarians, and did not obtain a consistent position of authority until the Liao Dynasty of the 10th century CE. It could not claim, like the ancient capitals of Xi'an or Luoyang further west, to be an original cradle of early Chinese civilisation. Nor was it a place that could be said to be a part of the classical Silk Road; again, if a thing as nebulous as the Silk Road could be said to have had an eastern terminus, Chang'an (Xi'an) or Luoyang have a better claim to that honour.

Like Moscow, Peking owes its enduring prominence to the irruption of the Mongol invaders. Moscow gained its position by becoming an agent for the Mongol Golden Horde, ruthlessly gathering tribute from the other Russian princedoms on their behalf and sending it to their capital of Sarai on the Volga River north of the Caspian Sea. Peking, however, under the Mongols became itself a great capital. It was first attacked by them in 1215, but with their longer term conquest of China in 1260, it became the seat of the Mongol Yuan Dynasty. It was then, in both importance and in fame, that Peking was able to outstrip the more ancient cities of China. Enlarged and beautified by the Emperor Kublai Khan, it was named Khanbalik (the Lord's City) or Dadu (the Great Metropolis). Turning into a centre of government, diplomacy and trade, it became a magnet for travellers from every corner of the world. Ambassadors and merchants resorted there not just from the countries bordering China, but from as far afield as the Middle East and Europe. Visitors began to leave accounts of the great wonders of the city, and the magnificence of its Khans. The most famous of these visitors, a contemporary of Kublai Khan, was none other than Marco Polo.

The controversy over Marco Polo, and whether he actually made any of the journeys recounted in his narrative, has never, and perhaps will never be resolved. However, whether or not he himself actually went any further east than the Black Sea coast, the description of Peking under Mongol rule left in his name not only tallies with his contemporaries in many details, but is perhaps the richest available for

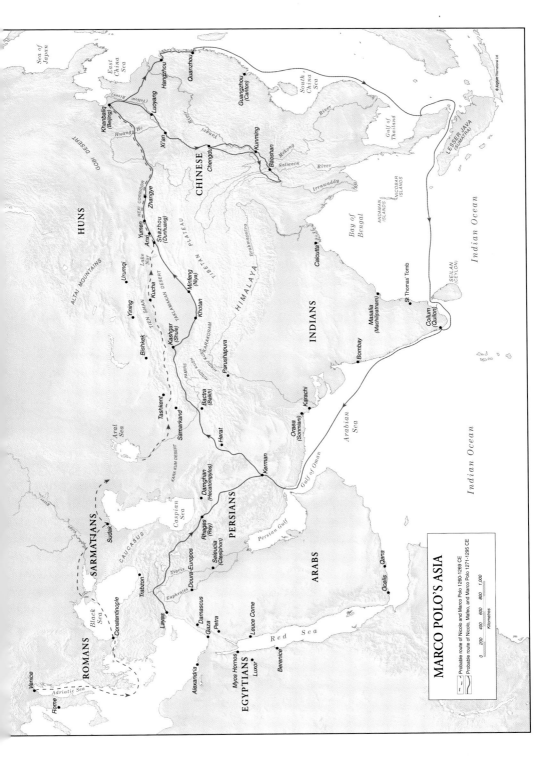

MARCO POLO'S ASIA

Probable route of Nicolo and Marco Polo 1260-1269 CE
Probable route of Nicolo, Matteo, and Marco Polo 1271-1295 CE

0 200 400 600 800 1,000
Kilometres

Sea of Japan

East China Sea

South China Sea

Gulf of Thailand

LESSER JAVA (SUMATRA)

Indian Ocean

Bay of Bengal

ANDAMAN ISLANDS

NICOBAR ISLANDS

SEILAN (CEYLON)

Arabian Sea

Gulf of Oman

Persian Gulf

Red Sea

Caspian Sea

Aral Sea

Black Sea

Adriatic Sea

Sea of Azov

GOBI DESERT

HUNS

ALTAI MOUNTAINS

TIEN SHAN

TAKLAMAKAN DESERT

HEXI CORRIDOR

CHINESE

TIBETAN PLATEAU

HIMALAYA

KARAKORAM

HINDU KUSH

PAMIRS

KARA KUM DESERT

CAUCASUS

SARMATIANS

ROMANS

PERSIANS

ARABS

EGYPTIANS

INDIANS

Khanbaliq (Beijing)
Luoyang
Hangzhou
Quanzhou
Guangzhou (Canton)
Xian
Chengdu
Kunming
Baoshan
Yumen
Anxi
Zhangye
Shazhou (Dunhuang)
Minfeng (Niya)
Khotan
Kucha
Urumqi
Yining
Bishkek
Kashgar (Shule)
Tashkent
Samarkand
Bactra (Balkh)
Herat
Purushapura
Karachi
Oraea (Sonmiani)
Kerman
Damghan (Hecatompylos)
Rhages (Rey)
Seleucia (Ctesiphon)
Doura-Europos
Sudak
Trabzon
Constantinople
Layas
Damascus
Gaza
Petra
Leuce Come
Alexandria
Myos Hormos
Luxor
Berenice
Qana
Ocelis
Bombay
Masalia (Machilipatnam)
St Thomas Tomb
Collum (Quilon)
Calcutta
Venice
Rome

Huang He
Yangtze
Mekong
Salween
Irrawaddy
Brahmaputra
Indus
Tigris
Euphrates
Lake Nur

Indian Ocean

colour and excitement. Much of the city he described was not long to survive the Mongols, and was demolished and rebuilt by subsequent dynasties. The account of Marco Polo, whatever its provenance, is the most vivid traveller's account we possess of an incarnation of the city which has long disappeared.

One of the sights of the Mongol city that was destroyed by the Ming Dynasty was the original palace of Kublai Khan. Marco Polo gives us a description not only of the buildings, but also of the life that was led there. The palace, he writes, "was the largest that was ever seen". It stood in the middle of square walls, a mile in length, ten yards high, battlemented and whitewashed. In the corners and on the sides of the square were smaller palaces, each of which served to store munitions. In one would be found the arms of Kublai's archers, bows and arrows, in another would be horse gear, saddles, bridles and stirrups, and so on, all the way round the walls. The great palace in the centre was also square, approached by great marble staircases that rose to a terrace like a ziggurat, affording entry to the building.

Inside, all was opulence on an unimaginable scale. The walls were covered with gold and silver, pictures of dragons and birds, horsemen and scenes of battle. The ceiling was similarly covered, so that no matter where one looked, there was "nothing to be seen anywhere but gold and pictures". The roof was a kaleidoscope of colours, scarlet and green, blue and yellow, and "so brilliantly varnished that it glitters like crystal and the sparkle of it can be seen from far away".

Another traveller, the Franciscan missionary Friar Odoric who visited the palace in the 1320s, confirmed this vision of magnificence. The walls were hung with "red skins, which are said to be the most costly in all the world". There were fourteen columns of gold, and also golden mechanical peacocks dotted through the palace that would spread their wings and fan out their tails, making as if to dance should someone clap their hands. Yet, it was not in any way a display of wealth without taste. "The whole building," says Marco Polo, "is at once so impressive and so well constructed that no man in the world, granted that he had the power to effect it, could imagine any improvement in design or execution... And [the] roof is so strong and so stoutly built as to last for many a long year."

The great hall in the midst of it was the scene for lavish banquets, made to mark various festivals throughout the calendar. The Khan sat on a high table, next to his "principal wife", sons and kinsmen, all seated in strict order of precedence. Some of the ranks of noblemen also ate at tables ranged below the Khan, but many of them sat to take their meals on carpets. The hall, says Marco Polo, had a capacity of 6,000, and outside there might be as many as 40,000 seated on carpets to join in the feast. Not only were there Chinese courtiers who held high office and sought further advancement, but "many visitors with costly gifts, men who have come from strange countries bringing strange things". In the centre of the hall, both Marco Polo and Friar Odoric both commented on a remarkable piece of furniture: a sort of drinks dispenser made out of jade and wreathed around with gold. At each corner was the image of a serpent "furiously shaking and casting forth his head". It was divided into sections, each with the capacity of a firkin (an ancient unit of volume equal to approximately 11 gallons or 41 litres). One section dispensed wine, another mares' milk, and another camels' milk. Huge stoups of gold were filled with these drinks, "enough to satisfy eight or ten men", but each was just shared between two.

Michie F.A. Fraser, of the British Legation at Pekin [sic], visited the Temple of Heaven and was hugely impressed with the symmetry of the Round Altar, as reported in The Illustrated London News, February 1873.

Round the hall "barons" acquainted with court etiquette would pass, showing the visitors, unfamiliar with the ways of the court, how to behave. They would also act as waiters, asking if the guests lacked anything, or if they wanted any more wine or milk to drink. Friar Odoric describes theatrical players, jesters and musicians who were enjoined to provide entertainment. At the doors stood two men of gigantic stature, who were charged with enforcing a strange rule. They clutched wooden staves in their hands, and would beat, or else tear off the clothes of anyone who should touch the threshold of the door. Although this was enshrined as a great point of court procedure, it harked back to the Mongols' life in the desert, where standing on the threshold of a *ger* (yurt) was taboo and thought to bring bad luck. Yet, the rule was not on every occasion so strictly enforced. "In leaving the hall, since some of the guests are overcome with drinking so that they could not possibly exercise due care, no such rule is enjoined." Thus was demonstrated the enlightened rule of the Mongols.

"Everything is arranged for [Kublai Khan's] comfort and convenience…" wrote Marco Polo. Within the palace, beyond the great hall, there were his private apartments where were stored his treasures, his gold and silver, pearls and precious stones. His harem of ladies and concubines were also there. "Outsiders are not admitted," lamented Marco Polo, but it was known that the competition to join the harem was fierce, with the criteria including virginity, clean breath, and not snoring.

Outside, there was a pleasant park with stately trees, grassland and raised paths. Game, such as white harts, musk deer, roebuck, stags and squirrels, were kept for the Khan to hunt at his pleasure,

A drawing of the Hall of Prayer for a Good Harvest, published in The Illustrated London News *in 1873. Today this is one of Beijing's main tourist attractions.*

and the ponds, fed by running streams, were rich with fish, swans and waterfowl. On the northern side, there stood a great mound of earth, "100 paces" in height and a mile in circumference, on which grew a dense forest of trees, all evergreen. If he heard of a particularly fine tree anywhere else in his domains, Kublai would, according to Marco Polo, have it pulled up at the roots, no matter how large, and have it transported to his palace to be planted here. The ground itself was inlaid with greenish stone, so there was no other colour to be seen, and in the midst of it a green palace – "and I give you my word that mound and trees and palace form a vision of such beauty that it gladdens the hearts of all beholders. It was for the sake of this entrancing view that the Great Khan had them constructed, as well as for the refreshment and recreation they might afford him."

Marco Polo has much to say about the city itself. Peking, in his time, was actually two cities side by side. The original city, called Yanjing by the Liao (Khitan) Dynasty (916–1125) and Zhongdu by the Jin (Jurchen) Dynasty (1115–1234), stood in rectangular walls to the south. To its eastern side was the great Temple of Heaven. However, Kublai built an entirely new city to the north. It was called Taidu by the Mongols, though later travellers referred to it as the "Mongol [or Tatar] City", and the older settlement as the "Chinese City".

The Mongol City was square in shape, 24 miles in circumference, enclosed by earthen ramparts 20 paces high and 10 paces thick at the base, battlemented, whitewashed, and pierced by three gates on either side. As with the Khan's palace, there were great buildings on the sides and at the corners, containing immense halls, and filled with weapons for the 1,000 soldiers who were detailed to stand guard at every gate. The city was laid out as a unity in straight lines. Symmetry and geometry were the guiding principles.

"All building sites throughout the city are square and measured by the rule," wrote Marco Polo. "Every site or block is surrounded by good public roads; and in this way the whole interior of the city is laid out in squares like a chess-board with such masterly precision that no description can do justice to it." A result of the emphasis on right angles was the creation of grand vistas. The main avenues were "so broad and straight that from the top of the wall above one gate you can see along the whole length of the road to the gate opposite".

The whole city was full of "fine mansions, inns and dwelling-houses". On every side were "ample courtyards and gardens", and although the city itself was densely populated, outside the walls the population was even more numerous. Outside every gate there was a suburb, and each had grown to touch the suburb belonging to the neighbouring gate, encircling the city in a great sprawl of dwellings which extended outwards for three or four miles. These should not be seen, however, as shanties. The suburbs boasted houses and mansions as fine as those within the city, "except of course for the Khan's palace".

It was to these suburbs that the great majority of travellers would initially resort. Situated around a mile from the city's gates on every side, there were hostels and lodgings for merchants and traders, each nationality having its own hostel. These hostels, according to Marco Polo, were luxurious and well appointed, and the visitors were able to pass their time in great comfort. One of the aids to this comfort was the army of 20,000 prostitutes who were licensed to practise their trade outside the city walls. "There are so many of them that no one could believe it." Their work was highly organised: as if a military regiment, their cohort was placed under a captain-general, and there were chiefs of hundreds and chiefs of thousands answerable to this high officer. Should a foreign ambassador arrive at the court of the Khan, the captain-general was required to provide a woman for his use, and one for each of his retinue. These were to be changed every night for the duration of their stay. For this work, the women were not paid. It was regarded as service in lieu of tax to the Khan. To Marco Polo, the number and ubiquity of the prostitutes was one of the greatest signs of the commerce and importance of the city. From it "you may infer the

number of traders and other visitors who are daily coming and going here about their business.

"Merchants and others come here on business in great numbers," Polo wrote, "both because it is the Khan's residence and because it affords a profitable market." No other

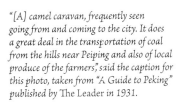

"[A] camel caravan, frequently seen going from and coming to the city. It does a great deal in the transportation of coal from the hills near Peiping and also of local produce of the farmers," said the caption for this photo, taken from "A Guide to Peking" published by The Leader in 1931.

city, he asserted, could rival it for the import of precious wares, or the sheer volume of commerce. Goods came not only from 200 other cities in China, but luxuries from as far afield as India were produced for sale in the Peking markets. 1,000 cartloads of silk would enter the city every day, and so plentiful was it that cotton, flax and hemp were scarcely used or known. Traders entering the city would surrender to the Khan great collections of precious stones, gold, silver, cloth of gold and silk; these would be assessed by a board of experts, and the traders would be repaid for these wares not in coin, but in paper money, a system which caused great wonder to Marco Polo. "I can tell you that the papers that reckon as ten bezants do not weight one." The notes, made of the bark of mulberry trees and stamped with the imperial seal, were current throughout the Khan's dominions. Traders who were returning abroad would use them to buy other goods, which they would then sell on at home.

But the rule of the Mongols, although flourishing and in many ways enlightened, was not of long duration. In 1368, the dynasty fell and much of Peking was ruined, briefly losing its status as the capital to Nanjing. However, at the turn of the 15th century, interest in the city re-emerged. It was first named as the Northern Capital (the literal meaning of "Peking") in 1403, by the Emperor Zhu Di, and in 1421, after many renovations, it was chosen as the principal capital, ranking in importance above Nanjing. An address to the Emperor on the subject neatly captures the abiding importance of the city: "Your ministers consider that Peking being a stronghold by virtue of its being sheltered by mountains and rivers, having sweet water and fertile soil, and having a populace of great simplicity and production in abundance, is a land naturally endowed… to be the capital of the empire. Your Majesty has already made elaborate plans for transforming the city into a lasting abode for your imperial descendants for 10,000 generations to come, and has also made frequent trips to the spot. Peoples from the four seas have assembled there and have enjoyed peace and prosperity. Moreover, canals have been newly cut or dredged, grain transportation is increasing rapidly, merchants gather there for trade with superabundance of goods, and treasures and big timbers and other excellent materials have been collected… To create a metropolis in Peking is but to abide by the dictate of Heaven and to follow the opinion of the populace and should therefore be carried out without delay."

The vision of magnificence embodied by the grand notion of transforming Peking into a city fit for 10,000 generations was not too wide of the mark. Like the Emperor Augustus with ancient Rome, Zhu Di found a city of clay, and left a city of marble. A grand programme of construction was inaugurated. The Forbidden City was built in place of the old Palace of Kublai Khan, along with a host of other palaces, halls, temples, city gates and bridges. A geometric pattern again became the basis of the layout of the wider city. And the city walls themselves, originally mud in the time of the Mongols, were faced with stone and brick.

Looking north towards a fanciful and distinctly understated Forbidden City in the 1870s, from The Illustrated London News.

However, the notion that the city was a haven for peoples of all lands and nationalities was perhaps overstating the case. Overland travel to China was not so much of note in the Ming Dynasty as it had been under the Mongols. For a start, the journey there, especially from Europe or even the Middle East, became much more difficult. By the beginning of the 15th century, the so-called Pax Mongolica had collapsed. The conquest of Asia by Genghis Khan and his successors in the 1200s, and its subjection, as a sort of grand federation, to the rule of his descendants, made it possible to travel in safety from the Levant all the way to Peking. It was this peace and security that allowed Western travellers such as Marco Polo, Friar Odoric and William of Rubruck, to make their various journeys far into the east. However, by the time of the Ming Dynasty, Mongol power and the order it had brought was no more. The Middle East and Central Asia were a ferment of strife, and the links, important but tenuous, which had been built up between China and Europe were severed.

Besides this, the change in dynasty was not propitious. The Ming Dynasty was a native Chinese dynasty, and it represented a backlash against the Mongols and the rule of a foreign elite. The Mongol mindset of tolerance was reversed with the accession of the Ming. Its customary openness to foreigners and foreign concepts was swept away. External influences were no longer welcome in Peking. As an example, the Christian Archbishopric of Peking, founded in the 1290s by another missionary Franciscan, John of Montecorvino, lapsed into abeyance. The Cathedral which he founded in the city was suppressed, and the emperor no longer listened to the hymns sung by its choir. The emphasis was now on excluding the ideas of outsiders, and curbing their influence in the Chinese Empire. It was not the most auspicious environment for the traveller.

Nonetheless, visitors still came to the city. Some of the earliest to leave an account of the journey to the Ming capital were ambassadors from Herat in modern-day Afghanistan, who arrived in Peking around 1420. Most of Afghanistan was by this time in the hands of the Timurid Empire, whose rulers claimed descent from Genghis Khan, and the embassy was an attempt to revive the transcontinental links that had evaporated with the end of Mongol hegemony.

The ambassadors left only a brief record of their visit, but it is enough to convey their astonishment at the wealth and magnificence of the city. Herat was an opulent metropolis, but the display of Peking was beyond anything they had ever experienced. When they arrived, it is likely that the work of rebuilding was still in progress. Up to 100,000 houses still lay in ruins. However, the Palace was ready for their reception. Outside the gate, five elephants stood guard on either side. Within, they found the complex thronging with people – 300,000 in their estimation – waiting for a reception with the Emperor. There were court officials charged with protocol. There were hordes of musicians singing hymns for the emperor's prosperity. There were also guards, armed with a fearsome variety of weapons, halberds, batons, darts, arrows, lances, swords and maces, charged with keeping back the surging masses of the crowd. When the time came for the people to be admitted to the presence of the emperor, drums and trumpets, flutes and shawms (a forerunner of the oboe) were sounded, a bell began to ring, the three consecutive gates to the place of audience were flung open, and the multitude surged forward.

The courtyard where they met the Emperor was immense. In the midst stood a great "kiosk" (pagoda) from which the Emperor would appear. On either side there were massed ranks of dignitaries and military officers, the commanders of hundreds, the commanders of thousands, and the commanders of ten thousands. Beyond them on every side were an "infinite" number of guards. There were rows of secretaries, charged with taking down every word of the Emperor. Over all, there hung a profound silence. Shortly, the Emperor made his entrance. He climbed nine steps of silver in the middle of the pagoda to his throne, an elaborate structure four cubits high, with trimmings of yellow satin, decorated with paintings of the phoenix, bright with gold. The ambassadors observed Zhu Di closely. A man of middle stature with a sizeable beard, they recorded, and 200–300 long hairs descending from his chin to his chest.

Amongst their letters, the ambassadors from Herat brought a rather formal and half-hearted suggestion that the Emperor of China should convert to Islam. Rather more concerted in their efforts however, were the Christian missionaries in the person of Jesuit Fathers, who were inspired to emulate

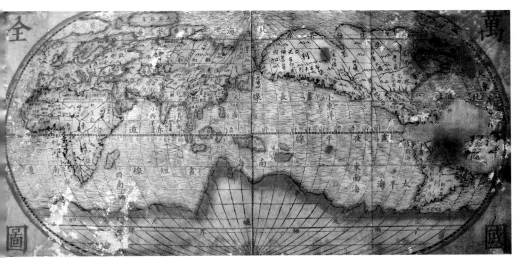

An early 17th century map of the world created by the Jesuits for the Chinese emperor, with China purposefully shown in a central position to pander to the belief that the Middle Kingdom was of paramount importance.

the travels of the 13th century Franciscan friars. Despite the avowed insularity of the Ming Dynasty, the Jesuits were able to gain an entrance to Peking, and, in many cases win a trusted place in the society of the Imperial court. The first of their number was Matteo Ricci, who came with the Portuguese traders to Macao at the end of the 16th century. Building on the work of earlier Jesuits, who had been established in Macao since 1577, he was able to travel on the Chinese mainland and live for a time in Nanchang, before receiving permission to set up a base in Peking in 1601.

Ricci's methods were those typical of his learned and intellectual order. He immersed himself in the culture of the city and of the people. He taught himself Chinese ideograms, studied Confucian texts, and grew to understand intimately the social and political ideas of the Chinese state. He won approval from the Chinese establishment not only for endowing them with the up-to-date scientific knowledge of the West, but also presenting it to them in a context of which they could approve. He published a map of the world in Chinese characters, but which placed China on the centre meridian rather than on the periphery, thus conforming to Chinese ideas. He was profoundly impressed by the concepts inherent in Confucianism, and attempted to syncretise the tenets of its philosophy with aspects of Christian dogma. In order to make Christianity acceptable to the Chinese, he sought to clothe it in Chinese customs, finding a way of incorporating such practices as ancestor worship into a Christian liturgy appointed for Chinese use. In his own behaviour he similarly emulated Chinese custom. He lived and dressed as a high official. He would not be seen in the streets on foot, and only travelled in a sedan chair. Only in this way, he understood, could he ensure respect for himself and his message.

Although by the time of Ricci, the operation of the overland Silk Road had ceased to have any great significance, the notion at Peking could be said to have found a latter-day incarnation. The Silk Road was as much a conduit for ideas as for trade, and with the work of the Jesuits ideas began to travel backwards and forwards from China to the West as they had done in no era since classical times. The only difference was that the way was by sea rather than land, down to Canton (Guangzhou) and Macao (Macau), or through the port of Tientsin (Tianjin). Through the Jesuits, the Chinese learned Western mathematics and science. They were furnished with ideas of astronomy, geography and physics. The Jesuits constructed for the Emperor a host of scientific and astronomical instruments, many of which are still to be seen in the city's observatory. They brought a knowledge of metallurgy, and cast cannon for use by the Chinese army. They acted as official astronomers, set the calendar, and were even responsible for diplomatic missions. It was the Jesuits who settled the original border between Russia and China with the Treaty of Nerchinsk in 1658, which stood until the Russian land-grab of the late 19th century.

In a lighter vein they composed music in Chinese style, which they played to the emperors on the spinet. A number were artists, painting murals and portraits for the Chinese court. Their triumph in the field was to design a Summer Palace for the emperors outside Peking, the Yuanming Yuan. This complex, built in a European style, boasted as its centrepiece a great hydraulic clock with 12 marble animals that would spout water in succession depending on the hour. In return, the Chinese furnished Europe with translations of its classics of philosophy and literature. Ricci had argued from the start that in many areas, such as economics, areas of technology, and various types of literature, China was just as advanced as Europe. European philosophers of the 17th and 18th centuries, such as von Leibniz, profess to have been influenced by ideas in these texts, and it is argued that tenets of Confucianism had a not insignificant role to play in the evolution of Enlightenment thought.

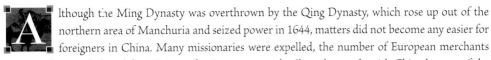

Although the Ming Dynasty was overthrown by the Qing Dynasty, which rose up out of the northern area of Manchuria and seized power in 1644, matters did not become any easier for foreigners in China. Many missionaries were expelled, the number of European merchants was strictly curtailed, and for 150 years foreigners were only allowed to trade with China by way of the port of Canton. Nonetheless, the Qing preserved and further beautified Peking as they had inherited it from the Ming Dynasty. The geometrical layout of the city was maintained, and it was enhanced with further palaces, courtyards and gardens.

Aside from the Jesuits who were permitted to remain in Peking until the beginning of the 18th century, the few Westerners who were granted the opportunity of seeing Peking in the summer of its prosperity were ambassadors from the Western powers. A number of Russian embassies were received in Peking over the course of the 17th century. Evert Ysbrants Ides, who led a mission there in 1695, left behind some of the most vivid accounts of their reception.

The way to Peking was through land that was meticulously kept and cultivated, rich in wealth and colour. The area round about was dotted with the houses and gardens of mandarins, enclosed behind high walls with carved gates. Paths led from house to house, sheltered with cypresses and cedars. The fields were rich with a multitude of produce – rice, barley and millet, wheat and oats, peas and beans. Processions were seen amongst the fields for the sake of blessing the crops. Marching bands carried trumpets, flutes and kettle drums making a "horrid noise", while pictures of the gods were held aloft. As for the roads, they were broad, straight and well kept. Although they were as busy as those of the city, with travellers, wagons and carts, the journey over them was not unpleasant. Street sweepers were employed to clear them of rubbish, and water troughs kept on the verge provided for the needs of the animals. The Russians would have found it an arresting contrast to the outskirts of Moscow.

Their reception at the city was not unlike that granted to ambassadors in the time of Kublai Khan. They were first greeted by the Emperor's uncle and several high nobles. The newcomers were transfixed by the opulence of their robes, dripping with silk and gold thread, embroidered with lions and tigers, dragons and cranes. Seated on carpets, they were then treated to a great banquet of 70 courses, with cold meats, roast geese, chickens, pork, mutton, and fruit. However, there was something more of frivolity in their sojourn at the Qing court. The number of amusements seemed endless, and at times passing the absurd. There were jugglers who juggled oranges and lemons. There were magicians who could bounce a glass ball the size of a man's head on the point of a sharp stick, propelling it this way and that without allowing it to shatter or fall. There were 10-year-old boys who scrambled up vertical bamboo poles and, laying themselves on their stomachs at the top of it, stretched out horizontally. On one occasion they were brought into the elephant stable, where the Emperor kept 14 of the animals, one of them white. All of them had been taught to perform not just tricks, but animal impersonations. One could roar like a tiger, "that all the stable trembled". Others could low like an ox, neigh like a horse, or even sing like a canary. On concluding their impressions, they were obliged to pay their respects to the visitors by sinking to their

(Left) *"Reception of the Foreign Ministers and consuls by the (new) Emperor of China at Pekin", from the September 1873 issue of* The Illustrated London News.

A drawing of Lord Macartney's infamous insult during the British embassy to China in 1793, when he was said to have refused to kowtow, or bow, upon greeting the emperor.

knees. Yet, it was not just the great of the animal kingdom that were trained to such indignities. There were apes that were trained to dress up in coloured coats and dance on tightropes. There were even mice that were taught to untangle themselves from chains, suggesting that the Chinese conceived of escapology long before the time of Houdini.

One of the few animals that was permitted to retain a modicum of self-respect was the goldfish. These were not seen outside of China before the modern age, and travellers, first seeing them in Peking, would often express their wonder. Ides was one of these. Having seen a tank full of them in a toyshop, he attempted to describe them for his Russian audience. They were a finger's length, he wrote, "and naturally looked as if they had been gilt with the finest gold; and the scales of some of them being fallen off, I discovered to my great surprise, the colour of the bodies to be the most beautiful crimson in the world."

A century later in 1793, the first ever British diplomatic mission to Peking, led by Lord Macartney, was received by the Chinese Emperor Qianlong. One of its officers, John Barrow, recorded vividly his impressions of the trip. As with the Russians 100 years earlier, he was also treated to displays of bamboo-climbing and plate spinning. There were even grand allegorical pageants with scores of performers dressed up in a multitude of elaborate costumes. One of the performances was intended to demonstrate the riches of the earth, and featured actors dressed as everything from rocks, oaks and pines, to dragons, elephants and tigers. The fowls of the air were represented by eagles and ostriches, while the abundance of the sea was displayed by players representing shells and sponges, corals, porpoises and sea monsters. The centrepiece of the pageant was a great whale, which spouted several tons of water from its mouth whilst making an obeisance before the emperor's box. Barrow was not much impressed: "...nothing comparable to Sadler's Wells," he wrote.

H e was less indifferent to the fireworks. There were boxes which would be hoisted 60 feet (18 metres) into the air and burst open to gush forth a hanging mobile of over 500 different coloured lanterns, cut with a wealth of intricate geometrical patterns, flashing like "prismatic lightning". There was also, to conclude the show, a "volcano… or general explosion and discharge of suns and stars, squibs, bouncers, crackers, rockets and grenades, which involved the gardens for above an hour after in a cloud of most intolerable smoke." This he could praise for its "novelty, neatness, and ingenuity of contrivance".

Macartney's mission got formal Anglo-Chinese relations off to a notably bad start when he refused to perform the traditional kowtow, or low bow, to the Emperor. Relations in the court were not of the easiest, and it was in the city outside the court that Barrow found most to interest him. Although apparently unmoved by much of the pomp of the court, the splendour of the city beyond it seemed genuinely to impress him. The first sight of the city from beyond the walls, he wrote, was not much calculated to raise expectations. In contrast to the spires of a European city visible from afar, not even a single chimney could be seen rising above the height of the rooftops. Everything being nearly the same height, one storey high, and the streets laid out in straight lines, the whole at first had the air of a military encampment. "If painted white," he wrote, "it would make the resemblance complete."

Yet once inside, it was a "singular and novel experience". The streets were lined with shops and warehouses, their sides – and those of the houses too – painted in brilliant colours, sky blue, green and gold. Before them stood tall wooden pillars, their pinnacles higher than the rooftops, festooned with flags,

The showroom of a lantern merchant in Peking, an engraving by renowned English artist and architect Thomas Allom (1804–1872), who travelled to China in the 1840s.

ribbons and brightly coloured streamers. Each of the posts was emblazoned with the name of the owner in golden letters, a description of the goods, and flamboyant testimonies of the good character of the shopkeeper. In front of these there were tents and booths where tea and rice were offered for sale. There were moveable workshops, where tinkers and blacksmiths plied their trade.

The street itself was a crush of every order of society. There were high-ranking mandarins with great cavalcades, surrounded by flags, umbrellas and lanterns. There were troops of camels, loaded with coal, ambling in the centre of the way. There were funeral processions bearing elaborately gilded and decorated coffins, followed by trains of lamenting relatives. There were also wedding processions bearing brides to the houses of their new husbands, followed by instrumentalists playing "squalling music". Both coffins and brides were carried on similar sorts of painted wagons, covered with ornamental canopies. (Often it was difficult to tell them apart.) Between them all there wove vegetable sellers with wheelbarrows and handcarts stuffed with all their produce, peddlers crying out a multitude of wares, jugglers, magicians, "mountebanks and quack doctors", all crushed so closely together that there was not a single piece of space in the street left unoccupied.

As with the roads leading into Peking, the city's environment was fastidiously maintained. The streets might often have been muddy or dusty, but at least, wrote Barrow, "no filth or nastiness creating offensive smells is thrown into streets". The sanitary arrangements were far ahead of many places in Europe at the time. Each family had a large earthen jar for the collection of their sewage, which would be regularly collected in exchange for money or vegetables. Nothing was put to waste, and all was done in the name of efficiency. The same cart even collected the sewage as distributed the vegetables that were given in return. And, despite the crush and level of population, the authorities were able to keep the city in "safety and tranquillity". At every crossroads there was a sentry box with a guard, and at night soldiers and vigilante watchmen patrolled the streets, striking together pieces of bamboo to let the population know that they were abroad.

Barrow and his contemporaries might have greatly admired Peking, but in his description of its opulence, there was also a note of fear. It was in the teeming markets full of every conceivable type of merchandise that the British and other visitors saw trouble for European commerce and the system of world trade. China was self-sufficient, and exported to Europe – by sea or by land – a wealth of luxury goods, tea, silk, textiles and porcelain. By contrast, aside from a few furs from Siberia, exotic foodstuffs and ingredients for traditional medicine, they had no cause to import anything. In the words of the Emperor Qianlong (reigned 1736–95), "The Celestial Empire possesses all things in prolific abundance and lacks no product within its borders. There is therefore no need to import the manufactures of outside barbarians in exchange for our own products."

Over the 18th and 19th centuries, the trade imbalance grew, as China accumulated more and more silver and bullion from the outside world. The ultimate consequence of this imbalance was military conflict and civil disturbance. The two Opium Wars (1840–42 and 1856–64) were the upshot of the British East India Company attempting to overcome Chinese objections to importing Indian-produced opium as a high-value product to right the trade imbalance. The results of the policy were long lasting and

Circular Street, and the Arrow Tower (at left), published in The Illustrated London News *in the 1870s.*

generally negative. European troops landed in China at several places along the coast. The Chinese army, facing the foreign invaders often with nothing more than bows and arrows, could put up little in the way of defence. The principal cities were besieged and attacked. Peking itself was not spared, and was sacked in 1860. The Emperor's Summer Palace outside Peking, the Yuanming Yuan, constructed by the Jesuits, was destroyed and burnt down in an orgy of looting perpetrated by a detachment of Anglo-French forces.

After the conclusion of hostilities, China was compelled to accept a series of terms that it found deeply humiliating. The country had to be opened up to foreign merchants; city quarters and shipping ports such as Hong Kong and Shanghai were conceded for the use of foreigners; Christian missionaries, until then scarcely tolerated, were given free rein to travel and operate as they pleased, their compounds being given special protection. Although they played a great role in the exploration of China, and were responsible for much in the way of healthcare and education, they showed little sensitivity to the intricacies of their setting or situation. They generally treated the native religions and customs with contempt, and were overbearing and haughty with the native clergy and converts that eventually they were able to recruit. Many acted also to open up areas to foreign trade, and their first appearance in the area was often a prelude to the appearance of foreign goods and merchants. The Chinese government itself was compelled to pay crippling indemnities to the European powers, and the consequent impoverishment of the peasant population who shouldered the greater part of the tax burden for these payments led to constant discontent and unrest, culminating in the Boxer Rebellion of 1900, when Chinese peasants attempted to eliminate every foreign influence within the country.

The terrible upheavals that China underwent in the 19th century left their mark on Peking. Its surroundings, previously so well kept, tended towards decay. The country houses were left empty, the roads, originally paved with granite slabs for many miles beyond the city, grew cracked and uneven. The city itself, although preserving in form its Ming architecture, customs and inheritance, suffered from impoverishment and neglect.

For the city's small population of resident foreigners, generally diplomats and missionaries, it was never reckoned as the easiest of postings. For diplomats, the duties might generally be light, ranging from monitoring the safety of missionaries in the field, to paying official calls, to mounting campaigns of espionage; the leisure might be manifold, ranging from dances and amateur theatricals to horseracing and endless rounds of tiffin parties, but life itself was not easy. Once outside the legation compounds, usually elegant Chinese palaces surrendered by former imperial princes, there was the risk of insult, abuse and even violence. As Archibald Colquhoun, a *Times* special correspondent at the end of the 19th century put it, "You may be thoroughly convinced of the sterling qualities of the Chinese and sincerely well disposed towards them as a nation, and yet a brick hurled from the city wall as you ride below, or a reflection on female relatives of whom you happen to be fond, may make the most forbearing angry."

Travellers to the city in this period dwelt on the worst aspects of its decline. None was more forthright than William Athenry Whyte, who was travelling overland from Hong Kong to England via Siberia in 1869, a spectator to the aftermath of the Opium Wars. To him, Peking was "without exception the most miserable, dirty, poverty-stricken town in China, and when that is said it means in the world." All one then found in the city was "decay and dilapidation... That China is rotten to the core, Peking is proof enough."

"*Curiosity Street, Pekin*," *from* The Illustrated London News, *16 February 1861.*

He railed against the state of the roads in the city. The main thoroughfares had elevated embankments running along the middle wide enough for two carts to pass abreast. On either side of these there were ditches which were meant to be used for heavy traffic but in fact acted as culverts in the rainy weather, turning into streams and filling up with sewage. Pigs, dogs and birds competed with humans to scavenge in the knee-deep mud and dust of the streets. "It cannot help striking the traveller what a miserable government the Chinese must be to permit such filth and abject misery, which, unless seen, could scarcely be imagined." And it was not only the roads that had sunk into such an abject condition. "In the Chinese city there is scarcely a decent looking house; they seem to consist mostly of old clothes shops, made of old rags and matting, where auctions take place. Here and there are the remnants of what might have been a fine building, but which is now in ruins. Such a miserable and truly god-forsaken place I never wish to see again," Whyte concluded.

In 1900, a British diplomat, A.B. Freeman Mitford, confirmed the picture painted by Whyte. There was always something "grotesque and barbarous" to be seen. The roads were unpaved and uncared for, filthy in both winter and summer. The hordes of people and carts, dogs and pigs in the streets raised clouds of dust which filled the "eyes, ears, hair, mouth and nose", destroying momentarily "any sense except touch". Beautiful palaces with their gardens and courtyards were going to rack and ruin, their walls tumbling down and the paving of the gardens shattered. Creatures normally found in the depths of the countryside, foxes and scorpions, polecats and weasels, made themselves at home in these derelict urban wildernesses. Most of all, it was the sight of the numberless beggars that he felt "would be a nightmare" for the rest of his life. An earlier traveller, David Field Rennie, recalled the professionalism with which boys had learned to beg. The Western traveller would be followed relentlessly with piteous tales and lamentations: "Oh your honour, save my life, send me down some money, I am hungry, my hunger is beyond toleration, I pray for your honour, I perform the kowtow to your Excellency, O relieve me from the suffering and save my life..." Rennie was cynical about their plight. They were "generally in very good condition, their appearance not being at all corroborative of their statements with reference to inanition."

With the onset of the 20th century, the impoverishment of Peking and its long-standing efforts to keep itself detached from the currents of modern life began to have a somewhat unexpected effect. There had been little development in any field, whether physical, in terms of architecture, or else in terms of customs and way of life. For travellers, who now had the benefit of improving rail and shipping communications, this gave the city an enchanting and bewitching allure. The travel firm Thomas Cook made this attraction the city's lead selling point in its 1917 Guidebook. "Peking is the one city in China where the traveller sees native life untouched and uninfluenced by foreign discipline and regulation..." A.R. Colquhoun spelt it out with greater eloquence. In Peking, "...we have no mere fossil remains, to be reconstructed and labelled for us by the archaeologist: we need pore over no cuneiforms and ransack no musty libraries in order to appreciate it. The Past itself confronts us – no mere dry bones, but the breathing flesh – in the city walls, still guarded by bow and arrow and painted cannon; in the ruins, still inhabited; and in the language, literature, dress, and manners of the citizens, practically unaltered since the period when our woad-stained British forefathers yet ran naked in the woods."

PEKING CAR

AMUSEMENTS ON THE ICE

This evocative drawing was used on the front cover of The Illustrated London News *in February 1861.*

For the travellers who visited Peking in these early years of the 20th century, the city became something of a living, breathing theme park; an "untouched world" in the words of the French novelist Abel Bonnard. It was not just the monuments and palaces, gardens and temples and gardens which filled the travellers with awe, the architecture which, again in Bonnard's words, was "devised for dignitaries and philosophers, and regulated by a harmony so subtle, that after having looked at it, you bend your head as if to listen to it". It was not just the fact that one could still see imperial pageantry, such as royal funerals, with processions over a mile long, in form, costume and style little changed for centuries. Nor was it the contemplations of the grandeur and the associations of the sacred sites such as the Temple of Heaven, where visitors would muse on the solemn ceremony of the Winter Solstice, in which the Emperor since time immemorial had on his own offered sacrifices to heaven to atone for the sins of his people. It was as much the colour of the everyday street life, unaltered for centuries, which brought rapture to the traveller. It is about this aspect of Peking that travellers left their most animated reminiscences.

To visit one of the street markets where cheap goods were sold was counted one of the greatest pleasures. Juliet Bredon, an inhabitant of Peking, described as an example a visit to a fair held in the grounds of a dilapidated Ming-era temple near the Eternal Happiness monastery. At the outer gates, the visitor "is besieged by men with Pekingese puppies. Some of them look like imitation dogs. They ought to have green wheels and red flannel tongues." Within, an endless array of merchandise was laid out on a long succession of stands. Crickets, confined in bamboo cages, were sold for use in cricket fights, a sport that was then still popular. Goldfish with triple and quadruple tails swam in murky tanks. A row of artificial flower stands was perused by Manchu women in search of hair ornaments. "It is fascinating to watch them with their slender, fine, faultlessly knit figures," wrote Bredon, "with just that suggestion of pliant elegance which the sight of a young bamboo gives when the wind is blowing."

There were stalls where false hair was sold in great tresses; stalls with red ceremonial candles ready for use in weddings; stalls for selling combs; stalls "with dozens of tiny but unusually sharp knives used for shaving cheeks, nose, brows and chin"; stalls with bamboo back-scratchers in the shape of tiny hands; and stalls that sold ribbon for winding round the ankles to keep the trousers in place. There were money-changers with racks of coins in grooved wooden trays; spectacle menders and razor grinders; herb sellers with their plants laid out away from the crush to avoid being trodden down; an old dentist occupied one of the corners, a stock of several dozen teeth laid out on a cloth, ready for purchase and use by the customers.

"The Lantern Painter" by M. Theodore Delamarre.

One of the most alluring stalls was that of the toy-seller. The toy-makers and toy-sellers, wrote Bredon, astonished foreign visitors with their ingenuity, making toys just as good and exciting as those in the West, but "at a cost too small to name". She explained: "Poverty ages ago taught them the secret of making pleasure the commonest instead of the costliest of experiences – the divine art of creating the beautiful out of nothing." There were paper butterflies that fluttered on light osier twigs. There were flocks of geese that would fly along a thread when one tightened an attached piece of bent bamboo. Paper figures would be made to stand on horsehair and dance on brass trays, animated by a little tap. Always, the cheapest materials were used, bamboo, straw, clay, scraps of wood or feathers, and yet, "each thing is so cleverly done – so expressive, often so humorous – that one is forced to buy".

The salesmen would often tell elaborate and usually spurious stories about their wares in order to encourage a sale. John Thomson, a photographer who travelled through China at the end of the 19th century, recorded one such example in the Peking markets. "This is the fur coat," cried one stallholder, "which, during the year of the great frost, saved the head of the illustrious family of Chang. The cold was so intense that people were mute. When they spoke, their words froze and hung from their lips. Men's ears congealed and were devoid of feeling, so that when they shook their heads they fell off. Men froze to the streets and died by their thousands; but as for Chang of honoured memory, he put on this coat, and it brought summer to his blood."

Amongst the stallholders, the traditional peddlers would ply their trade. These were some of the most distinctive and traditional sights of the Peking streets and markets. Their itinerant nature was in large measure a consequence of the custom of foot-binding. Women, who were unable to walk far on account of their bound feet, depended on the peddlers to pass along the streets in front of their houses in order to buy goods. This formed a large part of their trade. Each peddler usually had a very specific

Most of the Great Wall had fallen into disrepair by the 20th century, crumbling over time or being dismantled for local building materials. Some areas near Beijing have been reconstructed to their former glory, but others remain decrepit, like here in the Simatai area to the northeast of the city, and walking these sections can be a more satisfying way of appreciating the Great Wall.

remit: one might sell melon seeds, another almond tea, and another moon cake. They also had distinctive cries, and in many cases an assigned musical instrument to play, so that they might be heard approaching from far off. The rice flour cake peddler would shout "here come the rice cakes and sweet balls!" and strike a castanet with a stick. The dried fruit and nut peddler, by contrast, would clash two small brass bowls together like cymbals and cry "fruit paste and stuffed dates have arrived!" The toy-seller, around whom children would cluster, summoned them with the slogan "buy small man, they are lifelike, they have eyes and arms!"

On the northern side of Tiananmen Square a massive portrait of Chairman Mao adorns the Gate of Heavenly Peace, the main entrance to the Forbidden City.

(Top) *The magnificent Hall of Prayer for a Good Harvest was first built in 1545 but had to be rebuilt after an 1889 fire started by lightning. Its four new giant central columns were hewn from Oregon fir imported in the 1890s. (Bottom) The Great Wall near Beijing has been renovated in a number of locations – the result is a quintessential China experience for those who walk its ramparts. (Opposite top) "The Kingdome of China" – an early and somewhat inaccurate map of the Middle Kingdom. (Opposite bottom) A world map, made by Venetian monk Fra Mauro around 1450, shows Europe, Africa and Asia, and is inverted here because its original orientation was with south at the top, following the convention of Muslim maps of the time.*

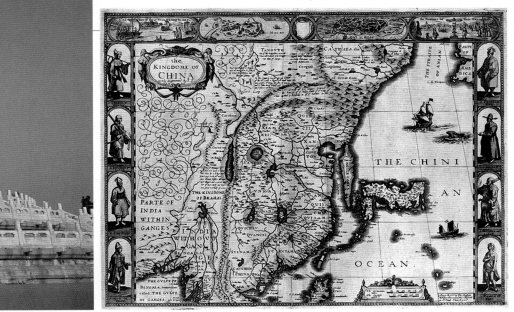

(Top) *"Jugglers exhibiting in the court of a Mandarin's Palace," an engraving based upon a mid-19th century drawing by Thomas Allom. (Above left) An ornate statue within the Lama Temple. (Above right) One of a pair of majestic marble lions guarding the pailou in front of the Hall of Heavenly Kings in Beihai Park. (Left) A pool filled with carp and lilies adds to the tranquillity within the Forbidden City's Six Eastern Palaces.*

A calligraphy brush vendor waits for customers in Beijing's Liulichang West shopping area.

Emperor Qianlong's Bronze Ox, just a stone's throw from the Seventeen-arch Bridge, with Longevity Hill on the horizon across the Summer Palace's Kunming Lake.

The White Pagoda stands on an island in Beihai Park's North Lake, surrounded by a lovely park-within-a-park that is part wilderness, part manicured garden.

Dongbianmen, the Gate of the North-East Angle, with the last remaining section of the magnificent Ming dynasty city wall.

The Summer Palace's exquisite Seventeen-arch Bridge leads to South Lake Island; according to the Dutchman Henri Borel, it was "to be trodden by none but shining angels and beatified souls".

(Clockwise from above) *Giant Buddha carvings at the Longmen Caves near Luoyang, capital of the Eastern Han Dynasty; a Tang Dynasty glazed pottery figurine of a court lady in Xi'an's National Museum of Shaanxi History; recently restored terracotta warriors stand ready for placement in Pit Number One of Xi'an's top attraction – the incredible Museum of Terracotta Warriors and Horses of Qin Shi Huangdi; Big Goose Pagoda shines out in symmetrical beauty even at night; a monk in the Big Goose Pagoda complex writes calligraphy for pilgrims; a simple cave dwelling carved from the loess sediment that covers much of the region between the Wei and Yellow rivers.*

A traditionally clothed and coiffured musician
performs at a Tang Dynasty evening show in Xi'an.

A group of one-third life-size pottery figures at the extraordinary Yang Ling complex, mausoleum of the fourth Han emperor Jingdi near Xi'an's airport. The figures once sported wooden arms and real clothes, but these have long since decayed.

(Top left) Beiyuanmen in the Muslim Quarter of Xi'an to the north of the Drum Tower is a vibrant area filled with shops and stalls. (Top right) Tang-era glazed pottery alluding to the influence of the Silk Road in that rich period of China's history. (Bottom) Xi'an's Bell Tower (with the Drum Tower at left behind), a major landmark by day and night, is constantly circled by traffic as the modern city thrives. (Opposite top) A pavilion on Xi'an's 14th century City Wall, the most complete remaining Ming wall in China. (Opposite bottom) Fan dancers move gracefully at a Tang Dynasty evening performance, one of many popular shows in the city.

The variety of the peddlers was legion. There were flower peddlers and fan peddlers, clay vessel peddlers and sesame oil peddlers. There were stove peddlers who cried out "stoves made of asbestos!" and old women peddling matches in exchange for broken bottles, carrying them away in large baskets over their shoulders. Many of the peddlers were seen only at certain times of year, and the sound of them was one of the harbingers of a new season. The reed horn peddler came out on the first day of the New Year, and was welcomed as a sign of warmth and longer days. The moon cake peddler was seen in the streets for the month around the Autumn Festival. The turnip and radish peddler, calling "compare my turnips with pears, if bitter I will exchange" and proudly displaying trays of turnips cut like lotus flowers, appeared with the onset of the winter cold.

Some of the peddlers were not so tied to the seasons. Many of them were performers, whose acts echoed the entertainments of the imperial court as described by travellers, stretching back all the way to the beginning of the Ming Dynasty and Marco Polo beyond. There were trained mice men, who travelled the streets with mice in

Horse sedan chairs were one method of transport for the wealthy...

...another was this, a mandarin's sedan chair complete with attendants, photographed by T. Child during the 1870s.

a large box slung over his back. The passers-by would gather round, and watch as his animals ran up and down small string ladders, jumped in and out of model pagodas, or chased round a wooden fish hanging

(Left) Pilgrims light votive candles and place them in an enormous holder in front of the Big Goose Pagoda, completed in 652 CE at the request of Tang monk Xuan Zang, who had journeyed on the Silk Road to India to bring back Buddhist scriptures.

from a string. There were trained monkey men, whose instrument was a gong, and who generally carried in their entourage a small goat in addition to the monkey. The monkey would rush round trying on hats hidden in boxes and climbing up poles, before concluding his act by riding on the back of the goat. There were also fortune-tellers. According to Marco Polo, no enterprise would be undertaken without the advice of a fortune-teller. This was still very much the case at the beginning of the 20th century; customers would beseech the fortune-tellers, many of them blind, for guidance, and receive counsel based on horoscopes or the *I Ching* or "Book of Changes".

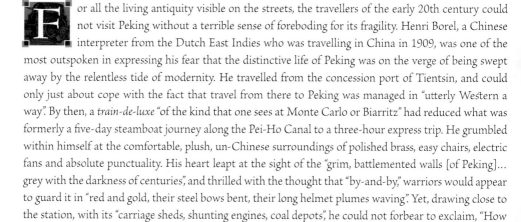

For all the living antiquity visible on the streets, the travellers of the early 20th century could not visit Peking without a terrible sense of foreboding for its fragility. Henri Borel, a Chinese interpreter from the Dutch East Indies who was travelling in China in 1909, was one of the most outspoken in expressing his fear that the distinctive life of Peking was on the verge of being swept away by the relentless tide of modernity. He travelled from the concession port of Tientsin, and could only just about cope with the fact that travel from there to Peking was managed in "utterly Western a way". By then, a *train-de-luxe* "of the kind that one sees at Monte Carlo or Biarritz" had reduced what was formerly a five-day steamboat journey along the Pei-Ho Canal to a three-hour express trip. He grumbled within himself at the comfortable, plush, un-Chinese surroundings of polished brass, easy chairs, electric fans and absolute punctuality. His heart leapt at the sight of the "grim, battlemented walls [of Peking]... grey with the darkness of centuries", and thrilled with the thought that "by-and-by", warriors would appear to guard it in "red and gold, their steel bows bent, their long helmet plumes waving". Yet, drawing close to the station, with its "carriage sheds, shunting engines, coal depots", he could not forbear to exclaim, "How comes this foreign steam-horse from the West to desecrate this seclusion with its rumblings and its foul fumes, disturbing the sacred silence of these immutable ramparts by the shrill screech of its whistle."

On entering Peking, his fear grew even greater. Leaving the station, which was outside the walls, he entered one of the gates and prepared for his first sight of the city. "The dream ends with a shock. I see a wide European street in glaring light, with European houses; a canal in the middle and quite near a large white building with bamboo scaffolding in front, as if it were being repaired or enlarged – a common, vulgar, modern European street, that's all."

The white building was the Grand Hotel des Wagons-Lits. Covered in scaffolding, it had been recently built but was already being extended, and the air was alive with the sound of construction. Inside, Borel could not tell if he were in Paris or Peking. The lobby was full of green wicker chairs in which lounged "European ladies and gentlemen" sipping coffee and conversing on the sights. "Exactly the people one sees at Ostend, Biarritz, Wiesbaden, Cairo – English, American, German, French, Italian – something of everything," he declared distastefully. The menu in the restaurant was consommé, carpe bleu and pâté de bécassines. As for his room, aside from the sight of rickshaws in the street outside, there was nothing to tell him that he was in the Chinese capital. "A trim English bed with silk eiderdown, lace curtains, a large wardrobe with mirror, electric light bulbs, a lavatory with taps for hot and cold water, a little lamp with a red silk shade on a small table by the bed, a comfortable easy-chair – everything in the best modern style."

"Thus appears Peking to me," he went on, "the holy city of the Emperors, the Sons of Heaven, tarnished by the snobbery of white globe-trotters and loafers, who have forced themselves by the fuming, screeching train through its sacred ramparts, which can no longer shield its virginity. And outside to the right and to the left, louder than the buzzing of voices, just overheard, I hear the hammering and knocking going on for ever – as if the modern had conquered, and were triumphantly erecting a new, vulgar, cosmopolitan town in the ancient holy fortress of the Tartars of the North."

A camel caravan passes through Peking's southern You'anmen Gate, circa 1920.

TOWARDS THE JADE GATE

To travel from Peking in the time of the Mongol emperors was not such a great travail as one might think, at least if one was travelling on government business. It was one of the works of Kublai Khan to enlarge and preserve the extensive road and postal network which he had inherited from his predecessors, allowing him to collect information throughout his empire from as far afield as possible. Peking was a great transport hub, from which roads radiated to the other Chinese provinces, and an endless stream of traders, travellers and imperial messengers made their way along them from the most distant corners of the empire to the capital. However, for all the great volume of traffic, the system was most adapted to the use of official travellers.

The finest description of the workings of the government postal network and transport arrangements again belongs to Marco Polo. "The whole system," he tells us, "is admirably contrived." At intervals of every 25 to 30 miles (40–48 kilometres) along the roads out to the provinces, there stood a post station, "which is called in their language *yamb* and in our language may be rendered 'horse post'". The imperial messengers, who rode on horseback, would take their rest at these every night, finding a "spacious and palatial hostelry for their lodgings". They boasted "splendid beds with rich coverlets of silk", and would well befit an emissary of high rank. Indeed, "if a king came," said Marco Polo, "he would be well lodged." In the morning, he would be able to choose from one of 400 horses that each station was meant to maintain, and take it to continue his journey.

In times of dire emergency, when news had to be conveyed to the capital of a rebellion by a subject province or vassal ruler, the messengers on horseback would ride post haste. The messenger would carry a tablet with a gerfalcon emblazoned on it as a sign of the urgency of his message, and sound a horn before reaching the post house, so that the best horse could be made ready before he arrived. On reaching it, he would change mounts without pause and carry on riding as quickly as possible. Nor would the couriers stop at night. If there were moonlight, they would ride by it. If not, runners would go before them bearing torches, allowing them to go on, but less quickly than before. In such a fashion, the messenger could travel 250–300 miles (400–480 kilometres) a day. However, there were few who had the stamina to travel in this fashion, and messengers who could endure the fatigue of such a ride were "very highly prized".

The emperor was not only dependent on the conventional horse messenger for his news. Urgent tidings could also be brought by means of running relays. The infrastructure of the post roads was designed to cater for this also. At intervals of every three miles, there were further postal stations. Although these could be extensive complexes, sometimes containing up to 40 buildings, they were set aside exclusively for the use of foot couriers. These would be entrusted with messages, and then set off to run as quickly as possible to the next post station, where another fresh courier would take up the message and perform the next stage. Such was done all the way from the provinces to Peking with urgent messages, and according

An 1875 watercolour by William Simpson depicts a group of Mongolians passing through the Great Wall on the way to Peking to present beautifully decorated horses to the emperor as wedding gifts.

to Marco Polo a message that would normally require 10 days' journey on foot could be conveyed to the capital within a day and a night. It was sometimes the case that these couriers were also used to send gifts to the emperor. Often, fruits would be collected in cities or provinces distant from the capital, and conveyed by means of the running relay still fresh to the imperial table.

The description Marco Polo gave of the Chinese government postal and transport system in the 13th century would probably be not dissimilar to the network as it was seen in the Han Dynasty (3rd century BCE) and even earlier. The system of post houses and depots is certainly known to have been in existence in those times, and was probably much the same. Certainly, his description of the official modes of travel was as true to life in the 19th century as it was in the 13th, with small details still little changed. The system was another piece of China's living antiquity. In the time of Marco Polo, the couriers would wear bells hanging from girdles which would jangle as they ran, giving the station ahead of them notice that another courier should be instantly made ready. In the 19th century, bells would also be rung, but they would be hand bells, instead of those worn on the clothing. The couriers of that age were also counselled not to use them at night, for fear of arousing any wild animals, such as wolves and tigers.

In the 13th century, a clerk at each station would record the time of arrival of each runner and the departure of his successor, so that if any were guilty of dawdling, the government inspectors could administer a punishment. In the 19th century, this aspect of the job was unchanged, and the regulations set out clearly the scale of punishments. If a runner arrived more than 45 minutes later than the period of time set for the stage, he would receive 20 strokes of the bamboo, and 40 strokes if he were an hour later than that. If the documents he carried were damaged, he faced 60 strokes of a heavy bamboo cane. However, there were considerable perks with the job. They were exempt from tax and richly rewarded for their work. They also received from the government the equipment necessary for travel: a raincoat and hat, a tasselled spear and baton for protection, and wooden boards with oil-cloth wrappers to prevent the documents they carried from being damaged or made wet on the journey.

Despite the excellence and efficiency of the government transport and postal networks, they were ultimately designed for the use of civil and military officials. This did not mean that ordinary travellers were entirely without benefit. Although the use of post houses and courier stations was generally confined to the imperial messengers and travellers on government business, the roads were for everyone to use. Trees were planted at short intervals along the way not only to provide shade, but also to mark out the path of the road. When it was not possible to plant trees, for example in desert regions or else on the sides of mountains, pillars would at least be erected so that travellers might know the way. However, according to Marco Polo Kublai Khan was eager to plant as many trees as possible, "because his sooth-sayers and astrologers declare that he who causes trees to be planted lives long."

Yet for all this solicitude, the roads, especially in the more isolated regions, were often poorly maintained and at the mercy of the seasons. Waterlogged and boggy during rainy periods, they were frequently difficult for wheeled transport, and were generally easiest to pass when the winter cold froze them solid.

For the traveller to whom the use of the Chinese post houses was forbidden, it was necessary to stay at an inn. This was never a particularly pleasant experience, at least for many of the Western visitors who left accounts of doing so. In fact, they seem to be close to unanimity on the subject. "I fancy I do not run much chance of being contradicted," wrote the artist Julius Price in 1892, "…when I say that for filth and general discomfort the average Chinese inn is probably without its equal in the world." Edwin J. Dingle, a British journalist who travelled on foot in China just under 20 years later, was equally vehement on the subject. "The traveller whom misfortune has led to travel off the main roads of Russia may probably hesitate in expressing an opinion as to which country carries off the palm for unmitigated filth; but with this exception, travellers in the Eastern Archipelago, in Central Asia, in Africa among the wildest tribes, are pretty well unanimous that compared with all these for dirt, disease, discomfort, an utter lack of decency and annoyance, the Chinese inn holds its own."

As a rule, wrote Price, the Chinese inn was built around a courtyard, always dirty, around which there stood a collection of outhouses, often tumbledown and dilapidated. The outhouses were partitioned off into sets of rooms, some of which would be reserved for the use of mules and baggage animals, and others set aside for human habitation. However, the distinction was not always observed, and men and animals could find themselves lodged in the same place. In such cases, the "removal of such trifles as foul straw and manure was deemed superfluous". The smell was the first thing that struck Julius Price, "which, as far as I could guess, seemed a conglomeration of sewage, garlic, decomposed animal matter and general human uncleanness all mixed up together". Vermin were *de rigueur*, and rats were frequent visitors, often not scorning to clamber over the bodies of the inmates as they slept. The floors were of earth which became mud during the wet weather, as water poured through the roofs which often suffered from "slight breaks… in continuity", as Dingle put it.

The furniture was generally composed of a bed made of planks placed between trestles, on occasion a table, and sometimes even some chairs. "If these are steady it is lucky, if unbroken it is the exception…" At one end of the room there was a hollow raised platform called a kang that was also covered with thick planks and matting, and in which a fire was lit during the winter. The guests would squat on top of it for warmth during these times, despite the enhancement of the native odour of the room with the fumes from burning fuel. As for privacy, it was nothing more than a forlorn hope. The windows were filled not with glass but with fragile tissue paper, which generally hung in shreds. Even if it was sound, it served little in the way of a defence. Henry Lansdell, who travelled in China in the 1890s, found that the native Chinese would poke holes through the tissue paper with their fingers in order to watch his every move. Others would just walk straight in and stare at him transfixed. On remonstrating with them, they would simply answer "cannot I come into a room in my own country?".

As with the government transport and postal system, the arrangements for private travel, as they were seen in the 19th century, had not changed for hundreds, and perhaps thousands of years. The Chinese inn would have been a familiar sight to travellers from previous dynasties, and the camel cart and the mule litter remained in service over many centuries. It was not until the advent of the railways in China that there was any innovation in the way that people travelled. However, their construction was often bitterly opposed and fraught with difficulty, and it was not until well into the 20th century that considerable travel over long distances became possible in China by rail.

It was in 1837 that Russia first started experimenting with steam railways by building a 29-mile (47-kilometre) track from the capital St Petersburg to the Tsar's summer palace. It was not for another 30 years that China was even to get thus far. The first proposals for building railways in China did not come until the end of the Second Opium War in 1864, when an Anglo-American consortium under Sir MacDonald Stephenson, who had worked on the Indian rail network, made a proposal to build a line from Shanghai to Nanking. This, however, was turned down by the Chinese government on the grounds that the presence of foreign builders in the interior would not be tolerated, and nor would the expropriation of land from Chinese peasants for the construction of the railways. Railways, maintained the government, would only benefit China if they were built and managed solely by the Chinese themselves.

Shortly afterwards, the Chinese people themselves were given the first opportunity to see a railway in action. A British merchant, hoping to drum up support for the construction of railways throughout the country, built a toy railway one-third of a mile long outside one of the gates of Peking as a public demonstration of the technology. It was not well received. The citizens of Peking reacted with suspicion and hostility, and the government, fearing that it would bring some malign influence to bear on the capital, ordered it to be dismantled.

Despite further entreaties, there the matter rested until December 1874, when the Anglo-Hong Kong firm Jardine Matheson, growing weary of the Chinese government's intransigence, decided to take matters into its own hands. Having itself bought the necessary land, it started to construct its own railway to connect the concession port of Shanghai to the nearby town of Woosung, 10 miles away. The Chinese government bitterly protested, but Jardine Matheson was unrepentant. It maintained that it could do whatever it pleased with land that had been legitimately purchased.

The construction work proceeded relatively briskly. Two thousand Chinese labourers were employed, a bed 15-feet (4.5 metres) wide was cut for the length of the route, and British materials were shipped in for the assembly of the track. Also from Britain was the first locomotive, christened the Pioneer, weighing a ton, and designed to run on the narrow 30-inch gauge of the track. By 1876 the line was up and running, and began to offer up to six return services every day for paying passengers. Crowds of suspicious onlookers came to watch the operation of the train. Initially they held themselves back from using it, but many were soon won over to its cause after being offered an initial free ride. Before long, the venture began to make money, and the weekly profit per mile reached around £27.

However, its popularity was short lived. In the August of its first year, the train struck and killed a Chinese solider on the line. The incident afforded a rallying cry for the opponents of the line to unite. Many peasants, through whose land the railway passed, complained that the noise and tumult of the line was disturbing the repose of their ancestors and the *feng shui* of their tombs. The government moreover remained suspicious of the whole notion of the railway, fearing that it would eventually be used for foreign infiltration. Using the furore surrounding the first railway death to bring diplomatic pressure to bear on Jardine Matheson, the Chinese government compelled the firm to close the line, and surrender it in return for compensation. Once this transaction had been completed at the end of 1878, the government moved in to restore the *status quo ante*. They removed the rails, grubbed up the roadbed and demolished the stations. The locomotives and track were shipped to Taiwan, dumped on one of the beaches and left to rust. The government officials who supervised the work of destruction were carried to watch it borne in sedan chairs, as if expressing their abhorrence at the intrusion into China of mechanical locomotion.

Despite their eagerness to keep out the miasma of the railway, the Chinese government was not ultimately able to prevent it from spreading. The new steamships on the great rivers demanded great quantities of coal, and the government ultimately allowed short stretches of track to be built from the mines to the shipping depots. The wagons on these lines were initially drawn by mules and pack animals, but small locomotives were furtively constructed within China and began to be used without official consent. When it was discovered that this was the only method that could possibly keep the steamships supplied with the necessary quantity of fuel, the number of locomotives began to multiply, and their use was winked at by the authorities. However, the railways in China still remained of a minimal extent, and by 1895 – when the Russians were redoubling their efforts to construct the Trans-Siberian – China could still only boast no more than 200 miles of track, set aside almost exclusively for the transport of coal and iron ore.

As was often the case, it was a war that brought about a sudden change of attitude. The Sino-Japanese War of 1894–5 exposed the terrible weakness of China, and its desperate need for modern communications and ease of movement in order to defend itself adequately against foreign aggression. On the conclusion of hostilities, a struggle broke out between traditionalist and progressive elements in the government. The former were hostile to the presence of foreigners and feared for the peace of their ancestors. The latter worried that without modern transport China would forever be at the mercy of outsiders. Ultimately, the progressives prevailed. However, on account of that same weakness stemming from the Opium Wars, their defeat by Japan and general unrest, China was in no position to finance such a grand project as the construction of a national rail network.

hina's distress was the opportunity that foreign investors had long been waiting for, and international governments scrambled for railway-building concessions. The process did little for China's battered self-esteem. Despite their attempts to pay for as much of the work as possible by public fund-raising and share offerings, they could only raise a small proportion of the required capital. They were compelled to borrow from a wide variety of international corporations and conglomerates, often at heavily disadvantageous terms. Foreign specialists and engineers were brought in, and the machinery necessary for the construction of the railways was imported rather than being manufactured in China.

Worst of all, the foreign governments involved in the enterprises used the concessions as an informal way of marking out their spheres of influence, not even troubling to consult the Chinese government. The Yangtze River basin was seen as a British Zone, Mongolia as Russian, and South Manchuria as Japanese. Yet, despite these humiliations, China was ultimately able to benefit from the development of the railways. By the turn of the century, Peking was linked into a network that led to South Manchuria and which ultimately led to the Trans-Manchurian branch of the Trans-Siberian. By the middle of the first decade of the 20th century, the railways had penetrated into areas such as Yunnan and Canton (Guangdong), and also linked great cities such as Nanking and Shanghai. By 1909, the railway line that was ultimately to tie Peking to the classical Silk Road, the Longhai Railway, had begun construction. It reached Luoyang, one of the ancient Chinese capitals, in 1910, and after an interval of 25 years, was brought all the way to Xi'an, the great capital of the Han Empire, and the eastern terminus of the classical Silk Road. (By 1911, China's railway network had increased in extent to 5,800 miles, or 9,334 kilometres, and by 1920 to nearly 7,000 miles, or 11,265 kilometres.)

The British journalist and travel writer Peter Fleming was one of the first Westerners to travel by the new train line to Xi'an. In 1935, when in Peking, he was made special correspondent of *The Times*, and set himself the mission of penetrating into northwestern China where the civil war between the Nationalist and Communist governments was raging fiercely. He planned to travel by rail to Xi'an, and then join a conventional caravan from there to follow the old Silk Road routes up to Xinjiang Province, before turning south and heading for the safety of British India. The journey would be especially dangerous – the Chinese Red Army were making night marches of astonishing rapidity and attacks were possible almost anywhere.

However, despite the threats, Fleming was not unduly concerned. He revelled in the lackadaisical way he prepared for the journey of over 2,400 miles (nearly 5,000 kilometres). His main equipment consisted of a rook rifle, six bottles of brandy, and a copy of Macaulay's *History of England*. This was supplemented by two compasses, two portable typewriters, two pounds of marmalade, four tins of cocoa, one bottle of Worcester sauce, one pound of coffee, three packets of chocolate, soap, tobacco, knives, and beads to hand out as presents along the way.

None of this was of any comfort to him on the train journey. The first leg from Peking to Zhengzhou was at least tolerable, travelling in a first-class carriage with little to rile him except a couple of other complaining British travellers: "Darling, I don't think I should eat that fish if I were you. It's much safer to stick to boiled food on these trains." However, his problems came when he had to change at Zhengzhou. No express was available, and he was compelled to join a third-class slow train, departing from the station in the middle of the night. Chinese third class in this time probably equated to Russian fourth class. The carriages were of the sort found on the Trans-Siberian marked "40 men or 8 horses". A Chinese officer ushered Fleming to the one in which he was to travel. It contained 72 people, mostly sleeping. The officer kicked some of them awake and then pushed a number back to allow Fleming and his travelling companion, Ella Maillart, a two-foot space on a bare wooden bench for themselves and their baggage. Treading on various of the sleeping Chinese to reach their place, they heaped up a mountain of suitcases and kitbags, and tried to settle themselves on top. It was not a comfortable experience. It was the midst of winter, but the doors of the carriage were missing "like so much public property in China," commented Fleming. The carriage was without lights, and a small guttering stove in the corner "did not appreciably affect the mean temperature". Fleming and Maillart tossed and turned on top of their baggage, twisting themselves into more and more contorted poses in a vain attempt to stave off numbness. The train lurched and juddered on the track, babies cried incessantly through the night, and when they entered a tunnel the whole carriage filled up with a pungent and gritty black smoke.

A view of the Great Wall showing encroaching sands, 1911 – now obsolete, the wall was left to fall into ruin.

Although Fleming and Maillart could barely tolerate the terrible conditions and the absolute absence of comfort, the Chinese travellers scarcely seemed to notice. They had, said Fleming, the "gift of making one cubic foot into two and running the Black hole of Calcutta into an only slightly overcrowded debating hall". They were impervious to lack of elbow or any other sort of room, and huddled together happily in a giant and indistinguishable mass. The "intricate pattern of humanity" of the mass of squashed passengers "had a surface as smooth and harmonious as a completed jigsaw puzzle". In the crush the Chinese slept, ate, conversed, nursed babies, hunted lice in their padded winter clothes, and "accepted the prospect of the journey with complete equanimity".

As the train crawled into Shaanxi Province, the view from the open doors at least provided a modicum of distraction. The terrain was composed of loess, the rich and fertile yellow earth so characteristic of the country, on which ancient Chinese civilisation had built its original agricultural prosperity. Certainly for Fleming, the landscape had an unnerving sense of antiquity. There was a "prehistoric look" to the land. It looked almost like an "antediluvian monster" in its colours and peculiar forms. The earth, ochre streaked with red, was formed into weird terraces "grotesquer than the most outlandish ant-hills", naturally occurring, but "which had enough of symmetry in them to suggest the artificial". There was about the earth a "strangely brittle air". It eroded easily, and even the smallest streams gouged out vertiginous chasms and gullies. The landscape, recorded Fleming, had "few houses, but many habitations". Easier than building somewhere to live was to scoop out a cave from the friable loess. The terraces and gullies were riddled with these troglodyte dwellings. Some of them were even equipped with doors and tattered paper windows, and smears of black soot that rose from above the entrances "commemorated on the yellow sandstone the house fires of many generations".

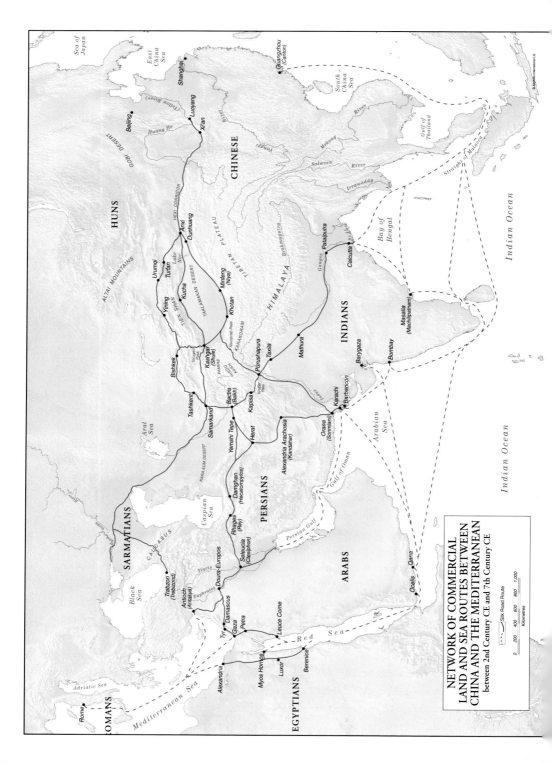

NETWORK OF COMMERCIAL
LAND AND SEA ROUTES BETWEEN
CHINA AND THE MEDITERRANEAN
between 2nd Century CE and 7th Century CE

- - - - Silk Road Route

0   200   400   600   800   1,000
Kilometres

The timelessness of the landscape seemed to find its apogee in Xi'an, the capital of the province. The place was not only the provincial capital, but had also been a capital of the Chinese Empire for various periods totalling over 1,100 years since the 2nd century BCE. It was the resting place, along with the Terracotta Army, of Qin Shi Huangdi, the great emperor who unified China and decreed the building of the Great Wall. Since his time, the city had seen countless dynasties rise and fall, the ravages of invading armies, and the coronation and assassination of many emperors. This sense of history, according to travellers, had a great and weighty bearing on the atmosphere of the city and the behaviour of its citizens.

One of the most acute observers of the city, Francis H. Nichols, an American traveller who made the journey there at the beginning of the 20th century to supervise the distribution of medical aid, commented on this at length. The city's apparent eternity, he wrote, was its peculiar and unique charm. The Xianese had a reckless way of referring to lapses of time that seemed hardly human. The Han or Tang dynasties were just as yesterday, and the people discussed events of the reign of Qin Shi Huangdi – who had died over two millennia previously – as if they had taken place just 50 years ago.

On top of this, the bearing of the people was refined and aristocratic. Many families there claimed to be able to trace their lineage back to the Han Dynasty and the era before Christ. The city was full of clubs and clubmen, societies of scholars, civil servants or military officers that were both exclusive and expensive. They would often meet to hold evening dinner parties of a "very slow" nature. Seldom were there more than 20 guests, and the functions would drag out half the night. Twelve to 15 courses would be slowly eaten, and the hours would be whiled away with "long discussions of a very serious character".

his aristocratic tendency was also manifested in the aloofness of the people, not just from foreigners, but also from people elsewhere in China. The post office, as an institution which brought Xi'an into contact with the outside world, was a place held in little esteem. According to Nichols, nine-tenths of the Xianese would never write a single letter from one end of the year to another. Even worse was the new telegraph line, which had been constructed to send orders to the mandarins from Peking. The opprobrium against this innovation was great, wrote Nichols, and it was heartily disliked by the citizens, many of whom felt that the "wire on the poles" was the abode of an evil spirit. Perhaps the best expression of the tendency to exclusivity was the obsession with the city walls. Rebuilt in their current form by the Ming emperors in the 14th century, the citizens still paid a large tax to keep them in good repair. Although not as great in length as those of Peking, being only 15 miles (24 kilometres) long, they were never less than 30 feet (nine metres) in height, and in some places rose to over 70 feet (21 metres). They were also enhanced by formidable towers four or five stories in height, pierced with dozens of windows for archers to shoot at attacking forces on the plain. The walls of the city, its well-maintained architecture, its compactness and its elegant arrangement were a great object of pride for the Xianese. They would often ask strangers if they didn't think that Xi'an was more pleasing and imposing than Peking. Nichols found himself unable to disagree.

The streets of Xi'an were broad and well laid, disposed at right angles, and each facing the cardinal points of the compass. There were no raised pavements or ditches at the edges of the streets, but the roadway itself stretched at a level from one side to the other. There was no mud or the danger of falling in

A modern-day view from Xi'an's Bell Tower towards the Drum Tower...

watery gullies, as in Peking. The whole was laid with thick stone slabs, which nevertheless, having been in use for centuries, were deeply worn and furrowed. Every day the streets were a bustle of activity, as traders with carts and mandarins in sedan chairs competed for space with customers heading for the many shops that lined the streets. In the centre, by the governor's residence, there was a fair held daily from sunrise to sunset. As in Peking, there were tents and booths with peddlers, jugglers and fortune-tellers. There was even, noted Nichols, a Chinese version of Punch and Judy, where puppets manipulated from behind a screen would quarrel, screech in falsetto, and cut off each other's heads. Every day the crowds would resort to the market for pleasure and entertainment, applauding the various shows and throwing cash at the performers to reward them.

The shops, wrote Nichols, had a different feel to those in many other Chinese cities. There was less of a sense of the bazaar about them. Silver jewellery, ivory carvings and pieces of jade were seldom traded, and the demand was for sturdier and more substantial goods – silk, cotton and tea. One thing that the city was particularly noted for was fur. The proximity of Xi'an to the wilds of Tibet made it one of the centres of the fur trade. The shops along several blocks of a long street were all dedicated to its sale. From here were drawn the supplies of mink and otter skins which mandarins throughout the empire used to line

...and the opposite view in the 1920s, this time from the Drum Tower across to the Bell Tower (archive photo by Osvald Siren).

their official robes. The prices, discovered Nichols, were absurdly cheap. A large leopard skin could be had for as little as seven dollars. Rarer, however, were foreign goods. The city did boast one department store at which it was said foreign goods would be sold, but on closer examination Nichols found that there was nothing of non-Chinese manufacture, save "a few cakes of French scented soap and about ten packages of American cigarettes".

The trade for which Xi'an was most noted in that time was banking. In Peking, the Xianese were often referred to as the "banking men". The city, on the western side, played host to a banking district with many dozens of institutions. The capital they dealt with was immense. A number had been in existence for centuries, but nevertheless they used modern methods of commerce. At home, domestic customers would be paid interest on their accounts. For those trading further afield, the banks maintained networks of correspondents in all the great cities, with whom funds were kept on deposit. With these could be traded drafts, promissory notes and bills of exchange. Travellers could deposit money in Xi'an, and pick it up elsewhere, on condition that they not only possessed the right bill of exchange, but also could satisfactorily identify themselves.

Y et despite these advanced practices, the methods used were thoroughly antique. There was not a hint of the cash till or typewriter. A Xianese banking hall was a minimalist place. Down one side would run a long counter on which there was nothing aside from, at one end, a set of scales for weighing coins. Behind this counter would sit a row of clerks, each issued with only a ledger book and an abacus. The capacity of the clerks for mental arithmetic was formidable. If one were to ask any of them the most complex of questions involving interest and rates of exchange, his fingers would immediately fly over the abacus "in a sort of lightning backgammon which lasts for about a minute", before he answered the inquiry correctly down to several decimal places. Never would he resort to scribbling down figures of calculations on paper, and certainly no other machinery was available to help him. The book-keeping also was simplicity itself: when a transaction was concluded, whether it was the sale of a bill of exchange, a deposit or a payment of interest, the clerk would do nothing but write down a few figures in a single ledger book with a brush. From this, he could give any customer a statement of his account "as readily and accurately as can any book-keeper in New York".

The southwest corner of Xi'an's city wall and West Gate, photographed by Osvald Sirén in the 1920s.

Although many in the city were of the banking profession, and although there were a number that one could describe as extremely rich, the city did not seem to suffer from the blight of social inequality. Despite the obvious inequalities in wealth, there was almost no one in the city who could be thought of as very poor. Nearly everyone in the city had a house and warm clothing. The vices of gambling and prostitution, which in Peking flourished as vigorously as under the Mongol emperors, seemed to be absent from Xi'an. There were no slum districts and no dives. Only a very small number of opium addicts appeared to be left out of the general prosperity. It was a matter of great surprise to Nichols that between the rich families who had fine villas in the fashionable district towards the southern wall and the poorest inhabitants, "there is not so wide a gulf of difference in education, opportunity, and environment as exists between a Fifth Avenue millionaire and the tenant of a Bowery lodging-house".

Xi'an's reputation as banking hub was only a function of its position as a great centre of travel and trade. For this, more than anything else, Xi'an was to earn its place in history. Xi'an has already been described as the eastern terminus of the classical Silk Road. Although such a definition is not a little problematic – the luxury trade of the ancient world certainly did not stop at Xi'an, and the trade routes were in existence, at least sporadically, long before the city had even been heard of – it nevertheless owes this accolade with some justification to one its citizens, Zhang Qian, one of the great travellers of the ancient world, and a pioneer of trade between China and the West.

In the second century BCE, Xi'an, then known as Chang'an, was the capital of China under the new Han Dynasty. The Han had only come to power at the beginning of the century, and in a short period of time they had achieved much. Following on from the work of Emperor Qin Shi Huangdi, the builder of the Great Wall, they had been able to unify the many warring Chinese states into a single empire, and had acted to standardise the systems of government, law,

The beautiful eighth century Little Goose Pagoda originally boasted 15 storeys, but two were lost to earthquakes in the 15th and 16th centuries.

coinage and written characters across the whole country. However, despite their successes, they still faced a considerable threat. On the steppes to the north of the empire dwelt the Xiongnu, a large confederation of Turkic nomads. The Xiongnu are thought to be the ancestors of the Huns, who after migrating west in later centuries were to bring the continent of Europe to the verge of collapse. In the time of the Han, the menace they bore to China was just as great. A formidable force of archers and cavalrymen, they used their mastery of guerrilla tactics to loot and pillage the Chinese cities, towns and agricultural settlements that had the misfortune to sit on the northern border. Coming under sustained and wearying attack, the Chinese found themselves unable to fight back. They neither had the military strength of the Xiongnu, nor did they possess the technology, wealth of horses, or the understanding of strategy to compete against their highly mobile methods of warfare.

The only solution, it seemed to the Chinese, was to seek out allies against the Xiongnu, and open up a war on two fronts. There was, they had heard, another nomadic horde called the Yuezhi, which had been displaced by the Xiongnu and had fled out to the far western regions. They would make, thought the Chinese government, ideal allies. They were certainly not well disposed to the Xiongnu. The skull of their leader, after their defeat at the hands of the Xiongnu, had been turned into a drinking vessel for the use of the Xiongnu chief. Not only would they be well disposed to the Chinese point of view about the Xiongnu, but they also understood the methods of nomadic guerrilla warfare. By working together and sharing their resources, thought the Chinese, they would be able to overcome their common enemy.

owever, there remained the basic problem of finding the Yuezhi. It was not a simple matter. It was known that they were vaguely somewhere in the west. But for the Chinese of this time, there was little known about the regions west of Xi'an. The knowledge of the modern-day region of Xinjiang, which at this time was a series of independent kingdoms that had never been under Chinese control, was nothing more than rumour. Beyond that, what could be said about Central Asia by the Chinese could be summed up in a handful of fantastical myths and legends. In Central Asia, they thought, would be found great monsters, isles of the blessed, and supplies of miraculous herbs which would confer immortality and restore eternal youth. The Persians and the Romans had never even been heard of.

The reason for this lack of knowledge was, of course, a lack of travel. There had been little in the way of official exploration, the sending of ambassadors or high-level trade. The presence of the Xiongnu and the instability of the regions to the west and northwest of Xi'an had, up to that point, been one of the principal restraints on the natural tendency to travel. The Xiongnu were known to have attacked travellers that they came across, often killing them without mercy and looting their property. If someone were to be sent to find the Yuezhi, they would have to contend with the fact that they did not know where to find them, that they did not know where they were going, and on top of that they would face the constant danger of capture by the Xiongnu.

In 139 BCE, Emperor Han Wudi decided to act. The situation for the Chinese was becoming increasingly difficult, and for all its perils the search for the Yuezhi would be worth the attempt. Therefore, the Emperor chose one of the Palace Guard, Zhang Qian, to mount an expedition to travel to the west to try and reach them. Zhang Qian at this time was 30 years old. Later accounts describe him as being courageous, strong and resolute, with the talent of winning men over to his side. He was given a detachment of 100 soldiers to accompany him, and also a Xiongnu renegade called Ganfu, a skilled archer who would act as a guide and advise him of the Xiongnu way of thinking.

After setting off from Xi'an, the expedition crossed the Yellow River and then entered the Hexi Corridor (in modern-day Gansu Province), a long and low-lying region between the Longshou and Qilian mountains leading northwest towards the Taklamakan Desert. Almost immediately, they ran into trouble – the area was under the control of the Xiongnu. For a time, they were able to evade the enemy, but after crossing the Great Wall they were discovered by a Xiongnu detachment, which captured them and led them into slavery. Zhang Qian was lucky not to have endured the same face as the Yuezhi ruler. After being brought before the Xiongnu chief, who asked contemptuously what business he had attempting to travel through Xiongnu territory when the same rights would not be accorded to his own people in China, Zhang Qian was put to work as a cattle herder in an aristocratic household.

For 10 years he lived in this fashion, even taking a Xiongnu wife and having a son by her. However, when a chance presented itself for escape, he, along with a number of his fellow Chinese captives, seized it. Nor did his wife neglect to follow him. They took with them supplies of dried food and water, and travelled westwards as quickly as they could, sleeping out in the open and relying on Ganfu and the other

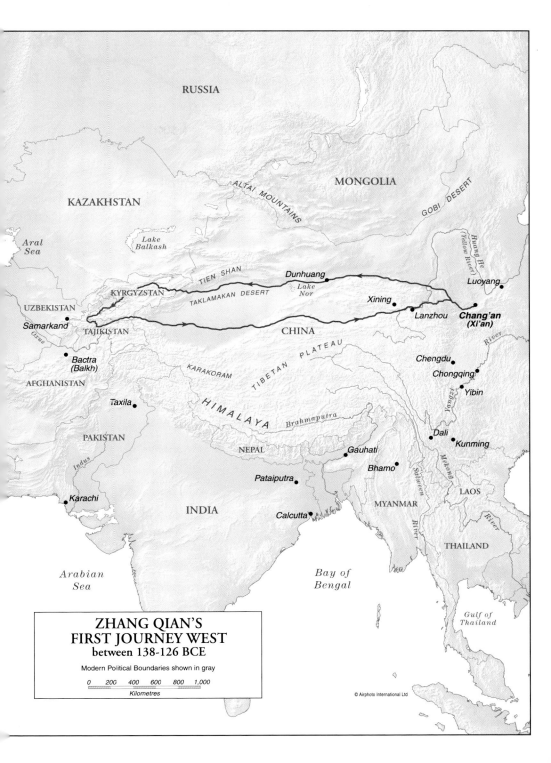

RUSSIA

MONGOLIA

KAZAKHSTAN

ALTAI MOUNTAINS

GOBI DESERT

Aral
Sea

Lake
Balkash

Huang He
(Yellow River)

TIEN SHAN

Dunhuang

Lake
Nor

Luoyang

KYRGYZSTAN

TAKLAMAKAN DESERT

Xining

UZBEKISTAN

Samarkand

Oxus

TAJIKISTAN

CHINA

Lanzhou

Chang'an
(Xi'an)

Bactra
(Balkh)

KARAKORAM

TIBETAN PLATEAU

Chengdu

River

AFGHANISTAN

Chongqing

Yibin

Yangzi

Taxila

HIMALAYA

Brahmaputra

PAKISTAN

Dali

Kunming

Indus

NEPAL

Gauhati

Mekong

Bhamo

Salween

LAOS

Pataiputra

MYANMAR

Karachi

INDIA

Calcutta

THAILAND

River

Arabian
Sea

Bay of
Bengal

Gulf of
Thailand

ZHANG QIAN'S
FIRST JOURNEY WEST
between 138-126 BCE

Modern Political Boundaries shown in gray

| 0 | 200 | 400 | 600 | 800 | 1,000 |

Kilometres

© Airphoto International Ltd

archers in the group to hunt down game for them to eat. Many of them perished along the way from hunger and thirst, but eventually they were able to reach the great salt lake of Lop Nor. Although in the midst of a wilderness, they were at least beyond the reach of the Xiongnu. Turning westwards, they passed along the northern fringe of the Taklamakan Desert in the modern-day province of Xinjiang, which was then divided into many petty kingdoms based around the small but prosperous oasis towns which dotted its length. Travel became somewhat easier, and Zhang Qian diligently noted the location, size and characteristics of each of the states through which he passed.

Beyond the Taklamakan, he was able to cross the Tian Shan or Heavenly Mountains via the Ili Valley and penetrate into Central Asia itself, where he was received hospitably by the King of the Dayuan, a kingdom based in the Ferghana Valley in present-day Uzbekistan. Zhang Qian here was able to learn not only the location of the Yuezhi – farther to the south in the northern regions of modern-day Afghanistan – but also much about the Western world which was new to Chinese understanding. He recorded the disposition and strength of the various kingdoms, and uncovered the existence of the Persians, Romans, and also the Indians. He was able to discover the location of roads, rivers and passes which connected the kingdoms and great cities. Finding Chinese goods for sale in the markets of Central Asia, such as cloth and bamboo, he even began to conjecture about the trade and links that might already exist at a low level between China and the West. Beyond this, he was presented with new varieties of fruit and vegetables, such as the turnip, garlic and sesame, as yet unknown in China. He also admired the horses bred in the region. These were not only strong, but also had the stamina to withstand long and arduous journeys. He noted how the conditions there were perfect for the cultivation of horses, and how they were fed on a variety of rich grass and alfalfa, which had never been grown in China. All of these potential resources were of great interest to the Chinese Empire, desperately short of horses and facing an enemy that had an abundance of them.

Zhang Qian was eventually conducted from the Ferghana Valley into northern Afghanistan, then called Bactria, where finally he was introduced to the long-sought Yuezhi. They listened to his proposal for an alliance against the Xiongnu with sympathy and considered his suggestion for over a year, but in the end they turned him down. They were happily settled in their new territories, did not wish to stir up old enmities, and also were not sure that the Chinese would make reliable partners, being so far distant.

Unable to secure the alliance, Zhang Qian eventually departed and began to make his way back to China, following a different route skirting the south of the Taklamakan Desert. Approaching his homeland, he was once more captured by the Xiongnu and this time kept as a prisoner in chains. However, on the death of the Xiongnu king his empire fell into a period of chaos, and Zhang Qian was again able to escape. At length he reached Xi'an in 126 BCE, 13 years after his departure. Only his wife and his companion Ganfu remained of the original travelling party. What happened to his son is unknown.

When Zhang Qian returned to Xi'an, the Emperor Han Wudi was still ruling in China. He was amazed at the return of his old envoy, and despite his failure to make a treaty with the Yuezhi, he showered him and also his companion Ganfu with honours, imperial titles and praise. Han Wudi had the insight to realise the importance of what Zhang Qian had achieved. He had been the first Chinese traveller in the era of recorded history to travel from China to the Western Kingdoms, chronicle his journey in detail so that the routes and locations would be available for future travellers, and also open relations with the kings of Western courts. Han Wudi understood that with this powerful information he would be able to set up communications with the outside world, search for other allies against the Xiongnu with far greater ease, garner military resources for the defence of China, and encourage trade to generate wealth.

Promptly he sent Zhang Qian to start exploring other routes to the West, and also to open more permanent relations with the Western kings. By around 110 BCE, the first Chinese embassy, led by one of Zhang Qian's colleagues, reached the Persian Empire. They presented the Persians with bolts of fine silk cloth, the first time that the fabric is known to have reached the Western world.

Before long, trade caravans were making their way along the newly opened roads between Persia and Xi'an. To China was brought an abundance of luxury goods. From Persia there came ostrich eggs and dishes of rock crystal, tables of jade from Khotan on the southern side of the Taklamakan, pearls, precious stones, and objects of tortoiseshell and rhino horn. There came animals, some ornamental such as Persian lions, peacocks and elephants, and also some for use, such as camels and the fine horses which Zhang Qian had so admired in the Ferghana Valley. Even more practically there came vines and alfalfa, sesame, hemp, carrots and coriander, onions, cucumbers, beans and saffron, the walnut tree and the pomegranate.

In the other direction China sent silk and high-quality iron – both of which were used by the Persians in their battles with the Romans, the silk for standards and the iron for weapons. They also sent lacquered woodwork and bamboo, bronze mirrors, ginger, cinnamon and rhubarb. Not only this, but metalworking technology and the knowledge to make a variety of metal alloys from tin, copper, nickel and silver, found its way westwards from China.

Before long, Chinese military garrisons and agricultural settlements began to spread up the Hexi Corridor towards Lop Nor and into the Taklamakan Desert. Peopled with convicts and settlers, merchants and low-ranking officials, they were responsible not only for securing the western flank of China against nomadic attack, but also for protecting the commerce which was now passing in great volumes along the trade routes. Xi'an itself had been transformed by the opening of the trade routes. Its population rose to over a quarter of a million. A first century CE Chinese chronicler, Ban Gu, described the opulence of the capital and its new-found reliance on international trade: "The walls were as of iron, a myriad spans in extent; the encircling moat dug deep as an abyss. Three stretches of highway were laid out, twelve gates of ingress and egress were erected. Within were the streets and cross-streets, the ward gates numbered a thousand. Nine market places were opened, the merchandise displayed, kind by kind in ordered rows."

This opulence, the opening of the trade routes ultimately linking China all the way to Persia, India and Rome, the spread of Buddhism, Christianity, Zoroastrianism and Islam into China and the spread of Chinese civilisation into the Xinjiang region of Central Asia, can all ultimately be traced back to that groundbreaking journey by Zhang Qian. There were earlier contacts between China and the West, but they were halting and slight, below the view of history. It was not until Zhang Qian endured his journey into the unknown that the West and China could in any way get to know each other, and the multitude of travellers on the Silk Road over the next 2,000 years could with any confidence make their way.

A s with elsewhere in China, the conditions for travellers beyond Xi'an did not significantly change between the time of Zhang Qian and the modern age. The railways did not follow Zhang Qian's route beyond Xi'an to Xinjiang and northwestern China until the end of the 1950s. Well into the 20th century, travel to these regions from the heart of China was conducted in a fashion that would be recognised by the early Silk Road traders.

One of the best accounts of travelling Zhang Qian's route out of China was left by Mildred Cable, a formidable Chinese-speaking missionary who traversed the route on several occasions in the 1920s. The region at this time was suffering not only from the ravages of civil war and warlords; the after-effects of the Muslim uprisings of the 1870s were still also being felt. In this way, there is a strange parallel between travel in her time, and Zhang Qian's careful negotiation of the marauding Xiongnu nomads.

Cable departed from Xi'an in a mule litter, such as was used between the Chinese frontier with Mongolia and Peking. She was not foolish enough, as were other Western travellers using these modes of transport, to keep out bottles of brandy and scotch to gladden the journey and expect them to survive unbroken. She was prudent in her packing, and prepared for the bumpy ride by ballasting the litter with heavy boxes, padding them down with wadded quilts, cushions and rugs. The mules were accompanied by a driver who walked on foot. In this region, the drivers had their own distinct ways of keeping the animals in order. Rather than using a stick or rope, they would drive them by throwing pebbles, each cast with a perfect aim. One on the nose was a warning to move backwards, and one on the hindquarters equivalent to an order to move on. Some drivers, who had grown up with mules from their early childhood, could boast an understanding of their psychology and way of thinking that was entirely without parallel. They could lead them entirely by noises and word of mouth. One sound might mean "water ahead", another "keep right", and another, as Cable put it, "you villain, if you do that again, when we get to the inn tonight I shall kill you, and spend a merry night eating your flesh boiled and fried".

The mule litter was by no means the only type of vehicle seen along the way. Gansu carts were conspicuous on the road, pulled by sturdy Urumqi horses. They were made entirely of wood, and so ingeniously crafted that not a single piece of metal, not even a nail, was used in their construction. They rode on great wheels, eight feet (2.5 metres) in diameter, tall enough to get them over any ford or along the muddiest highway. Their roofs, instead of felt or leather, were made of grass matting, and the whole contrivance seemed to Cable to be more redolent of rural France in the 19th century, rather than China.

The types of transport on the way could be identified just as easily by ear as by sight. Each vehicle had its own distinctive clamour. The carts of merchandise from the Taklamakan Desert, strung together into great caravans accompanied by up to 50 camels, could be heard more than half an hour before they were seen. Not only did the grumbling and cries of the camels go before them, but also the clanging of deep bells which served to warn other travellers of their approach. Lighter, tinnier bells also warned of the advent of the mail courier, travelling alone on horseback, and always riding at a fast canter. It was always a pleasure to meet him on the journey, recalled Cable. Not only was he unfailingly cheerful and friendly, but was full of vital information, relaying gossip and news about what might be encountered on the road ahead.

The scenery of the way from Xi'an into Gansu was often bucolic and picturesque. The plain around Xi'an, traversed by many tributaries of the Yellow River, was rich and fertile. At the right time of year, one would see vast fields of wheat, and late in autumn groves of persimmon trees with dark foliage and ripening golden fruits would add to the beauty of the picture. The wayside food in this region, according to Cable, was the best in China, and the local pears were beyond comparison. The spiritual was instinct in the landscape. The mills along the way served not only to grind flour, but also to turn prayer wheels. Plantations of trees clustered around shrines and carvings of the Buddha in the soft rock, and little booths sold carvings of wood from the jujube, red, dark and so tough as almost to be indestructible.

Yet, despite these beauties and constant motifs of interest, the signs of poverty and the aftermaths of war were ever present. Along the road, one would encounter a trail of empty towns, or suburbs with uninhabited and ruined houses. Fleeing from the Bolshevik Revolution and civil war beyond the northern border, White Russian refugees were to be found all along the trail, begging their way towards Peking. Russian women, despairing of making the journey, sold themselves as prostitutes or concubines in the cities.

Less conspicuous but more numerous were the Chinese beggars. They would congregate in their hundreds, especially outside city gates or the gates of temples. Clothed in tatterdemalion garments, they proffered an unending range of deformities in order to evoke sympathy from travellers and passers-by. In some places, they were less vulnerable than they seemed. Occasionally, they would band together to form a union, and impose a protection racket on the traders, against which the police were helpless. Yet, in other places, they were genuinely without succour. Despite their best efforts, however, there was often little pity or comfort for them. It was not uncommon, in the cold winter weather, to see a man, woman or child frozen to death on the side of the path, and no one would trouble to remove the corpse, unless it happened to be a tradesman in front of whose shop the beggar had died.

Even for a traveller with all the necessities of life, the everyday details of travel never ceased to be squalid. Frequently, the inns would be hollowed out of the loess cliffs. Their quality, however, did not improve with the distance travelled, and it was often difficult to tell them apart from stables. The walls were black, wrote Cable, with the dirt of generations, the floors were covered with manure, the luggage was kept in mangers, the doors were filthy hanging rags, and for light there was nothing but a flickering lamp of linseed oil. Often they would be a resort for opium smokers, and men insensible with the drug would huddle together in the recesses, eager for a draw on their pipe.

As one moved further northwest, inns run by Muslim Chinese began to appear. These were distinguished by the sign of a painted teapot outside their gates, and the words *kiao* men, "member of the assembly". They pretended to a cleanliness above the standards of other inns, but this, according to Cable, was a cleanliness not visible to the naked eye. It rather manifested itself in "endless bickering with the travellers on matters of purification connected with material or cooking utensils". Even in these inns, the fires to warm the rooms would be fuelled with horse dung. Their fumes were laden with so nauseating a smell that it permeated the traveller's bedding and clothing so as to be noticeable for weeks. But at least it had the effect of improving the décor of the rooms. The fumes so imbued the woodwork that they rapidly gained a surface equal in colour and polish to the best old oak.

According to his narrative, Marco Polo passed through Gansu and the Hexi Corridor, but of its cities he had little to report. According to his memoirs he spent a year in the capital of the region, Kanchau, the modern-day Zhangye, "but without any experiences worth recording". But he does at least speak of his abiding impression of the place as a "large and splendid city", full of adherents of many religions, both "idolaters, with some Mahometans… and also Christians". All faiths, not just the Christians, were endowed "fine large churches… many monasteries and abbeys", and the "idolaters" possessed a "vast quantity of idols", some "as much as ten paces in length…" made of wood, earthenware or stone, and "all covered with gold of excellent workmanship".

Entering this frontier area of China 600 years after the time of Marco Polo, Mildred Cable found in the cities that the diversity of faiths had by no means declined. Endlessly more extensive than Marco Polo in her descriptions of the region, she came across a profusion of people and practices. In Zhangye and Jiuquan, she found native Chinese and Chinese customs in the majority. In Zhangye as much as in Peking, the descendants of the first Chinese who settled there after Zhang Qian kept family shrines with names of their ancestors engraved on tablets. Incense would be burnt before them as offerings, and every day at sunset the women of the household would toll the bell over the shrine nine times, in three groups of three, and similarly beat the wooden drum "shaped like a crab" to recall them.

In Jiuquan, the last town within the Great Wall, she happened at one time to be present for the celebration of the Chinese New Year. Again, the festivities were just as she had seen in other parts of China, although they were celebrated on a different date to that decreed by the official almanac published by the Board of Rites in Peking. As elsewhere, the run-up to the celebration was marked by the sounds of "wrangling, quarrelling and violent invective". The 12th month of the year was the time usually set aside for debt collection, and as angry creditors banged at the doors, the debtors made their escapes by backdoors, apertures in the roof or holes in the floor. But as the fury for uncollected debt mounted to a crescendo and seemed ready to engulf the town in uproar, New Year's Eve fell upon them, and all the anger was forgotten. Obscene curses were put aside in favour of courtly bows. Families came together to feast, pay calls and make merry. The night was marked with crackers and fireworks, the ringing of temple bells, gongs and incense. By day, the rites of the New Year were celebrated. A cow was sculpted of mud, stuffed with dried fruits, to be a symbol of the spring and the return of fertility to the earth. Before it in his green sedan chair, the highest mandarin of the city burnt incense, and the workmen of the various trade guilds performed pageants.

After these religious duties were performed, the main street was turned into one long casino for an orgy and carnival of gambling. Croupiers spread out tables which surrounded with strings of cash, coins with holes, strung up hanging from red cords. For three days, such was the frenzy that the streets were completely clogged. People crowded onto the roofs to watch the pandemonium below. Everyone joined in the wagers around the tables, and around them swirled an endless throng of revellers with vividly painted faces, brilliant outfits of green, pink and scarlet, and garlands of artificial silk flowers in their hair.

And yet, despite the Chinese way of life being followed at the very fringe of the empire, Cable found other peoples and other ways of life in this border territory. The proximity to Tibet was deeply felt. Tibetan women were prominent amongst the travellers on the road. Their dress marked out their nationality, with clumsy top boots, gaudy embroideries, and headdresses with coral beads and seashells, turquoise and jade, hanging down from the nape of their neck to the knees. They were excellent riders, and all from young girls to 70-year-old women could leap on a horse bareback in pursuit of a runaway animal.

Beyond Zhangye were to be found Tibetan Buddhist monasteries and shrines. The roads in various valleys were lined not only with blue irises and edelweiss, but also dome-like roadside reliquaries, known as *chortens or stupas*. Prayer wheels and prayer flags lined the streams and wayside, and human bones engraved with prayers, hanging from trees, rattled in the wind. At the monasteries there were great pageants, just as many travellers had seen on the Russian borders and in Mongolia, watched by orange-robed lamas wearing diadems like triple crowns. Performers in the sacred mysteries wore fantastical masks with death's heads and harlequin outfits or satin robes, all accompanied by music suggestive of their character. Their costumes might represent deities of cattle and flocks, of the home and hearth, or else the powers of nature, the god and goddess of thunder. And after the performances, braziers were lit by the lamas, and as they rang bells they would feed into the fires the sacrifices of butter and wheat, chips of wood, fodder and poppies.

Just as much as the influence was being felt from Tibet, so also was it felt from the Turkic populations of Central Asia. The inns run by Muslims were not the only sign of one's impending departure from China. In Jiuquan, there was a whole Muslim suburb outside the city walls, from which the trade with the Taklamakan and Central Asia would be coordinated. Muslims had been forbidden from living inside the city since an uprising in 1862, and this suburb was as un-Chinese as the city itself was Chinese. The inhabitants, as well as the visitors who had travelled the trade routes from Central Asia, were dressed in the characteristic wadded coats of striped cotton or silk with loose trousers and high leather boots. On their heads they wore turbans, and many of them sported thick brown curly beards. The language was Turkic, not Chinese. Their markets were more reminiscent of what would be seen outside China further along the Silk Road. There were bales of cotton, along with rugs and fine saddlebags heaped up for sale on the stalls. They sat by great mounds of dried sultanas, apricots, and strips of dried melon. The whole proceedings of the market took place beneath the shadow of the dome and crescent of a whitewashed mosque, and the sound of students studying the Qur'an under the tutelage of a master mingled with the uproar of commerce.

Since the time of the Ming Dynasty in the 14th century Jiayuguan fortress, a little west of Jiuquan, had marked the traditional limit of the Chinese Empire and the western end of the Great Wall. Here, the Hexi Corridor narrowed to a strait defile no more than 10 miles (16 kilometres) in width, and sheer mountains hemmed the route in on both sides. "Jiayuguan" may be translated as "Barrier of the Pleasant Valley", and when Cable first reached it the name did not belie the nature of the place. On the Chinese side of the fort there were green meadows richly watered by springs and a small town. Above all this the mountains, covered in snow almost to the ground, provided an imposing backdrop to "the Earth's greatest barrier". The valley was stopped up by a clay wall several miles long; thus, all traffic had to pass through the fortress itself, a magnificent structure with a tall gate-tower, "splendid outer walls, loophole battlements, towers… and military barracks, still occupied", which "gave an impression of medieval importance to a place which otherwise would only be a tumbledown village".

However, as pleasant as the valley might have been, the border outpost was heavy with melancholy associations. For generations of Chinese, it was the gateway to the unknown. Looking from the pinnacles of the watchtowers across the old boundary line, the very sight of the territory was forbidding and without comfort. The area beyond the gate of Jiayuguan was known as Kow Wai – "the land beyond the mouth". The thought of journeying beyond this point brought horror to the Chinese. Beyond was no greenery but only the undulating expanse of the Gobi Desert. This was interrupted by the occasional abandoned settlement and, at 100 miles (160 kilometres) distance but still just visible, the ruined fort at Yumenguan or "Jade Gate Pass", where the Great Wall ended in Han times and which many Chinese once regarded as the very edge of the civilised world.

Sir Aurel Stein, one of the greatest explorers of the Silk Road, who travelled in the region in the first decade of the 20th century, felt a sense of "utter desolation" in this region. Cable, beholding the vista before her, was chilled not so much by the wintry wind that blew across the desert, but by the thought that this was the road by which one left China. Armies and merchants, heading for an uncertain future and years away from their families at home, would all have passed this way. Worse than this, an endless procession of outcasts over hundreds of years would have taken this route into exile. This thought was never far from Cable's mind. "If ever human sorrow has left an impress on the atmosphere of a place," she wrote, "it is surely here, through whose portals for centuries past a never-ending stream of despairing humanity has filed. Disgraced officials, condemned criminals, homeless prodigals, terrified outlaws, the steps of all these have converged to that one sombre portal, and through it have forever left the land of their birth."

The fear of exile and this very road to the unknown west was a consistent theme in Chinese legend and literature back to its earliest age. Many traditions hold that Laozi, the 7th century BCE semi-mythical founder of Taoism, followed the route along the Hexi Corridor to live as a hermit in the wilderness of the Gobi after China spurned his teaching. Legend also holds that he dictated his only surviving work, the I Ching, to one of the border guards in this region before he departed. Chinese poets of every period have also voiced their fear of departing along this route in their verses. Wang Zhihuan, a poet of the Tang Dynasty in the 8th century CE, expressed it thus:

The Yellow River soars to the white clouds,

The Great Wall disappears among ten thousand mountains,

Why does the Tartar flute play a lament for the willow trees?

The spring wind never passes Jade Gate Pass.

Surveying the walls of the fortress, Cable found many more recent, simple and heartrending examples of verse bidding farewell to China, scratched as graffiti by the many nameless travellers who passed before her: "When I leave thy gates of Jiayuguan/ My tears may never cease to run."

The actual moment of crossing the traditional threshold of China was also replete with customs. One of these, records Cable, was that travellers would throw a pebble on the outer side of the Great Wall. If the pebble rebounded towards the traveller, it meant that they would return to China in safety. If it fell to the ground, the traveller would never see China again. Cable noted that the wall by the gate had been worn away by these pebbles, and that a great heap of them lay at its foot.

INTO THE WESTERN REGIONS

aving passed the frontier of Jiayuguan, Cable found the desert territory beyond it towards the city of Anxi, the next major stop on the route, full of danger but enchantment. One of the first sights to catch her attention were the vultures, which preyed upon abandoned pack animals and even lost travellers. The first group of these that she saw sitting in the distance on the ground were so huge and statuesque that it was not until they were closely examined through binoculars that she could be sure they were really living creatures and not a row of rocks. They were of a tremendous size. When they moved on the ground they waddled like "small bears", but in flight they were grand and magnificent, bringing a sense of foreboding over any members of the caravan who caught sight of them above.

The way towards Anxi was dotted with the ruins of deserted villages, towns and even cities, speaking of a more prosperous past hundreds of years ago when the trade routes were flourishing in full vigour. Approaching these at night or towards daybreak, the sight of them plunged Cable into a speechless contemplation. "No words could evoke the extraordinary sensations crossing in moonlight, or the uncertain pallor of dawn, these abodes of the past, whose deserted streets are sometimes still clearly defined, and where abandoned houses, with yawning doorways, stand tenantless on either side." The largest of these abandoned settlements was Pulungki, about 35 miles (56 kilometres) beyond Jade Gate Pass. Once it had been a city of 50,000 people. When Cable visited, it was nothing but a collection of scattered ruins hemmed in by an immense encircling wall. A few inns eked out a living from the occasional passing traveller. In such places, she recorded, "nothing can be too fantastic for the imagination to devise, even after lingering in such surroundings only for a few hours".

Overawed travellers generated and attached a host of the most fantastic legends to the spot, which were carried up and down along the way. Some held that Pulungki was the original Eden of the human race. The land beneath it was replete with fantastic hoards of ancient treasure, protected by magic, or guarded by hosts of demons. Every hole in the ground was the entrance to a robber's den, or else an "Arabian Nights" grotto piled with glistering stones". There were stories of men digging in the ground and seeing stashes of gold, but when they reached down to gather it a rush of wings would throw the searchers violently to earth, and the gold would disappear.

The city of Anxi, the first major settlement beyond Jiayuguan, was not, when Cable visited it, a ruin, but it was not far off being one. The original old city had been destroyed in a series of Muslim rebellions against Chinese rule in the 19th century, and it had, by the 1920s, been only pitifully rebuilt. On arrival, she was given special permission to climb and walk round the city walls, a privilege only granted to women on special holidays. From the height of its battlements, the city revealed itself in "full decrepitude".

Large open spaces were heaped with accumulated rubbish, and not a single building was in good repair. Many large houses were crumbling away, leaving only single rooms out of entire buildings habitable. The disrepair spread even to the army barracks and the temples, which were falling to bits, the whitewash peeling off their shabby walls. The sense of abandonment and decrepitude was intensified by the climate. The place was "cold and storm-swept, exposed on every side". The winds were said to blow every day of the year, but in winter their onslaught was so terrible that all the shops shut, and everything came to a standstill. Coal and wood for fuel were unobtainable, and in the winter months everyone retreated indoors, eating and sleeping on the dung-fuelled kang, using the opium pipe to distract them from any thought of the freezing temperatures without.

Yet, this place was one of the vital stops on the ancient Silk Route. In Tang times the Chinese stationed troops there to ward off attacks from the desert nomads, calling it "The Western Protecting Garrison". It was a major crossroads, where the road from Xi'an split in two. One could choose the northern Silk Road, which led to the oasis cities on the northern edge of the Taklamakan Desert – Turfan (Turpan), Kuqa (Kucha) and Aksu. Alternatively there was the southern route, which led to Khotan (Hotan or Hetian) and Yarkand (Shache), before reuniting with the northern route at Kashgar at the western end of the Taklamakan. Also from Anxi there were even routes leading back east, passing north of the mountains through the Gobi desert back to Mongolia and Kalgan.

(Left) Tang Dynasty pottery of bearded Westerner with wineskin, part of the George Crofts collection in the Royal Ontario Museum. (Right) A Northern Wei Dynasty terracotta figure of a bearded foreigner on a camel, held at Paris's Cernuschi Museum.

It was therefore appropriate that at Anxi, amongst the decay, Cable found the traditional trade of the Silk Road had not yet been completely obliterated by the passing of time. The inns were still full of merchants and tradesmen, just as they had been for hundreds of years. Equally there were cart drivers and camel men who would use their stop in Anxi to rest and revel, joining makeshift travellers' clubs for the purpose of carousing and feasting; there would be no time on the long stretches of the journey ahead for any relaxation from effort.

The chief export in these winter months was wool. Cable saw caravans of hundreds of camels, each laden with heavy bales for shipment from Central Asia to the east. The merchants accompanying these goods knew all there was to know about the trade. They knew the prices that the wool would fetch in every city. They showed Cable how buyers would judge the quality of the wool by the feel and smell of samples; how the experts could tell by the texture of a handful whether the sheep had grazed on mountain pastures, lowland grass or the steppe, even whether the sheep had been fed on a north- or south-facing slope. They also showed her the old trick of inconspicuously weighing down the bales with fine Gobi sand, so as to get a better price when the wool was put on the scales. This same trick, it is known, was practised by wool merchants on the Silk Road 1,000 years before Cable saw it performed.

he task of unearthing the ancient life of the Silk Road, close in spirit but far removed in time from the beginning of the 1900s, was taken up in the late 19th and early 20th centuries by an intrepid and, one might say freebooting group of Western archaeologists and academics. One of the most prominent of this adventurous generation of scholars was Sir Aurel Stein (1862–1943). Hungarian by birth, he studied oriental languages at a number of European universities before gaining British citizenship and joining the Indian Civil service in 1887. In 1900, reading of the travels of Russian and other expeditions to the ancient frontiers of China, he determined to follow in their footsteps. He organised a number of his own expeditions to the region, and in 1907 came upon Dunhuang, one of the first stops on the Southern Silk Road, just four days journey out of Anxi. It was here at Dunhuang that he was to make one of his most important discoveries.

The way to Dunhuang shared the desolation of the region beyond Jiayuguan. The land was almost completely barren and bare of vegetation. The road, as Cable describes it, led over what seemed an expanse of salt that glittered brightly when illumined by starlight. The backdrop was a range of volcanic hills which seemed different every hour of the day, their colours changing according to the height of the sun from blue, to purple, to silver grey. Along the road itself there was scarcely a landmark to be seen. Stein recalled the occasional semi-derelict fort inhabited by cultivators trying to eke out a living, "so-called inns" full of opium fumes and the listless addicted, and little roadside shrines built of clay, festooned with votive offerings of papers and incense sticks.

However, the city itself made a sudden and agreeable contrast to the bleak surrounding landscape. It stood, surrounded by square walls, in the midst of an oasis. It was girded with farmland and large park-like orchards traversed with rushing streams. Many of the trees were pear trees, for which the city was celebrated. "So gay a place was it," writes Cable, that it had the nickname of "Little Peking". However, it was not just the sudden greenness which made the oasis pleasant. It was also a centre of trade, and an important

The ruins of a Han watchtower near Dunhuang – the distant dunes must have once been an ominous sight for those heading west

halt on the Silk Road. The first sign of it was meeting traders leading caravans from as far afield as Khotan in the west of the Taklamakan Desert. The inns bristled with merchants, "filthy Turkish traders from Kashgar and Yami", as Stein put it, who nevertheless ensured that the marketplace was always busy with goods and with buyers. Women in brightly coloured clothes came in from the farms in the outskirts for a day's shopping, and professional storytellers would circulate, working the crowds and providing amusement.

In these respects, the town had not changed for hundreds of years. Although it had passed through the hands of a number of different rulers many times throughout history – from the Chinese in the 1st century BCE, to the Tibetans, Mongols, Uighurs and then back to the Chinese in the 17th century CE – it remained a bastion of international trade. That trade brought not only prosperity, but also new ideas from abroad and the wealth to make them manifest. The Mogao Caves, or "The Caves of a Thousand Buddhas", located in a valley 16 miles (25 kilometres) to the southeast of the city, were the practical result of this mixture of money, travel, commerce and new ideas. In 366 CE, a Buddhist monk named Lie Zun came upon this valley and saw a vision of a thousand golden rays of light, "shining upon him like as many Buddhas". In commemoration of this vision, he hewed out and decorated a small cave in the side of the valley, consecrating it as a shrine and painting it with pictures of the Buddha and Buddhist images in order to win divine protection for his travels. Other travellers and pilgrims followed suit, and over a period of 1,000 years, the cliffs became honeycombed with a multitude of caves, becoming a great repository for Buddhist art.

The Caves, recorded Stein, the sight of which reminded him of the "troglodyte dwellings of anchorites... [from] early Italian paintings", betrayed the influences of every station on the Silk Road, and how truly international the place had been in its heyday. Some of the frescoes, with rich floral borders, graceful curves and ornate landscape backgrounds, bore Chinese influence; others, where there was a preponderance of deep greens and blues, the influence of Tibet. Some of the paintings echoed those Stein had seen in other of the nearby oases in the Taklamakan Desert; still others betrayed influences from much further afield, Indian and even Greek art. However, his detailed survey of the caves paled into insignificance in comparison to his discovery and removal of the Caves' greatest treasure: the Dunhuang Manuscripts.

Stein had heard a number of rumours that hidden in one of the caves in the Dunhuang complex was an enormous quantity of ancient scrolls. Knowing, he wrote, "what Indian experience had taught me of the diplomacy most likely to succeed with local priests usually as ignorant as they were greedy", he thought the same "might work on Chinese soil too". Therefore, he set to work attempting to bribe reliable information from the small community of monks and religious men who still lived at the shrine. At length, he found the truth of the matter. Not long before, when one of the caves was being restored, a bricked-up recess had come to light in which over 10,000 manuscripts had been found. They had probably lain there forgotten for around 1,000 years, hidden during one of the occasional moments of chaos which engulfed the oasis as different powers struggled for control. Samples of these manuscripts had been sent to the Chinese Viceroy of Gansu who recognised their importance, but lacked the resources to transport them to safety. He therefore ordered them to be concealed in their original resting place, and the recess to be fitted with a heavy lockable door. Armed with this information, Stein thought the way would be clear for him to prise the manuscripts from the grasp of the monks.

193. GIGANTIC ROLL OF PAPER, WITH SANSKRIT AND 'UNKNOWN LANGUAGE' TEXTS IN BRAHMI SCRIPT, FROM WALLED-UP TEMPLE LIBRARY, 'THOUSAND BUDDHAS,' TUN-HUANG.

Scale, one-fifth.

A shows the roll, which is over seventy feet long, partially opened.
B shows the silk painting on top of outer side.

Sanskrit writing on paper with a painted silk covering, part of Aurel Stein's haul from Dunhuang, now held by the British Library.

The leader of the community was a Taoist priest named Wang Yuanlu, who styled himself the *Tao-Shih*, or Abbot. Stein regarded him with little more than contempt. "As ignorant of what he was guarding as he was full of fears concerning gods and men, he proved at first a difficult person to handle." Although the Abbot did indeed want money, it was not for the sake of himself, but rather for his pet project, the restoration and maintenance of the shrines. However, even the "temptation of money for the shrine or personal gain was not itself likely to overcome his scruples". Even more important was his sheer reverence for the documents. He did not know what might be the fate of them should he surrender them to Stein, and feared even to let him see them. For a moment Stein was at a loss, until he realised that one of the frescoes in the cave complex was of one of the great travellers of the ancient Silk Road, a 7th century monk named Xuanzang. Stein remembered the story of Xuanzang, that

Wang Yuanlu, the Taoist priest who sold Stein the enormously valuable manuscripts for the equivalent of £130.

he had undertaken a perilous journey from China to India by way of Central Asia in order to obtain more and better texts of the Buddhist scriptures for his Chinese brethren. Inspired by this, he gestured to the fresco, which depicted Xuanzang leading a caravan of 20 donkeys, which were laden with sacred scrolls and relics. Surely, argued Stein, he himself was nothing less than a modern-day Xuanzang, who had ventured through many perils and hardship in the pursuit of knowledge and pure Buddhist texts. To allow him to take the scrolls would be an act of piety, for he would propagate them to the rest of the world, just as Xuanzang had done 12 centuries previously, rather than allowing them to languish forgotten in a distant cave.

Stein's meretricious appeal, which was as false in spirit as it was true in fact, found its mark. Before long, he was led to the cave, the doors were unlocked, and he was shown the astonishing wealth within. In the small recess, about nine feet square, there was a solid mass of manuscript scrolls, stacked to a height of 10 feet. Amongst them were rolled-up paintings on fine silk and linen, as well as temple banners festooned with silken streamers. As they were passed out to him, Stein inspected each item by the guttering light of a small oil lamp. The scrolls were made of good strong paper, a foot in width and some as much as 20 yards in length. They were written in a variety of languages, from Chinese to Indian and extinct Central Asian tongues. Their condition did little to betray their age. Some were as old as the 5th century CE. It was the same for the paintings of the Buddhist divinities, which displayed "perfect freshness, and remarkable fineness".

This discovery would be one of the most important of Stein's career. Although he was fully aware of the need for "diplomatic restraint", he could hardly conceal his eagerness. Working as quickly as possible to determine which were the most important items, like Xuanzang he filled 20 cases full of paintings, relics and manuscripts, pausing only to give "judiciously administered doses of silver" to Abbot Wang "to counteract his relapses into timorous contrariness". Despatching the cases to England, they arrived in London in 1908 to form the centrepiece of a huge collection of Silk Road documents that Stein would collect from China and Central Asia over the course of his expeditions.

Aside from Dunhuang, Stein excavated sites all the way from the Great Wall to the Taklamakan Desert. Digging in long-abandoned Chinese forts dating back in some cases to the 1st century BCE and the establishment of the classical Silk Road, he found a mass of artefacts and manuscripts which brought to life not only the region's broad history, but also many of the individuals who had passed that way many hundreds of years previously. "The thinnest layer of gravel" in these areas, recalled Stein, served

(Right) A 31-metre Sakyamuni Buddha carving and colourful murals date from the 4th century CE at the Thousand Buddha Cave, Shuilian Dong in Gansu Province.

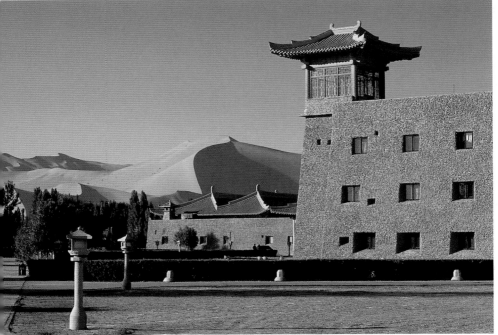

(Top) *Jiayuguan fortress stands guard at the western end of the Ming Dynasty Great Wall, for centuries the end of the known world for the Chinese. In the distance are the Qilian Mountains, which form the southern boundary of the Hexi Corridor. (Bottom) The beautiful Silk Road Dunhuang Hotel is a superb recreation of Han Dynasty architecture – beyond can be seen the famous Mingsha Dunes and next door the Yangguan Museum, which houses many interesting artefacts, including ancient war machines lined up outside the fortress-style walls. (Left) The Hongsha River cuts a gorge through the Qilian Mountains into the Hexi Corridor near Jiuquan. The camel caravan passing along the valley floor gives an idea of scale.*

(Above left) *A terracotta bodhisattva in one of the Mogao caves, near Dunhuang.* (Above right) *A beautifully carved seated wooden Buddha in th Gendharan style from the 5th century CE, discovered by Albert von Le Coq at Tumshuk, between Kucha and Kashgar.* (Below) *A camel caravan plods across parched land in front of the Flaming Mountains near Turpan.* (Left) *Within the extensive cave complex at Mogao, some of the cave entrances have been spruced up for visitors.*

(Top) The Bezeklik Caves are worth visiting just for their stunning location in a steep-sided valley that cuts through the Flaming Mountains. (Above) A 9th century mural originally from Cave 20 in Bezeklik showing Tokharians, Xinjiang's early settlers, offering gifts to the Buddha. (Right) The geometrically fantastic Emin Minaret on the edge of the town of Turpan.

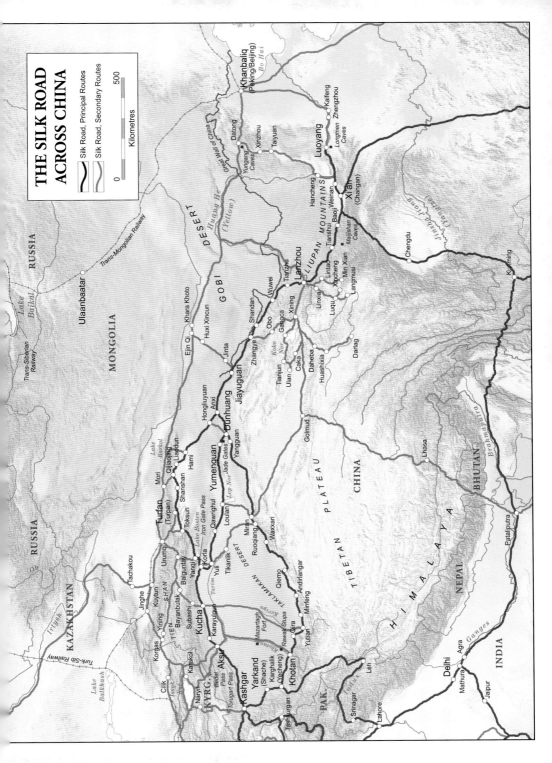

THE SILK ROAD ACROSS CHINA

Silk Road, Principal Routes
Silk Road, Secondary Routes

0   500
Kilometres

RUSSIA

Lake Baikal

Trans-Siberian Railway

Trans-Mongolian Railway

Ulaanbaatar

MONGOLIA

GOBI DESERT

Khara Khoto

Huang He (Yellow)

Khanbaliq (Peking/Beijing)

Bo Hai

Datong
Xinzhou
Taiyuan

Yungang Caves

Kaifeng
Zhengzhou
Longmen Caves

Luoyang

Hancheng
Baoji Weinan
Xi'an (Changan)
Tianshui
Majishan Caves
Lintao Min Xian
Xincheng
Xining
Langmusi

Chengdu

Yangtze (Chang Jiang)

Kunming

Great Wall of China

Ejin Qi
Huxi Xincun
Jinta

Hongliuyuan
Anxi
Dunhuang
Jiayuguan
Yangguan

Shandan
Zhangye
Obo
Gangca
Koko Nor
Caka
Tianjun
Ulan
Daheba
Huashixia
Darlag

Wuwei
Tiantzhu
Lanzhou
Linxia
Luqu

LIUPAN MOUNTAINS

PLATEAU

TIBETAN

CHINA

Golmud

Lhasa

Lake Barkol

Mori
Qijiaojing
Lladun
Shanshan
Hami

Turfan (Turpan)
Toksun

Urumqi
Balguntay
Yanqi

Tien Shan

Tachakou
Jinghe
Kuytun
Yining

KAZAKHSTAN

Irtysh

Turk-Sib Railway

Lake Balkhash

Korgas
Kalakol
Cilik
Naryn
Issyk Kul

KYRG.

Bedel Pass
Torugart Pass

Kashgar
Tashkurgan

Yarkand (Shache)
Karghalik (Yecheng)

PAK.

Leh

Srinagar

HIMALAYA

NEPAL

BHUTAN

Brahmaputra

Delhi
Agra
Mathura
Jaipur

Ganges

INDIA

Lahore

Kucha
Aksu
Karayulgun
Subashi
Bayanbulak
Yuli

Korla
Tikanlik
Loulan
Miran
Ruoqiang

Lop Nor

Lake Bosten

Qawrighul
Iron Gate Pass
Jade Gates

Yumenguan

Lop Nor

TAKLAMAKAN DESERT

Tarim

Keriya

Waxxari

Qiemo
Andir Langar
Minfeng
Niya

Yutian

Qira
Rawak Stupa
Mazartagh Fort
Khotan

Tarim

Indus

(Above) *An amazing satellite image showing the Tien Shan looking west towards Issyk Kul and the Ferghana Valley, with the ancient oases of Kucha and Aksu bordering on the Taklamakan Desert at lower left.* (Top right) *A Bactrian camel in northern Xinjiang; this fine specimen awaits tourists to take them on rides through the fantastical landscape of the Uryhe Ghost City north of Karamay.* (Bottom right) *The fertile Ili Valley, watered by glacial streams from high, protecting mountains, has been inhabited by waves of migrating Turkic tribes for millennia. Semi-nomadic Kazakhs are the current ethnic majority.*

A statue of Kumarajiva stands in front of the Kizil Caves near Kucha. A monk who lived at the height of the Kuchean Kingdom, Kumarajiva translated many Buddhist scriptures from Sanskrit to Chinese, thereby paving the way for Buddhism's rise in popularity in China.

(Top) *Traditional sericulture in Hotan (Khotan), which has been famous for silk production for more than 1,500 years. While the man bundles up the 25–30 silk threads into skeins, the woman winds the actual silk thread onto a reel.*

(Bottom) *The Buddhist stupa of Rawak near Hotan, built between the third and fifth centuries CE. The nine-metre-high, triple-floored stupa is crowned by a cylindrical building, to which steps lead from each of the four cardinal points. Though a permit is required to visit Rawak, this is one of the most evocative sites easily reached on the Southern Silk Road.*

(Above) A Yarkandi man in Kashgar, identifiable by his tall, fur-trimmed hat. (Left) A traditional Uygur woman wears a veil and embroidered cap. (Below left) Sacks of spice and nuts at a stall in Kucha old town – in many ways little has changed along this part of the Silk Road. (Below right) A mêlée of heads pack the sheep section of the Kashgar Livestock Market.

(Top) Worshippers exit the Idkah Mosque in Kashgar, the heart of Islam in Xinjiang and the largest mosque in China. (Bottom) Melon sellers in Xinjiang – an ubiquitous sight throughout Central Asia, and a delicious and refreshing snack for locals and travellers alike. (Left) Modern transport on the Southern Silk Road near Yarkand (Shache) – with petroleum now plentiful in the region, motorised vehicles are slowly gaining in popularity.

STUCCO IMAGE GROUP, REPRESENTING BUDDHA BETWEEN DISCIPLES, BODHISATTVAS, AND DVARAPALAS, IN CAVE-TEMPLE CH. III., 'THOUSAND BUDDHAS' SITE.

296. MY COMPANIONS AND MYSELF AT ULUGH-MAZAR, IN THE DESERT NORTH OF CHIRA.

(Above left) *A stucco Buddha and disciples in one of the caverns of the Mogao Caves complex in Dunhuang. (Right) Aurel Stein – at centre, with his terrier "Dash" – and field companions in the southern Taklamakan near Hotan in 1908.*

to preserve "in absolute freshness" not only papers, but "such perishable objects as shreds of clothing, wooden tablets, arrow shafts, straw and chips". All of these items had been preserved by "extremely scanty rainfall for the last 2,000 years... freezing gales... torrid heat... [and the absence of] any chance of irrigation or human interference". Hence, he was able to pick up "records of the time of Christ or before almost on the surface".

Often just by "scraping the ground with [his] boot", he was able to disclose where the ancient Chinese military detachments had put their refuse, which frequently contained a wealth of original documents. At Niya, excavating in an old rubbish heap which still smelled, after two millennia, of freshly deposited human waste, he found a host of writings on wood and leather adorned with strings and clay seals, some of which, astonishingly, were adorned with depictions of the Greek gods Pallas Athena, Eros and Heracles. Near the Jade Gate he found components for catapults and crossbows, ready for use, as well as all the accoutrements of the impoverished Chinese soldiers, coarse woollen rags for clothing, bags of arrowheads, hemp shoes and wooden eating bowls. Amongst this, perhaps more importantly, he also found an abandoned postbag full of letters in many languages, which had gone astray around 314 CE.

In other places, such as Turfan and Bezeklik farther to the west on the northern route, he found more waste papers, this time used to line the coffins of the departed. Not only the papers but also the bodies were in a perfect state of preservation. They wore peaked felt caps with big feathers and coarse woollen garments, just as ancient Chinese annals from the Han Dynasty had described the nomadic people of the region. It was a "strange sensation", wrote Stein, to look down on "figures which but for parched skin seemed like men asleep", and who had inhabited the area in the heyday of the Silk Road 2,000 years previously. Many of these relics, aside from the bodies themselves, now repose in the permanent collection of the British Library.

(Left) *A timeless sight in southern Xinjiang – donkey carts are still used to carry anything from firewood to mosque-bound pilgrims in heels and festive clothing.*

The behaviour of Stein, along with other Silk Road explorers of his generation such as Sven Hedin, Paul Pelliot and Albert von le Coq, even nowadays raises high passions, particularly among Chinese scholars. Their high-handed treatment of the native peoples, their conduct in removing a huge wealth of manuscripts and archaeological treasures, sometimes ineptly, and usually without the permission of the Chinese authorities, has earned for them a reputation among many as colonialist treasure-hunters rather than respectable archaeologists. Whatever the rights and wrongs of the case, it is undeniable that the audacity of these explorers, combined with their scholarship, was able to provide a huge impetus for the study of the Silk Road and inner Asia. The documents that they discovered, especially at Dunhuang, paint for us today a picture of the ancient Silk Road which is immediate and fresh, illustrating every aspect of life from the sacred to the thoroughly profane.

The papers which Stein unearthed at the military outposts conjured up for him the heaviness of a slow existence in the colonies, stuck in the western deserts, distant from the Chinese motherland, with nothing to relieve the monotony aside from the sight of trade caravans, the occasional attack by the Xiongnu nomads, and an incessant stream of garrison bureaucracy. Going through the discarded paperwork, Stein was afforded the glimpse of a bored and self-important army clerk from many aeons past, whose only distraction was the composition of a flood of self-important memoranda. All the details of camp life were to be found, daily orders, imperial edicts, reports of skirmishes, inventories, indents for deliveries of arrowheads and weaponry, and records of wages and the recruitment of indigenous troops. Officers, to beguile the time, paid endless calls on each other, and if absent left calling cards, their names inscribed on sticks, a testament to the social routines with which they attempted to defy the languor of the camp.

The postbag of letters from 314 CE casts light on the travels of the foremost traders of the ancient Silk Road, the Sogdians. Playing a similar role to the Armenians later on in Europe and the Middle East, they spread from their original homeland of Central Asia to become the middlemen *par excellence* of international commerce, stationing themselves all the way along the trade routes to China. The letters, which never reached their intended recipients, are hauntingly vivid. There are, as might be expected, the ordinary discussions of trade. A trader in Wuwei, named Frikhwataw, writes to his manager, "the chief merchant Aspandhat" to say that he has four bundles of white lead powder (used in drugs and cosmetics) ready to despatch, along with a load of pepper and a weight of silver, but such is the chaos on the roads because of nomadic attacks that "I have become isolated, and behold I stay here… and I do not go hither and thither, and there is no caravan departing from here… I am very wretched."

The disorder at the time through attacks of the Hunnish nomads appears throughout the letters. Nanaivandak, an employee of another merchant named Varzakk, wrote from Lanzhou that it was eight years since he had sent a party of Sogdian traders "inside" into China, but three years since he had heard anything from them. He feared the worst. The news from within the country did little to quiet him: "The last emperor, so they say, fled from Luoyang because of the famine, and fire was set to his palace and to the city, and the palace was burnt and the city [destroyed]. Luoyang is no more… if I were to write to you everything about how China has fared, it would be beyond grief: there is no profit for you to gain therefrom."

The travails of life on the Silk Road afflicted not only the Sogdian men. A woman named Miwnay, somehow abandoned in Dunhuang, writes piteously to her mother for help: "I live wretchedly, without clothing, without money; I ask for a loan, but no-one consents to give me one, so I depend on charity from the priest." There is no one in the city who is willing to lead her out of it back home. Later, there is a letter to her errant husband, Nanaidhat, saying that she has become the servant of a Chinese household because of her poverty. "Behold, I am living... badly, not well, wretchedly, and I consider myself dead. Again and again I send you a letter, but I do not receive a single letter from you, and I have become without hope towards you. My misfortune is this, that I have been in Dunhuang for three years thanks to you... I obeyed your command and came to Dunhuang and I did not observe my mother's bidding nor my brothers'. Surely the gods were angry with me on the day when I did your bidding! I would rather be a dog's or a pig's wife than yours!"

Beyond this, the 7,000 scrolls and manuscripts which Stein brought back from the Dunhuang caves are even more expansive about life on the Silk Road. Such is their number that one can scarcely begin to describe their variety. A small number of them are secular and about everyday affairs, just as the Sogdian letters from Jade Gate. One piece of correspondence orders the disposal of four dead camels from the road. One is from a man who had lent a traveller a donkey 10 months earlier, and was now pressing for its return. Another, from the wine-seller Teng Liu Ting to the melon-seller An A To, "to whom I supplied one tou of wine, I humbly beg to press for settlement". A mother writes to her son, a Buddhist official, begging him to return home after a long absence. A princess, about to start a journey, requests a votive lamp to be lit for her in a Zoroastrian temple. A minister submits a flustered report to a governor about the kidnap of his son on the road by brigands, and what he knows of their whereabouts.

However, the greater part of them is religious. Ideas from all shades of the world – Taoist, Zoroastrian, even Manichaean and Christian, are represented amongst the scrolls. However, most of them are copies of Buddhist scriptures and liturgies – eulogies, funeral lamentations, prayers, confessions, charms and vows. A number of them are duplicates of the same few sutras, which had been written out again and again on behalf of a sponsor, so that they might gain merit. Such recopied texts might have been of only theological interest, except that at the end of every scroll was a footnote, describing who commissioned it to be copied, when and why. Each scroll, therefore, throws open a small window onto the life of a distinct individual. In 550 CE, for example, a devout Buddhist, Tao Jung, "having cut down her expenses in food and clothing, caused [this] section of the Nirvana Sutra to be copied", and prayed that anyone who circulated it would "influence others to their enlightenment", and that she herself "might abide her present life in meditation, without further sickness or suffering...". One of the reasons for causing it to be copied, she holds, was that "she did something evil in a past life... and was reborn in the vile estate of woman... If she did not obey the wonderful decree of Buddha, how shall she find repose?"

The motives for having the scrolls copied are often far from meritorious. In 700 CE, one of the footnotes states that a certain assistant commissioner made a vow that, if he were promoted to the 6th official grade, he would pay for one roll to be copied every month, and if to the 5th grade, it would be two rolls every month.

The categorisation "religious" is very broad, and it encompasses medicine and magic as much as the divine. The superstitions under which every traveller and inhabitant of the ancient Silk Road would have laboured are described in the finest detail. There are almanacs and calendrical tables providing the propitious dates for everything from sacrificing and getting married, to cutting one's fingernails. There are remedies for all manner of illnesses and conditions. If the juice from the pounded leaves of a watermelon is rubbed on the scalp, for example, it will cause hair to grow where none was before. If the seeds and root of a lotus plant are eaten after being stored for a thousand years, it will prevent hunger and "so etherealise the body that it will be able to fly in a marvellous fashion". There were guides to *feng shui* and astrology, and others to unfold the meaning of every portent. If a cloud of white vapour should form in a certain shape in a man's house, "there will be grave illness". If its colour is blackish and the cloud expands to envelop the house, "the members of the family will perish in war, or the house itself will be destroyed". If, however, the white vapour should take the form of a wolf or tiger prancing or squatting on the ground, one of the sons of the household would reach the rank of general, duke or marquess within three years.

Some of the advice was more practical. "If you wish for filial duty from your sons and grandsons, your teaching must be enforced by physical correction: every day should witness a thousand beatings, and wrongdoings should be met with stern rebuke. To bring up a child, begin beating him from an early age, and don't let pity prevent you from using the cane... When your son grows up, do not allow him to get fond of wine; when your daughter grows up, do not allow her to go gadding about. If you encounter a drunken man on the footpath, clear out into the roadway; when he has passed you may come back again."

Tying the ancient times of the Silk Road to the life on the frontier of China as visitors observed it in the early 20th century are the accounts of ancient clubs in the Silk Road cities. These, although many hundreds of years in the past, were scarcely different to the clubs for travellers observed by Mildred Cable during her wanderings in the region in the 1920s. There were fines for turning up late to a meeting, half a beaker of wine, and a full beaker for failing to show up at all. There were rules on what could be discussed, and strict discipline was maintained against fighting and disorder. Three strokes of a bamboo cane could be administered for even wanting to leave the club. An understandable consequence of attending these clubs was the necessity of writing letters of apology for drunken behaviour: "...none of the rude or coarse language I used [last night] was uttered in a conscious state... I was overwhelmed with confusion and ready to sink into the earth for shame... I humbly trust that you in your wise benevolence will not condemn me for my transgression..." A letter in reply is given: "...yesterday Sir, while in your cups, you so far overstepped the observances of polite society as to forfeit the name of gentleman, and made me wish to have nothing more to do with you, but since you now express your shame and regret at what happened, I would suggest that we meet again for a friendly talk..."

The preparations for the journey from Anxi into the Desert of Lop and the Taklamakan would begin, in the summer, three hours before sunset. A call would be given by the leader of the caravan; instantly, the inn where its members were lodged would become a mass of activity. The pack animals, whether camels, donkeys or mules, were fed with handfuls of dried peas, which served better than anything to keep their appetites for the long road ahead; the courtyard was filled with the rhythmic sound of their jaws crunching

A satellite image of the Taklamakan Desert, its fringing oases and encircling ranges, to the north the Tien Shan and in the south the Kunlun Mountains. A sandstorm is sweeping from the east into the central heart of this harshest of lands.

up the hard feed. At the same time, the caravan leader would be calculating precisely the route they were to take, and the individual drivers arranging the loads on their animals.

Their commodities, on the whole, were conventional: anything from bales of cotton to melons, grain, fruit and vegetables from the oases, apricots and peaches, grapes and pears. However, some varieties of trade along this route were less agreeable to modern notions. Slaves, as much as fruit or cotton, could form a greater part of the caravans' commodities. It is likely that the trade played a part in the earlier history of the Silk Road, but at the beginning of the 20th century it featured as strongly as ever. Chinese families, displaced and dispossessed by the many years of civil strife in the northwest were led to sell their children, particularly daughters, in order to feed themselves. The going rate for a girl in the 1920s was one dollar each. These girls, some still infants but clad in muslin veils, might be found in the train of the caravans being hurried to the oases of the Taklamakan and Central Asia to be converted to Islam and married off. Otherwise, they might be seen among groups of travellers, or more commonly in the oases' inns, "thin, hawk-like" women in the words of Cable, with "painted lips, plucked and pencilled eyebrows, dyed fingernails, and elaborately dressed hair". They waited for the arrival of merchants or of soldiers to ply their trade as prostitutes, filling in the time by sitting listlessly on the heated kang, lighting vegetable oil lamps, and using these to smoke opium.

The desert, in the description of Cable, was variously "terrifying" and a "howling wilderness". For dozens, if not hundreds of miles, the land presented nothing but the uniform dismalness of a black pebble-strewn surface, a "limitless expanse of grey grit". To travel over it was an unending torment. The bleached bones of men and animals lay along the wayside. The cartwheels of their vehicles dragged heavily along the surface. The animals pulling them over the grit might be tired out after just 20 paces, and need to be urged on by the drivers. In some places, the gritty earth was covered in a treacherous crust of crumbling salt. As one walked over it, it broke off and settled upon the skin, making it desiccated and cracked. The dryness of the air meant that clothes, blankets and even the fur of the pack animals crackled with static electricity. Items of canvas grew so dry that they would turn brittle, even cracking and shattering down the creases. At the end of most stages, there was the mercy of a well, but every time, whether the water was found gushing from beneath a boulder in an apparently clear stream, whether it sat on the surface in a sluggish pool covered in repulsive scum, or whether it had to be fetched from a deep bore-hole by means of a bucket and rope, it was hardly a welcome blessing. Invariably, the water was brackish, tasting of the salts of magnesium and copper. To drink it encouraged thirst more than it quenched it, and to visit these desert wells was "always unsatisfying and always nauseating".

Along the way, the lodgings for travellers had little allure. At the end of every stage, a little settlement was usually to be found, often no more than a family overseeing a postal station with a single-roomed inn. According to Cable, these were even below the average of China for cleanliness. Indescribably filthy and devoid of comfort, their roofs were made of grass, covered with a mass of black deposits from the smoke of a dung fire in the middle of the room. A small hole in the roof would allow for ventilation and the smoke to escape. Although noisome, these hovels at least provided in their darkness a relief from the sun of the desert and the blowing sands, the attacks of flies and the danger of thieves. They were moreover somewhat preferable to the only other available accommodation, caves hollowed out in the hills on the wayside for travellers to shelter from sudden storms or blizzards. On their walls were scratched verses of previous travellers, which summed up the loneliness and hardship of life on the road:

> Today we came to Ansichow;
> Midday to more onward we go;
> All through the night carters' oil bottles flow;
> Heat, hunger, thirst, cold I now truly know;
> The mere sight of a cart makes my courage sink low!

and

> Though a man travels far, yet his heart bides at home;
> It is the prospect of wealth that still urges him on.
> But he looks for home joys when his hardships are past,
> And his wife's well-trimmed lamp guides his feet back at last.

It was melancholy for Cable to think on the lives of the families who ran these tiny complexes. Throughout the winter they would be quite isolated, and in the summer their only encounter with humanity would be the sight of a passing traveller. From the post offices at their stations they would run little shops to scrimp together money, offering matches, cigarettes and tobacco, as well as incense and paper for worship at the tiny wayside shrines. Although these stations acted as post offices and courier posts, there was nothing to be found in the way of postcards or stamps. Only opium seemed to be readily available. Nonetheless, in these places, squalid and near abandoned, could be found the most astonishing relics of the Silk Road trade at its height. At one of these stations, the keeper, an old man whose confidence Cable had won, produced from a hiding place under a heap of family bedding, a "mass of filthy wadded coverings of the most revolting description", inside which were "two of the choicest jade bowls that can be imagined". Porcelain and the finest of Ming ceramics were also to be found scattered throughout these otherwise poor stations, handed down within these hermit families as the "heritage of older generations".

The food on the way reflected the monotony of desert travel. The staple for travellers was dough strings, made simply from kneading flour and water into a stiff paste, which was then teased into noodles of varying thickness and boiled. The master of the caravan and the richer travellers would generally have their noodles made more thinly, but the drivers and men would prefer their servings, usually four bowls' worth, to be coarse and undercooked. In this way it tended to take longer to digest and was more satisfying. In the absence of fresh vegetables, the relish would be pickled turnip flavoured with garlic, pounded and mixed with linseed oil. Chopped chillies were also widely consumed. To conclude, the water in which the strings were boiled was also drunk. Drawn from the brackish wells, it had the advantage of losing its saltiness to dough, and thus becoming palatable.

here were variations in this staple Silk Road diet. Peter Fleming, who on his journey towards the Southern Silk Road took a route south of Xi'an through northern Tibet, fed daily on the staple of *tsamba*, or parched barley meal, a versatile substance that was perfect for the use of travellers. "It could be mistaken," wrote Fleming, "even in good light for fine sawdust." However, "it could be eaten in tea, with butter, with melted mutton fat, or neither". The procedure for making it was simplicity itself. One filled a shallow wooden bowl with tea, placed a good spoonful of butter to melt in it (usually rancid butter "with a good cheesy flavour") and then a handful of tsamba. "At first it floats, then, like a collapsing sandcastle, the foundations begin to be eaten by the liquid. You coax it until it is more or less saturated then become paste; then knead it until you have a doughy cake in your hand and the wooden bowl is empty and clean – breakfast is ready." It was neither, he claimed, as monotonous or unappetising as the recipe sounded, and he was happily able to live off the substance for three months on the road. One could vary the flavour and consistency at will. It could be made into cakes or porridge, flavoured with sugar, salt, pepper, vinegar, Worcester Sauce, or even cocoa. "I wouldn't say one wouldn't get tired of it," he concluded, "but you would get tired of anything else much quicker."

Yet, for all the apparent monotony of the desert, there was still a wealth of beauty to be found at closer sight. The granite rock of the hills in the distance, bare and rugged, would pass with the play of sunlight and shadow through a whole spectrum of colours, from blue and purple to green and grey.

The high jagged peaks were even dashed with blood-like specks of porphyry. Underfoot, there was an even greater plenitude of colour. Beyond the superficial uniformity of the plains, the pebbles and grit themselves were a feature of the desert's beauty. They presented a "matchless mosaic" in the view of Cable, passing through every shade from rose and pink, pistachio and tender peach, lilac, white, sealing-wax red and black. They formed a backdrop for the desert's most familiar creatures, the lizard, whose skin grew variegated, also like a grainy mosaic, to mimic the many hues of the desert floor. Every morning also, the sandier tracts would be found with a multitude of astonishing patterns, the trails of endless rodents, beetles and centipedes, which had come out at night to move silently and invisibly over the desert's surface. Most dangerous among these denizens were the snakes. Often a burnished yellow, they would lie hid in the ruts left in the sand by the carts. Drivers claimed that they could kill a horse or a mule with a single bite; on finding one, they would never hesitate to thrash it to death with whips or staves.

More benevolent and also more common of the animals which left trails was the jerboa or desert rat, a creature in many respects not dissimilar to a smaller version of the kangaroo, with long rear legs on which it could jump, an extended muscular tail ending in a tuft, and wide spreading ears. After sunset, it was not uncommon for a jerboa to pick up on the trail of any passing caravan. It would follow the wagons and the animals, jumping from side to side of the track left behind them, its agility keeping it safely out of the hunter's reach.

The desert was not only beautiful, but bountiful. For the experienced traveller, it was by no means a barren and infertile wilderness, but had the potential to supply them with a host of necessary supplies and even luxuries. Asparagus grew wild on the verges of the desert, and the discovery of wild chives along the track was always greeted with pleasure by the caravan drivers, who collected them eagerly to flavour their staple diet of dough strings. A more welcome addition to their diet would be the chance find of the hair vegetable (the edible blue-green alga *Nostoc commune var*). At first sight, this strange organism would appear to be nothing more than a large black wig sitting abandoned on the sand. However, on being soaked, parboiled and flavoured with vinegar, it became a delicacy, and could be used as an aromatic pickle to accompany other food. For the traveller who lost his way, his life could be saved by finding a sand millet bush (*Agriophyllum gobicum*), the only grain indigenous to the desert. This plant would grow to two feet in height, presenting nothing but a convoluted mass of hostile prickles. However, hidden inside were a group of small seedpods that could be collected by pushing the plant onto a cloth and then beating it with a rod. The grain within could be boiled to produce porridge, or ground to flour and cooked in a cake.

Other plants also aided the traveller. The camel thorn was gathered extensively for fuel – turned into charcoal and mixed with horse manure, it would carry on burning for hours. The sweet wormwood (Artemisia annua) could be used to keep away the insect life of the desert at night. The twigs would be picked up along the way, platted into ropes, and then set alight at sunset – smouldering throughout the darkness, it would repel sand flies and mosquitoes until close before dawn. Most versatile of all was the strong and fibrous desert grass. This could be collected and woven into baskets or fans, curry-combs for the mules, curtains, strings, ropes, hurdles to enclose animals and livestock, or even ladles for dishing out the dough strings from the boiling pot.

However, for many travellers the real exhilaration of journeying through the deserts on the frontier of China was not to be found in the observation of their subtle beauty or natural wealth, but rather the contemplative frame of mind that the emptiness of the vista and the slowness of the travel would induce. The average speed of the camel caravan in the desert was 2.5 miles an hour, slower than walking pace. In some travellers, such as Peter Fleming, this slow speed was only the cause of a temptation to sneak away from the caravan to have a smoke and catch them up later: "The sun was warm, the rock behind you impersonated adequately an arm-chair. Immobility alone was so exquisite a sensation that you were loath to dilute it..." However, the response of Mildred Cable was more conventionally poetic. For her, when there was nothing but the loneliness of the desert, the dull rhythmic pulse of the cartwheels against the sand of the road, and above the stars of the Milky Way like a "phosphorescent shower of myriad spots of light", then the perspective on life was radically changed. The speed of the desert was "the pace for talk – and no desert wayfarer is jarred by the annoyance of a hurried companion, nor delayed by the slackness of a fellow traveller. The human body, having found its natural swing, becomes strangely unconscious of itself, and releases the mind to its normal function of transmuting incident into experience. These are the conditions in which the philosopher becomes, according to his own measure, an observer, a philosopher, a thinker, a poet or a seer."

ore pleasant than to travel, at least for Peter Fleming, was to arrive. This, more than the emptiness of the Taklamakan or the rhythm of the cartwheels on the desert sand, moved him to near poetry. His description of reaching one of the oasis towns on the Silk Road, Cherchen, in the Taklamakan Desert, exchanging the hardships of wandering for the delights of the settled world, verges on the ecstatic. The first sign of the approach of the oasis was the sudden appearance of greenery. "We could not keep our eyes off the wall of vegetation which crowned its further bank. It looked extraordinarily dense, like the jungle. We could see as yet no signs of human life, only this opulent but non-committal screen... But as we came under the trees we ceased to speculate. Wonder and joy fell upon us. I suppose that the earth offers no greater contrast – except that between land and sea – than the contrast between desert and oasis. We stepped clean out of one world and into another. There was no phase of transition; we slipped into coolness and delight as smoothly and abruptly as a diver does."

It was as if he were not just reaching an oasis, but stealing into a bucolic paradise. "One moment we were stumbling in the open riverbed, plagued by glare and a grit-laden wind; the next we were marching down a narrow path under the murmurous protection of poplar and mulberry and ash. Trees lined the path, which threaded a patchwork of neat little fields of hemp and rice and barley. Men of gentle appearance in white robes lent on their mattocks to watch us pass... Hands were pressed, beards stroked, curious glances thrown at us. Everywhere water ran musically in the irrigation channels. A girl in a bright pink cap, washing her baby in a pool, veiled her face swiftly at the sight of infidels. Low houses with mud walls and wooden beams stood under the trees around courtyards half roofed over; women peered, or scuttled into the shelter of their doorways..."

The muffled, rare and subdued murmurings of the desert gave way to the joys of distinct and chaotic sounds: "A cock crowed... A familiar sound, unheard for nearly three months, asserted definitively our return to a world where men had homes; we began to think gloatingly of eggs. The sounds were the most vivid part of a strange and unforgettable experience. The wind in the leaves, the gurgling water, a dog barking, men calling to each other in the fields – these noises, and especially the wind in the leaves, changed the whole texture of our environment, filled the air with intimacy, evoked forgotten but powerful associations. Then a cuckoo called lazily; the essence of the spring we had missed, the essence of the summer that we had suddenly overtaken, were comprehended in its cry, and I had a vision of lawns picketed with great trees, young rabbits scampering into the gorse, a wall of ivy loud with sparrows: a vision that the cuckoo made oddly substantial, oddly near..."

There could be as many trials in an oasis town as out on the road itself. One of the most notorious of these for travellers was Turfan, in the Taklamakan's fringes on the northern branch of the Silk Road. Sandwiched between the eastern Tien Shan's 17,864-foot (5,445-metre) Bogda-ola (the Peak of God) to the north, and the trackless expanse of the desert to the south, Turfan sits in a depression that reaches 505 feet (154 metres) below sea level, the second lowest spot on the face of the Earth. Although a haven of greenery, the temperatures range from zero to 130 degrees Fahrenheit (-17°C to 54°C). The combination of heat and an abundance of water – drawn from the mountain slopes by underground canals called karez – have always made the place positively the Silk Road capital for every type of vermin. The German traveller, Albert von Le Coq, who visited Turfan in the early 1900s prior to excavating the nearby archaeological complex of Bezeklik, had a first-hand and stomach-turning experience of the unwelcome wildlife of the oasis. "There are scorpions whose sting is a very serious matter and, in addition, a kind of great spider that, in spite of its hairy body the size of a pigeon's egg, can take mighty jumps with its long, hairy legs. It makes a crunching noise with its jaws and is said to be poisonous, although I have never known any bitten by it." There was another type of spider, "very much smaller and black but hairy too", which "lives in holes in the ground. It is very greatly feared and its bite is said to be, if not deadly, at any rate extremely weakening and dangerous". The Turfan cockroaches were also equally displeasing: "...a repulsive pest, in size quite as long as a man's thumb, with big red eyes and formidable feelers." According to Cable, it had the habit of hiding in sleeping bags, or else in the rolls of one's clothing. Although not poisonous, it was by no means a pleasant experience to be suddenly surprised by such an apparition. "It was enough to make a man uncontrollably sick," wrote von Le Coq, "to wake in the morning with such a creature sitting on his nose, its big eyes staring down at him and its long feelers trying to attack its victim's eyes. We used to seize the creature in terror and crush it, when it gave off an extremely disagreeable smell."

To avoid the extremes of heat, the vermin, the scorpions that hid in shoes or dropped from the ceiling in the ordinary houses, people would retreat below ground in Turfan. The period from May to August would be spent in apartments hollowed out underground, reached by long flights of stairs and decorated simply with reed matting and grass-woven pillows. Francis Younghusband, one of the first English travellers to reach Turfan in July 1887, had heard rumours of such a way of life, but could scarcely believe it could be true. "I had read in some book that at Turfan it was so hot that people lived in holes underground. I never quite believed it, but today I found it was a real fact. Here in the inn yard is a narrow flight of steps leading underground. I went down them and found a room with a *kang*, and a

Chinaman lying on it smoking opium. It was perfectly cool below there, and there was no musty smell, for the soil is extremely dry. The room was well-ventilated by means of a hole leading up through the roof." People would eat and sleep in these subterranean apartments through the heat of the day for the summer months, emerging only at sunset, opening their shops and conducting their business by lamplight alone.

For all these ordeals in the oasis of heat and vermin, the pleasure for the traveller of a glimpse of settled life with its contingent luxuries far outweighed its tribulations. After weeks, or even months on a diet of undercooked dough strings enlivened only by the occasional find of chives or the hair vegetable, the joy of reaching the irrigated fields around the oasis to find an abundance of sweet and delicious fruits was near matchless. Such was the comment of almost every traveller throughout the history of the Silk Road. In the 7th century CE, the Chinese Buddhist monk Xuanzang praised the produce of the oases of the Taklamakan, the grapes and pomegranates, the many species of plums and pears, peaches and almonds. It was from Turfan, in these early centuries, that the Chinese emperors received their grapes, packed in ice, and also from Turfan that wine is supposed to have reached China. Marco Polo, whilst lamenting the cold of the place, concedes that, "the land produces grain and excellent wine".

The joy in the appearance of fruit was something as deeply felt by modern travellers as by the ancients. Mildred Cable waxed lyrical at the sight of the melon salesman. He sat on a mat surrounded by melons of every kind, from the "largest and most showy" – the watermelon weighing 20 pounds, with a glossy myrtle-green rind and a centre of rose-madder flesh – to the smaller and firm-fleshed cantaloupes. The customers would take infinite care to choose the best fruits, testing their ripeness by pressing them with their fingers, or else rapping them on the side and listening to the reverberations. The melons would be sliced and eaten greedily on the spot, the rinds thrown down and left to gather dust in the gutter.

The produce of the vineyards was just as prominent a feature. Outside the town itself, the greenness of the vines shone brilliantly, with their "vivid foliage at the base of the hills underneath the azure sky". The atmosphere, with the heat radiated back from the stone of the hills and the steamy humidity from the damp, irrigated ground, was as intense as a hothouse and caused the grapes to flourish; in the early summer, the fields were transfused with their perfume. As soon as they were harvested, they were hung up on horizontal poles in the grape-drying halls that were arranged amongst the vines. These were built of an open latticework of sun-baked bricks, and through the action of the heat and the wind, the grapes would dry into sultanas within 10 days. The best fruit would cling to the bunches and was bought up by the merchants for export; the poorer sort fell to the floor, and was swept up to be sold cheaply at the bazaar. The dried grapes in themselves possessed for the travellers great beauty. Their colours varied from oasis to oasis, those of Turfan being of a clear amber, whilst others from other towns of the route varied from pale gold to a clear green, the latter being esteemed as the best quality and fetching the highest price.

Strolling in the markets of the oasis towns, the extraordinary depth of trade which took place across the desert immediately became apparent. H.W. Bellew, a British traveller who visited the towns of Khotan and Yarkand (Shache) on the Southern Silk Road from India by way of Kashmir in 1873, left an account of the vibrant markets and bazaars he found on his way. There were butchers' and bakers' shops, drapers' markets and stalls with boots, hats and ready-made furs. One could find rice and corn, poultry and livestock, all available by barter or by coin. One might exchange horses for cows, or cows for sheep; a Kalmyk youth for a fur coat, or a Chinese girl for a silk robe. There was the cutler, selling knives from Andijan in modern-day Uzbekistan. The floor and counter of his shop were covered in sheath knives by the hundred, bright and sharp as a razor, and the shelves were heavy with brass and iron-plated flint and steel cases. There were chemists, surrounded by a close array of baskets full of drugs and medicinal spices, using scales to measure out the correct prescriptions, their weights little cubes of metal stamped with Chinese characters. They offered measures of Indian remedies: caraway and cardamoms, ginger, senna and long peppers, nuts of the water lily, fennel, pomegranate bark, asafoetida, dried poppy heads and the seeds of the castor oil plant. Aside from cannabis and opium, there were decoctions and tonics for dyspepsia, and powdered fungi used as a cataplasm for wounds. The ironmonger offered shovels and mattocks, locks, chains and hooks. There was salt that had been gathered in the desert, offered for sale on flat trays. Aside from this, there were crystals of alum used for dyeing cloth, lumps of copper and sticks of bar iron, yellow ochre, and nuggets of antimony wrapped in paper packets, used by the people as a cosmetic eyeliner.

The second-hand shops indicated not just the depth of the trade, but also its astonishing reach. Offered to Bellew were not only more conventional items, jade amulets and charms, patched sheepskin coats, chopsticks and old bits of china; also for sale was a cracked violin which had somehow reached this distant outpost of the Silk Road all the way from Europe, and a broken American clock. From the east were offered Chinese cloaks of costly fur, silk robes with flowers and dragons; from farther west came Turkic and Persian books, theological treatises in handwritten manuscripts, as well as lithographed books on medicine and history.

Each oasis, no matter how small, would offer its own speciality or local produce. One might offer liquorice, another, a heavy type of sand that was used for polishing jade. Jade itself was dug from the empty bed of the Yurungtash River at Khotan, whereas Turfan itself was famous for cottons and silks. The sellers of cotton goods at Khotan were numerous. In the markets they would sit cross-legged on low counters, teapot in hand, cooling themselves with dried-grass fans. Their stores were fronted with great unrolled lengths of vividly dyed material, horse cloths, saddlebags, rolls of bright chintz, or finer-quality stuffs patterned with flowers and butterflies. Rolls of silk in every colour were also available, and were much in demand for embroidering skullcaps. Aside from specialist goods, each oasis possessed its own distinct design of cap. Hami and Turfan had embroideries of variegated silk in different patterns, Aksu a cap of black velvet heavily embroidered with gold and silver. Only the stricter Muslims would spurn these designs, and resort to a cap of white stitched cotton.

With the variety of goods came a variety of peoples, characters and travellers. In the market itself, there was an endless succession of hawkers and peddlers. Some of them, such as the knife-grinder trundling his wheel, or the pie man wheeling a barrow full of pies, were so similar to those that might be found in Victorian England that Bellew for a moment thought himself in a strange byway of London rather than the Taklamakan; and that the cry of the pie man might as well have been: "Come buy! Come buy! Pies hot, pies cold! Pies new, pies old."

Other characters, however, were less redolent of the home country. There was the professional letter-writer, who waited at the door of the post office at a table with an ink slab, a writing brush, letter paper and a pad. He would listen to the tales that a customer might wish to relate to his friends or relatives in a distant city, and after bargaining a price, pull up his long sleeves, ink his brush, stroke its hair to a fine point, and then begin to transcribe the story in a high and flowery register. As he wrote a crowd would gather, and then cheer with approval at his art as he declaimed what he had composed, making suggestions for how it could further be improved.

There were professional singers and musicians, Muslims who wandered from oasis to oasis, playing the *dotar* (or dutar, a long-necked, two-stringed lute) and performing ballads of love and travel. "If I would have a red rose blooming/I must not pluck it in the bud;/If I want not to fall in love/I must not stay in this city." Or, "The road to Andijan is sandy/None has ever put sickle to it;/ we are two poor brothers/ None was ever so poor as we." To rival these in singing were the itinerant dervishes. Dressed in rags and tatters, but nevertheless carrying a high-peaked conical cap with an edging of fur, and bearing a leopard or antelope skin on their back, they danced wildly, and "drowned their cares in a wild song of calling". In their hands they would hold a great iron mace with jangling rings, and from this, rather than the dotar, they would draw an accompaniment for their song and the beat for the step of their dance.

Religious missionaries, professors and visionaries had made their way along the Silk Road ever since its inception, and even into the 20th century, long after the disappearance of Zoroastrianism, Buddhism and Manichaeism, the followers of Islam preserved the tradition. Aside from the dervishes, there were Peribashis, or spirit exorcists. Like the shamans of Siberia, with whom in the past they perhaps owned some spiritual inheritance, they were called to attend to the sick, and their methods of healing them were thoroughly redolent of those encountered in the Russian Far East. Sven Hedin, who travelled the Southern Silk Road in the early 1900s to discover and excavate ancient cities buried in the sands, witnessed the ceremonies they used to cure disease. If they were called to a house where someone lay ill, or a woman was on the verge of childbirth, they would wait until after dark, see to it that all the lights in the sick chamber, aside from some glowing coals, were extinguished, and then rush into the room. They would arrive in a group of three, bearded, wearing long *chapans*, and each carrying a drum of tightly stretched skin. These they would play in a long repeating rhythm, sometimes tapping them with their fingers, sometimes beating them with the flat of their hands or thumping them with their fists. The noise, according to Hedin, could be heard over six or seven miles away. Sometimes they would sit quietly in the room playing their instruments, and sometimes they would be seized with the music, getting up, dancing and throwing their drums in the air. They purported to be able to see any evil spirits present by gazing into the light of oil lamps which they would bring with them, and that by playing nine rounds of their drum music, a performance which would generally last for three-quarters of an hour, they would be able to drive the spirits away. If, however, the spirits should be able to abide the drumming, then they would resort to the use of a hunting falcon. This would be let loose in the sick chamber, and left until it should chase the spirits away.

As Buddhist shrines were prevalent along the early Silk Road, so in the Taklamakan, Islamic shrines, to which many would travel in pilgrimage, replaced them in their turn. Near Khotan, Sven Hedin found the complex of Kaptar Mazar, a shrine whose function was to provide a home for pigeons. According to legend, it marked the site of an ancient battle between Islamic fighters and Buddhists; the bodies of the Muslim dead were indicated in the carnage by pigeons which landed upon them, and hence the shrine was erected to protect and honour the birds. Whatever the truth of the matter, the place since time out of hand had been a shelter for pigeons, and when Hedin visited it, he found several thousand in residence, sitting on benches or perches on the walls, "...on the ridge of roof, rafters, eaves, everywhere, sitting in close serried rows, like beads on rosary". Fragments of skin hung from poles fixed to the gables to scare away birds of prey, yet should any hawk attack the birds, according to the custodian, it would fall down dead. The pigeons, however, were not at all afraid of humans. Visitors to the shrine would carry offerings of maize, which the birds would eat perched on their benefactors' shoulders and heads, and travellers would be suffered to sleep sharing rooms with the birds.

At Tuyok, a small village dependent on Turfan, Mildred Cable came upon a Muslim holy site that, like the Buddhist ones that came before them, consisted of a cave temple hollowed out of a rock. The entrance to it was festooned with the horns of Marco Polo sheep, yak tails, locks of human hair, sticks, bones, and within there were kept ancient silk banners of the Buddhist deities. The shrine attracted visitors from as far afield as Central Asia, and many of the devotees participated in strange ceremonies that had no place in conventional Islam. At evening prayer, as the Koran was chanted, a merchant stepped forward carrying his five-year-old son. The boy was handed to a mullah, who swung him backwards and forwards into the mouth of the cave, before finally catching him up and spitting on his forehead. No explanation could be found for this ritual, but it was performed without question whenever a boy was first brought to the shrine.

The life of the merchant, who travelled solely for the pleasure of business rather than religious devotion, was, in the eyes of Francis Younghusband, one of the most enviable to be had. A trader would buy up goods in some distant town, and engage a room in an inn for several months, even two years, until all the goods were sold. Then he would buy up new stock and move to a different place, going as he pleased. There was nothing better than this "independent wandering life interspersed with the hardship of travel and risks in strange countries, which give life a relish". Such a way of life made its practitioners "interesting, intelligent, shrewd, and full of information..." and cosmopolitan, not belonging to "any country except that in which they are living at the time". Their habit of "rubbing up against men of so many different countries gives them a quiet, even temperament, and a breadth of ideas which makes them charming company".

The nationalities which travelled through the Taklamakan for the sake of trade rather than religion were many. There were the Chinese, who by the 19th century administered the oases of the Taklamakan, and had built their own walled towns next to the original settlements to act as seats of government and garrison stations. There were Kalmyks (originally inhabitants of western Mongolia who migrated into Central Asia), their hair platted into pigtails, wearing round coloured caps with tassels and long coats. There were traders from the great cities of Central Asia further in the west – Samarkand, Bokhara and the Ferghana Valley. Tall in stature, they were immediately distinguished by their loose robes of cotton print, and long black leather boots with high heels, the same as worn by the Cossacks. Their trade was in the export of felts, furs and carpets along the oasis trade routes. Afghans were also frequently encountered, often engaged in the same line of trade. The Western travellers who encountered them often found them amongst the most congenial company on the way. Younghusband felt that they were much more "men of the world" than many others, and lauded them for being fearless enough to condemn the Chinese government in the oases as "oppressive". Peter Fleming came across an Afghan aksakal in Khotan named Rholam Mohammed Khan, an official appointed as a British deputy consul to look after the affairs of Indian traders in the region. His pride at holding the office knew no bounds. He wore a Union Jack pinned to his chest, and always carried with him a certificate of his British nationality, written in three languages. The gateway of his house also was draped in Union Jacks "of similar but by no means identical design". His little room, said Fleming, had more of civilisation than he had seen in three months of travel: "...a gramophone with Russian records in a variety of languages... oil lamps from Tashkent... an umbrella, and even a cuckoo clock."

Francis Younghusband was just as pleased to make the acquaintance of a Russian merchant, in spite of the rivalry between the British and Russian empires for trade in Central Asia in the 19th century. In the town of Hami at the time of his visit five Russian merchants maintained trading establishments. However, two of these were absent to buy goods, and two others were hunting down Mandarin debtors for payment. He found the last of the five in his shop, a building fronted by a sign in large Russian characters, from which the merchant sold cotton goods and ironware, pails, basins, knives – a business which he dolefully maintained was not profitable. Nonetheless, they exchanged hearty handshakes, and Younghusband invited him to dinner. It was a slightly fraught affair: neither spoke the other's language, and they had to communicate via a Chinese man speaking Mongol. Nevertheless, they spent a pleasant evening. Younghusband held up a glass and said "Czar" at which they drank together, then "'Skobeleff,' and so on through every Russian I had heard of. The Russian Guest knew very few Englishmen, but had grasped the fact we had a Queen, so at five-minute intervals he would toast Her Majesty."

The oases of Urumchi (Urumqi) and Kashgar, being close to the Russian and British borders and on the extreme edges of Chinese territory, were places where espionage and intrigue flourished. Throughout the 19th and early 20th centuries, rebels and secessionists plotted against the rule of the Chinese. The Russians, who had over the 1800s taken control of a great swathe of Central Asia, waited to see if an opportunity would appear to extend their power deep into the Chinese frontier as well; after the Communist Revolution, Urumchi became a resort for desperate White Russian refugees, who were nevertheless relentlessly pursued over the border by Bolshevik agents. Everyone seemed to be listening in on everyone else. Uprisings, coups and assassinations of officials were frequent, and the two towns became melting pots for the power-mad, the eccentric and the desperate.

Few of the travellers who reached Urumchi had a good word to say about it. Mildred Cable reported that it was crowded and dirty, with irregular narrow streets, and low formless buildings, devoid of architectural beauty. "Nothing draws men to the place but the prospect of good business or of political advancement, and the sordid streets are typical of its sordid civic life. In government circles friendly social intercourse has become impossible, as any visitor might be an informer. A secret report can always command a price, and promotion often depends on supplying it, therefore no man trusts his neighbour. For such reasons as these no one enjoys life in Urumchi, no one leaves the town with regret, and it is full of people who are only there because they cannot get permission to leave and may not leave without permission." Paul Nazaroff, a Russian refugee, spelt out plainly how dangerous everyday life in Urumchi could be: "Dinners are a particularly convenient occasion for packing off any unwanted person to the other world by means of poison. For this reason guests who have any grounds for expecting a dish specially prepared for them by their host always take the precaution of changing the dish served to them, either with that of the host himself if they can manage it, or with their next-door neighbour."

However, these very facets of Urumchi's character were what attracted an American traveller, Eleanor Holdgate Lattimore. The wife of Owen Lattimore, a prominent ethnographer and scholar of Central Asia, she visited the town at a similar moment to Cable in the 1920s: "I should like to live in Urumchi... full of intrigue and electric with rumours and uneasy with uncertainty and spicy with stories below stairs of those currently in the seats of the mighty... A delightful place, barbaric and civilised, medieval and modern all at once. There is a wireless station but no newspapers, electric lights but no printing press, no railways, but three motor cars, all owned by the governor, and only one works."

North of the Tien Shan mountains and outside the Taklamakan, Lattimore had a keen appreciation of the many aspects of the official capital of Xinjiang Province, with its proximity to Russian territory and the nomadic steppe of Central Asia. "It would look like any Chinese city if it weren't for the people and the things on sale in the shops... the streets swarm with... Kirgiz and Kazakhs, the shops are full of fascinating and crude things, brightly woven saddle bags and rugs and blankets and the coarse red and yellow cotton cloth, bridles and harnesses barbaric with pewter and enamel decorations, ropes and bags of brown and white wool woven like a coarse tweed. [There are many] Chinese shops whose fronts are open to the muddy streets, whose long gowned proprietors and clerks sit behind high black counters drinking tea and chattering about the price of things just as if they were at home, and whose shelves display a bewildering variety of straw hats, scented soaps, silks stockings, china bowls, enamel standard oil candles and Ruby Queen cigarettes. And a few tins labelled 'juice orange' containing a colourless pulp which tastes less like oranges than it does like the Chinese factory where they were tinned, a poisonous brand of tinned crab, a few bottles of Hennessy Three Star Brandy and an occasional one of spurious champagne."

The Russian district of the town, where many refugees had taken up residence, was of especial fascination. In the late afternoon in the midst of the squalor, "starched and beribboned Russian ladies lounge on benches in front of the shops or walk out for an airing, while the few prosperous families dash by in carriages drawn by huge galloping horses, paying calls on each other." Others however, even former aristocrats, were reduced to making a living by washing laundry in the streets. As many of the more wealthy families were "far from home with little to do but get into mischief", the Urumchi Russians became noted for their "strange marriages" and "amazing entanglements with each other's husbands and wives". She was particularly enthralled by a marriage she witnessed between a man of 70 and a girl of 21 – who had already had two previous husbands. Never had she enjoyed "so much gossip of domestic scandals".

A new mosque and contemporary minaret (paying homage to the Bukharan style) in the Uygur quarter of modern Urumqi.

I t was Kashgar, however, that held a place in the heart for many of the travellers on the Silk Road. This was the great market town where the northern and southern routes through the Taklamakan were reunited. It represented the conclusion of the desert and usually of a long and gruelling journey. It was, moreover, seen as the spiritual and almost geographical centre of the Silk Road; the threshold between Central Asia and China, where one might pause and recuperate before proceeding over the mountain passes to the great cities of the west – Bokhara and Balkh, Samarkand and Khiva – or else turning south via the Karakorum passes to India. To arrive there amongst the cultivated fields and pleasant surroundings was, for many centuries, a great joy for the traveller. Xuanzang, who leaves one of the earliest accounts of it, speaks of the "soft and agreeable climate" of the oasis, noting that the "winds and rain regularly succeed each other", that the ground was "regularly cultivated and productive", and that "fruit and flowers" were abundant. It was similarly the case when Marco Polo visited in the late 13th century: "They have very fine orchards and vineyards and flourishing estates. Cotton grows here in plenty, besides flax and hemp. The soil is fruitful and productive of all the means of life."

Little had changed by the end of the 19th century, either in terms of Kashgar's importance or the beauty of its environment. By this time, it sat close to one of the world's great watersheds of political power, the meeting point of the Chinese, Russian and British empires. It was also rocked by frequent revolutions and disturbances; at one point the city was seized by a rag-tag people's army headed by a pork-butcher, and at another by a Turkic secessionist against Chinese rule. Hence, it was inevitable that before long the great powers would install their own agent there to monitor developments and the machinations of their rivals. The first British official sent there on such a permanent mission was George Macartney, who was charged with opening a consulate in the city. Arriving in 1890, he was able to acquire a native courtyard house known as Chini-Bagh "the Chinese Garden", which over time became a near-legendary haven for all manner of travellers.

Travel between Kashgar and Urumchi (Urumqi) in the 1920s was an arduous affair, with many bruises and stops for repairs.

View of Kashgar and the Range of Mountains that Divides it from the Russian Possessions, painted by Robert Shaw in 1868.

Macartney's wife Catharine described in detail their arrival at Chini-Bagh, and her ceaseless work in turning the originally ramshackle buildings into a place worthy to be thought of as a British Consulate. Her first impressions of the spot were as pastoral as those of Marco Polo or Xuanzang before her. The courtyard house sat on the edge of a small cliff, with a view of the snow-topped Pamir Mountains in the far distance to the south and west. Closer to hand in the plains below there was a continuous stream of loaded donkeys and horses passing on their way. The fields in the summer were rich with melon and rice, cotton and clover. Around the Kashgar River there were countless tableaux of activity: horses were watered by naked boys by riding them without saddles into the river; dyers were at work laying out on the ground long strips of cotton cloth dyed a deep red from black hollyhock flowers; millers at mills all along the river would call, by blowing through rams' horns, for more grain to grind. All day long people jostled to cross the bridge over the river with the animals and carts, shouting and singing. The whole performance was framed by loess cliffs and terraced fields, the desert on one side in the distance, and the white peaks of the Tien Shan to the north.

The work of decorating Chini-Bagh so that it would, in the words of a later consul, Claremont Skrine, impress visitors "with the dignity of the British Empire", was long and arduous. One of Catharine's first priorities was to acquire glass and pierce the walls with windows. Both of these, even by this time, were little known in Central Asia; houses were lit by skylights, and windows, when extant, were covered in the Chinese fashion with paper, sometimes oiled. The problem was initially solved by the Russian consul, who presented the Macartneys with a pane as a mark of friendship. However, he shortly afterwards demanded it back in retaliation for some perceived slight. Yet, the sudden arrival not long afterwards of a Russian merchant with a caravan full of window panes meant that they could glaze Chini-Bagh to their hearts' content, and that the power of British diplomacy in the city would appear by no means inferior.

Furniture was knocked together by a Dutch missionary, one Father Hendricks, who in a previous life had a vocation as a cabinet-maker, and although paint and varnish were unobtainable, Catharine sewed together cushions and shades for the paraffin lamps from material bought in the bazaar. Her greatest triumph, however, was the transportation of a piano from London, which was brought across the wilds of Central Asia and hauled over the mountain passes of the Pamirs. It had not arrived in perfect condition. It had been sealed in a zinc case, which the Russian customs officers had opened but not closed again properly or securely. Hence, as it had forded the icy rivers of the Pamir Mountains, water had leaked into the case, and swilled around the piano for days. When it reached Chini-Bagh, the keys were swollen and would not move, whilst the metal parts and springs were thick with rust. Nonetheless, nothing daunted, after it had been taken to pieces and reassembled, it was teased again to life, and Catharine was able to fill the house with parlour music and song.

Kashgar itself had many of the same sights as the other oasis towns of the Taklamakan. It consisted of the old city, and the walled Chinese garrison several miles to the south. Both were surrounded with thick, crenellated walls, but the former was the place where all the real interest resided in terms of life and things to see. Its streets were narrow and dirty, full of ups and downs, muddy from the water spilled by water-carriers and donkeys laden with pails. Beggars and lepers, the faces horribly eaten away by disease, clustered about looking for alms. The women, dressed in bright and colourful outfits, mainly went about unveiled. Some, who ostensibly sold milk, were in fact on offer as "temporary wives" to travellers, who were able to marry them just for the duration of their stay; such, it was thought, would preserve the morality of the town.

The roads were lined with "dark little shops" with awnings of reed mats drawn from one side of the road to the other for shade. The shopkeepers, never apparently anxious for trade, would squat inside amongst their goods. They would however fully come to life on Thursday, which was market day. Then, according to Catharine, all the ways were clogged with crowds so that one could hardly move. Not only were there people, but also donkeys and horses so loaded with goods that only a nose and four hooves were visible. The market itself, the *id-gah*, was great and picturesque, presided over by the chief mosque. Ranged around were fruit stalls in the summer piled high with crimson peaches, apples and mulberries, grapes and melons, purple and yellow figs. Colourful caps stood on tall stands like flowers. Amongst the blacksmiths, silversmiths and teahouses, storytellers and singers entertained the crowds, and red-legged partridges or ground larks in wicker cages engaged the passers-by with their melodies.

But perhaps as enthralling were the strange characters, the flotsam of civilisation, who had ended up as resident in this frontier of empires. Sven Hedin left the most detailed sketches of many of them. There was a Roman Catholic missionary, a Polish man named Adam Ignatieff, a "...fine old man, clean shaven with snow white hair", a rosary and cross around his neck. He had arrived in Kashgar at around the same time as the Macartneys, but in the 10 years between that time and Hedin's visit, he was unable to point to a single convert, nor any serious attempt to make one. He claimed to have made one convert, a Tajik woman who was won over on her deathbed, but others maintained that she was dead when he converted her. Nonetheless, his lack of success did not seem to distress him, and he

Sketch of a Kashgar road scene, *a drawing by T.E. Gordon during his Central Asian sojourn in the 1870s.*

was jovial and contented in his lot, so much so that Hedin claimed to have seen him drink 17 cups of brandy on one occasion at a banquet hosted by the Chinese governor. Very different to him was Father Hendricks, who had helped Catharine to construct the furniture for Chini-Bagh. A man who spoke 12 languages and was highly cultured, he lived in a caravanserai in grinding poverty on scanty fare. Forgotten by Europe, he seldom received letters. Often he would be seen striding through the market in a long cloak, broad-brimmed clerical hat and big glasses. Heedless of the bustle of caravans, he would recite mass daily in his room – his altar was a packing case covered with a dirty lace cloth, and the communion wine was home-made – before going on to read or sing songs in French. He sat philosophising, said Hedin, and seemed to have it as a mission to share the travellers' loneliness.

But for the many travellers who reached Kashgar – Stein, Hedin, von Le Coq – the city spelt more of a return to civilisation than an escape from it. To reach Chini-Bagh with its Western comforts and air of serenity was, after the Taklamakan, almost to reach a promised land. Peter Fleming recalled the shock of the sudden transition: "One night we slept on the floor, drank tea in mugs, ate doughy bread, argued with officials, were stared at, [and] dreaded the next day's heat... [The] next day [we were] in comfortable armchairs with long drinks and illustrated papers and a gramophone playing, all cares and privations banished." Fleming was able to have his first bath in five and a half months, and found sleeping in an ordinary bed an "eccentric and amusing procedure". His travelling companion Ella Maillart, felt similarly. On seeing the "English lawn" on which the consul's pet ducks strode, the verandah, the cool hall, well-polished furniture and armchairs covered with chintz, she felt obliged to be on her best behaviour. Presented with a "table piled high with sandwiches and hot scones swimming in melted butter", she struggled to keep her cup of tea straight on a slippery saucer, and in response to the solicitous enquiries of her hosts as to her time in the wilds of the Taklamakan, responded with her "best society smile 'two lumps please... yes thanks, we had an excellent journey'".

THE HEART OF CENTRAL ASIA

o make the journey from the eastern to the western half of the Silk Road, there were many routes from which the traveller could choose. If one had taken the route north of the Tien Shan Mountains towards Urumchi, one might continue westwards towards the Ili Valley before debouching into the area around Almaty in modern-day Kazakhstan in the Tien Shan's northern foothills. More usual, however, in terms of the historical Silk Road, was to leave from Kashgar, exchanging desert-suited pack animals such as camels and horses for the sturdier mountain yak, and turn towards the southwest, first to reach a point known as the "Stone Tower" or Tashkurgan, which the classical geographer Ptolemy identified as the midway point of the road to the kingdom of the Seres, or Chinese.

The exact location of the Stone Tower has not yet been discerned. However here, according to various ancient historians, Chinese and western merchants would meet to trade their bundles of silk. Having no common language, the Chinese would come forward and deposit their bales of silk in the tower with their prices marked, and then retire to allow the western merchants to inspect the wares, and signal with sign language what they wished to buy.

Beyond Tashkurgan, one would proceed westwards by the mountain passes in the Pamir Mountains to reach the Wakhan Corridor in modern-day Afghanistan, before descending towards the ancient city of Balkh close to the banks of the Oxus River. Otherwise, one might select from a multitude of alternative routes through other passes (including the Irkeshtam, Torugart or Kulma passes), which would lead, by way of trails over the Pamirs and across modern-day Tajikistan or Kyrgyzstan, into the heart of Central Asia.

The mountain ranges which separated the eastern or Chinese section of the Silk Road from the western portions were always considered to be one of the most formidable obstacles in the way of travellers, perhaps even more gruelling than the crossing of the Taklamakan. Marco Polo is brief but outspoken in his opinion of this part of the journey. For this whole region, "…there is no habitation or shelter, but travellers must take their provisions with them. No birds fly here because of the cold, fire is not so bright here nor of the same colour as elsewhere, and food does not cook well". As for the few inhabitants, "they are idolaters and utter savages, living entirely by the chase and dressed in the skins of beasts. They are out and out bad".

The various Chinese pioneers of the Silk Road, primarily the Buddhist monks travelling over 1,500 years ago in search of original scriptures from the heartland of India, left perhaps the most arresting descriptions of the travails of ascending the Pamir passes. According to Faxian, who travelled at the beginning of the 5th century CE, in these regions there was "snow both in winter and summer. Moreover, there are poison dragons, who when evil-purposed spit poison, winds, rain, snow, drifting sand, and gravel stones; not one of ten thousand meeting these calamities escapes…" The territory through which the traveller passed, unlike the Taklamakan, was unremittingly harsh, without food or forage. According to Xuanzang, who travelled in the 7th century CE, "day and night the wind rages violently. The soil is impregnated with salt and covered with quantities of gravel and sand. The grain which is grown does not ripen, shrubs and trees are rare; there is but a succession of desert without any inhabitants."

It is amongst the brief travel memoirs of these Chinese pilgrims that the first records of snow blindness are to be found. Sung Yun, another Buddhist monk who travelled in the 6th century CE, recalls after making his way up a road of "one continuous ascent of the most precipitous character", where for many miles there were "overhanging crags, 10,000 fathoms high, towering up to the very heavens", one reached, after creeping up, "step by step" for four days, the peak of the range. It was a spot where it seemed "as though one was poised in mid-air". Here, "a mischievous dragon took up his residence... and caused many calamities... Travellers by his influence are subjected to all sorts of inconveniences. The snow is so brilliant that it dazzles the sight; men have to cover their eyes, or they would be blinded by it; but if they pay some religious service to the dragon, they find less difficulty afterwards."

What specifically this "religious service" was that enabled them to escape the effects of snow blindness, the travellers did not care to chronicle. However, their records also give a first historical indication of the incidence of altitude sickness. A Chinese official, Too Kin, when travelling in the mountains around 30 BCE, names the various locations in the range as "Big Headache" and "Little Headache" Mountains, and also "Red Earth" and "Swelter" Hills. Their exact location is unknown, but the official was explicit about their effect on him: "They make a man so hot his face turns pale, his head aches, and he begins to vomit. Even the swine react this way."

One of Faxian's travelling companions was even more gravely afflicted: "On the north side of the mountains, in the shade, they suddenly encountered a cold wind which made them shiver and unable to speak. Hwuy-Ring could not go any farther. A white froth came from his mouth and he said to Faxian 'I cannot live any longer. Do you go immediately away, that we do not all die here'; and with these words he died."

rom thousands of years before the birth of Christ until the end of the 19th century, a traveller entering Central Asia would have found its essential nature and constitution unaltered. Empires and dominions would come and go, rulers and conquerors would flourish and disappear, even terrible armies of conquest such as the Mongols might ravage the land and kill millions; yet, the fundamental patterns and way of life that governed the existence of the people continued there unchanged. Had a traveller ventured all the way along the Silk Road from China, he would immediately have recognised the same polarity which had kept in tension the inhabitants of China proper and of Mongolia: the clash between the sedentary dweller and the nomad.

Central Asia for all of this time in essence consisted of a string of great and wealthy cities, often situated in fertile valleys or oases, linked by a complex web of trade routes. Between them in the desert places lived the nomads, usually dependent on the pasturing and transhumance of sheep and livestock. The cities were the cradle of trade and artisanship, and as a result of this they grew, over time, to wealth and luxury. The nomads, by contrast, maintained themselves in sturdy poverty. Central Asian history, although it consists of the rise and fall of many empires, can to all intents and purposes be summed up in the tension and interplay between these two opposites. As the cities grew decadent and effete thanks to their opulence, a new wave of nomads, tempted by the wealth of the cities and the ultimate inability of the city dwellers to defend themselves, would be drawn to sweep down on the cities, plunder their wealth, and set themselves up as their new rulers and inhabitants. In time, they themselves, having taken to the life of the city and having lost the original vigour of their nomadic origins, would be destroyed in their turn by the next onslaught of nomadic invaders.

And yet, it does not paint the full picture of Central Asian life to describe the conflict between the two modes of existence as a "clash". For the most part, the city dwellers and nomads would live in a useful symbiosis. The cities would provide the nomads with a variety of essential goods that they could not themselves manufacture or obtain: highly wrought metal ware, horse tack, grains, silks and varieties of clothing. In return, the nomads would bring to the city a variety of goods from their livestock: wool, felt, carpets and milk. Some of them might also bring captured slaves to the city as the highest item of luxury they could offer. However, more important than the wares they could offer was that they also formed part of the city's protection, and more relevantly to the Silk Road, they provided the manpower, animals and expertise for the transport of goods to take place between cities. Although the impetus for international trade might originate from businessmen and merchants in the cities themselves, they would not have been able to bring their plans to fruition without the cooperation of the nomads in providing horses and camels, their ability to rule a caravan, and their detailed knowledge of the roads and trails.

This stable equilibrium between nomadic and city life continued for the most part unaltered right up until the 19th century. It was at this point that the influence of the Russian Empire began to be felt most strongly in Central Asia. Just as it had been drawn east into the vacuum of Siberia, so also without a fixed land border with the south, Russian dominion expanded over time to fill the regions all the way up to the River Oxus and Afghanistan.

Russia's growth into Central Asia could be attributed to many factors. It feared the instability which the nomads on its southern steppe, if unchecked, might bring. Not possessing a clear boundary with the Central Asian steppe, it was drawn almost automatically to press on in search of a defensible line for the sake of security. It wanted to ensure that its manufactures would reach the markets of the Central Asian cities, and that it would have the option of more easily purchasing luxury goods for its own use. Aside from this Russia was apprehensive about the expansion of the British Empire in India. The British, who originally ruled just a small number of bases and territories on the subcontinent, were being drawn to expand their possessions for reasons very similar to those of the Russians. The Russians, worried that the British might be able to gain possession of the weak states in Central Asia, were drawn on to conquer them before their rivals were able to do so.

This conflict was at the heart of the "Great Game" rivalry that dominated Anglo-Russian relations in the East throughout the 19th century. Yet, its consequences for the everyday way of life in Central Asia are just as important as its effects on diplomatic and military history. Russia's conquest of the great Central Asian cities of Bokhara (Bukhara), Khiva and Samarkand, often by force of arms, brought – at least until

An 1898 group shot during one of German explorer Willi Rickmer Rickmers' expeditions into the western Pamirs, then part of the Bukharan emirate, but today the modern state of Tajikistan.

the Bolshevik Revolution – a close to the endless changes of ruler and civil conflicts which weakened the territories. However, with the advent of Russian railways, the establishment of Russian colonial towns alongside the original ancient oasis cities, and the influx of new ideas, goods and technologies, the old ways of life began to totter. The new Russian towns became the focus of trade, and the vitality of the old cities was extinguished. The railways did away with the role of the nomads as the labour force for transport, and the tradition of the long-distance camel caravan, the staple of the Silk Road, was made obsolete. By the end of the 19th century, the two conflicting modes of life in Central Asia came to be not so much the sedentary and the nomadic, but the unequal struggle between the old and the new. The travellers who saw Central Asia in this time were witnesses to this inevitable transition.

To those travellers of the 19th century who had just crossed from Chinese territory into Central Asia by the Ili route, this contest between old and new would be immediately apparent. This area had fallen under Russian control in 1853, and shortly after its conquest the Russians had moved to construct a string of fortifications and settlements in the region. One of these was Fort Verniy, on the site of an old Silk Road settlement, Almata (Almaty). This town, which was later to become the capital of modern-day Kazakhstan, was one of the first that would greet any traveller crossing from Chinese territory by way of the Ili Valley. An early account of it is given in the 1870s by Eugene Schuyler, an American journalist who, being a citizen of a then neutral power, was able to travel round the region with relative freedom.

In the construction of the town, there was little of Central Asia. It was an astonishing contrast to the many native villages of mud-brick that stood nearby. There was a suburb that had been built by local inhabitants, which seemed like a straggling appendage to the town, but altogether it was the sort of place that could have been found anywhere in Russia or Siberia, and many of the inhabitants had settled from the motherland. There were wide and regular streets; along them there were shops festooned with hoardings and brash signs. There were large official buildings, a cathedral, governor's palace, schools, "dirty little hotels", a club, and "all things that make a Russian town". There were sawmills, brick kilns, distilleries and breweries, and public gardens where families attended musical evenings in an illuminated pavilion with dancing and supper.

Yet, many of the people who filled the town were quite unfamiliar with these Russian and European pastimes. There were Persian-speaking Sarts or "City dwellers", Kazakhs and Kyrgyz, as well as Kalmyks from the region north of the Caspian Sea. Chinese merchants were prospering in the new environment, "much to the annoyance of the careless Russians", and labourers from China had arrived to offer their services to the incipient industries. The nomads, leading their caravans, made the town one of their major stopping-off points; yet the town, its industries, and the railway that eventually it was to bring would soon put an end to their visits.

Beyond Almaty, Schuyler was able to visit and observe the life of many of the steppe nomads, the Kazakhs and Kyrgyz, some of the last generations to pursue the wandering existence of their ancestors before the pressure of modernity drew it to an eventual close. The nomadic peoples of Central Asia at this period still occupied a colossal swathe of territory. For generations, the tribes had used a huge portion of the Central Asian steppe for grazing their livestock. Nonetheless, even though by the 19th century the Russians had begun to regulate closely the allocation of lands that each tribe had available for summer and

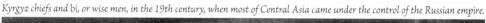

Kyrgyz chiefs and bi, or wise men, in the 19th century, when most of Central Asia came under the control of the Russian empire.

winter pasture, the areas set aside for their use were at least as large as Western Europe, extending from the Tien Shan and Altai mountains in the east to the Aral Sea in the west. Yet despite the size of this area, the travellers found, no matter where they happened to be on the steppe, there was little or no variation in their mode of life or customs, and indeed their way of life closely mimicked that of other nomadic peoples elsewhere in the world.

Like the nomads that other travellers had encountered in Mongolia, the Kazakhs and Kyrgyz lived in yurts. A description of their simple but elegant construction by Januarius MacGahan, a correspondent for the *New York Herald* who travelled in the region in 1873, shows how closely they echoed those found far to the east. The yurt, he wrote, was "...composed of a number of thin strips of wood six feet long, loosely fastened together in the form of a vine-trellis; this frame opens out and folds up compactly, so that it may be placed on a camel. The sticks forming this frame are slightly curved in the middle, so that upon opening out it naturally takes the form of a segment of a circle. Four of these frames complete the skeleton sides of the tent. On the top of this are placed some 25 or 30 rafters, curved to the proper shape, the upper ends of which are placed in a hoop, three or four feet in diameter, serving as a roof tree."

The ease with which they could be constructed, allowing the nomads to establish themselves or ready themselves for travel within a matter of minutes, was greatly admired by MacGahan. "As soon as the camel carrying the felt and framework of a [yurt] arrived, he was made to kneel down, two women seized the framework, set it up on end, and stretched it out in form of a circle, one holding it while the other fastened the different parts together. Then the doorposts were set up, and a camel's hair rope was drawn around the whole, to bind it tightly together. One of them then took the wooden hoop and elevated it inside the tent... while the other immediately commenced inserting the rafters, some 20 or 30 in number, the bases of which are fastened to the lower framework by means of loops. The heavy rolls of felt are then drawn over this skeleton, and the [yurt] is complete... The whole operation only requires about 10 minutes, and it is so solid that any wind short of a tornado will not budge it."

It was as much of a pleasure too for a weary traveller to enter a Kazakh yurt as it was for the travellers in Mongolia. There they would find, according to MacGahan, "a bright fire flashing up out of the darkness and throwing a ruddy light over bright coloured carpets, rugs, and cushions". The walls of white felt were hung with the few possessions with which the nomads were encumbered, "utensils and various articles of household use, a sword and gun, saddles and bridles", as well as a "three-stringed tartar guitar, thrown carelessly aside..."

A traveller would be greeted by the entire household, not just the men – such were the rigours of nomadic life that the purdah of the cities was never enforced. The fashion in which the women would greet MacGahan was deeply beguiling. With "downcast eyes" they would take his hand between both of theirs, and lay it on their heart "with a pretty modest meekness that was perfectly bewitching". When staying with them, he "never lost a pin", and saw that the people "rode miles to restore lost goods". They displayed to a remarkable degree "the qualities of honesty, virtue, hospitality", and it grieved him "to see these simple happy people" on the verge of being "inoculated with our civilisation and its attendant vices".

Many of the customs of the nomads of Central Asia closely emulated those that had been seen in Mongolia. The nomadic dress consisted of, in the words of Schuyler, "immense baggy leather breeches" and a "coarse shirt with wide flapping collars" over which was a long cotton or woollen *khalat*, like a "dressing gown with long sleeves". Various chiefs might be seen wearing robes of red velvet, which the Russians would send as a mark of honour or distinction. On their feet they would wear leather boots covered with galoshes, and on their heads embroidered caps, "fantastically pointed hats of felt, or a busby of sheepskin", depending on the season. Their greatest adornments

were "belts, saddles and bridles, often so covered with silver, gold and precious stones, as to be almost solid". The women dressed similarly to the men, but had their heads and necks "swathed in loose folds of white cotton cloth, making a sort of bib and turban at the same time". Their hair might be platted into small braids from which dangled coins if they were rich, but if they were poor a random collection of metallic ornaments. One traveller of the period noted a Kyrgyz lady's hair adorned with a set of old keys and a broken brass tap.

Many aspects of their behaviour were also similar. The men were immensely lazy. Most of the work, from constructing the yurt, to keeping the household and animals in order, spinning, making clothes, weaving, embroidering and cooking, fell to the women. The principal activity of the men was to see to the horses, after which they devoted themselves to the pursuit and propagation of gossip. Deeply sociable, they would ride great distances across the steppe to seek out and pass on fresh news. Information travelled for hundreds of miles in these places, wrote Schuyler, "as if almost by telegraph". Their recreations were primarily song – it was not unusual for a nomad travelling to sing to himself – and equestrian competitions. Marriage, funerals and circumcision feasts provided excuses, not that any were needed, to travel for many days to participate in racing contests of anything from 10 to 20 miles (16–32 kilometres), and then to indulge themselves in extreme gluttony at the expense of their hosts. Their staple diet was mutton, sometimes enhanced with horseflesh, accompanied by brick tea and the fermented mare's milk kumiss. As with the Mongolian nomads, Kazakhs and Kyrgyz had the most astonishing powers of endurance when it came to eating. For several days they could go without food if none were to be had, and then "gorge themselves to repletion" when it became available.

Though the women might have found themselves the losers in such a domestic situation, their condition was not entirely without dignity or stature. When it came to the job of choosing a husband, the "love chase" was still known on the steppe in the 19th century. The bride, armed with a whip, would mount a "fleet horse", according to Schuyler, and be pursued by "all the young men who make any pretensions to her hand". She however was allowed, in this contest, "to use her whip to the utmost", and spur her horse to great speed. In the melee, she would probably "favour the one whom she has already chosen in her heart", and the other unlucky suitors might well be sent injured away. As for the marriage ceremony, there were few mullahs in the steppe, and therefore there was not much in the way of an organised religious rite.

Dina and Zhambyl, *by Abram Cherkasski* (left), *and* Kokpar, *by Kanafia Telzhanov* (right), *both housed in the Museum of Fine Arts, Almaty. They illustrate two important cultural elements for the Turkic nomads of Central Asia: music and equestrian skill.*

In a yurt the bride and her friends would congregate, along with the friends of the groom. The bride's friends would sing her virtues, the groom's of his exploits – how many cattle he had stolen, in how many marauding expeditions he had been engaged – before the man himself had to break into the yurt and, in a relic of an older custom of marriage by capture, drag off his bride as her friends desperately resisted.

As for religion, according to Henry Lansdell, the English missionary who had travelled both in Siberia and the Taklamakan, although the nomads called themselves Sunni Muslims, they were "indifferent and ignorant of doctrine". The few mullahs whom they did have could only stumble through certain prayers learned by heart from the Qur'an in Arabic, a language which they did not understand, and their mosques were even fewer than the number of mullahs. Nonetheless, all believed firmly in the "invisible world". To them, the tops of the mountains were peopled with spirits; such spirits could cause illness or intervene for good or ill in the affairs of human life, and countless ceremonies and shrines existed in order to honour and conciliate them.

According to Schuyler, few had heard of Mohammed, and still fewer knew any of the prayers or practised the observances of Islam; yet, shamanism, such as was found in Siberia, was still rampant. Shamans would wear long hair, with caps and sleeves of swans' down, and act not only as repositories of music, poetry and traditional epics, but also see to rituals of communion with spirits and healing. For medicine, sympathetic magic was still practised. If one had jaundice, one would wear on one's forehead a piece of gold, or spend the whole day staring at a yellow brass basin; if one had a fainting fit, one would utter obscenities in order to drive away the spirit that was thought to cause it. Tombs and rock carvings were venerated with offerings of tallow, and most peculiarly it was taboo to utter the names of one's male relatives in the presence of others: the possession of someone's name conferred the power to conjure, and circumlocutions had to be used to avoid the names falling into the hands of an enemy. If, as Schuyler cites as an example, "a wolf had stolen a sheep and taken it to the reedy side of a lake" and any member of the family rejoiced in the name of "wolf", "sheep" or "lake", then the problem would have to be reported with the words "in the rustling beyond the wet a growler gnaws one of our woollies".

he routes that trade caravans would pursue across Central Asia were many and complex. Linking the ways from the east, they fanned out into a great delta, connecting in a web the great mercantile cities of Bokhara, Samarkand, Khiva, Balkh and Herat, before narrowing to two main routes that proceeded from Central Asia to the West. The first passed from Khiva north of the Caspian Sea to Astrakhan, from whence one could travel into Russia by way of the Volga, or else carry on by land towards Trebizond on the Black Sea. The second went by way of the old city of Merv towards Mashhad, and then continued westwards south of the Caspian through Persia and thence into the Ottoman Empire and Asia Minor.

Nevertheless, as with the life of the nomads, the form and fashion of caravan travel throughout the whole region remained constant, no matter whether one was on the banks of the Oxus, or else nearing the foothills of the distant Tien Shan. The camel was the essential vehicle of the road. Although horses might be faster and mules somewhat more pliable, in the desert neither animal was so useful, and such animals would generally be used for the merchants or more privileged travellers to ride. The camel could carry three times the load of a horse, and its requirement for water and fodder on the journey was next to nothing. They would be laced together in a line by a thin cord which was fastened on the equipage of one animal and passed through a hole pierced in the nose of the animal behind it. The cord was thick enough so that one camel would be able to support the camel behind and prompt it to move forward, but thin enough to snap should one of them stumble and fall. Generally, the animals were tied into groups of seven, the seventh out of every group being used to carry provisions, and the rest devoted to merchandise.

The camel would often provoke the most extravagant eulogies of praise from travellers, in awe of its resilience and forbearance. Armin Vambery, a Hungarian scholar of oriental languages who disguised himself as a dervish to travel through the Middle East and Central Asia in the 1860s, made perhaps one of the most fulsome tributes. "It is no wonder," he wrote, "that the wanderers over the desert praise the camel as surpassing all other beasts of the field, and even love it with an almost adoring affection. Nourished on a few thorns and thistles, which other quadrupeds reject, it traverses the wastes for weeks, nay, often for months together. In these dreary, desolate regions, the existence of man depends upon that of the camel. It is, besides, so patient and obedient that a child can with one 'tshukh' make a whole herd of these tall strong beasts kneel down, and with a 'berr' get up again. How much could I not read in their large dark blue eyes! When the march is too long or the sand too deep, they are accustomed to express

A late 19th century photo of a loaded camel. These beasts of burden could carry heavy loads but they travelled at a slow, if steady, pace.

their discomfort and weariness. This is especially when they are being laden, if too heavy bales are piled upon their backs. Bending under the burden, they turn their heads round towards their master; in their eyes gleam tears, and their groans, so deep, so piteous, seem to say 'Man, have compassion upon us!'"

They had, however, their detractors in more than equal measure. Schuyler was the first among these. It was all very fine "to speak of them as ships of the desert, and other poetical expressions, but they are practically the most disagreeable, unpleasant animals that I have ever seen; ungainly, unamiable and disgusting in odour, they seem to be a sort of cross between a cow and a cassowary. Seen in the distance they make one think of a big over-grown ostrich, with their claw feet and long necks, which they turn about so as always to observe everything which comes by, and stare at you with their big vacant eyes until you have passed fully out of sight." More blunt on the subject was Fredrick Augustus Burnaby, a British army officer and adventurer who in 1876 contrived to travel from Orenburg, north of the Caspian, to Khiva and beyond: "There is a good deal of nonsense talked and written about the patience and long-suffering of these so-called ships of the desert. I should much like any individual who thus sings the virtues of these huge animals to ride a thousand miles on a camel, as the writer of these lines has done, and find his patient quadruped either running away, or else suddenly lying down without any forewarning motion. This latter camel eccentricity is most disagreeable, as the rider has his back-bone nearly dislocated, or otherwise feels as if his body had been split up by the unexpected concussion..."

For all their sins, however, Vambery was quick to defend them: "...as is well known, they have not the pleasantest smell. It often happens that the saline fodder and water which these animals feed upon produce palpable consequences for such as sleep in their immediate neighbourhood. I myself often woke up with such frescoes. But no-one takes any notice of such things, for who could be angry with these animals, who, although ugly in appearance, are so patient, so temperate, so good-tempered, and so useful?"

The time of travel and departure was generally dependent on the season. In summer, one might often set out at midnight or else an hour after sunset. In winter, the caravan would frequently wait until a few hours after midnight, or even stay until daybreak. More of the journey was made by night rather than by day, since it was easier to pitch camp, look after the animals and prepare food whilst daylight was still available. The time for departure was determined by the *caravanbashi*, or leader of the caravan. He would rise before everyone else and, when he gave the signal, all the members of the convoy would rapidly prepare themselves for the journey. Only a little tea, taken around a fire, would be allowed in the way of breakfast. All haste was used to ready the caravan for departure. Even the camels, according to Vambery, would understand the caravanbashi's signal for departure, and without being driven they would return to the very bales of merchandise with which they were laden on the previous day. Within a quarter of an hour, all had found their place in the line of march, and nothing was left behind save the remains of small bonfires and a scattering of bones gnawed clean.

The order of march would also depend on the time of day. During daylight, the caravan would consist of one single long, unbroken chain. The lead camel would bear a loud and booming bell to signal its coming, and the rearmost animal would carry a set of smaller jangling bells to indicate its passing. Yet, at night the arrangement was different. The single line was broken up into six or eight smaller lines, which would march in parallel in the form of a close square, the outer lines being marshalled by the sturdiest and boldest men. This was necessary to protect from the danger of banditry in the midst of the inky blackness. "During the dark starless night," recalled Vambery, "everything is full of horror, and to go one step from the side of the caravan is equivalent to leaving the home circle to plunge into a desolate solitude."

The length of the march would usually be determined by the distance to the next well or source of water. This might range between six and 12 hours. The changing scenes of travel did much to absorb the attention, and, should there be a starlit night, the sight of "Jupiter above the horizon, and Venus [shining] gloriously upon the desolate wild", in the words of one traveller. "The impressive, endless silence of the desert – a silence as of the grave – cast a most powerful spell over my soul," said Vambery. The silence, the hypnosis of the steady pace of the caravan, the cramp of remaining in the saddle, and often, during winter nights, the cold – icicles would form on the beards of travellers and the whiskers of camels – would often lull the traveller on horse or camelback to sleep.

hatever their tiredness, the members of the caravan could by no means relax their vigilance. To travel by caravan in Central Asia was to court danger from any number of sources. Provisions might run low, and one of the baggage animals might have to be slaughtered from necessity. Grasping princes and petty sultans might detain any merchants and exact a tithe of their goods in return for their release or safe conduct. And on the road itself, banditry perpetrated by roving groups of armed men was a danger that lay ever in store.

Anthony Jenkinson, the pioneer of the Muscovy Company and the first Englishman known to have travelled in Central Asia, who made a commercial journey to Bokhara from Russia in 1558 by way of the Volga, Caspian Sea and then caravan, left one of the most vivid accounts of a desert encounter with such brigands. Not long after leaving Urgenj (Urgench), his caravan of 1,000 camels had been warned by a group of Hajjis travelling with it that they would encounter danger but overcome it; such, they had discovered by casting the shoulder bones of sheep. Jenkinson and his entourage refused to credit such "sorcerie", but he was later surprised to find it true, for within three hours of their prophecy they "escried farre off divers horsemen which made towards us, and we (perceiving them to be rovers) gathered our selves together, being 40 of us wel appointed, and able to fight, and we made our prayers together every one after his lawe, professing to live and die one with another, and so prepared our selves. When the theeves were nigh unto us, we perceived them to be in number 37 men well armed, and appointed with bowes, arrowes and swords, and the captaine a prince banished from his Countrey. They willed us to yeelde our selves, or els to be slaine, but wee defied them, wherewith they shotte at us all at once, and wee at them very hotly, and so continued our fight from morning until two houres within night, divers men, horses and camels being wounded and slaine on both partes: and had it not bene for 4 handgunnes which I and my companie had and used, we had bene overcome and destroyed: for the theeves were better armed, and were also better archers then we; But after wee had slaine divers of their men and horses with our gunnes, they durst not approch so nigh, which caused them to come to a truce with us untill the next morning, which we accepted, and encamped our selves upon a hill, and made the fashion of a Castle, walling it about with packes of wares, and laide our horses and camels within the same to save them from the shotte of arrows…"

A Kyrgyz herdsman, wearing the distinctive embroidered felt cap known as a kalpak, takes a goat to market in central Kyrgyzstan. The Kyrgyz were originally nomadic pastoralists who migrated south to the Tien Shan from the Yenisei region of northern Mongolia and Russia.

The heart of Central Asia as seen from space. In the centre is the lush, fertile Ferghana Valley, watered by meltwaters from the Tien Shan to the north (among which lies iridescent blue Issyk Kul) and the mighty ramparts of the Pamir Mountains to the south. In the east can be seen the western extremity of the Taklamakan Desert and the Kashgar oasis, while in the far southwest the Amu Darya (the Oxus to the ancient Greeks and Romans) courses out of the Pamirs, and in the northwest the Syr Darya (Jaxartes) flows north after irrigating the Ferghana. The legendary city of Samarkand lies at the end of the mountain spur at mid-left of this image.

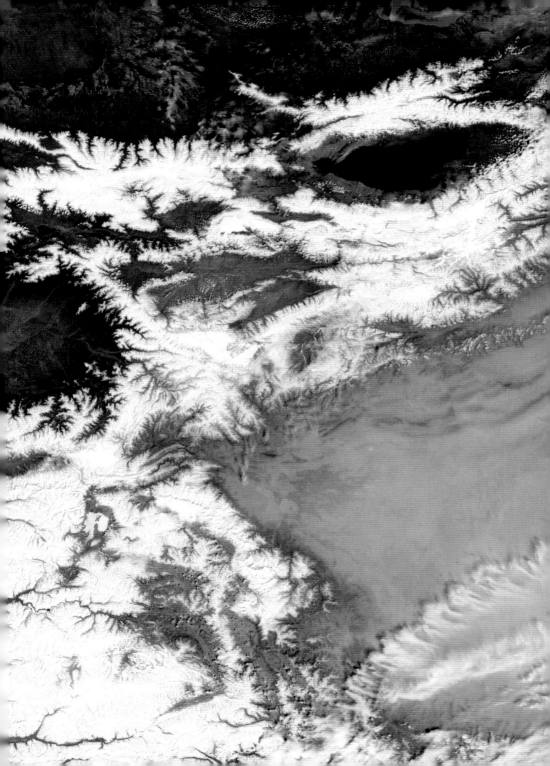

(Right) *A nomadic Kyrgyz summer camp at Tash Rabat near the Torugart Pass, one of the main routes for traders journeying between Kashgar and the Ferghana Valley.*

(Below) *An aerial view of the Tien Shan from the northern Kazakhstan side looking south towards the Chong Kemin Valley in Kyrgyzstan; just beyond is Issyk Kul, 6,236 square kilometres of clear blue water that is the second largest mountain lake in the world.*

(Opposite) *The first Kolsay Lake in Kazakhstan's Kungey Alatau range near Almaty. Trekking is possible from here over the Sarybulak Pass to Issyk Kul, a wonderful experience taking you through incredibly biodiverse alpine landscapes.*

(Top left) *The beautiful ribbed dome of the Mausoleum of Khoja Ahmed Yasawi in Turkistan, Southern Kazakhstan.*
(Top right) *The imperial Russian splendour of the Holy Ascension Cathedral in Almaty.* (Bottom) *The massive southeastern portal of the Mausoleum of Khoja Ahmed Yasawi.* (Opposite top left) *A Tajik offering of bread and salt is a traditional greeting to visitors.* (Opposite top right) *A Kazakh grandmother and child in the Zhetisu region of Kazakhstan known as the "Land of Seven Rivers."* (Opposite bottom) *A Kyrgyz horseman with his prized golden eagle; hunting with eagles and falcons has been practised throughout Central Asia for millennia.*

The road near Karakol, at the eastern end of Issyk Kul in Kyrgyzstan. Today most main routes through Central Asia are tarmac, but their condition varies considerably, and you don't have to go far off a main road to encounter dirt tracks that may have changed little in centuries.

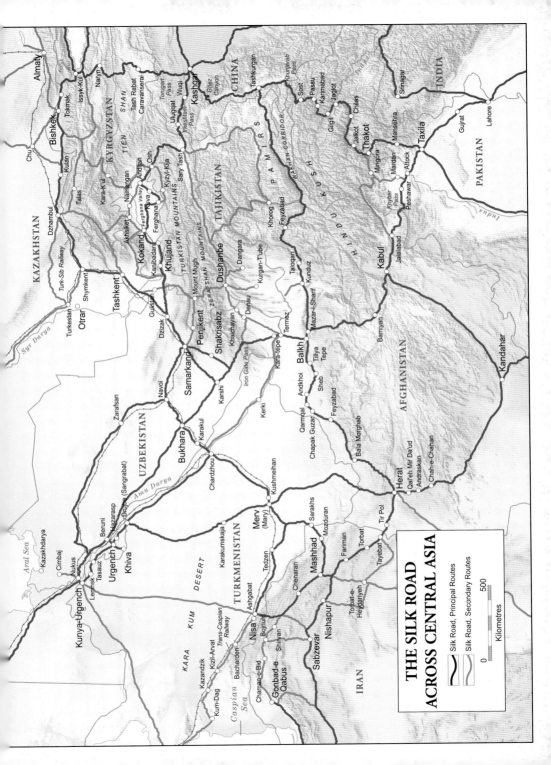

THE SILK ROAD
ACROSS CENTRAL ASIA

Silk Road, Principal Routes
Silk Road, Secondary Routes

0   500
Kilometres

KAZAKHSTAN

Almaty
Bishkek
Tokmak
Kulan
Talas
Dzhambul
Chu
Issyk-Kul
Naryn
Kara-Kul
KYRGYZSTAN
TIEN SHAN
Tokmak

CHINA
Kashgar
Tash Rabat
Tash Rabat
Caravanserai
Torugart Pass
Uluqqat Pass
Wuqia
Threshtam Pass
Tashkurgan
Sost
Passu
Khunjerab Pass
Chez Canyon
Karimabad
Jaglot
Gilgit
Jalkot
Chilas
Thakot
Srinagar
INDIA
Mansehra
Taxila
Attock
Lahore
Gujrat
PAKISTAN
Indus

Shymkent
Tashkent
Turkestan
Otrar
Turk-Sib Railway

Akhsiket
Namangan
Andijan
Osh
Kokand
Kanibadan
Ferghana
Kyzyl-Kja
Sary Tash
Ferghana Valley
Ava
Khujand
Turkestan
TURKISTAN MOUNTAINS
TAJIKISTAN
Mount Mugh
ZERAFSHAN MOUNTAINS
Dushanbe
Dangara
Kurgan-Tube
Khorog
Feyzabad
PAMIRS
WAKHAN CORRIDOR
Mingora
Mardan
Peshawar
Khyber Pass
Jalalabad
Kabul

Gulistan
Dzizak
Penjikent
Samarkand
Shakrisabz
Khalchayan
Denau
Termez
Kara-tepe
Iron Gate Pass
Talogan
Kunduz
Mazar-i-Sharif
Bamiyan
HINDU KUSH

Navoi
Zaratsan
Bukhara
Karakul
Karshi
Kerki
Qarmqal
Chapak Guzar
Andkhoi
Sheb
Tillya Tepe
Feyzabad
Balkh
Bala Morghab
AFGHANISTAN
Kandahar

UZBEKISTAN
Chardzhou
Amu Darya

Kazakhdarya
Cimbaj
Nukus
Aral Sea
Beruni
Mazarasp
Duya (Sangrabat)
Urgench
Khiva
Leninsk
Tasauz
Kunya-Urgench

Syr Darya

Karakumskaja
Kushmeihan
Merv (Mary)
Sarakhs
Mozduran
Fariman
Torbat
Tir Pol
Herat
Qaleh Mir Da'ud
Andraskan
Chah-e-Chahan

KARA KUM DESERT
Trans-Caspian Railway
Ashgabat
Tedzen
Chenaran
Mashhad
Nishapur
Torbat-e-Heydariyeh
TURKMENISTAN

Nisa
Bojnurd
Shirvan
Sabzevar
Tayebat
IRAN

Kum-Dag
Kazandzik
Kizil-Arvat
Bacharden
Chamae-Bid
Gonbad-e Qabus

Caspian Sea

The life-giving Panj River forms the border between Afghanistan and Tajikistan near the Vanch Valley. Though here the Pamirs are starting their descent to the Central Asian desert plains, the surrounding peaks are still more than 5,000 metres high.

(Above) *Panjshanbe Market in Khudjand, founded by Alexander the Great and one of the Ferghana Valley's most historically important towns. Markets like this can be found throughout modern Central Asia, usually on the sites of older market areas. (Top left) The ancient fortress town of Hissar close to Dushanbe, with the old caravanserai at bottom right. (Bottom left) A bridge in Tajikistan's Yagnob Valley, illustrating an ingenious and enduring wood and stone building tradition.*

Р. Зоммеръ

(Top left) *Bronze Age petroglyphs at Sarmysh in modern-day Uzbekistan. Rock art sites can be found at numerous sites throughout Central Asia and Mongolia.* (Top right) *A gold-toothed Uzbek woman sells delicious bread in Samarkand bazaar.* (Bottom) *Three faces of Central Asia show the blending of Eastern and Western features that has occurred down the ages.* (Left) *Kirghiz on a camel, an oil on canvas painting by Richard Karlovich Zommer (1866–1939); at that time the term "Kirghiz" referred to both Kazakh and Kyrgyz tribes.*

Three hundred years later, it was still the custom for travellers to protect themselves and the caravans when endangered by making such a "castle", placing the goods in the centre, and encircling them with the camels facing outwards, seated on the ground. The camels, according to Vambery, could perceive any threat from afar off, and would raise the alarm by making a dull rattle in the throat.

When the dangers of the stage had been negotiated and a source of water was near, the caravanbashi would give directions for a halt. As quickly as camp had been struck in the morning, the convoy came to a halt, and the travellers dismounted and unpacked. The younger members would rush off to collect scrub and dried roots for fuel, and others would untie the heavy burdens of merchandise from the camels. These would be piled up and used as shades from the sun, whilst the camels were turned loose to enjoy whatever pasture they could find nearby. As the animals departed, the whole caravan would be filled, according to Vambery, with a "solemn stillness", a sort of intoxication resulting from the sudden absence of movement, and the prospect of rest and refreshment.

This refreshment came first in the form of tea. This moved Vambery to as much a paean of praise as did the fortitude of the camels. "It is nothing more than a greenish warm water, innocent of sugar, and often decidedly turbid; still human art has discovered no food, has invented no nectar, which is so grateful, so refreshing in the desert, as this unpretending drink. I have still a vivid recollection of its wonder-working effects. As I sipped the first drops a soft fire filled my veins, a fire which enlivened without intoxicating. The later draughts affected both heart and head; the eye became peculiarly bright and began to gleam. In such moments I felt an indescribable rapture and sense of comfort. My companions sank in sleep; I could keep myself awake and drink with open eyes."

Once the tea had been consumed, there followed food, which was eaten by large groups sitting in circles, smoking. It was prepared in a way that would not please the most fastidious. "Here, they are baking bread. A Hadji in rags is actively kneading the black dough with dirty hands. He has been so engaged for half an hour, and still his hands are not clean, for *one* mass of dough cannot absorb the accumulations of several days." It was not much better with the meat, which formed the desert staple. "In order to know what is being cooked, it is not necessary to look round. The smell of mutton-fat, but especially the aroma, somewhat too piquant, of camel or horse cutlets, tells its own tale." There was nothing, in any ordinary circumstances, that would be found inviting about such cuisine. Yet, "in the desert a man does not disturb himself about such trifles. An enormous appetite covers a multitude of faults, and hunger is notoriously the best of sauces."

The leisure hours of the caravan towards the end of the day were spent simply. One amusement was to shoot at targets, for which the prize would be a quantity of gunpowder and lead shot. Another was to attempt to catch and mount one of the wild asses that would roam in groups throughout the desert. On one of Vambery's journeys, three spoonfuls of sheep's-tail fat was put up for anyone capable of such a feat. "Three spoonfuls of mutton fat is a tempting prize for Hadjis in the desert, so that many were seduced by the prospect of gaining it." Yet, as they attempted to mount a captured animal, they found that "...they could make nothing of this uncivilised brother of Balaam's charger..." and the "unfortunate Hadjis had no

(Left) Street Scene in Samarkand, *by Richard Karlovich Zommer – the same alley can be visited today, and little has changed.*

sooner seated themselves on its back than they were stretched sprawling in the sand". Otherwise, the time was devoted to religious exercises, the reading of the Qur'an, sleep, or the pursuit, not in too particular a fashion, of hygiene. The primary concern was to keep the beard and facial hair in order by means of plucking with small pincers. As for anything else in the way of washing, there was nothing excessively elaborate. "As to the toilet of the Hadjis, and, indeed, my own," wrote Vambery, "it is so simple and so prosaic as to be scarcely worth alluding to. The necessary requisites were sand, fire, and ants. The manner of application I leave as a riddle for the reader to solve."

Sir Alexander Burnes, a British soldier and spy, dressed in local attire to avoid detection.

As primitive as the toilet facilities might have been, as unappetising and repetitive the fare, the Western travellers who left accounts of travel through Central Asia by caravan had much to say for the experience. It was the sheer feeling of camaraderie and communality which beguiled them. Alexander Burnes, a young British army officer and spy who travelled through Afghanistan into Central Asia and Bokhara in the early 1830s, was drawn to comment on this aspect of the travelling life in Central Asia again and again: "A caravan is a complete republic; but I do not believe that most republics are so orderly... In the society of the caravan, there is much good fellowship, and many valuable lessons for a selfish man." Despite the number of people in the convoy and their competing wealth and ranks, there was never any disputing about the arrangement or order of march. All would, at all times, look out and wait for all other members of the caravan. If a single camel threw down its load, the whole line would halt until it was replaced. Everything that everyone possessed in the way of food and victuals was shared out in common, and no one cared to eat until everyone was in possession of a meal. "The khan fares as simply as the peasant; and never offers to raise a morsel to his lips till he has shared it with those near him... It is a pity that civilisation, with all its advantages, does not retain for us these virtues."

The air of content about the caravan also left a deep impression on Vambery. "At evening prayers, in which the whole company took part, this peace of mind struck me most forcibly. They thanked God for the benefits they enjoyed. On such occasions the whole caravan formed itself into a single line, at whose head stood an imam, who turned towards the setting sun and led the prayers. The solemnity of the moment was increased by the stillness which prevailed far and wide; and if the rays of the sinking sun lit up the faces of my companions, so wild yet withal so satisfied, they seemed to be in the possession of all earthly good, and had nothing left them to wish. Often I could not help thinking what would these people feel if they found themselves leaning against the comfortable cushions of a first-class railway carriage, or amid the luxuries of a well-appointed hotel. How distant, how far distant are the blessings of civilisation from these countries!"

The arrival of a caravan in one of the great trading cities of Central Asia was often likened to the arrival in port of a ship from the ocean. In many ways, both great and small, the comparison was apt. Seasickness, whether the traveller rode on the back of a camel, or hunched in wicker panniers slung over its sides, was common. For the latter stages of its journey, a caravan was guided to the city, at least at night, by fires burning at the top of minarets, like lighthouses, the only thing visible on the horizon in the midst of a trackless and hostile wilderness. And the joy on reaching the city, the abandonment of austerity, the freedom to leave behind the close confines of caravan life for the opulence and sensual pleasures of the city, were just the same for desert travellers as sailors reaching a great harbour, where all things were available, and everything was full of news and novelty, many of the others sojourning there being also travellers from different lands.

For travellers from the West, a visit to the Central Asian metropolises had perhaps even more of a relish than for those who traversed the Silk Road and trading routes in the course of ordinary business. Aside from the traditional allure of the luxury of the East, they had the added attraction of being places little known. The Westerners who were able to reach Central Asia, even late into the 19th century, were few, and those who left accounts of any sort were even fewer. After Anthony Jenkinson of the Muscovy Company reached Bokhara in 1558, there is little to go on until the seminal visit of the British explorer and spy Alexander Burnes in 1833. Even after Burnes, the number of travellers remained slight. It included journalists such as MacGahan, eccentric spies such as Vambery, and pure eccentrics such as Dr Joseph Wolff, an English clergyman of German origin, who visited Bokhara in 1843, marching up to the city wearing the full Anglican clerical dress with a bible in his right hand, declaring himself to be the "Grand Dervish" of all England.

Russian occupation and the later Bolshevik revolution made the cities of Central Asia little easier for foreign travellers to visit. Again, the greater number of accounts from this time are from fugitives and spies. Most notable amongst them was F.M. Bailey, who infiltrated the Communist establishment in Tashkent in the early 1920s in a series of ludicrous false identities which were so effective that he eventually receiving an executive

A large-wheeled cart in the Ferghana Valley – the size of the wheels probably lessened the jolts to the cargo as the horse pulled it along potholed tracks.

order to arrest his British alter-ego, who was thought to be hiding in the vicinity. The allure of these little known but much fabled cities was best summed up by Lord Curzon, who wrote in 1889 that "the traveller who has made a periplus of the universe, and like Ulysses, *Much has seen and known; cities of men/And manners, climates, councils, and governments*, may yet confess to a novel excitement as he threads the bazaars of remote Bokhara, or gazes on the coronation stone and sepulchre of Timur at Samarkand."

For travellers coming from China and other Far Eastern countries, Central Asia was similarly held to be a place of abundance, and almost of paradise. In early Chinese myths, it was a place where a holy race lived on an archipelago of blessed isles, guarding the elixir of everlasting life. When the first known Chinese explorer to reach these places, Zhang Qian, made his way to them in the 2nd century BCE, he found that the rulers of the Central Asian cities possessed "blood-sweating" horses, far more resilient than anything possessed by China, and the rich grass, alfalfa, with which to pasture them. And, although later Chinese travellers could detect no trace of the mythical blessed isles, they still found the Central Asian cities and their oases places of bliss and great contentment. Ye-lu Ch's Ts'ai, Genghis Khan's counsellor, who travelled in his retinue in the early 13th century, eulogised the pomegranates of Khujand in modern-day Tajikistan, "large as two fists and a sour sweet taste. People take three to five of this fruit and press out the juice into a vessel... delicious for slaking thirst."

is contemporary K'iu Ch'ang Ch'un reserved his praise for the city of Samarkand. Although he was doubtful about the women, whom he recorded as having moustaches, and who covered their heads in embroidered black or red gauze coverings "like Buddhist nuns", he considered it a delicious place. Being present at the spring equinox, the city was embowered with peach trees in full blossom. He went for a walk outside the great walls in the company of an astronomer – the cities were also great seats of scientific learning – and took a bottle of wine. The

Tashkent in the 1870s – horses, ponies and donkeys were all used as mounts rather than have to walk under the hot desert sun.

air was fine and clear, "the flowers and the trees in full freshness. Everywhere we saw lakes and orchards, towers and tents. We lay down on the grass and were all very happy together, talking about matters sublime. Even Chinese gardens cannot be compared with Samarkand; but there was no singing of birds."

Yet, the travellers who reached these cities might also hold them to be the worst of places, as well as the best. They were often stricken not only by external invaders, but also civil conflict. Jenkinson complained of the Central Asian ruling dynasties in 1558 that "every one will be King of his owne portion, and one brother seeketh always to destroy another", because the sons of kings were often born of different mothers in the royal harem. This conflict led, he complained, not only to occasional collapses of trade and demand in the cities, but also to renegade members of the royal families fleeing and living in the wilderness. The renegade prince, he continued "...so robbeth and spoileth as many Caravans of Marchants and others as he be able to overcome, continuing in this sort his wicked life, until such time as he may get power and aide to invade some of his brethren againe… For it is marvell, if a King reigne there above three or foure yeres, to the great destruction of the Countrey, and marchants."

As for the rulers actually in power, travellers often found them to be dangerous and tyrannical. The most notorious example of such behaviour was the captivity and execution in Bokhara in 1842 of two British envoys, Charles Stoddart and Arthur Connolly. Stoddart, on account of his committing a number of *faux pas* in the presence of the Emir – he had not been trained in the niceties of Central Asian diplomacy – was bound and flung into a dungeon below the Emir's *Ark*, or palace. This dungeon, according to a later account, in which Stoddart and later his friend Connolly, who had come to intercede for him, were confined, "swarmed with innumerable ticks and every disgusting species of vermin, which are especially reared to annoy the wretched prisoners; and should this prison by any extraordinary chance be without inmates, that the vermin might not perish they are supplied with rations of raw meat."

Yet, the main complaint made by travellers about the cities of Central Asia was the strictness with which the laws of religion were maintained. Islam, as many travellers had already observed, lay as little more than a veneer over the ancient customs of the steppe. Such were the rigours of nomadic life that the

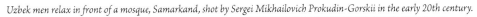

Uzbek men relax in front of a mosque, Samarkand, shot by Sergei Mikhailovich Prokudin-Gorskii in the early 20th century.

strict application of Islamic law was not possible; indeed, its doctrines were scarcely even known to the nomads. It was a different matter, however, in the cities. More and more after the 16th century, strictness in religion became the order of the day.

Bokhara, amongst all others, was particularly noted in this regard. An ancient proverb ran that in other parts of the world light descended from the sky, but in Bokhara, the light of day arose from the city itself, such was the depth of its piety. Citizens who had committed crimes, out of zeal for the faith would confess their misdeeds and demand before judges the full punishment required by law, even if that should be death. The city abounded with over 350 religious colleges, built like caravanserais with little cells around the central square, not dissimilar in design to the colleges of Oxford or Cambridge. To these, students would resort from all over Asia to study the Qur'an. Islamic traditions, philosophy and law, for periods of up to seven or eight years. During term-time, the students and professors would sit in the quadrangles from sunrise to sunset, disputing on fine points of theology. "One person says 'Prove there is a God!'" said Alexander Burnes, who witnessed the spectacle during his stay in Bokhara, "and about five hundred set arguments are adduced." This devotion to learning, however, did not open the minds of the Bokharans, he asserted, but rather narrowed them. The learning was nothing but the parroting of received formulas handed down without challenge, and their erudition was nothing but the "unprofitable maze of polemical discussion".

The practical consequences for the traveller of this spirit of literalist piety were many. The absence of alcohol was the first complaint. "And yet," wrote Jenkinson on his first visit to Bokhara, "it is there forbidden to drinke any other thing than water, & mares milke, and whosoever is found to break that law is whipped and beaten most cruelly through the open markets, and there are officers appointed for the same, who have authoritie to goe into any man's house, to search if he have either Aquavitae [or] wine… and finding the same, doe breake the vessels, spoile the drinke, and punishe the masters of the house most cruelly, yea, and many times if they perceive but by the breath of a man that he hath drunke, without further examination he shall not escape their hands."

Women were kept closely confined in their own quarters of their houses, and it was a point of honour to let no one unconnected with their family have sight of them. Husbands kept a suspicious watch on the balconies of surrounding houses, fearful that neighbours might snatch an illicit glimpse of their wives. With travellers such as

Jews in Samarkand in the late 19th century – as in so many countries in Eurasia, Jews were permitted to live here only under many strictures.

Prokudin-Gorskii captured this shot of a teacher and Jewish children during his trip to Bukhara (Bokhara) and Samarkand.

Alexander Burnes in town, they were right to be worried. "The house in which we lived was exceedingly small, and overlooked on every side, but we could not regret it, since it presented an opportunity of seeing a Toorkee beauty, a handsome young lady, who promenaded one of the surrounding balconies, and *wished to think* she was not seen. A pretended flight was not even neglected by this fair one, whose curiosity often prompted her to steal a glance at the Firingees. Since we had a fair exchange, she was anything but an intruder, though unfortunately too distant for us to indulge in 'the sweet music of speech.'"

Non-Muslim travellers often laboured under many disadvantages. The Jews of Bokhara, who had dwelt there for many generations, were compelled to live under many strictures, and these the Western travellers were often compelled to imitate. They were not allowed to go on horseback in the city, but could only travel on foot. In the fields, if they were riding on an ass, they were required to dismount as a mark of respect to any Muslim they should pass; and it was the right of the Muslim citizen to strike a Jew but not of the latter to retaliate. The difference of religions was also marked by different dress. Jews were not allowed to wear garments of silk or turbans, but only cotton robes and black calico hats. The broad sashes that Bokharans would wear around the waist were also substituted for a belt of rope, or else just a piece of string; this stood to symbolise, according to various travellers, that the wearer might be arbitrarily hanged under the laws of the city. Bathing, within the city, was also fraught with difficulty. Alexander Burnes was forbidden entry to many of the city's opulent public paths on account of the popular belief that their water might "change into blood if polluted by a woman or an infidel". These strictures were nowhere drawn from the authority of scripture, but had become customary within the city.

These difficulties for travellers, however, were not the entire story. The inheritance of the Silk Road inclined the inhabitants of the Central Asian cities to boundless hospitality towards the traveller. Islam also enjoined hospitality towards the visitor. "O brother, respect the guest and look after him," wrote the poet Hafez, "For the guest is the gift of God;/For the guest brings blessings and removes the sins of the host;/He who respects the guest respects the Prophet and God…"

Ibn Haukal, a 10th century Arab traveller, confirmed that these precepts had very much been taken to heart. "Such is the generosity and liberality of the inhabitants that no one turns aside from the rites of hospitality; so that a person contemplating them in this light would imagine that all the families of the land were but one house." Such was the addiction to the display of hospitality that it could even lead to ruination for the host. "When a traveller arrives there, every person endeavours to attract him to himself that he may have opportunities of performing kind offices for the stranger; and the best proof of their hospitable and generous disposition is that every peasant, though possessing but a bare deficiency, allots a portion of his cottage for the reception of a guest. On the arrival of a stranger, they contend one with another for the pleasure of taking him to their home, and entertaining him. Thus, in acts of hospitality, they expend their incomes."

Thus, even the Western and Christian traveller could be hopeful of receiving a welcome of great liberality. Perhaps the most outrageous example of this was the reception given to Ruy Gonzáles de Clavijo, an ambassador sent by Henry III of Castile to the Emperor Tamerlane. Arriving at Samarkand in September 1404, Clavijo and his party were received in tents of rich crimson cloth, embellished with hangings of gold, of silk and of jewels. For days, they were entertained with displays of fighting elephants, drinking bouts – such then was permitted, at least in private, to Tamerlane's nobility – and an unwearying succession of great banquets.

Clavijo chronicled them in his diary in full detail. The description of one will stand well for all others: "After the lord [Tamerlane], and his women, had drunk a great deal, they began to eat many sheep and horses, roasted whole, which were served up on very large skins, like printed leather, which men carried round; and there was so much that it took three hundred men and more to bring it, and there was a great noise when they brought it before the lord. They then put it into the basins, and served it up without bread, according to the custom; and all this time cartloads of meat did not cease to arrive, and camels with panniers full of meat, which was placed on the ground, in great heaps, and eaten by the rest of the people. Afterwards they brought many tables, without cloths, on which were dishes of meat cooked with rice, and bread made with sugar. As night came on they placed many lighted lanterns before the lord; and they commenced eating and drinking again, as well the men as the ladies, so that the feast lasted all night; and during the night two relations of the lord were married. When the ambassadors saw that this would last all the night, and they had had as much as they wanted, they returned to their lodgings, while the lord and his ladies continued their revelry."

t was not for the pleasures of diplomacy but rather for the sake of trade that most travellers would make their way to Central Asia's cities; the bazaars and caravanserais, rather than the indulgences of the court, were the main focus of their attention. Anthony Jenkinson was one of the first to describe the goods that were seen in the markets, and the countries from which they all came. "The Indians," he wrote, "doe bring fine whites, which the Tartars do all roll about their heads, & al other kinds of whites, which serve for apparell made of coton wooll and crasko, but golde, silver, precious stones, and spices they bring none." These latter, found Jenkinson, which earlier would have been brought by the traditional Silk Road routes overland, were now exported by sea from India by the Portuguese. At Bokhara, the Indian merchants would buy "wrought silkes, red hides, slaves, and horses, with such like," but when he attempted to interest them in his British narrow-cloth, he found that there were no takers.

There were three other main sources of trade: Persia, Russia, and China. "The Persians," he recorded, "Craska, wollen cloth, linnen cloth, divers kindes of wrought pide silkes, Argomacks, with such like, and doe carie from thence redde hides with other Russe wares, and slaves, which are of divers countries..." The Russian contribution to the markets, aside from hides and sheepskin, was "woodden vessels, bridles, saddles, with such like," and they would return to the north laden with silks and fine woollen cloth. The most glamorous imports came from China, at least when the roads were open. The goods of the "Cathay" merchants included "musk, rubarbe, satten [and] damaske"; yet Jenkinson was able to see none of these exposed for sale, as for three years "great warres... had dured betwixt two great Countries & cities of Tartars," Tashkent and Kashgar, not to mention "certain barbarous fielde people... Cassaks of the law of Mahomet... [who had] so stopped up the way" that it was impossible "for any Caravan to pass unspoiled".

Although the rise of the sea trade from India and China, as well as chronic instability in the steppe, put paid to a great proportion of the overland trade, it was by no means extinguished or without vigour even in the 19th century. Alexander Burnes, on his visit to Bokhara, could identify as many nationalities, if not more, than Jenkinson 300 years earlier. Seating himself in the bazaars or on a bench of the

Paper sellers in an unknown Central Asian city in the late 19th century. Paper originated in China and had spread to Central Asia by the 7th–8th centuries CE.

Registan, "where idlers and newsmongers assemble round the wares of Asia and Europe", he found he could "converse with the natives of Persia, Turkey, Russia, Tartary, China, India and Cabool". Here, the traveller would meet with "Toormuns, Calmuks, and Kuzzaks, from the surrounding deserts, as well as the natives of more favoured lands. He may contrast the polished manners of the subjects of the "Great King" [of Persia] with the ruder habits of a roaming Tartar".

The bazaars themselves could display an equal depth of diversity in the variety and provenance of their goods. Forty years after the time of Alexander Burnes, Schuyler gave his own account of the same markets. In Tashkent, the bazaar was extensive and intricate. There was a street allotted to every trade, for example silk sellers, jewellers or brass workers. The number of trades was reckoned as being 32; by Islamic tradition, there were 32 parts of the body, and consequently the categorisation of trades and trade guilds was made to reflect this. Looking down from the entrance gate over the whole bazaar above the flat mud roofs of the shops overgrown with grass and poppies, the streets were so thronged with visitors riding on horses or asses that it was difficult to see how anyone escaped from being trampled. Over various of the walls skeins of cotton and silk cloth were hung to dry, having just been dyed

Knife vendors were found in every town or city – carrying a knife was de rigueur for all men in Central Asia.

in a range of colours. Descending into the bazaar itself, one might find an equal claustrophobia in the merchants' shops. Most of them were so small that they scarcely allowed space for the shopkeeper and two visitors. They were composed of nothing more than a square room open to the street, with another smaller storeroom leading off at the back. The merchant would sit cross-legged on a carpet, and his wares would be laid out around him. He affected to be more willing to show his merchandise to the passer-by for *tomasha*, or amusement, rather than to sell it; indeed, if anyone offered to purchase his entire stock at once, he would refuse, saying that he would be left with little else to do.

here was indeed much in the way of tomasha to be found by merely browsing. There were shoemakers, tanners and dye-sellers, saddles, bridles and harnesses. There were the sellers of the products of nomads, camel's-hair cloth, ropes, carpets, rugs, tent frames and felt. There were jewellers selling turquoise and precious stones, silver rings, belt clasps and amulets. There were ironmongers, each dedicated to a small area of expertise, some selling ornamented knives and sabres, some just the bottom of ewers, others the handles for cooking pots. In the midst of their outlets, the workshops of blacksmiths and jewellery-makers were arranged, where boys sweated to pump hand-operated bellows to heat furnaces, and skilled craftsmen wove gold and silver wires to lay down filigree in grand dishes and ewers.

Among the merchants whose wares were dedicated to pure utility were those whose services were dedicated to ornament. The barber surgeons would offer a range of cosmetics, used as much by men as by women: black powder of antimony to heighten the eyelashes or paint the two eyebrows into one; white lead, imported from Russia; rouge, henna and a preparation of the gall of the pistachio tree mixed with the scales from a blacksmith's forge used for painting the teeth black. One of the few preparations to be absent, noted Schuyler, was anything in the way of hair pomade. The method of washing hair was to rub it with sour milk, before rinsing it in warm water, and perfuming it excessively with rosewater.

The signs of international trade in the bazaars of Central Asia were just as clear in the time of Schuyler as they were in the time of Jenkinson. In Tashkent, the metalworkers would improve on Russian samovars and teapots, and Uzbek jewellers would repair Russian watches. In Bokhara, there were Russian calicoes and Persian swords, finer than those made locally. Imported from the United States, a selection of revolvers made the other weaponry available in the bazaar – chain armour and matchlocks – seem miserably obsolete. English, French and German manufactured goods, chiefly cloth, were brought up from India by way of Afghanistan, a trade ultimately overseen by firms founded by Greek families operating out of Calcutta – Ralli and Co, Petrococchino and Schillizzi. Alongside these wares, native Indian commodities would arrive in the bazaar – dyestuffs and drugs, muslin, silver and pepper, printed and written books. From other cities in Central Asia, for example Khiva, would come fur and linseed oil, mutton tallow, wheat and rice, apples, sheep, poppy heads, copper, and Russian sugar candy in conical lumps. For export, Bokhara

returned amongst other items gold and silk, lambskins, camel and goat hair, madder, velvet and cotton, satin and fur robes, opium and tobacco, horses, asses, cats and nightingales. The total value of the trade annually in Bokhara, reckoned Schuyler, was worth at least £5.5 million annually at the time of his visit, a sum which translates very approximately into £2.5 billion (US$4.13 billion) in current values.

For all the frenzy of trade, there was still plenty to be had in the way of leisure and recreation in the midst of the bazaar. This primarily revolved around

A typical Central Asian tea stall, an ubiquitous sight throughout the region – tea drinking was an essential part of daily life.

the consumption of tea. "In every part of the bazaar," wrote Burnes, "there are people making tea…" and no one in the city – "and the remark applies indeed universally to all Central Asiatics" – continued Vambery, could ever "pass by a second or third tea-booth without entering, unless his affairs are very urgent indeed". Vambery found that in the bazaars the etiquette and rules surrounding the consumption of tea were as great, if not far greater, than in a London drawing room. Every man carried with him his own bag of green tea, a part of which he would give to the proprietor of the teahouse on entering; it was only the business of the teahouse to supply hot water, but not the tea itself. An *amuse-bouche* (a small hors d'oeuvre), such as small cakes of flour and mutton suet, for which Bokhara was famous, would be served while the visitor waited for his brew. When it arrived, any attempt to cool it down by blowing on it was regarded as "highly indecorous, nay as an unpardonable offence". The usual method was to swill the tea around the cup until

A view over a street dedicated to tea stalls in Samarkand.

the temperature became tolerable. "To pass for a man *comme il faut*, one must support the right elbow in the left hand, and gracefully give a circular movement to the cup; no drop must be spilt, for such an awkwardness would much damage a reputation for *savoir faire*." Once the teapot had been drained, the used tealeaves would be fished out and passed round all in the teahouse to be nibbled. "Etiquette forbids any one to take more than he can hold between finger and thumb, for it is regarded by connoisseurs as the greatest dainty."

One section of the Central Asian bazaars that brought no pleasure at all to the later Western visitors was that part set aside for the sale of slaves. Slavery had been long established in the Central Asian cities, it having been an institution condoned by Islamic law for many generations, and even in the later 19th century it continued to flourish unabated. Most of the slaves were Persians, captured by the nomadic Turkomans from travellers' caravans or else raids on the northeast of Persia. Their adherence to Shi'a Islam made them worse than unbelievers in the eyes of the orthodox Sunni Muslims of Central Asia, and therefore legitimate fodder for the slave trade. However, a small number were Russians, both men and women, who had been captured when straying too far from the safety of Orenburg, the Russian imperial outpost on the Kazakh steppe. Their presence gave one of the pretexts for the Russian invasion of the Central Asian cities in the 1860s and 1870s, and before that time a number of travellers, partly out of horror of the trade, but also to remove this pretext for invasion, made strenuous efforts to have them released. On a couple of occasions, they were even successful. For example, one late summer's day in 1840, the Russian commandant of Fort Alexansdrovsk on the Caspian was astonished to see 416 freed Russian slaves being led towards the gates by an English army captain, Richmond Shakespeare, who by means of careful diplomacy had managed to emancipate them from their owners in Khiva. Yet despite these one-off events, the trade continued, and even managed to survive for a time the Russian occupation of Central Asia, with one of its avowed aims of destroying the slave trade; the merchants merely moved their business from the bazaars behind closed doors into the upper storeys of private houses.

Travellers such as Burnes and Vambery were able to see the trade in the open air. The day for buying slaves in Bokhara, noted Burnes, was Saturday, and those for sale could be seen penned up in "thirty or forty stalls, where they are examined like cattle, only with this difference, that they are able to give an account of themselves *viva voce*". Once the purchaser had satisfied himself on the main point – that the intended purchase was a heretic Shi'a – he proceeded to inspect the specimen, finding out what might be his or her strengths and weaknesses, and ensuring that they were free from disease, particularly leprosy, which was then especially prevalent.

As with second-hand car dealers or estate agents, the slave traders were notorious for trying to cover up any defects in their wares, and it was the custom that the buyer was permitted to seek a refund within three days in case he should discover any fault with the goods, "for, although the buyer at the time of sale examines him carefully all over like a beast of burden, makes him show the strength of his arms, chest, back and voice, he is still obliged to be on his guard against the tricks of the broker". Buyers were most commonly deceived over the age of their slaves. The slave traders would usually dye their beards black if there was any hint of grey hair to be seen. "It is thus possible," recorded Vambery, "to make a mistake of twenty, nay, even of thirty years, and it sometimes happens that a slave who, when bought, had a fresh, youthful appearance, and a coal black beard, a few days afterwards turns out to be a grey-haired old man."

After the completion of the business day, the attention of the city dwellers would turn to leisure and recreation. The traveller Eugene Schuyler once asked a mullah in Tashkent what were the amusements of the people in Central Asia. The mullah replied that he himself read, made translations or said prayers, but that the people of Central Asia had no amusements. The men, he claimed, might occupy themselves in horseracing or shooting, but aside from the occasional festival where dancing might occur, there were no amusements to be had of any kind. Religion, he claimed, only allowed people to train for the observance of religion and war, and any toys or amusements would be an expression of impiety.

Schuyler however found in fact that, despite the mullah's definition and protestations of piety, that there was plenty to occupy one's time in the Central Asian cities. The children were well supplied with toys, knucklebones, balls and rag dolls. With the older men, chess was popular, as was playing cards, a pastime which had spread to Central Asia from Russia, the games they played being the same as those popular among the Russian peasants. Another popular game, probably indigenous, was for old men to sit in the street and lay out coins in front of them, and then bet on which would be the first to have a fly land on it. There were performers and comedians who would mimic various scenes of life – the

A falconer in Tashkent. The saker falcon was the preferred bird of prey for hunting.

judge and the suitor, the teacher and student, the doctor and patient, as well as imitating cats, dogs and other animals. Wrestling was common, particularly in the spring, as was falconry, and quails also were trained to fight; indeed, according to Schyuler, "every youth of fashion" would carry a quail or similar small bird on his hand or nestled in his bosom.

A dancing boy and musicians – since women were forbidden to dance in public, effeminate young boys were used in their place – if talented, they could rise to positions of great celebrity.

Music also was popular. Resorting to gardens outside the city, performers would sit singing for hours, both day and night, strumming dotars or sitars (two- and three-stringed instruments, like lutes or guitars) as well as reed pipes like clarinets, drums and small trumpets. Earlier in the day, there might be half-chanted recitations of poems, but as the twilight drew on the music would grow livelier and more frenzied. Wilder songs would be sung to the clapping of hands or the beating of tambourines, brass salvers being struck if tambourines happened not to be available.

It was however in the inescapable accompaniment to music – the dance – which travellers to Bokhara and the other Central Asian cities saw them painted in their twin extremes of virtue and depravity. Dervishes marked one of these poles, dancing boys the other.

It was held by the religious establishment that Islamic law forbade women from dancing in public. The prohibition, however, was circumvented by resorting to boys and beardless youths to provide such open entertainment. Late into the 19th century, they were numerous in large towns – no place that had any pretensions to position or grandeur would be without one. Even men with low incomes would club together to procure one to amuse themselves in their hours of rest and recuperation. Teashops would vie for their services, and if, adds Schuyler, they should be pretty, the proprietor would be ensured business all day long. Throughout the cities, they were respected as great artists and occupied a position much the same as a modern celebrity, being fêted, followed and indulged. According to Schuyler, he had never seen such breathless interest as they aroused, and the whole crowd would "devour them with their eyes". If a boy should coquettishly offer one of the spectators a bowl of tea, the lucky recipient "bows to take it with a profound obeisance, and returns the empty bowl addressing him as 'taxir', Majesty, 'Kulluk', I am your slave."

Such was the ubiquity of the dances that Schuyler was able to describe the procedure extensively. At the time appointed for a performance, the boys would arrive at the venue in twos and threes. Seated on the edge of the carpet, they would be presented with tea, fruits and sweets, whilst the musicians tuned their instruments and heated the tambourines over hot charcoal to increase their resonance. This done, each boy would then rise to begin his dance. This, said Schuyler, was difficult to describe. "Clad in flowing robe of bright-coloured variegated silk, and loose trousers, with bare feet, and with two long tresses of hair streaming from under his embroidered skullcap, the [boy] begins to throw himself into graceful attitudes, merely keeping time with his feet and hands to the beating of the tambourines and the weird monotonous song of the leader. Soon his movements become wilder, and the spectators all clap their hands in measure; he circles madly about, throwing out his arms, and, after turning several somersaults, kneels facing the musicians. After a moment's pause he begins to sing in reply to the leader, playing his arms in graceful movements over his head. Soon he rises, and, with body trembling all over, slowly waltzes about the edge of the carpet, and with still wilder and wilder motions again kneels and bows to the spectators. A thrill and murmur of delight runs through the audience, an extra robe is thrown over him, and a bowl of tea handed to him as he takes his seat."

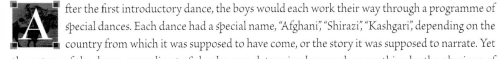fter the first introductory dance, the boys would each work their way through a programme of special dances. Each dance had a special name, "Afghani", "Shirazi", "Kashgari", depending on the country from which it was supposed to have come, or the story it was supposed to narrate. Yet the nature of the dance, according to Schuyler, was determined as much as anything by the physique of the dancer. The younger and more supple would dance in a more gymnastic fashion with somersaults and handsprings. The elder and taller would devote themselves to posturing, slow movements, and amatory and lascivious gestures. The most popular, observed Schuyler, were those who dressed as girls "with long braids of false hair and tinkling anklets and bracelets". Few boys in a dance troupe could carry off such an exhibition. Once they had donned female attire, it would not be removed for the entire evening. Frequently they would mime the action of seizing their heart in their hands, and then pretending to throw it to the members of the audience, "like throwing kisses". Sometimes he would go amongst them, choosing a spectator and offering a bowl of tea in the most provocative manner possible. The spectator would go forward to embrace the boy, but he would slip away at the last moment, flirtatiously moving his attentions to another enthralled admirer. These, if generous, would drop some coppers into an empty bowl, but some might even offer a gold coin to the boy between his lips, which the boy in the same way would take.

s much as dancing could lead to depravity, it was also the way to the heights of the mystic communion with God. Outside the city, especially towards the evening, particularly by the tombs of saints and holy men, the traveller would frequently come across dervishes and devotees enacting Sufi rituals and dances, entrancing themselves to a state of ecstasy. Schuyler was as much a witness of these events as of the dancing boys, and was able to recall them thoroughly. He watched one such ceremony, conducted by a Sufi brotherhood, in a mosque near Tashkent. Late one Thursday evening inside the mosque, a crowd of 30 men, both young and old, knelt to pray facing the direction of Mecca. Others joined them, taking off their robes and turbans as they entered the mosque, standing round them in a circle two or three deep, writhing and exclaiming a litany of short prayers: "My defence is in the Lord, may God be magnified... There is nothing but God in my heart... My light, Mohammed, God bless him..." The prayers were chanted semi-musically, and in time to the chant each worshipper tossed his head violently from the left shoulder down to his chest, to the right shoulder and then back down on to the chest. The texts were repeated hundreds of times, perhaps for a number of hours. At first the movements were slow, but gradually according to the will of the Ishan, or master in charge of proceedings, they would accelerate and grow move violent. If anyone failed to keep up, the Ishan would strike them on the head and they would be hauled out, only to have one of the spectators eagerly take his place. Others, according to another traveller, Henry Lansdell, would jump out of the mêlée, shouting and slapping themselves. Everyone was wet with perspiration, and the voices began to grow hoarse with the chanting. Soon, all joined in the simple cry "*hai hai Allah, hai*," and everyone in the room put their hand on the shoulder of their neighbour, forming several concentric rings which rushed around and leapt from side to side of the mosque wailing "*hai Allah hai*". At last, as the leaping and the chanting grew more wild, the worshippers broke out in a frenzy. Their bodies acted automatically as if almost independent of their minds, and they sprinted in all directions about the room gyrating, convulsing, hauling the bystanders into the thick of the dance. At length, when their bodies were utterly exhausted, the worshippers stumbled and sunk to the floor, and, as the Ishan recited prayers or the poetry of Hafez they embraced, groaned and wept, beating their breasts, stroking their beards, and lying on the ground enwrapped in contemplation.

The dervishes and the dancing boys, the emirs and courtiers in their palaces, the slave markets and chaos of the bazaars, the caravans and camel drivers, all of these things managed to survive in Central Asia even into the 20th century, and some even to this day. However, the vigour of their spirit belonged to the past, and it was the conquest by the Russians that brought their era to a close.

The magnificent interior of Tillya Kari Madrassah, in Samarkand's Registan, is replete with gold leaf – hence its name, Tillya Kari, which means "gilded". The madrassah's exterior is just as impressive, in fact the Registan is possibly the most magnificent public square in the world, its three edifices all architectural masterpieces in their own right but, when combined, one of Central Asia's greatest man-made treasures.

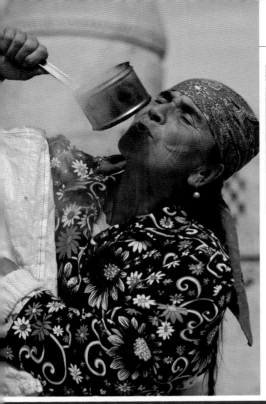

(Above) A multitude of Samarkand's buildings are blessed with incredible tile detail that amazes both from a distance and when examined close up.

(Left) A colourfully dressed Uzbek woman cools a freshly boiled drink for refreshment during a visit to Samarkand's many pilgrimage sites.

(Below) Gloriously intricate and symmetrical tiling graces a dome at the Bibi Khanum Mosque, Tamerlane's attempt to create the greatest mosque in the 14th century world.

(Opposite) The Shir Dor Madrassah shines in the afternoon sun at the Registan in Samarkand.

Samarkand's Tillya Kari Madrassah faces south across the Registan, its 75-metre façade flanked by corner turrets rather than minarets, its main portal a feast of colourful mosaics including bright sun symbols above the entrance.

(Left) A melon seller in Samarkand Bazaar, 1905–15; Sergei Prokudin-Gorskii's classic image could almost have been taken yesterday.

(Below) The Bazaar in Samarkand, an oil on board painting by Alexei Vladimirovich Issupoff (1889–1957), showing a Kazakh couple arriving by camel at the Registan beside the Ulug Beg Madrassah.

(Opposite top) The Mir-i Arab Madrassah in Bukhara; a traditional saying has it that "Samarkand is the beauty of the earth, but Bukhara is the beauty of the spirit".

(Opposite bottom) Catching the train at Tashkent Station – if only the merchants and camel drivers of old could see how easy it is to cross the desert wildernesses of Central Asia today!

(Left) *The 10th century Ismael Samani Mausoleum is Bukhara's oldest building, a fascinating brick cube with elements of early Sogdian architecture.*

(Below) *The Gur Emir, Tamerlane's Mausoleum in Samarkand, is lit up to atmospheric effect by night.*

(Opposite top) *Young musicians in Shakhrisabz (known as Kesh in antiquity) in front of a statue of the town's most famous son, Tamerlane.*

(Opposite bottom) *Cotton production in Chinaz near Tashkent – along with wheat, cotton is the region's most significant crop, although it requires a lot of irrigation and water resources have been severely depleted in the process, leading to political tensions between the countries through which the many rivers coursing out of the mountains pass.*

(Top) The Ark Fortress, home to the rulers of Bukhara for more than a thousand years. (Bottom) Phoenix motifs and Koranic writing grace the portal of the Nadir Divan-Beghi Madrassah in the Lyab-I Hauz complex, Bukhara. (Left) Bukhara's incredible Kalon Minaret, a defining symbol of the city and at 48 metres high, a beacon for caravans toiling through the desert.

(Above) At the Fortress Walls. "Let Them Enter!" by Vasily Vereshchagin, 1871, illustrating the defence of Samarkand's central fortress – against odds of 80 to one – by its imperial Russian garrison after an uprising by the native population.

(Left) The Emir of Bukhara, Muhammad Alim Khan, poses for Sergei Mikhailovich Prokudin-Gorskii in 1911 – the last of Bukhara's emirs, he was to rule until 1944.

(Opposite) The Islam Khoja Minaret and its madrassah in Khiva were the last major architectural achievements of the Central Asian khanates, named after the much-loved grand vizier who commissioned them in 1908 and 1910. Sadly, Islam Khoja – an educational reformist – was assassinated in 1913 with the passive approval of his master, Isfandiyar Khan (see page 368).

(Right) *Ruins of the Kepter Khana within the UNESCO World Heritage site of ancient Merv; it is thought this may have been part of a library and the recesses may have once held books.*

(Below) *The Kalta Minaret, Amin Khan Madrassah and Ark in Khiva, probably the best-preserved Central Asian city, and one of the most remote.*

(Opposite top) *A Desert Fort, by Aleksandr Evgen'evich Yakovlev (1887–1938), showing a typical fortress in the region of Karakalpakstan. Surrounded by the Kizil Kum and Kara Kum deserts, historically this was home to the Khorezm civilisation.*

(Opposite bottom) *A Turkmen (Turcoman) camel driver with loaded camel, an image taken in the early 20th century by Sergei Prokudin-Gorskii. Even at this time, travel through the desert towards Iran was a difficult and dangerous proposition.*

THE TRANS-CASPIAN RAILWAY

The great cities of Central Asia fell to the Russians, one by one, over a period of about 30 years in the latter part of the 19th century; Bokhara and Samarkand in 1868, Khiva in 1873. Of the conquest of the latter, there was an eyewitness in the person of the reporter, James MacGahan, an American who worked for the *New York Herald*. Disregarding the prohibition by the Russian government against foreign travellers or war correspondents travelling or reporting from Central Asia, MacGahan doggedly played a game of cat and mouse with the Russian army throughout the territory. MacGahan was able to speak Russian and understood Russian customs on account of his Russian wife. Consequently, he was able to ingratiate himself with the ordinary soldiers, who helped him, in spite of their orders, to survive and covertly continue his pursuit. In the end, the Russian commander, so impressed by MacGahan's doggedness, relented, and allowed him to join the Russian forces as an early embedded correspondent to observe the conquest of Khiva.

The Emir of Khiva, fearful of the power of the Russian artillery, decided against a long and bloody siege, and surrendered the city to his opponents, himself fleeing into the desert. MacGahan and the Russians were therefore able to enter the city unopposed. To a certain extent, the city presented to them the exotic east of their imaginations. Its oasis was lush with vegetation, a welcome sight after several months marching in the desert. So thickly was the city surrounded with trees that its high battlemented walls only became visible when they came within half a mile. Within there were minarets and domes, grand squares, and the great tower of Khiva – a turret 125 feet (38 metres) tall, entirely jewelled with rich porcelain tiles in blue, green, purple and brown, and covered over with sayings from the Qur'an. After dark, the sight of the cityscape became even more arresting. Near midnight, wrote MacGahan, "...the silent, sleeping city lay bathed in a flood of glorious moonlight. The palace was transformed. The flat mud roofs had turned to marble; the tall slender minarets rose dim and indistinct, like spectre sentinels watching over the city. Here and there little courts and gardens lay buried in deepest shadow, from which arose the dark masses of mighty elms and the still and ghostly forms of the slender poplars. Far away, the exterior walls of the city, with battlements and towers, which in the misty moonlight looked as high as the sky and as distant as the horizon. It was no longer a real city, but a leaf torn from the enchanted pages of the *Arabian Nights...*"

The close reality of the conquered city, however, was an entirely different matter. The army made a glorious entrance. Marching bands playing the national anthem as they strode through the gates, and the banners of the regiments were paraded in the streets. Such were their numbers that they raised huge clouds of dust as they entered the city's portals. Yet, aside from the small parts of the city adorned with grand architecture, according to MacGahan, there was a palpable sense of disappointment. None had

(Left) A classic image by Sergei Prokudin-Gorskii of Isfandiyar Jurji Bahadur, Khan of Khiva in the early 20th century.

seen a city so forlorn. "We began to see small groups of men in the lateral streets, in dirty ragged tunics and long beards, with hats off, bowing timidly to us as we passed. These were the inhabitants, and they were not yet sure whether they would be massacred or not. With what strange awe and dread they must have gazed upon us as we passed, dust-covered and grimy after our march of 600 miles over the desert, which they had considered impassable. Grim, stern, silent and invincible, we must have appeared to them like some strange, powerful beings of an unknown world."

The Persian slaves still held in the city were at least pleased at the advent of the Russians. They ran out into the streets whooping and shouting for joy; they knew that the Russians would see to their release. However, the sense of the city, forlorn and forsaken, was most intense in the palace abandoned by the Emir. MacGahan and his Russian companions took the opportunity to explore it. The grand audience chamber, a great hall with an arch rather like a theatre stage, where the Emir would sit with his ministers to dispense justice, was empty, for the courtiers had fled. All that remained was an elderly official, who brought the Russians tea. In the treasure room, a room garishly frescoed with flowers and vines, they found the accumulated riches of the khanate. In the midst was an ancient old chair, low-backed and leathered, which was said to be over 700 years old, the khan's throne. Around it were iron chests, some emptied, which contained masses of silver, saddles and bridles covered in gold and rubies, emeralds and turquoise. There was a rifle which had been sent as a gift from Lord Northbrook, the Governor-General of India, Persian scimitars, silken robes of honour, several hundred ancient books, chain mail rusted with dust, telescopes, pottery, bows and arrows, and suits of armour so ancient that they might well have dated back to the Crusades. All had been abandoned. It was the same with the harem. All of the Emir's wives, concubines and their household had been left behind without protection. Looking into their quarters, MacGahan saw "women of all kinds", old and young, pretty and ugly, infants and adults, "sweet young girls of fifteen" and "old toothless hags, apparently a hundred and fifty". All cried and wrung their hands "in the most despairing way".

With the Russians came the inevitable railways. The great line – the Trans-Caspian – which in the end was to stretch from the Caspian Sea to Almaty, and eventually to be the basis for a Central Asian rail network connecting Iran to the Central Asian Cities, to southern Russia and even eastern Siberia, had its beginnings long after its cousin, the Trans-Siberian, and its origins were far more humble.

Primarily, it was envisaged as a short military train line. As the Russians extended their influence into Central Asia, the supplies for their military campaigns became ever more problematic. Particularly in the Kara Kum Desert, east of the Caspian, there was little forage to be had from the land, and every army had to be dependent on taking all of their food by camel caravan. This made them vulnerable not only to attack by the local nomadic tribes, the Turcomans, but also to the vicissitudes of the weather, and the health of their baggage animals. The problems stretched back as far as 1839, when the Imperial Russian forces had made their first attempt to capture Khiva. Their invasion force, marching over winter, was hit by unexpectedly fierce snowstorms, and of the column of 5,000 men and 10,000 camels, 1,000 men perished and only 1,000 camels survived. The rest of the column was plagued by frostbite, snow-

Women sell sturgeon meat at the market in Turkmenbashi on Turkmenistan's Caspian coast.

blindness, scurvy and wolves. Forty years later, although the Russians were more militarily successful, overcoming both their Turcoman enemies and the Khanate of Khiva, they still suffered difficulties and losses of baggage animals on a similar or even worse scale. With such consistent attrition of their supplies, their more certain control of Central Asia, and also their potential interest in threatening Afghanistan and British India to the south, the building of a railway became ultimately unavoidable.

The original nature of the line might have turned out differently. In the mid-1870s, ambitious plans were put forward by members of the Russian government to build a railway line all the way from Peshawar in British India, across Afghanistan and Central Asia, via Samarkand and Orenburg, to Europe and England. The work, according to the Russian plan, would be shared between the British and the Russians, the former taking responsibility for the track from India to Samarkand, and the Russians being responsible for the rest. The Russians, according to one of their Central Asian commanders, General Ignatieff, were particularly keen on the project as it would demonstrate "the essentially pacific and civilising character of Russian influence in those regions". This would be, rather than a military undertaking, a means of promoting trade and commercial relations. The British, however, suspecting otherwise, received the plan, in the words of Lord Curzon, not with much alacrity. This first project for a Central Asian railway therefore lapsed. However, with Russian military action against the Turcoman tribes at the end of 1879 and 1880, the plans were soon resurrected. Yet, the location of the line was changed, as was its character. The need for logistical support was greatest in the Kara Kum Desert, and thus the new line was envisaged as only a military supply route, leading the short way from the Russian port of Krasnovodsk (today called Turkmenbashi) on the east coast of the Caspian, to the oasis of Kyzyl Arvat, a distance of 145 miles.

The station of Bahmi on the Trans-Caspian Railway, circa 1890. To the north stretches the lifeless Kara Kum Desert.

Like the original proposals for the Trans-Siberian, the Trans-Caspian line was first planned as more of a tramway. The gauge of the tracks would be a mere 20 inches, and the carriages would be pulled by horses rather than locomotives, on account of the lack of coal or firewood in the desert. However, the plans became considerably more ambitious when the great pioneer of the line, General Mikhail Annenkov, who had been responsible for transport arrangements in the Russo-Turkish War in 1877, was appointed to oversee its construction. Annenkov was full of ambition. Promptly, he scrapped the notion of a narrow-gauge line, and instead began work on a fully fledged five-foot gauge track, following the standard of the rest of the Russian network. He also set aside the notion of the carriages being drawn by horse as hopelessly antique. Instead, he looked to the near boundless supply of crude oil now being extracted across the Caspian Sea at Baku, and lighted upon the idea of using one of the by-products of the refining process, naphtha, as a fuel for modern locomotive engines.

Lord Curzon, who travelled on the line some 10 years after it had been constructed, described it as "the easiest and simplest railway that has ever been built". Certainly, Annenkov did not face anything like the engineering difficulties that beset the builders of the Trans-Siberian in the isolated mountains, ground-shifting tundra or the vermin-ridden swamps between Irkutsk and Vladivostok. As Curzon explained in his account of the line, "The region which it penetrates is as flat as a billiard table for almost the entire distance, the steepest gradient met with being only 1 in 150... There are no tunnels, and only a few insignificant cuttings in the sandhills. Sometimes the rails run in a bee line for 20 or 25 miles without the slightest deviation to right or left." Nonetheless, the building of the line was certainly not without its problems, and the achievements of Annenkov should not be treated as lightly as did Curzon. The main trouble was the sand. In the howling wilderness of the desert, wrote Curzon, "The sand, of the most brilliant yellow hue, is piled in loose hillocks and mobile dunes, and is swept hither and thither by powerful winds. It has all the appearance of a sea of troubled waves, billow succeeding billow in melancholy succession, with the sand driving like spray from their summits, and great smooth-swept troughs lying between, on which the winds leave the imprint of their fingers in wavy indentations, just like an ebb-tide on the sea-shore."

In some areas, Annenkov attempted to combat the danger of the line and earthworks being swallowed up by spraying it with seawater; this, after evaporated, solidified and held it in check. In others, it was padded down underneath a layer of protective clay. Plants and long-rooted desert shrubs were introduced along stretches of the line, and nurseries set up to cultivate them for use on the railway. Failing these, a type of woven fence, originally used in Siberia for blocking the onset of snowdrifts, was adapted for desert use and laid by sections of the track. Yet, despite all these precautions, the line could still be swiftly inundated, and parties of workmen had to be quickly despatched to dig out the line from the dunes.

Then, there was the matter of supplies. There was little that could be had or manufactured locally that was required for the construction of a railway line. Every piece of timber, iron and steel had to be made in Russia, generally in industrial plants in the south of the country, shipped down the Volga and then across the Caspian to Krasnovodsk. Also, for a 100-mile stretch of land from the coast of the Caspian to the small oasis of Kazanjik fresh water was not to be found. At first, primitive desalination equipment was set up to distil seawater, but later water was collected in huge vats from the few oases and shipped up and down the line. Water, along with food and construction materials, had to be despatched to the workers at the head of the line by rail twice a day. It was not such a difficulty, however, with bricks for stations and other outbuildings. Stone could be quarried from the nearby Persian mountains, or, more easily, sun-baked bricks could be removed from the many ancient ruins in the vicinity and incorporated into the modern building work.

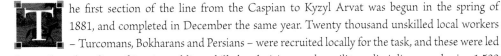

he first section of the line from the Caspian to Kyzyl Arvat was begun in the spring of 1881, and completed in December the same year. Twenty thousand unskilled local workers – Turcomans, Bokharans and Persians – were recruited locally for the task, and these were led by a railway battalion of Russian soldiers, skilled technicians under military discipline, numbering 1,500 men. The conditions for all were considerably better than those endured by the engineers constructing the Trans-Siberian. For many of the native workers, the wages paid by the Russian army – in some cases reaching a quarter of the wages paid to the Russian soldiers – were the first regular salaries they had ever received. This was particularly the case with the nomadic Turcomans, who previously had been accustomed to deriving their livelihood from sheep-rearing and slave-stealing. Such were the effects of giving them gainful occupation in the construction of the line that arguably it contributed much more to their pacification than any military campaign.

As for the Russian workers, they were accommodated in a remarkable double-decker working train, which advanced at the head of the line as it was built. This train included not only quarters for 1,500 men, but also food supplies, kitchens, a mess, medical facilities, a blacksmith's workshop and a telegraphy room. Nor were the working hours too onerous. The 1,500 men were divided into two equal brigades, one of which worked from 6am to midday, and the other from midday to 6pm. The native workers would go ahead flattening the area for the line, building embankments and making cuttings where necessary, and the Russians would follow them laying the sleepers and track. The fact that the sleepers were not ballasted and the rails held down only with spikes made early travel on the line a slow affair – the average speed was 10 to 20 miles an hour (16–25kph) – but it did allow for the line to be constructed at an unprecedented rate. At best, when the weather was favourable and everything was running smoothly, as much as four miles of track could be laid every day.

The Trans-Caspian line was eventually extended to Ashkhabad (Ashgabat) in 1885, the ancient Silk Road city of Merv (Mary) in 1886, and Samarkand in 1888. The first train, decked with flags and loaded with soldiers, pulled into Samarkand station on 27 May that same year, saluted by cannons and the music of marching bands. The advent of the railway, much more than the Russian conquest, had a profound effect of the ancient cities of Central Asia. As in both China and parts of Siberia, there was an initial hostility on the part of the local population. The railway was regarded as not only a dangerous foreign innovation, but as almost against religion. In Bokhara, it was dubbed *Shaitan's Arba*, or the "Devil's wagon", and the strong feeling of the citizens ensured that the railway station was built 10 miles outside the city.

However, the Russians in this and other similar cases turned the local hostility to their advantage. With railway stations far outside the original cities, they could establish and build new towns around the new transport links to rival them and ultimately to diminish their original importance and power. With Bokhara, Curzon was able to see the process in its earliest stages. A station was being built with imported stone, and all around it plots of land had been eagerly bought up by prospectors and local trading companies, who looked forward to moving their premises out of the old city into new and Western-style accommodation. Streets were about to be laid out and barracks to be built for the Russian soldiers, who could be accommodated with much greater ease in the Russian city, enflaming far fewer sensibilities on the part of the native population, but still able easily to keep them in check. Before long, the full panoply of Russian life would descend on the ancient cities, along with hotels and libraries, clubs and ballrooms. Restaurants would soon offer seven-course meals with menus printed in French, and dances would be held where Russian women paraded in low-cut evening gowns, with jewels and diamonds in their hair.

As soon as the trains began to reach the Central Asian cities, the local people began quickly to overcome their original hostile antagonism towards the line. "Already when the first working train steamed into Bokhara," wrote Curzon, "with rolling stock and material for the continuation of the line, the natives crowded down to see it, and half in fear, half in surprise, jumped into the empty wagons. Presently apprehension gave way to ecstasy. As soon as the line was in working order they would crowd into the open cars in hundreds, waiting for hours in sunshine, rain, or storm, for the engine to puff and the train to move."

Quickly, business began to drain from the old city centres and the old caravan routes to the railway towns and the railways. Shortly after its establishment in 1888, the Bokhara station was taking over £300 (worth about £23,000 today) every day in passenger fares and goods traffic. European trade, which before was a difficult, uncertain and even dangerous prospect, became an easy undertaking. Merchants arrived immediately in droves, some to buy live sheep for export by rail and others to buy fine lambskins for sale in Moscow. French traders from Asia Minor, Armenians and Jews came to buy walnut trees or else great quantities of carpets, forcing prices to soar.

In their wake they brought all manner of European goods, both valuable and commonplace, but little before seen in Central Asia. To the bazaars were introduced porcelain, lamps, glasses, mirrors, coffee, preserves and biscuits. At the railway stations could be procured playing cards and cigars, beer, wine and brandy, the latter for sale in "the fantastic glass bottles, shaped like animals, that the Russian taste affects". The prohibition against drinking alcohol, which from the time of Jenkinson had been sternly enforced, now began to lose its rigour. It was not a new import of which Curzon approved: "The Russian soldier in Central Asia has an excuse for insobriety in the loneliness of his life and the want of more elevating pastime. But his example is unhappily contagious... Already the Khans of Merv, habituated to European entertainment, sip their glass of vodka, and toss off their bumper of champagne. Where costliness does not intervene, the licence of an upper class is soon apt to become the law of a lower. Western civilisation in its Eastward march suggests no sadder reflection than that it cannot convey its virtues alone, but must come with Harpies in its train, and smirch with their foul contact the immemorial simplicity of Oriental life."

ravel on the Trans-Caspian line in general presented less in the way of luxury than was possible on the Trans-Siberian. Only one first-class carriage existed on the line, and this was reserved for the use of General Annenkov and other high dignitaries. Most of the traffic was restricted to the transport of freight, soldiers and settlers, and little thought was given to luxury. Often, the carriages were little more than baggage wagons with windows and seats. However, an ordinary passenger train, consisting of second-, third- and fourth-class carriages would set out from Krasnovodsk three times a week, where a few more concessions were made to comfort. Each carriage was divided into closed compartments with benches and upper berths that could be let down at night and converted into bunks. Those passengers who were travelling at night were compelled to bring their own bedding, linen and towels. As with the Trans-Siberian, the carriages were heated by iron stoves, and the toilets were placed at one end of the gangway. These were, according to one traveller, Francis Skrine, who travelled just before the turn of the century, "on the most primitive model". However, Lord Curzon, who travelled slightly before, said of the second-class wagons, "more comfortable carriages I never travelled in". Unlike the Trans-Siberian, the carriages were not colour-coded according to class, but all were painted white, even the locomotive, and thus the trains presented, according to another American traveller, John Bookwalter, "a neat and pleasing appearance".

While some trains were furnished with restaurant cars, food was more generally taken in the stations along the route. These varied highly in quality and design. Some, such as those in the main settlements such as Krasnovodsk, Ashkhabad or Samarkand, were relatively grand complexes built out of brick and stone and whitewashed with lime, often two storeys high. Others, in the middle of small desert oases, might be nothing more than a set of dingy wooden huts, often half buried in the sand. Yet, at any of these, it was possible to obtain an excellent meal. The main stations were equipped with proper restaurants, but even at the smallest stations in the middle of the wilderness, the arrival of a train would cause a flurry of local residents to appear by the side of the track, offering roast chicken, bottles of fresh or fermented milk, bread, butter, and hot samovars for tea.

A British intelligence officer, Captain Roland Teague-Jones, who was travelling in the area in the summer of 1918 when the area was suffering from civil war, recorded in his diary the scramble for lunch made by the passengers at one of these wayside stops, Kaahka near the Persian border: "Never have I seen such a sight. It might well have been a scene from one of the London musical comedies. There were Russian peasants in red shirts, Armenians and Persians, Cossacks and Red soldiers, Sart traders and Bokhariotes, Turkmans in their giant *papkhas*, while among the crowd there were a number of pretty young girls and women in the latest Paris summer fashions. All this medley came crushing into the buffet and clamoured for glasses of tea, hunks of black bread and platters of soup. Somehow or other they all seemed to get served and Asiatic and European, Mongol and Muscovite, sat down literally cheek by jowl, and satisfied their hunger."

The Trans-Caspian line could not compete with its younger cousin, the Trans-Siberian, in terms of scale. However, it could certainly match and even exceed it in terms of the desolation and emptiness through which it passed. Away from the oases and in the middle of the Kyzyl Kum Desert, there was nothing but featureless and rolling hills of sand covered occasionally in scrubby greenery, depending on whether rain had recently fallen. It might possess, conceded some travellers, a certain austere beauty. However, such beauty, according to James MacGahan, was thoroughly deceptive. The verdure which covered the sand dunes "hides horrors as great as those covered by the roses that twine themselves over sepulchres". The greenery was always short lived, and the blooms would "shoot up, ripen, die and rot, in the course of a few days". If touched, they immediately would droop, and emit a most disgusting odour. Beneath their foliage lurked "scorpions, tarantulas, immense lizards, often five to six foot long, turtles and serpents and the putrefying bodies of dead camels". Once lost in "this desert ocean, without guide or water, you may wander for days, until you and your horse sink exhausted to die of thirst, with the noxious week for bed, winding sheet and grave... This world of desolate life, this plain of charnel house vegetation, we enter with a sickening feeling of depression."

Travelling by rail, Lord Curzon's feelings were scarcely different. "On the train... The fire-horse, as the natives have sometimes christened it, races onward, panting audibly, gutturally, and shaking a mane of sparks and smoke. Itself and its riders are all alone. No token or sound of life greets eye or ear; no outline redeems the level sameness of the dim horizon; no shadows fall upon the starting plain. The moon shines with dreary coldness from the hollow dome, and a profound and tearful solitude seems to brood over the desert. The returning sunlight scarcely dissipates the impression of sadness, of desolate and hopeless decay, of a continent and life sunk in a mortal swoon. The traveller feels like a wanderer at night in some desecrated graveyard, amid crumbling tombstones and half-obliterated mounds. A cemetery, not of hundreds of years but of thousands, not of families or tribes, but of nations and empires, lies outspread around him; and ever and anon, in falling tower or shattered arch, he stumbles upon some poor unearthed skeleton of the past."

t the forefront of Curzon's mind when he wrote this description would most likely have been the ancient city of Merv. When Curzon travelled through it in the 1880s, it was not much more than a recently captured Russian frontier town. Beyond the remains of about 100 native huts, there was a railway station, some rapidly constructed Russian hotels (which stewed at 40°C and crawled with scorpions), businesses, a clubhouse and a music hall which offered "the airs of Offenbach and the melodies of Strauss". Yet this was the place which in ancient times had been known as the "Queen of the World", and, for miles around, extensive ruins bore witness to this title.

Once, the River Oxus (Amu Darya) had flowed past it into the Caspian Sea, before changing course at some unknown moment and diverting into the Aral. Up to that time, the area around had been a rich and fertile alluvial plain, and even afterwards painstakingly constructed irrigation systems near the city managed to preserve this fertility. Not only did it grow rich from agriculture, but it also occupied a vital spot at the nexus of trade routes between Bokhara, Khiva, Persia and Afghanistan. Much local trade passed by the spot, and a grand bazaar was still held regularly in the locale late into the 19th century, even after the city was a ruin. The combination of agriculture and trade had originally made it one of the wealthiest settlements in the region. Yet, this opulence made the city a target for constant attack, and several times over it had suffered devastation at the hands of invaders. Each time it was rebuilt in a slightly differing location, more lavishly and beautifully than before, until it and the irrigation works that sustained its agriculture were utterly destroyed at the orders of Genghis Khan in 1221, a blow from which it was never fully to recover.

Few sights in the region could exercise as powerful an effect on travellers as this vision of a once famous city lying desolate and in ruins. No traveller described the vision of it from the windows of the Trans-Caspian Railway as well as Michael Myers Shoemaker, an American who travelled the line at the beginning of the 20th century:

"The glaring hot day draws to its close as our train approaches the ancient city. Already the atmosphere has taken on that wonderful golden glow which in the still air of the desert heralds the approach of night and marks the passing of the sun. As I gaze from the carriage window… as far as the eye can reach spread the ruins of the wonderful city – mile after mile of crumbling arches, tottering towers, and ruined mosques. In the clearness of this air distances are annihilated and ruins miles away are as distinctly visible as those nearer at hand. One stands awe-struck as one's eye roves over the vast desolation. The silence is so intense that even the puffing engine of our train seems impressed by it and grumbles in a monotone.

"No sign of life [shows] in all the desolate prospect save some lonely floating vultures, and even they, turning from the desolation of Merv, soon vanish in the distance, and as they go the day departs, while from the vast ocean of black sand stretching away to the eastward far beyond the city the moon rises slowly.

"Two millions of people lived here once, and now you cannot even find their graves, while these ruins of the palaces and houses they once inhabited are sadder than any grave. All is vanity. Truly as I gaze outward into the deepening shadows tonight I fully appreciate that all is and has ever been – vanity."

This 19th century etching of a Persian slave in Khiva evokes something of the fear engendered by the Turcoman slave traders.

Before the conquest by the Russians and the advent of the railway, it was a fearful thing to make the crossing from the Central Asian khanates and the Kyzyl Kum Desert into the lands of the Empire of Persia. It was not so much the ordinary perils that faced every traveller and every caravan throughout Central Asia – the dangers of losing one's way, of running out of provisions, of being unable to find water, of being attacked by thieves – but on the frontier of Persia the terror which occupied every moment of the traveller's attention was the threat of enslavement. The slave markets which prospered so well in Bokhara, Khiva and Tashkent were all fed primarily from this region. The harvesting of slaves was perpetrated by the nomadic Turcoman tribesmen, who for the most part lived like other nomadic peoples of the steppe, but for whom slave raiding was additionally an integral part of their way of life. Their victims were in the main Shi'a Muslims – whom the nomadic Sunni Turcoman regarded as heretics and infidels – travelling as traders or pilgrims to the holy city of Mashhad.

Joseph-Pierre Ferrier, a French mercenary who travelled through Persia to Afghanistan in the 1840s, described better than any the procedures for the organisation of a raid. When a Turcoman chief decided that he wished to stage a slaving expedition, he would go out of his tent and plant a lance with his colours in the ground, and invite his fellow tribesmen, in the name of the Prophet of Islam, to join in an attack against the Persian misbelievers. Usually, they would name a date for setting out weeks in advance. This would give them time to collect companions in sufficient numbers, and to condition their horses for the rigours of the expedition. For over a month this would form their chief concern. They would keep their horses to a limited diet of barley and hay, riding them at top speed for over half an hour every day and allowing them to drink very little. Towards the end of the month, they would be taken on long forced marches as a final preparation, being allotted a diet of barley flour kneaded together with sheep fat, fed to them in large balls.

Once the horses had been conditioned and a force of men collected, the party would set out. Their first concern was to gather intelligence. They would scout about for caravans travelling in the desert, and when they had done so, some of the Turcomans would join with it, masquerading as ordinary wayfarers.

After finding out the strength of the caravan, the number of armed men, the nature and value of its merchandise, they would suddenly disappear, and convey this news to their leaders. Sometimes they could also obtain such information from Persians on the frontier, who were willing to betray their countrymen, or else the force of Kurdish border guards, who had been stationed on the northeastern frontier to ward off Turcoman attack, but were happy to collude with it.

Once they had chosen their target, they would appoint a spot suitable for an ambush. Half a dozen of the men would be left behind in a safe place to guard the baggage animals, and the rest would go on to the attack. Their tactic was to ride as quickly as possible against the caravan with full force, taking it by surprise and devastating it within moments, rushing away before their victims could mount any defence. The only hope of the caravan was to make a great show of force and be ready to fight in time – the Turcomans were happy to ambush, but not to engage in hand-to-hand combat. Alexander Burnes related how his own caravan quickly reacted to the threat that Turcomans might be about to attack: "About midnight the braying of a donkey intimated to some palpitating hearts that we were in the neighbourhood of human beings where none should exist. The shout of 'Allaman, Allaman! [a raid! a raid!]' spread like lightning; and the caravan, in a moment, assumed the appearance of a regiment in open column, closing up in double march to form a square. The foremost camels squatted instantly, and the others formed behind them. Matches were lit on every side, swords were drawn, pistols loaded, and the unhappy merchants capered in front of their goods, half mad with fear and fury. The unarmed portion of the caravan took post among the camels... The anxiety was intense, it was general; the slaves were more terrified than the rest, for they knew well the fate of capture by the Toorkmuns..."

In Burnes' case, the caravan was lucky; it was nothing more than a false alarm caused by a couple of wandering shepherds. However, had it not been so then the fate faced by anyone captured by the Turcomans would indeed have been terrible. Prisoners would have been taken on captured horses, or if they were few, thrown over the Turcomans' own. The animals were driven for 30 or 40 miles towards the attackers' base camp, and would be forced on until they dropped or were knocked up. The captives were treated with equally little mercy. If their horses dropped then the prisoners were attached by a long cord to his saddle by their captor, who would then drag them along, sometimes walking, sometimes running, depending on the pace he chose to set for his horses. Any prisoner who showed signs of fatigue would be spurred on by the point of a lance; and any who gave out entirely would be killed on the spot. Only a third of the prisoners captured would thus reach the slave markets in the cities of Turkistan.

For a Turcoman to return empty-handed from a slaving expedition was regarded as an inexcusable disgrace. He would be subject to mockery by the old men of his encampment and the scorn of his wives. Indeed, these would present him with petticoats as a mark of their contempt as they spurred him to return to the fray. Those who came back with slaves and booty were by contrast treated with honour. The slaves were kept in the camp until an Uzbek slave trader could visit the camp – typically, they would call on each camp two or three times a year – and buy up the slaves for the city market. The prices paid to the Turcomans were in inverse proportion to the age of the slave. For a boy of 10, they would receive 40 tomans; for a man of 30, 25 tomans; and for a man of 40, 20 tomans.

Persia: Civilisation Reached

he boundary between the Turcoman Desert and the Persian Empire marked one of the great watersheds of the Silk Road. It was the same sort of contrast between the Mongol steppe and the Chinese heartland: the dividing line between the nomadic world and the settled, between pasturing sheep and fields under the plough, and between a desert wilderness of tents and an ancient land of cities. This boundary between the Persian Empire and the desert nomads, as with China and Mongolia, was originally also marked by a great wall. The *Sadd-e Iskander*, (Alexander's Barrier) originally extended for around 150 miles (241 kilometres) east from the Caspian Sea in the province of Gorgan. It was originally almost a Herculean work, 10 metres high and clad in stone, further protected by a 30-metre-wide ditch and 40 interval forts. Persian legend attributed it to Alexander the Great. Myth held that he had built it to keep out the legendary peoples of Gog and Magog, a horde of barbarian tribes mentioned in the Bible and Qur'an, who were prophesied to attack the civilised world from somewhere in the northeast, bringing the onset of a millennial cataclysm. In reality, it was probably built hundreds of years after Alexander's time, in the 3rd century CE, but its function was not dissimilar to that described in the legend, to ward off the attacks of nomads from settled society.

By the time that modern travellers began to travel this route, the wall had dwindled almost to nothing, its stone ransacked for other buildings and other parts of it subsumed in the desert sand. Yet the line it traced still described a visible contrast. The desert was left behind. The quality of soil improved, and water was suddenly more readily available. There were lakes, ploughed fields and, into the 20th century, harvesting by hand, the corn cut with scythes and threshed on mud floors outside farm walls. The land became hillier and more varied. Deer and goats ranged on the hillsides, and all along the route could be found trees in full blossom, barberries and rhubarb.

It was from the summits of the hills that the traveller would catch his first sight of Mashhad. Mashhad for generations had been one of Persia's easternmost cities and its greatest place of pilgrimage. In 816, it became the burial place for Imam Reza, one of the leaders of the Shi'a Muslim community, whom many believed had been poisoned by a Sunni rival. Before long, Shi'a Muslims came to regard it as sacred, and many would travel there to pray at the shrine of their leader. Although attacked many times over the centuries, especially by nomadic invaders, it grew in stature as wealth poured in from visiting pilgrims, and Islamic rulers endowed the shrine and built ever more elaborate complexes of mosques, colleges and places of prayer to mark the spot.

When the pilgrim or pious traveller first saw Mashhad in the distance, like a wanderer approaching Rome, he would stop to make a prayer. Even for Western and non-Muslim travellers, there was a sense of the sacred about the sight. Curzon recalled straining his eyes to catch in the distance the "glint of the

A group of mullahs and students pose for the camera, circa 1910–15, part of the George Grantham Bain Collection.

golden cupola" and the "minarets of the Holy Imam". "Slowly the mist curled upward as though a silken window blind were being delicately raised by cords, and first a sparkle, and then a steady flash, revealed at a distance that must have been twelve and fifteen miles the whereabouts of the gilded dome." Muslim travellers would dismount if they were travelling on horseback or mule, shout "Ya Ali, Ya Husein, Ya Imam Reza" in invocation of the holy figures of Shi'a Islam, and prostrate themselves before the city. Besides this, in a fashion reminiscent of Buddhist pilgrims on the early Silk Road, they would also add pebbles onto stone cairns by the roadside, or tear strips off their garments and tie them like streamers to the trees.

The arrival at Mashhad was for the pilgrim one of the most sacred moments of their life, and at least for other travellers journeying from Central Asia a respite from the dangers and hardships of desert travel. Despite all this, the city was far from free of trials. The main problem, according to many travellers, was its filth and its decay. It was surrounded by a nine-foot-high mud wall, topped with ramparts and parapets, but by the beginning of the 20th century all was crumbling and in disrepair. Within, cutting across the city, there was a canal, 12-feet wide, and lined with an avenue of mulberries, elms and willows. It might once have been pleasant, but in the avenue of trees there were many irregular gaps, and the remaining specimens looked ill and forlorn; the handsome stone kerbs which once faced the footbridges (which had for the most part been replaced with rickety planks) had been removed; and the canal itself, in the words of Lord Curzon, united the uses of a "drinking fountain, a place of bodily ablution, and washing of clothes, a depository for dead animals, and a sewer". The city's water was particularly noisome. Curzon was alarmed to find that his razor, left to stand in a glass overnight, had turned "gunmetal black".

One particularly depressing aspect of Mashhad was its enormous concentration of beggars. They were attracted to the city by the presence of pilgrims, who would gain merit in the eyes of Islam by giving alms. James Bailie Fraser, a Scottish traveller who visited Mashhad in the 1820s, painted a picture of their misery that was Dickensian in the extreme:

"Hundreds and thousands of the most miserably squalid objects beset every approach to the shrine, waylaying the pilgrims who flock to worship, principally in the evening. Old men and women in the most abject states of want, and wretchedness, and sickness, pressed upon us at every step, beseeching for relief in the name of all the Imauns; but what was that – what was all the misery of manhood, or even of age, to the sufferings of withering childhood and helpless infancy! The way was actually strewed with creatures that could not, many of them, be more than from three to four years old; not standing or sitting by the wayside, but grovelling in the dust and dirt, naked, like the vermin we were treading under foot. Living skeletons they were; more like the starved young of animals than human creatures; there they lay, strewed in the very paths, so that you could scarcely help trampling on them; some crying and sending forth piteous petitions, with their little half-quenched voices, for help for bread! Others silent, lying like dead things, or only giving symptoms of life by the sobs that would now and then issue from their little breasts, or the shudders of pain that shook their wasted frames. Some sat listless and motionless, with half-closed eyes, and countenances on which death seemed already to have put his seal; while the wolf-like glare from the sunken eyes of others, gave terrible evidence of the pangs of hunger which gnawed them."

Mashhad shared many features with the cities to the northeast in Central Asia. There were the winding backstreets with elegant courtyard houses concealed behind great and forbidding curtain walls. There was the bazaar with its narrow and crowded lanes in which could be seen every nationality and every class of person. Curzon observed the "stately white-turbaned mullah... the half-caste dervish... portly merchant... tattered and travel stained pilgrim... [and the] supercilious sayyed in green turban". There was the "cowering Sunni" from Central Asia, who had "ventured into the stronghold of the [Shi'a] enemy", the "black-eyed Afghans and handsome Uzbegs, wealthy Arabs and wild Bedouins, Indian traders and Caucasian devotees", as well as Turks, Mongols and Tajiks. The trade was similar to the Central Asian cities, if a little poorer. The bazaars were full of silk, cotton and velvet, carpets, turquoise and precious stones, as well as sword blades and cups, bowls, basins and ewers.

One way in which Mashhad differed from the other cities was its principal industry, the burial of the dead. The city was hallowed by the presence of the body of Imam Reza, and the devotees of Shi'ism were eager not only to visit the city in life, but also to be laid near his sepulchre in death. The corpses of the faithful constituted the chief import of the city, and unlike the other cities of Central Asia, a traveller might turn the corner in one of the labyrinthine alleyways to be met suddenly with a vast and expansive graveyard. Perhaps unsurprisingly, many travellers found the sight of them far from uplifting. Many

A studio photograph of a Kurdish chief, taken in the late 19th century by the Abdullah Frères, three brothers who were commissioned by the sultan to document the Ottoman Empire.

reported them as being drab and unkempt. The English artist and traveller Fred Richards, who visited Mashhad in the late 1920s, described them as being like a ploughed field hardened in the sun, without a trace of a blade of grass. The earth upon the graves themselves was sunken and depressed, and it seemed almost as if an earthquake had struck the area, so crazy were the angles at which the headstones jutted out. The graves were not dug deep, and on occasion dogs and jackals would worry up the bones. Openings and cavities yawned out all over the ground, and crowds of lizards, grey, green and yellow, would swarm about the cracked memorials.

specially on Thursday evenings, the day before prayer day, families and women would come to sit by the tombs and weep, talk or drink tea, and mullahs would sit under white awnings to read the scriptures and say prayers. Around the edge of the graveyards, masons in sheds would work all day to chisel inscriptions to the dead out of the coarse granite quarried from the hills nearby. The headstones were in general were small and unostentatious, often not unlike milestones. They recorded the name and profession of the deceased, and usually displayed also a verse of the Qur'an. They were designed not to be long lasting. Such was the demand for space, that graves would be reused as quickly as possible, and old broken stones were left littering the ground in disorder.

For many Western travellers, the visit to Mashhad was often as much of a pilgrimage as for the devout Shi'a Muslims. The object of their interest, out of curiosity rather than motives of religious piety, was to see the interior of the holy precinct, and the shrine to Imam Reza. This was an object, however, that was fraught with considerable danger. Entrance to the area around the shrine was barred to non-Muslims, and the only way they could enter was by means of deceit. Should they be detected in their intrusion, they would be subject to forced conversion, or else to an immediate and frenzied execution.

James Fraser was one of the first Westerners to visit the shrine, smuggled in by a Persian friend. However, he did not dawdle there, too conscious of the danger to observe much of the scene. Arthur Conolly, a British army officer who was travelling through Persia and Afghanistan in the 1830s, was a little bolder. He also was smuggled in by a Muslim guide, who taught him to imitate the actions of Islamic prayer. Conolly's attention was taken not so much by the buildings, but the sight of the devotees. In the Mosque of Gawhar Shad, next to the shrine of Imam Reza, he watched as a preacher in a low pulpit narrated by candlelight the martyrdom of Hosein (the son of the Prophet's son-in-law, Imam Ali). The preacher, he wrote, "was gifted with a deep melodious voice, and had entire sway over the feelings of those whom he addressed. When, dealing with the cruelty with which Hossein's son was murdered in his very arms, he spoke of the lamentations of the mother – all were softened and wept; but as, after a pause, he went on to tell of the youthful courage of his sister Zeinab's two sons, their sorrow gradually gave way to admiration, which they expressed in a deep hum of applause; and when he described the noble firmness with which the martyr met his death... they caught the enthusiasm of the speaker and burst into a proud and prolonged shout of 'Hossein!'"

A young Iranian woman is captured in golden evening light above superb Achaemenian carvings at the ancient site of Persepolis.

(Top) An exquisite container from Esfahan; artesan's have always prospered in Persia, their works appreciated and rewarded by a procession of rulers and dynasties.

(Bottom) A 20-stater gold coin minted by 2nd century BCE Greco-Bactrian king Eucratides the Great – unearthed in Bukhara, this is the largest antique gold coin ever discovered.

(Right) An engraved map of Persia created in 1814, at a time when Imperial Russia and the British Empire were vying for control over the region.

PERSIA.

Engraved by J. Smith, Clement's Inn, Strand.

British Statute Miles

Persian Farsangs or Parasangs

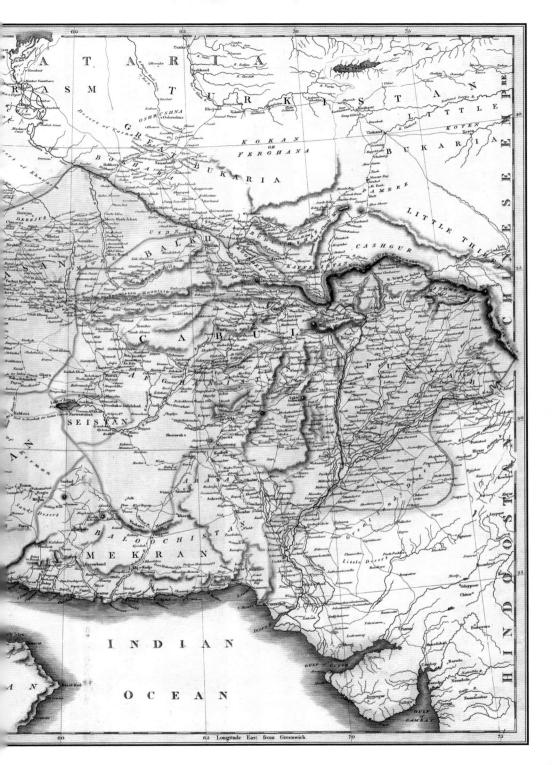

The tomb of 17th century Imam Reza in Meshhad, one of Islam's great pilgrimage sites.

Marking the entrance to Tehran, the amazing Azadi Tower is 50 metres tall and entirely clad in marble. It was built in 1971 to commemorate the 2,500th anniversary of the Persian Empire.

Intricately worked metal plates on sale at a stall in Esfahan – beautiful souvenirs can be found round every corner in Iran's bazaars.

The Stairway of the Apadana, the great audience hall at Persepolis, built during the 6th–5th centuries BCE. Here, representatives and delegates from vassal nations came to be heard by the Achaemenian ruler.

(Above) Isfandiyar Fights with the Wolves, *a miniature painting in the School of Tabriz style.* (Left) Unusual *haft rangi* tilework used in the building of the Royal Mosque in Esfahan.

(Below) Within the Regent's Bazaar, Kerman; though considered a poorer region of Iran, its architecture is still impressive.

(Opposite) The Royal Mosque, Esfahan, built by Shah Abbas in 1611 – he considered it his masterpiece.

(Top) Two modern Iranian women combine traditional headscarves with stylish sunglasses. (Bottom) The Hunter's Rest, by 19th century artist Frants Alekseevich Rubo (Roubaud), illustrates a Muslim (Moslem) piously performing salat, or daily prayer, standing barefoot on his prayer mat, which faces Mecca. Note his gun laid within easy reach. (Opposite top) Modern Tehran lies against the southern slopes of the Alborz Mountains. (Opposite bottom) Tehran bazaar is as frenetic and bustling as it was in centuries past.

The caravanserai of Deir-i Gachin between Rey (Tehran's early name) and Qom, founded by the Sasanians but later used by the Seljuks and Safavids.

(Above left) *A Kurdish woman makes unleavened flatbread.* (Above right) *A Kurdish mother near Lake Van in 1973.* (Below)
A satellite image shows the Kurdish and Armenian controlled lands between Persia and Constantinople; the Caucasus Mountains are strung between the Caspian and Black seas, and Lake Van is the farthest left of the three small turquoise lakes in the centre.

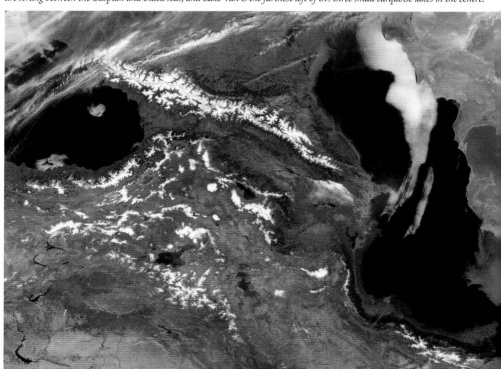

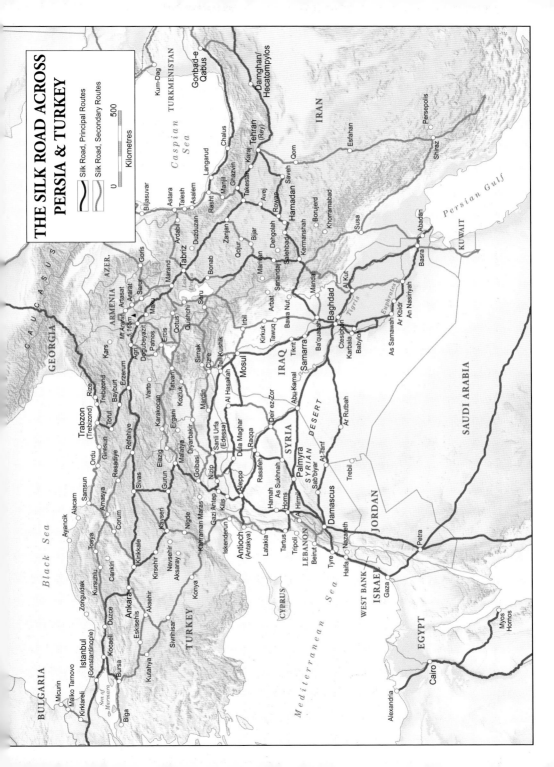

THE SILK ROAD ACROSS PERSIA & TURKEY

Silk Road, Principal Routes
Silk Road, Secondary Routes

Kilometres
0   500

Conolly did not enter the shrine where the Imam Reza was buried, contenting himself with looking through the door before passing on to the Mosque of Gawhar Shad. Robert Byron, who travelled in the 1930s, was altogether more bold. Byron had a particular fascination with the architecture of the 15th century, the time of the Timurid Empire, and in particular the buildings commissioned by Gawhar Shad, the wife of Tamerlane's youngest son. To penetrate the shrine itself, he resorted to a disguise of darkening his skin with burnt cork, as well as concealing his face by affecting a perpetual sneeze. In spite of having to keep his nose buried in his handkerchief, he was able to describe the scene around him:

"Amber lights twinkled in the void, glowing unseen from the mighty arch before the sanctuary, reflecting a soft blaze over the gilded entrance to the Tomb opposite, and revealing, as the eye adapted itself, a vast quadrilateral defined by ranks of arches. An upper tier rose out of reach of the lights, and passing through a zone of invisibility, reappeared as a black parapet against the stars. Turbaned mullahs, white-robed Afghans, vanished like ghosts between the orbits of the lamps, gliding across the black pavement to prostrate themselves beneath the golden doorway. A sound of chanting was heard from the sanctuary, where a single tiny figure could be seen abased in the dimness, at the foot of its lustred mihrab.

"Islam! Iran! Asia! Mystic, languid, inscrutable!!

"One can hear a Frenchman saying that, the silly fool – as if it was an opium den in Marseilles. We felt the opposite; that is why I mention it. Every circumstance of sight, sound and trespass conspired to swamp the intelligence. The message of a work of art overcame this conspiracy, forcing its way out of the shadows, insisting on structure and proportion, on the impress of superlative quality, and on the intellect behind them. How this message was conveyed is difficult to say. Glimpses of arabesques so liquid, so delicately interlaced, that they looked no more like mosaic than a carpet looks like stitches; of larger patterns lost in the murk above our heads; of vaults and friezes alive with calligraphy – these were its actual words. But the sense was larger. An epoch, the Timurids, Gohar Shad herself, and her architect Kavam-ad-Din, ruled the night."

(Above) *A portrait of one Mullah Kudai, taken by an unknown photographer circa 1865–72; Persia's religious clerics ranged from the uneducated to highly schooled – however, they were often charismatic, and fervent devotion and conviction would light up their eyes. (Left) The Armenian St Thaddaeus Church near Maku on the Iran-Turkey border.*

P ersia, unlike the variable states of Central Asia, had been a coherent empire for most, although certainly not all parts of its history. A result of this relative unity was a greater ease of travel. Like all empires, Persia was dependent on a fast and effective network of communication that could allow information about any trouble or dissent to be brought as quickly as possible to the centre. Hence Persia, like Russia and China, was compelled to develop and maintain a coherent system of roads, and also a postal network for the swift transfer of information.

The Achaemenid Empire, which ruled Persia from the 6th–4th centuries BCE, is generally credited with the development of the world's first postal system. They established post-roads between the major centres, most famously the "Royal Road" between the Persian capital of Susa and Sardis in Asia Minor, and also a body of messengers trained to traverse these routes at speed. The historian Herodotus, describing the war between the Greeks and the Persians in 480 BCE, gave an admiring account of the way in which they worked: "Now there is nothing mortal which accomplishes a journey with more speed than these messengers, so skilfully has this been invented by the Persians: for they say that according to the number of days of which the entire journey consists, so many horses and men are set at intervals, each man and horse appointed for a day's journey. These neither snow nor rain nor heat nor darkness of night prevents from accomplishing each one the task proposed to him, with the very utmost speed. The first then rides and delivers the message with which he is charged to the second, and the second to the third; and after that it goes through them handed from one to the other…"

The postal system persisted into the modern age, and was as much a benefit to ordinary travellers as to governments and their messengers. Aside from travelling as part of a conventional caravan, the option was open of using the official post network, travelling by its horses, and staying overnight at the *chaparkhanehs*, or post-houses that lined the routes. The principle was similar to travelling by government post on the *trakt*, or Siberian post-road. *Chaparkhanehs* were established every 20 miles (32 kilometres) or so along the main roads (from Tehran to Mashhad, Resht, Tabriz, Kerman and Bushire), and at each were kept a number of government-owned post-horses, which could be hired out, at the end of the 19th century, at the rate of 2½ pence per mile.

The advantage of travelling by *chapar* was its speed. Riding on post-horses, various travellers reported being able to cover on average 50 to 70 miles (80–112 kilometres) a day, rising to over 100 miles in case of emergency. A caravan, by contrast, would never travel more than 25 miles (40 kilometres) a day. Travelling by chapar, wrote Lord Curzon, who travelled the route at the end of the 19th century, entailed "rapid if exhausting and sometime painful physical progress", where the traveller was treated as a piece of "animate baggage"; whereas the caravan, although allowing one the leisure to dawdle and investigate the world around, was apt to be "unutterably tedious" and "unconscionably slow".

The speed at which the post-horses were able to journey along the post-roads was often a matter of great surprise to many travellers. It is not just that the roads were often no more than mere caravan-tracks, frequently covered in sand or drifting snow. It was more the fact that the horses were some of the most wretched creatures that the travellers had ever come across. "Given a good horse and fine weather, Persian travel would be delightful," wrote Harry de Windt, who also travelled extensively across Persia as much as Siberia, "but the former is, unfortunately, very rarely met with." Most of the post-horses were in the job because they were suitable for nothing better, and each possessed some vice which "nothing but constant hard work" would keep under. "Kickers, rearers, jibbers, shyers, and stumblers" were all too common, wrote de Windt, and falls were an almost daily occurrence.

Curzon was even more outspoken on the subject. On the Mashhad-Tehran road, he often found fewer than half-a-dozen post-horses at each station, and these, he found "...to be for the most part underfed, broken-down, and emaciated brutes, with ill-regulated paces, and open sores on their backs that sometimes made it almost unbearable to bestride them. The best that were supplied to me would anywhere else be classified at a low level of equine mediocrity. To ride the worst was a penalty to which any future Dante might appropriately condemn his most inveterate foe in the lower circles of hell."

A night spent in the post-houses was not much more inviting than a day spent on the post-horses. The post-houses, marking the end of each stage on the road, might be found almost anywhere: at the heart of a village, on its outskirts, or even in the apparent wilderness, nowhere near a settlement at all. Their location was primarily dictated by the availability of water. From outside, it had the appearance of a small square fort built of mud. Each side was a blank curtain wall of mud, a low tower would rise above a gateway, and each corner was marked with a bastion. Indeed, the post-houses were intended to be as secure as a fort, to ward off the danger of banditry and theft, or even the possibility of a Turcoman attack. Yet, although they might have been safe, they were by no means sanitary.

On passing through the gate, the traveller would find a courtyard, at one end of which was a mud platform, or *chabutra*. Usually, this was occupied by "fowls and filth", but the traveller had the option of sleeping on it al fresco in the warm nights of the summer. All around there were mangers full of chopped barley and tethers for the post-horses. Here, during the summer also, the horses would be left overnight; in winter, they would be taken indoors and sleep in the long stables on the ground floor. These chambers, dark, poorly ventilated and "reeking with accumulated refuse", also doubled as accommodation for the post-boys.

For the Western traveller, the best room in the post-house, the *bala-khaneh* or high chamber in the tower above the gateway, was always available. He would be ushered up there by the keeper of the post-house – a government employed official "who sometimes wears the semblance of an official dress" – climbing mud staircases "of almost Alpine steepness" to reach it. The room generally had windows without glass, open to the elements on all sides, and thus was generally "not much less draughty than the rigging of a ship". Lord Curzon had wide experiences of the post-houses' bala-khanehs:

"The interior has at one time been plastered and whitewashed. Its only decorative features are a number of shallow niches in the walls, in which Persian visitors have sometimes scrawled the most fearful illustrations, and occasionally, but not always, a fireplace. Of furniture it is absolutely destitute. To have the floor swept clean of vermin, to spread a felt or carpet in the corner and one's sack of straw upon it, to buy firewood and light a fire, to stuff up the open windows and nail curtains over the ramshackle doors – all these are necessary and preliminary operations, without which the dingy tenement would be simply uninhabitable, but which it is sometimes hard work to undertake in a state of extreme stiffness and exhaustion after a long day's ride upon a freezing winter's night... In half an hour's time, however, when the work has been done, as the genial warmth begins to relax stiff joints and weary limbs, and as the samovar puffs out its cheery steam, a feeling of wonderful contentment ensues, and the outstretched traveller would probably not exchange his quarters for a sheeted bed in Windsor Castle. But it is upon the following morning, when, aroused at four or five A.M. in the pitchy darkness and amid biting cold, he must get up to the light of a flickering candle, dress and pack up all his effects, cook his breakfast, and finally see the whole of his baggage safely mounted in the dark upon the steeds in the yard below, that he is sometimes tempted to think momentarily of proverbs about game and candles, and to reflect that there are consolations in life at home."

The caravanserais, which were given primarily for the use of those travelling in caravans, were generally similar in design to the post-houses, but larger. Many were built during the early part of the Safavid Empire in the 16th century for the encouragement of trade, and early travellers report that although they were generally better built and cleaner than those in the neighbouring Ottoman Empire (modern-day Turkey), they still left much to be desired. John Fryer, a medical doctor who travelled to Persia in the 1670s, made a list of complaints that were scarcely different to those of Curzon: "Coming to our Inns, we have no Host, or young Damosels to bid us Welcome, nor other Furniture than Bare Walls; no Rooms Swept, nor Cleanly Entertainment, Tables neatly Spred, or Maidens to Attend with Voice or Lute to Exhilarate the Weary Passenger; but instead of these, Apartments covered with Filth; Musick indeed there is, of Humming Gnats pricking us to keep an unwilling Measure to their Comfort: So that here is neither Provision for Man or Beast, only an open House, with no enlivening Glass of Pontack, or Poinant Cheer to encourage the Badness of the March; but every [20 miles] on the King's High way, a *Caravan Ser Raw* [caravanserai], as dirty as Augeus his Stable, those before always leaving the next comer work enough to cleanse where they have been; that after coming in Tired, they are more intent to spread their Carpets for Repose, than remove the incrustated Cake of Sluttery, the constant Nursery of Flies and Bees, they often bringing their Horses into the same Bed-Chamber..." Whilst a night in such conditions might have been difficult for the more aristocratic traveller to bear, they were still regarded as a great amenity by the great multitude of poor travellers, who were able to stay for as long as they wished without charge.

The road from Mashhad to Tehran has been described by more than one traveller as one of the world's great "corridors of history". It was the leading route of the Silk Road connecting Central Asia to Byzantium and the Mediterranean. It was the route which generation after generation of conquerors pursued, from Alexander the Great to the Parthians, the Arab Muslim invaders, the Seljuk Turks from Central Asia and later the Mongols. Along it were also dotted once great cities which were formerly cradles of wealth and high civilisation, wealthy not only from trade, but also from mines of turquoise and copper, and the formerly rich agricultural land all around. Nishapur, a city "whose marvels", in the words of Henry Filmer, "were once reckoned by dozens and multiples of dozens" was the home of the great poet and mathematician Omar Khayyam; and Tus nearby was the birthplace and burial place of the Iranian equivalent of Homer, the writer of the Persian epic the *Shahnameh* or "Book of Kings".

Yet later in history, the road became less inviting to traverse, particularly for European travellers. Its intrinsic attractions, wrote Lord Curzon, were so small that "no one would ever be found to traverse it but for the necessity of getting from one place to the other." For the route's entire 560 miles, there was "scarcely a single object of beauty and but few of interest." The scenery, he held, at least when he travelled in late autumn, was "colourless and desolate", and that the only sight to see was the road itself as it wound over stony plains, "unlovely mountains" and deserted villages and towns. Many of the villages still standing were built as fortifications, and little turrets dotted the landscape "like chessmen" for locals to take refuge in case of a Turcoman attack. Other travellers also commented on the many ancient cities that had crumbled into indistinct and compacted heaps of clay along the wayside, and Filmer noted of one of the cities still standing, Nishapur, that the "Sultan's turret" no longer caught the rays of the rising sun.

Despite this, for Persian and especially for Shi'a travellers, the route retained its importance and its allure. It was still the main pilgrim route for travellers to visit the shrine of the Imam Reza at Mashhad, and this ensured a constant flow of traffic, even despite the hardships of travel and the peril of the Turcomans. The shrine, to a certain extent, rivalled not only Mecca, but also other Shi'a pilgrimage sites in modern-day Iraq such as Kerbela and Najaf, and like pilgrims to Mecca who would receive the title "Hajji", those who made the journey to Mashhad would rejoice in the title "Mashhadi".

Pilgrim caravans for the journey to Mashhad were often assembled in Tehran and other towns by a *sayyed*, or descendant of the Prophet. He might advertise for up to two months to assemble a suitable number of people for the journey. In doing so, he would promise, for a small consideration, not only to conduct them to the pilgrim site in safety and stay at only the best and cheapest stops, but also to preserve them from the effects of the evil eye, the machinations of bad *jinns*, to consult the stars about the road, and only to leave on a propitious day.

Arthur Conolly recalled the sight of such a pilgrim caravan about to leave a town in Gorgan on the way to Mashhad. All the walls by the road leading out of the town were picketed with horses and other pack animals, and the entire traffic between the main gate and the well just beyond it were men and horses. Within, there was hardly a way to be had amongst the crowds of expectant pilgrims, horses and camels. Everywhere, horses were neighing and fighting as their owners scrubbed or shod them, mended saddles ready for the journey, or rushed around haggling for corn and chopped straw. Outside the houses, some pilgrims sat reading the Qur'an out loud as they waited to depart. Amongst them circulated fakirs and dervishes, clothed in ragged outfits with brightly coloured sugar-cone caps, calling on the crowds to remember that they were about to embark on a journey of spiritual service, and to give them alms in the name of the Imam Reza for whom they travelled.

The animals were loaded up with bedding and extra clothing. Food such as lamb, chicken, eggs, fruit and bread would usually be bought along the way, along with chopped barley for the animals, but the kitchen utensils all had to be brought along with the baggage. The sight of a tiny donkey, absurdly overloaded, was quite usual, and the smallest animals would be seen staggering under a great mass of pots and pans, furniture, water bottles, guns, and not infrequently perched on top might be a live chicken, taken for the pot. Another piece of unusual luggage might be a corpse. Pilgrim caravans were often responsible for the conveyance of dead bodies to Mashhad in order that they might be buried near the shrine. Two corpses might even be wrapped up in black felt and hung over either side of a donkey so as to balance each other out. It was a burden that many were willing to undertake. The expenses paid for conveying one corpse to Mashhad would usually cover the cost of the entire journey.

Western travellers usually stuck to more conventional cargoes. Lord Curzon, delighted that they had by the end of the 1880s reached Tehran, encumbered his luggage further with "Crosse and Blackwell's tinned soups… easily prepared and a meal in themselves"; a flask that held a quart bottle of spirits "ample for the requirements of a journey of many hundreds of miles"; and a frock coat and formal suit in case he should meet any "royal personages". "Were I setting out tomorrow either for Lhasa or for Timbuctoo,

A satirical US cartoon from 1923 tells its own story about Persia's relationship with the Russian bear, while the British lion looks on.

they should accompany me; for I am convinced that I should find them equally useful were I to meet in audience either the King of the Negroes or the Dalai Lama of Tibet."

In the regions towards the east, there was always the threat of an attack by the Turcomans. However, on top of this there was equally the danger of ordinary thieves. The security on the roads varied from age to age, but in the time of the Safavids, stern provisions were made to protect travellers. Guards were posted at every stage of the journey, ready for pursuit should any uproar be heard. Should any thieves be apprehended and caught, the penalties were severe. They might be tied to the tail of a camel set to wander; have their stomachs torn open; be buried up to the neck and left to starve to death; or else stretched out and tied down, and then have lighted candles placed all over them, which were then left to burn down into them. According to Tavernier, the thieves who had been buried would beg passers-by to cut off their heads; and when he met two convicts enduring death by candles who beseeched him to end their lives, all he could do was to offer them "a pipe of tobacco".

Once the pilgrims had embarked on the actual journey, and they were not in the regions where they laboured under the fear of a Turcoman attack, the journey, although tough, became much more pleasant and good-natured. The pilgrims would unfurl pennons and flags, and the clergy would smile and even exchange jokes with all around them. Others would dance around the wayfarers, mimicking fights or rushing ahead to stand on small hills by the roadside and shouting at the crowds to whip up excitement: "Upon the rose of the cheek of Mohamed, may the blessing of God momentarily rest", to which the travellers would call in reply "O God, bless Mohammed, and the issue of Mohammed", crying it again and again until they were satisfied that the shout was loud enough: "Better than that – sweeter than that – dust on your heads, is this your [blessing]? Now one hearty shout that will ring to the tomb of the blessed Imam Reza – angels join with you – shout!"

Lord Curzon, when encountering pilgrim caravans, would similarly find his own forms of amusement. One game he enjoyed was to ride up very quickly behind heavily veiled women travelling slowly by donkey, startling the animals so that the women's veils rose up with a shriek. Such a pastime, he recalled, "was to crack one's side with sorely needed and well-earned laughter".

Some travellers would sit on their animals and chant the Qur'an in a low monotone. Others, in less solemn groups, would recite verses of Persian poetry and tell stories to each other. All travellers were particularly solicitous of the sayyed leading the caravan. Everyone vied to perform some service for him, whether cooking his dinner, washing his clothes, driving away flies from his person, or even shielding him from the rays of the sun. The only remuneration the travellers expected for these services was to be allowed to kiss the hem of his garment or his hand, and, wrote Ferrier, "this he grants with the coldness of ascetic pride, appearing to consider that the kind offices which he receives are nothing more than what is due to his meritorious and holy life". The sayyed did in fact repay the travellers by means of storytelling. In this, he was usually a skilful practitioner, and like the preachers in the Mosque at Mashhad, he could easily rouse the emotions of the travellers. When he reached the climax of any tale, wrote Ferrier, "his voice falters, he is overcome by feigned emotion, and a deluge of tears is seen to flow down the cheeks of his audience". His own tears were always at his command. "If he is telling a tale, he is sure to shed them at the proper moment; for example, when his hero sprains his ankle, or wants to smoke and there is no kailoon; but if he is dying of thirst, or falls into the hands of his enemy, oh then the groans and lamentations are past belief; the men cry like calves, the women like he does, and the children bawl loud enough to make deaf men hear..."

Whilst the journey was full of all sorts of amusement, the greatest pleasure was perhaps the sense of unity amongst the travellers. The pilgrims might be drawn from all levels of society. At one end there might be travellers and merchants on fine horses, officials and soldiers, mullahs on sleek and well-groomed mules; at the other there would be poor men who clubbed together to buy just one donkey, taking turns to ride it throughout the journey, or, even below them, beggars in rags accompanying the travellers on foot as they went. There would be families, and also women travelling in wicker baskets (known as *khajavehs*) balanced on the backs of camels, or muffled in blue cotton veils. Nonetheless, travel caused them to transcend all of these differences. "A social feeling pervades all members of the caravan," observed Ferrier. "They have their food in common... the noble, tradesmen, peasant, and fakir sit in same circle and eat same dish." In such circles of travellers, there would be full liberty of speech, and the stranger would be welcomed. The fact that they were Muslims and that they were pilgrims were sufficient enough to bring them together.

he Tehran of today is a polluted and sprawling megalopolis. Its population is nearly eight million, and it is one of the largest cities in the Middle East. However, it is only in relatively recent times that it took on its current size, status and appearance. Vita Sackville-West, who travelled to Tehran in the 1920s with her husband, the diplomat Sir Harold Nicholson, recalls on her first approach to the city that even when she came within 20 miles of it, the place was scarcely visible. "Where was that city? A patch of green trees away to the left, a faint haze of blue smoke; otherwise nothing, only the open country, the mountains, the desert, and little streams in flood pouring at intervals across the road. It all seemed as forlorn and uninhabited as the loneliest stretches of Kurdistan. Yet there stood a gate, suddenly, barring the way; a gate of coloured tiles, a wide ditch, and a mud rampart, and a sentry stopping us, notebook in hand."

Earlier travellers recall their first sight of Tehran in a similar light. In the early 19th century, James Bailie Fraser held Tehran's most notable aspect to be its mud walls, with their low bastions and "formidable ditch". Otherwise, there was "scarce one attractive or marking feature". All to single out the city in the distance were a couple of small gilded domes. Unlike the other magnificent cites of Persia, such as Esfahan or Shiraz, Tehran was a place of "little show". There was no "great minaret or tower to give effect to the distant view", and the whole scene was "without brilliancy or splendour". The main distinguishing mark of the place was the sight of Mount Damavand, the tallest mountain in Iran, standing high above the city to the north.

The reason for this apparent lack of grandeur is Tehran's late rise to prominence in comparison with other Persian cities. Although it occupies what another 19th century British traveller, Sir Robert Ker Porter, described as "a position of general surveillance" – strategically located within reach of the troublesome frontiers with the Turcomans on the one hand and the Georgians on the other – it only became the Persian capital in the early 1800s. It is not a city with the great antiquity possessed by many of the other cities in the region. To be sure, the locality was an important stop on the main east-west Silk Road route, but it was the nearby city of Rey (also known as Rhages) to which travellers would resort. Many legends relate the opulence of this now vanished city. Jean Chardin, the 17th century French traveller, was told by local residents that the city in its glory days was second only to Babylon in wealth, and that it possessed 96 quarters, with 6,400 colleges, 16,600 baths, 15,000 minarets, 12,000 mills, 1,700 water channels and 13,000 inns. Whatever the truth of the matter, the city was certainly prominent for many hundreds of years until its destruction at the hands of the Mongols in the 13th century. It was mentioned in the Bible, and a series of ruins a short distance out of Tehran, now mostly obliterated, bore witness to its past magnificence.

Tehran, at the time of Rey's splendour, was scarcely a place of any great account. The 12th century Arab geographer Yakut al-Hamawi wrote of Tehran that its inhabitants lived in houses underground, and were permanently at war not only with their ruler, but also with each other. The place, he recorded, was divided into 12 quarters, and a man living in one quarter could never enter the neighbouring quarter. It was surrounded with pleasant gardens and orchards, but the thickets and hedges around them served more as defensive walls, and fearing that anything they might harvest would be looted by their townsmen, they never cared to put their fields to the plough.

The Spanish ambassador Ruy Gonzáles de Clavijo, who passed through Tehran at the beginning of the 15th century, declared it to be delightful and well supplied, but unhealthy, finding fevers to be prevalent in the area. This was a point on which many travellers concurred, for example Sir Robert Ker Porter, who held that the spring torrents that washed down from the mountain heights gave the place an unhealthy and stifling humidity. Dustiness was also a terrible problem, and a great incentive to be outside of the city. The streets were often clogged with members of the nobility on horseback, and sometimes on elephants, smoking water-pipes, surrounded by great entourages of servants, making their way to take the air in the mountains above, where, in the words of Vita Sackville-West, it was as "pure as the note of a violin".

The easy availability of water at least ensured that it preserved its reputation as a city of gardens. The Italian traveller Pietro della Valle, who visited Tehran in the 1620s, said that an infinity of streams flowed through the gardens in the city, that fruit ripened there as in no other place, and that its roads were shaded with a such multitude of plane trees that he would remember the city as the "City of the Plane".

Otherwise, he agreed with many of the other visitors that there was no building or monument of much note in the city. As the great Persian scholar and traveller of the late 19th century, E.G. Browne said, it was a "pleasant place to stay in, rather than an interesting place to see". If it featured largely in the travel narratives of many of the writers of the 19th and early 20th centuries, this is perhaps because it was the place where they had the fortune to obtain an audience with the Shah. Usually more engaging than their long descriptions of the somewhat down-at-heel accoutrements of the palace and the chaotic administration of court protocol were their accounts of the flattery they produced in the presence of the King of Kings. The most extreme example was perhaps that of Sir Alexander Burnes: "After a little break in the conversation, the Shah, with some interest in what he said, enquired for the greatest wonder which I had seen in my travels. The opportunity was too favourable in so vain a court, and I replied in a loud voice, 'Centre of the universe, what sight has equalled that which I now behold, the light of your Majesty's countenance, O attraction of the world!'"

The greatest interest of the place for the more everyday traveller was generally to be found in the observation of everyday life. The most sympathetic of such observers was perhaps Vita Sackville-West. Sitting beside one of the city gates, which was gaudily decorated in blue and yellow tiles with depictions of scenes from Persian legend, she found that she could watch the "life of the city streaming disconnectedly in and out..." The trail of passers-by offered an entertaining view: "...a string of camels, a drove of donkeys, some pedestrians, some veiled women, a car or two; some bicyclists – for everyone in Persia rides a bicycle, and falls off it the moment he sees another vehicle approaching..."

In the age that motor transport was just beginning to become known in Persia, and the caravanserai was beginning to be made obsolete by the garage, Sackville-West's observations captured the spirit of the moment of transition, and the intimations of a changing way of life:

"Camels arrive with boxes and bales from Baghdad, having been six or eight or ten weeks on the way; they arrive with petrol from the south, and very odd it is to see the English words on the crates 'Highly Flammable.' Then the donkeys come in, tiny grey donkeys, almost invisible, but on four poor little legs, under an enormous load of camel thorn for fuel, then a flock of sheep, brown and black, their hard little hooves pattering just like rain over the gravel. Then a gaggle of geese, driven by a child, then a man carrying two chickens. It is most remarkable, the extent to which the Persians carry chickens. Why they should walk about carrying them, in the way they do, is a mystery I never could fathom. They might walk down the street, a chicken tucked under each arm, as a child might affectionately carry puppies. The fowls too, display a special mentality in this country, for at any street corner you may see a man squatting beside a brass tray, on which sit two or more hens beside a couple of dozen eggs in a contented fashion quite unknown to the hen in England."

Travelling a little earlier, Lord Curzon was similarly able to portray something distinctive in Tehran – the creeping influence of Westernisation, and the fashions in which the way of life in Tehran was beginning to accommodate the innovations of the West, which had still not stolen further east into Central Asia:

"A sign-board with *Usine à Gaz* inscribed upon it will suddenly obtrude itself in a row of mud hovels, ostentatiously Asiatic. Tram-lines are observed running down some of the principal thoroughfares. Mingled with the turbans and *kolahs* of the Oriental crowd are the wide-awakes and helmets of Europeans. Through the jostling throng of cavaliers and pedestrians, camels, donkeys and mules, comes rolling the two-horsed brougham of some Minister or grandee. Shops are seen with glass windows and European titles. Street lamp-posts built for gas, but accommodating dubious oil-lamps, reflect an air of questioning civilisation. Avenues, bordered with footpaths and planted with trees, recall faint memories of Europe. A metalled and watered roadway comes almost as a shock after weeks of mule track and rutty lane. Strange to say, it does not appear to be mistaken by the inhabitants for the town sewer. We, ride along broad, straight streets that conduct into immense squares and are fringed by the porticoes of considerable mansions. In a word, we are in a city which was born and nurtured in the East, but is beginning to clothe itself at a West-End tailor's."

he cities on the road from Tehran towards the northwest have always benefited from royal connections. The first, and perhaps most famous, were mythical. Marco Polo, always searching for signs of Christianity in unconverted lands, declared that this region was the home of the Three Kings from the Christmas story, and held that Zoroastrian traditions of fire-veneration had their origins with these figures. Otherwise, in more verifiable historical record, these northwestern cities were once the seats of royal power. Tabriz functioned as the capital of the Persian Empire from the time of the Mongol Ilkhanid Dynasty in the 13th century until the rise of the Safavids in the 1500s, and nearby Qazvin fulfilled this role during the middle of the 16th century until Esfahan became the home of the court.

The region, when it was the residence of the kings, could easily overwhelm travellers with its opulence. Adam Olearius, who acted both as an ambassador from the Dukes of Holstein to Persia as well as to Russia, was overawed by the tomb complex of the Mongol ruler Oljaitu Khodabandeh, with its dome over 50 metres high and its great gates, taller than those of St Mark's in Venice, "not of brass or copper but steel, wrought and polished Damask-wise". Before him, Friar Oderic of Pordenone, a Franciscan missionary who travelled in Persia in the 1320s, reacted similarly to Tabriz, writing that it was the "best city for merchandise in the world". There was not on the face of the Earth, "any kind of provision, or any species of goods, but you will find great store thereof at Tabriz... for the whole world almost hath dealings with that city for merchandise... and the Christians there will tell you that the Emperor there... has more revenue from that one city than the King of France from his whole realm."

Marco Polo concurred: "The people of Tabriz live by trade and industry; for cloth of gold and silk is woven here in great quantity and of great value. The city is so favourably situated that it is a market for merchandise from India and Baghdad, from Mosul and Hormuz, and from many other places; and many Latin merchants, especially Genoese, come here to buy the merchandise imported from foreign lands. It is also a market for precious stones, which are found here in great abundance. It is a city where good profits are made by travelling merchants."

Travel through these regions possessed

Ruins of the Blue Mosque in Tabriz, 1881.

as many dangers and inconveniences as were to be found on the road further east. The road became more hilly and precipitous. Adam Olearius complained of the journey over the terrain in the khajavehs, or wicker panniers balanced one on each side of a camel. Whilst on the route he was put to "two great inconveniences, one proceeding from the violent motion caused by the going of that great beast [the camel] which at every step gave us a furious jolt, and the other, from the insupportable stink of the camels, whereof there being but one boy to guide eight or ten, they were ty'd one to another, and went all in a file, insomuch that the infectious smell of all that went before, came full into our noses."

New types of vermin were also encountered, in particular the Mianeh bug, named after one of the towns on the route. Its bite was supposed to be fatal. Travellers on the route would inoculate themselves against it in a homœopathic fashion, grinding up a portion of the red-spotted insect and eating it with bread. It was perhaps a preferable solution to many of the remedies for the bite. The affected area of the flesh might be wrapped in the flesh of a newly slaughtered bullock, or the patient might be made to drink a glass of sour milk, be suspended by cords from the ceiling, wound up and spun round until violently sick, thus causing the poison to be expelled.

Tabriz city in the early 20th century – it would take the discovery of oil and natural gas to fuel the leap into modernity.

Yet, on reaching the cities of the northwest, there is a great note of delight in the accounts of the travellers. They were places where one could take his pleasure. Jean Chardin recalled how in Tabriz, towards evening the great Maidan, or square, would be filled with people who had repaired there "for sport and pastime". There were those who went "for gaming... some for tricks of activity, some for seeing Jack-pudings and mountebanks act their drolleries, some for wrestling, others for bull and ram fighting, others for repeating verses, some reciting stories in prose, and some to see wolves dance." The dancing wolves were so popular in Tabriz, according to Chardin, that they would change hands for over "500 crowns a piece" and that great disputes would arise over their ownership, "which are not easily appeased". In Qazvin, by contrast, dancing elephants were more to the people's taste. Olearius saw one such on his visit: "He could do many tricks, and was governed by a little boy, who by touching him on the forehead with a little poleaxe guided him, and made him lye down and rise up as he pleased..."

In the daytime, there were the options of taking one's leisure at any of the city's coffee houses, teahouses or wine taverns. Olearius described the difference between them: "In the scire Chanes, they sell wine, but those who have the least tenderness for their reputation, will not come into those places, which are infamous, and the common receptacles of a sort of people who divert themselves there with musick, and the dancing of some of their common drabs, who having, by their obscene gestures, excited the brutalities of the spectators, get them into some corner of the house, or draw them along into some public places, where they permit the commission of those abominations as freely as they do that of ordinary sins."

However the *chai-khanehs*, or teahouses, were more respectable: "They are only persons of good repute who drink of this, and frequent these houses, where, in the internals of their drinking, they spend the time at a certain game somewhat like our tick-tack. But they commonly play at chesse, at which they are excellent, and go beyond the Muscovites, whom I dare affirm to be the best gamesters at chesse of any in Europe." However, for the most intellectual, there were the coffee houses: "Cahwa Khane are those places where they take tobacco and drink of a certain black water which they call Cahwa... Their poets and historians are great frequenters of these places and contribute much to the divertissement of the company. These are seated in a high chair in the midst of the hall, whence they entertain their auditors with speeches, and tell them satirical stories, playing in the mean time with a little stick, with the same gestures, and after the same manner, as those do who show tricks of ledgermain among us."

As much as the cities gave to the travellers after their journey the opportunity to refresh their minds, it offered them a similar chance to do so with their bodies. Sir Robert Ker Porter took advantage of his time in Tabriz to enjoy the Persian baths. The visit was replete with sensuality. The bathers would enter the marbled halls, warmed with an elaborate system of boilers and steam flues, not only to be washed, soaped and scrubbed with gloves of woven hair, but also to have their beard dyed with henna and indigo, their feet rubbed down with a pumice stone, their joints cracked, their bodies pinched and rubbed all over, and finally their hair and nails stained black, and their feet bright red. All the while they would smoke up to a dozen waterpipes of tobacco, and luxuriate among rose petals.

There were other bodily needs that the travellers would see to in the cities. Prostitutes were available, and of all classes. Olearius, of all travellers, gave the frankest account of his encounters with them. On reaching Qazvin, within 500 paces of the city he met "15 young ladies, exceedingly well mounted, very richly clad in cloath of gold and silver, etc, having necklaces of great pearls about their necks, pendants in their ears, and abundance of other jewels. Their faces were to be seen, contrary to the custom of honest women in Persia. Accordingly we soon found, as well by their confident carriage, as the accompt given us of them, that they were some of the eminent curtezans about the city, who came to entertain us with the Divertisement of their musick. They march'd before us, and sung, to the sound of certain hawboyes, and bag-pipes, that went before them, making a very extravagant kind of harmony." Within the city, he found the "common traders", the ordinary prostitutes "to any that will take them up".

"All sit in a row, having their faces covered with a veil, and behind them stands a bawd... who hath by her a bed, and a quilted coverlet, and holds in her hand a candle unlighted, which, when any customer comes, she presently lights that he may look the wench in the face, and order her to follow him, whom he likes best among them."

The Arg of Tabriz, which dates back to Mongol times.

he sight of Mount Ararat, going westwards from Persia, announced the limits of the Persian Empire, and the arrival in the realm of the Ottoman Turks. Ararat itself stood between not just these two powers, but a third – the Armenians to the north, for whom the mountain has always been a sacred symbol, originally the home of the pantheon of the Armenian gods, and later, after their conversion to Christianity, the resting place of Noah's Ark after the flood. It is this latter association that has always ensured the interest of travellers in the mountain. Of all of them, Sir Robert Ker Porter wrote most vividly on the approach to it:

"A vast plain peopled with countless villages; the towers and spires of the churches of Eitch-mai-adzen, arising from amidst them; the glittering waters of the Araxes, flowing through the fresh green of the vale; and the subordinate range of mountains skirting the base of the awful monument of the antediluvian world. It seemed to stand, a stupendous link in the history of man, uniting the two races of men before and after the flood. But it was not until we had arrived upon the flat plain, that I beheld Ararat in all its amplitude of grandeur. From the spot on which I stood, it appeared as if the hugest mountains of the world had been piled upon each other to form this one sublime immensity of earth, and rock and snow. The icy peaks of its double heads rose majestically into the clear and cloudless heavens; the sun blazed bright upon the crown; and the reflection sent forth a dazzling radiance, equal to other suns. This point of the view united the utmost grandeur of plain and height. But the feelings I experienced, while looking on the mountain, are hardly to be described. My eye, not able to rest for any length of time upon the blinding glory of its summits, wandered down the apparently interminable sides, till I could no longer trace their vast lines in the mists of the horizon; when an irrepressible impulse, immediately carrying my eye upwards again, refixed my gaze upon the awful glare of Ararat; and this bewildered sensibility of sight being answered by a similar feeling in the mind, for some moments I was lost in a strange suspension of the powers of thought."

For all the majesty of the view and the holiness of the spot, the journey became even more perilous. The traveller now entered the realm inhabited by the Kurdish tribesmen, who posed as serious a threat to his safety as the Turcomans had farther to the east. The Kurds lived primarily as nomads, although some had settled and built villages for themselves in the isolated reaches of the valleys and mountain passes between Persia and Ottoman Turkey. As with the Turcomans, they were dependent on plunder to make a living. In general outside the effective control of the empires around them, travellers were dependent, either by bribes or by friendship, on winning their good favour before proceeding through areas under their power.

The traveller might find the sight of the Kurdish tribesmen picturesque in the extreme. James Creagh, an Irish traveller who passed through the region in the 1870s, wrote, "The sight of a band of roving Koords, wandering in single file along the ledge of a precipice overlooking a roaring brook, winding among rocks down the side of a steep mountain-side, or marching through one of those dark little valleys enclosed all round by overshadowing and dismal snow-capped heights, with which the Armenian highlands are everywhere indented, carries the imagination of a traveller back to the days of Abraham."

In dress and custom, they had scarcely altered over the ages, and according to Creagh, "the modern Koord differs very little from the swarms of light horsemen who resisted so successfully the arms of the Crusaders. He is mounted on a hardy, spirited, and well-bred horse, capable of enduring the extremes of both fatigue and hunger. His saddle is decorated with every imaginable kind of caparison or ornament, which dangles down towards the ground... His flowing garments of the brightest and most fantastic hues, his voluminous turban of a sombre colour, his long flowing locks reaching half-way down his back, his immense moustachios, black and piercing eyes, insolent expression and proud display of pistols, knives, yataghans, scimitars, blunderbuss, long gun and sword besides an enormous spear about twelve feet long, ornamented... with a bundle exactly resembling in size and shape an ordinary football, from which

Kurdish warriors on horseback; the Kurds were feared as brigands by merchants transporting cargo between Constantinople and Tabriz.

several strings or streamers are dependent – give him a truculent and aggressive aspect..."

However, it was as much from the female of the species as the male that the traveller could expect danger. A British explorer, Major Fredrick Millingen, who travelled in the Ottoman Empire in the 1860s, described how troops of women would club together and contrive to rob the solitary male traveller:

"A troop of fair bandits takes up a station at the side of the road, there patiently to wait for the arrival of the doomed traveller. As soon as the *vedettes* announce his approach, the fair troop starts off to meet him, welcoming him with dances and with fiery glances of irresistible power. He is compelled to stop, as a matter of course, and the fair maids then politely request him to alight from his horse. No sooner has the bewildered victim, unconscious of his fate, put his foot on the ground than he finds himself at close quarters with the whole troop. Immediately he is stripped of all he has on his back, and is left in that primitive state in which Adam was at one time. Then begins a series of dances and fascinating gestures in the style of those performed by the maids at the Lupercalian festival, the object of which is to make the unfortunate traveller lose his self-control. An attempt, however, on the part of the victim to reciprocate the advances of his alluring tyrants becomes instantly fatal, as the troop get hold of him in a summary way, declare him to have made attempts on the virtue of one of the fair maids, and condemn him to be pricked with thorns on a very sensitive part of his person."

Despite all these dangers, the Kurds were by no means incapable of lavish hospitality. Their villages might be poor and the people themselves in want, but when they chose to receive a traveller they did so as well as anyone else on the entirety of the Silk Road. James Bailie Fraser, despite his original reservations that the Kurds "might not prove the safest and most disinterested of hosts", several times in his journeys was compelled to rely on their generosity, and in few cases found it wanting.

A Kurdish family in the early 20th century – the lives of such villagers was often a struggle, and they made do with little.

At first sight, the Kurdish villages appeared to be the most poverty-stricken in all of Asia. They set a pattern that was to be found for much of the way towards Constantinople. Many of the dwellings were subterranean, or even set into cavities on the sides of cliffs. From a distance, the villages in the plain appeared like "heaps of horse-dung in a farm-yard in winter, smoking and steaming at a great rate, but without anything that could lead a stranger to suspect the existence of a human dwelling among them". Often, the houses themselves, covered by snow in the mountains, could not be seen, and their entrances were nothing more than "black-looking holes". Inside the cottages, it was not untypical to find "a confused assemblage of buffaloes, horses and cows, men, women and children, who were all mingled higgledy-piggledy". The dwellings would typically be divided into three parts: one end for "*mal*", the cattle and property; the opposite end for "*zan o bacheha*", the women and children; and an apartment in the middle for the master. However, this rule did not always hold good, and the traveller might find himself "amidst a lowing and bleating of beasts, a crying of children, and a gabble of women, that might have made one fancy he had got into a sort of Noah's ark in a gale of wind".

The walls were crudely made of stones, wood and mud, and the roofs often of huge wooden beams covered in earth, which put Fraser in mind of the old crofters' cottages of Highland Scotland. Nonetheless, the Kurdish dwellings seemed to him to be much more cheerful and comfortable. The people might sing and play the flute; mats and carpets were spread on the floor, oil lamps provided light, and heat came from a fire at one end of the ensemble, fuelled sometimes with briars but principally with cow dung. This was also the fuel for the tandoor, or oven, which was sunk into the floor, and in which the food would generally be cooked. Bread would be baked spread out in flat cakes on its inside walls, and the traveller could also look forward to fried eggs, roast lamb (killed on the spot and cooked in the melted fat of its own tail), or thick meat soup. The tandoor served the double purpose of allowing the travellers to thaw out their frozen limbs, which they would stick inside the oven to warm up at the same time as the food was cooking.

Sleep, however, was not so easy in such a place for the traveller unused to the atmosphere. Each inhabitant would lay himself down to sleep wherever he happened to be sitting, "and the whole floor was covered in a trice... with snoring black heaps. What with the effluvia of men and beasts, and the remains of an ample fire, the heat became intense, the air suffocating." Even if one could get over the depth of the fug, there was still one insurmountable barrier to sleep: the "multitude of fleas" which infested every corner of the hovel, could more than anything banish rest from the traveller.

Hosap Castle, near Lake Van, was built in 1643 by the Kurdish chief Mahmudi Suleyman as a base from which to prey on passing caravans.

(This page) *The 4th century Sumela Monastery between Trabzon and Erzurum has survived many changes in ruling kingdoms and empires. Although many of the frescoes within the monastery's Rock Church have been badly damaged, some beautiful work still remains, such as this saint being attacked by lions, and nearby an angel fresco. (Opposite top) The Isak Pasa Palace guarded the mountain passes around Mt Ararat. (Opposite bottom) The Hagia Sophia in Trabzon (Trebizond) on the Black Sea coast.*

The Hagia Sophia was built in 532–537 CE by Byzantine emperor Justinian, and was the largest cathedral in the world for more than a thousand years. When Constantinople was conquered by the Ottoman Turks in 1453, Sultan Mehmed II ordered it to be converted into a mosque – Islamic elements such as the minarets were added, and murals were plastered over. Finally, in 1935 the Republic of Turkey turned it into a museum.

(Clockwise from top left) *Superb interior dome decoration in the Selimiye Mosque in Edirne, Thrace, the original capital of the Ottoman Empire before Constantinople; a satellite image of Istanbul and the Bosphorus; the bane of the Byzantine Empire, Sultan Mehmed II, titled "the Conqueror"; The Entry of the Crusaders into Constantinople, 1840, by Ferdinand Victor Eugene Delacroix; occupying a strategic position between the eastern Mediterranean and Black Sea, Turkey has always been seen as a cultural and commercial bridge between East and West.*

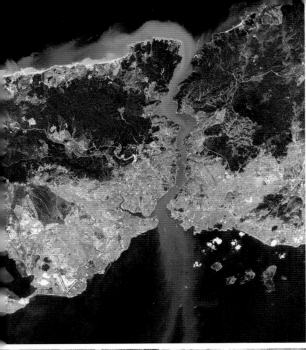

(Top) A modern panorama of the Golden Horn and its minaret-spiked skyline.

(Above) An older and broader panoramic photo of Istanbul shows how busy sea trade was in the early 20th century.

(Left) Four Ottoman Officers and Court Officials, a watercolour by Jean Brindesi (1826–1888), showing notables of the court of Mahmud II, the 30th sultan of the Ottoman Empire.

(Far left) Constantinople from the Entrance to the Golden Horn, a famous watercolour by Thomas Allom (1804–1872), showing the full panoply of vessels that plied its busy waters, from cargo rafts to oceangoing sailing ships and steamboats, as well as ornate longboats used by the wealthy for leisure jaunts up and down the waterfront.

Yeni Cami Mosque, an oil on panel painting by
Robert Charles Gustave Laurens Mols (1848–1903)
that vividly portrays Constantinople's exotic blend
of everyday seaport life with the grandeur of its
architectural edifices.

(Opposite) Yalis (or villas) line the European shore of
the Bosphorus in Istanbul's Arnavutkoy district.

(Above) Sultan Ahmed III meets the Dutch ambassador in the Topkapi Palace, *a painting by Jean Baptiste van Mour in 1727.*

(Right) *A luminous 6th century fresco of the Virgin Mary and Baby Jesus on an interior wall of the Hagia Sophia; many of these images were plastered over by the Ottomans, but careful restoration work has brought some back to light.*

(Opposite top) *The massive Sultan Ahmet Mosque, also called the Blue Mosque.*

(Opposite bottom) *The Bay of Constantinople, by Rudolf Hellgrewe (1860–1935).*

The interior of the Hagia Sophia, a building with a long, rich and varied history. Early Western travellers took great risks to gain entrance during its incarnation as a mosque, but today the general public can wander at will, gazing in awe at its many wonders.

CONSTANTINOPLE: ROAD'S END

he road from the Armenian centre of Ezerum westwards across Asia Minor towards Constantinople was, on account of the climate and terrain, one of the most difficult parts of the journey towards the west. Fraser himself summed up the thoughts of many travellers when he described it as "a continued period of discomfort and fatigue and anxiety, such as I never before, under any circumstances, experienced". The land had once been flourishing, but wars with Russia throughout the 19th century had led to depredation and depopulation. Ezerum itself was in a "miserable condition", with half of the houses in ruins, and the other half standing in "squalid disrepair". Beyond it, the road might pass along dangerous cliffs and mountain roads, or else over mile-long duckboard causeways through muddy fields and waterlogged swamps.

Travel in winter caused the greatest problems, as the roads were frequently snowbound, and travellers, contending with driving snow and blocked roads, and themselves encrusted with ice, had to flog their horses through every obstacle in the attempt to reach the next village. Frequently the traveller would encounter the bodies of dead horses, half eaten by wolves on the wayside. The need to press on with such haste was made more intense by the infrequency of stopping places, particularly in the east. Fraser noted that in Persia there were more villages on the route, although dilapidated and ruinous, but on the Turkish side that although the villages were better kept, they were few and far between.

Such were the perils facing the traveller in this part of the journey that they became deeply dependent on their guides. These were usually part of the postal establishment, which was similar to that over the border in Persia. The guides would live in the post-houses, which were arranged at intervals of between three to 16 hours' ride along the road, and accompany the post-horses which had been hired from them by the travellers as a groom. Trained from childhood to such work, they were brilliant horsemen, well able to deal with the road in all weather. They were a striking sight on the journey; they wore embroidered riding breeches, a short jacket of green or purple velvet, a striped silk or cotton vest, long boots, and a turban "wound in a peculiar loose and rakish style, generally over the fez". From a leather girdle and sash, they carried huge pistols, a shoulder bag for dispatches, a chain from which hung a steel knife and flint, and finally they carried a fearsome whip, with which they would "belabour [their] unhappy steeds".

Thus attired, it is little wonder that they had a "saucy and impudent" air, and a sense of "brutal surly assurance". Yet, when disaster struck the traveller, it was then that they would display their worth. "...If you would see the true value of the Soorajee [guide]," wrote Fraser, "look at him in times of danger and exertion; when the snow is deep, when the road is lost, when the load-horses stick in the mud, or flounder over head and ears in the snow; or roll, luggage and all, down a hill-face, carrying the snow with them like

(Top left) *The Bosphorus Bridge spans Europe and Asia, as today's Istanbul continues to take advantage of its cross-cultural perspective.* (Left) *As the sun sets, modern ferries combine with a resplendent mosque to capture a quintessential Istanbul scene.*

an avalanche. See then the fellows spring from their nags, plunge into the mud or snow, extricate the fallen animals and set them on their legs, or relieve them of their burthens, carrying the luggage on their own shoulders to firmer and safer ground; and when you have witnessed their vigour and alertness in spite of drifting snow and freezing fingers, you will confess, as I did to myself, that no men on earth could be more suited for their work, or do it better, than these same Turkish Soorajees."

For all travellers, no matter whether from the West or the East, they had never seen anything quite like Constantinople. It was not merely the fact that it had been the capital of the eastern Roman Empire and later the Byzantine Empire, nor the fact, especially important for Christians and particularly Orthodox Christians, that it was one of the great seats of the faith and the site of one of its grandest churches, St Sophia. The city's magnitude, its position and even its shape, spread out like a triangle on the shores of the Bosporus (Bosphorus), was enough to call forth their amazement. Before its fall to the Turks in 1453, its size could only be compared to Baghdad in its heyday; such was the strength of its walls, enhanced with nearly 100 towers, it was commonly believed an angel on horseback rode round them constantly in their defence; and such was its wealth that it was difficult to find any comparison.

Benjamin of Tudela, a Jewish traveller from southern Spain who visited Constantinople in the mid-12th century, rightly linked this wealth to the city's position on the Bosporus as a great conduit for trade. "Great stir and bustle prevails at Constantinople in consequence of the conflux of many merchants, who resort thither, both by land and sea, from all parts of the world for purposes of trade, including merchants from Babylon and Mesopotamia, from Media and Persia, from Egypt and Palestine, as well as from Russia, Hungary, Patzinaika [the land north of the Black Sea], Budia, Lombardy, and Spain… They say that the tribute of the city alone amounts every day to 20,000 florins, arising from the rents of hostelries and bazaars, and from the duties paid by merchants who arrive by sea and by land."

The signs of this lavish opulence were everywhere. "The tribute, which is brought to Constantinople every year from all parts of Greece, consisting of silks, and purple cloths, and gold, fills many towers… The

Greeks who inhabit the country are very rich, and possess great wealth in gold and precious stones. They dress in garments of silk, ornamented with gold and other valuable materials. They ride upon horses, and in their appearance they are like princes."

As for the princes themselves, their wealth could scarce be imagined. Benjamin was admitted to see the

Constantinople's Bosphorus waterfront, with the Blue Mosque behind, by Thomas Allom, circa 1834.

Blachernae Palace, which had been constructed in the period before his visit. "The pillars and walls are covered with pure gold, and all the wars of the ancients, as well as [the current emperor's] own wars, are represented in pictures. The throne in this palace is gold, and ornamented with precious stones; a golden crown hangs over it, suspended on a chain of the same material, the length of which exactly admits the emperor to sit under it. This crown is ornamented with precious stones of inestimable value. Such is the lustre of these diamonds, that, even without any other light, they illumine the room in which they are kept."

Everything to be seen was a matter for wonder among the travellers. In the Hippodrome, the ancient racetrack where horse races and games were conducted, there were endless extravagant public spectacles which would transfix the attention of the travellers. Aside from chariot races, Benjamin of Tudela spoke of the displays that would be put on at Christmas: "On these occasions you may see there representations of all the nations who inhabit the different parts of the world, with surprising feats of jugglery. Lions, bears, leopards, and wild asses, as well as birds, which have been trained to fight each other, are also exhibited. All this sport, the equal of which is nowhere to be met with, is carried on in the presence of the King and Queen."

A Norwegian traveller, Sigurd, who visited at the beginning of the 12th century, also described how this was accompanied by fireworks, acrobatics, harp-playing, singing, and all manner of other musical instruments. Yet the architecture and decoration of the hippodrome was even more a matter for amazement. The huge extent of the racetrack, nearly 400 metres long, around which there were up to 40 rows of seats, was marked with columns of semiprecious stone. From the earliest times, it had been adorned with the arts and trophies of antiquity. The *spinae*, or turning posts in the centre of the track, had been decorated by emperors since the time of Constantine with the finest statues taken from all parts of the Roman Empire. Sigurd described the figures on the spinae – men, horses and lions – as being so ingeniously cast that they gave the impression of being alive and joining in the competition. An Arab traveller, al-Idrisi, wrote of the figures that they were so skilfully made that they threw even the best of artists into despair, and a French crusader, Robert de Clari, held that the statues had been made as dolls, charmed into life so that they played and moved, but were then frozen in the midst of their movement.

For most of travellers, especially those from the West, it was the Christian associations of the city which were of greatest interest. When the Spanish ambassador Ruy Gonzáles de Clavijo passed through the city in 1403 on his journey to meet Tamerlane, his greatest concern was to visit the churches and other holy places of the city. The ubiquitous ostentation in these places – the mosaics, the gold, the columns in precious jasper and porphyry – might have gained his attention, but his veneration was reserved for the great store of relics which they possessed. Shortly after he and his retinue's arrival at the end of October, one of the first things they determined to see was the church of St John by the Emperor's palace, which contained the left arm of John the Baptist, "from the shoulder to the hand". The arm was withered, recalled Clavijo, so that the skin and bone alone remained, but in true Byzantine fashion the joints of the elbow and the hand were adorned with jewels set in gold.

On another day, when they had been able to secure the keys to a particular reliquary from the Emperor himself and the ecclesiastical dignitaries had had more time to prepare themselves, they were

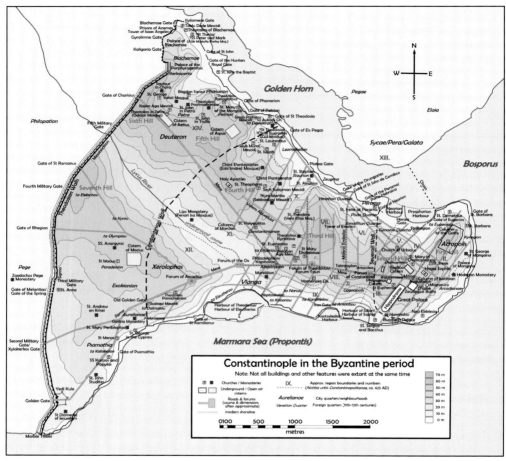

Constantinople in the Byzantine period

Note: Not all buildings and other features were extant at the same time

⊞ ▣ Churches / Monasteries	IX. Approx. region boundaries and numbers
▢ ▭ Underground / Open air cisterns	- - - - - (Notitia urbis Constantinopolitanae, ca. 425 AD)
▤ Roads & forums (course & dimensions often approximate)	*Aurelianae* City quarters/neighbourhoods
modern shoreline	*Venetian Quarter* Foreign quarters (11th–12th centuries)

0 100   500   1000   1500   2000
metres

treated to a more spectacular display of the church's artefacts. When they arrived, the monks robed themselves, lighted many candles, took the keys from Clavijo and proceeded to the tower where the most precious relics were preserved. Shortly afterwards, they returned "chanting very mournful hymns", carrying lighted tapers and swinging thuribles full of smoking incense, carrying before them a box of relics which they set on a high table in the midst of the church.

Once its seals were broken and the box opened, the monks began to lay out the relics on platters of silver gilt. The first was a finely spun cotton bag containing the piece of bread which Christ gave to Judas at the Last Supper as a sign of his betrayal. This was followed by a crystal vial containing the blood of Christ collected at the Crucifixion. Another glass case housed preserved hairs from the beard of Christ, and attached to a board was the iron from the centurion's lance which pierced Christ's side at the Crucifixion: "It was as fine as a thorn, and of well tempered iron... and the blood on it was as fresh as if the deed which was done with it had just been committed." On top of all of this was the garment of Christ for which the

Roman soldiers cast lots after the Crucifixion. "The garment was of a red dimity, like muslin, and the sleeve was narrow, and it was doubled to the elbow. It had three little buttons, made like twisted cords, like the knots on a doublet, and the buttons, and the sleeve, and all that could be seen of the skirt, seemed to be of a dark rose colour; and it did not look as if it had been woven, but as if it had been worked with a needle, for the strings looked twisted in network, and very tight."

The exhibition of the relics to the party of Spanish travellers caused as much excitement among the people of Constantinople as to Clavijo himself. As they watched this exhibition in the church, the people of the city, who knew what was happening, rushed to join them, "and they all cried very loudly, and said their prayers."

Clavijo was one of the last travellers to behold the city in such a Christian guise. Fifty years after his visit, Constantinople, already long enfeebled by the attack of the Western crusaders in 1204, fell to the Muslim armies of the Ottoman Turks, and became for the next 500 years the capital of their empire. St Sophia, originally one of the greatest churches in Christendom, along with many other of the holy places of the city, were turned over to Islamic worship, and put beyond the bounds of Christian visitors, of which there were many.

Constantinople (or Istanbul), as the seat of a great European power, was courted by many Western ambassadors as they attempted to secure its diplomatic and military support. Moreover, the great stream of traders and merchants from all corners of the world persisted, as did their interest in the city, whose opulence, with their support, continued despite the change in government. The suburbs of Pera and Galeta, outside the walls of the main city, were set aside for the use of Italians and Germans, the English and French, and other quarters were conceded to the Greeks, Jews and Armenian traders.

The fact that the once Christian monuments had now been put beyond their reach in the service of another faith intensified the desire of Western travellers to see them. Just as Muslims before the Turkish conquest had been denied entrance to St Sophia unless they genuflected before the great crucifix within, so afterwards Christians were forbidden to enter it without special permission from the Turkish Sultan. As with Mashhad, the penalty for any Western Christian traveller would be summary execution at the hands of an enraged mob.

For some travellers, such danger was an inducement rather than a deterrent. Perhaps the most daring of these was Julia Pardoe. Born in Yorkshire in 1806, she travelled extensively with her father in Europe and Near Asia for the sake of her health, and wrote prolifically about her experiences. Coming to Constantinople in her late 20s, she set her sights on St Sophia. "What European traveller, possessed of the least spirit of adventure, would refuse to encounter danger in order to stand beneath the dome of St Sophia?" she asked, and even more provocatively, "what wandering Giaour [Western infidel] could resist the temptation of entering a mosque during high prayer?"

Like Robert Byron with the shrine of the Imam Reza, it was a venture that had to be undertaken in disguise. It was a prospect that delighted Pardoe, for no costume more than the Turkish "[leant] itself more readily or more conveniently to the purposes of disguise". She stained her light eyebrows with dark dye, shrouded herself in a great pelisse lined with fur, and pulled a fez low down on her brow. Thus attired, having told her father that she was going on a walk to see the Bosporus by moonlight, she set off with a male Turkish dignitary who was in on the deception, and servant bearing a lantern, to intrude on the midnight prayers.

On entering the covered peristyle outside the main body of the building, she little suspected how overwhelming would be the sight within. In the peristyle, the floor was covered in fine matting, and the lamps which hung from the ceiling half illumined the many recesses in which beggars lurked, holding out their begging bowls in the hope of a coin. All around there lounged a crowd of servants, waiting for their masters to exit from their prayers. But when her own attendant moved forward and pulled open the curtains which veiled the entrance to the nave, she "involuntarily shrank back before the blaze of light that burst upon me".

"Far as the eye could reach upwards, circles of coloured fire, appearing as if suspended in mid air, designed the form of the stupendous dome, while beneath, devices of every shape and colour were formed by myriads of lamps of various hues: the Imperial closet, situated opposite to the pulpit, was one blaze of refulgence, and its gilded lattices flashed back the brilliancy, till it looked like a giant meteor!

"As I stood a few paces within the doorway, I could not distinguish the limits of the edifice – I looked forward, upward – to the right hand and to the left – but I could only take in a given space, covered with human beings, kneeling in regular lines, and at a certain signal bowing their turbaned heads to the

An image of the monumental Hagia Sophia taken some time between 1880 and 1900 by the Abdullah Frères company.

earth, as if one soul and one impulse animated the whole congregation; while the shrill chanting of the choir pealed through the vast pile, and died away in lengthened cadences among the tall dark pillars which support it.

"And this was St Sophia! To me it seemed like a creation of enchantment – the light – the ringing voices – the mysterious extent, which baffled the earnestness of my gaze – the ten thousand turbaned Moslems, all kneeling with their faces turned towards Mecca, and at intervals laying their foreheads to the earth – the bright and various colours of the dresses – and the rich and glowing tints of the carpets that veiled the marble floor – all conspired to form a scene of such unearthly magnificence, that I felt as though there could be no reality in what I looked on, but that, at some sudden signal, the towering column would fail to support the vault of light above them, and all would become void."

A Scottish traveller, John Reid, who visited Constantinople in the 1830s, and who was dependent on the Sultan's permission to enter St Sophia, took a differing view as to its merits:

"Much has been said and written regarding St Sophia, but I think the new twaddler merely catches the former twaddler's opinion, and, without taking the trouble of thinking, exclaims or writes down – sublime, beautiful, without considering the value of the words. St Sophia, in my opinion is a building sacred to the eye of every member of civilisation, but sacred from nothing that is in it as a building; sacred solely from its being the only entire building of Greece that remains, amid the wreck of former ages; and sacred from the materials of which it is composed, connected as they are with everything great in the ancient grandeur of Greece and Rome. The building itself looks like a huge giant, whose head, sunk between his shoulders, seems as if he was nearly suffocated by a confused and irregular cluster of wens [boils or cysts] growing up on all sides; and if any admiration can be felt for the building, as a building, it must be akin to that felt by looking at an overgrown ox, or the fat boy. It is a remnant of ancient Greece, and I revere it because it is so, for it is evidently the work of an age when the arts were in decline, and when, to raise an enormous edifice, not a fine one, was the taste of the day. It is a confused gathering of marble, granite, porphyry, and freestone, built without a leading design, by various hands, full of beauties, full of faults, and embellished with pillars of all heights, colours, and diameters, evidently torn from other temples, by those who could not see the sin of so doing, and huddled together by those who did not know their value."

Female travellers often had the edge on male travellers in the extent that they were able to penetrate local society. Unlike men, they were able to enter the harems of Turkish households with ease and give a picture of domestic life that male travellers were unable to discover except by hearsay. Pardoe was no exception in this. Shortly after her arrival in Constantinople she was given admission to the harem in a Turkish merchant's house, and was able to record her impressions accordingly.

The room was large and warm, laid with fine carpets, and surrounded on three sides with a low sofa in rich crimson velvet. The floor was scattered with silk cushions embroidered in gold, and in the corner of the room a copper tandoor full of charcoal provided heat. At one end, closely latticed windows allowed in light, and the only other furnishings were a large jug, "classically shaped" of water, a goblet in a glass saucer, and on a rosewood bracket in a niche, a copy of the Qur'an beneath a handkerchief of cloth of gold.

The family consisted of a father and mother, a son and his wife, a daughter and her husband. The ladies of the ensemble, who were present in the harem as Pardoe was introduced, were huddling around the tandoor. They were dressed in silk chemisettes trimmed with ribbons, wide trousers of printed cotton, dresses of printed cotton in the "brightest colours", blue and yellow fringed with pink and green, and cashmere shawls. They went about the room barefoot, although sometimes wearing "little yellow slippers that scarcely covered their toes, in which they moved over the floor in greatest ease".

Their customs, according to Pardoe, were "luxurious and indolent", except for their habit of early rising, which she accounted as a mixed blessing, as it only served to add "two or three hours of ennui to each day". Their time was occupied by "dressing themselves, and varying the position of their ornaments", as well as in bathing and sleeping. Their talent for the latter was a wonder to Pardoe. They appeared to have sleep entirely at their beck and call, "as a glass of water". They only had to nestle by the tandoor in the winter, or to bury themselves amongst the cushions in the summer, "and in five minutes they are in the land of dreams". "Indeed so extraordinarily gifted are they in this respect that they do not unfrequently engage their guests to take a nap, with the same *sang-froid* with which a European lady would invite her friends to take a walk."

Pardoe sensed a certain lack of self-esteem on the part of the women of the harem. Aside from the more conventional questions, such as asking her age, why she did not marry, could she read and write, and did she like Constantinople, they constantly remarked "how I must find everything in Turkey inferior to what I had been accustomed to in Europe: and they lost themselves in wonder at the resolution that had decided me to visit a part of the world where I must suffer so many privations".

Yet, she also found that a far greater liberty had been accorded to the women by their way of life than she had expected. The visits of men to the harem, even those of the family, were always announced beforehand. Every day, when the paterfamilias returned home, he was obliged to deposit some token of esteem on the table of the harem, whether it be a bunch of grapes, sweets, some fish or a salad. Not to do so would be taken as a grave insult or a sign of repudiation. But just as the men were expected to give some daily sign of their regard, it was just as open to the women to stray in their affections. Should they so please, they could go out into the street in the company of their slaves, either on foot or in a carriage, from which their flirtations could be conducted. "Such finished coquetry I never before witnessed as that of the Turkish ladies in the street... should a group of handsome men be clustered in the pathway, that instant is accidentally chosen for arranging the *yashmac* [face veil]. The dark-eyed dames of Spain, as accomplished as they are in the art, never made more graceful use of the veil than do the orientals of the jealous *yashmac*."

Shopping also was a great outlet for the energy of the dwellers of the harem. "The taste for shopping," wrote Pardoe, "is as great among the eastern ladies as with their fair European sisters; but it is indulged in a totally different manner. Constantinople boasts no commercial palace like those of Howell and James, or Storr and Mortimer; and still less a Maradan Garson: no carriage draws up at the door of an Ebers or a Sams for 'the last new novel'; nor does a well-warmed and well-floored bazar tempt the satin-slippered dame to wander among avenues of glittering gewgaws and elaborated trifles: the carriage of the veiled Osmanli stops at the door of some merchant who has a handsome shopman: and the name of the latter, having been previously ascertained, Sadak or Mustapha, as the case may be, is ordered by the *arabafhe*, or coachman, to exhibit to his mistress some article of merchandize, which he brings accordingly, and, while the lady affects to examine its quality and to decide on its value, she enters into conversation with the youth, playing upon him meanwhile the whole artillery of her fine eyes. The questioning generally runs nearly thus: 'What is your name?' 'How old are you?' 'Are you married?' 'Were you ever in love?' and similar misplaced and childish questions. Should the replies of the interrogated person amuse her and his beauty appear as great on a nearer view as when seen from a distance, the merchandize is objected to and the visit repeated frequently 'ere the fastidious taste of the purchaser can be satisfied."

An earlier traveller to Constantinople, Lady Mary Wortley Montagu, the wife of Sir Edward Wortley Montagu who acted as the British ambassador from 1716–18, was able to enter the Imperial Harem [Seraglio] in the Topkapi Palace. The occasion of her visit was a call on the dowager Empress, the Sultana Hafise, who was the widow of the Sultan Mustafa II. She found the way of life similar to that discovered by Pardoe in the more modest harems, but the wealth surrounding her person similar to the Greek monarchs who had ruled hundreds of years beforehand:

"...her dress was something so surprisingly rich, that I cannot forbear describing it to you. She wore a vest called dualma, which differs from a caftan by longer sleeves, and folding over at the bottom. It was of purple cloth, strait to her shape, and thick set, on each side, down to her feet, and round the sleeves, with pearls of the best water, of the same size as their buttons commonly are... This habit was tied, at the waist, with two large tassels of smaller pearls, and round the arms embroidered with large diamonds. Her shift was fastened at the bottom with a great diamond, shaped like a lozenge; her girdle as broad as the broadest English ribband, entirely covered with diamonds. Round her neck she wore three chains, which reached to her knees; one of large pearl, at the bottom of which hung a fine coloured emerald, as big as a turkey-egg; another consisting of two hundred emeralds, close joined together, of the most lively green, perfectly matched, every one as large as a half-crown piece, and as thick as three crown pieces, and another of small emeralds, perfectly round. But her ear-rings eclipsed all the rest. They were two diamonds, shaped exactly like pears, as large as a big hazle-nut. Round her talpoche she had four strings of pearl – the whitest and most perfect in the world, at least enough to make four necklaces, every one as large as the duchess of Marlborough's, and of the same shape, fastened with two roses, consisting of a large ruby for the middle stone, and round them twenty drops of clean diamonds to each. Besides this, her head-dress was covered with bodkins of emeralds and diamonds. She wore large diamond bracelets, and had five rings on her fingers (except Mr Pitt's) the largest I ever saw in my life. 'Tis for jewellers to compute the value of these things; but, according to the common estimation of jewels, in our part of the world, her whole dress must be worth a hundred thousand pounds sterling. This I am sure of, that no European queen has half the quantity..."

I t was still to trade and the city's mercantile culture that the Imperial court could attribute its wealth. As for the bazaars, in terms of their pattern and the way in which business was conducted, they differed little from those to be found further down the Silk Road in the towns and cities of Persia or Central Asia. However, the Grand Bazaar in Constantinople, which was begun in the mid-15th century by Sultan Mehmed II, trumped these by its sheer extent. Its streets extended for several miles, and the varieties of merchandise sold there were legion. Their copious nature was the great attraction for many of the city's visitors. J.B. Fraser was a case in point: "The bazars are the things I could dwell on for months – so large, so grotesque, so filled with everything strange and attractive – so perfectly Oriental and Caliph Haroon-ul-Rasheed-ish." Pardoe, by contrast, was less easily impressed. "Rudely paved, disagreeably dirty, plentifully furnished with égouts [sewers], of which both the sight and the scent are unpleasing, badly lighted, clumsily built, and so constructed as to afford no idea of the space they cover, until you have wandered through the whole of their mazes, your involuntary impression is one of wonder at the hyperboles which have been lavished on them by travellers, and the uncalled for extacies of tour-writers."

Different streets of the Bazaar were given to different trades. Fraser's first interest was taken by the section called the Bezestein, "a very large sort of caravanserai, or covered bazar, which is what might be called the fancy mart, the Strand the Ludgate-hill or, perhaps, rather the Soho Bazar of Constantinople". Here, the merchants sold great quantities of "arms and accoutrements, sabres, spears, old extraordinary matchlocks, bows and arrows, shields, battle-axes, spears, yataghans, daggers, pistols... with rich apparel, strange old watches, clocks, cabinets, and curiosities of all sorts..." However, his excitement was also equally aroused by the ladies' slipper shops "of which there are whole ranges, filled with the most beautiful *papooshes*, for the delicate supporters of the fair ones of Constantinople, the elegant *fabrique* and rich embroidery of which would, I think, go far to tempt the British ladies to imitate their sisters of Islam in this particular."

Pardoe agreed that the shoe bazaar, where the slippers, worked with seed pearls, velvet, gold and silver thread, "made a very handsome and tempting appearance"; however, the perfume bazaar proved of greater allure. That quarter, she wrote, was "indeed a miniature embodiment of 'Araby the blest'," the air rich with everything from the Western scent of Eau de Cologne to the Eastern rosewater and attar gul. "Nor less luxurious was the atmosphere of the spice bazaar, with its pyramids of cloves, its piles of cinnamon and its bags of mace – and, while the porcelain dealers allured us into their neighbourhood by a dazzling display, comprising every variety of ancient and modern china; silks, velvets, Broussa satins and gold gauze in their turn invited us in another direction..."

In the middle of the 19th century, slaves were still traded in Constantinople. Pardoe visited the slave market expecting to be shocked and disgusted, but her opinions on the matter were changed by her experience, and she left the market "only with an increased conviction of the great moral beauty of the Turkish character". The slave market, she wrote, was "a square court, three of whose sides are built round with low stone rooms, or cells, beyond which projects a wooden peristyle. There is always a painful association connected with the idea of slavery, and an insurmountable disgust excited by the spectacle of money given in exchange for human beings; but beyond this (and assuredly this is enough) there is nothing either to distress or to disgust in the slave market of Constantinople. No wanton cruelty, no idle insult is permitted: the slaves, in many instances, select their own purchaser from among the bidders; and they know that when once received into a Turkish family they become members of it in every sense of the word, and are almost universally sure to rise in the world if they conduct themselves worthily. The negroes only remain in the open court, where they are squatted in groups, until summoned to show themselves to a purchaser; while the Circassians and Georgians, generally brought there by their parents at their own request, occupy the closed apartments, in order that they may not be exposed to the gaze of the idlers who throng the court. The utmost order, decency, and quiet prevail. And a military guard is stationed at the entrance to enforce them, should the necessity for interference occur, which is, however, very rarely the case..."

Reid characteristically took a different viewpoint. The sight of slaves being herded to the bazaar at sunrise "attended by masters and assistants", put him in mind of the droves of sheep or black cattle sent on their way to Smithfield meat market, "but the difference [being] that sheep are well clothed", yet the slaves had nothing but dirty rags.

he ultimate conduit for all of this trade was the Bosporus (Bosphorus). All goods coming from the great routes to the east had to cross it, and most of the merchandise leaving from Constantinople for the West – whether it was silk in the time of the Byzantines, spices, carpets or tempered steel blades – departed by way of the river for the Mediterranean or the Black Sea.

Many travellers, such as Fraser, maintained that it was better to survey the city from the vantage of the water to avoid the crowded dirty streets, the odours of the sewers, the low eating houses and butchers which filled the centre and the suburbs. Although others maintained that such an opinion was overly fastidious, none dissented that the sight of Constantinople from the sea, and the approach to the city by boat, was one of the great joys of travel to the place. Nowhere else, and few other places on the land journey from the east, would have presented such a variety of sights. All about the water darted seagulls, wild ducks and water hens, and below there swam porpoises, showing their "white bellies to the light". The rocky hills along the Bosporus were topped at their heights with houses and gardens, fields and enclosures, and nearer their base the waterfront was lined an endless procession of buildings and palaces painted primarily in green and white, and mosques and towers. From some of the Imperial palaces, the sound of music could be heard near the water, the sound of stringed instruments and tambourines, so that near them the boatmen slowed down, and "you are almost ready to fancy," as Pardoe wrote "...that Apollo must have first swept his lyre in a Turkish harem". Closer at hand, one could also see tokens entwined in the latticework windows of the harems, an orange with a lock of hair, or a marigold suspended by a red ribbon, partially concealed. Beyond these, there were handsome burial grounds surrounded with cypresses, little concealed bays with creeks and little villages and pleasure grounds where people on excursions sat around kiosks and drank coffee.

However, such was the volume of traffic on the river that one was likely to see as much life on the water as in the crowded city streets. Every day, the river was a mass of fishermen, rowing boats, and a diversity of vessels under sail. The principal vessel to be seen was the caïque, a long narrow rowboat, which was adapted to a multitude of uses. The grandest were the imperial barges, set aside for the use of the Sultan and his immediate retinue. These were brightly gilded and decorated, and had a deck with a kiosk set aside for the Sultan. In the eyes of Pardoe, these were the most alluring objects on the Bosporous, "looking as though its model had been cut out of gold paper in an hour of luxurious indolence, and carried into execution during a fit of elegant caprice".

Other ranks of imperial officials and their households could be identified by the splendour of their vessels. The pasha travelled hidden beneath a red umbrella on his caïque. His wife, on another, kept a more elaborate waterborne establishment. Her caïque was "a light buoyant glittering thing, with a crimson drapery fringed with gold flung over its side, and almost dipping into the water", and she herself reclined on a pile of cushions in the bottom of the boat, attended by three slaves and "a collection of yellow slippers strewn about her".

More formidable was the Admiralty barge, which cast a long shadow before it on the water. It claimed 14 rowers in red caps and white jackets, and behind them, seated at the stern was the High Admiral, surrounded by junior officers, a pipe bearer and a secretary taking dictation; it was customary to conduct much business on the river. It was similarly the case for the British Ambassador. His caïque of seven rowers was immediately recognisable by the large Union Jack which trailed from behind, as was the man himself, who sat on the water reading the newspapers in a red fez, always marked out by his "aristocracy of bearing".

The caïque was as much for the ordinary tradesmen as the high officers of the city, and darting between the gilded vessels one might see caïques heaped with any sort of merchandise. Caïques laden with fruit protected from the sun by coverings of leaves would be rowed up to the houses overhanging the water by Greek traders to sell their wares to the inhabitants. Others would be adapted to carry passengers, taking them the length of the river into the port of Constantinople for less than two pence. This small sum would be discounted for those who would travel in the amphibious seats, with their legs hanging over the side by the water.

In the port itself, innumerable vessels jostled and weaved across the water, from the caïques to small sailboats, to the greater many-decked vessels of the Turkish fleet. Similarly, all about there rang the languages and calls of many nationalities, sailors, merchants and travellers, signifying those who had arrived, or those who were about to depart. "Here the deep 'brig-ahoy!' of the British seaman boomed along the ripple; there the shrill cry of the Greek mariner rang through the air: at intervals the full rich strain of the dark-eyed Italian relieved the wild monotonous chant of the Turk; while the cry of the sea-boy from the rigging was answered by the stern brief tones of the weather-beaten sailor on the deck." It was a scene recorded by Pardoe that would have changed little throughout the centuries, and would have answered for the 4th century CE when the western Romans established the city, or when the Christian Byzantines in later centuries stood at the gateway to the riches of the East and the Silk Road.

Amongst the cries of the sailors was to be heard the folk song of the Turkish fishermen. This was more often than not of a "melancholy tone... in the minor mode", but never unpleasant to hear as the fishermen drew in their nets. Lady Emelia Hornby, who spent time in the city over the period of the Crimean War in 1856, recorded a number of these, many of which brought to mind the sights of departure to the West or to unknown lands – a theme always to be apprehended in the port of Constantinople.

Didst thou not see the fair one?
Alas, I too beheld her yesterday,
When she stepped into a little boat,
And departed for foreign parts.

The wind blew, and the sea was rough.
The sails filled
Like the plumes of a little pigeon
When it spreads its wings.

Her friends stood on the shore
With mingled grief and joy,
And she with a handkerchief
Returned their adieux.

And a sad adieu
I also would have said,
But the cruel one
Denied me even this.

I weep not for the boat,
I weep not for the sails,
But I weep for the fair one
Who is gone to foreign parts.

(Top) *The narrowest point of the Khyber Pass, guarded by the Ali Masjid Fort. This broad cleft in the Hindu Kush was for thousands of years the main route into the fabled lands of India from Central Asia and the West.* (Above left) *"Beloochis in the Bolan Pass", the frontispiece of* Sketches in Afghaunistan *[sic], by James Atkinson, 1842.* (Above right) *The British army passes through the entrance to the Bolan Pass near Quetta in March 1839.* (Opposite top) *Herat citadel in 1969, and* (opposite bottom) *at the camel market in Balkh, 1974 – these were the last of the peaceful days when Western travellers could traverse Iran and Central Asia by land with impunity.*

THE MUGHAL ROUTE
THE WAY TO INDIA

Throughout history, travellers have followed three major routes from Central Asia into India.

The first, and certainly most practical from the point of view of both merchants heavy-laden with goods and commanders leading strong armies, is that which passes through Afghanistan. Through here, the traveller would have the choice of a flatter, more circuitous route, or one more hilly but direct. The former went by way of Herat and Kandahar, keeping between the well-watered foothills of the Hindu Kush on the left and the perishing wilderness of the Dasht-i Margo (Desert of Death) on the right. The other dropped more directly by way of Balkh or Mazar-i Sharif in the north of Afghanistan into the lower ranges of the Hindu Kush, reaching Bamiyan before turning east towards Kabul. Both routes then cut through the dangerous and convoluted screen of mountains, the Suliman Range, which divide Afghanistan from present-day Pakistan. The former route would generally conclude with the Bolan Pass, and the latter with its more famous

cousin, the Khyber, before debouching into the wider plains of the Punjab.

These routes saw perhaps some of the most famous conquerors in history, not least of whom were Alexander the Great, Tamerlane and Genghis Khan. It was by means of the Afghan route in the 16th century that Babur, originally one of Tamerlane's heirs to princely rule in Central Asia, managed to outdo his predecessors and carve out a kingdom in India, the Mughal Empire, which lasted until the days of the

British Raj. Beyond these, they also saw over the centuries a wealth of international trade. In the heyday of the Silk Road, in the centuries after the birth of Christ, the goods trafficked along these routes included not only silk, but also rubies and lapis lazuli, spices, silverwork, gold, cut gems, glass vessels, amber, frankincense, asbestos cloth, amphorae and even Roman statuary.

Not less than these were traded ideas, styles of art, and even religions. The ruins of the Buddhas of Bamiyan, and the Rock edicts of King Asoka, second century BC inscriptions on the Buddhist faith in Greek and Aramaic, are perhaps two of the most conspicuous examples of this cultural exchange. Yet this route, which was most traversed of all, is now one of the most difficult for foreigners to follow. The fragile state of Afghanistan, and the fighting endemic in the Tribal Regions on the Pakistan border, have all but closed the routes except to the most intrepid or foolhardy.

Contemporary politics are also responsible for similar difficulties on the second major route. This linked India to the southern branch of the Silk Road on the fringes of the Taklamakan Desert (in modern-day Xinjiang), in the region that during the first millennium CE was part of the Buddhist kingdom of Khotan, and later came under Islamic rule centred around Yarkand. Indeed, until the second half of the 20th century this remained as large and influential a city as Kashgar as a result of its direct connection to the exotic riches of the subcontinent. The route

(Top) *Nomadic Kuchi tribespeople at the Blue Mosque, 1974.*
(Above) *The large Buddha at Bamiyan in 1974, destroyed by the Taliban in 2003.*

started from Yarkand (today also known as Shache) and made its way south over not one but three mighty mountaintain ranges – the Kunlun, Karakoram and Himalaya – by way of the high mountain region of Ladakh (a stronghold of Buddhism still known as "Little Tibet"), before reaching the capital of Kashmir, Srinagar.

(Right) *A Hazara horseman at the Band-i-Amir lakes north of Bamiyan.*

(Clockwise from right) *The astonishing Band-i Amir lakes near Bamiyan are volcanic craters with walls of pumice stone – note the ice waterfalls leaking from this lake's wall, and the horse nearby; the cliffs of Bamiyan, site of the famous giant Buddhas, in 1974 – this fertile soil has been farmed for many centuries, but the fortified farms show that danger from attack has always been an issue; an Afghan musician in a tea shop in Balkh; the Blue Mosque in Mazar-i Sharif, site of the Shrine of Hazrat Ali, the Prophet's son-in-law; the Bala Hissar, or High Fort, in Kabul in 1972 – for many centuries, this fortress contained the seat of the local rulers; nomads decorate their camels with colourful tackle.*

An Indian cargo truck at the Zoji-La pass from Ladakh into Kashmir – historically this was the main route from Leh to Srinagar, and today a hairpin road follows much the same path.

This south-facing satellite image shows the ancient "Five Passes" trade route from the southern Silk Road oasis kingdom of Khotan (seen here at bottom) into India, first crossing the Kunlun Mountains, next traversing the high-altitude plain of Aksai Chin, then tackling the Karakoram range before descending into the Indus Valley, following it downstream, and turning southwest to cross the Himalaya into the Kashmir Valley, which here appears like a grey misty lake in the upper right of the picture.

Thikse Monastery, near Leh in the upper Indus Valley
– known as "Little Tibet", the Buddhist kingdom of
Ladakh had close contact with the desert oases fringing
the Taklamakan Desert to the north, despite the
mighty mountain ranges that intervened.

Incredible mountain scenery at the Passu Cathedral,
on the descent from the Kunjerab Pass towards
Hunza and the plains of Pakistan and India.

Karakul Lake in southwestern Xinjiang, on the Karakoram Highway leading to the border with Pakistan at the Kunjerab Pass.

The picturesque Hunza Valley has inspired travellers for centuries. Surrounded by the immense peaks of the Karakoram range, its fertile soil and strategic location on the Indus River route south to the plains of the Punjab allowed it to prosper.

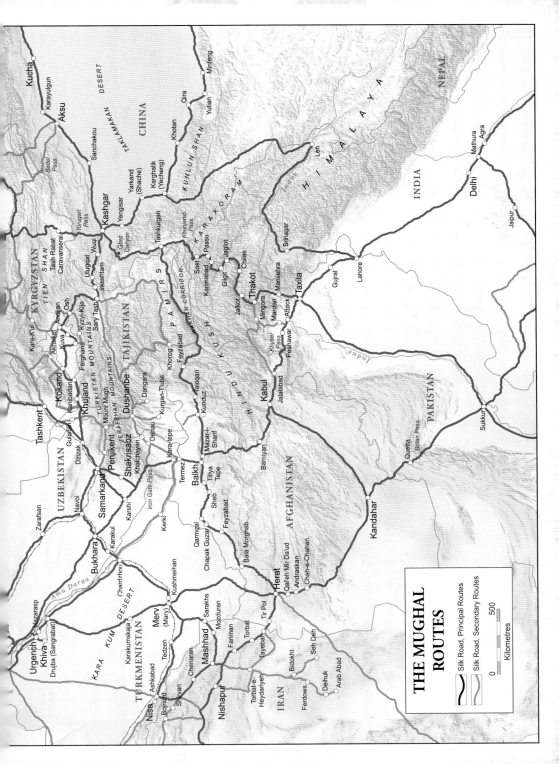

THE MUGHAL ROUTES

Silk Road, Principal Routes

Silk Road, Secondary Routes

0   500
Kilometres

CHINA
INDIA
NEPAL
PAKISTAN
AFGHANISTAN
IRAN
TURKMENISTAN
UZBEKISTAN
KYRGYZSTAN
TAJIKISTAN
TAKLAMAKAN DESERT
KARA KUM DESERT
HIMALAYA
TIEN SHAN
KUNLUN SHAN
KARAKORAM
HINDU KUSH
PAMIRS
TURKISTAN MOUNTAINS
ZERAFSHAN MOUNTAINS
WAKHAN CORRIDOR

Kucha
Karayulgun
Aksu
Sanchakou
Kashgar
Yengisar
Yarkand (Shache)
Karghalik (Yecheng)
Khotan
Qira
Yudian
Minfeng
Leh
Srinagar
Mathura
Agra
Delhi
Jaipur
Lahore
Gujrat
Taxila
Attock
Peshawar
Mardan
Mingora
Mansehra
Thakot
Jalkot
Chilas
Jaglot
Gilgit
Karimabad
Passu
Sost
Feyzabad
Khorog
Jalalabad
Kabul
Bamiyan
Kunduz
Taloqan
Mazar-i-Sharif
Balkh
Termez
Kara-tepe
Kurgan-Tube
Dangara
Denau
Khalchayan
Kerki
Chardzhou
Karakul
Bukhara
Karakumskala
Merv (Mary)
Kushmeihan
Tedzen
Ashkabad
Nisa
Bojnurd
Shirvan
Chenaran
Mashhad
Sarakhs
Mozduran
Fariman
Torbat
Tir Pol
Torbat-e-Heydariyeh
Tayebad
Bidokht
Ferdows
Seh Deh
Deihuk
Arab Abad
Nishapur
Herat
Qal'eh Mir Da'ud
Andraskan
Chah-e-Chahan
Bala Morghab
Feyzabad
Qamqal
Chapak Guzar
Sheb
Tillya Tepe
Kandahar
Quetta
Sukkur
Srinagar
Khunjerab Pass
Tashkurgan
Ghez Canyon
Bedel Pass
Torugart Pass
Tash Rabat
Caravanserai
Uluqqat
Wuqi
Irkeshtam
Sary Tash
Kyzyl-Kija
Osh
Andijan
Kuva
Ferghana
Akhsiket
Kokand
Kanibadan
Gulistan
Dzizak
Khujand
Mount Mugh
Penjikent
Shakrisabz
Samarkand
Karshi
Navoi
Zarafsan
Zarafshan
Kara-Kul
Tashkent
Khiva
Urgench
Nazarasp
Drujba (Sangrabat)
Tashkurgan
Dushambe
Kara-Kul
Iron Gate Pass
Khyber Pass
Bolan Pass

Amu Darya
Indus
Indus

(Top) *Constructed in the reign of Mughal emperor Aurangzeb, the 17th century Badshahi Mosque in Lahore was the largest mosque in the world until 1986 – it can hold 10,000 worshippers within its main prayer hall and 100,000 in its courtyard and porticoes.* (Bottom) *Humayun's Tomb in Delhi was the first Mughal garden tomb in India, built by a Persian architect in 1562.* (Opposite) *A shikara is reflected perfectly on beautiful Nagin Lake in Srinagar, Kashmir, with houseboats on the far shore, and in the distance the foothills of the Himalaya. Once an idyllic tourist destination, Kashmir today is a troubled land.*

(Top) *Built by Sha Jahan in the 17th century, Delhi's Red Fort showcases some of the most wonderful Mughal architecture, combining elements of Persian, European and Indan art.* (Bottom) *The Hall of Public Audience, or Diwan-i Am, in Agra Fort, which predates Delhi's Red Fort and was home to six of the great Mughal rulers.* (Opposite top) *The Amber Fort just north of Jaipur is a breathtaking blend of Hindu and Mughal architectural and artistic styles.* (Opposite bottom) *Two miniature Mughal paintings show Emperor Akbar on an elephant, and presiding over his court.*

(Above) *Mist from the Yamuna River veils the Taj Mahal at dawn. Built by Emperor Shah Jahan in memory of his favourite wife, Mumtaz Mahal, the Taj Mahal is considered the pinnacle of Mughal architecture, and is one of the most famous tourist attractions in the world, for good reason. It took more than 20 years to complete, employing thousands of artisans and workers.*

(Right) *Flower and vine marble detailing on the walls of the Taj – depending on the time of day, the polished white marble can appear pink, white or golden.*

(Opposite) *The Taj Mahal at dawn, its minarets and front portal turned salmon pink as the sun rises from the surrounding plain. More than any other historic building, this one requires repeated visits at different times of day to fully appreciate its magnificence.*

Approach to Yarkand, *an 1868 drawing made by Robert Shaw during his adventurous journey into Chinese Turkestan.*

This was originally one of the most difficult routes of the Silk Road; in the mountain roads beyond Srinagar, travellers were dogged by perpetual blizzards and avalanches. Between Leh, the capital of Ladakh, and Yarkand there were five passes of more than 16,000 feet (4,877 metres) to cross, and on account of the scarcity of settlements travellers had to carry 14 days' worth of food not just for themselves but for their baggage animals also. There were the dangers of crossing many mountain rivers in spate, and scores of ponies and other pack animals were guaranteed to be lost as a result of the thinness of the air.

For all this, through history right up to the time before Indian Independence it was the major conduit for Indian tea, spices and sugar, as well as an extensive trade in British cloth, manufactured in Bradford and Manchester and exported via India to the bazaars of western China; while in the opposite direction came gold, silks and carpets from Khotan. Indeed, its extreme remoteness and lack of human habitation made the "Five Passes" route more appealing to merchants and travellers than the physically less arduous routes farther west, which passed through regions notorious for banditry – most preferred to battle the natural elements rather than bloodthirsty brigands. Sadly, today, thanks to political and actual fighting in this region between China, India and Pakistan (ceasefire lines demarcate the disputed mountain borders), as well as its termination in troubled Kashmir, and the ongoing instability in the region as a result, it is now not possible to use this route for international travel.

(Top left) *The Hawa Mahal, or Palace of Winds, in Jaipur, was designed in the form of the crown of Krishna, and was part of the women's quarters of the main palace, from where the royal ladies could watch everyday life in the street below.*
(Bottom left) *A camel driver and his mount in the Thar Desert, Rajasthan.*

he third route was that which is traced by the modern-day Karakoram Highway. This, although not quite as demanding as the way via Ladakh, had the disadvantage of being unsuitable for heavy traffic or armies heavy-laden, and hence in comparison with the other routes historically it was neglected. Besides this, it was also an infamous haunt of thieves who preyed on passing travellers. It was perhaps most notable as a route of pilgrimage more than anything else, used especially by Buddhist monks travelling from China to India in order to seek more authentic texts or relics from the heartland of the faith. The rocks on the side of the way, inscribed with Buddhist inscriptions and other ancient graffiti, bear witness to this traffic. Yet, after the journey of the Chinese monk Faxian, who is thought to have traversed it in the 4th century CE, we have few literary notices of the region until Western explorers began to pass through it towards the end of the 19th century.

Starting from Kashgar, the Karakoram Highway traces the old trade route from Kashgar directly south, crossing the Pakistan border at the Kunjerab Pass, and working its way towards Islamabad through the high valleys and isolated mountain settlements of the Hindu Kush. Today, out of the three main routes between Central Asia and India, it the easiest to follow and the most frequented, primarily on account of the modern 800-kilometre highway which was built by the governments of Pakistan and China – and at the cost of the lives of hundreds of labourers – in 1978. But up to that point, it was still one of the most difficult routes to traverse of the entire Silk Road. Faxian wrote that the snow rested upon the way both in summer as well as in winter, and that among the mountains dwelt "venomous dragons, which, when provoked, spit forth poisonous winds, and cause showers of snow and storms of sand and gravel". Not one in 10,000 travellers, according to his account, was able to survive the perils of the journey.

His observations were all but confirmed by travellers of the modern age. Algernon Durand, a British frontier officer who served in and around Gilgit towards the end of the 19th century, wrote of the frequent avalanches and rock slips which Faxian himself must have suffered: "Thousands of feet above you are the mountain tops, shattered by frost and sun into the most fantastic outlines, from whose rugged summits fall masses of rock… Whenever there is heavy rain, or snow begins to melt in the spring, rock avalanches come down, and I have lain at night for hours listening to the thundering roar of great fragments plunging down from thousands of feet above one's camp. In the day-time you have to keep a sharp look-out when marching. There are many places well known as extremely dangerous, in crossing which it is prudent not to loiter. I have never seen a man killed, but I have seen a man's leg broken a few yards in front of me by a falling stone, and have witnessed very narrow escapes. There was one particularly nasty stone shoot at Shaitan Nara, where stones fell all day long, the smaller whizzing by like a bullet, and the larger cannonading down in flying leaps, the last of which frequently carried them nearly across the Astor River."

More unsettling than the threat of avalanches were the paths themselves. Often, when the roads by necessity had to run along precipitous cliffs which dropped sheer into the mountain rivers hundreds of feet below, two tracks would be made to circumvent them. One, winding and rising over the top away from the cliff edge, would be wider, intended for baggage animals and mounted traffic. Another path, however, lower down and more direct, was intended for foot passengers. These were never more than a

The stone fort, dating to the 6th century CE, in Tashkurgan, which means "Stone City" in Tajik.

foot wide, and carried on little more than narrow ledges, which clung to the sheer cliff face itself. Durand recalled their rickety construction: "Taking advantage of a ledge in the rock here, supported on pegs driven into its face there, carried across a bad place on a single shaky plank or light bundle of tamarisk, ascending fifty feet up a cleft in the rock by a series of small tree-trunks notched to give a foothold, and polished by years of use... [there] is often a sheer drop of a hundred feet from the path on to the rocks below." For all the danger of these paths, they caused little terror to the local inhabitants, who, according to Durand, had "no nerves", and thought nothing of ascending or descending "some obviously impossible rock staircase" which would have caused the uninitiated to quail with fear.

The last major Chinese town on the route before the border crossing was Tashkurgan, south of Kashgar. This had always been a significant stop on the Silk Road, and was the site of the near-legendary Stone Tower, which ancient authorities reported as marking the halfway point of the route from the west to China. For all its weight of history, and the fact that it was little more than a grand mud fort, many travellers seemed prey to a certain light-heartedness when reaching it. Peter Fleming, who traversed the route towards India, recalled it as the quintessential frontier town, which had "the air of living on passers-by, on people from outside". The inns were full of Afghan and Indian merchants, delayed by the requirements of paperwork and border officials. The shops were dedicated to the needs of travellers, and "sold mainly the things you needed on the road – ropes, boots and fur hats and victuals – leavened with such finery, sweetmeats, and medicines as might attract men to whom the inconsiderable town was what a port is to a sailor". C P. Skrine, a British official making his way in the opposite direction towards Kashgar in 1922, recalled in the vicinity that even though it was a place devoted to travel and trade, the locals' understanding of the use of baggage animals was slight. He complained in a letter home:

A precarious track leads from Nanga Parbat out to the Indus Valley – the tiny figure on the left provides some scale.

"The people of this country have no idea how to load a camel. They seem to think it ought to be done by perching as many packages on top of the beast's spine as possible, then tying a single rope round the whole and finishing up by hanging a lot more odd articles from any projecting corner they can find; the result is that before the animal has gone half a mile, various tin cans, lanterns, baskets, hat-boxes and other odds and ends have become unshipped and the balance of the load, such as it was, is destroyed.

Round slips the whole affair under the camel's stomach, whereupon he takes fright and bolts. Now a camel bolting at the ungainly, lumbering trot of the species with several hundredweight of assorted luggage raining off him like leaves in autumn is one of the funniest sights imaginable when it is somebody else's luggage; but when it is one's own cases of whisky, medicine chests or favourite yakdans that are dangling from the beast's tummy, the humour of the situation is not so striking."

A road in Baltistan, trapped between fast-flowing river and sheer cliff, with concrete blocks attempting to prevent fatal accident.

Yet beyond Tashkurgan, trepidation often overtook the traveller as the last comforts of civilisation, such as they were, were left behind, and the difficulties of the way became apparent. The plain of Central Asia, with its "vast indefinite expanse, pale yellow and brown with wide shadows lying on it where the oases were", sank into the distance, and all was replaced with snow, glaciers, and the dangers of the mountain paths. Fleming recalled on crossing the 15,600-foot (4,755-metre) Mintaka Pass – a more frequently used alternative to the Kunjerab (Khunjerab) Pass before the construction of the Karakoram Highway – that the way was strewn with the whitening bones of dead pack animals. Circling above were snow partridges and lammergeyers. There was no sound to be heard aside from the clink of horses' hooves on the rock, and the cursing of the Turki servants as they struggled to climb along the path. Fleming noticed their practice, upsetting at first sight, of stabbing the horses between the eyes and the nostrils with long iron skewers, which purportedly helped them to breathe more easily in the high passes. C.P. Skrine, standing on the watershed between Indian and Chinese territory looking northwards to the lower ranges of the Pamirs, found that "[what] strikes one at once… is their cleanness and their spaciousness. The soil, the water, the contours of the hills are all cleaner and purer than the crumbling, decaying rocks, the muddy rivers and the black sinister mountains of the terrible country to the south of Mintaka."

For all this, the beauty and fascination of the route belied these first impressions. There was nothing monotonous about the road towards Gilgit, wrote Fleming, and "no lover of the picturesque could be disappointed by the day's march" towards the area of Hunza, high in the mountains beyond the border crossing. Not only did the toils of the march and the giddy winding of the narrow tracks lead to a sense of exhilaration, but also the variety of the landscape and the fascinating and isolated cultures to be found among the mountain peoples. E.F. Knight, a British journalist who travelled in the region in the 1890s, recalled the sights he saw on just a single day's march in the region: "The first part of the way was through pine forest, the glades covered with marguerites, violet and white; then the path ran along hillsides one mass of spirea, the air thick with its honey – like scent; and dropped gently down, passing a chain of small lakes, grass and willow bordered…"

C.P. Skrine was perhaps the most eloquent on the beauty of the region:

"The charm of the Hunza valley lies in its amazing combination of the most diverse elements in a landscape; in its villages embedded in foliage and neat terraced fields overhung by glaciers and needle-peaks ribbed with ice; its orchards perched on dizzy cliff-tops, and romantic castles built on crags above the gorge; its plume-like waterfalls spraying vineyards cocked at terrifying angles; its irrigation-channels carried along the face of vertical cliffs to homesteads where merely to stroll in the garden after dinner must require a good head.

"The Baltit reach of the Hunza valley is the finest of all. At Murtezabad you cross from the south or Nagar side of the river by a suspension bridge (the northernmost and last of the Indian Public Works Department bridges on this road) to the Hunza side. All is bare and terrible here, and the sides of the deep gorge are unstable and gashed with landslides. The tiny orchards and neatly terraced cornfields begin once more; suddenly you turn a corner and – there in front of you is the heart of Hunza. Imagine a spacious valley with sides from ten to eighteen thousand feet high, a winding canyon with a fierce pale-brown

Nanga Parbat's northern Rakhiot face, from the popular trekking region of Fairy Meadows. Though beautiful from a distance, this is a very dangerous mountain.

river threading it below, its sides green-clad up to two thousand feet or more above the stream; four miles away, right opposite you, an ancient castle on a hill covered with flat-roofed houses and trees, behind which rises a seemingly vertical mountain-face three miles high, crowned with ice-cliffs and snow cornices away up in the blue heavens..."

The crowning glory of the region, south of Hunza and Gilgit, was the great peak of Nanga Parbat, towering over the region at a height of 26,660 feet (8,126 metres). For E.F. Knight, it was an experience not soon to be forgotten: "...a huge white mass, such a mountain as I had never beheld before: not a solitary sharp pinnacle... but shaped like a hog's back; a long rolling height sloping steeply at either end; a prone Titan. The snowy domes were piled one on the other, and flashing glaciers leagues in length streaked the furrowed sides."

It was even more beautiful by night: "The air was perfectly clear, and the moon shone full upon the side of the mountain that faced me, revealing every detail of the pure snows, the steel blue glaciers, the stupendous crags. The dark shadowed chasms had an awful appearance. It was the barrier of the unknown world, and it might have been the wall of fairy land itself, so mysteriously lovely did those lifeless wastes appear."

The region around Hunza and Gilgit first came to the attention of the British Government in India at the end of the 19th century on account of its strategic location. They knew little of its geography, and as with Afghanistan, feared that the Russians, in pursuit of their purported ambition of gaining a foothold in India, would find some way of making the area a conduit for invasion. The royal families which ruled the settlements throughout it were not viewed as the most stable, being prey to endemic fratricide, intrigues with Tsarist agents, and collaboration with the various bandits who targeted the few travellers who attempted to make the journey in those earlier times.

Annexation to British rule was inevitable, and in the 1890s the area became notorious for some of the most fiercely fought engagements of the time, with half a dozen Victoria Crosses being won in one campaign alone. Yet, once the region had been pacified, it became better known not for the military efforts to subdue it, but rather for aspects of the people's culture. One of the most prominent of these is the predilection for the sport of polo – as strong today as ever. The region contains some of the highest and most ancient polo grounds in the world, and preserves a form of the game somewhat more primal than that familiar to the West. C.P. Skrine had the privilege of attending a game whilst on his travels. He recorded in his diary:

"Never have I played such strange polo, nor on so romantic a ground. Any number can play at the same time; the sticks used have heavy fish-shaped heads set at a sharp angle, almost impossible to hit the ball with when you first try; the ground is very long but (of necessity in a country like Hunza) narrow, and is bounded by four-foot walls of rough stones, off which the ball comes at remarkable angles; there is no penalty for 'crossing' or any other foul; after one side has scored a goal, its captain picks up the ball in the same hand in which he holds his stick, gallops full speed up the ground followed by his side and at the half-way mark throws the ball up and smites it full-pitch towards the enemy's goal. I saw the veteran Mir (ruler), who in spite of his years is still a wonderful player, perform this feat, known as the tambok, eight times in succession, and never once did he hit the ball less than a hundred yards. There are no chukkers, the game continuing until one side or the other has scored nine goals. The result is that the ponies, though many of them are of the Badakhshi breed famed for their stamina and spirit, become dead-beat and the game flags somewhat after the first twenty minutes or so. While they last, however, the game is a most exciting and invigorating one."

It was also a land rich in music and dance. E.F. Knight noted that it was the practice of all the leading men of the area to maintain a musical establishment, and their playing was, to his mind, "excellent in their way". The melodies were "barbaric and in the minor key, often singularly impressive" and the songs they sang were "not the melancholy lamentations of a subject and oppressed race, but the spirited war-chants of a conquering people, in which the bard triumphantly celebrates old fights, successful forays, and the raids on caravans of treasure…" As they sang and beat the drums, all around would "clap their hands and energetically join, with flashing eyes, in the savagely exultant chorus – the sort of thing to quicken the pulses of men and excite in them the lust for battle".

The intervals between singing were occupied with dance. This was reserved to the men, but all ranks, from the princely families downwards, would engage themselves in the performance. Some of the dances, observed Knight, were stately and graceful, but others were fiercely energetic. "Now one man alone, now two or four, would step into the ring and engage in the pleasing figures… there were some dances furious as those of hemp-intoxicated dervishes, when the drums and tomtoms would keep up a tremendous rolling, while the tribesmen shouted and clapped their hands to excite the dancers to still more frantic efforts." The fiercest of these exhibitions was the sword dance. C.P. Skrine was treated to one such in the evening after his polo match: "I had never seen such a dance – it was thrilling, finer even than the well-known Cuttack [Pashtun] dancing of the North-West Frontier. By the light of three bonfires, with the sixteen-thousand-foot precipices behind the Castle gleaming above them in the moonlight, those Hunza guardsmen danced like men possessed, and yet in perfect time and with every step, every twist and whirl of their swords correct. The wild music, the flickering light of the fires, the rows of watching faces, the swaying of the tall dancers and the rhythmic, inexorable sweep of the swords were for us a never-to-be-forgotten experience."

THE MUGHAL CARAVAN

The travellers from Central Asia, whether they came by way of Afghanistan, the route from Kashgar over the Mintaka Pass, or else from Yarkand through the Buddhist stronghold of Ladakh, would be likely before long to join the great route which led to the leading cities of India, what during the days of the British Raj was titled the Grand Trunk Road. In its genesis, this route can claim as great an antiquity as any other in the web of the Silk Road. Before 200 BCE, trade was conducted on routes paralleling that of the Grand Trunk Road between the ancient cities in northern Pakistan, the Gangetic Plain, and Afghanistan. This continued to be the case in the following centuries, with the route shifting or being extended depending on the rise or fall of cities and empires in India throughout time.

It served as a route of conquest as much as trade. Most famously, it was the route that Babur followed from Afghanistan in his quest to carve out a dominion in the Subcontinent. His victory on the field of Panipat in 1526 at a strategic point near the route allowed him to establish the Mughal Empire, which would endure as the greatest power in India until the rise of the British. Later in the 16th century, Babur's successors were to re-establish and lay down the route afresh, calling it the *Sadak-e-Azam*, or "Great Road", and it was on this foundation that the modern trunk road came to be built during the period of British rule. Rudyard Kipling, in his evocative and much-loved book *Kim* (set against the backdrop of the Great Game in the 1880s), describes it thus: "Look! Brahmins and chumars, bankers and tinkers, barbers and bunnias, pilgrims and potters – all the world going and coming.

Beautiful Buddha sculptures at Jaulian monastery in Taxila, centre of the Buddhist Gandharan Empire (6th century BCE–5th century CE), now part of Pakistan.

The lifelike head of the bronze Fasting Buddha in Lahore Museum.

It is to me as a river from which I am withdrawn like a log after a flood. And truly the Grand Trunk Road is a wonderful spectacle. It runs straight, bearing without crowding India's traffic for fifteen hundred miles – such a river of life as nowhere else exists in the world." Today, in its latest incarnation as a motorised highway, it retains its position as one of the great transport arteries of the Subcontinent.

If the Grand Trunk Road can own an equal antiquity with the routes further afield in Central Asia, in the person of the Mughal emperors it can almost certainly lay claim to the most splendid encountered by the Silk Road's travellers. The wealth of the country, and indeed of its rulers, was needless to say proverbial. After making his conquest, Babur observed in his diary, the *Baburnama*, the first pleasant thing about India was that it was "a large country and has masses of gold and silver". It was part of the work of the emperors to display this wealth by means of gift-giving, magnificence, and the employment of a vast retinue. Such was their duty since it was not only an expression of power but also an economic necessity. The wealth of India was great, but so was its population. Not only did the colossal size of the population allow for a supply of cheap and plentiful labour, but it also compelled the emperors, as the great fount and controllers of the country's riches, to share this wealth widely for the sake of social stability by employing as many people as possible.

The emperors were the leading means of livelihood for the residents of the capital. Such was their dependence on the one hand, and the emperors' need for display on the other, that when the emperor desired to move, his entire establishment was required to move with him. François Bernier, a French doctor in the service of the Emperor Aurangzeb in the mid-17th century, wrote that the whole population of Delhi followed the Great Mughal, "because deriving its employment and maintenance from the court and army, it has no alternative but to follow them in their march or to perish from want during their absence". Hence, the emperor's travel along the Indian roads partook less of the character of travel, and more of that of a migration.

A bullock cart on the Grand Trunk Road in 1895, taken by William Henry Jackson.

The Delhi Gate of that city's Red Fort, built by Mughals, but used by the British as a military camp until Indian independence.

The numbers involved were truly colossal. Everything that the emperor might need, whether by way of work, protection or pleasure, was included in his train. The record office and scribes, the nobles and the treasury, the military escort, artillery and huntsmen were by his side, as were his wives and his harem, artisans and musicians, engineers and labourers, bazaar-traders and merchants – all that was necessary to make such an enormous movement of people possible and, for the emperor, agreeable. With these also came their wives and their families. To reckon up the size of the march was near impossible. "All I can confidently assert," said Bernier, "is that the multitude is prodigious and almost incredible."

At the beginning of the 17th century, Edward Terry, the chaplain of the British Mission to the Emperor, held the numbers involved in such travels to be "no lesse then two hundred thousand men, women, and children." Bernier himself was unwilling to venture a precise figure. "Many are of the opinion that the camp contains between three and four hundred thousand persons; some believe this estimate to be too small, while others consider it rather

A Delhi street scene in 1907 .

exaggerated." Even this did not take account of the baggage animals required to assist in the enterprise. Bernier, attempting to make a reckoning, thought it was in the region of 250,000: "more than one hundred and fifty thousand animals, comprising horses, mules, and elephants; that besides these, there cannot be much less than fifty thousand camels, and nearly as many oxen or horses employed to carry the wives and children, the grain and other provisions..."

For the Mughal emperors, it was not at all seemly to travel light. The notion of travelling clothes did not occur to them, and they arrayed themselves in the same costume as they would wear in the stationary court. A Mughal emperor on the road was an item on display as much as a traveller, and the sight of his opulence was calculated to remind the people of his power. Sir Thomas Roe, the Ambassador who led the mission of which Edward Terry was chaplain, described how the Emperor Jahangir was dressed for the road. On his head he wore a rich turban plumed with long heron feathers; "on one syde hung a ruby unsett, as bigg as a walnutt; on the other syde a diamond as great; in the middle an emralld like a hart, much bigger..." He wore a coat of cloth of gold, a sash adorned with pearls, rubies and diamonds, a chain set with triple rows of pearls, armlets set with diamonds, a gold ring on every finger, and a sword and buckler "sett all over with great diamonds and rubyes". His footwear also was hardly calculated to endure the rigours of a long and difficult journey: "on his feete a payre of embrodered buskings with pearle, the toes sharp and turning up".

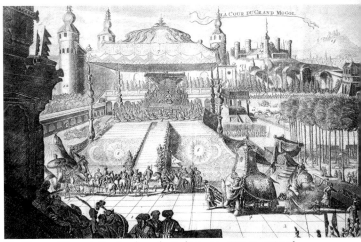

The Voyage of Francois Bernier, *drawn by Paul Maret in 1710, is captioned* "The Court of the Great Mogul" *in French.*

Not, of course, that the Great Mughal had to worry about exertion in the course of travel. His conveyances, in general, allowed him to pass the journeys in the greatest of ease. His manner of travel was various. According to the Emperor Jahangir, it was customary for the great of India when going east "to ride on an elephant with long tusks; when towards the west, to ride a horse of one colour; when towards the north, to go in a litter or palki [palanquin]; when towards the south, to go in a carriage drawn by bullocks". As picturesque was the rule, it seems to have been a custom more honoured in the breech than in the observance; the conveyances were chosen according to convenience, and the horse-drawn carriage was also apt to make an appearance.

Most commonly used to convey the Emperor, according to Bernier, was the *takht-ravan*, or field throne. This was a grand litter or "species of magnificent tabernacle", as Bernier put it, "with painted and gilt pillars and glass windows, that are kept shut when the weather is bad. The four poles of this litter are covered either with scarlet or brocade, and decorated with deep fringes of silk and gold. At the end of each pole are stationed two strong and handsomely dressed men, who are relieved by eight other men constantly in attendance."

Similar to the takht-ravan was the hauze, or howdah. This was "an oval chair with a canopy on pillars... superbly decorated with colours and gold", carried not by attendants but by an elephant. If, however, the emperor chose that he wished to sleep whilst on the journey – and it seems that the lilting

rhythm of the elephant's pace would often persuade the emperor to slumber – it was more convenient for him to be transferred to the *mekdambar*. Again, this was mounted on the back of an elephant, but was far more elaborate than the howdah. It was, in fact, "a small house or square wooden tower, gilt and painted", in which the emperor could lie down on a bed. These two means of transport, in the mind of Bernier, were "by far the most striking and splendid style of travelling, as nothing can surpass the richness and magnificence of the harness and trappings". Of these contrivances, spares were always kept. According to Manucci, an Italian traveller in India at the end of the 17th century, in addition to the travelling throne, there were also three palanquins of different shapes, and five elephants with different litters for him to use "whenever he desired".

The howdah – generally considered to be the most regal way to travel in India.

Besides these, for his greater comfort, there were "eight mules carrying small tents, which are used on the march when the king desires to rest, or to eat a little something, or for any particular necessity. Along with them are two mules carrying clothes, and one mule loaded with essences of various odoriferous flowers".

The grandeur of the emperor's conveyance was much magnified by the extent of his entourage. Ahead of him, there were three divisions of cavalry, each numbering 8,000 men, one forming the vanguard, and one to guard each wing. Around his person, equal columns of men and horsemen in ordered files brandished silver staves "with which they drove off the people when anyone made so bold as to draw near". Others among them carried a multitude of flags and standards with diverse colours and designs so as to represent the virtues of the emperor. Elephants bore on their backs insignia displaying Qur'anic inscriptions to proclaim the emperor's piety; a great spear to signify that the emperor was a conqueror; the model of a crocodile to show that the emperor was lord of the rivers, and another a fish to show that he was lord of the sea. Behind these were a crowd of musicians, some with kettledrums, some with pipes and others with trumpets, all charged with playing loudly, that everyone might know the emperor was approaching.

A grand state entry to the Delhi Durbar in 1903.

Richly caparisoned elephants for the Maharaja of Gwalior.

ravelling behind the party of the emperor, usually up to a distance of half a mile, was the harem. The order of march around it paralleled that of the section around the emperor himself. Manucci, who was able to witness its passing, saw the Emperor Aurangzeb's sister Roshanara Begum at its head, ensconced on an elephant-borne throne similar to a howdah, covered with a dome "made all of enamelled gold, and highly adorned". Instead of being flanked by soldiers, as was the emperor, she was surrounded by 150 female servants, "riding handsome horses, and covered from head to foot with their mantles of various colours, each with a cane in her hand". To the head of these, there marched "a number of bold and aggressive men on foot to drive away everybody, noble or pauper, with blows from sticks and with pushes". Attended also in the midst of the train by a retinue of "several sour-faced eunuchs on horseback, with others on foot", a multitude of other great ladies followed close by on elephants or in palanquins "covered with different nettings of gold thread". The intention of all of this was to keep the "princesses and nobles' wives… shut up in such a manner that they cannot be seen", although they could observe the passers-by. "Truly," wrote Bernier, "it is with difficulty that these ladies can be approached, and they are almost inaccessible to the sight of man. Woe to any unlucky cavalier, however exalted in rank, who, meeting the procession, is found too near. Nothing can exceed the insolence of the tribes of eunuchs and footmen which he has to encounter, and they eagerly avail themselves of any such opportunity to beat a man in the most unmerciful manner."

But far beyond the members of his harem, the emperor was treated with a carefulness and veneration which verged almost on the sacral. No man was permitted to mount before the emperor. His nobles were only permitted to ride horses when the emperor himself was travelling by elephant, but when he was borne in the palanquin they were all expected to go on foot, thus preserving on the journey the exaltation of his rank. As with the Prophet of Islam, whom many stories reputed to have had dozens of secretaries to record his every word and movement, so it was the case for the Mughal Emperor with respect to the progress of his journey. The moment the emperor set forth from the royal pavilion to begin the day's journey, the threshold would be marked, and from here, the emperor's progress would be measured by means of men marching with a rope: "The man in front who has the rope in his hand makes a mark on the ground, and when the man in the rear arrives at this mark he shouts out, and the first man makes a fresh mark, and counts 'two'. Thus they proceed throughout the march, counting 'three', 'four', and so on. Another man on foot holds a score in his hand, and keeps count. If perchance the king asks how far he has travelled, they reply at once, as they know how many of their ropes go to a league." The time that was spent on the journey was similarly measured. Responsible for this was "another man on foot who has charge of the hourglass, and measures the time, and each time announces the number of hours with a mallet on a platter of bronze".

Besides this, his attendants were assiduous in preserving the emperor from any sights that might cause him distress. Emperor Jahangir once ordered that whenever he left his palace his servants should "keep away defective people, such as the blind and those whose noses and ears had been cut off, the leprous and the maimed, and all kinds of sick people, and not permit them to be seen". Hence, whilst on the road not only did his attendants go ahead to water the roads and scent the air with perfumes, but others would go ahead with a white cloth "which is used to cover over any dead animal or human being found on the road".

The journeys might have seemed to the Great Mughal mere expeditions of ease, but to preserve the emperor in his pleasure, let alone look after the needs of such a vast number of people on the road together, was a huge logistical challenge. For example, just to feed the emperor after his accustomed manner required the labour of dozens of servants, working to a tight and wearisome timetable. "It is the custom of the court," wrote Manucci, "when the king is to march the next day, that at ten o'clock of the night the royal kitchen should start. It consists of fifty camels loaded with supplies, and fifty well-fed cows to give milk. Also there are sent dainties in charge of cooks, from each one of whom the preparation of only one dish is required. For this department there is an official of standing, whose business it is to send in the dishes sealed up in bags of Malacca velvet…" Similarly, the emperor travelled with not one but two private camps, one of which would travel a day in advance of the other so that he should be guaranteed to find at the "end of every journey a camp fully prepared for his reception". The statistics of even one of these private camps, known as *pish-khanehs* or "before-houses" because they went ahead of the emperor, stretch credibility. To transport them, recorded Bernier, "the aid of more than sixty elephants, two hundred camels, one hundred mules, and one hundred men-porters is required". The elephants would be entrusted with the carriage of the large tents and their heavy poles, the smaller tents by the mules, the general luggage and kitchen utensils by the camels, and to the porters "the lighter and more valuable articles" such as the "porcelain used at the King's table" or else his "painted and gilt beds".

Should there be any unevenness or blockage in the road, or should there be any need to ready a place for the camp, there travelled close to the baggage "one thousand labourers, with axes, mattocks, spades, and pick-axes to clear any difficult passage…" And should the emperor decide in the course of the journey to go

A hunting leopard, carried in a cart with a lord's retinue until such time as he decided to go on a hunt.

hunting, it was by no means a spontaneous matter, but rather the ground had been prepared long before. Near Delhi and Agra, and along great courses of the Jumna (Yamuna) River close by the Great Road all the way to Lahore, wide tracts of uncultivated land were set aside as royal game reserves, and were protected by gamekeepers. In them flourished amongst other things antelope, which were hunted with tame cheetahs, grey oxen, which were pursued with "arrows, short spikes, swords, and musketoons", and cranes, which were caught with hawks and other birds of prey. Yet to the mind of the Mughal princes, the greatest sport was afforded by the pursuit of the lion, which however required a protracted contrivance on the part of the gamekeepers long before the emperor was due to pass by on the road:

"As a preliminary step, an ass is tied near the spot where the gamekeepers have ascertained the lion retires. The wretched animal is soon devoured, and after so ample a meal the lion never seeks for other prey, but without molesting either oxen, sheep, or shepherds, goes in quest of water, and after quenching his thirst, returns to his former place of retirement. He sleeps until the next morning, when he finds and devours another ass, which the gamekeepers have brought to the same spot. In this way they contrive, during several days, to allure the lion and to attach him to one place; and when information is received of the King's approach, they fasten at the spot an ass where so many others have been sacrificed, down whose throat a large quantity of opium has been forced. This last meal is of course intended to produce a soporific effect upon the lion. The next operation is to spread, by means of the peasantry of the adjacent villages, large nets, made on purpose, which are gradually drawn closer... Everything being in this state of preparation, the King appears on an elephant protected in places with thin plates of iron, and attended by the Grand Master of the Hunt, some Omrahs [Amirs, or Lords] mounted on elephants, and a great number both of gourze-berdars [macebearers] on horseback and of gamekeepers on foot, armed with half-pikes. He immediately approaches the net on the outside, and fires at the lion with a large musketoon. The wounded animal makes a spring at the elephant, according to the invariable practice of lions, but is arrested by the net; and the King continues to discharge his musketoon, until the lion is at length killed."

A justification was made of the time that the emperor spent on his journeys hunting, which was also used as a justification of the journeys themselves. Hunting was always a way, in the view of Bernier, for the emperor to increase his knowledge of his domains. It gave him an opportunity to disappear incognito for a time from the cumbersome equipage of his travel, and enquire into the conditions of the people and the army, the revenues and taxation of a region, or else the quality of its government and administration. Similarly, when he was back on the road, an official travelling with him "provided a description of the provinces, lands, and villages through which the king must pass, in order to explain at once if the king asked what land and whose province it was through which he was then passing. These men," wrote Bernier, "can give him an account of everything down to the petty villages, and the revenue obtained from the land." Thus it was that the emperor, by means of his travels, might "[lift] up such as are oppressed, and [punish] the oppressors."

A classical miniature painting of Sha Jahan – he liked to be shown with a halo around his head, implying a connection to a higher plane.

At the end of a day of travel, a night of rest beckoned in the camp. However, not suitable for the emperor was any village or caravanserai that they might find along the way. Such was the scale of the travelling establishment that even were anything of sufficient luxury to be discovered, it would by no means be sufficient for the colossal size of the emperor's entourage. Every time the emperor came to the end of a day's stage, usually between ten and twelve miles, a new camp was built. However, such a creation had less the character of an encampment and more, in the words of the Mughal historian Abraham Eraly, of "a moveable city". Such was the view of the travellers who accompanied the emperor on his travels. Some held that it was of the same extent as 17th century London. Thomas Roe went further, and ventured that its circumference was "little lesse then twenty English miles". Bernier disagreed, holding that in general it was not less than five miles, but said nothing to contradict Roe's assertion that the Mughal camp on the march "may equall almost any Towne in Europe for greatnesse".

It was the job of the Emperor's Grand Quartermaster to travel one day ahead of the main convoy and choose a spot suitable for the encampment. At first, in the centre of it he would mark out a square, 300 paces in length, which 100 pioneers would immediately clear and level, raising high platforms of earth for the pitching of the royal tents. Around it he would erect screens, seven or eight feet in height, of the thickest and finest calico decorated with patterns of flowers. Aside from this, the complex was guarded with an encirclement of canons, and an empty *cordon sanitaire* of nearly 1,000 feet, where only guards were permitted to patrol.

Within the royal complex, the arrangement of tents would replicate everything that was to be found in a Mughal palace, and be equally suitable for the discharge of imperial government. Aside from the emperor's private tents, and tents for the use of the harem, there were grand pavilions for audiences with noblemen and officials, a smaller tent for the meeting of the emperor's privy council, where "all the important concerns of the kingdom are transacted", tents where fast horses were kept in case of emergencies, and tents where the emperor's lords kept guard. Within the great tents of audience, the emperor was presented on a stage under "under a spacious canopy of velvet or flowered silk". The tents themselves, recorded Bernier, were similarly sumptuous. Externally, they were covered with "a strong and coarse red cloth, ornamented with large and variegated stripes; but the inside is lined with beautiful hand-painted chintz... the ornamentation of which is set off by rich figured satin of various colours, or embroideries of silk, silver, and gold, with deep and elegant fringes. Cotton mats, three or four inches in thickness, are spread over the whole floor, and these again are covered with a splendid carpet, on which are placed large square brocade cushions to lean upon. The tents are supported by painted and gilt pillars."

(Top) *Snake charmers in 1903 – they are still a popular entertainment today.*
(Bottom) *Professional dancing girls in Delhi, 1903.*

An exquisite pavilion in Delhi's Red Fort illustrates the perfect symmetry, from grand design to intricate detail, that is a hallmark of classic Mughal architecture.

fter the Quartermaster had dealt with the emperor's own precinct, he would mark out a network of streets radiating from the royal encampment, but usually tending in the direction that the next stage of travel was to follow. A royal bazaar, from which the army and camp followers were provisioned, was established along the first main street leading from the royal tents, and other bazaars "neither so long nor so spacious" were laid out perpendicular to it. These supplied "forage, rice, butter, and other necessary articles of life". Specific areas were assigned to specific products, so that "every man knowes readily where to seeke his wants". The locations of the bazaars were marked with "extremely long poles stuck in the ground at the distance of three hundred paces from each other, bearing red standards, and surmounted with the tails of the Great Tibet cows [yaks], which have the appearance of so many periwigs". The yak tail standard, showing the royal association of the bazaar, was since the earliest days of Central Asian history an emblem of royal dignity, and camp bazaars continued to be so marked well into the days of the British Raj.

Amongst the bazaars, at regular intervals, were laid out the precincts of the noblemen, or omrahs. These were laid out after the fashion of the emperor's enclosure, but never on so grand a scale. A number of the omrahs perhaps might have had the resources to challenge the emperor in splendour, but were careful not to do so, lest "the King perceive it and command that the tents be thrown down". For the same reason,

they avoided the use of the colour red in their decoration, it belonging wholly to the use of the emperor. Finally, in amongst all of these noblemen's precincts and bazaars were permitted to encamp the other members of the convoy, the soldiers, tradesmen, labourers, and their collected family members.

With so many people coming together to encamp at one, despite the best efforts of the Quartermaster to demarcate the camp – and according to travellers this was a process that the practised officials and engineers were able to accomplish within four hours – chaos was only to be expected. Dust kicked up by the travellers arriving at the site would obscure the boundary marks for the royal and noble enclosures, the progress of camels and men was impeded by others pitching their tents, and minor officers whose areas were not marked out by the Quartermaster came to blows as they fought over the best spots for their own camp. This was intensified as they objected to any "strange" tents being fixed near their own, or those of their wives. Once you were in the midst of the morass of these lower officials setting up their tents, "a horde of their lusty varlets, with cudgels in their hands" would not allow anyone to interfere with the ground marked out by their masters, recalled Bernier; "you then naturally retrace your steps, and find that while you have been employed in unavailing efforts to pass at one end, your retreat has been cut off at the other. There is now no means of extricating your laden camels but by menace and entreaty; outrageous passion, and calm remonstrance..."

However, the time of greatest annoyance in the camp, decided Bernier, was perhaps the evening, "when business calls you to any distance. This is the time when the common people cook their victuals with a fire made of cow and camel dung and green wood. The smoke of so many fires of this kind, when there is little wind, is highly offensive, and involves the atmosphere in total darkness." Such was the thickness of the smog that it was easy to lose one's way, and travellers had to be guided by the "aguacy-du" [Akasdiah, or Light of the Heavens], a great light suspended from a pole around 12 metres high like a ship's mast, which was the only thing visible when every other object in the camp was "enveloped in impenetrable darkness". Such conditions were also perfect for thieves, and despite the employment of scores of watchmen carrying torches and shouting "Kaber-dar!" (Beware!), and other soldiers patrolling and blowing trumpets, robberies were frequent.

For all this, the Mughal camp, in terms of its opulence and sheer extent was without parallel both in Asia and also perhaps in history. Certainly there has been little to compete with it in modern times, and similar phenomena were only to be found in the ancient world, with the progress of Persian monarchs with their wealth, harems and myriad armies – if, that is, the figures of historians are to be believed. At any rate, it was with justification that Bernier found the sight of the royal encampment "striking and magnificent"; that Edward Terry held that it was "spacious and glorious... very beautiful to behold"; and Thomas Roe declared that the camp was "one of the wonders of my little experience".

MODERN-DAY HIGHLIGHTS

ST PETERSBURG TO
VLADIVOSTOK AND BEIJING

ew countries in the world capture the imagination with as much fervour as Russia. We think of Russians as all passion and cultural creativity, their artistic achievements filled with an intense emotional strength, from soul-stirring classical music to romantic literature that is truly epic in scale. In its architecture as well the Russian spirit soars towards the sublime, from the modest but beautiful window carvings that grace most country peasants' *dachas* to the grandiose 18th century edifices of Imperial Russia and the fantastical towers, onion domes and sky-piercing spires of its cathedrals and palaces.

There is no better way to explore the Russian way of life, character and cultural legacy than by visiting its two greatest cities, St Petersburg and Moscow, and riding the equally epic Trans-Siberian Railway that spans this, the world's largest country. Therefore, as the great 19th century dramatist Nikolai Gogol put it:

On with the journey!…
Russia! Russia!
When I see you… my eyes
are lit up with supernatural power. Oh what a
glittering, wondrous infinity of space… What a
strange, alluring, enthralling, wonderful world!

Catherine's Palace – an essential day trip from St Petersburg.

St Petersburg is, as its name suggests, the legacy of Peter the Great, who wanted to create a brand-new Russian capital to rival the great metropolises of Western Europe that he had visited as a younger man. Rising from the marshes of the Neva River, this somewhat improbable vision was indeed realised in the most impressive fashion, and soon St Petersburg was being dubbed the "Venice of the North". Today, it remains an astonishingly beautiful city, one that begs to be explored on foot. A stroll along the canal embankments and channels of the Neva, which wind around and through the streets of the city, is an enchanting experience, the water reflecting rows of glorious 18th century façades.

Must-see sites include the needle-like spire of the **Peter and Paul Cathedral**, which stands out like a beacon in the midst of the original citadel, the **Peter and Paul Fortress** on the north bank of the Neva. The south bank boasts the wonderful **Hermitage Museum**, housed in the buildings that once comprised the tsar's Winter Palace. The Hermitage is one of the world's greatest museums, and is worthy of more than a single day's exploration. Beside it is the **Palace Square**, a work of architectural genius with the **Alexander Column** at its centre, and to the west is the **Admiralty** and **Senate (Decembrist's) Square**, where the magnificent **Bronze Horseman** stands, with golden-domed **St Isaac's Cathedral** facing it to the south.

Still the city's main thoroughfare, **Nevsky Prospekt** offers a walk through 300 years of history, with the **Church of the Savior on the Blood** a favourite stopping-off point. St Petersburg's collection of museums and theatres also deserve mention, though they are too numerous to name individually.

Almost 30 kilometres west of the city is Peter the Great's Summer Palace, **Peterhof (Petrodvorets)**. This superb complex was designed to resemble Versailles in France, and rivals it in ambition and grandeur, with the great **Cascade Fountain** in its gardens a highlight. An excellent way to reach Peterhof in summer is by hydrofoil from the Neva River in front of the Hermitage, but it is accessible by train and bus as well.

(Left) Downtown St Petersburg is intersected by three main canals, the Moika, Griboyedov and Fontanka, lined by beautiful 19th century façades. (Right) Astonishing gilt towers crown exquisite Catherine's Palace.

Twenty-four kilometres south of St Petersburg is another imperial monument to architectural splendour: **Catherine's Palace** in the town of **Tsarskoye Selo (Pushkin)**. This Baroque masterpiece was the longest palace in the world (300 metres) when completed, and its glorious blue façade and golden domes are matched by the incredible gilded halls and rooms of its interior. Beyond Tsarskoye Selo is **Pavlovsk Park**, the old royal hunting grounds, and if you continue south you will come to **Novgorod**, one of the oldest towns in Russia, whose riverside Kremlin fortress dates back to about 1000 CE.

s the capital of the Middle Age principality of Muscovy, **Moscow** was Russia's political, cultural and commercial centre in the 15th century. Under Ivan the Great it became the capital of the Russian Empire, the largest empire in the world, and he brought in Europe and Russia's greatest architects to turn it into a city so wondrous that "reality embodied fantasy on an unearthly scale".

Although much of that heavenly splendour was destroyed by fire, a host of wonderful sights remain or have been rebuilt, and Moscow still symbolises the soul of the nation. Alexander Pushkin, one of the great Russian poets, said of it: "...in the shimmer and light of the white walls and golden domes, Moskva lies great and splendid before us... O Moskva have I thought of you! Moskva how violently the name plucks at any Russian heart!"

Initial perceptions of the modern city of Moscow may not tally with this heartfelt emotion, but once you enter the city centre and stand in front of the gilded domes of the palaces and churches of the former tsars, rising up from within the mighty walls of the **Kremlin**, you will start to perceive the effect it had on Russians and other visitors of times past. Outside the citadel's crenellated walls lies Red Square, site of **Lenin's Mausoleum** and dominated by Ivan the Terrible's fairytale creation, **St Basil's Cathedral**.

Moscow epitomises Russia's new paradox: hyper-consumerism sitting cheek-by-jowl with profound spirituality. You can browse the high-priced shops of GUM, the state department store and the largest shopping centre in Russia, stretching 2.5 kilometres in total on its three levels, linked by ornate bridges and topped by an enormous glass roof. Exiting, you are then within walking distance of at least a dozen ornate churches and cathedrals, from the gleaming **Kazan Cathedral** on the northeast corner of Red Square (reconstructed in 1993) to the **Cathedral of the Assumption** within the Kremlin itself, where the tsars were crowned.

The area east of Red Square is called **Kitai-Gorod**, and was the merchant area of old Moscow, where most foreigners lived. All the city's main roads radiate out from Red Square, linking up with the ring roads like spokes of a wheel – a walk along **Nikolskaya Street** and **Ilyinka Street**, with side trips into the alleyways between, will still uncover shopping gems, with everything from Gucci to old book stores.

Lovers of museums will be in heaven in Moscow (and St Petersburg) – highlights include the **Armory Palace**, Russia's oldest museum, situated in the Kremlin grounds and housing a fantastic collection of weaponry and kingly gifts to the tsars that date back to the 13th century; the **Pushkin Museum of Fine Arts** just west of the Kremlin; and the **State Historical Museum**, at the northern end of Red Square. And no trip to Moscow would complete without a visit to either the **Bolshoi Theatre** or the **Moscow State Circus** – or both, depending on your tastes.

he immensity of the distance between Moscow and Vladivostok on Russia's Pacific coast must have seemed almost insurmountable in the days before the Trans-Siberian rail line. Today, however, it's possible to cross the Russian heartland to the Ural Mountains, traverse the seemingly endless steppe to the Altai Mountains and Lake Baikal, and navigate the wilderness of eastern Siberia to Vladivostok by the Pacific shore in a matter of just six days, should you so wish. In doing so, though, you would be missing a host of exciting opportunities.

Heading east from Moscow's Yaroslavsky Terminal, the first major town is **Yaroslavl**, 250 kilometres northeast of the capital at the confluence of the Volga and Kotorosl rivers. The historic section of the city is a World Heritage site, with the **Transfiguration of Our Saviour Monastery** and its 16th century cathedral the main sights – it was from here that an army set out to liberate Moscow from Polish invaders in the 17th century. In 2010 the city celebrates its 1,000th anniversary.

Here the railway crosses the mighty **Volga River**, Europe's longest river system that winds south to the Caspian Sea, along the way accumulating a number of major towns and cities that owe their existence to its life-bringing flow. Both **Nizhny Novgorod** and **Kazan** lie on its banks, and both boast illustrious pasts, when they were strongholds of historical principalities – as such they each boast atmospheric, protected Kremlins of their own. During the 19th century Nizhny Novgorod became a major trading centre between East and West, while Kazan is the capital of the Republic of Tatarstan and is the centre of Tatar culture in Russia.

Moving east, the Trans-Siberian arrows towards the Ural Mountains, the natural boundary between Europe and Asia. Still on the western, European side is **Perm**, one of Russia's largest cities situated in hilly territory by the **Kama River**. Few travellers stop here – indeed the majority of foreigners riding the train never stop off at any towns between Moscow and Irkutsk – but Perm, and other "remote" cities in Siberia can still boast impressive buildings and culture, as well as a rare and fascinating insight into "provincial" Russian life.

On the eastern side of the Urals, at the beginning of the open steppe lands that lead into Siberia, lies **Yekaterinburg**, a modern city renowned for its theatres and general artistic bent, but most famous to foreigners as the place where the last royal family of Russia – the Romanovs – were murdered by Bolsheviks after the Russian Revolution in 1918. The Ipatiev House, where the killings took place, is no more; on the site now stands a beautiful church, the **Church on Blood in Honour of All Saints Resplendent in the Russian Land**.

Tyumen claims to have been the first Russian outpost in Siberia, as the empire spread inexorably east. Another early 17th century Russian town to the south is **Kurgan** (on a secondary Trans-Sib rail line connecting Omsk with Samara in southern Russia); both these urban centres are situated on pancake-flat steppe, an indication of what lies eastwards.

The next major town is **Omsk**, which lies by the **Irtysh River** about halfway along its meandering course from the Altai Mountains to the Arctic Ocean. Omsk is the second largest Russian city east of the Urals, but is 2,700 kilometres away from Moscow, and despite being among Russia's most landlocked urban centres, is only 87 metres above sea level. Already a major city during the second half of the 19th

(Above) *Yekaterinburg's Church on Blood, constructed on the site of the Ipatiev House where the Russian royal family, the Romanovs, were executed by Bolsheviks.* (Above right) *A Trans-Siberian train skirts Lake Baikal on a misty day.*

century, Omsk boasts an array of impressive Imperial architecture along **Lubyinsky Prospekt** and **Lenin Street**, and happily has kept some of the old wooden merchant's houses that once filled the town.

The city of **Novosibirsk** was only founded in 1893, at the site where the Trans-Siberian Railway was to cross the might **Ob River**. This spelled disaster for **Tomsk**, the former main town of the region, for with the railway came rapid development. Today, Novosibirsk is a modern, skyscraper-strewn city of 1.5 million, but few travellers stop here, unless it is to visit the lovely **Altai Mountains** region to the south, or switch to the **Turkestan-Siberian Railway** line which from here heads south into Kazakhstan and Central Asia.

The Trans-Sib continues east across the Siberian taiga to the next major river crossing, arriving at **Krasnoyarsk** on the Yenisei River (you will notice a pattern emerging of major cities located always on the banks of the largest rivers that course across the Siberian plain). Some adventurous souls jump off in this fairly industrial city in order to follow the Yenisei upstream into the **Tuvan People's Republic**, an incredibly remote and little-visited region rich in early human history. Tuvans are a Mongolized Turkic people famous for their ancient oral tradition, epitomised by the emotive throat-singing.

Taishet (Tayshet) is a major rail junction, where the **Baikal Amur Mainline** junction cuts off to the northeast towards Tynda, while the main Trans-Sib line heads southeast towards Irkustk and Lake Baikal. The city of **Irkutsk** is 5,185 kilometres east of Moscow, and by now the flat steppe of western Siberia has been left far behind – the city, situated along the banks of the Angara River, lies within rolling hills covered by thick taiga forest. This topography, combined with the fact that it is smaller than many of the cities through which the railway has passed in the west, makes it far more appealing to travellers. Add to this the fact that it is conveniently close to the obvious attractions of **Lake Baikal**, and said lake exerts a tempering influence on its otherwise continental climate, and it's understandable that this is a must-stop destination on any Trans-Siberian journey.

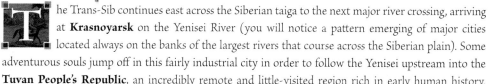

(Right) *The colourful brickwork and onion domes of an Orthodox cathedral make a striking landmark in Omsk.* (Far right) *A massive bust of Lenin's head in Ulan-Ude – a number of Soviet-era monuments remain in the cities of the Russian Far East.*

The city itself is quite pleasant, with some streets still sporting **traditional wooden houses**, complete with exquisite carved ornamentation around the windows and gables. The 18th century **Church of the Epiphany** has an unusual mixture of cultural elements, and the **Decembrists Museum** is worth a visit, as is **Znamensky Monastery**, **Gagarin Boulevard** and the riverfront promenade.

Outside the city, there are a number of side trips worth considering. To the north, halfway up the western coast of Lake Baikal is **Olkhon Island**, the lake's largest at more than 700 square kilometres. This is a sacred place for the indigenous inhabitants, filled with legend and tradition. Its coastline alternates between rocky cliffs and sandy bays, and just offshore is the deepest point in the lake. Seventy kilometres south of the city, where the **Angara River** emerges from the lake and starts its course to meet up with the Yenisei, is the village of **Listvyanka**, once a busy port filled with cargoes of tea, meat, fish and furs. Today it offers a lovely rustic atmosphere, as well as superb views of the lake from the surrounding hills, and the **Baikal Museum**, devoted to the history, flora and fauna of this unique body of water. Between here and Irkutsk is the **Taltsy Museum of Traditional Siberian Architecture**, whose highlight is a recreation of the 17th century fortress of Ilimsk that was transported from its original site when the Angara Valley was flooded to create a dam in the 1970s.

The train journey itself is a great pleasure in this region. After the relatively monotonous steppe and taiga, the train line's course along the southern lakeside is a stunning visual feast across cerulean water to snow-capped mountain peaks on the far side. The next major stop is at Ulan-Ude, where the Trans-Mongolian Railway line turns south into Mongolia (more of this later). **Ulan-Ude** is the capital of the Buryat (Buriat) Republic, the traditional home of the Mongol **Buriats** and the Siberian **Evenks** – tours to visit and spend time with these hospitable nomadic tribes can be arranged in the city or Irkutsk.

he Trans-Siberian Railway now enters the Russian Far East, running through the eastern Siberian towns of **Chita** (where the Trans-Manchurian Line cuts directly east into China and Harbin, and on to Vladivostok or south to Beijing) and **Skovodorino** as it follows the **Amur River** on its northern side. This is a land of thick taiga forest wilderness, often swathed in mist and fog. At the confluence of the Amur and Ussuri River stands the city of **Khabarovsk**, only 30 kilometres from the Chinese border and 800 kilometres north of Vladivostok, which is now only an overnight ride away. Originally a military outpost, it changed hands between the Russian Cossacks and the Chinese Qing Dynasty but finally settled as part of Russia, with the Trans-Sib rail line bringing increasing prosperity. Khabarovsk is a surprisingly cosmopolitan place, probably due to investment from Korea and Japan, and the constant flow of Chinese who travel north for business. **Amursky Boulevard** is a vibrant, bustling street, and the city's **Orthodox cathedral** is a beautiful site, its tall, narrow façade almost skyscraper-esque.

And so the Trans-Siberian Railway enters its final leg, as it turns sharply south to its conclusion on the Pacific coast at **Vladivostok**. This strategically important port is the home of the Russian Pacific Fleet, but was little more than a military stronghold until the railway allowed it to boom as a trading metropolis. Before the Cold War its population was a mix of Korean, Chinese and Russians, but between 1958 and 1991 it was closed to foreigners, with non-Russians being deported. When it was opened to tourism in 1992, through the 1990s it once again became an international melting pot, and imports and investment from Korea, China and Japan fuelled a frenzy of growth.

Today, Vladivostok is a city of paradoxes. Its location and history give it an air of romance and excitement, the city centre's waterfront promenade replete with grand old buildings and the Central Square, **Ploschad Bortsov Revolutsy**, dominated by two massive memorial statues. But it suffers from terrible pollution because of the many industrial sites around the city, and in recent years it has become horrendously expensive, as "new money" floods in from the Far East's tiger economies. For those spending a couple or more days in town, a trip to the **Arsenev Regional History Museum** is recommended, and to the **C-56 Submarine** that has been placed on dry land near the Naval Memorial and is open for visitors to wander around and inside.

For some transcontinental travellers, an attractive alternative to the eastern section of the Trans-Sib is instead to take the **Trans-Mongolian Railway** south from Ulan-Ude, traversing the mountains, steppe and desert of **Mongolia** before crossing into China and heading straight to Beijing. The train crosses the border at the small border towns of **Naushki** on the Russian side and **Sukhbaatar** on the Mongolian side – the old road border crossing at **Kiakhta** is 25 kilometres to the east, facing Altanbulag (known as Maimachin during its Chinese-controlled period) across a river.

Once on Mongolian soil, the train rumbles through Mongolia's northern Selenge *aimag* (province), today its breadbasket, as this is a major wheat-growing region. It's a straight run of 280 kilometres southeast to the country's capital, **Ulaanbaatar**, from where you can base yourself for tours into Mongolia's diverse environments. The city is a sprawling, pleasant place to spend time, with plenty of attractions in itself. The central **Suhbaatar Square** is a good place to start, surrounded by the massive edifices of the **Ceremonial Hall**, where a huge seated statue of Chinggis Khaan (Genghis Khan) gazes outwards, the **State Palace** parliament building, the **Cultural Palace** and the colonnaded **Opera and Ballet House**. In the middle a statue of the Mongolian hero Suhbaatar sits astride a horse, arm raised as he faces east, towards China.

Ulaanbaatar has some beautiful temple complexes, including the **Choiijin Lama Temple**, the **Gandan Monastery** (complete with a 25-metre-tall golden statue of Janraiseg), and the **Ondor-Gegeen Temple**. Also well worth visiting are the **National Museum of Mongolian History**, the **Zanabazar Museum of Fine Arts**, and the beautifully preserved **Bogd Khaan Palace Museum**, the old winter palace of the religious leader of Mongolian Buddhism. Just outside town, on the southern slopes of **Bogd Khan Uul** (mountain) is the **Zaisan Memorial**, a large circular mosaic illustrating the friendship between Mongolia and Russia. The view of the city from here is excellent – but it will only serve to highlight the natural splendour of the land on its doorstep.

Even those with the shortest of stopovers must try to make a foray out into the Mongolian countryside. Within easy reach of the city are beautiful grasslands where nomadic *gers* (yurts) stand near grazing herds of horses, cattle, fat-tailed sheep and cashmere goats. The **Bogd Khan National Park** sports hill steppe and thick forests of pine, birch larch and cedar, and an hour northeast of the city is **Gorkhi Terelj National Park**, at the southern end of the Hentii Mountains, a beautiful region of stunning rock formations (such as **Turtle Rock**, see page 174), larch forests, sweeping grasslands and swift-flowing streams.

If you have more time on your hands, Mongolia is a treasure chest of natural and cultural wonders – from the historic and architectural beauty of the **Amarbayasgalant Monastery** and **Erdene Zuu Monastery** near ancient **Karakorum**, to the natural wonderland of the Altai Mountains and **Altai Tavan Bogd National Park** in the far west, where Kazakhs live and still hunt with eagles; the gorgeous **Hovsgol Lake** in the north; or the dinosaur fossil mecca of the **Flaming Cliffs** in the **Gobi Desert**, where you can also visit the mighty sand dunes of the **Khongoryn Els**.

Once back on the Trans-Mongolian, however, the train courses southeast through rolling steppe and into scrub desert, finally entering the Gobi proper, a vast, inhospitable landscape of rock and sand. Passing through **Saynshand** it arrives at the border, where at the Chinese town of **Erenhot** (Ereen or Erlian) the train must switch tracks to the Chinese "standard" gauge from the Mongolian "Russian" gauge. From there, it's a nine-hour ride across China's autonomous province of **Inner Mongolia** to the old fortress town of **Zhangjiakou** near the **Great Wall**, long known as Kalgan and through which camel caravans would pass on the ancient Tea Road from Dadu (Beijing) to Urga (Ulaanbaatar). The final stretch of rail line crosses a vast plain where fields of rice and vegetables are interspersed with modern Chinese towns, and roads are lined with poplar trees as wind breaks. Mountain ridges loom on the horizon, the train whistles into a number of tunnels carved through rugged hills, and finally the train's terminus is reached: **Beijing**.

(Above) *The Zaisan Memorial is a huge mural on a hill just outside Ulaanbaatar, commemorating Russo-Mongolian friendship and offering great views over the city. (Right) Horse trekking on the Mongolian steppe in summer can be an inspirational experience. (Below) A girl of the Evenks tribe wears traditional dress – Evenks are a Tungusic people and one of the Russian north's indigenous tribes. (Below right) Ancient deer stones near Lake Hovsgol in the Mongolian north – these monumental stelae can be up to 3,000 years old.*

The Silk Road: Beijing to Istanbul

Anyone who has read tales of Silk Road merchants, Buddhist pilgrims and Central Asian explorers, or marvelled at the exploits of Alexander the Great, Sven Hedin or Marco Polo, will at some point have wondered what it must be like to travel in their footsteps to those distant, exotic and almost mythical lands. Most of us who have fondled a creased map of Inner Asia have traced our fingers in wonder over its monochrome yellow deserts and white glacial peaks. Murmuring the words "Samarkand", "Bactria" or "Kashgaria", names so resonant with history that they simply define the exctic and remote, is enough to quicken the pulse of a certain type of traveller.

Today's travellers need not raise an expedition to reach the cave art of Dunhuang, nor dodge bands of roving slave traders to taste Turkestan's forbidden fruits. Tourists to Central Asia can sleep in a converted caravanserai or ride one of Ferghana's famous horses out to an ecofriendly yurt camp. Anyone with the requisite fistful of visas can take the golden road to Samarkand, travel by rail across the Eurasian landmass or journey by jeep over the high snow-swept passes of the Tien Shan.

Central Asia is indeed an epic canvas crisscrossed by the ghosts of past travellers. From hardy pilgrims like Xuanzang and Faxian to marauding figures like Tamerlane and Genghis Khan, the modern tourist travels always in the footsteps of history. Stand at the base of Bukhara's Kalon (Kalyan) Minaret and feel a frisson of excitement when you remember that Genghis Khan once stood less than a stone's throw away. It's not difficult to catch echoes of a Sogdian trader in the faces of today's Tajik merchants, or glimpse the Turkic hordes in the eyes of a Kyrgyz or Kazakh nomad.

The Silk Road is more than a string of tourist sites – it's a journey between cultures. As you progress along the Silk Road the land shifts and faces change; cheekbones rise and fall and noses become more prominent; eyes change hue and hats change shape. Chinese yields to Indo-European, and Turkic mixes with Persian, as Central Asia bleeds into the Middle East.

 he classic route along the Chinese Silk Road generally starts in **Beijing**, a city drenched in history. A site for important cities since the Warring States Period of 473–221 BCE, it has had many names over the centuries, but came to real prominence under the Mongol Yuan Dynasty of Kublai Khan, when it was rebuilt as **Dadu**, the "Great Capital". The Ming and Qing dynasties built on this, and the People's Republic of China protected much of the city's historical wonders, so today any visitor would be wise to allow at least three or four days to take in the best of its attractions. A trip out to the **Great Wall** is a priority, though choose between the reconstructed perfection and attendant crowds of **Badaling**, 65 kilometres north of the city, the slightly farther and less crowded **Mutianyu**, or the more distant and dilapidated – but atmospheric – section between **Jinshanling** and **Simatai**. In the city centre the **Forbidden City** is just as essential, and deserves a full day of exploration, while the same is true of the **Summer Palace** in the city's northwest and the **Temple of Heaven** in the south. In between these major sites, take time to stroll around any of the city's many other small parks, and wander the *hutong* alleys to the north of the Forbidden City before heading to the **Bell and Drum Towers** and the **Hou Hai** lake area in the evening.

Although most travellers head straight from Beijing to Xi'an, between these two historical powerhouses are a few destinations worth considering. **Kaifeng**, on the south bank of the Yellow River near Zhengzhou, is one of the Seven Ancient Capitals of China (it was the seat of the Northern Song Dynasty, 960–1127 CE), and boasts the 57-metre **Iron Pagoda**, as well as many reconstructed buildings. To the west is another ancient capital, **Luoyang**, which has been an important site since Neolithic times. Near the city are the **Longmen Caves**, an amazing set of Buddhist rock carvings, statues, pagodas and steles set on both sides of the Yi River that date to the 5th century CE.

Though it can be argued that the Silk Road began in Beijing, Kaifeng and Luoyang at various times through China's history, most still consider its original source to be in **Xi'an**, China's first true imperial capital. Xi'an is famously home to the **Terracotta Warriors** of Qin Shihuangdi, the unifying emperor of the Qin Dynasty in the 3rd century BCE. The three pits of the complex, an hour outside the city, need most of the day to be fully appreciated, and like Beijing, Xi'an has so many archaeological treasures to offer that it's wise to allow at least a couple of days here. There's the **Banpo Museum**, built on the site of a Neolithic village discovered in 1953; the **National Museum of Shaanxi History**, which houses an astounding collection of fantastic exhibits; the **Yang Ling** burial complex out near the airport, where an army of third life-size figures was buried, à la Terracotta Warriors, by the Han emperor Jingdi; and of course the **Big Goose Pagoda** within the grounds of the Da Cien Temple. Don't forget also to walk the mighty **Ming City Wall**, and shop your way through the **Muslim Quarter** to the **Great Mosque**.

From Xi'an, the Silk Road travels – as it always did – along the Hexi Corridor, edging between the Gobi Desert and the Tibetan Plateau, up into Chinese Turkestan, now known as Xinjiang. An overnight train brings you to **Lanzhou**, on the dusty banks of the Yellow River, where you can visit the provincial museum and night market. From June to October it's possible to take a two-hour boat trip to the Buddhist caves of **Bingling Si**. From Lanzhou the train runs to **Jiayuguan** and the spectacularly located fortress that marked the symbolic end of the Chinese Empire at Jiayuguan Pass. A half-day side trip to one of the most westerly sections of the Great Wall offers a fine counterpoint if you visited the eastern wall near Beijing.

Another overnight train (or summertime flight) replaces the three-week plod faced by Silk Road camel caravans, passing through the ruined beacon towers of the **Jade Gate (Yumen)** to Dunhuang via an extension rail line from Liuyuan. **Dunhuang** features one of the artistic highlights of western China, the **Mogao Caves**, where you should plan at least a full day to see the caves, and also get out into the monumental **Mingsha Sand Dunes** for a taste of the desert.

Next stop Xinjiang. Yet another overnight train or flight takes you 400 kilometres to Urumqi or Turpan. **Urumqi** is a modern Chinese city that rarely stirs the soul, though the beautiful Tien Shan mountain regions of **Heavenly Lake** and **Nan Shan**, with their Kazakh nomadic encampments, are within easy reach. **Turpan** is a charming and relaxed Uygur town, lined with shady trellises covered in vines. Excellent and easily arranged side trips to the ruins of **Gaochang** (Karakhoja), **Jiaohe** (Yarkhoto), the **Bezeklik Caves** and **Astana Tombs** offer plenty of diversions, and you can reward your sightseeing efforts with a cold Xinjiang beer or a bottle of locally produced sweet and fruity red Loulan wine.

From Turpan or Urumqi there are two main routes to Kashgar. The northern route is the more established, passing through Kucha and Korla, especially since the railway link to Kashgar was opened in 2000, offering a comfortable overnight train ride from Urumqi. If you want to break that journey, stop at **Kucha**, which has an exciting Friday bazaar and is the base from which to visit the wonderful cave complexes of **Kizil**, **Kumtura** and the ruined city of **Subashi**, centre of the powerful Buddhist Kuchean kingdom of the first millennium CE.

The southern route is more arduous, passing along the southern underbelly of the Taklamakan Desert and passing the archaeological sites of the Southern Silk Road frequented by Aurel Stein and Albert von Le Coq. Most of these sites are extremely expensive and difficult to obtain permission to visit, but the town of **Hotan (Khotan)** is a rewarding destination, with a Sunday market that rivals Kashgar's and feels more authentic, while the nearby ruined Silk Road towns of **Melikawat** and **Yotkan** are relatively easy to visit with a taxi driver and guide. Perhaps the most satisfying trip in this vicinity is to the evocative ruins of **Rawak Stupa**, which requires special permission (and a fee) from the authorities in Hotan but not only allows you to visit a fascinating archaeological site but also places you in the midst of genuine Taklamakan desert landscape. Overnight buses run from Urumqi along the peripheral and cross-desert highways, and

(Above) Camel trips can be arranged from various towns fringing the Taklamakan Desert, giving a real sense of what the old traders had to endure. (Right) Terracotta warriors line up in Pit One of Xi'an's top tourist attraction. (Below) The Uygur way of life is in many ways unchanged in the Turpan region. (Below right) Shipton's Arch is difficult to get to, but an awesome lesson in Mother Nature's stark beauty.

mercifully there are also daily flights. Buses run on to Kashgar but it's better to stop in the interesting Uygur bazaar towns of **Karghalik** (Yecheng) and **Yarkand** (Shache) en route.

Kashgar is without doubt one of the most interesting towns in Central Asia. Its fantastic **Sunday Bazaar** and **Livestock Market**, the most interesting in Asia, may now be overrun with tourists but the town's backstreets shelter the cultural soul of the Uygur people, making this an endlessly fascinating city. Sadly, the destruction of much of the Old City by the Chinese government in 2009 has left few areas undamaged, but the **Idkah Mosque**, China's largest, remains the heart of Islam in Chinese Central Asia. Travel agencies in Kashgar run tours to remote **Tushuk Tash**, also known as **Shipton's Arch** after mountaineer (and then Consul-General in Kashgar) Eric Shipton, who discovered the arch in the 1940s. Remote and difficult to reach, this is the world's tallest natural arch.

ravelling overland between China and Central Asia you currently have several choices. The most reliable route is the direct train between Urumqi and Almaty in Kazakhstan, which takes about 40 hours. From Urumqi the train skirts the northern edge of the Tien Shan then heads through the **Dzungarian Gate**, a gap between the Tien Shan and Tarbagatai mountains that historically was the main route for invading Mongol armies into the west. After crossing the China-Kazakhstan border at Alashankou, the train crosses the windy Kazakh steppe past Alakol Lake to link up with the Turkestan-Siberian Railway line at Aktogay near Lake Balkhash, then turns south to the cosmopolitan city of **Almaty**. This was the Kazakh capital until 1998, and it boasts a wonderful natural setting; the Tien Shan rises immediately to its south, and day trips into the mountains are easy to arrange. The city itself is very pleasant, with broad, tree-lined avenues and parks that are always popular with locals. **Panfilov Park** is the location of the exquisite **Holy Ascension Cathedral** and the **Museum of Folk Musical Instruments**; just to the west of the park are the **Arasan Baths**, a public sauna and bathhouse that offers a great "local" experience, and in the south of the city **Republic Square** and the **Central State Museum** are worth a visit. A cable car in the southeast of town takes you to the top of **Koktobe Hill** for panoramic views towards the mountains, over the city and onto the flat steppe beyond. (From Almaty the rail line continues southwest through the old trading centres of **Taraz** and **Shymkent** to Tashkent in Uzbekistan.)

An interesting alternative to the Urumqi-Almaty train follows one of the old northern Silk Road trade routes, veering off to the south before the Dzungarian Gate and passing gorgeous **Sayram Lake**, where Kazakh nomads graze their flocks and herds, before descending into the fertile **Ili Valley** and its historic capital **Yining**. This traditionally Kazakh stronghold is lush with farmland, pasture and flanking forest-blanketed mountains – a big change from the usual preconceptions of Xinjiang – and from here you can exit China at Khorgas and travel onward to Almaty. Although a train spur line is being built to Yining and Khorgas, the current method of travel for this excursion is by bus or private jeep.

From Kashgar there are three main onward routes: to Pakistan over the **Khunjerab Pass** and down the spectacular **Karakoram Highway** (see later in this chapter); or to Kyrgyzstan over either the **Torugart** or **Irkeshtam** passes. The Torugart is one of the most exciting and scenic ways into Central Asia but finicky border requirements mean travellers need to arrange transport in advance on both sides of the border through a travel agency in order for border guards to allow you to cross.

1000 YEARS "ŠĀH-NĀMA"

Current stamps from Tajikistan focus on its rich culture, that stretches back to Sogdian times.

In 2003 the Irkeshtam Pass between China and Kyrgyzstan opened, thus allowing a more direct (and authentic) Silk Road route between Kashgar, Osh and the Ferghana Valley of Uzbekistan. The route offers glimpses of such Pamir giants as Peak Lenin (7,134 metres) and best of all, there are none of the logistical complications attached to the Torugart Pass (public buses run between Osh and Kashgar for around US$50). This route allows the traveller to take the **Pamir Highway** from Dushanbe in Tajikistan to **Sary Tash** in the Kyrgyz Alai Valley, cross the Irkeshtam Pass to Kashgar and then take the Karakoram Highway to Tashkurgan and Pakistan, making this probably the world's greatest mountain drive. (The Torugart and Irkeshtam passes are closed on weekends and Chinese public holidays, including the May and October holiday weeks.)

A minor detour from this road would take you along the **Wakhan Corridor** and the Shugnan branch of the Silk Road – but sadly the current political situation in this region means this is not possible. Marco Polo travelled along this valley before crossing the Sarikol Pamir into what is now modern-day Xinjiang. A fourth road exists between the Karakoram Highway in China, north of Tashkurgan, and **Murghab** in the Gorno-Badakhshan region of **Tajikistan**, over the 4,362-metre **Qolma (Kulma) Pass**. The Chinese authorities have not yet opened this road to international traffic but if and when they do travellers will be able to journey directly along the Pamir Highway from Dushanbe to Murghab and then join the Karakoram Highway near Tashkurgan, making this another superbly scenic option.

For ancient traders, simply getting across the formidable ramparts of the Tien Shan, Karakoram, Hindu Kush and High Pamir was reward enough for their endeavours, and few would tarry to explore the natural beauty of the mountain regions. Today's tourists and travellers have a different agenda, however, and there is much to see. In **Kyrgyzstan** the highlight is huge **Issyk-Kul**, a 170-kilometre-long deepwater lake surrounded by rich pastureland and high mountains, and making use of the **local homestay programmes** is a wonderful way of gaining insight into the warmth and hospitality that is a trademark of Central Asian nomadic culture. The fascinating and authentic market in the ancient trading town of **Osh** has a history stretching back thousands of years, and trekking by foot or on horseback is *de rigueur* in such a picturesque alpine environment. If you are headed to or from the Torugart Pass, a stop at the almost perfect **Tash Rabat Caravanserai** is an absolute must (you can stay in a basic yurt camp here for a few dollars). **Son-Kul** is a beautiful high-altitude lake, fringed with shepherds' yurts and herders, a short detour off the main highway from the pass to the capital Bishkek, and along this route you could also visit the **Burana Tower** and the petroglyphs of **Cholpan-Ata**.

Tajikistan, if anything, has even more impressive trekking credentials, though the **High Pamir** offers a more austere and awe-inspiring outback experience, with massive, bare valleys flanked by scree-faced mountain slopes, and the occasional ruined caravanserai to set the mind thinking of the travails the ancient traders faced. The **Fan Mountains** to the north of Dushanbe offer beautiful hiking, with the turquoise splendour of **Iskander-Kul** a popular stopover point.

But for Silk Road khanates, beaconing minarets, cloistered bazaars and epic Islamic architecture, the heartland of Central Asia is very much the **Ferghana Valley** and the lands around and between the ancient **Oxus** and **Jaxartes** rivers, today called the **Amu Darya** and **Syr Darya** respectively. The majority of this territory is now part of **Uzbekistan**; **Tashkent**, its capital, is a largely Soviet creation, rebuilt after a massive 1966 earthquake. Tamerlane's capital at **Samarkand** contains the region's most audacious architecture and the name alone resonates with romantic allure. The town's huge **Registan Square** and ruined **Bibi Khanum Mosque** are joined by some of the region's most exquisite artistic touches at the tombs of the **Shah-i-Zindah**, and you can also descend the steps into the crypt of the **Gur-i-Emir** to touch Tamerlane's tomb.

Tamerlane's hometown of **Shakhrisabz** is a good day trip from Samarkand; this traditional Uzbek town has the ruins of some of Tamerlane's most monumental architecture. With travel agency help (and a Tajik visa) another day trip runs to the Sogdian city of **Penjikent** just over the border.

Nan bread is an ubiquitous sight throughout Xinjiang and the Central Asian countries – and makes for a cheap and delicious snack.

The most atmospheric of the Silk Road cities is without doubt **Bukhara**, whose old town backstreets hide a wealth of hidden tombs, shrines and madrassahs. Must-sees include the **Ark**, formerly home to the Emir of Bukhara; the **Kalon Minaret**, which stopped Genghis Khan in his tracks in 1220; and the gorgeous decoration of the **Ismael Samani Mausoleum** – it's worth planning a couple of extra days here. Stay in one of the many stylish bed and breakfasts in the old town and take tea with the *aksakals* ("white beards", or elders) of the poolside **Lyab-i-Hauz** teahouse.

he remotest of the khanates was **Khiva** and today it's a flight or long drive of 450 kilometres across the monotonous and stony Kara Kum Desert from Bukhara. The most intact of the Central Asian citadels, it's also the most sterile, having been preserved by the Soviets as an open-air museum. A long day trip from Khiva could take you to **Kunya-Urgench**, once one of the Islamic world's major intellectual centres until razed by Mongols in the 13th century, but this raises some bureaucratic headaches as it requires a Turkmenistan visa. Those with a special interest in archaeology have two options for some exploring. From Khiva it's possible to hire transport to the 2,000-year-old ruined desert city fortresses of **Toprak Kala** or **Ayaz Kala**, where you can stay in desert yurts.

From Uzbekistan, many travellers finish their Silk Road sojourn and take advantage of Tashkent's international air connections, but the development of rail lines linking Russia's heartland with the "Stans", originally by Imperial Russia in the late 19th century, then the Soviets and finally, after independence, by the various countries of the Commonwealth of Independent States (CIS), now allows for a range of entry/exit opportunities for Central Asia. As already mentioned, from Almaty in Kazakhstan the **Turkestan-Siberian Railway**, more commonly called the **Turk-Sib**, travels north across open steppe to **Semey** (Semipalatinsk) in the East Kazakhstan Region, a city infamous for the nuclear bomb testing performed by the Soviets in the mid-20th century, but gateway to the beautiful mountains of the **Kazakh Altai**. The Turk-Sib crosses the Russian border to the north and passes through **Barnaul** on its way to link up with the Trans-Siberian line at **Novosibirsk**, making this an interesting way of combining a Trans-Siberian trip with a Silk Road experience.

From Almaty the Turk-Sib skirts the northern slopes of the Tien Shan down to Tashkent, but at **Shymkent** a major junction links it with the older line that was built during imperial times to connect Moscow with the wealth of the Ferghana Valley. Within a few hours of Shymkent are the ruins of the ancient city of **Otrar**, a major Silk Road centre dating back to the 2nd century BCE but destroyed in a vengeful campaign by Chinggis Khaan in 1219. Also in this region is **Turkistan**, site of the hugely impressive **Mausoleum of Khoja Ahmed Yasawi**, designed by Tamerlane but left unfinished after his death. The rail line travels north, following the course of the Syr Darya River to **Aralsk**, once a port town on the coast of the Aral Sea, but today a desert town a dozen kilometres from the once-shrinking sea's water (recent damming is saving the northern section) – the **ship's graveyard** of abandoned vessel hulks lying in desert scrub has now become something of a tourist destination. From here, it crosses the Sary Arka, the Great Steppe, to **Aktobe**, then on to **Orenburg** in Russia, and so to **Samara** where it links up with the southern branch line of the Trans-Siberian. Samara stands on the eastern bank of the Volga River, and owes its prosperity over the centuries to its position on that watery thoroughfare. Indeed, the riverfront embankment is considered to be Samara's most beautiful attraction.

A third rail route makes its way north from Central Asia, this one following the course of the Amu Darya from a junction near Bukhara (on the Trans-Caspian Railway line), stopping at Urgench, then Nukus (near to Kunya-Urgench just across the Turkmenistan border) before passing south of the Aral Sea and crossing the barren desert steppe between that body of water and the much larger Caspian Sea to the west. It stops at **Atyrau**, Kazakhstan's oil capital, then crosses the Russian border to the Volga River delta at **Astrakhan**. Though it traverses vast tracts of seemingly inhospitable land, this rail line does in fact closely follow a well-trod trading route from the golden days of the Silk Road. The Astrakhan region, rich in natural resources thanks to the **Volga Delta**, and a natural gateway to the Orient, has been fought over for centuries, being home to the Golden Horde, the nomadic **Kalmyks** (still represented today in the nearby Republic of Kalmykia) and subject to invasion down the years by Tamerlane, various Cossack forces, Ivan the Terrible and the Ottomans, before Imperial Russia finally consolidated its hold.

Northwards, the railway reaches **Volgograd**, more famously known as Stalingrad, and site of some of the most terrible fighting during WWII. On a hill in the city – the **Mamayev Kurgan** that saw some of the most intense fighting – a memorial complex to the Battle of Stalingrad is dominated by an astonishing 82-metre-high allegorical sculpture of Mother Russia, titled "**The Motherland Calls!**" – when it was built in 1967, this was the world's tallest freestanding sculpture. From Volgograd the railway heads north to meet up with the Trans-Siberian Railway's southern branch and so arrives in Moscow.

Back on the classical Silk Road, it is also possible to continue your journey from Uzbekistan on the **Trans-Caspian Ralway** into the bizarre republic of **Turkmenistan**, for years dominated by the personality cult of President Saparmurat Niyazov, self-styled Turkmenbashi or "Father of the Turkmen", until his death in December 2006, and now controlled in a slightly more relaxed way by his successor, Gurbanguly Berdimuhamedow. With a visa (a letter of introduction is necessary) it's not too difficult to follow the Trans-Caspian, with a stop in **Merv** (modern name **Mary**) to visit the impressive **Seljuk-era Sultan Sanjar Mausoleum**. The Turkmen capital **Ashgabat** holds few draws except for its colourful **Tolkuchka Bazaar** and the chance to shop for a "Bukhara" carpet.

With travel through Iran an on/off option these days, an offbeat alternative is to travel westwards from Turkmenistan via the Caucasus – though this raises its own visa and security problems. The Trans-Caspian Railway stretches northwest from Ashgabat all the way to the Caspian Sea coast at **Turkmenbashi** (formerly known as **Krasnovodsk**). Ferries sail across the Caspian Sea from here to **Baku** in **Azerbaijan**, from where you can wind your way through the mountain valleys of Mtskheta to **Tbilisi** in **Georgia** and either on to the Russian Volga or to the beautiful northeastern region of Turkey, with its ruined Armenian cathedrals and Black Sea port at **Trabzon**. The **Selim Caravanserai** in the Vayots Dzor region of southern **Armenia** is probably the best-preserved Silk Road site in this region.

A word is due here about **Afghanistan**. Serious security issues within Afghanistan in 2010 make travel even to Kabul and Herat very risky. At this time it is virtually impossible to undertake any leisure travel within the country – it can only be hoped that eventually this wonderful land will find peace and some semblance of stability, allowing adventure travellers entry once again. Should that happen, there are three major west-east routes through the country, all starting at one of the legendary cities of

A painting by the Kazakh artist Abylkhan Kasteyev documents the opening of the Turk-Sib Railway in 1930.

Central Asia: Herat. The northernmost runs via Balkh and Mazar-i-Sharif; the central via Bamiyan; and the southerly, via Kandahar. The former two meet at Kabul and the traveller proceeds from there to Faisabad, from where one tracks Marco Polo through the original "Roof of the World", the **Wakhan Corridor** which leads to China through the **Yuli Pass**.

Herat has historically looked more towards Iran than Afghanistan. It reached its apogee during the 15th century Timurid period, many of whose monuments can still be seen. The great **Musallah of Gohar Shad**, despite its ruinous state is of great interest, and the tiling on the **Friday Mosque** is awe-inspiring – tiles are still produced at the mosque in the world's oldest tile factory. For those tracing the Silk Road, the Sufi shrine of **Gazargah** is of interest; Robert Byron identified the decorative effects in the *iwan* as showing Chinese influence.

The northern route passes through **Balkh**, Alexander the Great's headquarters and site of the ruined **Noh-i-Gumbad**, one of the world's oldest mosques, and **Mazar-i-Sharif**, reputed to be the final resting place of the Prophet's son-in-law, before heading up into the mountain-locked valleys of **Badakhshan**. The central route follows the Hari Rud river upstream, past the famous **Minaret of Jam**, and to the Buddhist centre of **Bamiyan**, site of the great Buddha carvings that were tragically destroyed by the Taliban in 2001. There are still many sites of interest here, however, and the landscape is stupendous, particularly the astonishing cyan lakes of **Band-i-Amir**.

D espite the ethnic, historical and artistic links that bind Central Asia to **Persia**, crossing from Turkmenistan into Iran remains a little-travelled option. The easiest way (assuming you have an Iranian visa) is to fly from Ashgabat to the holy Shia city of **Mashhad**, from where you can continue overland. By land there are two road border crossings (again if you have the requisite visas), at Serakhs and Bajgiran. You'll need to arrange transport or take one of the shared taxis to/from both borders.

One interesting diversion from Mashhad is to the fine **Rabat Sharif Caravanserai** near Serakhs on the Turkmen border. Farther west is the town of **Nishapur** and the tomb of Persian poet **Omar Khayam**. Also worth a stop en route to Tehran is the **Gonbad-e-Kabus**, a remarkable funeral tower that rises sheer from the Turkmen plain. **Tehran** is a modern city whose ancient settlement was located to the south, when it was

Ancient Van Fortress, near Turkey's Lake Van, an impregnable stone fortification from which the surrounding land could be controlled.

called **Rey**. Not much remains of those early days, and attractions in the city today focus on the vibrant **bazaar** and **Emam Khomeini Mosque**, located near the **Golestan Palace** and gardens. The monumental **Azadi Tower** displays the modern face of Iran.

Iran's most glorious sites – **Esfahan**, **Shiraz**, **Persepolis**, **Yazd** and the ruined city of **Bam** – lie well south of the most direct overland route across Iran but shouldn't be missed, so this is the time for some detours. (Tragically, Bam was levelled by an earthquake in December 2003.) Despite media perceptions of the country the Iranian people are some of the most hospitable and welcoming in the world, though women should respect certain dress codes.

With Iraq currently off-limits to travellers, the main overland route swings northwest to **Tabriz**, the capital of East Azerbaijan Province and a major trading city for centuries. The Mongol Il-khan ruler Ghaza Khan made it his capital in the late 13th century, and it retained that status until the 16th century, when the Safayids moved their capital to Esfahan. Tehran's 15th century **Blue Mosque** is its most famous attraction, considered a masterpiece of Iranian decorative tilework, though an earthquake caused serious damage and today it is still in ruin, though beautiful nevertheless.

The route now crosses into Turkey's Kurdish southwest, passing to the south of historic **Mt Ararat**, 5,156 metres high and the reputed final resting place of

The tiny people around her base show the immensity of Volgograd's 82-metre-high "The Motherland Calls!" statue.

Noah's Ark. The mountain can be climbed by adventurous souls, but expansive views of the landscape are also to be had at the romantic **Isak Pasa Palace** complex, built by a Kurdish chieftain in the 18th century to guard the mountain passes through which both benign traders and warring hordes had to pass.

To the west lies beautiful **Lake Van**, Turkey's largest lake, 119 kilometres at its widest point. With no outlet river, it is strongly alkaline from sodium carbonate and other salts and therefore hosts only a single species of hardy fish. This region has seen much conflict, and the ruins of Seljuk mosques and Armenian churches, monasteries and tombstones can be seen in the surrounding area, including the medieval **Fortress of Van** and the 17th century Kurdish **Hosap Castle**. On **Akdamar Island** near Van's southern shore stands the picturesque 10th century Armenian **Church of the Holy Cross**.

On the Black Sea coast, the trading port of **Trabzon** (historically Trebizond) was an important early link in Silk Road trade both from Persia to the southeast and from the Volga region across the Caucasus Mountains. A melting pot of religions and cultures, it boasts a host of old churches and mosques, the highlight being the **Ayasofya**, or **Hagia Sophia**, built in the 13th century as a Byzantine church, converted to a mosque under the Ottomans, and now a museum. In the mountains 46 kilometres south of Trabzon at an altitude of 1,200 metres lies the **Sumela Monastery**, a complex built at the foot of a vertiginous cliff in beautiful countryside. Founded in the 4th century CE, its current form dates to the 13th century, and it is most famous for the vivid frescoes of its **Rock Church**, created in a cave in the cliffside.

The routes through Anatolia were many and various, but the city of **Ankara** dominated the region. Inhabited since the Bronze Age, this ancient city has been through many incarnations, controlled by Phrygians and Persians, Celtic Galatians and Roman, Byzantines and the Turkic Seljuks and Ottomans, before finally becoming the capital of modern Turkey. Although very modern in initial appearance, its archaeological sites and museums are legion, the pick perhaps being the culturally mixed **Ankara Citadel**, the **Temple of Augustus and Rome**, and the **Column of Julian**, erected in 362 CE. The **Museum of Anatolian Civilisations** and the **Ankara Ethnography Museum** are both recommended.

Finally, the Silk Road – or more accurately the countless interweaving braids that made up the network of the Silk Routes – comes to its conclusion in the majestic city of **Istanbul (Constantinople)**, like Beijing at our journey's other extremity more than once the capital of a powerful empire, and still an economic force and cultural centre. To name only a few of its numerous sites and experiences seems futile, but mention must be made of the mighty **Hagia Sophia** and its Islamic counterpoint, the **Sultan Ahmet Mosque**, also called the **Blue Mosque**. The **Topkapi Palace** is a must-see, as is the **Grand Bazaar**, and don't forget to take a ferry across the **Bosphorus** or round the **Golden Horn** for a seafarer's view of this most exotic of cities.

THE MUGHAL ROUTE:
CENTRAL ASIA TO INDIA

 n times of yore, the trade routes favoured by merchants would shift and change as tyrannical rulers conquered new lands, neighbouring kingdoms warred, or groups of brigands destabilised mountain passes, forcing caravans to seek out the least perilous trail to their destination. The same is true today, with nations such as China, India and Pakistan squabbling and fighting over boundaries, while civil conflict and the war on terror in Afghanistan have effectively closed that country to simple travel.

Thus, when it comes to the historic routes between Central Asia and the subcontinent, there is little choice for the modern traveller. The old "hippy trails" through Afghanistan, from **Herat** to **Kandahar** and the **Bolan Pass** into southern Pakistan, or from **Mazar-i-Sharif** to **Bamiyan** and **Kabul**, and thence through the **Khyber Pass** to **Peshawar** and the Indus Valley, are simply out of the question at the present time. Equally, the old **Five Passes route** from the Southern Silk Road towns of **Hotan** (**Khotan**) or **Shache** (**Yarkand**) across the Kunlun and Karakoram ranges to **Leh** in **Ladakh** is forbidden due to India and China's ongoing antagonism over the intervening **Aksai Chin** region, and there are no signs that this will change.

However, it is certainly possible to visit Ladakh and pick up the ancient trading route in Leh, the capital of this Tibetan Buddhist region – indeed you can backtrack slightly on the route by visiting the starkly beautiful **Nubra Valley** to the north. The upper Indus Valley is worth exploring, with the atmospheric **Thikse** and **Hemis** monasteries providing full explanation of why they call this corner of India "Little Tibet". The modern-day tarmac road follows the old tracks trodden by caravans of pack animals, tracing the Indus downstream, or northwest, before crossing it and climbing past **Lamayuru Monastery**, perched like an eagle's nest on a mountain ridge, then winding up and over the main range of the majestic Himalaya, through Kargil and Drass to the **Zoji-La** pass, where the road descends in nerve-jangling hairpins to the floor of the **Sonamarg Valley** and so into the verdant Vale of Kashmir.

Kashmir is another of those names redolent with romance and history, a destination spoken of with excited, reverent tones by those who have spent time there. It deserves its fame, for this is one of the most beautiful valleys in the subcontinent, lush and green, filled with fields of saffron crocus, rice, wheat and barley, well-watered vegetable gardens and fruit orchards.

Tragically, the spectre of political violence still roams Kashmir after 20 years of armed insurgency, and as a result most governments strongly advise travellers to stay away. Should the day come when Kashmir is once again safe to be explored, travellers will no doubt flock to revel in the superb trekking

(Clockwise from above) Wooden architecture and an old houseboat beside one of the canals linking Srinagar's Dal and Nagin lakes; young monks call their colleagues to prayer from the roof of the Tibetan Buddhist Thikse Monastery in the upper Indus Valley region of Ladakh; Tajik women shop in the main street of Tashkurgan, on the Chinese side of the Karakoram Highway; a Kyrgyz yurt in the High Pamirs; the Jantar Mantar astronomical observatory in Jaipur; dawn bathes one of the Taj Mahal's minarets in soft, golden light.

areas of **Sonamarg**, **Pahalgam** and the **Amarnath Temple**, wander the meadows of **Gulmarg** in summer (or ski there in winter), and luxuriate in the ornate colonial comfort of the houseboats on **Dal** and **Nagin** lakes in the capital, **Srinagar**, taking time to float in a *shikara* through the waterways to the manicured Mughal gardens of **Shalimar Bagh** and **Nishat Bagh**.

e are therefore left in the present day with a single safe – and unbroken – land route from the desert oases into India: the spectacular **Karakoram Highway**. This 1,284-kilometre road links Kashgar with Islamabad in Pakistan, following one of the Silk Road routes from the Taklamakan Desert to the valleys of Hunza, Gilgit and the Indus River, and so into the plains of the Punjab and the grand cities of India. The modern highway, begun in 1967, is an amazing feat of engineering by Chinese construction teams, and survives frequent rock slides and flash floods through constant maintenance, allowing both leisure travellers and, more significantly, today's version of the trade caravans – convoys of trucks filled with merchandise – to travel across the inhospitable roof of the world between China and the subcontinent.

From Kashgar it's a clear, easy run south to the looming ramparts of the Karakorams. The road enters the precipitous **Gez Defile** and appears to be heading for a sheer jagged wall of rock thousands of metres high, but veers off and winds its way up onto a high-altitude permafrost plain leading to beautiful 3,500-metre-high **Karakul Lake**, by whose shores Kyrgyz nomads live and rent out yurt space to visitors. Above the lake towers 7,546-metre **Muztagata**, the "Father of Ice Mountain". Further along the road is the interesting Tajik town of **Tashkurgan**, meaning "Stone City", perhaps for the impressive stone fortress that sits on the southern side of town overlooking the broad valley. Chinese visa formalities take place here, and then it's on to the **Khunjerab Pass**, a broad break in the Pamirs 4,733 metres above sea level.

On its southern side the highway descends swiftly to 2,500 metres and progresses to Sost; you are now in Pakistan, and from here the mountain scenery on show from the roadside ranks as some of the most awesome in the world. The **Passu Cathedral** is a jaw-dropping sight, a monstrous mass of bare, pinnacled rock (see pages 454–455), but the Hunza Valley garners most praise, wide and fertile but hemmed in by huge peaks like 7,788-metre **Rakaposhi**. Little wonder that some claim it as the inspiration for James Hilton's Shangri-la, and its rulers, the Mirs, controlled the trade route and surrounding region from the relative opulence of **Baltit Fort** near the modern capital **Karimabad**.

The highway moves on to **Gilgit**, the British Empire's headquarters in the Northwest Frontier and in modern times a thriving trekking centre, then curves to finally meet the Indus River as it emerges from the shoulder of mighty **Nanga Parbat**, 8,126 metres high and the westernmost mountain in the Greater Himalaya. The trekking in and around the **Fairy Meadows** near its northern face is stupendous. Farther south the Karakoram Highway is blasted from the precipitous walls of the gorge created by the power of the Indus. It passes **Chilas**, with its concentration of ancient petroglyphs carved by travellers over millennia, and finally breaks free of the mountains to end in Islamabad, Pakistan's modern capital, from where a slight detour will bring you to the ruins of ancient **Taxila**, centre of the Gandharan kingdom that ruled eastern Afghanistan and northern Pakistan from the Vale of Peshawar between the 6th century BCE and 5th century CE.

For today's traveller heading for India, the route is simple, taking you south on the historic **Grand Trunk Road** to **Lahore**, with its beautiful Mughal **Badshahi Mosque** and the fascinating **Lahore Museum**. A short distance south is the border with India, and not far across it you reach **Amritsar**, holy city of the Sikhs and site of the **Golden Temple**. From here, by road or train the way leads inexorably towards **Delhi**, centre of Indian culture and history for most of the last 3,000 years. Highlights focus on the incredible artistic achievements of the Delhi Sultanate and subsequent Mughal rulers, from the **Qutub Minar**, the world's tallest free-standing brick minaret (72.5 metres), to **Humayun's Tomb**, the magnificent **Red Fort** and the **Jama Masjid**, India's largest mosque. Of course Delhi's bazaars are worth a wander, filled with exotic colours, sights and smells, and the **National Museum** should not be missed.

A popular triangular route beginning and ending in Delhi is easy and guaranteed to fulfil the most rapacious culture vulture's desires. A slow, trundling train ride southeast brings you to **Agra**, sight of the peerless **Taj Mahal**, about which no words of praise are adequate. Visit it at dawn, midday and sunset to truly grasp its heavenly beauty – but don't forget also to visit the Agra Fort a few kilometres upriver of the Taj, which rivals Delhi's Red Fort in splendour.

From Agra, journey west to the edge of the **Thar Desert** of **Rajahstan**, where **Jaipur**, the "Pink City", waits to seduce you. Its most famous sight is the small but gorgeous **Hawa Mahal**, or "Palace of Winds", built to allow the ladies of the royal court to watch the everyday life of the city folk from the haven of their harem quarters, and part of the **Royal Palace**, a wonderful fusion of Hindu Rajput and Islamic Mughal architecture. The astronomical observatory called the **Jantar Mantar** is a fascinating complex, the largest of three built in the 18th century by Maharaja Jai Singh II. Finally, in the hills just to the north of the city is the ridge-top **Amber Fort** with panoramic views out over the landscape – the better to see danger coming.

A short ride west from Jaipur the pilgrimage town of **Pushkar** lies around holy Pushkar Lake on the very edge of the Thar Desert. This is the site of the annual November **Camel Fair** that draws camel traders – and tourists – from great distances. Wandering through the cacophany of sights, sounds and smells, the urgent calls of stall vendors, the roaring complaints of camels being loaded or unloaded, the hustle and bustle of buyers and sellers, you will be transported to a timeless place that – in many ways – could as well be in Samarkand, Herat or Tabriz, in Almaty, Osh or Kashgar.

At the end of the five-day fair the camels will be loaded with goods or hitched to large wooden-wheeled carts piled high with merchandise and travellers, and the people will depart along dusty trails into and around the desert, heading home or to some other marketplace. The tracks will become almost invisible as they cross the barren wilderness, but the camel drivers will know the way. And in this modern, sometimes antiseptic world of high technology and high-altitude jets, it's good to know that in a multitude of places throughout Eurasia this link with the past is still very much alive for us to experience and enjoy – if we have courage and imagination enough to take that first step of exploration.

Specialising in Asia Overland

since 1964

As the world's leading **Trans Siberian Railway** and **Silk Road** operator our aim is simple; offer the best journeys possible for anyone with a passion for discovery.

Small Group Journeys, Independent Adventures, Tailor Made Experiences, Premium & Deluxe Tours and Private Trains.

Call for a free brochure or visit our website.

China	Kazakstan	Iran
Mongolia	Uzbekistan	Armenia
Russia	Turkmenistan	Georgia
Siberia	Kyrgyzstan	Turkey
Tuva	India	Vietnam
Japan	United Arab Emirates	

www.sundownersoverland.com

LONDON
1 St.George's Court, 131 Putney Bridge Rd London SW15 2PA
E   europe@sundownersoverland.com
T   +44 20 8877 7660

MELBOURNE
Level 1, 51 Queen St Melbourne 3000
E   mail@sundownersoverland.com
T   +61 3 9672 5300

ADVICE FOR THE TRAVELLER

WHEN TO GO

entral Asia and the majority of Russia are subject to a continental climate, which translates into extremes of temperature. If you don't mind the cold, and are wrapped up properly, winter can be a great time to visit the Russian cities of St Petersburg and Moscow, with fewer tourists, an atmospheric blanket of snow and no accommodation problems. Summer nights in St Petersburg are spectacular, and autumn is a popular time to visit Moscow.

Siberia's name is synonymous with cold, and it's true that the cities along the Trans-Siberian Railway can reach some mind-numbingly low temperatures in the long cold months. Summer is the most popular time to take the train across Eurasia, autumn is the most picturesque, with the taiga forest offering blazes of gold as the trees prepare for winter – but each season offers its own benefits and rewards.

Summer brings sizzling heat to much of Central Asia, particularly the deserts of Xinjiang, Uzbekistan, Turkmenistan and Iran, while it freezes solid in the sub-Siberian winters. April/May and September/October are the premium times to make a trip if high-altitude trekking is not in your itinerary. The catch is that the mountain passes are generally only open or traversable between May and October (though the Torugart and Irkeshtam crossings are technically open year-round).

Turkey's Mediterranean-influenced climate is amenable at any time of the year, while the Indian subcontinent suffers from debilitating heat in the build-up to the summer monsoon – most people prefer to travel in India early in the year or in September/October at monsoon's end.

WHAT TO WEAR

The trick here is layers. The combination of continental climate and radical changes in altitude (if you're negotiating Central Asia's intimidating mountain ranges) results in the need to be prepared for wild swings in temperature, often between day and night but sometimes from one hour to the next! Today's bevy of high-tech fabrics are a blessing: they allow your skin to breathe while blocking wind, insulate without adding kilos to your luggage, or offer waterproof protection even in severe storms. Pack accordingly, mixing T-shirts and light cotton shirts with a fleece, windbreaker and waterproof jacket. In winter gloves, a scarf and woollen hat are essential, and if you are heading for the desert or high mountains in summer be sure to bring good sunglasses and a wide-brimmed hat for protection from the sun.

ESSENTIAL ITEMS TO BRING

On an extended transcontinental trip through some fairly remote regions it pays to be prepared. Having the following items in your luggage brings peace of mind and can easily resolve potentially difficult situations:

- A decent medical kit, including diarrhoea, rehydration and antibiotic medication, a pack of disposable syringes and water purification tablets or drops.
- A torch, or perhaps two – tiny credit card sized ones make useful back-ups.
- Plenty of spare batteries, preferably rechargeable – solar-powered battery chargers are not cheap to buy, but can be invaluable.
- An international electrical adapter plug.
- Rechargers for your digital camera/iPod, etc.
- Photocopies of all your important documents, kept separately – should you be unlucky enough to have your bag stolen, these will speed up and ease the subsequent bureaucratic quagmire.
- A small Swiss Army or other multipurpose knife.
- High-factor sunscreen, sunglasses and hat – don't be fooled by low temperatures, and don't underestimate the debilitating effects of severe sunburn.
- A small collapsible umbrella or waterproof covering for your luggage.
- Toiletries and some toilet paper for emergencies.
- Plenty of reading material for the long journeys that lie ahead (see Recommended Reading).
- Ear plugs for those nights when noisy co-passengers or hotel room neighbours make sleep impossible.
- A water bottle and personal mug for drinking, and a plastic bowl or plate can also be useful.
- A few sealable plastic kitchen bags to protect cameras and other delicate items from the fine dust of the deserts, which is often whipped into a frenzy by the strong winds that sweep across the Eurasian landmass.

TRAVEL INSURANCE

Whether you're on a package tour or travelling independently, having good travel insurance is imperative. Your policy should provide good cover for loss of personal items, cancellation of flights and especially potential medical expenses. Make sure you use a reputable company with good contacts and expertise in the regions where you will be travelling. For lists of relevant UK companies, try **www.travel-quest.co.uk/shop_insurance.htm** or **www.travel-lists.co.uk/lk2ins.html**; in the US try **www.squaremouth.com**; and in Australia try **www.covermore.com** or **www.worldnomads.com**.

ACCOMMODATION: MODERN-DAY CARAVANSERAIS

Standards of accommodation along the Trans-Siberian and Silk Road have improved greatly in recent years. Major cities from St Petersburg to Beijing, from Delhi to Istanbul all offer everything from five-star splendour and boutique hotels to functional hostels. Most mid-sized towns have comfortable three-star accommodation which, though not luxurious, offers clean rooms, hot water and decent dining. There has been a trend towards traditional-style accommodation that highlights local culture; an example of this is the Silk Road Hotel Management Co. Ltd., which offers a unique experience of "culture hotels" in

Dunhuang, Xining and Turpan (**www.the-silk-road.com**). Look out for this type of accommodation when researching what's available, and it's also worth considering homestays and local bed and breakfasts in Siberian Russia and the Central Asian countries (see **www.lyabi-house.com** or **www.emirtravel.com** for an idea of such places in Samarkand or Bukhara).

The Internet is the best destination today for up-to-date information on what your options are, what's best or within your price range. There are plenty of forums once you start researching, but a good general idea can be garnered from the following websites:

www.wikitravel.com	www.tripadvisor.com	www.allrussiahotels.com
www.hotelsinrussia.com	http://english.ctrip.com	www.travelchinaguide.com
www.smarttravel.com	www.indiahotels.com	www.chinaplanner.com

TRAVELLING BY TRAIN

Those of us who eschew plane travel as much as possible when planning an adventurous holiday – or the trip of a lifetime – usually agree with the maxim that "the journey is a large part of the adventure". It's generally accepted that of all modern long-distance land travel, the train is the most sensible, convenient and comfortable, as well as being the most evocative and romantic, linking us with a golden age and transporting us to exotic realms at a clanking but curiously comforting 60 kilometres per hour.

Although your personal space on a train – whether sitting in a crammed carriage or sharing a sleeper cabin – can be limited and sometimes claustrophobic, once you're settled in and have your gear stashed as you like it, there's a homeliness to your "berth" for the next few days. Trains often elicit a feeling of camaraderie among their passengers, all "in it together" and going the same way regardless of individual circumstance or status. Making friends on a train journey is one of the great experiences of travel in both Russia and Asia, whether you're in it for the long haul from Moscow to Vladivostok, crossing the Kara Kum Desert from Bukhara to Ashgabat, or riding the Mail train from Delhi to Agra. Language difficulties become irrelevant – sign language will do fine – and once the food is broken out to be shared, possibly with a bottle of vodka, then you know you're in for a fine time.

The rail network in Asia is evolving and improving even today. There are now a host of sinuous route options for traversing the continents – in many ways mirroring the ancient Silk Road's crisscrossing network of trails. There are branch lines of the Trans-Siberian line at both its western and eastern extremes; the Mongolian Railway line is a fascinating alternative entry point into China; and three lines connect Russia – and by extension Europe – with Central Asia.

From Beijing, the train is definitely the most convenient way to travel by land along the Silk Road. China's rail network is massive, and from Xi'an the rail goes first to Lanzhou, then up the Hexi Corridor to Dunhuang, Turpan, Urumqi, Korla, Kucha, Aksu and Kashgar. There are plans to blast and tunnel a new track from Kashgar through the Tien Shan into Kyrgyzstan and thence to Uzbekistan's railway system, but when this will actually materialise is anyone's guess. For now, from Urumqi there are two trains a week to Almaty (a 40-hour trip), via part of the Turk-Sib Railway that comes south from Novosibirsk.

(The Turk-Sib is a surprisingly little-used link between the Trans-Siberian line and Central Asia, and also has the benefit of opening up the beautiful Altai Mountains region to exploration.) From Almaty, lines continue via Taraz and Shymkent down to Tashkent and on to Khiva, Ashgabat and Turkmenbashi.

High-level talks about a rail connection from Tashkent/Ashgabat to Iran have stalled, with endless wrangling over transit regulations meaning that, sadly, the single international test run has never been repeated; the wait continues for that unbroken train run from Istanbul to Beijing.

In general, Central Asian trains are not as safe or comfortable as those in China. Currently the only trains frequented much by tourists are the overnight run from Tashkent to Bukhara, and the routes within Kazakhstan, which boasts a more stable government and greater prosperity. Occasional tourist charter trains traverse the region in style.

CULTURAL DOS AND DON'TS

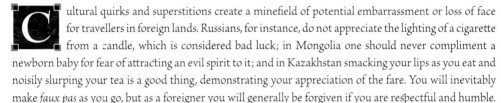

ultural quirks and superstitions create a minefield of potential embarrassment or loss of face for travellers in foreign lands. Russians, for instance, do not appreciate the lighting of a cigarette from a candle, which is considered bad luck; in Mongolia one should never compliment a newborn baby for fear of attracting an evil spirit to it; and in Kazakhstan smacking your lips as you eat and noisily slurping your tea is a good thing, demonstrating your appreciation of the fare. You will inevitably make *faux pas* as you go, but as a foreigner you will generally be forgiven if you are respectful and humble. However, here are a few general rules to follow.

When visiting a Russian home, always try to bring a small gift, perhaps some food or drink. Indeed, the act of gift-giving when invited to someone's house or yurt/ger is a wise practice throughout Central Asia too, from Mongolia to Kazakhstan to Afghanistan. This can be some cake or a local bottle of drink, chocolates or flowers, but something small from your homeland, like a simple badge, postcards or pens/pencils will be hugely appreciated. Many cultures also like to give a small gift to a guest upon leaving – this should always be accepted with grace.

In Russia, Mongolia and the former Soviet Central Asian republics, all now independent states, the drinking of vodka is an intrinsic part of socialising. (Drinking in China also follows this pattern, though beer, wine and hard liquors are preferred to vodka.) You will be plied with vodka (or brandy) wherever you go, and it can be hard to refuse politely, leading to some very heavy sessions and sore heads the next day. If you firmly but politely decline to drink alcohol, this will be accepted, but you are less likely to be taken "to heart". The making of many toasts is a remnant of nomadic culture in Kazakhstan and Kyrgyzstan in particular. Be prepared to be invited to make a toast to your host, and don't think to refuse. If you are not drinking alcohol then the omnipresent tea is a perfectly acceptable substitute with which to toast.

Although the precepts of Islam forbid the consumption of alcohol, the form of Islamism practised in Xinjiang, and across the border in some of the CIS countries, has been diluted to the extent that it is acceptable to the majority to drink beer and hard liquor. It is wise not to draw attention to this apparent flouting of Islamic code, since this may be perceived as a questioning of your dining partners' faith, which is highly rude and, in some situations, can be dangerous.

Among nomadic society, never finish all the food on your plate, as it will be refilled on the assumption that you haven't had enough. When you are replete, leave a small amount on your plate to show that you have had your fill. Never enter a nomad's yurt or ger encampment without attracting attention – call out a greeting as you approach. If invited in, wait to be seated – this will often be in the position of honour facing the entrance.

In deference to Muslim sensibilities, trousers or long skirts should be worn whenever possible – shorts are disapproved of for both women *and* men, even in baking-hot locations. Also, in many places it is normal to remove your shoes upon entering a house, apartment or yurt. In Central Asia women should carry a small headscarf with them if they intend to visit holy sites.

Taking photos can be a delicate business. The large, cosmopolitan cities present few problems in general, but be culturally sensitive in the usually more conservative countryside. It is always best to ask permission first, and respect the potential subject's wishes if he/she says no. You can get natural portraits by using a long telephoto zoom lens, but be discreet. Always check before taking photos in a mosque or church, and never do so during prayers.

FOOD & DRINK

ampling a country's local cuisine is one of the most enjoyable ways of getting to know its people, and provides an insight into one of the core elements of its culture. It really pays to be adventurous, and very often the best food to be had is actually in a cheap local restaurant. Don't be afraid to eat from streetside or market stalls – when you can see the food being prepared and cooked in front of you, you can be more confident that you won't get sick as a result of dinner.

Russian food is traditionally based on simple fare, using potatoes, cucumbers, cabbage, onions and bread, spiced up with sour cream and dried herbs. Borsch and beef stroganov are the most well-known dishes, but there are plenty of regional variations, involving pickles, cold meats and sausage. In the Volga Delta and Lake Baikal regions, fish is on the menu more often – there are countless ways to cook fresh sturgeon, and Baikal's cuisine is based around fish such as omul, whitefish and grayling.

Mongolian food is high in meat (mostly mutton), flour and dairy products, designed to fill you up and keep you warm. Make sure you try the steamed dumplings filled with meat called *buzz*, or *khuushuur*, dumplings fried in mutton fat. Stews are filled out with potatoes and carrots, and meat is often served with fresh noodles or rice. Milk tea is drunk constantly, often with dried dairy products such as the dried cheese curds called *aarul*. The fermented mare's milk known as *airag* (called *kumis* in Central Asia) is a traditional drink that you will most likely be offered – slightly fizzy and sharp, it is about as alcoholic as weak beer.

The typical food of northern China and Beijing is not rice based, but uses steamed bread, dumplings and many different types of noodle as a base, with northern vegetables such as cabbage, spinach and turnip as accompaniments. Street food is delicious and filling, from steamed sweet potatoes called *hongshu* to pancake-like *jianbing* or *mala tang*, a spicy noodle soup. Without a doubt, though, the signature dish that must be tried if you're in Beijing is Peking Duck.

In Gansu and Xinjiang you'll find Hui (Chinese Muslim) food, based around noodles – Lanzhou-style noodles are famous throughout the country; watch the noodles being stretched and pulled by hand as they have been since before pasta was even a glimmer in an Italian mind.

The quintessential Xinjiang meal runs along the lines of a round of grilled mutton *shashlyk* (kebabs) on a plate of hot sesame seed *nan* bread, followed by sweet Turpan grapes or a Hami melon, washed down with a cold beer or a pot of green tea (*kok chai*). The introduction of Middle Eastern spices like cumin are just one thing you can thank the Silk Road for. Xinjiang-style *suoman* is available everywhere and mixes Mediterranean tomatoes and peppers with Chinese noodle squares, stir-fried in a wok – an early form of fusion cuisine. Hot *gizhde nan* are bagel-like rolls, delicious when hot straight out of the oven.

The cuisine of the Central Asian "Stans" blends and merges so it is hard to identify one country's food from another's. Mutton, beef and horsemeat are fried, grilled, boiled and baked, forming the central foundation around which pasta, potatoes, vegetables and bread are added. A popular dish for special occasions in Kazakhstan and Kyrgyzstan is *beshparmak*, or "Five Fingers", a stew of meat, onions, potato and herbs served on a bed of flat square noodles and traditionally eaten with the fingers, hence the name. The national dish in Uzbekistan and Tajikistan is *plov* (pilaf or pilau), a rice dish fried in oil or mutton fat and cooked in a seasoned broth with meat and vegetables. *Manty* are delicious large pasta dumplings filled with minced meat and onions, and sometimes sweet pumpkin.

In case the idea of so much fatty food is unappealing, remember it's still possible to eat pleasurably and healthily, especially if you supplement the vast quantities of meat on offer with the wonderful fruits (both fresh and dried) and diverse bread creations that augment most dinner tables. Iran brings a more sophisticated cuisine, benefiting from the introduction of rose water, pistachio and saffron. Kebabs are joined by yoghurt, stews (*khoresht*) and fragrant pilaus.

But a growing popularity of Turkish restaurants in all the Central Asian countries gives a hint as to the culinary riches on offer in Turkey, and Istanbul in particular. Turkish cuisine is rightly placed alongside that of France and China in terms of its innovative delights. Drawing inspiration from both East and West, it offers something for everyone, from grilled kebabs and minced lamb *koftas* to honeyed deserts like *baklava*. And of course the food of northern India, with its Mughlai cuisine of *makhni* and *korma* curries, its Punjabi *masalas* and exotic sweets, is worthy of much experimentation on your travels.

A final word about the most important cross-cultural beverage: tea. From Russia to China and Turkey to India, drinking tea is more than simply a way to take liquid on board – it is an intrinsic part of each respective culture. It may be prepared in wildly different forms – from the milk tea of Mongolia to the hot green tea of Central Asia; from the Russian tea drunk through a rock of sugar held in the teeth, to the countless varieties drunk in refined Chinese teahouses; from the fragrant black tea of Istanbul to the sweet milk *chai* of Delhi – but the social importance attached to the sharing of a cup or glass of tea with others, whether in a teahouse or at home, cannot be overstated. Therefore, take the time to "take tea" wherever you go; the rewards are many.

Festivals and Public Holidays

Timing your trip to coincide with festivals or significant public holidays can be a double-edged sword. The benefits are obvious: the chance to see a country's annual cultural highlight is not to be missed. But travelling during and around festival time is a nightmare, and accommodation can be impossible to find, so plan carefully.

Russia celebrates **Labour Day** on 1 and 2 May, with parades in St Petersburg and Moscow and a festive atmosphere in every town, but much of the country shuts down for the first two weeks in May as a result. The **Russian Winter Festival** from 25 December till 5 January is also an event-filled time. Mongolia's two main festival periods are **Tsaagan Sar**, the Lunar New Year held in January or February, and the **Naadam Festival**, or "Three Manly Games", held in July. The **Chinese New Year** also takes place some time in January or February, according to the phases of the moon, and travel in China during this period can be hellish.

In Islamic states and regions, **Ramadan**, the month of fasting, occurs in the ninth lunar month of the Islamic calendar, generally in August/September. This can have a major effect on your travel plans and experience, though Ramadan is practised with wildly varying degrees of enthusiasm from one region to the next. The week following the end of Ramadan is a time of great festivity. **Nowruz** (or **Nevruz**), traditionally the Persian New Year, falls on the March equinox, the first day of spring, and is celebrated from Turkey through to Xinjiang and south as far as Kashmir. The Islamic "Festival of Sacrifice", **Eid al-Adha** or **Korban**, takes place slightly earlier each year than the last, according to the Gregorian calendar – in 2009 it took place on 27 November. In India, the five-day **Diwali** or "Festival of Lights" takes place between mid-October and mid-November.

Visas

Tourist visas for Russia are relatively easy to procure, though they can take 10–15 working days to be issued. The easiest way is of course to let a travel agent do it for you; a few websites that can help are **www.gotorussia.com**; **www.russiagateway.com**; and **www.russia-travel.com**. Mongolia too has a simple visa system – applications can be made at its embassies and consulates; visit **www.mongolianconsulate.com.au/mongolia/embassies.shtml** to find one relevant to you.

As far as red tape is concerned for Silk Road journeys, the high point for travellers came just after the Mongol invasions in the 13th century. The subsequent *pax mongolica* meant that a traveller could travel the breadth of Asia with only one "visa", a golden plaque issued by the Mongol khans. If only it were that simple today.

Even the splintering of the Soviet empire has done little to facilitate entry requirements in the region, which run the gamut from a convenient formality (Kyrgyzstan, India and China) to requiring advance planning (Tajikistan) to downright obstructionist (Iran and Turkmenistan). Currently citizens of most Western countries do not need an invitation to get visas for Kazakhstan (a pricey "visa on arrival" service is available for direct flights into Almaty airport), Kyrgyzstan, China, India, Turkey and, most recently, Uzbekistan. Invitations are required for Iran, Turkmenistan and Tajikistan.

It's therefore best to research current requirements well in advance, either by phoning your nearest embassies or visiting their websites. Travel agents can help for a fee, particularly if you book some travel arrangements with them. A multi-country Silk Road trip will require months of visa hunting, so leave plenty of time.

TRAVEL ADVISORIES

he journeys covered in this book traverse some volatile parts of the world, especially along the Silk Road, which has indeed always been this way. Silk route travellers have for centuries adapted their travel routes to avoid bandits and detour around hostile empires, and today's travellers will have to do likewise. War and strife are almost as current in the 21st century as they were in the fifth.

To get an idea of the security in the areas you intend to travel through, it's necessary to piece together information from various sources. Do a search on news stories for those regions to get a feel for the political climate. Check the British Foreign and Commonwealth Office (**www.fco.gov.uk/travel**), US State Department (**http://travel.state.gov/travel/cis_pa_tw/tw/tw_1764.html**) or Australian Department of Foreign Affairs and Trade (**www.smartraveller.gov.au**) for up-to-the-minute advice, travel warnings and consular information sheets. They offer a detailed breakdown of regions, not just states, though they tend to err on the side of caution. Currently, all three advise against travel to Afghanistan and Iraq, and all three recommend caution when travelling to Tajikistan, particularly the border areas.

USEFUL WEBSITES

The cyber-world is a labyrinth of information, some accurate and interesting, some error-strewn and fatuous. The best advice is to spend some time "surfing", and compare what you read or discover from one site to the next before coming to a consensus of opinion about the destinations you're interested in. Below are some recommendations and a short list of interesting or useful websites on relevant regions and cultures. However, the usual caveat applies: websites come and go all the time, so we cannot guarantee that all the following will be up and running when you hit the button.

Russia & Mongolia

www.baikalnature.com – an Irkutsk-based company specialising in adventure trips in the Lake Baikal region.

www.cityvision2000.com – St Petersburg at Your Fingertips.

www.interknowledge.com/Russia – the Russian National Tourist office website.

www.irkutsk.org – general information on the Baikal region.

www.mongoliatourism.gov.mn – the official website of the country's Tourism Department.

www.mongolia-web.com – regular news and feature stories on Mongolia, including useful links.

www.moscow-guide.ru – official tourist site of the Moscow government.

www.russia-tourism.com – extensive travel and tourism links.

www.sundownersoverland.com – a wide range of information from a long-distance travel specialist.

www.trans-siberia.com – a personally biased but useful site about Trans-Siberian travel.

www.travel.spb.ru – information on St Petersburg for tourists.

http://vladivostoktimes.ru – online site of the *Vladivostok Times*.

www.waytorussia.net – guides to major Russian cities, including Vladivostok.

China

www.aboutxinjiang.com – an excellent authorized online guide to Xinjiang (the English version of Tianshannet's website), with comprehensive news and travel information.

www.bjreview.com.cn – comment and features from the long-established monthly *Beijing Review*.

www.chinaexpat.com – offers a huge amount of information on cities and regions throughout the country.

www.chinatt.org – an invaluable English-language Chinese Railway Timetable available to buy online (pdf electronic format US$20, A4 printed size US$40).

www.chineseculture.about.com – informative and comprehensive guide to the arts, culture and history of China.

www.gansu.gov.cn – Gansu Provincial People's Government website.

www.mychinastart.com – offers a vast number of links to all major regions and cities in China.

www.thatsbeijing.com – Beijing site of Asiaxpat.

www.thebeijingguide.com – a well-designed site, steeped in cultural delights, with traditional music, 360° vistas, videos and more.

www.thexianguide.com – the online China Guide's Xi'an pages.

www.travelchinaguide.com/silkroad – tourist information and photos from the Chinese Silk Road.

www.visitbeijing.com – site of the Beijing Tourism Industry Bureau featuring nationwide travel news, shopping guides and bizarre travel tips.

www.wildwall.com – the best site for the Great Wall and how to visit, with an emphasis on conservation.

Central Asia

www.bukhara.net – tourist information on the city.

www.cbtkyrgyzstan.kg – Kyrgyzstan's Community-based Tourism site.

www.ecotourism.kz – Ecotourism Information Resource Centre in Kazakhstan.

www.eurasianet.org – news stories, cultural items and some travel links.

www.exkz.org – an online community for expatriates in Kazakhstan.

www.freenet.kg/kyrgyzstan – an online Kyrgyz site with information about the country.

www.khiva.info – an interactive online guidebook.

www.neweurasia.net – lively comment and debate from a Central Asian network of blogs.

www.pamirs.org – good information on Tajikistan.

www.samarkand.info – an independent online guide.

www.steppemagazine.com – a high-quality glossy periodical covering all Central Asia.

www.timesca.com – online site for the English-language *Times of Central Asia*.

www.tourism.uz – Uzbekistan's Department of Tourism information.

www.turkmens.com – general site on Turkmenistan.

www.uzbekworld.com – contains a good travel section.

Iran & Turkey

www.allaboutturkey.com – professional tour guide Burak Sansal's wide-ranging site, excellent on history and culture.

www.goturkey.com – the Turkey Official Tourism Portal.

www.irpedia.com – travel and tourism information on Iran.

www.istanbulcityguide.com – the Istanbul City Guide.

www.itto.org – the Iran Tourism & Touring Organisation.

www.tehrantimes.com – online site of the *Tehran Times*.

www.tourismturkey.org – site of Turkey's Ministry of Tourism.

The Subcontinent

www.incredibleindia.org – India's Ministry of Tourism site, with many links.

www.kabulcaravan.com – excellent travel site on Afghanistan.

www.kabulguide.com – focused practical information on visiting Kabul

www.mapsofindia.com – general travel and tourism information on all major cities.

www.pakistan4ever.com – a comprehensive travel site for the country.

www.rajasthantourismindia.com – travel info from the state's tourism authority.

www.thehindu.com – online version of The *Hindu*, a quality broadsheet.

www.timesofindia.com – online version of the *Times of India* newspaper.

www.tourism.gov.pk – official site of Pakistan Tourism.

www.travelgodelhi.com – good information on the city's heritage sites.

General Silk Road sites

http://depts.washington.edu/silkroad/index.html – online information on the Silk Road in Central Asia.

http://idp.bl.uk – the British Library's International Dunhuang Project contains excellent links to aspects of Silk Road history.

www.silkroadfoundation.org – The Silk Road Foundation, Saratoga, California has a vast amount of useful information.

www.silkroadproject.org – The Silk Road Project, an organization founded by classical cellist Yo-Yo Ma, aims to "illuminate the Silk Road's historical contribution to the diffusion of art and culture".

www.unesco.org/culture/silkroads – the UNESCO pages relevant to the Silk Road.

Health & Safety

www.cdc.gov – Centers for Disease Control and Prevention.

www.fitfortravel.nhs.uk – travel health information.

www.healthinchina.com – medical advice and contacts for travellers.

www.mdtravelhealth.com – general recommendations for travel to different countries.

www.who.int/ith – the World Health Organization's online version of *International Travel and Health*.

General sites

www.cia.gov/library/publications/the-world-factbook/index.html – the CIA's encyclopaedic online country fact book.

www.infoplease.com – contains a huge amount of factual information on countries around the world.

www.lonelyplanet.com – its Thorn Tree Travel Forum can be a good source of up-to-the-minute travel information.

www.odysseypublications.com – information on Odyssey's wide range of historical and cultural guides.

www.seat61.com – an award-winning site dedicated to train travel and packed with essential information.

www.virtualtourist.com – an up-to-date feedback and forum for travellers.

www.wikipedia.org – the "Free Encyclopedia" online, with monumental amounts of useful cultural and historical information.

http://wikitravel.org – a constantly updated and enlarged database of info on all aspects of tourist travel.

www.world66.com – "The Travel Guide You Write"; an open-content site for individual travellers to share up-to-date information.

www.worldtravelguide.net – comprehensive tourism and business travel info by country.

Lastly, for general accommodation websites with customer feedback, try the following:

www.asiahotels.com   **www.hotelclub.net**

www.sinohotel.com   **www.tripadvisor.com**

RECOMMENDED READING

O ne constant of travel on any of the routes this book has described is that you'll find yourself with plenty of spare time – in waiting rooms, train carriages or on long-distance buses – in which to read up on and absorb something about your destinations. Below is just a small selection of literature that could fill that time in an enjoyable, satisfying and useful way. A full Bibliography and more extensive reading list can be found on the Odyssey website at **www.odysseypublications.com**.

Russia, Mongolia and the Trans-Siberian Railway

Andrews, Roy Chapman, *Across Mongolian Plains* (first published 1921, Carveth Press, 2008)

Cronin, Vincent, *Catherine: Empress of All the Russias* (William Morrow and Co., 1978)

Dobbs, Michael, *Down with Big Brother: The Fall of the Soviet Empire* (Vintage, 1998)

Dostoevsky, Fyodor, *Crime and Punishment* (Bantam, 1982)

Feinstein, Elaine, *Pushkin: A Biography* (Ecco Press, 1999)

Figes, Orlando, *Natasha's Dance: A Cultural History of Russia* (Picador, 2003)

Fraser, John Foster, *The Real Siberia* (London, 1901)

Gogol, Nikolai, *Dead Souls* (Penguin, 1997)

Kennan, George, *Tent Life in Siberia* (first published 1870, University Press of the Pacific, 2001)

Lincoln, W. Bruce, *The Conquest of a Continent* (Random House, 1994)

Man, John, *Genghis Khan: Life, Death and Resurrection* (St Martin's Press, 2004)

Massie, Robert, *Peter the Great* (Ballantine, 1980)

Murphy, Dervla, *Through Siberia by Accident* (John Murray, 2005)

Newby, Eric, *The Big Red Train Ride* (Picador, 1978)

Nordbye, Masha, *Moscow, St Petersburg & the Golden Ring* (Odyssey Books & Guides, 2007)

Pasternak, Boris, *Dr Zhivago* (Ballantine, 1988)

Robinson, Carl, *Mongolia: Nomad Empire of Eternal Blue Sky* (Odyssey, 2010)

Steinberg, Mark and Khrustalyov, Vladimir, *The Fall of the Romanovs* (Yale University Press, 1995)

Theroux, Paul, *The Great Railway Bazaar* (Penguin, 1995)

Thomas, Bryn, *The Trans-Siberian Handbook* (Trailblazer, 2007)

Thubron, Colin, *In Siberia* (Harper Perennial, 2000)

Tolstoy, Leo, *Anna Karenina* (Penguin Classics, 2004))

Ure, John, *The Cossacks* (Overlook Press, 2003)

Weatherford, Jack, *Genghis Khan and the Making of the Modern World* (Crown, 2006)

Wenyon, Charles, *Across Siberia on the Great Post Road* (London, 1896)

Chinese Silk Road

Barrow, J, *Travels in China* (1802)

Becker, Jasper, *The Chinese* (John Murray, 2003)

Bonavia, Judy, *The Silk Road: Xi'an to Kashgar* (Odyssey, 2008)

Boulnois, Luce, translated by Helen Loveday, *Silk Road: Monks, Warriors & Merchants* (Odyssey, 2008)

Bredon, Juliet, *Peking* (Oxford University Press China, 1983)

Cable, Mildred, *The Gobi Desert* (London, Hodder & Stoughton, 1950)

Cable, Mildred, *Through Jade Gate and Central Asia* (London, Hodder & Stoughton, 1927)

Chan, Charis & Tredinnick, Jeremy, *China: Renaissance of the Middle Kingdom* (Odyssey, 2008)

Cohn, Don J., *Beijing Walks: Exploring the Heritage* (Odyssey, 2008)

Fleming, Peter, *News from Tartary: A Journey from Peking to Kashmir* (Northwestern University Press, 1999)

Hedin, Sven, *My Life As an Explorer* (Kodansha International, 1996)

Hedin, Sven, *Through Asia* (General Books LLC, 2009)

Johnston, Reginald Fleming, *Twilight in the Forbidden City* (Amerion, 1995)

Lansdell, Henry, *Chinese Central Asia* (London, 1893)

Lattimore, Eleanor Holgate, *Turkestan Reunion* (Kodansha Globe, 1995)

Lattimore, Owen, *The Desert Road to Turkestan* (Kodansha Intl., 1995)

Maillart, Ella, *Forbidden Journey* (Hesperides Press, 2008)

Mooney, Paul and Hibbard, Peter, *Beijing & Shanghai: China's Hottest Cities* (Odyssey, 2006)

Mooney, Paul, Maudsley, Catherine and Hatherly, Gerald, *Xi'an, Shaanxi and the Terracotta Army* (Odyssey, 2009)

Shipton, Diana, *The Antique Land* (Oxford Paperbacks, 1988)

Skrine, Sir Clarmont Percival, *Chinese Central Asia* (first published 1926, Vanguard, 1999)

Spence, Jonathan, *The Search for Modern China* (WW Norton, 2001)

Stein, Aurel, *Ruins of Desert Cathay* (first published 1907, Dover Publications, 1987)

Warner, Marina, *The Dragon Empress* (Atheneum, 1986)

Whitfield, Susan, *Life Along the Silk Road* (University of California Press, 2001)

Wriggins, Sally Hovey, *Xuanzang: A Buddhist Pilgrim on the Silk Road* (Westview Press, 1998)

Central Asian Silk Road

Byron, Robert, *The Road to Oxiana* (Oxford University Press, 1982)

Danziger, Nick, *Danziger's Travels: Beyond Forbidden Frontiers* (Harpercollins, 2002)

Glazebrook, Phillip, *Journey to Khiva: A Writer's Search for Central Asia* (Kodansha Intl., 1996)

Hopkirk, Kathleen, *A Traveller's Companion to Central Asia* (John Murray, 1993)

Klass, Rosanne, *Land of the High Flags: Afghanistan When the Going Was Good* (Odyssey, 2007)

Knight, E.F., *Where Three Empires Meet* (London, 1903)

Kremmer, Christopher, *The Carpet Wars: From Kabul to Baghdad: A Ten-Year Journey Along Ancient Trade Routes* (Ecco Press, 2002)

MacLeod, Calum & Mayhew, Bradley, *Uzbekistan: The Golden Road to Samarkand* (Odyssey, 2008)

Middleton, Robert and Thomas, Huw, *Tajikistan and the High Pamirs* (Odyssey, 2008)

Omrani, Bijan and Leeming, Matthew, *Afghanistan: A Companion & Guide* (Odyssey, 2007)

Schreiber, Dagmar and Tredinnick, Jeremy, *Kazakhstan: Nomadic Routes from Caspian to Altai* (Odyssey, 2008)

Shaw, Robert, *Visits to High Tartary, Yarkand and Kashgar* (Oxford University Press, USA, 1985)

Stewart, Rowan, *Kyrgyz Republic* (Odyssey, 2008)

Thubron, Colin, *The Lost Heart of Asia* (Perennial, 2000)

Thubron, Colin, *Shadow of the Silk Road* (HarperCollins, 2007)

Yamashita, Michael, *Marco Polo: A Photographer's Journey* (White Star Publishers, 2002)

Younghusband, Francis, *Among the Celestials* (first published 1898, Adamant Media Corp, 2003)

Persia & Turkey

Curzon, George Nathaniel, *Persia and the Persian Question* (London, 1892)

Fraser, J.B., *A Winter's Journey* (London, 1838)

Freely, John, *Istanbul: the Imperial City* (Penguin, 1998)

Harris, Jonathan, *Constantinople: Capital of Byzantium* (Continuum, 2009)

Horobin, Gilbert, *Turkey* (Odyssey, 1999)

Loveday, Helen, Wannell, Bruce, Baumer, Christoph and Omrani, Bijan, *Iran: Persia Ancient and Modern* (Odyssey, 2010)

Pamuk, Orhan, *Istanbul: Memories and the City* (Vintage, 2006)

Pardoe, Julia, *The City of the Sultan and Domestic Manner of the Turks* (London, 1837)

The Subcontinent

Coll, Steve, *On the Grand Trunk Road: A Journey into South Asia* (Penguin, 2009)

Dalrymple, William, *City of Djinns: A Year in Delhi* (Penguin, 2003)

Dalrymple, William, *The Last Mughal: The Fall of a Dynasty – Delhi, 1857* (Vintage 2008)

Davidson, Robyn, *Desert Places* (Penguin, 1997)

Eraly, Abraham, *The Mughal Throne: The Saga of India's Great Emperors* (Phoenix, 2004)

King, John, *The Karakoram Highway* (Lonely Planet, 1998)

Kipling, Rudyard, *Kim* (Barnes and Noble, 2003)

Koul, Sudha, *The Tiger Ladies: A Memoir of Kashmir* (Beacon Press, 2003)

Margolis, Eric, *War at the Top of the World: The Struggle for Afghanistan, Kashmir and Tibet* (Routledge, 2002)

TOUR AND
TRAVEL OPERATORS

The inevitably linear nature of the Trans-Siberian Railway between the Russian West and Far East means that the planning and execution of a journey along it is a relatively simple affair for the individual traveller – research through the Internet will provide answers to virtually all your questions (see Advice for the Traveller section on page 512). However, for those wanting to minimise the hassles, booking a group trip with a tour company is a sensible idea – there are a number of specialist operators out there, such as **Sundowners Overland** and **GW Travel Ltd** (see listing below).

If your fascination lies along the Silk Road, but you are not quite sure where to start or what to plan for, the first conundrum to come to terms with is that there is no Silk Road; at least no single route, or road. Modern travellers have to cobble together a route based on issues such as transport, budget, security and visas – just as the original traders did more than 2,000 years ago. If you decide to make a Silk Road journey under your own steam, you should expect frequent problems and difficulties, from some pretty mediocre hotels, to questionable food and volatile politics, all of which must be endured with good grace or overcome in the right spirit. But come prepared also to be seduced by amazing nomadic hospitality, the graceful hand-over-heart greeting of a turbaned Uzbek elder, or the sophistication of an azure Timurid dome. Few journeys shimmer in the distance with such romance and expectation.

In addition, bear in mind that the Silk Road was a transcontinental network of routes that stretched for thousands of miles. The traders of bygone ages would never cover more than one or two legs at a stretch before handing over to other local middlemen, and the modern traveller would be wise to take heed. A rushed dash across the continent will not suffice for many, so concentrate on a particular section, and leave wanting to come back for more. (The **Silk Road Tour Operators Group**, **www.silkroadtog. com**, has a newsletter and links to member travel agencies, which give a good overview of what's possible. **Oxiana** is an email forum devoted to travel in Central Asia; once you've joined – send a blank message to **oxiana-subscribe@yahoogroups.com** – you can read articles pertaining to the region and post travel-related queries.)

But in today's turbulent political and economic world the risks and hassles do seem to pile up, so the option of signing on to a package tour either for some or all of your trip can be a smart move. A good tour operator will arrange visas, partner with experienced local companies in destination countries, and offer a range of routes and trip styles to choose from, or even allow you to join up for certain sectors but go your own way in between. With this in mind, here is a by no means exhaustive list of international and regional tour operators who cover some or all of Eurasia's great land routes:

INTERNATIONAL COMPANIES

Abercrombie & Kent International, 1411 Opus Place, Executive Towers West II, Suite 300, Downers Grove, IL 60515-1182, USA, tel: 800 554 7016 or 630 725 3400, website: www.abercrombiekent.com

Archaeological Tours, 271 Madison Avenue, Suite 904, New York, NY 10016, USA, tel: (212) 986 3054 or (866) 740 5130, fax: (212) 370 1561, email: archtours@aol.com, website: www.archaeologicaltours.com – Xi'an to Kashgar and Central Asia tours, featuring lectures by leading scholars.

Asia Transpacific Journeys, 2995 Center Green Court, Boulder, Colorado 80301, USA, tel: (1) 303 443 6789 (toll free: 1-800-642-2742), fax: (1) 303 443 7078, email: travel@asiatranspacific.com, website: www.asiatranspacific.com

Audley Travel, New Mill, New Mill Lane, Witney, Oxfordshire OX29 9SX, UK, tel: 01993 838 000, website: www.audleytravel.com

Exodus, Grange Mills, Weir Rd, London SW12 0NE, UK, tel: (020) 8675 5550, email: info@exodus.co.uk, website: www.exodus.co.uk

Explore, Nelson House, 55 Victoria Road, Farnborough, Hampshire GU14 7PA, UK, tel: 0845 013 1537, email: info@explore.co.uk, website: www.explore.co.uk

Geographic Expeditions, 1008 General Kennedy Avenue, PO Box 29902, San Francisco, CA 94129, USA, tel: 1 800 777 8183, fax: 1 415 346 5535, email: info@geoex.com, website: www.geoex.com

Golden Bridge International, 6/F, Tak Woo House, 17-19 D'Aguilar St. Central, Hong Kong, China, tel: (852) 2801 5591, fax: (852) 2523 7293, email: info@goldenbridge.net, website: www.goldenbridge.net

Go Russia, Boundary House, Boston Road, London W7 2QE, UK, tel: (020) 3355 7717, email: info@justgorussia.co.uk, website: www.justgorussia.co.uk

GW Travel Ltd, Denzell House, Denzell Gardens, Dunham Road, Altrincham WA14 4QF, UK, tel: 44 (0)161 928 9410, fax: 44 (0)161 941 6101, email: mail@gwtravel.co.uk, website: www.gwtravel.co.uk – the world's leading provider of private rail tours through Russia and the CIS. Its flagship tour is the Trans-Siberian Express, but it also operates in China and India.

Helen Wong's Tours, Level 11, 99 Bathurst Street, Sydney, NSW 2000, Australia, tel: 612 9267 7833, fax: 612 9267 7717, email: hwtaus@helenwongstours.com, website: www.helenwongstours.com

Journey Anatolia Ltd, 37A Rosendale Road, London SE21 8DY, UK, website: www.journeyanatolia.com – unusual and intimate tours of Turkey.

MIR Corporation, Suite 210, 85 South Washington Street, Seattle WA 98104, USA, tel: 1 206 624 7289 or 1 800 424 7289, fax: 1 206 624 7360, email: info@mircorp.com, website: www.mircorp.com

On the Go Tours, tel: (44) 207 371 1113, fax: (44) 207 471 6414,
email: info@onthegotours.com, website: www.onthegotours.com

Peregrine Adventures, 380 Lonsdale Street, Melbourne VIC 3000,
tel: (61 3) 8601 4444, fax: (61 3) 8601 4422,
email: websales@peregrineadventures.com, website: www.peregrine.net.au

Regent Holidays, Mezzanine Suite, Froomsgate House, Rupert Street, Bristol BS1 2QJ, UK,
tel: 0845 277 3317, fax: (44) 117 925 4866, email: regent@regent-holidays.co.uk,
website: www.regent-holidays.co.uk

The Russia Experience, 1D The Court, Lanwades Business Park, Newmarket CB8 7PN, UK,
website: www.trans-siberian.co.uk

Silk Road and Beyond, 371 Kensington High Street, London, W14 8QZ, tel: (020) 7371 3131, fax:
(020) 7602 9715, email: sales@silkroadandbeyond.co.uk, website: www.silkroadandbeyond.co.uk

Silk Road Tours, 300-1497 Marine Drive, West Vancouver, B.C. V7T 1B8, Canada,
tel: (1 888) 881 7455 or (604) 925 3831, email: canadian32@gmail.com,
website: www.silkroadtours.com – specialists in Iran and Central Asia.

Silk Road Travel Management Ltd, Suite 1602, Chinachem Century Tower, 178 Gloucester Road,
Wanchai, Hong Kong, tel: (852) 2736 8828, fax: (852) 2736 8000,
email: travel@the-silk-road.com, website: www.the-silk-road.com

Silk Steps, Odyssey Lodge, Holywell Rd, Edington, Bridgwater, Somerset TA7 9JH, UK,
tel: (01278) 722 460, email: info@silksteps.co.uk, website: www.silksteps.co.uk

Steppes Travel, 51 Castle St, Cirencester, Gloucestershire GL7 1QD, UK,
tel: (01285) 880 980, fax: (01285) 885888, website: www.steppestravel.co.uk

Sundowners Overland, 1 St George's Court, 131 Putney Bridge Road, London SW15 2PA, UK,
tel: (44) 20 8877 7660, fax: (44) 20 8877 9002, and
Level 1, 51 Queen Street, Melbourne 3000, Australia,
tel: (61 3) 9672 5300, fax: (61 3) 9672 5311, website: www.sundownersoverland.com

TCS & Starquest Expeditions, Suite 1400, 1000 Second Avenue, Seattle WA 98104, USA,
tel: 1 800 454 4149 or 727 7477, email: info@tcsandstarquestexpeditions.com,
website: www.tcsandstarquestexpeditions.com

Travelsphere Ltd, Compass House, Rockingham Road, Market Harborough, Leics LE16 7QD, UK,
tel: 0870 240 2460 or 0800 567 7372, website: www.travelsphere.co.uk

Voyages Jules Verne, 21 Dorset Square, London NW1 6QG, tel: 0845 166 7003, website: www.vjv.co.uk

Wild Frontiers Adventure Travel, Unit 6, Hurlingham Business Park, 55 Sulivan Rd, London SW6
3DU, UK, tel: (020) 7736 3968, fax: (020) 7751 0710, email: info@wildfrontiers.co.uk,
website: www.wildfrontiers.co.uk

World Expeditions, 78 George Street, Ottawa (ON) K1N 5W1, Canada, tel: 1 613 241 2700,
   fax: 1 613 241 4189, email: info@worldexpeditions.ca, and
   81 Craven Gardens, Wimbledon, London SW19 8LU, UK, tel: 020 8545 9030,
   fax: 020 8543 8316, email: enquiries@worldexpeditions.co.uk, website: www.worldexpeditions.net

REGIONAL TRAVEL COMPANIES

he following local agencies can organize part or all of your trip through the Siberia, Central Asian
and subcontinent regions. They and their websites are a good source of general information,
travel information and visa invitations (if necessary), and can also help with accommodation
and transport bookings. Many are used by the large international tour operators as in-country partners.

Afghanistan

Travel Afghanistan, tel: 01962 738492, email: travel@matthewleeming.com,
   website: www.travelafghanistan.co.uk

Georgia

Caucasus Travel, 44/II Leselidze Street, 0105 Tbilisi, Georgia, tel: (995 32) 987400,
   email: online@caucasustravel.com, website: www.caucasustravel.com

India

Wild Frontiers India, 1/Floor, 20/230A, Masjid Moth (near Jain Dadabari), South Extension Part II,
   New Delhi 49, India, email: info@wildfrontiers.co.uk, website: www.wildfrontiers.co.uk
   – the Indian office of UK-based Wild Frontiers Adventure Travel.

Indian Luxury Tours, Suite T-305, Sector 5, Plot 7, Dwarka, New Delhi 110075,
   tel: (91) 011 4557 2470, fax: (91) 011 2508 4950, email: castleandking@vsnl.net,
   website: www.indianluxurytours.net

Iran

Pasargad Tours, 146 Africa Avenue, Tehran, 19156, Iran, tel: (98 21) 2205 8833,
   email: info@pasargad-tours.com, website: www.pasargad-tours.com

Pars Tourist Agency, Zand Street 71358, Shiraz, Iran, tel: 0098-9171118514,
   email: sales@key2persia.com, website: www.key2persia.com

Kazakhstan

Ecotourism Kazakhstan, 71 Zheltoksa Street, 050000 Almaty, tel/fax: (7727) 2798146,
   email: ecotourism.kz@mail.kz, website: www.ecotourism.kz

Stantours, Kunyaeva 163/76, Almaty, Kazakhstan, email: info@stantours.com,
   website: www.stantours.com

Turan-Asia, 66/8 Ablay Khan Avenue, Almaty, 480004, Kazakhstan, tel: (727) 266 3687,
   email: turanincome@belight.net, website: www.turanasia.kz

Kyrgyzstan

Asia Silk Tours, 34b-29, Sixth Microdistrict, Bishkek, Kyrgyzstan, tel: (996 312) 469 923,
    email: centralasia@sify.com, website: www.centralasiatravel.com

Celestial Mountains, Kievskaya 131–2, Bishkek, Kyrgyzstan, tel: (996 312) 311 814,
    email: celest@infotel.kg, website: www.celestial.com.kg

ITMC Tien-Shan, 1–a Molodaia Gvardia Street, Bishkek, Kyrgyzstan, tel: (996 312) 651 404,
    email: itmc@elcat.kg, website: www.itmc.centralasia.kg

Kyrgyz Concept, 100 Razzakov Street, Bishkek, Kyrgyzstan, tel: (996 312) 661 331 or 210 556,
    email: akc@elcat.kg, website: www.concept.kg

Mongolia

Juulchin World Tours Corporation, Marco Polo Place, Jamyan Gunii, Street 5/3 Ulaanbaatar,
    Mongolia, tel: (976) 11 319401, fax: (976) 11 319402, email: info@juulchinworld.com,
    website: www.juulchinworld.com

Look Mongolia, Look Mongolia Building, Chinggis Khan Avenue 98, Ulaanbaatar 210136, Mongolia,
    tel: (976) 11 344488, fax: (976) 11 687122, email: info@ lookmongolia.com,
    website: www.lookmongolia.com

Nomadic Expeditions, Building 76, Suite 28, 1-40 000 Peace Avenue, Chingeltei-3, Ulaanbaatar
    210644, Mongolia, tel: (976) 11 313396, fax: (976) 11 320311,
    email: mongolia@nomadicexpeditions.com, website: www.nomadicexpeditions.com

Pakistan

Sitara, Waheed Plaza, 3rd Floor, 52 West Jinnah Avenue, Blue Area, P.O. Box 1662 Islamabad, Pakistan,
    tel: (92 51) 287 3372 75 or 227 4892 93, fax: (92 51) 227 9651, email: islamabad@sitara.com,
    website: http://sitara.com

Russia

Baikal Nature LLC, Office 1, 53 Krasnoyarskaya Street, 664023 Irkutsk, Russia,
    tel: (7) 3952 974501, fax: (7) 3952 546743, email: travel@baikalnature.com,
    website: www.baikalnature.com – specializes in adventure travel in the Lake Baikal area,
    with local guides leading cruises, trekking, climbing and cultural excursions, available in several
    foreign languages.

Tajikistan

Great Game Travel, 16 Malone View Park, Belfast BT9 5PN, Northern Ireland, UK,
    tel: (028) 9099 8325, website: www.greatgametravel.co.uk, and
    Pulod Tolis 5/11, Dushanbe, Tajikistan, website: www.traveltajikistan.com

Pamir Adventure, 43 Bukhoro St, Dushanbe, Tajikistan, tel: (992 372) 235 424 or 276 524,
    email: info@pamir-adventure.com, www.pamir-adventure.com

Turkey

Anatolian Adventures, Sogutlucesme Cadessi Karatekin Is Mrk No. 65, Kat 3, 1 Kadikoy, Istanbul, Turkey, tel: (90 216) 418 5222, fax: (90 216) 550 1400, email: info@anatolianadventures.com, website: www.anatolianadventures.com

Byzas Tours, Ergenekon Cadessi No. 20, Kat 2, Pangalti, Istanbul 34373, Turkey, tel: (90 212) 225 7670, email: info@byzastoursturkey.com, website: www.byzastoursturkey.com

Fez Travel, Akbiyik Cadessi No. 17, Sultanahmet, Istanbul 34400, Turkey, tel: (90 212) 516 9024, email: feztravel@feztravel.com, website: www.feztravel.com

Turkmenistan

Ayan Travel, 108-2/4 Magtumkuli Ave, Ashgabat, Turkmenistan, tel: (993 12) 352914, 350797, email: info@ayan-travel.com, website: www.ayan-travel.com

DN Tours, 48/1 Magtumguly Ave, Ashgabat, Turkmenistan, tel: (993 12) 26312 or 226320, email: dntour@online.tm, website: www.dntours.com

Latif, 19 Bitarap Turkmenistan, Ashgabat, Turkmenistan, tel: (993 12) 392 808, email: latif@online.tm, website: www.turkmenistan-latif.com

Uzbekistan

Asia Travel, 97 Chilanzrskaya Street, Tashkent, Uzbekistan, tel: (998 71) 273 5107, email: info@asia-travel.uz, website: www.asia-travel.uz

Dolores Tour, 27 M. Torobi Street, Tashkent, Uzbekistan, tel: (998 71) 220 8883, email: info@sambuh.com, website: www.sambuh.com

Sairam Tourism, 13A Movarounahr Street, Tashkent, Uzbekistan, tel: (998 71) 233 7411 or 233 3559, email: info@sairamtourism.com.uz, website: http://sairamtour.com

Salom Travel, 9 Sarafon Street, Bukhara 705018, Uzbekistan, tel: (998 65) 224 4148, website: www.salomtravel.com

Xinjiang/China

CITS China International Travel Service Ltd, Room 700, CITS Building, 1 Dongdan Beidajie, Beijing 100005, China, tel: (86 10) 6522 2991, email: support-en@cits.com.cn, website: www.cits.net

CYTS Xinjiang International Tour Company, 3rd Floor, 2 Jianshe Road, Urumqi, Xinjiang, China 83002, tel: (86 991) 281 845, email: silkroad-cyts@vip.sina.com, website: www.seexj.com.cn

WildChina, 801 Oriental Place, No. 9 East Dongfang Road, North Dongsanhuan Road, Chaoyang District, Beijing 100027, China, tel: (86 10) 6465 6602, email: info@wildchina.com, website: www.wildchina.com

Xinjiang Caravan International Travel Service, 18 North Jiefang Road, Kashgar, China, tel: (86 998) 283 8988, email: caravan_travel@yahoo.com.cn, website: www.caravantravel.cn

INDEX

User's Note: Page references to illustrations, such as photographs and maps, are printed in bold type, ie **383**. Where references are made to subject matter in captions to illustrations, the entry comprises the page number followed by "c", ie 234c.

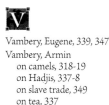

Make the most of your journey with ODYSSEY books, guides and maps

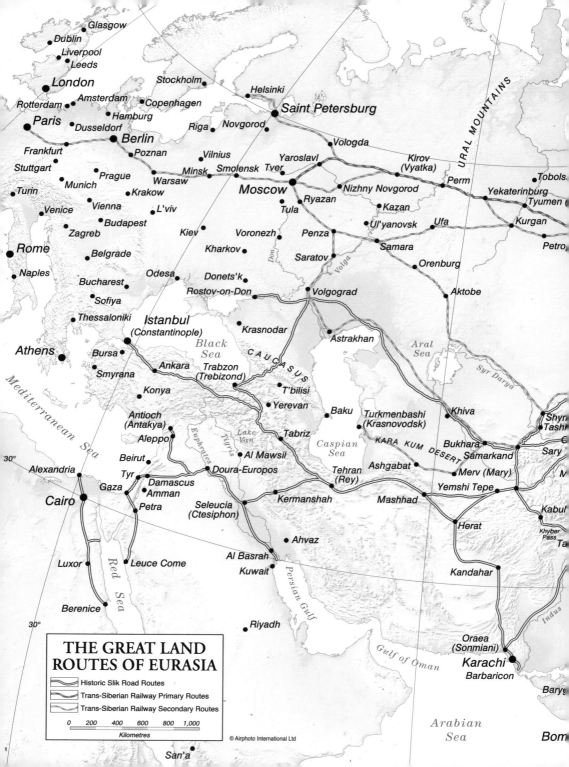

THE GREAT LAND ROUTES OF EURASIA

〰	Historic Silk Road Routes
〰	Trans-Siberian Railway Primary Routes
〰	Trans-Siberian Railway Secondary Routes

0   200   400   600   800   1,000
Kilometres

© Airphoto International Ltd